THE INTERNATIONAL STANDARD BIBLE ENCYCLOPEDIA

THE INTERNATIONAL STANDARD BIBLE ENCYCLOPEDIA

FULLY REVISED • ILLUSTRATED • IN TWELVE VOLUMES

VOLUME TWELVE: W–Z

GENERAL EDITOR

Geoffrey W. Bromiley
Church History and Doctrine

ASSOCIATE EDITORS

Everett F. Harrison
New Testament

Roland K. Harrison
Old Testament

William Sanford LaSor
Biblical Geography and Archeology

CONSULTING EDITOR

Gerald H. Wilson
Old Testament

PROJECT EDITOR

Edgar W. Smith, Jr.

CrossAmerica Books

Crossings Book Club Edition

William B. Eerdmans Publishing Company

First published 1915;

Completely revised and reset.

Printed in the United States of America

Published by CrossAmerica™ Books, an imprint of Crossings Book Club, Box GB, 401 Franklin Avenue, Garden City, New York 11530

Crossings Book Club Edition first printing 1998

CrossAmerica™ Books trademark registration pending on behalf of Crossings Book Club

ISBN 1-56865-421-9

Previously published by Wm. B. Eerdmans Publishing Co. as a four-volume set.

Cover art: *Christ's Charge To Peter* by Giuseppe Vermiglio
Christie's Images/© SuperStock

Contributors†

Allen, George H.*
Ph.D., Editor of *Forum Conche*, or *Fuero de Cuenca*, the Medieval Charter and Bylaws of the city of Cuenca, Spain.

Anderson, Ray S.
B.S., M.Div., Ph.D., Professor of Theology and Ministry, Fuller Theological Seminary, Pasadena, California.

Anderson, Robert T.
B.A., S.T.B., Ph.D., Chairperson, Department of Religious Studies, Michigan State University, East Lansing, Michigan.

Angus, S.*
M.A., Ph.D., Professor of New Testament and Historical Theology, St. Andrew's College, University of Sydney, Australia.

Archer, Gleason L., Jr.
B.A., B.D., A.M., Ph.D., LL.B., Professor of Old Testament and Semitic Languages, Trinity Evangelical Divinity School, Deerfield, Illinois.

Aune, David E.
B.A., M.A., M.A., Ph.D., Professor of Religion, Saint Xavier College, Chicago, Illinois.

Balchin, John A.
M.A., B.D., Pastor, First Presbyterian Church, Papakura, New Zealand.

Baly, A. Denis
B.A., Late Professor of Religion, Kenyon College, Gambier, Ohio.

Bandstra, Barry L.
B.A., B.D., M.A., Ph.D., Assistant Professor of Religion, Hope College, Holland, Michigan.

Bartchy, S. Scott
B.A., M.Div., Ph.D., Adjunct Associate Professor of Early Christian History, University of California; Resident New Testament Scholar, Westwood Christian Foundation, Los Angeles, California.

Beitzel, Barry J.
B.A., M.A., Ph.D., Associate Academic Dean and Professor of Old Testament and Semitic Languages, Trinity Evangelical Divinity School, Deerfield, Illinois.

Biggs, David W.
Th.B., M.Div., M.A., Graduate Student in Biblical Studies, Fuller Theological Seminary, Pasadena, California.

Birch, Bruce C.
B.A., B.D., M.A., M.Phil., Ph.D., Professor of Old Testament, Wesley Theological Seminary, Washington, D.C.

Block, Daniel I.
B.Ed., B.A., M.A., Ph.D., Professor of Old Testament and Hebrew, Bethel Theological Seminary, St. Paul, Minnesota.

Blomberg, Craig L.
B.A., M.A., Ph.D., Assistant Professor of New Testament, Denver Conservative Baptist Seminary, Denver, Colorado.

Borchert, Gerald L.
B.A., LL.B., M.Div., Th.M., Ph.D., Professor of New Testament Interpretation, Southern Baptist Theological Seminary, Louisville, Kentucky.

Brisco, Thomas V.
B.A., Ph.D., Assistant Professor of Biblical Backgrounds and Archaeology, Southwestern Baptist Theological Seminary, Fort Worth, Texas.

Bromiley, Geoffrey W.
M.A., Ph.D., Emeritus Professor of Church History and Historical Theology, Fuller Theological Seminary, Pasadena, California.

Bube, Richard H.
Sc.B., M.A., Ph.D., Professor of Materials Science and Electrical Engineering, Stanford University, Stanford, California.

Buehler, William W.
B.S., B.D., D.Th., Professor of Biblical and Theological Studies, Gordon College, Wenham, Massachusetts.

Bullard, Reuben G.
B.A., Th.B., M.A., M.S., Ph.D., Professor of Ancient History and Geology, Cincinnati Bible College & Seminary, Cincinnati, Ohio.

Burdick, Donald W.
A.B., B.D., Th.M., Th.D., Professor Emeritus of New Testament, Denver Conservative Baptist Seminary, Denver, Colorado.

Burge, Gary M.
B.A., M.Div., Ph.D., Assistant Professor of Biblical Literature, North Park College, Chicago, Illinois.

Burke, David G.
A.B., B.D., Th.M., Ph.D., Editor for Scripture Resources, American Bible Society, New York, New York.

†An asterisk (*) indicates a contributor to the 1915/1929 *ISBE* whose work has been retained with editorial changes.

BURTON, KELLY L. C. RUSSELL
B.A., M.A., Graduate Student in Old Testament, Fuller Theological Seminary, Pasadena, California.

BUSH, FREDERIC W.
B.A., M.Div., Th.M., M.A., Ph.D., Associate Professor of Old Testament, Fuller Theological Seminary, Pasadena, California.

BUTLER, JAMES T.
B.A., M.Div., Instructor of Old Testament, Fuller Theological Seminary, Pasadena, California.

CAMPBELL, E. F.
B.A., B.D., Ph.D., Professor of Old Testament, McCormick Theological Seminary, Chicago, Illinois.

CAMPBELL, ROBERT C.
A.B., M.A., B.D., Th.M., Th.D., President, Eastern Baptist Theological Seminary, Philadelphia, Pennsylvania.

CARMIGNAC, JEAN
D.Th., Editor, *Revue de Qumrân,* Paris, France.

CARPENTER, EUGENE E.
A.B., M.Div., Ph.D., Professor of Old Testament Literature and Languages, Asbury Theological Seminary, Wilmore, Kentucky.

CARTLEDGE, TONY W.
B.S.Ed., M.Div., Doctoral Candidate in Old Testament, Duke University; Pastor, Oak Grove Baptist Church, Boone, North Carolina.

CHAMBERLAIN, GARY
B.A., M.Div., Ph.D., Assistant Professor of Biblical Studies, University of Dubuque Theological Seminary, Dubuque, Iowa.

CLEMONS, JAMES T.
A.B., B.D., Ph.D., Professor of New Testament, Wesley Theological Seminary, Washington, D.C.

COCHRANE, MICHAEL R.
B.A., M.Div., M.Th., Graduate Student, Fuller Theological Seminary, Pasadena, California.

COOK, EDWARD M.
B.A., M.Div., M.A., Ph.D., Adjunct Faculty, Fuller Theological Seminary, Pasadena, California; Managing Editor, *Maarav: A Journal of the Northwest Semitic Languages and Literatures.*

CORLEY, KATHLEEN E.
B.A., Doctoral Student in New Testament, The Claremont Graduate School, Claremont, California.

COUCH, AARON J.
B.A., M.A., M.Div., Pastor, Grace Lutheran Church, Ridgecrest, California.

COUGHENOUR, ROBERT A.
B.S., M.Div., M.A,. Ph.D., Professor of Old Testament, Western Theological Seminary, Holland, Michigan.

CRAIGIE, PETER C.
M.A., Dip.Th., M.Th., Ph.D., Late Professor of Religious Studies and Vice President (Academic), University of Calgary, Calgary, Alberta, Canada.

DAANE, JAMES
A.B., Th.B., Th.D., Late Professor of Theology and Ministry, Fuller Theological Seminary, Pasadena, California.

DANKER, FREDERICK W.
B.D., M.Div., Ph.D., Professor of New Testament, Lutheran School of Theology at Chicago, Chicago, Illinois.

DAY, ALFRED ELY*
M.A., M.Sc., Professor of Natural Sciences, American University of Beirut.

DECLAISSÉ-WALFORD, STEPHEN G.
B.A., M.A., Doctoral Student in Ancient Near Eastern Studies, University of California at Los Angeles.

DEHOOG, JOHN W.
A.B., Former Project Editor, *ISBE* Revision.

DEMENT, BYRON H.*
Th.D., Professor of Sunday School Pedagogy, Southern Baptist Theological Seminary, Louisville, Kentucky.

DERAUD, MARK E.
B.A., Student, Fuller Theological Seminary, Pasadena, California.

DE VRIES, BERT
B.A., B.D., M.A., Ph.D., Professor of History, Calvin College, Grand Rapids, Michigan.

DEVRIES, CARL E.
B.S., M.A., B.D., Ph.D., Former Research Associate (Associate Professor), Oriental Institute of the University of Chicago, Chicago, Illinois.

DEVRIES, LAMOINE
B.A., M.Div., Th.M., Ph.D., Campus Minister, Baptist Student Union and Adjunct Instructor, Old Testament and Archaeology, Southwest Missouri State University, Springfield, Missouri.

DILLMAN, CHARLES N.
A.B., B.D., Th.M. Ph.D., Professor of Religion and Biblical Studies, Spring Arbor College, Spring Arbor, Michigan.

DOLPHIN, LAMBERT T.
A.B., Senior Research Physicist, SRI International, Menlo Park, California.

DONALDSON, TERENCE L.
B.Sc., M.Rel., Th.M., Th.D., Professor of New Testament Language and Literature, College of Emmanuel and St. Chad, Saskatoon, Saskatchewan, Canada.

DORMAN, THEODORE M.
B.A., M.Div., Ph.D., Adjunct Professor of New Testament, Fuller Theological Seminary, Pasadena, California.

DORSEY, DAVID A.
B.A., M.A., Ph.D., Professor of Old Testament, Evangelical School of Theology, Myerstown, Pennsylvania.

DOZEMAN, THOMAS B.
B.A., M.Div., M.Phil., Ph.D., Assistant Professor of Old Testament, Calvin College, Grand Rapids, Michigan.

DUKE, RODNEY K.
B.A., M.C.S., Doctoral Candidate in Old Testament, Emory University, Atlanta, Georgia.

EADES, KEITH L.
B.A., M.A., M.A., Doctoral Student in Old Testament, The Claremont Graduate School, Claremont, California.

EASTON, BURTON SCOTT*
D.D., Ph.D., Professor of the Interpretation and Literature of the New Testament, General Theological Seminary, New York, New York.

EDWARDS, RUTH B.
M.A., Ph.D., Lecturer in New Testament Exegesis, University of Aberdeen, Scotland.

ELLIS, E. EARLE
B.S., M.A., B.D., Ph.D., Research Professor of Theology, Southwestern Baptist Theological Seminary, Fort Worth, Texas.

ELLISON, HENRY LEOPOLD
B.A., B.D., Late Senior Tutor, Moorlands Bible College, Dawlish, England.

EMMERSON, GRACE I.
M.A., Dip.Or.Lang., Recognised Lecturer, Department of Theology, University of Birmingham, England.

ESKENAZI, TAMARA C.
B.A., M.A., Ph.D., Assistant Professor of Judaic Studies and Director of the Institute for Interfaith Studies, Center for Judaic Studies, University of Denver, Denver, Colorado.

FENSHAM, F. CHARLES
B.A. B.D., M.A., D.D., Ph.D., Professor of Semitic Languages and Head of the Department, University of Stellenbosch, Republic of South Africa.

FRANK, PHILIP A.
B.A., M.A.T.S., M.A., Production Editor, Hendrickson Publishers, Peabody, Massachusetts.

FULLER, DANIEL P.
B.A., B.D., Th.M., Th.D., D.Theol., Professor of Hermeneutics, Fuller Theological Seminary, Pasadena, California.

GAEBELEIN, PAUL W., JR.
B.A., Ph.D., Ph.D., Adjunct Faculty in Semitic Languages, Fuller Theological Seminary, Pasadena, California.

GARBER, PAUL LESLIE
Th.M., Ph.D., Professor Emeritus of Bible and Religion, Agnes Scott College, Decatur, Georgia.

GARCÍA, WILLIAM HENRY
B.A., Student, Fuller Theological Seminary, Pasadena, California.

GARLAND, DAVID E.
B.A., M.Div., Ph.D., Associate Professor of New Testament, Southern Baptist Theological Seminary, Louisville, Kentucky.

GASQUE, W. WARD
B.A., B.D., M.Th., Ph.D., Vice Principal and Professor of New Testament, Regent College, Vancouver, British Columbia, Canada.

GAY, GEORGE A.
B.A., B.D., Th.M., Ph.D., Senior Associate Professor of New Testament, Fuller Thelological Seminary, Pasadena, California.

GERHARDSSON, BIRGER
Th.D., Professor of Exegetical Theology, University of Lund, Sweden.

GHIRSHMAN, ROMAN
Late Member of the Académie des Inscriptiones et Belles-Lettres, Paris, France.

GLOER, W. HULITT
B.A., M.Div., Ph.D., Associate Professor of New Testament Studies, Midwestern Baptist Theological Seminary, Kansas City, Missouri.

GORDON, VICTOR R.
A.B., M.Div., Ph.D., Chaplain and Assistant Professor of Biblical Studies, Wheaton College, Wheaton, Illinois.

GREENLEE, J. HAROLD
A.B., B.D., M.A., Ph.D., Missionary of OMS International; Translation Consultant for Wycliffe Bible Translators; Former Professor of Greek New Testament, Asbury Theological Seminary, Wilmore, Kentucky.

GWINN, RALPH A.
B.A., B.D., Ph.D., Former Professor of Religion and Philosophy, Tarkio College, Tarkio, Missouri.

HAGNER, DONALD A.
B.A., B.D., Th.M., Ph.D., Professor of New Testament, Fuller Theological Seminary, Pasadena, California.

HAMMOND, PHILIP C.
B.A., B.D., M.A., Ph.D., Professor of Anthropology, University of Utah, Salt Lake City, Utah.

HANSON, K. C.
M.A., Ph.D., Assistant Professor of Biblical Studies, Episcopal Theological School at Claremont, California.

HARRIS, BRUCE F.
M.A., B.A., B.D., Ph.D., Associate Professor of History, Macquarie University, North Ryde, New South Wales, Australia.

HARRISON, EVERETT F.
B.A., Th.B., M.A., Ph.D., Professor Emeritus of New Testament, Fuller Theological Seminary, Pasadena, California.

HARRISON, ROLAND K.
B.D., M.Th., Ph.D., D.D., Professor Emeritus of Old Testament, Wycliffe College, Toronto, Ontario, Canada.

HARTLEY, JOHN E.
B.A., B.D., M.A., Ph.D., Chair, Department of Biblical Studies, Professor of Old Testament, Graduate School of Theology, Azusa Pacific University, Azusa, California.

HASEL, GERHARD F.
M.A., B.D., Ph.D., Professor of Biblical Theology and Dean, Andrews University Theological Seminary, Berrien Springs, Michigan.

HAWK, L. DANIEL
B.A., M.Div., Doctoral Student in Old Testament, Emory University, Atlanta, Georgia.

HAWTHORNE, GERALD F.
B.A., M.A., Ph.D., Professor of Greek, Wheaton, College, Wheaton, Illinois.

HAYDEN, ROY E.
B.A., B.D., Th.M., M.A., Ph.D., Professor of Old Testament, Graduate School of Theology and Missions, Oral Roberts University, Tulsa, Oklahoma.

HEIDEL, WILLIAM ARTHUR*
M.A., Ph.D., Research Professor of Greek Language and Literature, Wesleyan University, Middletown, Connecticut.

HEMER, COLIN J.
M.A., Ph.D., Late Research Fellow in New Testament History, Tyndale House, Cambridge, England.

HERION, GARY A.
B.A., M.A., Ph.D., Adjunct Assistant Professor, Program in Studies on Religion, University of Michigan, Ann Arbor, Michigan.

HERR, LARRY G.
B.A., Ph.D., Associate Professor of Religion, Canadian Union College, College Heights, Alberta, Canada.

HESS, RICHARD S.
B.A., M.Div., Th.M., Ph.D., Research Fellow, Tyndale House, Cambridge, England.

HICKCOX, ALICE
B.A., M.A., M.Div., Doctoral Student in Old Testament, Emory University, Atlanta, Georgia.

HILDEBRAND, DAVID R.
B.A., M.A., Ph.D., Dean of Academic Affairs, Briercrest Bible College, Caronport, Saskatchewan, Canada.

HILGERT, EARLE
B.A., B.D., M.A., D.Th., Professor of New Testament, McCormick Theological Seminary, Chicago, Illinois.

HILL, ANDREW E.
B.A., M.A., M.Div., Ph.D., Assistant Professor of Old Testament Studies, Wheaton College, Wheaton, Illinois.

HOEKEMA, ANTHONY A.
A.B., M.A., Th.B., Th.D., Professor of Systematic Theology, Emeritus, Calvin Theological Seminary, Grand Rapids, Michigan.

HOFFMEIER, JAMES K.
B.A., M.A., Ph.D., Associate Professor of Archaeology and Old Testament Studies, Wheaton College, Wheaton, Illinois.

HOFFNER, HARRY A., JR.
B.A., M.A., Th.M., Ph.D., Professor of Hittitology, The Oriental Institute, University of Chicago, Chicago, Illinois.

HOLWERDA, DAVID E.
A.B., B.D., D.Th., Professor of New Testament, Calvin Theological Seminary, Grand Rapids, Michigan.

HORSNELL, MALCOLM J. A.
B.A., B.D., Th.M., Ph.D., Associate Professor of Old Testament Interpretation, McMaster Divinity College, Hamilton, Ontario, Canada.

HOWARD, DAVID M., JR.
B.S., M.A., A.M., Ph.D., Assistant Professor of Old Testament, Bethel Theological Seminary, St. Paul, Minnesota.

HUBBARD, DAVID A.
B.A., B.D., Th.M., Ph.D., President and Professor of Old Testament, Fuller Theological Seminary, Pasadena, California.

HUBBARD, ROBERT L., JR.
A.B., B.D., M.A., Ph.D., Associate Professor of Old Testament, Denver Conservative Baptist Seminary, Denver, Colorado.

HUDDLESTUN, JOHN
B.A., Doctoral Student in History and Culture of Ancient Israel, University of Michigan, Ann Arbor, Michigan.

HUGENBERGER, GORDON P.
B.A., M.Div., Adjunct Professor of Old Testament, Gordon-Conwell Theological Seminary; Pastor, Lanesville Congregational Church, Gloucester, Massachusetts.

HUNT, LESLIE
B.A., B.D., M.Th., D.D., Principal Emeritus and Professor of New Testament, Wycliffe College, Toronto, Ontario, Canada.

HURTADO, LARRY W.
B.A., M.A., Ph.D., Associate Professor of Religion, University of Manitoba, Winnipeg, Manitoba, Canada.

IRVIN, DOROTHY
B.A., M.A., D.Theol., Consultant and Lecturer in Scripture and Women's Studies, Durham, North Carolina.

ISAACS, ELLA DAVIS*
M.A., Cambridge, Massachusetts.

ISAACS, NATHAN*
Ph.D., LL.B., S.J.D., Professor of Business Law, Harvard University, Cambridge, Massachusetts.

JACOBS, HENRY E.*
D.D., LL.D., Norton Professor of Systematic Theology, Lutheran Theological Seminary, Philadelphia, Pennsylvania,

JEFFORD, CLAYTON N.
B.A., M.Div., Th.M., M.A., Assistant Director, Institute for Antiquity and Christianity, The Claremont Graduate School, Claremont, California.

JEWETT, PAUL K.
B.A., Th.B., Th.M., Ph.D., Professor of Systematic Theology, Fuller Theological Seminary, Pasadena, California.

JOHNSON, THOMAS F.
B.Ph., B.D., Th.M., Ph.D., Professor of New Testament, North American Baptist Seminary, Sioux Falls, South Dakota.

JORDAN, GREGORY D.
B.A., M.A., M.Div., Ph.D., Associate Professor of Old Testament, King College, Bristol, Tennessee.

JUDGE, EDWIN A.
M.A., M.A., Professor of History, Macquarie University, New South Wales, Australia.

JUNG, KURT GERHARD
Th.D., U.S. Army Chaplain, Berlin, Germany.

KELLY, ROBERT A.
B.A., M.Div., Ph.D., Assistant Professor of Systematic Theology, Waterloo Lutheran Seminary, Waterloo, Ontario, Canada.

KELM, GEORGE L.
B.A., B.D., M.A., Ph.D., Professor of Biblical Backgrounds and Archaeology, Southwestern Baptist Theological Seminary, Fort Worth, Texas.

KEOWN, GERALD L.
B.S., M.Div., Ph.D., Associate Professor of Old Testament Interpretation, Southern Baptist Theological Seminary, Louisville, Kentucky.

KINSELLA, ARTHUR JAMES*
M.A., Instructor in Greek, University of Cincinnati, Cincinnati, Ohio

KITCHEN, KENNETH A.
B.A., Ph.D., Professor of Egyptian and Coptic, School of Archaeology and Oriental Studies, University of Liverpool, England.

KLEIN, RALPH W.
M.Div., Th.D., Christ Seminary-Seminex Professor of Old Testament, Lutheran School of Theology at Chicago, Chicago, Illinois.

KNAPP, GARY L.
B.A., M.Div., Th.M., Editorial Associate, *ISBE* Revision.

KNIGHT, GEORGE A. F.
M.A., B.D., D.D., Retired Principal of Pacific Theological College, Suva, Fiji.

LADD, GEORGE ELDON
Th.B., B.D., Ph.D., Late Professor of New Testament Exegesis and Theology, Fuller Theological Seminary, Pasadena, California.

LASOR, WILLIAM SANFORD
A.B., A.M., Th.B., Th.M., Ph.D., Th.D., Emeritus Professor of Old Testament, Fuller Theological Seminary, Pasadena, California.

LEE, GARY A.
B.A., M.T.S., Editor, Reference Books, William B. Eerdmans Publishing Company.

LIEFELD, WALTER L.
Th.B., A.M., Ph.D., Distinguished Professor of New Testament, Trinity Evangelical Divinity School, Deerfield, Illinois.

LINTON, CALVIN D.
A.B., M.A., Ph.D., Professor Emeritus of English and Dean Emeritus, Columbian College of Arts And Sciences, The George Washington University, Washington, D.C.

LIVERANI, MARIO
Professor of Ancient Near Eastern History, University of Rome, Italy.

MACDONALD, BURTON
B.A., M.Th., M.A., Ph.D., Associate Professor of Theology, St. Francis Xavier University, Antigonish, Nova Scotia, Canada.

MACLEOD, MURDO A.
M.A., Director and General Secretary, Christian Witness to Israel, Kent, England.

MADVIG, DONALD H.
A.B., B.D., Th.M., M.A., Ph.D., Senior Pastor, The Evangelical Covenant Church, Springfield, Massachusetts.

MARTIN, RALPH P.
B.A., M.A., Ph.D., Professor of New Testament and Director of the Graduate Studies Program, Fuller Theological Seminary, Pasadena, California.

MASTERMAN, ERNEST W. G.*
M.D., F.R.C.S., F.R.G.S., Honorary Secretary of the Palestine Exploration Fund, London, England.

MATTHEWS, VICTOR H.
B.A., M.A., Ph.D., Associate Professor of Religious Studies, Southwest Missouri State University, Springfield, Missouri.

MCCANN, J. CLINTON, JR.
A.B., D.Min., Th.M., Ph.D., Assistant Professor of Old Testament, Eden Theological Seminary, St. Louis, Missouri.

MCCARTER, P. KYLE, JR.
B.A., M.Div., Ph.D., William Foxwell Albright Professor of Biblical and Ancient Near Eastern Studies, The Johns Hopkins University, Baltimore, Maryland.

MCDONALD, LEE M.
B.A., B.D., Th.M., Ph.D., Senior Pastor, First Baptist Church, Santa Clara, California; Adjunct Professor of New Testament, Fuller Theological Seminary Extension.

MCKENNA, JOHN E.
A.B., M.Div., Ph.D., Adjunct Professor of Biblical Hebrew and Aramaic, Fuller Theological Seminary, Pasadena, California.

MICHAELS, J. RAMSEY
B.A., B.D., Th.M., Th.D., Professor of Religious Studies, Southwest Missouri State University, Springfield, Missouri.

MILLARD, ALAN RALPH
M.A., M.Phil., Rankin Reader in Hebrew and Ancient Semitic Languages, University of Liverpool, England.

MILLER, DONALD G.
B.A., S.T.B., S.T.M., M.A., Ph.D., Formerly Professor of New Testament, Union Theological Seminary, Richmond, Virgina and President of Pittsburgh Theological Seminary, Pittsburgh, Pennsylvania.

MORGAN, DONN F.
B.A., B.D., M.A., Ph.D., Professor of Old Testament, Church Divinity School of the Pacific, Berkeley, California.

MORRIS, LEON
B.Sc., B.D., M.Th., Ph.D., Former Principal of Ridley College, Melbourne, Australia.

MOSIMAN, SAMUEL K.*
Ph.D., Litt.D., President of Bluffton College, Bluffton, Ohio.

MOULDER, WILLIAM J.
B.A., M.Div., Ph.D., Associate Professor of Bible, Trinity College, Deerfield, Illinois.

MOUNCE, ROBERT H.
B.A., B.D., Th.M., Ph.D., President, Whitworth College, Spokane, Washington.

MOUNCE, WILLIAM D.
B.A., M.A., Ph.D., Associate Professor of New Testament, Azusa Pacific University, Azusa, California.

MOYER, JAMES C.
A.B., M.Div., M.A., Ph.D., Professor and Head of the Department of Religious Studies, Southwest Missouri State University, Springfield, Missouri.

MULLER, RICHARD A.
B.A., M.Div., Ph.D., Associate Professor of Historical Theology, Fuller Theological Seminary, Pasadena, California.

MURRAY, JOHN
M.A., Th.B., Th.M., Late Professor of Systematic Theology, Westminister Theological Seminary, Philadelphia, Pennsylvania.

MYERS, ALLEN C.
B.A., M.Div., Editor, Reference Books, William B. Eerdmans Publishing Company.

NEUSNER, JACOB
A.B., M.H.L., Ph.D., University Professor and Ungerleider Distinguished Scholar of Judaic Studies, Brown University, Providence, Rhode Island.

NORTH, ROBERT
B.A., M.A., S.S.D., Editor, *Elenchus Bibliographicus Biblicus*; Professor of Archeology, Pontificio Istituto Biblico, Rome, Italy.

OLIVIER, J. P. J.
Th.M., D.Litt., Associate Professor of Old Testament, University of Stellenbosch, South Africa.

OPPERWALL-GALLUCH, NOLA J.
A.B., M.Div., Editorial Associate, *ISBE* Revision.

ORR, JAMES*
M.A., D.D., Professor of Apologetics and Theology, Theological College of United Free Church, Glasgow, Scotland.

OSBORNE, GRANT R.
B.A., M.A., Ph.D., Professor of New Testament, Trinity Evangelical Divinity School, Deerfield, Illinois.

PAAS, PATRICK F.
B.R.E., M.Div., Student, Calvin Theological Seminary, Grand Rapids, Michigan.

PATTEN, B. REBECCA
B.S., B.A., M.A., Ph.D., Professor of New Testament and Academic Dean, Patten College, Oakland, California.

PATTEN, PRISCILLA CARLA
B.S., B.A., M.A., Ph.D., President and Professor of New Testament, Patten College, Oakland, California.

PAYNE, DAVID F.
B.A., M.A., Academic Registrar, London Bible College, Northwood, Middlesex, England.

PAYNE, J. BARTON
B.A., B.D., M.A., Th.M., Ph.D., Late Professor and Chairman of the Department of Old Testament, Covenant Theological Seminary, Saint Louis, Missouri.

PECOTA, DANIEL B.
B.A., M.Div., Th.M., D.Min., Professor of Greek and Theology, Northwest College, Kirkland, Washington.

PIERCE, RONALD W.
M.Div., Th.M., Ph.D., Associate Professor of Biblical Studies and Theology, Biola Univerity, La Mirada, California.

PINNOCK, CLARK H.
B.A., Ph.D., Professor of Systematic Theology, McMaster Divinity College, Hamilton, Ontario, Canada.

PLANTINGA, CORNELIUS, JR.
A.B., B.D., Ph.D., Professor of Systematic Theology, Calvin Theological Seminary, Grand Rapids, Michigan.

POLLARD, EDWARD BAGBY*
M.A., D.D., Ph.D., Professor of Homiletics, Crozer Theological Seminary, Chester, Pennsylvania.

PRATICO, GARY D.
B.A., M.Div., Th.D., Assistant Professor of Old Testament, Gordon-Conwell Theological Seminary, South Hamilton, Massachusetts.

PRATT, RICHARD L., JR.
B.A., M.Div., Th.D., Assistant Professor of Old Testament, Reformed Theological Seminary, Jackson, Mississippi.

PREWITT, J. FRANKLIN
B.A., B.Th., D.D., Professor of Bible and History, Western Baptist Bible College, Salem, Oregon.

PROVENCE, THOMAS E.
B.A., M.Div., Ph.D., Co-Pastor, First Presbyterian Church, Lafayette, Louisiana.

RAINEY, ANSON F.
B.A., M.A., B.D., M.Th., Ph.D., Professor of Ancient Near Eastern Cultures and Semitic Languages, Tel Aviv University, Tel Aviv, Israel.

REDDITT, PAUL L.
B.A., M.Div., M.A., Ph.D., Chairman of the Department of Religion and Professor of Old Testament, Georgetown College, Georgetown, Kentucky.

RENWICK, A. M.
M.A., B.D., D.L.H., D.D., Late Professor of Church History, Free Church of Scotland College, Edinburgh, Scotland.

ROBECK, CECIL M., JR.
B.S., M.Div., Ph.D., Assistant Professor of Church History and Assistant Dean for Academic Programs, Fuller Theological Seminary, Pasadena, California.

SAARISALO, AAPELI A.
Th.D., Late Professor of Oriental Literature, Helsinki University, Helsinki, Finland.

SCALISE, PAMELA J.
B.A., M.A.T.S., M.A., M.Phil., Ph.D., Assistant Professsor of Old Testament, Southern Baptist Theological Seminary, Louisville, Kentucky.

SCHARLEMANN, MARTIN H.
M.Div., Ph.D., Th.D., Late Graduate Professor of Exegetical Theology, Concordia Seminary, St. Louis, Missouri.

SCHLEY, DONALD G.
B.A., M.T.S., Ph.D., Instructor in Western History, Dekalb College, Clarkston, Georgia.

SCHNEIDER, DALE A.
B.A., B.D., S.T.M., Ph.D., Homemaker; Proprietor, Schneider Werke, Deep River, Connecticut.

SCHOVILLE, KEITH N.
B.A., M.A., Ph.D., Professor of Hebrew and Semitic Studies, University of Wisconsin, Madison, Wisconsin.

SCHREINER, THOMAS R.
B.S., M.Div., Th.M., Ph.D., Assistant Professor of New Testament, Bethel Theological Seminary, St. Paul, Minnesota.

SCHULTZ, SAMUEL J.
Th.D., Emeritus Professor of Biblical Studies and Theology, Wheaton College, Wheaton, Illinois.

SEGERT, STANISLAV
Ph.Dr., C.Sc., Professor of Biblical Studies and Northwest Semitics, Department of Near Eastern Languages and Cultures, University of California, Los Angeles, California.

SHEA, WILLIAM H.
B.A., Ph.D., Research Associate, Biblical Research Institute, General Conference of Seventh-Day Adventists, Washington, D.C.

SHEPPARD, GERALD T.
B.S., M.Div., M.A., M.Phil., Ph.D., Associate Professor of Old Testament, Emmanuel College of Victoria University in the University of Toronto, Canada.

SIMPSON, JOHN W., JR.
B.A., M.A., Editorial Asssociate, Reference Works, William B. Eerdmans Publishing Company.

SITTERLY, CHARLES FREMONT*
M.A., Ph.D., S.T.D., Professor of Biblical Literature, Drew University College of Theology, Madison, New Jersey.

SMICK, ELMER B.
B.A., Th.B., S.T.M., Ph.D., Professor of Old Testament, Gordon-Conwell Theological Seminary, South Hamilton, Massachusetts.

SMITH, DUANE E.
B.S.E.E., M.A., M.Th., Biblical Scholar and Lecturer, Pomona, California.

SMITH, EDGAR W., JR.
B.A., B.D., Ph.D., Project Editor, *ISBE* Revision.

SMITH, GARY V.
B.A., M.A., Ph.D., Professor of Old Testament, Bethel Theological Seminary, St. Paul, Minnesota.

SODERLUND, SVEN K.
B.A., M.A., M.C.S., Ph.D., Registrar and Associate Professor of Biblical Studies, Regent College, Vancouver, British Columbia, Canada.

SPINA, FRANK A.
B.A., M.Div., M.A., Ph.D., Professor of Old Testament, The School of Religion, Seattle Pacific University, Seattle, Washington.

SPITTLER, RUSSELL P.
B.A., M.A., B.D., Ph.D., Associate Professor of New Testament, Fuller Theological Seminary, Pasadena, California.

STEELE, FRANCIS R.
B.A., M.A., Ph.D., Minister-at-Large, North African Mission, Upper Darby, Pennsylvania.

STEIN, ROBERT H.
B.A., B.D., S.T.M., Ph.D., Professor of New Testament, Bethel Theological Seminary, St. Paul, Minnesota.

STUART, DOUGLAS K.
B.A., Ph.D., Professor of Old Testament, Gordon-Conwell Theological Seminary, South Hamilton, Massachusetts.

SUN, HENRY T. C.
B.A., M.A., M.A., Doctoral Candidate in Old Testament, The Claremont Graduate School, Claremont, California.

SWEET, RONALD F. G.
B.A., Ph.D., Professor, Department of Near Eastern Studies, University of Toronto, Ontario, Canada.

TENNEY, MERRILL C.
Th.B., A.M., Ph.D., Late Professor of New Testament and Dean, Graduate School of Theology, Wheaton College, Wheaton, Illinois.

THIELE, E. R.
B.A., M.A., Ph.D., Late Professor of Antiquities, Andrews University, Berrien Springs, Michigan.

THOMPSON, JOHN ALEXANDER
A.B., M.Div., Th.M., Ph.D., Former Research Consultant, Translations Department, American Bible Society.

THOMPSON, JOHN ARTHUR
B.A., B.Ed., M.Sc., M.A., Ph.D., Former Reader and Chairman, Department of Middle Eastern Studies, University of Melbourne, Australia.

THOMPSON, WINFIELD L., JR.
M.A., M.A., Adjunct Faculty, Fuller Theological Seminary, Pasadena, California.

TREVER, JOHN C.
B.D., Ph.D., Director, Dead Sea Scrolls Project, School of Theology at Claremont, Claremont, California.

VAN ALSTINE, GEORGE A.
B.A., B.D., Th.M., Pastor, Altadena Baptist Church, Altadena, California.

VAN DAM, CORNELIS
B.A., B.D., Th.M., Th.D., Professor of Old Testament, Theological College of the Canadian Reformed Churches, Hamilton, Ontario, Canada.

VANELDEREN, BASTIAAN
A.B., B.D., M.A., Ph.D., Professor of Theology, Free University, Amsterdam, The Netherlands.

VANGEMEREN, WILLEM A.
B.A., B.D., M.A., Ph.D., Professor of Old Testament, Reformed Theological Seminary, Jackson, Mississippi.

VAN LEEUWEN, RAYMOND C.
A.B., M.A., B.D., Ph.D., Assistant Professor of Old Testament, Calvin Theological Seminary, Grand Rapids, Michigan.

VAN SELMS, ADRIANUS
Dr.Theol., Late Professor of Semitic Languages, University of Pretoria, South Africa.

VERHEY, ALLEN D.
B.A., B.D., Ph.D., Professor of Religion, Hope College, Holland, Michigan.

VIVIANO, PAULINE
B.A., M.A., Ph.D., Associate Professor of Theology, Loyola University, Chicago, Illinois.

VÖÖBUS, ARTHUR
M.A., D.Theol., Director of the Institute for Syriac Manuscript Studies and Professor Emeritus of Church History, Lutheran School of Theology at Chicago, Chicago, Illinois.

VOS, CLARENCE J.
A.B., Th.B., Th.M., Th.D., Professor of Religion, Calvin College, Grand Rapids, Michigan.

VOS, HOWARD F.
B.A., Th.M., Th.D., M.A., Ph.D., Professor of History and Archaeology, The King's College, Briarcliff Manor, New York.

WALLACE, RONALD STEWART
B.S., M.A., Ph.D., Professor Emeritus of Biblical Theology, Columbia Theological Seminary, Decatur, Georgia.

WALTON, JOHN H.
A.B., M.A., Ph.D., Assistant Professor of Bible, Moody Bible Institute, Chicago, Illinois.

WARING, DAWN E.
B.S., M.A., Ph.D., Adjunct Assistant Professor of Old Testament, American Baptist Seminary of the West, Southwest Branch, Covina, and Fuller Theological Seminary, Pasadena, California.

WATSON, DUANE F.
B.A., M.Div., Ph.D., Pastor, Tri-Church Parish United Methodist Church, North Western, New York.

WAY, R. J.
M.A., M.A., Minister, St. Columba's United Reformed Church, Leeds, England.

WEAD, DAVID W.
A.B., B.Th., B.D., Th.D., Minister, First Christian Church, Nashville, Tennessee.

WEDDLE, FOREST
A.B., M.S., Ph.D., Late Professor of Biblical Archaeology and History, Fort Wayne Bible College, Fort Wayne, Indiana.

WEIR, THOMAS HUNTER*
B.D., M.A., M.R.A.S., Lecturer in Arabic, University of Glasgow, Scotland.

WENHAM, GORDON J.
M.A., Ph.D., Senior Lecturer in Religious Studies, The College of Saint Paul and Saint Mary, Cheltenham, Gloucester, England.

WESTERHOLM, STEPHEN
M.A., D.Th., Assistant Professor of Religious Studies, McMaster University, Hamilton, Ontario, Canada.

WHALEY, E. BOYD
B.A., M.Div., Doctoral Student in Old Testament at Emory University; Director of Pastoral Services, Metro Atlanta Recovery Residences, Clarkston, Georgia.

WIEBE, JOHN M.
B.A., M.Div., Adjunct Professor, American Baptist Seminary of the West, Covina; Teaching Fellow, Fuller Theological Seminary, Pasadena, California.

WILLIAMSON, H. G. M.
B.A., M.A., Ph.D., Lecturer in Hebrew and Aramaic, University of Cambridge, England.

WILSON, GERALD H.
B.A., M.A., M.Div., M.A., Ph.D., Associate Professor of Biblical Studies, George Fox College, Newberg, Oregon.

WILSON, MARVIN R.
B.A., M.Div., M.A., Ph.D., Ockenga Professor of Biblical and Theological Studies, Gordon College, Wenham, Massachusetts.

WISEMAN, DONALD J.
B.A., M.A., D.Lit., Emeritus Professor of Assyriology, University of London; Chairman and Former Director, British School of Archaeology in Iraq.

WOLFF, ROBERT J.
B.A., M.A., Ph.D., Associate Professor of Biology, Trinity Christian College, Palos Heights, Illinois.

WRIGHT, CHRISTOPHER J. H.
M.A., Ph.D., Tutor and Lecturer in Old Testament, All Nations Christian College, Ware, England.

WRIGHT, G. ERNEST
B.A., B.D., Ph.D., Late Professor of Divinity, Harvard University, Cambridge, Massachusetts.

WYATT, ROBERT J.
B.A., M.A., Ph.D., Former Editorial Associate, *ISBE* Revision.

WYPER, GLENN
B.A., B.D., Th.M., Registrar, Professor in the Biblical/Theological Studies Department, Ontario Bible College, Willowdale, Ontario, Canada.

YAMAUCHI, EDWIN M.
B.A., M.A., Ph.D., Professor of History, Miami University, Oxford, Ohio.

YOUNG, BRADFORD H.
B.A., M.A., Ph.D., Lecturer in Early Christianity and Judaism, Hebrew University, Jerusalem, Israel.

YOUNGBLOOD, RONALD F.
B.A., B.D., Ph.D., Professor of Old Testament and Hebrew, Bethel Theological Seminary, West Campus, San Diego, California.

ZORN, WALTER D.
B.A., M.Div., Ph.D., Professor of Biblical Languages and Old Testament, Great Lakes Bible College, Lansing, Michigan.

Abbreviations

GENERAL

A	Codex Alexandrinus (*See* Text and MSS of the NT I.B)
abbr.	abbreviated, abbreviation
act.	active
Akk.	Akkadian
Amer. Tr.	J. M. P. Smith and E. J. Goodspeed, *The Complete Bible: An American Translation*
Am.Tab.	el-Amarna Letters (*See* Amarna Tablets)
Apoc.	Apocrypha
Apost. Const.	Apostolic Constitutions
Aq.	Aquila's Greek version of the OT (*See* Septuagint)
Arab.	Arabic
Aram.	Aramaic
art.	article
Assyr.	Assyrian
ASV	American Standard Version
AT	Altes (or Ancien) Testament
AV	Authorized (King James) Version
b.	born
B	Codex Vaticanus (*See* Text and MSS of the NT I.B)
Bab.	Babylonian
bk.	book
Boh.	Bohairic (dialect of Coptic)
ca.	*circa,* about
Can.	Canaanite
cent., cents.	century, centuries
CG	Coptic Gnostic (*See* Nag Hammadi Literature)
ch., chs.	chapter(s)
Chald.	Chaldean, Chaldaic
col., cols.	column(s)
comm., comms.	commentary, commentaries
Copt.	Coptic
d.	died
D	Deuteronomist (*See* Criticism II.D.4); also Codex Bezae (*See* Text and MSS of the NT I.B)
diss.	dissertation
DSS	Dead Sea Scrolls
E	Elohist (*See* Criticism II.D.4); east
E.B.	Early Bronze (Age)
ed., eds.	editor, edition, edited (by), editors, editions
Egyp.	Egyptian
E.I.	Early Iron (Age)
Einl.	*Einleitung* (Introduction)
Eng. tr.	English translation
ERV	English Revised Version (1881-1885)
esp.	especially
et al.	and others
Eth.	Ethiopic, Ethiopian
f., ff.	following
fem.	feminine
fig.	figuratively
ft.	foot, feet
gal., gals.	gallon(s)
gen.	genitive
Ger.	German
Gk.	Greek
gm.	gram(s)
H	Law of Holiness (Lev. 17–26; *See* Criticism II.D.5)
ha.	hectare(s)
Heb.	Hebrew
Hist.	History
Hitt.	Hittite
Hom.	Homily
impf.	imperfect (tense)
in.	inch(es)
in loc.	at/on this passage
inscr.	inscription
intrans.	intransitive
intro., intros.	introduction(s)
J	Yahwist (*See* Criticism II.D.4)
JB	Jerusalem Bible
K	*kethibh* (*See* Text and MSS of the OT)
km.	kilometer(s)
l.	liter(s)
L	Lukan source (*See* Gospels, Synoptic V)
Lat.	Latin
L.B.	Late Bronze (Age)
lit.	literally
loc. cit.	in the place cited
LXX	Septuagint
m.	meter(s)
M	Matthaean source (*See* Gospels, Synoptic V)
masc.	masculine
M.B.	Middle Bronze (Age)
mg.	margin
mi.	mile(s)
mid.	middle voice

Midr.	Midrash
Mish.	Mishnah (*See* TALMUD I)
Moff.	J. Moffatt, *A New Translation of the Bible* (1926)
MS, MSS	manuscript(s)
MT	Mas(s)oretic Text (*See* TEXT AND MSS OF THE OT)
N	north
n., nn.	note(s)
NAB	New American Bible
NASB	New American Standard Bible
n.d.	no date
NEB	New English Bible
neut.	neuter
N.F.	*Neue Folge* (New Series)
NIV	New International Version
NJV	New Jewish Version
no., nos.	number(s)
N.S.	New Series
NT	New (Neues, Nouveau) Testament
Onk.	Onkelos (Targum)
op. cit.	in the work quoted
OT	Old Testament
Oxy. P.	Oxyrhynchus papyrus
p	papyrus (used only with superscript number of the papyrus)
P	Priestly Code (*See* CRITICISM II.D.5)
par.	(and) parallel passage(s)
para.	paragraph
part.	participle
pass.	passive
Pent.	Pentateuch
Pers.	Persian
Pesh.	Peshito, Peshitta (*See* VERSIONS)
pf.	perfect (tense)
Phoen.	Phoenician
pl.	plural
prob.	probably
pt., pts.	part(s)
Q	*Quelle* (*See* GOSPELS, SYNOPTIC V)
Q	*qere* (*See* TEXT AND MSS OF THE OT)
repr.	reprinted
rev.	revised (by)
RSV	Revised Standard Version
RV	Revised Version (ERV or ASV)
S	south
Sah.	Sahidic (dialect of Coptic)
Sam.	Samaritan
Sem.	Semitic
sing.	singular
sq.	square
subst.	substantive
Sum.	Sumerian
supp.	supplement(ary)
s.v.	*sub voce* (*vocibus*), under the word(s)
Symm.	Symmachus' Greek version of the OT (*See* SEPTUAGINT)
Syr.	Syriac
Talm.	Talmud
T.B.	Babylonian Talmud
Tg., Tgs.	Targum(s)
Th.	Theodotion's revision of the LXX (*See* SEPTUAGINT)
T.P.	Palestinian (Jerusalem) Talmud
TR	Textus Receptus (*See* TEXT AND MSS OF THE NT IV)
tr.	translation, translated (by)
trans.	transitive
Ugar.	Ugaritic
v., vv.	verse(s)
v.	*versus*
var.	variant
vb., vbs.	verb(s)
viz.	namely
vol., vols.	volume(s)
Vulg.	Vulgate (*See* VERSIONS)
W	west
yd., yds.	yard(s)

SYMBOLS

א	Codex Sinaiticus (*See* TEXT AND MSS OF THE NT I.B)
<	derived from (etymological)
=	is equivalent to
*	theoretical or unidentified form
§	section

PUBLICATIONS

AASOR	*Annual of the American Schools of Oriental Research*
AB	*Anchor Bible*
ADAJ	*Annual of the Department of Antiquities of Jordan*
AfO	*Archiv für Orientforschung*
AJSL	*American Journal of Semitic Languages and Literatures*
Alf.	Henry Alford, *Greek Testament* (4 vols., 1857-1861)
ANEP	J. B. Pritchard, ed., *The Ancient Near East in Pictures* (1954; 2nd ed. 1969)
ANET	J. B. Pritchard, ed., *Ancient Near Eastern Texts Relating to the Old Testament* (1950; 3rd ed. 1969)
ANT	M. R. James, *The Apocryphal New Testament* (1924; repr. 1953)
AOTS	D. W. Thomas, ed., *Archaeology and Old Testament Study* (1967)
AP	W. F. Albright, *The Archaeology of Palestine* (1949; rev. 1960)
APC	L. Morris, *Apostolic Preaching of the Cross* (3rd ed. 1965)
APOT	R. H. Charles, ed., *The Apocrypha and Pseudepigrapha of the Old Testament* (2 vols., 1913; repr. 1963)
ARAB	D. D. Luckenbill, ed., *Ancient Records of Assyria and Babylonia* (2 vols., 1926-1927)
ARI	W. F. Albright, *Archaeology and the Religion of Israel* (4th ed. 1956)
ARM	*Archives Royales de Mari* (1941–)
ATD	*Das Alte Testament Deutsch*
ATR	*Anglican Theological Review*
BA	*The Biblical Archaeologist*
BANE	G. E. Wright, ed., *The Bible and the Ancient Near East: Essays in Honor of William Foxwell Albright* (1961; repr. 1965, 1979)
BASOR	*Bulletin of the American Schools of Oriental Research*
Bauer	W. Bauer, *A Greek-English Lexicon of the New Testament,* tr. W. F. Arndt and F. W. Gingrich (1957; rev. ed.

[tr. F. W. Gingrich and F. W. Danker from 5th Ger. ed.] 1979)

BC — F. J. Foakes Jackson and K. Lake, eds., *The Beginnings of Christianity* (5 vols., 1920-1933)

BDB — F. Brown, S. R. Driver, and C. A. Briggs, *Hebrew and English Lexicon of the Old Testament* (1907)

BDF — F. Blass and A. Debrunner, *A Greek Grammar of the New Testament*, tr. and rev. R. W. Funk (1961)

BDTh — *Baker's Dictionary of Theology* (1960)

BH — R. Kittel, ed., *Biblia Hebraica* (3rd ed. 1937)

BHS — K. Elliger and W. Rudolph, eds., *Biblia Hebraica Stuttgartensia* (1967-1977)

BhHW — *Biblisch-historisches Handwörterbuch* (1962–)

BHI — J. Bright, *A History of Israel* (1959; 2nd ed. 1972; 3rd ed. 1981)

Bibl. — *Biblica*

BJRL — *Bulletin of the John Rylands Library*

BKAT — *Biblischer Kommentar, Altes Testament*

Bousset-Gressmann — W. Bousset, *Die Religion des Judentums im späthellenistischen Zeitalter*, rev. H. Gressmann (*HNT*, 21, 1926)

BZ — *Biblische Zeitschrift*

BZAW — *Beihefte zur Zeitschrift für die alttestamentliche Wissenschaft*

BZNW — *Beihefte zur Zeitschrift für die neutestamentliche Wissenschaft*

CAD — I. J. Gelb, *et al.*, eds., *Assyrian Dictionary of the Oriental Institute of the University of Chicago* (1956–)

CAH — *Cambridge Ancient History* (12 vols., rev. ed. 1962; 1970)

CBC — *Cambridge Bible Commentary on the New English Bible*

CBP — W. M. Ramsay, *Cities and Bishoprics of Phrygia* (1895-1897)

CBQ — *Catholic Biblical Quarterly*

CBSC — *Cambridge Bible for Schools and Colleges*

CCK — D. J. Wiseman, *Chronicles of Chaldaean Kings* (1956)

CD — K. Barth, *Church Dogmatics* (Eng. tr., 4 vols., 1936-1962)

CD — See Biblical and Extrabiblical Literature: Dead Sea Scrolls

CERP — A. H. M. Jones, *Cities of the Eastern Roman Provinces* (1937)

CG — P. Kahle, *The Cairo Geniza* (2nd ed. 1959)

CGT — *Cambridge Greek Testament* (20 vols., 1881-1933)

CHAL — W. L. Holladay, *A Concise Hebrew and Aramaic Lexicon of the Old Testament* (1971)

CIG — *Corpus Inscriptionum Graecarum* (1825-1859; index 1877)

CIL — *Corpus Inscriptionum Latinarum* (1862–)

ConNT — *Coniectanea Neotestamentica*

CRE — W. M. Ramsay, *The Church in the Roman Empire Before A.D. 170* (1903)

DBSup. — L. Pirot, *et al.*, eds., *Dictionnaire de la Bible: Supplement* (1928–)

DCG — J. Hastings, *Dictionary of Christ and the Gospels* (2 vols., 1906, 1908)

Deiss.*LAE* — G. A. Deissmann, *Light from the Ancient East* (Eng. tr., 2nd ed. 1927 [from German 4th ed.]; repr. 1978)

Dessau — H. Dessau, ed., *Inscriptiones Latinae Selectae* (3 vols., 2nd ed. 1954-1955)

DJD — *Discoveries in the Judean Desert*

DNTT — C. Brown, ed., *Dictionary of New Testament Theology* (3 vols., Eng. tr. 1975-1978)

DOTT — D. W. Thomas, ed., *Documents from Old Testament Times* (1958)

DTC — *Dictionnaire de Théologie Catholique* (15 vols., 1903-1950)

EAEHL — M. Avi-Yonah and E. Stern, eds., *Encyclopedia of Archaeological Excavations in the Holy Land* (4 vols., Eng. tr. 1975-1978)

EB — T. K. Cheyne and J. S. Black, eds., *Encyclopaedia Biblica* (4 vols., 1899)

Enc.Brit. — *Encyclopaedia Britannica*

EQ — *Evangelical Quarterly*

ERE — J. Hastings, *Encyclopaedia of Religion and Ethics* (12 vols., 1908-1926)

EtB — *Études Bibliques*

EvTh — *Evangelische Theologie*

Expos. — *The Expositor*

Expos.B. — *The Expositor's Bible* (3rd ed. 1903; rev. 1956)

Expos.G.T. — *The Expositor's Greek Testament*

Expos.T. — *Expository Times*

FRLANT — *Forschungen zur Religion und Literatur des Alten und Neuen Testaments*

FSAC — W. F. Albright, *From the Stone Age to Christianity* (2nd ed. 1957)

GAB — L. H. Grollenberg, *Atlas of the Bible* (1956)

GB — D. Baly, *Geography of the Bible* (1957; 2nd ed. 1974)

GJV — E. Schürer, *Geschichte des jüdischen Volkes im Zeitalter Jesu Christi* (3 vols., 4th ed. 1901-1909) (Converted to *HJP* when possible; but Eng. tr. not complete)

GKC — W. Gesenius, E. Kautzsch, and A. E. Cowley, *Gesenius' Hebrew Grammar* (2nd ed. 1910)

GP — F.-M. Abel, *Géographie de la Palestine* (2 vols., 2nd ed. 1933-1938)

GTTOT — J. Simons, *Geographical and Topographical Texts of the Old Testament* (1959)

HAT — *Handbuch zum Alten Testament*

HBD — M. S. Miller and J. L. Miller, eds., *Harper's Bible Dictionary* (1952; 2nd ed. 1961; 8th ed. [rev.] 1973)

HDB — J. Hastings, ed., *Dictionary of the Bible* (4 vols., 1898-1902, extra vol., 1904; rev. one-vol. ed. 1963)

HGHL — G. A. Smith, *Historical Geography of the Holy Land* (rev. ed. 1932)

HibJ — *The Hibbert Journal*

HJP — E. Schürer, *A History of the Jewish People in the Time of Jesus Christ* (Eng. tr. [of Ger. 3rd ed.] 1892-1901)

*HJP*² — E. Schürer, *The History of the Jewish People in the Age of Jesus Christ*, ed. G. Vermes and F. Millar (Eng. tr. and rev. 1973–)

HNT — *Handbuch zum Neuen Testament*

HNTC — *Harper's New Testament Commentaries = Black's New Testament Commentaries*

HNTT	R. H. Pfeiffer, *A History of New Testament Times with an Introduction to the Apocrypha* (1949)
HR	E. Hatch and H. A. Redpath, *Concordance to the Septuagint* (1897)
H-S	E. Hennecke and W. Schneemelcher, eds., *New Testament Apocrypha* (2 vols., Eng. tr. 1963, 1965)
HST	R. Bultmann, *History of the Synoptic Tradition* (Eng. tr., 2nd ed. 1968)
HTK	*Herders Theologischer Kommentar zum Neuen Testament*
HTR	*Harvard Theological Review*
HUCA	*Hebrew Union College Annual*
IB	*Interpreter's Bible* (12 vols., 1952-1957)
ICC	*International Critical Commentary*
IDB	*Interpreter's Dictionary of the Bible* (4 vols., 1962; Supplementary Volume, 1976)
IEJ	*Israel Exploration Journal*
ILC	J. Pedersen, *Israel: Its Life and Culture* (vols. I-II, Eng. tr. 1926; III-IV, Eng. tr. 1940)
Interp.	*Interpretation: A Journal of Bible and Theology*
IOTG	H. B. Swete, *Introduction to the Old Testament in Greek* (1902)
IP	M. Noth, *Die israelitischen Personennamen in Rahmen der gemeinsemitischen Namengebung* (1928)
ISBE	J. Orr, *et al.*, eds., *International Standard Bible Encyclopaedia* (2nd ed. 1929)
JAOS	*Journal of the American Oriental Society*
Jastrow	M. Jastrow, *Dictionary of the Targumim, the Talmud Babli, and the Midrashic Literature* (2 vols., 1950)
JBL	*Journal of Biblical Literature*
JBR	*Journal of Bible and Religion*
JCS	*Journal of Cuneiform Studies*
JEA	*Journal of Egyptian Archaeology*
JETS	*Journal of the Evangelical Theological Society*
Jew.Enc.	*Jewish Encyclopedia* (12 vols., 1901-1906)
JJS	*Journal of Jewish Studies*
JNES	*Journal of Near Eastern Studies*
JPOS	*Journal of the Palestinian Oriental Society*
JQR	*Jewish Quarterly Review*
JR	*Journal of Religion*
JSS	*Journal of Semitic Studies*
JTS	*Journal of Theological Studies*
KAI	H. Donner and W. Röllig, *Kanaanäische und Aramäische Inschriften* (3 vols., 2nd ed. 1966-1968)
KAT	E. Schrader, ed., *Die Keilinschriften und das Alte Testament* (3rd ed. 1903)
KD	K. F. Keil and F. Delitzsch, *Commentary on the Old Testament* (Eng. tr. 1864-1901; repr. 1973)
KEK	*Kritisch-exegetischer Kommentar über das Neue Testament*
KoB	L. Koehler and W. Baumgartner, *Lexicon in Veteris Testamenti Libros* (1953)
KS	A. Alt, *Kleine Schriften zur Geschichte des Volkes Israel* (3 vols., 1953-1959)
KZAT	*Kommentar zum Alten Testament*
KZNT	*Kommentar zum Neuen Testament*
Lange	Lange Commentaries
LAP	J. Finegan, *Light from the Ancient Past* (1946; rev. 1959)
LBHG	Y. Aharoni, *Land of the Bible: A Historical Geography* (Eng. tr. 1967)
LCC	*Library of Christian Classics*
LCL	*Loeb Classical Library*
LSC	W. M. Ramsay, *Letters to the Seven Churches of Asia* (1905)
LSJ	H. G. Liddell, R. Scott, H. S. Jones, *Greek-English Lexicon* (9th ed. 1940)
LTJM	A. Edersheim, *Life and Times of Jesus the Messiah* (8th ed., rev., 1904; repr. 1977)
LTK	Herder, *Lexicon für Theologie und Kirche* (2nd ed. 1957–)
MM	J. M. Moulton and G. Milligan, *The Vocabulary of the Greek New Testament* (1930)
MNHK	E. R. Thiele, *The Mysterious Numbers of the Hebrew Kings* (1965 ed.)
MNTC	*Moffatt New Testament Commentary*
MPB	H. N. and A. L. Moldenke, *Plants of the Bible* (1952)
MSt	J. McClintock and J. Strong, *Cyclopaedia of Biblical, Theological and Ecclesiastical Literature* (1891)
NBC	F. Davidson, ed., *New Bible Commentary* (1953)
NBD	J. D. Douglas, ed., *New Bible Dictionary* (1962)
NHI	M. Noth, *History of Israel* (Eng. tr. 1958; 2nd ed. 1960)
NICNT	*New International Commentary on the New Testament*
NICOT	*New International Commentary on the Old Testament*
Nov.Test.	*Novum Testamentum: An International Quarterly*
NTD	*Das Neue Testament Deutsch*
NTS	*New Testament Studies*
ODCC	*Oxford Dictionary of the Christian Church* (1957; 2nd ed. 1974)
ORHI	W. O. E. Oesterley and T. H. Robinson, *History of Israel* (2 vols., 1932)
OTG	H. B. Swete, *The Old Testament in Greek According to the Septuagint* (4th ed. 1912)
OTL	*Old Testament Library*
OTMS	H. H. Rowley, ed., *The Old Testament and Modern Study* (1951)
Pauly-Wissowa	A. Pauly and G. Wissowa, eds., *Real-Encyclopädie der classischen Altertumswissenschaft*
PEF	*Palestine Exploration Fund Memoirs*
PEQ	*Palestine Exploration Quarterly*
PG	J. P. Migne, ed., *Patrologia Graeca* (162 vols., 1857-1866)
PIOT	R. H. Pfeiffer, *Introduction to the Old Testament* (1952 [1957] ed.)
PJ	*Palästinajahrbuch*
PL	J. P. Migne, ed., *Patrologia Latina* (221 vols., 1844-1864)
PSBA	*Proceedings of the Society of Biblical Archaeology*
QHJ	A. Schweitzer, *The Quest of the Historical Jesus* (1906; Eng. tr., 2nd ed. 1936)
RAC	*Reallexikon für Antike und Christentum*

PSBA	*Proceedings of the Society of Biblical Archaeology*
QHJ	A. Schweitzer, *The Quest of the Historical Jesus* (1906; Eng. tr., 2nd ed. 1936)
RAC	*Reallexikon für Antike und Christentum*
RB	*Revue Biblique*
RGG	*Religion in Geschichte und Gegenwart* (5 vols., 3rd ed. 1957-1965)
RGJ	K. L. Schmidt, *Der Rahmen der Geschichte Jesu* (1919)
RHR	*Revue de l'histoire des religions*
RQ	*Revue de Qumran*
RRAM	D. Magie, *Roman Rule in Asia Minor* (2 vols., 1950)
RTWB	A. Richardson, ed., *A Theological Word Book of the Bible* (1950)
SB	H. L. Strack and P. Billerbeck, *Kommentar zum Neuen Testament aus Talmud und Midrasch* (5 vols., 1922-1961)
SBT	*Studies in Biblical Theology*
Sch.-Herz.	*The New Schaff-Herzog Encyclopedia of Religious Knowledge* (2nd ed. 1949-1952)
SE	*Studia Evangelica*
SJT	*Scottish Journal of Theology*
SPT	W. Ramsay, *St. Paul the Traveller and Roman Citizen* (1920)
SQE	K. Aland, ed., *Synopsis Quattor Evangeliorum* (2nd ed. 1964)
SSW	G. Dalman, *Sacred Sites and Ways* (Eng. tr. 1935)
ST	*Studia Theologica*
SVT	*Supplements to Vetus Testamentum*
SWP	C. R. Conder, *et al.*, eds., *Survey of Western Palestine* (9 vols., 1881-1888)
TDNT	G. Kittel and G. Friedrich, eds., *Theological Dictionary of the New Testament* (10 vols., Eng. tr. 1964-1976)
TDOT	G. J. Botterweck and H. Ringgren, eds., *Theological Dictionary of the Old Testament* (1974–)
THAT	E. Jenni and C. Westermann, eds., *Theologisches Handwörterbuch zum Alten Testament* (2 vols., 1971-1976)
Thayer	Thayer's *Greek-English Lexicon of the New Testament*
ThHK	*Theologischer Handkommentar zum Neuen Testament mit Text und Paraphrase* (7 vols., 1928-1939; rev. 1957–)
TLZ	*Theologische Literaturzeitung*
Torch	*Torch Bible Commentaries*
TR	*Theologische Rundschau*
TU	*Texte und Untersuchungen zur Geschichte der altchristlichen Literatur*
TWOT	R. L. Harris, *et al.*, eds., *Theological Wordbook of the Old Testament* (2 vols., 1980)
UT	C. Gordon, *Ugaritic Textbook* (*Analecta Orientalia*, 38, 1965)
VC	*Vigiliae Christianae*
VE	*Vox Evangelica*
VT	*Vetus Testamentum*
WA	Luther's *Werke*, Weimar Ausgabe (1883–)
Wace	H. Wace, ed., *Apocrypha* (*Speaker's Commentary*, 1888)
WBA	G. E. Wright, *Biblical Archaeology* (rev. ed. 1962)
WC	*Westminster Commentaries*
WHAB	G. E. Wright and F. V. Filson, eds., *Westminster Historical Atlas to the Bible* (1956)
WMANT	*Wissenschaftliche Monographien zum Alten und Neuen Testament*
WTJ	*Westminster Theological Journal*
ZAW	*Zeitschrift für die alttestamentliche Wissenschaft*
ZDPV	*Zeitschrift des deutschen Palästina-Vereins*
ZNW	*Zeitschrift für die neutestamentliche Wissenschaft*
ZTK	*Zeitschrift für Theologie und Kirche*

ANCIENT AUTHORS AND DOCUMENTS

Appian *Syr.*	*Syrian Wars*
Aquinas *Summa Theol.*	*Summa Theologica*
Aristotle *De an.*	*De anima* (*On the Soul*)
Eth. Nic.	*Nicomachaean Ethics*
Eth. Eud.	*Eudemaean Ethics*
Meta.	*Metaphysics*
Phys.	*Physics*
Pol.	*Politics*
Anal. post.	*Posterior Analytics*
Anal. pr.	*Prior Analytics*
Rhet.	*Rhetoric*
Poet.	*Poetics*
Augustine *Civ. Dei*	*De civitate Dei* (*The City of God*)
Conf.	*Confessiones*
De trin.	*De trinitate*
Ench.	*Enchiridion*
Ep.	*Epistulae*
Retr.	*Retractiones*
Calvin *Inst.*	*Institutes of the Christian Religion*
Chrysostom	
Hom. in Gen.	Homily on Genesis
Hom. in Heb.	Homily on Hebrews
Hom. in Jn.	Homily on John
Hom. in Mt.	Homily on Matthew
Clement of Alexandria	
Misc.	*Miscellanies* (*Stromateis*)
Paed.	*Paedagogus*
Curtius Rufus	Quintus Curtius Rufus
Digest	*See* ROMAN LAW II.G
Dio Cassius *Hist.*	*Roman History*
Hist. Epit.	Epitome of the *History*
Diodorus	Diodorus Siculus, *Library of History*
Diogenes	Diogenes Laertius, *Vitae philosophorum*
Epiphanius *Haer.*	*Adversus lxxx haereses* (*Panarion*)
Eusebius *HE*	*Historia ecclesiastica*
Onom.	*Onomasticon*
Praep. ev.	*Praeparatio evangelica*
HE	*Historia ecclesiastica* (*Church History*)
Herodotus	Herodotus *History*

Hippolytus *Ref.*	*Refutatio omnium haeresium (Philosophoumena)*
Homer *Il.*	*Iliad*
Od.	*Odyssey*
Irenaeus *Adv. haer.*	*Adversus omnes haereses*
Jerome *Ep.*	*Epistula(e)*
De vir. ill.	*De viris illustribus*
Adv. Pelag.	*Dialogi adversus Pelagianos*
Josephus *Ant.*	*Antiquities of the Jews*
BJ	*Bellum Judaicum (The Jewish War)*
CAp	*Contra Apionem*
Vita	*Life*
Justin Martyr *Apol.*	*Apologia*
Dial.	*Dialogus contra Tryphonem*
Livy *Epit.*	Epitomes of *Annals of the Roman People*
Origen *De prin.*	*De principiis*
Orosius	Orosius *Historiae*

ABBREVIATIONS

Pliny (the Elder) *Nat. hist.*	*Naturalis historia*
Pliny (the Younger) *Ep.*	*Epistulae*
Ptolemy *Geog.*	*Geography*
Sallust	*Bellum Catilinae*
Strabo *Geog.*	*Geography*
Sulpicius Severus *Chronicorum*	*Historia sacra*
Tacitus *Ann.*	*Annals (Annales ab excessu divi Augusti)*
Hist.	*Histories*
Tertullian *Adv. Judaeos*	*Adversus Judaeos*
Adv. Marc.	*Adversus Marcionem*
Adv. Prax.	*Adversus Praxean*
Apol.	*Apologeticum*
De orat.	*De oratione*
De praescr. haer.	*De praescriptione haereticòrum*
De res.	*De resurrectione carnis*
Vergil *Aen.*	*Aeneid*

BIBLICAL AND EXTRABIBLICAL LITERATURE

OLD TESTAMENT

Gen.	Genesis
Ex.	Exodus
Lev.	Leviticus
Nu.	Numbers
Dt.	Deuteronomy
Josh.	Joshua
Jgs.	Judges
	Ruth
1, 2 S.	1, 2 Samuel
1, 2 K.	1, 2 Kings
1, 2 Ch.	1, 2 Chronicles
Ezr.	Ezra
Neh.	Nehemiah
Est.	Esther
Job	Job
Ps.	Psalm(s)
Prov.	Proverbs
Eccl.	Ecclesiastes
Cant.	Canticles (Song of Songs)
Isa.	Isaiah
Jer.	Jeremiah
Lam.	Lamentations
Ezk.	Ezekiel
Dnl.	Daniel
Hos.	Hosea
	Joel
Am.	Amos
Ob.	Obadiah
	Jonah
Mic.	Micah
Nah.	Nahum
Hab.	Habakkuk
Zeph.	Zephaniah
Hag.	Haggai
Zec.	Zechariah
Mal.	Malachi

NEW TESTAMENT

Mt.	Matthew
Mk.	Mark
Lk.	Luke
Jn.	John
	Acts
Rom.	Romans
1, 2 Cor.	1, 2 Corinthians
Gal.	Galatians
Eph.	Ephesians
Phil.	Philippians
Col.	Colossians
1, 2 Thess.	1, 2 Thessalonians
1, 2 Tim.	1, 2 Timothy
Tit.	Titus
Philem.	Philemon
He.	Hebrews
Jas.	James
1, 2 Pet.	1, 2 Peter
1, 2, 3 Jn.	1, 2, 3 John
	Jude
Rev.	Revelation

APOCRYPHA

1, 2 Esd.	1, 2 Esdras
Tob.	Tobit
Jth.	Judith
Ad. Est.	Additions to Esther
Wisd.	Wisdom of Solomon
Sir.	Sirach (Ecclesiasticus)
Bar.	Baruch
Ep. Jer.	Epistle (Letter) of Jeremiah
Song Three	Song of the Three Young Men
Sus.	Susanna
Bel	Bel and the Dragon
Pr. Man.	Prayer of Manasseh
1, 2 Macc.	1, 2 Maccabees

PSEUDEPIGRAPHA

Asc. Isa.	Ascension of Isaiah
Asm. M.	Assumption of Moses
2 Bar.	2 (Syriac Apocalypse of) Baruch
3 Bar.	3 (Greek Apocalypse of) Baruch
1, 2 En.	1, 2 Enoch
Jub.	Jubilees
Ps. Sol.	Psalms of Solomon
Sib. Or.	Sibylline Oracles
XII P.	Testaments of the Twelve Patriarchs
T. Reub.	Testament of Reuben
T. Sim.	Testament of Simeon
T. Levi	Testament of Levi
T. Jud.	Testament of Judah
T. Iss.	Testament of Issachar
T. Zeb.	Testament of Zebulun
T. Dan	Testament of Dan
T. Naph.	Testament of Naphtali
T. Gad	Testament of Gad
T. Ash.	Testament of Asher
T. Jos.	Testament of Joseph
T. Benj.	Testament of Benjamin

APOSTOLIC FATHERS

Barn.	Epistle of Barnabas
1 Clem.	1 Clement
2 Clem.	2 Clement
Did.	Didache
Ign.	Ignatius of Antioch
Eph.	Epistle to the Ephesians
Magn.	Epistle to the Magnesians
Trall.	Epistle to the Trallians
Rom.	Epistle to the Romans
Philad.	Epistle to the Philadelphians
Smyrn.	Epistle to the Smyrnaeans
Polyc.	Epistle to Polycarp
Polyc. Phil.	Polycarp of Smyrna, Epistle to the Philippians
M. Polyc.	Martyrdom of Polycarp
Shep. Herm.	Shepherd of Hermas
Vis.	Visions
Mand.	Mandates
Sim.	Similitudes
Diogn.	Epistle to Diognetus

DEAD SEA SCROLLS

Initial arabic numeral indicates cave number;
Q = Qumrân; p = pesher (commentary).

CD	Damascus Document (Zadokite Fragment)
1QapGen	Genesis Apocryphon
1QH	Thanksgiving Hymns
1QIsa^{a}	First copy of Isaiah from Qumrân Cave 1
1QIsa^{b}	Second copy of Isaiah
1QM	War Scroll
1QpHab	Pesher (Commentary) on Habakkuk
1QpMic	Pesher on Micah
1QpPs	Pesher on Psalms
1QS	Manual of Discipline
1Q*34*^{bis}	Prayer for the Feast of Weeks (Fragment of Liturgical Prayer Scroll = 1Q Prayers)
1QDM (or 1Q*22*)	Sayings of Moses
3QInv (or 3Q*15*)	Copper (Treasure) Scroll
4QFlor	Florilegium (eschatological midrashim) from Cave 4
4QPBless	Patriarchal Blessings
4QpIsa$^{a, b, c, d}$	Copies of Isaiah pesher from Cave 4
4QpNah	Pesher on Nahum
4QpPs37	Pesher on Ps. 37
4QSam$^{a, b, c}$	Copies of Samuel
4QTestim	Testimonia text from Cave 4
6QD (or 6Q*15*)	Fragments of the Damascus Document

Transliteration Scheme

GREEK

α	*a*	ζ	*z*	λ	*l*	π	*p*	φ	*ph*
β	*b*	η	*ē*	μ	*m*	ϱ	*r, rh*	χ	*ch*
γ	*g, n*	θ	*th*	ν	*n*	σ	*s*	ψ	*ps*
δ	*d*	ι	*i*	ξ	*x*	τ	*t*	ω	*ō*
ε	*e*	ϰ	*k*	ο	*o*	υ	*y; u*	̔	*h*

HEBREW
(Consonants)

א	ʾ	ו	*w*	כ	*k, ḵ*	ע	ʿ	שׂ	*ś*
ב	*b, ḇ*	ז	*z*	ל	*l*	פ	*p, p̄*	שׁ	*š*
ג	*g, ḡ*	ח	*ḥ*	מ	*m*	צ	*ṣ*	ת	*t, ṯ*
ד	*d, ḏ*	ט	*ṭ*	נ	*n*	ק	*q*		
ה	*h*	י	*y*	ס	*s*	ר	*r*		

(Vowels)

ַ	*a*	ָה	*â*	furtive pataḥ	*(a)*
ָ	*ā*	ֶי	*e(y)*		
ֶ	*e*	ֵי	*ê*	vocal shewa	ᵉ
ֵ	*ē*	ֵיּ	*êy*	ֲ	ᵃ
ִ	*i*	ִי	*î*	ֱ	ᵉ̆
ָ	*o*	ִיּ	*îy*	ֳ	ᵒ
ֹ	*ō*	וֹ	*ô*		
ֻ	*u*	וּ	*û*		

Pronunciation Key

a	at, sad	i	in, lid	o͞o	fool, rude	y	yes, beyond		
ä	arm, father	ī	idea, by	ou	out, how	z	zeal, fuse		
ā	ate, face	j	jaw, ridge	p	pan, map	zh	vision, treasure		
â(r)	air, spare	k	keep, lake	r	ran, far				
b	ball, tab	l	leaf, meal	s	see, pass				
ch	church, match	m	meet, team	sh	share, push	ə	used for very		
d	door, bid	n	new, run	t	take, sat		short vowels		
dh	th in then, bathe	ng	angle, thing	th	thank, wrath		with the sound of:		
e	end, met	o	odd, top	u	up, love		a in about		
ē	evil, be	ō	obey, go	ū	use, few		e in system		
f	find, calf	ô	organ	û(r)	urn, fern		i in rarity		
g	get, tag	oi	oil, boy	v	very, wave		o in lemon		
h	hear, ahead	oo	book, pull	w	wipe, away		u in focus		

WADI wä'dē [Arab. *wâdī*]. A valley through which water runs during the rainy seasons and which is dry the rest of the year. The term frequently is used in the names of watercourses (e.g., Wâdī en-Nâr, "river of fire," which is the valley through which the confluence of the Kidron and Hinnom valleys flows). The Hebrew equivalent is *naḥal,* whose translation "torrent, torrent valley" is appropriate only during flash floods (cf. Jgs. 5:21). W. S. L. S.

The Wadi Shuʿaib in the as-Salt vicinity, Amman (R. H. Smith)

WAFER [Heb. *rāqîq*–'thin cake' < *rqq*–'be thin' (Ex. 29:2, 23; Lev. 2:4; 7:12; 8:26; Nu. 6:15, 19; 1 Ch. 23:29), *ṣappîḥiṯ*–'flat cake' (Ex. 16:31)]; AV also CAKE (1 Ch. 23:29); NEB also FLAT CAKE. All references to "wafer" in the RSV (except Ex. 16:31) are associated with various offerings. *See* SACRIFICES AND OFFERINGS IN THE OT; BREAD IV.

WAGES [(vb.) Heb. *śāḵar* (Hag. 1:6); (subst.) Heb. *śāḵār* (Gen. 30:28; Ezk. 29:19; Mal. 3:5), *maśkōreṯ* (Gen. 29:15; 31:7, 41), *peʿullâ* (Lev. 19:13), *pōʿal* (Job 7:2), *meḥîr* (Dt. 23:18 [MT 19]; Gk. *misthós* (Rom. 6:23), *opsṓnion* (Lk. 3:14)]; AV also HIRE (Gen. 30:32f.; 31:8; 1 K. 5:6 (MT 20); Zec. 8:10; Mt. 20:8; Lk. 10:7; Jas. 5:4), PRICE (Zec. 11:12), WORK (Job 7:2), REWARD (Rom. 4:4; 1 Cor. 3:8; 1 Tim. 5:18), LABOR (Prov. 10:16); NEB also PAY (Ex. 2:9; Jn. 4:36), PROFIT (Prov. 11:18). Recompense for services rendered.

The Hebrew verb *śāḵar* and its derivatives, *śāḵār* and *maśkōreṯ,* in the OT always refer to literal payment, although money, per se, dates only to the introduction of coinage in the late 8th cent. B.C. Thus while Zechariah can speak of his wages as thirty shekels of silver (Zec. 11:12 — a passage applied to Jesus' betrayal by Judas in Mt. 27:9), earlier wages include Laban's cattle (and daughters!) for Jacob (Gen. 29:15; 30:28), wheat and oil for King Hiram (1 K. 5:11), and the land of Egypt and its booty for Nebuchadrezzar's army (Ezk. 29:19).

From the Hebrew verb *pāʿal* ("make," "work") derive the substantives *pōʿal* and *peʿullâ*. The former often refers to God's mighty acts in history or to a person's moral actions. Thus Prov. 11:18 speaks of "deceptive wages" that the wicked earn. Elsewhere, though, only ordinary recompense seems in view — the slave longing for his day's wage (Job 7:2) and the neighbor not receiving payment for his service (Jer. 22:13). *Peʿullâ* is used twice as a clear synonym for *śāḵar* (in the otherwise antithetical parallelism of Prov. 11:18, and as the pay which a hired servant must receive before nightfall each day lest he go hungry in Lev. 19:13).

The origin of Heb. *meḥîr* is uncertain, perhaps from the root *mḥr* (see BDB, pp. 563f.). Its basic meaning seems to be "price" or "reward" (cf. Job 28:15; Isa. 45:13; 55:1; Mic. 3:11).

In the NT all but one of the occurrences of "wages" translate the Gk. *misthós*. Again the term may refer to literal payment, as in the parable of the vineyard laborers (Mt. 20:8), where the only scriptural reference to a standard wage appears — the daily denarius for a common field laborer (v. 2). So too Jesus cites Levitical precedent (cf. Jgs. 17:10) to argue that "the laborer deserves his wages" (Lk. 10:7 — in this context food and drink for the seventy itinerant preachers), a saying quoted by Paul (as Scripture!) encouraging churches to provide for their elders (1 Tim. 5:18). James echoes a common complaint of OT prophecy — the rich are defrauding the poor of a decent wage (Jas. 5:4; cf. esp. Mal. 3:5). Ancient Israel regularly had a large working class exploited by a few rich landowners with very little "middle class" in between.

On the other hand, the NT "wage" frequently takes on spiritual or symbolic overtones. Paul declares that "to one who works, his wages are not reckoned as a gift but as his due" (Rom. 4:4), applying the literal meaning of "work" and "wage" to the spiritual realm, and contrasting justification by legalism with that of grace. In his famous dictum, "the wages of sin is death" (Rom. 6:23), only this symbolic usage remains, as eternal death is directly contrasted with the free gift of eternal life. Similarly, Jesus' disciples receive "wages" as they accomplish the work of God and "gather fruit for eternal life" (Jn. 4:36).

In one instance, however, *misthós* in this symbolic sense seems to refer to more than just eternal life and death. Paul speaks of the rewards Christians will receive according to the type of works they have erected upon the foundation of faith in Christ (1 Cor. 3:8-14). Many interpreters believe that Paul envisaged different levels of reward above and beyond life in heaven itself. But this seems to contradict the conclusion of the above-mentioned parable of Jesus that graphically illustrates how first and last shall receive equal "pay" (Mt. 20:16). It is better, therefore, to see the reward for good works as the endurance rather than destruction of those works when tested by fire, and of the satisfaction of seeing one's activity produce lasting results, rather than to interpret it as degrees of further recompense in heaven.

The final NT use of "wages" translates *opsṓnion,* which originally referred to payment for food, primarily in military contexts. This is how John the Baptist uses it when he tells a soldier to be content with his rations (Lk. 3:14). In sum, Scripture strongly supports fair payment for human labor, but recognizes that for spiritual work, merit pay can lead only to condemnation. Only God's intervening grace can save, but subsequent Christian living produces rewards of many types in this life.

See also HIRE; MONEY.

Bibliography.–*DNTT,* III, 138-144; *TDNT,* IV, *s.v.* μισθός κτλ. (Preisker, Würthwein); *TWOT,* I, 500; II, 730, 878; A. C. Bouquet, *Everyday Life in NT Times* (1953), pp. 123-141.

C. L. BLOMBERG

WAGON [Heb. *ʿagālâ*–'chariot, cart' (Gen. 45:19, 21, 27; 46:5; Nu. 7:3, 6-8), *galgal*–'chariot wheel' (Ezk. 23:24; 26:10)]; AV, NEB, also WHEEL. *See* CART.

WAHEB wä'heb. In Nu. 21:14 Heb. *wāhēḇ bᵉsûpâ* is apparently the first of a group of lines (vv. 14f.) from "the Book of the Wars of the Lord" identifying a region centered on the Arnon River, the northern boundary of Moab (cf. v. 13). RSV "Waheb in Suphah" and NEB "Vaheb in Suphah" take it as such and understand the two terms as place names. In this they are most likely correct, although precise identification of the places represented is not possible (see the comms.). The LXX (*Zōob*) and Old Latin versions reflect a Hebrew text reading *zāhāḇ,* one of the places mentioned in Dt. 1:1. AV "what he did in the Red Sea" follows Vulg. (which follows, in turn, early Jewish treatment of the words reflected in the Targum) and may take *wāhēḇ* as a form of the root *yhb,* which is, however, known not in Biblical Hebrew but in later Aramaic, Syriac, and Arabic. (The AV reading also takes *sûpâ* as *yam sûp,* "Red Sea.")

See also SUPHAH.

J. W. S.

WAIL; WAILING [Heb. hiphil of *yālal,* (noun) *yᵉlālâ*] (Isa. 15:2; Jer. 4:8; Joel 1:5; etc.); AV HOWL; NEB also HOWL, "derided" (Isa. 52:5, reading *yᵉhullᵉlû* [from *hālal*] for *yᵉhêlîlû*), etc.; [Heb. *mispēḏ*] (Am. 5:16f.; Mic. 1:11); AV also MOURNING; NEB also LAMENTATION; [Heb. *nāhâ, nᵉhî, nî*] (Jer. 9:10, 18f. [MT 9, 17f.]; Ezk. 27:32; 32:18; Mic. 2:4); AV also LAMENT; NEB also LAMENT(ATION); [Heb. *zāʿaq*] (Est. 4:1; Ezk. 27:30); AV CRY; NEB CRY, EXCLAIM; [Gk. *thrēnéō*] (Mt. 11:17 par. Lk. 7:32); AV MOURN; NEB WEEP AND WAIL; [Gk. *alalázō*] (Mk. 5:38); [Gk. *klauthmós*] (Mt. 2:18); AV WEEPING; [Gk. *kóptō*] (Rev. 1:7; 18:9); AV and NEB also LAMENT. In Hos. 10:5 RSV "wail" and NEB "howl" are based on emendation of MT *yāgîlû* (from *gîl,* "rejoice," followed by AV) to *yaylîlû* (from *yālal*).

"Wail" in the RSV most often represents the Hebrew root *yll* (hiphil of *yālal* and the noun *yᵉlālâ*), which is found only in the prophetic books (except for *yᵉlēl* in Dt. 32:10). *Yll* designates a scream or cry of agony or despair and appears where the people of Israel are called to the community's assembly for prayer and repentance responding to or anticipating disaster (Jer. 4:8; 25:34; Joel 1:13; Zeph. 1:10f.; Zec. 11:2f.). *Yll* is not used in connection with mourning for the dead; a consistent feature of its use is that a disaster affecting a whole community elicits the wail of despair (Isa. 52:5; Jer. 25:36; 47:2; Ezk. 21:12; Joel 1:5, 11; Am. 8:3; Mic. 1:8). But Jer. 51:8 (cf. Rev. 18:2, 9) suggests that it might have been used outside Israel in reference to mourning for individuals. Its use in relation to idolatry in Hos. 7:14 again suggests that *yll* might have been associated with foreign practices. The summons to community wailing also appears in oracles against foreign nations — as a part of a prediction of unavoidable catastrophe rather than as a call to repentance (Isa. 13:6; 14:31; 16:7; 23:1, 6, 14; Jer. 48:20; 49:3; Ezk. 30:2; cf. Isa. 15:2f., 8). Isa. 65:14 distinguishes between the obedient and the rebellious in a single community, referring to the latter as those who will wail.

Other OT words translated "wail" or "wailing" also signify lamentation for disasters experienced by entire communities (Est. 4:1; Jer. 9:10, 18f.; Ezk. 27:30, 32; 32:18; Am. 5:16f.; Mic. 1:11; 2:4).

In the NT "wail" is generally used in references to practices of community mourning for the dead (Mt. 2:18; 11:17 par. Lk. 7:32; Mk. 5:38; Rev. 1:7). Matthew's use of Jer. 31:15 in Mt. 2:18 has provoked much discussion, for Matthew seems to misapply that prophecy. But as several commentators have noted, Matthew has reapplied this OT text to a NT situation in a way that emphasizes the key theme of salvation (cf., e.g., R. E. Brown, *Birth of the Messiah* [1977], pp. 216f., 221-23; R. H. Gundry, *Matthew* [1982], pp. 35-37).

See also BURIAL; LAMENT; WEEP.

Bibliography.–*TDOT,* VI, *s.v.* "yll" (Baumann); H. W. Wolff, *ZAW,* 76 (1964), 48-56.

J. W. SIMPSON, JR.

WAIT [Heb. niphal, piel, and hiphil of *yāḥal* (Jgs. 3:25; 1 S. 13:8; Job 6:11; 14:14; Ps. 31:24 [MT 25]; Isa. 42:4; Lam. 3:26; etc.), piel of *ḥāḵâ* (2 K. 7:9; Job 32:4; Ps. 106:13; Isa. 8:17; 30:18; 64:4; Dnl. 12:12; Hos. 6:9; Hab. 2:3; Zeph. 3:8), qal and piel of *qāwâ* (Gen. 49:18; Job 30:26; Ps. 27:14; 56:6 [MT 7]; 119:95; Isa. 25:9; Lam. 3:25; etc.), hithpalpel of *māhah*–'linger' (2 S. 15:28), piel of *śāḇar*–'hope,' 'wait' (Ruth 1:13), *yāšaḇ*–'sit' (Ruth 3:18; 1 S. 1:23), *ʿāmaḏ*–'stand' (Nu. 9:8; 2 S. 17:17; 1 K. 1:2; 20:38), *šāmar*–'watch' (Job 24:15; Prov. 8:34), *nû(a)ḥ*–'rest,' 'wait' (1 S. 25:9; Hab. 3:16), hithpael of yāšaḇ–'take one's stand' (Ex. 8:20 [MT 16]), niphal of *nāṣaḇ*–'stand' (Ex. 5:20; 7:15), *hāyâ*–'be' (Ex. 24:12; 2 K. 5:2), *dāmam*–'stand still' (1 S. 14:9), *dûmîyâ*–'silence' ("wait in silence," Ps. 62:1, 5 [MT 2, 6]), piel of *šārat̲* ("wait on," Gen. 40:4), *ṣāḏâ* ("lie in wait," Ex. 21:13), *yāšaḇ ʾereḇ* ("lie in wait," Job 38:40), *ʾāraḇ* ("lie in wait," Dt. 19:11; Jgs. 9:32; Prov. 1:11; Lam. 3:10; etc.); Gk. *aphíēmi*–'let go,' 'leave' (Mt. 27:49 par. Mk. 15:36), *ekdéchomai*–'wait for' (Acts 17:16; 1 Cor. 11:33; He. 10:13; Jas. 5:7), *apekdéchomai*–'expect eagerly' (Rom. 8:19, 23, 25; 1 Cor. 1:7; Gal. 5:5; He. 9:28; 1 Pet. 3:20), *prosdéchomai*–'accept,' 'expect' (Lk. 12:36; Acts 23:21; Jude 21), *ménō*–'stay,' 'wait' (Acts 20:5), *anaménō*–'wait for' (1 Thess. 1:10), *periménō*–'wait for, endure' (Acts 1:4), *méllō*–'be about to' (Acts 22:16), *prosdokáō*–'wait for, expect' (Lk. 1:21; 8:40; Acts 28:6; 2 Pet. 3:12-14), *enedreúō* ("lie in wait," Lk. 11:54), *proskarteréō* ("wait on," Acts 10:7)]; AV also TARRY, STAY, STAND STILL, LET BE, WATCH, etc.; NEB also LINGER, DELAY, WATCH, LAY SNARES, etc.

The verb "wait" occurs in different contexts and has a variety of meanings. The distinctions among these various senses often, but not always, reflect different underlying biblical terms.

Several Hebrew verbs, primarily *qāwâ* (usually piel), *ḥāḵâ* (piel), and *yāḥal* (usually piel or hiphil), signify waiting with hope or expectation. Heb. *qāwâ,* the most clearly defined of the group (cf. the derived noun *tiqwâ,* "hope"), occurs only in poetry, being common especially in Isaiah (25:9; 26:8; 33:2; etc.) and the Psalms (25:5, 21; 27:14; 37:34; etc.). Its object is almost always "the Lord" (*see also* Look I). In Ps. 56:6 (MT 7) and 119:95, however, this verb seems to mean waiting in ambush. Similarly, in Hos. 6:9 *ḥāḵâ* seems to mean "lie in wait (for ambush)" (although the text is open to question), but elsewhere this verb means to wait patiently. Although it is used in a variety of contexts, in the Psalms and prophetic books it often has Yahweh as its object. *Yāḥal* (cf. derived noun *tôḥelet̲,* "expectation, hope") is often used in synonymous parallelism with *qāwâ* (cf. Job 30:26; Ps. 130:5; Isa. 51:5; Lam. 3:25f.; etc.). Although it is sometimes used with other objects (e.g., human beings, Job 29:21, 23; Mic. 5:7 [MT 6]) or with no object (e.g., Gen. 8:10, 12; 1 S. 10:8), this verb also occurs frequently with Yahweh or God as its object (2 K. 6:33; Ps. 37:7; 38:15 [MT 16]; 69:3 [MT 4]; etc.).

Underlying the expression "wait for the Lord/God" is the faith that Yahweh is a God who delivers those who put their Hope in Him. But this expression also implies a faith that is willing to operate on God's time rather than one's own. The emphasis may be on waiting with endurance and patience (which does not exclude the frequent cry, "How long, O Lord?") or on confident assurance (e.g., cf. Ps. 27:13f.). But in each case the biblical author recognizes that it is God's people who must conform to God's design for history.

In the NT the expression "wait for the Lord/God" does not occur, but the theme of expectant waiting is strong, particularly with reference to the eschatological hope. Christian expectation centers on the return of Christ (1 Cor. 1:7; 1 Thess. 1:10; cf. Lk. 12:36; Jude 21), on the "coming day of God" that will usher in "new heavens and a new earth" (2 Pet. 3:12-14), and on the full manifestation of those who have been adopted as "sons of God" (Rom. 8:23; cf. vv. 19, 25). (*See also* Eschatology IV, X.)

"Wait" has negative connotations when it is used in the expression "lie in wait." This is a common translation of Heb. *ʾāraḇ,* which has the same overtones of violence and treachery that the phrase "lie in wait" has in English. Its NT counterpart, Gk. *enedreúō,* is used only twice: once literally, of the Jews' plot to assassinate Paul (Acts 23:21; RSV "lie in ambush"), and once figuratively, of the Pharisees' attempt to trap Jesus with words (Lk. 11:54). Heb. *ṣāḏâ,* on the other hand, might be translated more generally as "go hunting," with either stalking or ambush as a possible meaning. The RSV supplies "lie in wait" in Jer. 5:26; here the context refers to evildoers trapping the innocent, but the text is corrupt.

The third major sense of "wait" is that of domestic service, to "wait on" someone. Although in Gen. 40:4 Heb. *šārat̲* (piel) is used of Joseph's service to other prisoners, it is more commonly used of the temple service of the priests and Levites. To "wait on" someone can also be expressed with the Hebrew verbs for "stand" (*ʿāmaḏ,* 1 K. 1:2) or "be" (*hāyâ,* 2 K. 5:2) in someone's presence. The NT equivalent is Gk. *proskarteréō* (lit. "adhere to," "attach oneself to"; Acts 10:7).

Bibliography.–*TDOT,* III, *s.v.* "dāmāh II" (A. Baumann); IV, *s.v.* "chākhāh" (C. Barth); VI, *s.v.* "yāḥal" (C. Barth); *TDNT,* II, *s.v.* δέχομαι κτλ. (W. Grundmann).

G. CHAMBERLAIN N. J. O.

WALK [Heb. *hālaḵ*–'go, walk' (Gen. 24:65; Ex. 18:20; Lev. 18:3; etc.), *sāḇaḇ*–'march around' (Ps. 48:12 [MT 13], *ʾāšar*–'walk straight (ahead)' (Prov. 9:6), *ṣāʿaḏ*–'step, march' (Jer. 10:5), tiphel of *rāgal*–'teach to walk' (Hos. 11:3), *ʿāḇar*–'go by, pass' (Zeph. 3:6); Aram. *hᵃlaḵ* (haphel, Dnl. 3:25; 4:37 [MT 34]); pael, 4:29 [MT 26]); Gk. *peripatéō*–'go about, walk around', *poreúomai*–'go, proceed, travel' (Lk. 1:6; Acts 9:31; 14:16; Jude 11), *stoichéō*–'hold to, agree with, follow' (Gal. 5:25; 6:16), *proágō*–'go before, lead, precede' (Mk. 10:32)]; AV also GO, PASS BY, etc.; NEB also FOLLOW, BEHAVE, CONFORM, GO, etc.

I. In the OT.–*A. Terminology.* The term most frequently translated "walk" in the RSV OT is Heb. *hālaḵ,* which occurs in various forms: in the qal nearly two hundred times, in the piel eleven times (e.g., Ps. 81:13 [MT 14]; 86:11; 89:15 [MT 16]; Prov. 6:28; 8:20; Eccl. 11:9; Ezk. 18:9), in the hithpael ("go to and fro," "go about") thirty-three times (e.g., Gen. 3:8; 5:22, 24; 6:9; 17:1; Lev. 26:12; 2 K. 20:3; Job 1:7; 2:2; Ps. 26:3; Prov. 6:22), and in the hiphil ("cause to go," "bring") three times (Lev. 26:13; Jer. 31:9; Ezk. 36:12). It refers literally to the walking of persons or animals, but it can also be used figuratively in the sense of "live," especially in regard to one's moral or religious life. "Walk" also appears in anthropomorphic statements (e.g., Gen. 3:8; Job 1:7; 2:2).

In Hos. 11:3 the form of the Hebrew verb *rāgal,* "teach to walk," may be a tiphel (see GKC, § 55h; but cf. F. I. Andersen and D. N. Freedman, *Hosea* [*AB,* 1980], p. 579).

B. OT Use of Hālaḵ. *1. Literal Uses.* Examples that indicate the concrete spatial meaning include walking backward (Gen. 9:23), through the land (13:17), in a field (24:65), beside a river (Ex. 2:5), on dry ground (14:29; 15:19), upon a roof (2 S. 11:2), in a house (2 K. 4:35), on hot coals (Prov. 6:28), or in the streets (Lam. 4:18).

2. Figurative Uses. Ps. 1:1 declares "Blessed is the man who walks not in the counsel of the wicked." This represents only one of many references for the figurative use of *hālaḵ.* Others include walking in darkness (Ps. 82:5;

Prov. 2:13; Isa. 59:9), in fellowship with another person (Ps. 55:14 [MT 15]), in the midst of trouble (138:7), with sinners (Prov. 1:15), and in pride (Dnl. 4:37 [MT 34]). Figurative uses of "walk" occur in the following common phrases.

a. Walking in God's Laws/Statutes/Commandments/Ordinances/Truth. "Walk" frequently occurs in phrases referring to walking in God's law (Heb. *tôrâ*); e.g., those who walk in the law of the Lord are blessed (Ps. 119:1). Obedience to the Lord characterizes a proper walk (Ex. 16:4). 2 Ch. 6:16 states that the Lord made certain promises to David if his sons would "walk in my law as you [David] walked before me." Ps. 78:10 says that the Ephraimites "did not keep God's covenant, but refused to walk according to his law" (cf. Neh. 10:29 [MT 30]). Jer. 26:4f. indicates that those who did not obey God's voice or walk in His law would receive His judgment (also see 32:23; 44:23; cf. 2 K. 10:31).

"Walking in God's statutes" (Heb. *ḥuqqâ*, "something prescribed") also appears frequently (e.g., Lev. 18:4; 26:3; 1 K. 6:12; Ezk. 11:12; 18:9, 17). Ezk. 5:6f. indicate that God's people (Jerusalem) had not walked in His statutes or kept His ordinances; 20:13, 16 say that Israel rebelled in the wilderness and refused to walk in His statutes (cf. 20:18f., 21); but God's gracious provision of a new heart and a new spirit would give new motivation to His people to walk in His statutes, keep His ordinances, and obey Him (Ezk. 11:20; cf. esp. 36:26f.).

Several other phrases also occur, including "walking in God's commandments [Heb. *miṣwâ*]"; e.g., in 1 K. 6:12 the Lord affirms to Solomon that He will dwell with His people if Solomon walks in His statutes; Prov. 6:22 says that a father's commandments guide the walk of a faithful son. Ps. 89:30 (MT 31) states that punishment awaits those who fail to walk in God's ordinances (Heb. *mišpāṭ*). In Ps. 86:11 the psalmist prays for guidance: "Teach me thy way, O Lord, that I may walk in thy truth [*'ᵉmeṯ*, "faithfulness"]."

Although the ideal conduct is to walk in the laws of God, it is also possible to walk in the "statutes" (Heb. *ḥuqqâ*) of foreign gods (Lev. 18:3), as well as the "customs" (*ḥōq*) of other gods (Lev. 20:23; 2 K. 17:8, 19; see esp. 2 K. 17:7-18).

b. Walking in God's Way(s). This phrase occurs quite frequently (e.g., Dt. 5:33; 8:6; 11:22; 19:9; 26:17; 1 K. 2:3; 3:14; 8:58, 61; 2 Ch. 6:31; Isa. 30:21; Jer. 6:16; 7:23; Zec. 3:7). The term "way" (Heb. *dereḵ*) in this phrase refers to the conduct required by God. In 1 K. 3:14 God promises longevity to Solomon if he walks in His ways; 1 K. 11:33 reveals Solomon's failure to do so. Ps. 81:13 (MT 14) parallels listening to God with walking in His ways. Ps. 119:3 testifies, "Blessed are those . . . who also do no wrong, but walk in his ways," while 128:1 declares, "Blessed is every one who fears the Lord, who walks in his ways!" Similarly, in Jer. 7:23 God commands His people to walk in His way, "that it may be well with [them]." "In the last analysis, what we are concerned with here is adherence to Yahweh alone and exclusive fidelity to him" (*TDOT*, III, 396).

c. Walking before the Lord. In Gen. 17:1 the Lord commands Abram to "Walk before [Heb. *lᵉpānay*, lit. "to the face of"] me, and be blameless" (see esp. 1 K. 2:4; 3:6; 8:23, 25; 9:4 and par. in 2 Ch. 6–7). "God orders Abraham (now representing Israel) to live his life before God in such a way that every single step is made with reference to God and every day experiences him close at hand" (C. Westermann, *Genesis 12–36* [Eng. tr. 1985], p. 259). Gen. 24:40 and 48:15f. testify to the faithful walks of Abraham's servant (Eliezer?), Abraham, and Isaac before the Lord. In 2 K. 20:3 (par. Isa. 38:3) King Hezekiah claims that he also walked before the Lord in faithfulness. "By itself *hālakh*/*hithhallēkh* means "live"; in conjunction with *liphnê yhvh* . . . it refers to the way of life God requires" (*TDOT*, III, 393).

d. Walking after the Lord. Appearing in a context of warnings against idolatry, Dt. 13:4 (MT 5) commands, "You shall walk after the Lord your God and fear him, and keep his commandments and obey his voice, and you shall serve him and cleave to him." Also, in 2 K. 23:3 Josiah agreed "to walk after the Lord and to keep his commandments and his testimonies and his statutes, with all his heart and all his soul, to perform the words of this covenant that were written in this book; and all the people joined in the covenant." In the phrase "walk after the Lord" the word "after" translates Heb. *'aḥᵃrê*, which means "in accordance with"; thus in this phrase it indicates a relationship that is governed by a norm. When it applies to other gods "following after" means cultic worship, but "when it applies to Yahweh, it means fulfilment of God's law, especially the commandments to accept Yahweh exclusively" (*TDOT*, III, 395; also see I, 204-207).

e. Walking with God. The OT mentions several notable individuals who "walked with God," e.g., Enoch (Gen. 5:22, 24) and Noah (6:9). In Enoch's case this expression may suggest that he "stood in a direct and immediate relationship to God" (C. Westermann, *Genesis 1–11* [Eng. tr. 1984], p. 358). Noah, who was "righteous" (Heb. *ṣaddîq*) toward human beings and "blameless" (*tāmîm*) before God, also "walked with God." This seems to imply a very intimate and personal fellowship between God and Noah. The LXX uses the Greek verb *euarestéō*, "be well pleasing," to translate Heb. *hālaḵ*. In Mic. 6:8 one of the Lord's requirements is "to walk humbly with your God," a stipulation that "goes beyond the summons to do justice and love kindness; it means setting God at the center of human life" (*TDOT*, III, 395). Also, "peace and righteousness" characterized Levi's walk with the Lord (Mal. 2:6).

f. Walking contrary to God. This particular phrase appears only in Lev. 26, a chapter that concludes the Holiness Code (chs. 17–26) with various divine warnings and promises. The RSV has "contrary" for Heb. *qᵉrî*, "(hostile) encounter, meeting" (KoB, p. 855), a term that implies fighting against another person. The passages state that if God's people "walk contrary to [Him]" (vv. 21, 23, 27, 40), then He will "walk contrary to [them]" (vv. 24, 28, 41), i.e., He will mete out various punishments to discipline His people.

g. Walking in One's Integrity. Both Psalms and Proverbs refer to individuals who walked in integrity; e.g., David maintained that he walked in his integrity (Ps. 26:1, 11). In this phrase in the RSV "integrity" translates Heb. *tōm* and *tāmîm*, both of which are cognate with the verb *tāmam*, "be complete." In the OT "integrity" essentially means "'soundness of character and adherence to moral principle,' i.e., uprightness and honesty" (*ISBE*, II, 857). OT individuals who possessed this noble quality included Abraham (Gen. 20:5f.), David (1 K. 9:4), Job (Job 2:3, 9; 4:6; 27:5; 31:6), and psalmists (Ps. 7:8; 25:21; 41:12; 101:2). In Proverbs "integrity" typifies the upright person; e.g., God protects those who possess it (2:7); those who walk in it are assured security (10:9; 28:18; cf. 2:21; 20:7); it is preferable to material wealth (19:1; 28:6).

h. Walking in the Ways of Israel's Rulers. The OT frequently mentions the failures of Israel's leaders and kings. Samuel's sons, e.g., did not walk in his (righteous) ways, but "took bribes and perverted justice" (1 S. 8:3, 5). Jgs. 2:17 rehearses Israel's apostasy, viz., how they failed to walk like their fathers, who had obeyed God's commands. Very often the OT speaks about the kings of Israel and Judah who "walked in the [evil] way(s) of his father" (e.g., Nadab, 1 K. 15:26; Ahaziah of Israel, 22:52; Amon, 2 K. 21:21), or "in the sins/way of Jeroboam" (e.g., Baasha, 1 K. 15:34; Zimri, 16:19; Omri, 16:26; Ahab, 16:31; Jehoahaz, 2 K. 13:6; Jehoash, 13:11; the people of Israel, 17:22), or "in the way of the kings of Israel" (e.g., Jehoram, 2 K. 8:18 par. 2 Ch. 21:6; Ahaz, 2 K. 16:3). The OT makes occasional reference to a king who did act righteously, e.g., Jehoshaphat, who "walked in all the way of Asa his father; he did not turn aside from it, doing what was right in the sight of the Lord" (1 K. 22:43); yet even he did not take down the "high places." Also, King Josiah "did what was right in the eyes of the Lord, and walked in all the way of David his father" (2 K. 22:2 par. 2 Ch. 34:2).

II. In the NT.–A. Terminology. In the RSV NT "walk" most frequently translates Gk. *peripatéō,* which means "go about, walk around." This is the customary meaning in the LXX and the almost exclusive meaning in classical Greek. This verb occurs nearly one hundred times in the NT, although it is not always translated "walk"; its NT usage is almost evenly divided between literal and figurative meanings (see below).

In the RSV NT "walk" translates Gk. *poreúomai* only four times. Like *peripatéō* it may also include both literal and figurative meanings, but where the RSV translates *poreúomai* as "walk," it reflects only the figurative sense, "conduct oneself, live, walk"; e.g., Lk. 1:6 applies a familiar OT form of expression to Zechariah and Elizabeth: "they were both righteous before God, walking in all the commandments and ordinances of the Lord blameless." Also, in Acts 9:31 Luke describes the early Palestinian church as "walking in the fear of the Lord." Acts 14:16 states that God previously allowed the Gentiles to conduct their lives ("walk") as they wished (see 17:30), yet not without a witness to divine truth. In Jude 11 one may understand the phrase "walk in the way of Cain" as either the imitation of Cain's sin or as a euphemism for death (see R. J. Bauckham, *Jude, 2 Peter* [*Word Biblical Comm.*, 1983], pp. 80f.).

The RSV translates Gk. *stoichéō* as "walk" twice. Gal. 5:25 manifests the typical Pauline interaction of the indicative and the imperative: "we live by the Spirit (granted); therefore let us keep in step [*stoichéō*] with the Spirit" (F. F. Bruce, comm. on Galatians [*NIGTC,* 1982], p. 257; see also Gal. 6:16).

In Mk. 10:32 Gk. *proágō* (RSV "walking ahead"; lit. "go before, lead, precede") portrays Jesus' resolute decision to "go up to Jerusalem" and do God's will; this portrayal of Jesus vividly contrasts with the disciples who hesitantly and fearfully followed behind.

B. NT Use of Peripatéō. *1. Literal Uses.* In a number of instances the RSV NT uses "walk" (*peripatéō*) in the literal sense, e.g., walking by the sea (Mt. 4:18), on the sea (Mt. 14:25f.; 14:29 [Peter]; Mk. 6:48f.; Jn. 6:19), and in the temple (Mk. 11:27; Jn. 10:23). The RSV also uses "walk" in the absolute sense (e.g., Jn. 1:36); where this is so, the context frequently involves the miraculous healings of lame human beings, events that proclaim the coming of God's kingdom (e.g., Mt. 9:5-7 par.; 11:5 par.; 15:30f.; 5:42; Jn. 5:8f., 11f.; Acts 3:6-10; 14:8, 10).

2. Figurative Uses. When used figuratively, *peripatéō* means one's conduct or walk of life, i.e., the manner in which one conducts oneself (cf. 2 K. 20:3; Prov. 8:20). This use is especially characteristic of Paul, who further qualified it and grouped it into two categories that fundamentally oppose one another; e.g., he speaks about walking according to the Spirit or according to the flesh (Rom. 8:4; see also Gal. 5:16; cf. v. 25, *stoichéō*); accordingly, one may walk in good works (Eph. 2:10), in love (Rom. 14:15; Eph. 5:2), as children of light (Eph. 5:8), in new life (Rom. 6:4), or "by faith, not by sight" (2 Cor. 5:7); or one may walk in sins (Eph. 2:2; Col. 3:7). Cf. RSV "lead a life" for Gk. *peripatéō* in Eph. 4:1; Col. 1:10; 1 Thess. 2:12.

Bibliography.–R. Bultmann, *Theology of the NT,* I (Eng. tr. 1951), 330-340; *DNTT,* III, 943-47; *TDNT,* V, *s.v.* πατέω (Seesemann, Bertram); VI, *s.v.* πορεύομαι C. 6 (Hauck, Schulz); VII, *s.v.* στοιχέω (Delling); *TDOT,* III, *s.v.* "hālakh" (Helfmeyer).

G. L. KNAPP

WALL. In a number of places AV has "hedge(s)" where RSV has "wall(s)" for Heb. *gāḏēr* (Ps. 80:12 [MT 13]; Eccl. 10:8; Ezk. 13:5; 22:30; otherwise, AV usually has "wall" for *gāḏēr*) and *geḏērâ* (Ps. 89:40 [MT 41]; cf. Heb. *gāḏar* in Lam. 3:7; AV "hedged about"; RSV "walled about"). *Gāḏēr* and related words most often refer to defensive walls built of stone, whether a simple structure built around a vegetable plot or the walls of a city.

See FORTIFICATION; GALLERY (Ezk. 41:15); HOUSE IV.A.

WALLET. *See* BAG.

WANDER [Heb. *tā'â* (Gen. 20:13; 21:14; 37:15; Job 12:24; 38:41; Ps. 107:4, 40; Prov. 21:16; Isa. 47:15; Lam. 4:14), *nû(a)'* (Nu. 32:13; 2 S. 15:20; Ps. 109:10; Prov. 5:6; Jer. 14:10; Lam. 4:14f.; Am. 4:8; 8:12), *nāḏaḏ* (Job 15:23; Ps. 55:7 [MT 8]; Hos. 9:17), *šāgâ* (Ps. 119:10, 21; Ezk. 34:6), *nûḏ* (Gen. 4:12, 14; 2 K. 21:8; Jer. 49:30), *hālaḵ*–'walk' (1 Ch. 16:20 par. Ps. 105:13; Eccl. 6:9), *nāsa'* (Jer. 31:24; Zec. 10:2), *yāraḏ*–'descend' (Jgs. 11:37), *na'ar*–'youth' (Zec. 11:16), *'āḇaḏ* (Dt. 26:5), *bāḏaḏ* (Hos. 9:9), *ṭā'â* (Cant. 1:7, following Syr., Vulg., Symm.; MT *'ōṭyâ*–'veiled' < *'āṭâ*); Gk. *(apo)planáō* (1 Tim. 6:10; He. 11:38; Jas. 5:19), *planḗtēs* (Jude 13), *apostréphō* (2 Tim. 4:4), *ektrépomai* (1 Tim. 1:6)]; AV also BE MOVEABLE, BE A VAGABOND, GO UP AND DOWN, ERR, MOVE, GO, GO FORTH, GO DOWN, TURN (ASIDE), "the young one" (Zec. 11:16), "ready to perish" (Dt. 26:5), "alone" (Hos. 9:9), etc.; NEB also TAKE LEAVE OF, STUMBLE OFF, BE A VAGABOND, "croak" (Job 38:41), "lost their way" (Ps. 107:4), etc.

Words translated "wander" are used in three significant contexts: for the nomadic life of the patriarchs (Gen. 20:13; 21:14; 37:15; Dt. 26:5; cf. Jer. 31:24; He. 11:38), for the Israelites' experience in the wilderness before their entry into the Promised Land (Nu. 32:13; 1 Ch. 16:20 par. Ps. 105:13), and metaphorically for life characterized by sin, sometimes despite exposure to God's truth (Ps. 119:10, 21; Prov. 5:6; 21:16; Eccl. 6:9; Jer. 14:10; Zec. 10:2; Jude 13; Jas. 5:19). The Pastoral Epistles use the same metaphor, but with more specific identification of the direction of the wandering, which is generally doctrinal (1 Tim. 1:6; 6:10; 2 Tim. 4:4). Being made to wander in the desert is regarded as a punishment for sin (Gen. 4:12, 14; 2 K. 21:8; Job 12:24; Ps. 107:40; 109:10; cf. Lam. 4:14), as is the wandering of the Diaspora (Lam. 4:15; Hos. 9:17). But to wander in the wilderness could also be thought of as a way of finding refuge from the conflicts of settled areas (Ps. 55:7 [MT 8], in contrast to Ps. 107:4).

See also WILDERNESS. J. W. S.

WANDERINGS OF ISRAEL. The formative religious experiences of Israel occurred in the context of a series of journeys termed the "wanderings of Israel." The primary biblical materials giving the specifics of the journeys are found in Ex. 12–19; Nu. 10–22; and Dt. 1–2. Other scattered references supply a few more details. Nu. 33 gives a comprehensive list of the encampments along the way, but the precise nature of this chapter is much debated. The journeys began in the northwest Delta of Egypt and concluded in the plains of Moab just NE of the Dead Sea.

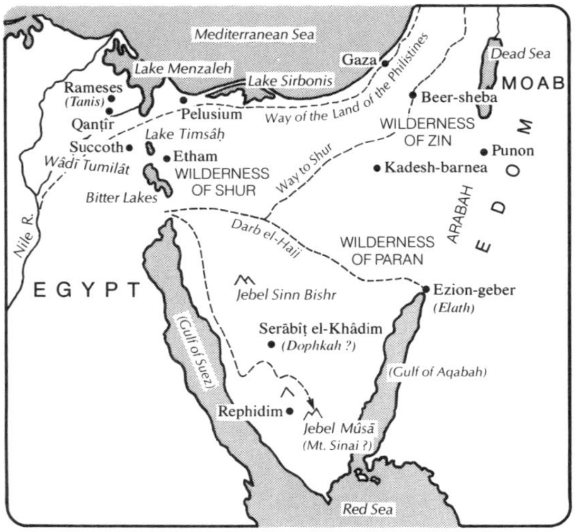

I. Preliminary Concerns
   A. Southern Route Theory
   B. Number of Participants
II. Geographical and Historical Background
   A. Geographical
      1. Sinai
      2. Kadesh-barnea
      3. Arabah and Southern Transjordan
   B. Historical
III. Journey from Egypt to Sinai
   A. From Rameses to the "Sea of Reeds"
   B. From the "Sea of Reeds" to Mt. Sinai
IV. From Mt. Sinai to Kadesh-barnea
   A. Route to Kadesh-barnea
   B. Sojourn at Kadesh-barnea
V. From Kadesh-barnea to the Plains of Moab
   A. Possible Approaches
   B. Archeological Discoveries

I. Preliminary Concerns.–A. *Southern Route Theory.* This article is a continuation of the article EXODUS, ROUTE OF THE, which describes and briefly evaluates the major route theories proposed for the Exodus, and it should be read in conjunction with that article.

Any attempt to trace the itinerary of these journeys faces formidable critical and geographical problems that render all such attempts hypothetical (*see* esp. EXODUS, ROUTE OF THE I). The widely varying options given by competent authorities demonstrate the complexity of the issues. In an article such as this no attempt can be made to deal with all the alternatives. Rather, this article assumes the position that the narrative of the journeys as it presently stands supports the theory of a southern route. Some of the basic reasons for this assumption must be summarized.

The key issue is the location of Mt. Sinai. The beginning of the journeys at Rameses is well established, as is the location of a major hiatus in the journeys at Kadesh-barnea. Further, although the journey from Kadesh-barnea to the plains of Moab presents its own difficulties, the general area and some precise locales are well known. It is the uncertainty regarding the location of Mt. Sinai that permits different route theories.

That Mt. Sinai should be located in the southern part of the peninsula seems to be indicated by the following observations. First, most of the sites mentioned are found only in the Exodus narrative. This suggests they were distant from the areas normally controlled by Israel or used in travel to Egypt. Even the precise location of Mt. Sinai was lost after the time of Elijah (9th cent. B.C.). At times the land under Israel's control extended to Kadesh-barnea and Ezion-geber, but no mention is made of these sacred sites. Second, a northern locale for the route and Mt. Sinai seems to be precluded by the specific statement that the Israelites were not to travel by the "way of the land of the Philistines" (Ex. 13:17), a reference to the great trunk route through the coast of Sinai connecting Sile with Gaza. Third, the statement that Mt. Sinai was n eleven days' journey from Kadesh-barnea (Dt. 1:2) best fits a locale in the south. Fourth, the probability that a few of the encampments (e.g., Dizahab, identified with Dhahab, and Jotbathah, identified with Ṭabeh) can be plausibly located in central or southern Sinai argues for a location in the south. Finally, although the Christian tradition placing Mt. Sinai at Jebel Mûsā dates only from the 4th cent. A.D., this tradition conflicts with the normal practice of locating sacred sites in easily accessible areas. It now appears certain that the tradition of a sacred mountain in south Sinai is older than the 4th cent. A.D., and that Christians built upon previously existing traditions. (*See also* EXODUS, ROUTE OF THE IV.C.).

But how far south was Mt. Sinai? Harel developed the view that Mt. Sinai should be located at Jebel Sinn Bishr, about 48 km. (30 mi.) SE of Suez. This view accommodates the inference that Mt. Sinai was a three days' journey from Egypt (Ex. 5:3), avoids the problem of Amalekites appearing so far south, and presents plausible identifications of the encampments between the crossing of the sea and Elim. Only a few scholars (e.g., Wenham) have adopted this theory. It is difficult to accommodate the numerous stations listed in the itineraries; nor does Jebel Sinn Bishr fit well the statement in Dt. 1:2 that Horeb (Sinai) was eleven days' journey from Kadesh-barnea. A mountain located farther south seems to be required.

B. Number of Participants. Scholars continue to debate how to interpret the figures given concerning the number of participants involved in the wanderings. Ex. 12:37 mentions the figure 600,000 — a number that agrees closely with the two census figures given in Numbers (chs. 1, 26). Since these figures apply only to adult males, it has been traditionally assumed that the total number of participants including women and children, was on the order of 2.5 million. To many scholars such a large figure seems troublesome at several points. First, the sheer size of the group presents serious logistical problems in the Sinai. Second, estimates of the strength of the Egyptian army at the battle of Kadesh in 1286 B.C. suggest a figure of twenty thousand — a number that presents a striking contrast to the fighting men available to Israel. Third, some biblical materials are hard to understand if the group was so large, e.g., the implication that only two midwives served the needs of the group (Ex. 2:15), or the statement that Israel represented a nation of few people (Dt. 7:7).

These reasons and others have led some scholars to propose other ways to understand the figures. Some have argued that the Hebrew term *'elep* normally translated "thousand(s)," originally carried another meaning such as "family" (Petrie) or a tribal subunit upon which a military draft was levied (Mendenhall). Thus Petrie suggested, e.g., that the number of 74,600 for the tribe of Judah meant seventy-four families comprising a total of six hundred people. Mendenhall believed that the figures signified seventy-four sub-sections of the tribe, with a combined military levy of six hundred fighting men. Albright proposed that the figures are basically correct but represent the population of Israel at the time of David. Still others have argued that the numbers are purely symbolic and have employed gematria or some other scheme to derive the meaning of the figures. None of these theories is free of difficulty; it is fair, however, to say that the majority of scholars favor some interpretation of the figures that results in a much smaller group than 2.5 million people.

II. Geographical and Historical Background.–A. *Geographical. 1. Sinai.* For a brief description of the geography of the Sinai Peninsula *see* EXODUS, ROUTE OF THE II. This article will amplify the description of some conditions of the peninsula and describe the major routes that cross the region. The latter point is of particular importance, since travel in Sinai by a group of any size is limited to certain geologically defined tracks.

The lack of available water in the Sinai is a point emphasized by the biblical writers. Today the entire region receives less than 10 cm. (4 in.) of rainfall yearly. This rainfall tends to be confined to brief, often violent cloudbursts occurring in the winter months. Most of the water evaporates or runs off along the innumerable wadis, such as the system forming the Wâdī el-ʿArîsh, which drains the vast central section of the peninsula northward to the sea. At least one-quarter of the rainfall, however, percolates downward to form a considerable reservoir of water or aquifer. Interestingly, a few records have noted that the collapse of thin rock material in the Sinai has resulted in immediate access to this underground reservoir; this brings to mind the incidences in the wanderings in which a rock was struck and water produced (Ex. 17:1-7; Nu. 20:8-13). In a few areas this water flows to the surface in the form of springs, allowing an oasis to break the monotony of the arid landscape. Important springs are found in the south of the peninsula in the Wâdī Feiran and beneath Jebel Mûsā. Smaller springs are scattered over the north and south of the peninsula but are rarer in the central region known as the Badiyat et-Tīh.

Movement within the Sinai Peninsula is restricted by the nature of the terrain to a few routes or tracks capable of use by significant groups of people. The major routes are all located in the northern third of the peninsula. As the connecting link between Egypt and Palestine, this was the most heavily traveled region. The major artery was the coastal road that began at Sile (Pelusium) and continued to Gaza, apparently referred to as the "way of the land of the Philistines" (Ex. 13:17). The Egyptians secured this route by maintaining a series of fortified outposts along the way; the pharaohs of the New Kingdom used this road often for military operations in Palestine and Syria. Another important route began near modern Ismailia (Wâdī Tumilât) and led to Beer-sheba, perhaps the "way to Shur" (Gen. 16:7) generally favored by the patriarchs in their migrations to and from Egypt. A third route led from modern Suez to Elath and is today known as the Darb el-Hajj, a Moslem pilgrim-route connecting north Africa to Mecca. Little evidence suggests that this route was used extensively in antiquity, although branches of the route extend NE to the region of Kadesh-barnea.

Southern Sinai, much more isolated, has no routes comparable to those in the north. During the Bronze Age the Egyptians mined turquoise at Serābîṭ el-Khâdim. Later, during the Roman period, the Nabateans traveled in south Sinai, probably in their trade endeavors. Christian pilgrimages to the region began during the 4th cent. A.D. Access to the southern peninsula from Egypt is gained down the east coast of the peninsula along the gulf of Suez. This route intersects two east-west tracks that lead to the granite peaks that form the heart of southern Sinai. The most important of these tracks is the Wâdī Feiran, which leads to the region of Jebel Mûsā by the Wâdī esh-Sheikh and the Watiya Pass. The wadis Baʿbaʿa and Mukattab join this system from the north. A less direct and more difficult approach to the southeast mountains is via Wâdī Ṭaiyiba and the sandy plain Debbet er-Ramleh. On the other hand, two possibilities exist for movement from the region of Jebel Mûsā to the east or northeast. Wâdī Naṣb extends almost due E to Dhahab. The second route leads northwest by the Watiya Pass along the wadi Saʿal, Ṣafra, Haggag, Hudera, Ghazala to Wâdī Watīr, thence to Elath.

An aerial view of the Red Sea and the east coast of the Sinai Peninsula (L. T. Geraty)

2. Kadesh-barnea. As indicated, the location of Kadesh-barnea has been established with reasonable certainty at ʿAin el-Qudeirât, approximately 88 km. (55 mi.) SW of Beer-sheba. Israel spent a considerable amount of time in this region as the faithless generation perished (Nu. 14:33; Dt. 1:46). Several important events are connected with the stay at Kadesh-barnea, including the reconnoitering of the land (Nu. 13), an abortive attempt to enter Palestine from the south (Nu. 14; Dt. 1:41-44), and the death of Miriam (Nu. 20).

The immediate environs of Kadesh-barnea provide adequate resources for a prolonged stay. Although ʿAin el-Qudeirât possesses the largest spring in the area, two other good sources of water are located at ʿAin Qedeis, 8 km. (5 mi.) SW, and ʿAin Qoseimeh. The former site retains the ancient name, and some favor identifying it with Kadesh-barnea. Possibly all of the springs in the immediate vicinity were included in the name Kadesh-barnea. Winter rains could be collected and conserved, allowing some small scale crop production, and areas for grazing can be found. Routes passed nearby to allow movement in several directions. The "way to Shur" gave access to Beer-sheba, another route led from Kadesh to Arad, while yet another linked Kadesh with the top of the Gulf of Aqabah. The latter probably is the "way to the Reed Sea" (*yam sûp*) taken by the Israelites upon leaving Kadesh (Nu. 21:4; Dt. 2:1).

The broader region in which Kadesh-barnea is located is quite inhospitable. Kadesh is variously described as being in the desert wastes known as the Wilderness of ZIN or the Wilderness of PARAN. The former term refers to the area N and E of Kadesh, which is practically devoid of vegetation, lacks significant water supplies, and never was permanently settled. The deep wadis that criss-cross the region make travel difficult.

3. Arabah and South Transjordan. For a description of the geography of the lands through which the Israelites journey after leaving Kadesh-barnea, *see* ARABAH; EDOM; MOAB.

B. Historical. To appreciate the obstacles posed by an attempted escape from Egypt, a few historical observations are important. The northeast Delta, the biblical land of Goshen, had long attracted seminomadic groups that are variously referred to in Egyptian sources as Asiatics or Shasu. These peoples came to Egypt across the Sinai with their herds and flocks, seeking the abundant water resources and pasturage afforded by the Delta. Trade between these groups also occurred, as depicted in the Beni-hasan tomb drawings. This migratory activity became troublesome for the Egyptians, especially after the First Intermediate Period. To monitor the migrations, the rulers of the Middle Kingdom (12th Dynasty) built the "Wall of the Prince," referring to a system of checkpoints using fortified outposts, or possibly to a system that used a (rediscovered) canal as a barrier to control access (see Sneh and Weissbrod). Egypt's vulnerability to infiltration across the Sinai from the northeast was highlighted during the Hyksos Period (*see* EGYPT VIII.F). Upon the expulsion of the Hyksos by the 18th Dynasty, the New Kingdom pharaohs continued to monitor closely access to and from the Delta.

In addition, New Kingdom pharaohs like Thutmose III, Amenophis II, and Ramses II asserted Egyptian influence in Palestine, Syria, and Transjordan. Through a series of campaigns launched from the northeast Delta and utilizing the coastal road across Sinai, the New Kingdom rulers ranged northward to southern Syria and beyond. Control of the eastern border and the major routes of Ṣinai were important matters to Egypt both militarily and economically.

The Exodus began in the northeast Delta probably during the resurgent 19th Dynasty (but *see* EXODUS, DATE OF THE). This powerful group of rulers included Seti I (*ca.* 1305-1290 B.C.), Ramses II (*ca.* 1290-1224), and Merneptah (*ca.* 1224-1214). During their reigns the administrative capital of Egypt was moved to the eastern Delta. This move was designed to enhance access to Palestine and Syria in the face of mounting pressure from the Hittites. New building projects were initiated by Seti I and energetically continued by his son and successor Ramses II.

III. Journey from Egypt to Mt. Sinai.–A. From Rameses to the "Sea of Reeds." The administrative focus of the 19th Dynasty was Rameses, Egyp. *pr-rʿ-ms-sw* ("house of Rameses"), the originating point of the Exodus (Ex. 12:37). Once there was much debate about whether the correct site of Rameses was at Tanis (Ṣân el-Ḥagar) or at Qanṭîr/Tell el-Dabʿa, but excavations at the latter site have confirmed it as the logical choice (see Bietak). The new capital was an impressive expansion of the older Hyksos capital Avaris, which had been neglected by the 18th Dynasty. At Qanṭîr a large palace begun by Seti I has been identified, along with houses belonging to high officials under Seti I and Ramses II. Although the remains have been seriously disturbed, it is clear that within the larger area centering upon Qanṭîr/Tell el-Dabʿa, the rulers of the 19th Dynasty built palaces and temples worthy of the capital. Also constructed were support facilities necessary for provisioning the royal household and bureaucracy, as well as military facilities. In this sense Rameses and Pithom could be described accurately as Heb. *ʿārê miškᵉnōṯ* ("store-cities," Ex. 1:11), a term perhaps derived from Akk. *maškantu* or *maškattu,* meaning "provision" (Soggin, p. 111).

From Rameses the Israelites moved SE to Succoth (Ex. 12:37; Nu. 33:5), a site conceded by most to be the Egyp. *Ṯkw* (*see* SUCCOTH 2). Identified with Tell el-Maskhûṭah, the site lies in the eastern portion of Wâdī Ṭumilât. This wadi was a major conduit extending from the eastern Nile branches to the frontier near Ismailia. Groups crossing the Sinai by the "Way of Shur" entered Egypt by this wadi. A papyrus document dating *ca.* 1190 B.C. details the passage of Shasu tribes with their herds from Edom via *Ṯkw* — an event dutifully recorded by a frontier official (*ANET,* p. 259). The same document mentions a *Pr-Tm,* probably PITHOM.

The narrative of the journey from Succoth to the crossing of the sea contains some detailed geographical information that is unfortunately susceptible to varying interpretations (for details see Cazelles, de Vaux, and Davies). Four sites are mentioned in connection with two encampments: Etham, Pi-hahiroth, Migdol, and Baal-zephon (Ex. 13:20; 14:2). None can be identified with certainty, and the last two terms could have been used to describe more than one site in the region. Papyrus Anastasi V (*ANET,* p. 259), however, relates the story of two fugitive slaves and their pursuit by a frontier official. Their route took them S of *Ṯkw* (Succoth). The official tracked them until his arrival at *Ḫtm* (Etham?), where he learned that the slaves had slipped past the Migdol of Seti, presumably into the desert; hence the pursuit was discontinued. Possibly three of the sites mentioned in the Exodus account are found here in order: *Ṯkw* may be Succoth, *Ḫtm* may be Etham, and Migdol of Seti I may be Migdol. Unfortunately, the equation of Egyptian *Ḫtm* with Etham is philologically difficult. The document does, however, suggest two important points: (1) the way S of *Ṯkw* was known and used by fugitive slaves, and (2) a Migdol was located S of *Ṯkw*.

Many scholars, however, prefer to identify Migdol with Tell el-Ḥeir, 13 km. (8 mi.) S of Pelusium, and Baal-zephon with either Mohammediyeh or Râs Qasrun, both located on the narrow bar of land N of Lake Sirbonis. It is probable that Tell el-Ḥeir was known as Migdol, perhaps the one mentioned later in the prophetic writings (Jer. 44:1; Ezk. 30:6). But the fact remains that such a line of march would invite Egyptian intervention, and it would fail to account adequately for Ex. 13:17. Acceptable, even preferable, alternatives can be given for Migdol and Baal-zephon in the central portion of the isthmus. Several Migdols are mentioned in and around the eastern Wâdī Ṭumilât. Baal-zephon can be located at Tell Defneh near Qantrah or perhaps even further south (Davies, p. 81). It seems preferable to assume that the Hebrews proceeded S of *Ṯkw* (Succoth) along a route similar to that of the two slaves.

The miraculous deliverance occurred at the *yam sûp,* best translated as "Sea of Reeds." A clue to the location of *yam sûp* may be found in the command to "turn back" (Ex. 14:2). This probably meant that the group changed directions and headed north — but how far north? Since only one encampment is mentioned prior to the crossing of the sea, the distance could not be great (perhaps 16 km. [10 mi.]). This would mean that the miracle should be located at one of the bodies of water between Lake Menzaleh and the Bitter Lakes. The area near Lake Menzaleh is in the vicinity of the marsh regions referred to in Egyptian documents as the "papyrus region" (*Pa-Tjouf(y)*) which may be related to the Hebrew term *yam sûp*. But the Lake Menzaleh region appears to be too far north; a better candidate would be Lake Timsâḥ near Ismailia in the center of the isthmus. Another possibility is the Bitter Lakes somewhat further south, but this is difficult to harmonize with the command to "turn back."

B. From the "Sea of Reeds" to Mt. Sinai. After the miraculous sea crossing, the Israelites journeyed for three days without water in the Wilderness of Shur (Ex. 15:22). The term refers to the northwest Sinai Peninsula, where some of the characteristics of the coastal plains intrude south. Sand and scrub dominate the area and water is scarce; the region contrasts sharply with the abundant water of the Delta lying just to the west.

The journey south followed the route along the east coast of the Sinai Peninsula. Nu. 33 lists seven stops between the sea crossing and Mt. Sinai (although Mt. Sinai is not actually mentioned). Exodus records information about four of the encampments. None can be identified with certainty, but several springs and small oases along the coast have invited attempts to locate sites mentioned in this portion of the journey. Marah (Ex. 15:23) traditionally has been placed at ʿAin Ḥawârah, a small spring, but some prefer the more copious spring at ʿAin Mûsā, 14 km. (9 mi.) S of Suez. Wâdī Gharandel, some 95 km. (60 mi.) S of Suez fits the description given of Elim with its twelve springs and seventy date palms (Ex. 15:27). The encampment by the sea (Nu. 33:10) has been placed either at the entrance to Wâdī Ṭaiyiba or near el-Merkhah, 8 km. (5 mi.) S of Abu Zeneimeh. At the latter site have been found the remains of a small Egyptian settlement used in the Late Bronze Age.

Within the area the Israelites first experienced the divine provision both of manna and of quail (Ex. 16). Both miracles may have been related to natural phenomena known to occur within the Sinai. The scale and timing of the phenomena revealed to the Israelites the sustaining hand of Yahweh. The yearly migration of quail between Europe and Arabia is well known. In the fall the quail land on the coast of northern Sinai, exhausted after their flight over the Mediterranean Sea. The appearance of the quail so far south may be explained by the fact that the Israelites encountered them in the spring not the fall. Also, in another instance (Nu. 11:31) the text indicates that the quail were brought to the Israelites by a wind, suggesting that the quail were blown off their normal migration route.

Upon departure from the encampment by the sea, the group continued into the Wilderness of Sin before reaching Rephidim. Nu. 33:12-14 mentions two stations, Dophkah and Alush, along the way. This clearly implies a turn in a more easterly direction and penetration into the rugged terrain of the interior peninsula. Two possible routes for this segment of the journey are feasible. The group could have entered the interior by the Wâdī Ṭaiyiba or the Wâdī Baʿbaʿa and moved past the Egyptian turquoise mining center at Serābîṭ el-Khâdim into the sandy tract known as Debbet er-ramleh. Dophkah has been identified with Serābîṭ el-Khâdim on the supposed basis of a philological similarity with the Egyptian word for turquoise. This appears to be an unacceptable philological argument, however, and it has now been abandoned. On the other hand, Debbet er-Ramleh is a suitable locale for the Wilderness of Sin. Yet, access to the interior of southern Sinai is more easily achieved through the wadis Sidri and Mukattab, which bypass the more difficult terrain to the north and east and interconnect with Wâdī Feiran. This seems preferable logistically, but it leaves Dopkhah unidentified.

The Wâdī Feiran is the most important track from the west leading to the center of the southern Sinai. The name Feiran recalls the more general term Paran. The wadi is rather wide in the west and narrows as it gently slopes upward to the east. The largest oasis of the southern peninsula is found at Pharan, some 26 km. (16 mi.) E of the point where Wâdī Mukattab joins Wâdī Feiran. Rephidim must be located in this area, possibly in or near the Wâdī Refâyid, which may still preserve the name. The obvious problem with identifying Rephidim with Pharan, as was often done earlier, is that Israel complained at Rephidim about the lack of water. This complaint is difficult to harmonize with the abundant water sources at Pharan. Interestingly, the similar episode in Nu. 21 (if it is not a doublet, as many would contend) occurs at Kadesh-barnea, where water sources are abundant. In both cases the people's complaint is underscored by the use of onomastic etiologies: Massah, "test," and Meribah, "contend" (Ex. 17:7; Nu. 20:13; cf. Dt. 6:16; 9:22).

At Rephidim the Amalekites attacked Israel (Ex. 17:8-13). Since the Amalekites normally are associated with northwest Sinai and the Negeb, this incident is used to support a northern route theory. The Amalekites are well known for their seminomadic character, however; possibly they were attempting to control access to the large oasis at Pharan and hence came into conflict with the Israelites.

The passage from Rephidim to Mt. Sinai probably was accomplished through the Wâdī esh-Sheikh and the Watiya Pass. Over six weeks after leaving Egypt the Israelites arrived at Mt. Sinai in the Wilderness of Sinai (Ex. 19:1f.). The site of the theophany and of Israel's covenanting with Yahweh must be sought on one of the several majestic red granite peaks situated at the apex of the peninsula. Among these peaks some of the more impressive are: Jebel Katerīn (2634 m., 8641 ft.), Jebel Umm Shomar (2585 m., 8482 ft.), and Jebel Mûsā (2281 m., 7482 ft.). The latter has traditionally been equated with Mt. Sinai. The small plain er-Râḥa below Râs es-Ṣafṣefeh affords space for encampment, while numerous springs in the area make a long-term stay feasible.

***IV. From Mt. Sinai to Kadesh-barnea.**–A. Route to Kadesh-barnea.* Leaving the peaks of southern Sinai, the Israelites headed toward Kadesh-barnea, a distance of approximately 240 km. (150 mi.). The main narrative gives very little information concerning this segment; in fact, only three place names are mentioned. On the other hand, Nu. 33 lists twenty encampments between Mt. Sinai and Kadesh-barnea. Aside from the paucity of information, a key question is whether the Israelites came to Ezion-geber before arriving at Kadesh-barnea, as stated in Nu. 33. Those who hold a northern route theory find such a detour impossible, and some have adopted Ewald's suggestion that Nu. 33:36b-41a has been dislocated and originally stood after v. 30a. But the apparent difficulty is removed if a southern route is accepted.

Before the Israelites left Sinai, Yahweh gave them a plan of encampment and method of march (Nu. 1:52-2:34; see diagram). The arrangement clearly assumes that representatives of all twelve tribes were involved in the theophany at Mt. Sinai. Since many critical reconstructions will not admit this assumption, the arrangement is widely regarded as being artificial, intended to symbolize that Israel as the people of Yahweh was gathered in His presence. But if one allows that representatives of all twelve tribes were at Mt. Sinai, then additional evidence for this camp arrangement has been discovered in a contemporary parallel from the time of Ramses II, in which pharaoh's tent is the central focus and the various military units form a square around it.

The line of march from Mt. Sinai to Kadesh-barnea would again be determined by the available routes. Two

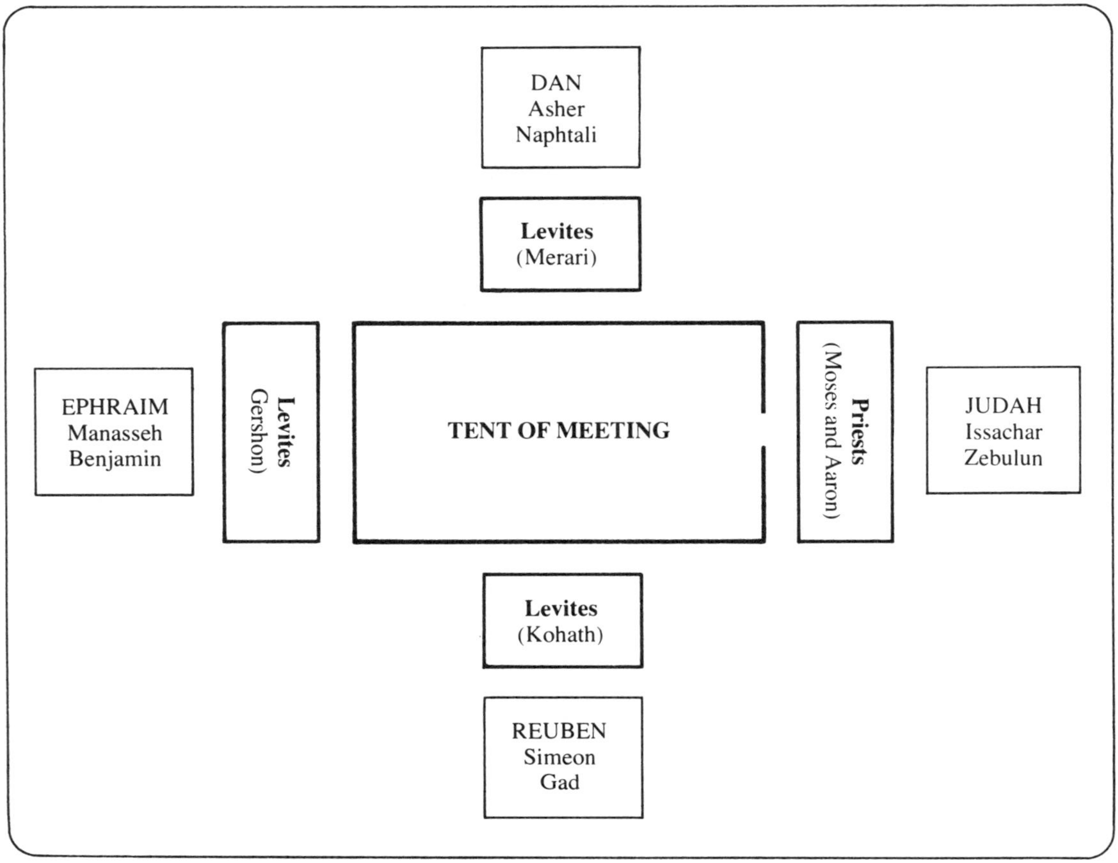

possibilities exist. A track to the east of Jebel Katerīn, Wâdī Naṣb, leads to the area of Dhahab on the Gulf of Aqabah. From Dhahab, access to Ezion-geber could be obtained along the coast. This line of march would be strongly suggested if Dizahab could be equated with Dhahab (Dt. 1:2). This route is more difficult than the alternative, however, and initially moves away from the intended goal of Kadesh-barnea.

A second and more likely alternative is an inland route that stays W of a longitudinal range of mountains along the east coast of Sinai. Leaving the central granite region by the Watiya Pass, this route continues northeast by wadis Saʿal and Ṣafra past Wâdī Haggag and Wâdī Hudera to Wâdī Ghazala. The Wâdī Watīr intersects Wâdī Ghazala NW of Nuweibe and affords relatively easy access to either Kadesh-barnea or the coast. Numerous Nabatean, Jewish, and Christian inscriptions have been found along this route, especially in Wâdī Haggag (see Negev). Moreover, the name Hazeroth (Nu. 11:35; 33:17) may well be preserved at ʿAin Hudera in the Wâdī Hudera. The pleasant spring and relatively wide wadi make such an identification attractive.

Along the way several incidents occurred, including a second visitation of quail (Nu. 11:31-35) and the continued provision of manna (Nu. 11:4-9). Again, the murmuring motif appears prominently in connection with these provisions, resulting in further onomastic etiologies, e.g., Taberah, "burning" (Nu. 11:3), and Kibroth-hattaavah, "graves of greediness" (Nu. 11:35; cf. Dt. 9:22). Both Miriam and Aaron rebelled at Hazeroth, and Miriam suffered an affliction as punishment (Nu. 12).

The term "wilderness of Paran" occurs with some frequency in this section (Nu. 10:12; 12:16). The Israelites' first contact with Canaan originated in the Wilderness of Paran as the spies were sent out (Nu. 13); the same account places Kadesh-barnea in the wilderness of Paran to which the spies returned. Both Aharoni and de Vaux regard the term as a general name, perhaps ancient, which was applied to large portions of the Sinai. This would account for its frequency of occurrences, but it would also explain the vagueness with which it is used.

B. Sojourn at Kadesh-barnea. According to Nu. 33:35f. the Israelites arrived at Kadesh-barnea from the southeast by way of Ezion-geber, a site identified with Tell el-Kheleifeh at the top of the Gulf of Aqabah or with the Jezirat Faraun, an island in the gulf 16 km. (10 mi.) south. Kadesh-barnea is the site of an important cluster of traditions that detail how Israel rejected the leadership of both Moses and Yahweh, with the result that Yahweh forbade the faithless generation to enter Canaan, necessitating a prolonged stay in the region. (Nu. 14:26-35; Dt. 1:26-40). Both Miriam and Aaron died in or near Kadesh, although the precise location of Mt. Hor, upon which Aaron died, is much debated.

It is not necessary to insist that all of the Israelites stayed at Kadesh; undoubtedly smaller family or tribal units sought pasturage and water in the surrounding springs and wadis in the region. Similarly, Dt. 2:14 refers explicitly to extended wanderings during the thirty-eight years preceding the crossing of the Zered. This suggests a complex historical process that positioned the tribes for penetration into the settled territories — a process from which only a few paradigmatic events are narrated.

Among the recorded incidents was an unsuccessful attempt to enter Canaan from the south (Nu. 14:39-45; Dt. 1:41-46). This effort was beaten back by the seminomadic Amalekites and the settled Canaanites inhabiting the Negeb, who defeated the Israelites at Hormah in the general vicinity of Beer-sheba. This episode represented a rebellion against Yahweh in that He had previously condemned those involved to perish before Israel could possess Canaan (Nu. 14:20-35).

The motif of rebellion appears again in the account of how Korah led some 250 people to resist Moses, resulting in their death (Nu. 16:1-35). The narrative states that the earth opened up and swallowed the leaders of the rebellion (vv. 31-33). Some have tried to explain this incident in terms of a peculiarity of the Arabah region: mud flats crust over in the heat, forming a thin surface that masks a treacherous condition (Hort). This feature, it is suggested, accounts for the earth "swallowing" the leaders of the rebellion along with their possessions. This explanation seems forced, however, and it is difficult to harmonize with the narrative.

*V. **From Kadesh-barnea to the Plains of Moab.**–A. Possible Approaches.* The final segment of the wanderings of Israel began at Kadesh-barnea and terminated in the plains of Moab with Israel poised to penetrate Canaan from the east. The basic description of this part of the journey occurs in Nu. 20–21; 33; Dt. 1–2; and Jgs. 11:12-28. The narrative describes a rather lengthy detour around the territories of the Edomites and Moabites to a point N of the Arnon and then details a series of conflicts with certain Amorite kingdoms occupying land promised to Israel. Once the Arnon was crossed, Israel entered a new phase of history as the promise of land began to become a reality.

Yet the information in the biblical texts is often difficult to harmonize with a single line of march. Especially problematic is the relationship between the itinerary of Nu. 38:37-49 and that in chs. 20–21. Several proposals have been developed to deal with the problems. One hypothesis favored by several Israeli scholars posits that the accounts relate two different routes taken by different groups at different times (Mazar; *LBHG*). According to this theory Nu. 33 describes a route that crossed the Arabah at Zalmonah and continued to Punon. From Punon it joined the King's Highway northward through Edom and Moab. Since no protest from either Edom or Moab is mentioned, it is assumed that the group that took this route did so before the settlement of these kingdoms in Transjordan, probably in the 14th cent. B.C. On the other hand, it is argued that chs. 20–21 (supplemented by Dt. 2 and Jgs. 11), which presume the presence of Edom and Moab, detail a great detour S to Ezion-geber and then E along the desert's edge. The group that took this route is dated to the 13th cent. B.C. and is associated with the conquest of the Amorite kingdoms and the figure of Moses.

Another approach regards the attempt to trace a continuous journey in these narratives as useless, since the narratives reflect originally disparate tribal or clan traditions that have been combined much later and given an "all Israel" orientation (Noth). While not denying that some of the material contains valid recollections of tribal life in the desert steppes, this approach emphasizes that these traditions reflect a prolonged, gradual movement of various groups out of the steppes into more settled territory — a process that by its very nature could not involve a continuous journey. De Vaux affirmed the existence of mutually exclusive routes embedded in the narratives, parts of which were perhaps borrowed or invented to fill in gaps. He maintained that the data permits no firm conclusion as to the route taken by Moses from Kadesh to the Arnon (de Vaux, pp. 551-564).

A final approach does not regard the attempt to reconstruct a line of march as futile and attempts to reconcile the various traditions (*GTTOT*; *GP*). While recognizing the complexity of the material and the possibility that the larger group may have broken up at times, this approach seeks to establish a general route involving a detour of Edom and Moab.

Because the issues are so complex, an analysis of the strengths and weaknesses of these various positions is impossible in a brief article. The discussion will be limited to a few remarks regarding the narratives. The biblical texts affirm that the Israelites attempted both unsuccessfully and successfully to enter Palestine from the south (Nu. 14:39-45; 21:1-3). Yet there remains the strong tradition that Canaan could not be penetrated permanently from that direction and that a major effort was made from the east. This is consistent with the presence of strongly fortified sites in the south that undoubtedly deterred the advance. Also, at several points the narrative presents a tradition that Israel was not permitted to pass through the territories of Edom and Moab, and that this necessitated a lengthy detour (Nu. 20:14-21; Dt. 2:8f.; Jgs. 11:17f.). Admittedly the itinerary in Nu. 33, with its description of a direct line of march from Kadesh through the Arabah, Edom, and Moab to the plain of Moab, appears to go against this tradition; but discussions regarding the nature of this list suggest that such an interpretation might not be necessary (see below). Further, a persistent tradition indicates a line of march following the "way to the *yam sup*" (Nu. 14:25; 21:4; Dt. 2:1), which in this case must refer to the Gulf of Aqabah; Ezion-geber is also mentioned in connection with this route (Dt. 2:8).

That the Israelites moved from Kadesh to near Ezion-geber is thus strongly suggested, but the exact route is not clear. Since, as Aharoni has pointed out (*LBHG* [rev. ed. 1979], pp. 201f.) Mt. Hor should be located NE of Kadesh, an initial movement in that direction must have ended in a turn to the southeast, perhaps as a result of the Edomite refusal. It is possible that the sites mentioned in Nu. 33:30b-36a belong to this section (*GTTOT,* p. 259). This might account for the mention of (Beeroth) Bene-jaakan (cf. Dt. 10:6), which is sometimes identified with el-Birein, 19 km. (12 mi.) N of Kadesh.

At Ezion-geber a command to "turn north" (Dt. 2:3) can be interpreted in two ways. The more likely alternative is that the group headed north along the eastern Arabah to the area of Punon, almost certainly in or near modern Feinân; then they continued between Edom and Moab along the Zered (Wâdī el-Ḥesā), near which Oboth and Iye-abarim must be located (Nu. 21:10-12). This theory permits the bronze serpent episode (vv. 4-9) to be located in the Arabah, where copper deposits are available. An alternative theory is that the group skirted E of both Edom and Moab and only penetrated the settled lands N of the Arnon. In this case it is possible that they attempted to enter Moab by traveling W down the Zered (thus accounting for the references to Oboth and Iye-abarim) but were forced back to the desert and later traveled to the Arnon.

A Red Sea shoal near Elath on the Gulf of Aqabah (W. Braun)

The events N of the Arnon involving Heshbon and Dibon are more easily followed; both places were located on the King's Highway. In the high fertile tableland N of the Arnon the Israelites defeated Sihon, an Amorite king who evidently had seized Moabite territory somewhat earlier (Nu. 21:21-35; Dt. 2:26-35). The detailed list of Nu. 21:16-20 diverges from that of ch. 33, and this has led to some speculation that at this point the larger group split. In any case, the wanderings ended in the plains of Moab, where the Israelites made a final encampment between Beth-jeshimoth and Abel-shittim (33:49). Nearby on Mt. Nebo Moses died after being allowed the privilege of viewing the land promised to his ancestors (Dt. 34:1-8).

B. Archeological Discoveries. At least two archeological discoveries are of interest in relation to Israel's wanderings from Kadesh-barnea to the plains of Moab. First is Rothenberg's excavation of the smelting site of Timnaʿ in the southern Arabah. The excavation uncovered the remains of a small temple used by the Egyptians, which had been destroyed and subsequently reused. Rothenberg concluded that the Midianites were responsible for this reuse and that the structure was converted to a tent shrine. Moreover, among the votive gifts and offerings Rothenberg found a 12-cm. (5 in.) copper serpent with a gilded head. In the light of the relationship that Moses sustained with the Midianites, the tent shrine and copper serpent are remarkable, the former recalling the tent of meeting used in the wanderings and the latter the episode of the bronze serpent (Nu. 21:6-9).

Even more surprising are the Aramaic texts found at Tell Deir ʿallā, which include prophetic materials of Balaam the son of Beor. This must certainly be a reference to the same figure hired by Balak to pronounce a curse upon the Israelites (Nu. 22–24; 31:8, 16; Dt. 23:4f.; Josh. 13:22; 24:9f.). The texts, dated to the 7th cent. B.C., were found in a building interpreted as a sanctuary and testify to the importance of the ancient seer (see Hoftijzer and Van Der Kooij).

Finally, archeological work in Transjordan suggests that Glueck's theory regarding settlement in the region is in need of revision. Contrary to his theory, parts of Transjordan did contain settled urban populations during the Middle and Late Bronze ages, although more data and further analysis are required before the precise patterns can be established. Moreover, there appears to have been no upsurge of urban sites connected with the 13th cent., as proposed by Glueck and others. In fact, all arguments concerning the date or routes of the Exodus based upon a sudden emergence of Edom and Moab in the 13th cent. B.C. cannot be considered valid. On the other hand, the narratives of Israel's wanderings do not require a settled urban population; tribal groups led by a primary figure or "king" could have effectively refused passage through their lands.

Bibliography.–W. F. Albright, *BASOR,* 109 (1948), 5-20; M. Bietak, *Tell el Daba II* (1975); H. Cazelles, *RB,* 62 (1955), 321-364; G. W. Coats, *CBQ,* 34 (1972), 135-152; G. I. Davies, *Way of the Wilderness* (1979); R. H. Dornemann, *Archaeology of the Transjordan in the Bronze and Iron Ages* (1983); H. Ewald, *Geschichte des Volkes Israel* (3rd ed. 1864-1868); A. H. Gardiner,

JEA, 6 (1920), 99-116; N. Glueck, *Other Side of the Jordan* (2nd ed. 1970); *GP; GTTOT;* M. Harel, "Route of the Exodus of the Israelites from Egypt" (Diss., New York University, 1964); S. Herrmann, *Israel in Egypt* (Eng. tr., *SBT*, 2/27, 1973); *History of Israel* (Eng. tr. 1975); J. Hoftijzer and G. Van Der Kooij, *Aramaic Texts from Deir Alla* (1976); G. Hort, *Australian Biblical Review*, 7 (1959), 2-26; C. S. Jarvis, *Yesterday and Today in the Sinai* (1936); *LBHG;* B. Mazar, ed., *World History of the Jewish People*, III: *Judges* (1971), pp. 69-79; A. Negev, *Inscriptions of Wadi Haggag* (1977); M. Noth, *History of Pentateuchal Traditions* (Eng. tr. 1981); *Numbers* (*OTL*, Eng. tr. 1968); E. H. Palmer, *Desert of the Exodus* (1871); W. M. F. Petrie, *Researches in Sinai* (1906); E. Robinson, *Biblical Researches in Palestine, Mount Sinai, and Arabia Petraea* (3rd ed. 1841); B. Rothenberg, *Timna: Valley of the Biblical Copper Mines* (1972); B. Rothenberg and Y. Aharoni, *God's Wilderness* (1961); H. H. Rowley, *From Joseph to Joshua* (1950); A. Sneh and T. Weissbrod, *Science*, 180 (1973), 59-61; J. A. Soggin, *History of Israel* (Eng. tr. 1984); H. C. Trumbull, *Kadesh-Barnea* (1884); R. de Vaux, *Early History of Israel* (Eng. tr. 1978); G. J. Wenham, *Numbers* (*Tyndale OT Comms.*, 1981); *see also* Bibliography in EXODUS, ROUTE OF THE.

T. V. BRISCO

WANTON [Heb. *neḇālâ* ("wanton crime," Jgs. 20:10; "wanton folly/fools," 2 S. 13:12f.), *peṯayyûṯ* (Prov. 9:13), *pûš*–'(playfully) paw the ground' (Jer. 50:11), qal part. of *zānâ*–'be unfaithful' (Ezk. 6:9), qal part. of *pāḥaz*–'be insolent, loose' (Zeph. 3:9); Gk. *katastrēniáō* (1 Tim. 5:11), *strēniáō*–'live in luxury, live sensually' ("played the wanton," Rev. 18:7; "were wanton," v. 9)]; AV also FOLLY, FOOL, SIMPLE, WHORISH, LIVE DELICIOUSLY (Rev. 18:7, 9), etc.; NEB OUTRAGE, SIMPLETON, RECKLESS, WALLOW IN LUXURY (Rev. 18:7, 9), etc.; **WANTONLY** [(verb) Heb. qal part. of *zānâ*–'have illicit intercourse' (Nu. 15:39; Ezk. 6:9), hiphil of *pāra'*–'let grow without restraint' ("dealt wantonly," 2 Ch. 28:19), piel part. of *śāqar*–'ogle' ("glancing wantonly," Isa. 3:16), (adverb) *rêqām*–'in a vain manner' (Ps. 25:3), *ḥinnām*–'without cause, undeservedly' (Prov. 1:11)]; AV WHORING, "made naked" (2 Ch. 28:19), "without cause," "wanton eyes" (Isa. 3:16); NEB also "had been unbridled" (2 Ch. 28:19), "without cause," "wanton glances" (Isa. 3:16), etc.; **WANTONNESS** [Heb. *rāṣôn*–'desire, will' (Gen. 49:6), *neḇālâ* (Jgs. 20:6); Gk. *strēnos*–'sensuality, luxury' (Rev. 18:3)]; AV SELFWILL, FOLLY, DELICACY; NEB also BLOATED. In Ps. 106:14 the RSV "wanton craving" (AV "lusted exceedingly") translates the cognate accusative of Heb. *wayyiṯ'awwû ṯa'awâ* (lit. "desire a desire").

The terms that are translated "wanton" and its derivatives in the OT and the NT often refer to actions that are both selfish and contrary to the will of God, whether by direct opposition to Yahweh through idolatrous actions (Zeph. 3:4), or in senseless and willful harm of human beings (2 Ch. 28:19) or animals (Gen. 49:6).

The Hebrew words often have sexual/sensual connotations (Gen. 49:6; Jgs. 20:6, 10; 2 S. 13:12f.; Prov. 9:13; Isa. 3:16), but also are used figuratively to refer to Israel's idolatrous practices (2 Ch. 28:19; Ps. 25:3; Ezk. 6:9; Zeph. 3:4), to the arrogance with which Babylon brought havoc upon Judah (Jer. 50:11), to insatiable desire which has selfish intent (Nu. 15:39; Ps. 106:14), and also to the evil intent of one lying in wait to kill another (Prov. 1:11).

In the NT Gk. *katastrēniáō* in 1 Tim. 5:11 refers to younger widows whose loyalty to serving Christ may be threatened by the possibility of remarriage. In the OT those who pull back from serving the Lord are sometimes likened to an unfaithful wife (Ezk. 6:9; Zeph. 3:4). Here also this comparison is made with those who would retreat from faithful service to Christ in the church. In Rev. 18 the cognates *strēnos* and *strēniáō* refer to the excessive self-indulgence and luxurious life-styles of Babylon (vv. 3, 7) and the kings of the earth (v. 9). L. M. McDONALD

WAR; WARFARE.

I. Terminology
II. Purposes of War
III. Personnel of War
IV. Paraphernalia of War in Antiquity
V. Military Operations
VI. Warfare in the Intertestamental Period
VII. War in the NT

I. Terminology.–In the RSV OT the term most frequently translated "war" is Heb. *milḥamâ*, "fight, battle" (e.g., Gen. 14:2), a word that occurs over three hundred times in the Hebrew OT. Cognate to *milḥamâ* is the verb *lāḥam*, "fight, do battle," whose niphal form is often rendered "make war" (e.g., Dt. 20:19; Josh. 10:5; Jgs. 11:4f.; etc.). Heb. *ṣāḇā'*, "service in war," also is translated "war" (esp. in Nu. 1). The RSV also renders *qerāḇ* ("hostile approach, fight") as "war" (e.g., Ps. 55:21 [MT 22]; 68:30 [MT 31]; 144:1; etc.).

The RSV NT usually renders the Greek noun *pólemos* as "war." This term applies both to armed conflicts (e.g., Mt. 24:6; He. 11:34; Rev. 11:7; 12:17; 13:7; 19:19; etc.) and to interpersonal quarrels or strife (e.g., Jas. 4:1). The cognate verb *poleméō*, "make war, fight," also refers both to intense wars (e.g., Rev. 2:16; 17:14; 19:11) and to interpersonal hostilities (Jas. 4:2). In 2 Cor. 10:3; Jas. 4:1; and 1 Pet. 2:11 "war" translates Gk. *strateúomai*, "do military service, serve in the army." The latter two verses apply the term figuratively to personal internal struggles. In Rom. 7:23 the Greek verb *antistrateúomai*, "be at war," refers to the battle waging between the authority of the law of God and the power of sin. In 2 Cor. 10:4 and 1 Tim. 1:18 the RSV "warfare" translates the Greek noun *strateía*, "military campaign," a term used only figuratively in the NT.

II. Purposes of War.–Wars are fought between groups of people. The purposes that move a collection of individuals to engage in armed conflict reflect the motives in the individual. As early as the story of Cain and Abel (Gen. 4:1-16) the Bible reveals the human tendency toward violence against another person. The general explanation is that unfulfilled desire and envy lead to aggression and murder (Jas. 4:1f.). Transferred to social groups — clan, tribe, and nation — this human tendency results in war.

Depending upon the level of group organization, the purposes of war vary from tribe to kingdom to empire. All three levels of sociopolitical organization are reflected in biblical wars. Conflicts may occur between small groups, such as families, clans, or tribes, over matters of food, territory, self-preservation, domination, independence, and the maintenance of social solidarity within the group. For larger groups, such as kingdoms and nations, the drives toward wars are predominantly over territory, for adventure, to dominate another people, and to maintain a ruling class in power. The latter involves an individual sense of identity with the ruling social group. Religious factors permeate the idea of social solidarity and group loyalty. These drives toward conflict on the part of one group induce a defensive action by the threatened group. *See* WAR, IDEA OF.

III. Personnel of War.–The first reference to war in the Bible is of a coalition of four Mesopotamian kings who invaded and sacked the five cities of the plain in the Dead Sea region (Gen. 14:1-12). Abraham marshaled a force of 318 men who pursued the invading force and rescued the captives and the booty (vv. 13-16). Although the leaders of the coalition are called kings, their combined forces

A relief from Zenjirli (*ca.* 8th cent. B.C.) showing two soldiers in a chariot: one drives in the front and the other with a drawn bow and a spear stands in the back. Beneath the horse is an enemy pierced with arrows (Archaeological Museum, Istanbul)

were apparently little more organized than a major raiding party. Abraham's rescue team consisted of retainers who were loyal to him as essentially a tribal leader.

The tribal leader determined when to go to war and functioned as the leader in combat. The men of the tribe, who normally were herdsmen and hunters, were obligated to follow the leader. The famous wall painting of the Beni-hasan tomb in Egypt, depicting Middle Bronze Age Semites entering Egypt under the leadership of a certain Ibsha, is a reminder of clan and tribal organization in which the men of the group were responsible for its defense and for aggressive activities. The weapons and training of tribal warriors were unsophisticated and traditional since they were only occasional soldiers.

Before Israel's conquest of Canaan, the sociopolitical organization was primarily that of the small city-state, consisting of a walled urban area with outlying villages and fields and pasture land within a moderate walking distance from the city and villages. City-state organization tends to break down family, clan, and tribal loyalties, replacing them with loyalty to the larger group and allegiance to the ruling family and king. Petty kings of Late Bronze Age Canaanite city-states maintained small armies of professional soldiers, including foot-soldiers and charioteers. At Ugarit each village was required to supply a number of men for military service on a regular basis, thereby supplementing the professional forces. The number of professional soldiers was apparently small in Canaan. In several of the Amarna Letters Canaanite princes request that Pharaoh send "one hundred garrison troops" to Megiddo (Am.Tab. 244:34f.), a garrison of "fifty men" to Jerusalem (Am.Tab. 289:42f.), and one troubled prince mentions fifty chariots from Acco and Achshaph that have come to his help in Hebron (Am.Tab. 366:20-25; see *ANET*, pp. 485, 487, 489). The specifics of military organization are lacking, although they must have existed. The numbers "fifty" and "one hundred" suggest an organization along the lines of Israel under Moses (Ex. 18:25).

The Israelites were organized as military units based on the tribal structure. Under the leadership of Moses and Joshua this tribal confederation functioned as a formidable fighting force in the conquest of Canaan. With the division of the land among the tribes (Josh. 13–21), military organization reverted to the tribal pattern (cf. Jgs. 5:12-18). No organized army existed during the period of the Judges until the time of Samuel and Saul. Instead several tribes might be united in a military force to confront a common threat, as in the case of Manasseh, Asher, Zebulun, Naphtali, and Ephraim under the leadership of Gideon (Jgs. 6:35; 7:24), and the tribes that were called to arms by Deborah and Barak (4:6f.; 5:14f.). When the horrible incident at Gibeon occurred (ch. 19), all the tribes of Israel joined in the retaliation except the men of Jabesh-gilead (21:8f.). One of the results of the tribal condition, when "every man did what was right in his own eyes" (21:25), was the military weakness that permitted the organized army of the Philistines to threaten Israel. In part, the people demanded a king to provide strong military leadership (1 S. 8:20).

David learned the arts of war both as a fugitive outlaw leader (1 S. 22:1f.) and as a refugee among the Philistines (27:1-3; 29:1-11), who were better organized and equipped than the Israelites during Saul's reign. Later, under David, who is described as "a warrior" (1 Ch. 28:3), the Israelite army developed into the most powerful force in the region with a core of exceptional fighting men, apparently professional soldiers (2 S. 23:8-39), and a contingent of mercenaries from the conquered Philistines (2 S. 8:18; 15:18; 20:7, 23; 1 K. 1:38, 44), including six hundred men from Gath (2 S. 15:18). Solomon added a contingent of chariotry (1 K. 10:26) to the professional army, which had previously consisted of foot soldiers.

The innovations of both David and Solomon were in line with the military practices of the Canaanites, Egyptians, Hittites, and Assyrians. The use of both chariot forces and mercenaries in Judah was practically eliminated after the conquest of Sennacherib in 701 B.C., so that the Judean forces were primarily conscripts. The annals of Nebuchadrezzar mention only "men of war," rather than mercenary or chariot forces. Only in the Hasmonean period do sources mention cavalry as a part of the Jewish army (1 Macc. 16:4, 7), and in the early Roman period Herod had at his disposal thirty thousand infantrymen and six thousand cavalry (*BJ* i.17.9 [346]). In this period provincial military forces reflected the organization and training of the Roman legions throughout the empire and existed only with the permission of the central government.

IV. Paraphernalia of War in Antiquity.–The weapons of combat consisted of personal offensive and defensive arms for the individual soldier. Cain may have slain Abel with a stone from the field. The sling must have been used by hunters from the very earliest times. Among the earliest manufactured weapons were flint knives and spearheads followed by the invention of the bow during the Natufian period (*ca.* 15,000-8,000 B.C.). Gradually warriors improved the sling, knife, and bow and arrows, and developed new weapons such as composite and compound bows, improved arrows, javelins, spears, swords, maces, and battle axes. These new weapons enabled the individual warrior to strike a piercing blow to the enemy in hand-to-hand combat or at a distance.

For defense against an opponent's blows an individual warrior might carry a shield, usually a wooden frame covered with leather that required maintenance with oil (2 S. 1:21). Helmets and armor made of tough leather and metal scales were also developed for personal protection (1 S. 17:5).

Apart from the individual soldier, more complicated war machines were invented. The wheel and axle were invented a little before 3000 B.C. in the vicinity of the Tigris and Euphrates Valley. The earliest carts had two or four solid wheels. Both models had a central pole, indicating they were powered by a team (of oxen or wild asses). By 3000 B.C. people used these vehicles for war as well as domestic purposes, as indicated in models, reliefs, and cylinder seals from Sumer.

Chariot warfare was revolutionized in the M.B. Age (*ca.* 2000-1800 B.C.) by the introduction of spoked wheels and the use of horses. This new development has been attributed to the Hittites in Anatolia, who brought the technology with them in their migration from central Asia. The new war machine soon spread to the Assyrians, the Achaeans, and the Egyptians, and it became a major factor in the development of early empires (*see* pictures in BABYLONIA; HORSE). In Gen. 41:43 Pharaoh raised Joseph to power and provided a chariot for his use. The NT mentions chariots several times with the last reference alluding to the thunderous sounds of horses and chariots (Rev. 9:9), but the predominant period for Israelite chariot warfare was that from Solomon to Hezekiah. Until Solomon, the Israelites burned captured chariots and lamed the war horses (Josh. 11:6; cf. 2 S. 8:3f.). *See* CHARIOT.

Domesticated asses and horses were used as pack animals and carried riders, but the earliest evidence of a mounted warrior is a decoration on a Cretan burial urn dating to the Mycenaean period. Cavalry were introduced into warfare by the end of the 2nd millennium B.C., but chariotry continued to be the predominant form of highly mobile forces throughout the biblical era.

The battering ram in a primitive form may have been in use by the middle of the 3rd millennium B.C. The first illustrations of this war machine appear in the Beni-hasan tomb paintings (*ca.* 1900 B.C.), and the improved offensive

Ashurbanipal's assault on a city using a six-wheeled battering ram with wicker shields and a metal-tipped battering-pole. Behind the battering ram is a mobile assault tower with two archers who provide cover fire for the battering-ram operators (orthostat from Ashurnasirpal II's northwest palace at Nimrûd, 883-859 B.C.) (courtesy of the Trustees of the British Museum)

weapon, designed to aid in the penetration of city walls, is confirmed for Syria-Palestine by the appearance of the ramparted city walls of the M.B. II A/B period, dating to the same era as the Egyptian tomb painting (*see* FORTIFICATION). A visual representation of the Iron Age II Assyrian battering ram appears on the reliefs recovered from the palace of Sennacherib in the Nineveh excavations (*see* picture in LACHISH; *see also* SIEGE).

Concurrent with the employment of the battering ram, the siege tower was often used. Another important attack weapon against city walls was the ladder (*see* picture in HAMATH). In combination with the personal weapons of the combat forces, the mechanical and structural war engines advanced the art of ancient warfare.

Every army has the problem of logistics, and a certain number of personnel in an armed camp are noncombatants, left behind to guard the baggage while the main force goes forth to engage the enemy. In the more primitive style of warfare carried on with tribal units from the time of Joshua to the establishment of the monarchy, the men were summoned to war by the call of the trumpet (Jgs. 3:27), the word of a messenger (6:35), or even by a symbolic act (1 S. 11:7). They brought with them their own simple weapons, usually swords and slings. Jgs. 5:8 indicates that in Deborah's day neither shield nor spear was to be found among the forty thousand of Israel. Apparently the men took a small supply of food with them, but in the field they lived off the land, supplemented from time to time with food from home (1 S. 17:17). With the establishment of a professional army in the reign of David, the army was equipped with supplies from the store-cities before departure to the field (1 K. 9:19; 20:27).

An integral part of ancient warfare was the plundering and collection of booty by the conquering warriors. They carried off everything of value: flocks (1 S. 14:32), possessions of dead soldiers (31:8), booty in the enemy camp (2 K. 7:16), and people (5:2).

The booty was shared according to custom (Nu. 31:26-47; Jgs. 5:30), but David liberalized the share of booty that the camp guards were to receive (1 S. 30:24f.). The most valuable articles became the possessions of the king or were placed in the sanctuary (2 S. 8:7f., 11f.).

V. Military Operations.–Warfare in the Bible reflects a wide variety of operations, depending upon the historical period in which each conflict took place, the geographical setting, the objectives of the attackers and the defenders, the weapons and training of the combatants, and especially the motivation of the warriors.

A powerful motivating force for war was the link between religion and war that permeated all the peoples of antiquity. Because Israel saw itself as the chosen people of God, all of its institutions were vested with religious significance, including war (*see* WAR, IDEA OF). Thus preparations for war included religious rites to sanctify the military activity (1 S. 7:8-10; 13:9), and the prophets saw armies as summoned and consecrated by God to the avenging task (Isa. 13:3; Jer. 6:4-6). The armed camp of Israel was holy because of the Lord's presence within it, and only the ritually pure could participate in it (Dt. 23:10-14). This was the reason why Uriah could not go in to Bathsheba, even though David urged him to do so (2 S. 11:9-11). The combatants went forth certain of victory, for the Lord had already given the enemy into their hands (Josh. 6:2; Jgs. 3:28; 1 S. 23:4; etc.). The warriors had to have faith and be without fear (Josh. 8:1), and in battle they believed that the Lord fought for Israel (10:14; 1 S. 7:10). The ark of God represented the presence of the Lord. It was taken into battle at Ebenezer with unexpected and disastrous results (4:1-11) because of the sins of Eli's sons Hophni and Phinehas, but at Michmash a notable victory was won (14:18). Later the prophet of the Lord might be consulted to determine the divine will on a projected campaign (1 K. 22:5-12; 2 K. 3:11).

An armed force could move into the field organized in units of one thousand, one hundred, fifty, and ten men (2 S. 18:1; 2 K. 1:9; 2 Ch. 25:5; etc.) and divided into groups (1 S.11:11; 2 S. 18:2; etc.). One group acted as a rear guard (Nu. 10:25; Josh. 6:9), and the main body was likely preceded by an advance party. The clash with a hostile force could occur either in open terrain or in conjunction with a siege operation.

Israel's first military engagements were wars of con-

Galloping over dead enemies, Assyrian horsemen armed with spears pursue a camel rider (relief from Nimrûd, Tiglath-pileser III, 744-727 B.C.) (courtesy of the Trustees of the British Museum)

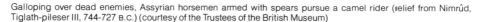

quest, taking possession of the Promised Land with God's help (Nu. 21:21-35; 31:1-12; Josh. 1–12; etc.). The Israelite troops were primitive desert warriors pitted against the occupants of cities "great and fortified up to heaven" (Dt. 1:28) with professional troops who fought from iron-clad chariots (Josh. 17:16-18). By various stratagems the Israelites defeated the superior Canaanite forces, conquering and destroying even fortified cities. Ai was conquered by a combination of ruse and ambush (Josh. 8), while a spy operation contributed to the fall of Jericho (ch. 2; 6:15-27). A surprise attack combined with the intervention of God defeated the southern coalition of Canaanite kings (10:9-14).

The Israelites fared badly in open battles in the period of the Judges (1 S. 4:1-11; 31:1-7), but frequently succeeded with daring attacks, bold tricks, and ambushes by small groups of armed men (Jgs. 6:33–7:22; 1 S. 14:1-23). In this fashion they occupied the highlands but stopped short of the plains where fortified cities and chariots were major obstacles (Josh. 17:12, 16; Jgs. 1:19, 27-35). As late as the 9th cent. B.C. the Syrians believed the Israelites were practically unbeatable in the hills but vulnerable in the plain (1 K. 20:23).

The conflicts of Israel during the period of the Judges and early monarchy were defensive wars against the counterattacks of the Canaanites and later against the encroachments of the Philistines, who were professional military men and armed with superior weapons (1 S. 13:19-23). But David adopted a policy of conquest with the professional army and mercenaries (see III above). His military operations included raids and sorties while he was in the service of Saul (18:25-29) and the Philistines (27:8-12). His fight with Goliath illustrated the ancient alternative to a general battle — the contest between two champions (ch. 17).

David's army fought in open battle, defeating both foot soldiers (2 S. 5:17-21) and chariot forces (10:17-19). Information about combat tactics in such battles remains quite scanty. Trumpets were used for signaling, and the infantry, chariots, and cavalry were coordinated in the attack. The battle opened with a battle cry on signal (1 S. 17:20; Jer. 4:19; 49:2; etc.), and the din of battle (Nah. 3:2f.) filled the air until the vanquished fled (cf. 2 S. 10:13f.).

David's forces under the command of Joab also besieged cities; the siege of the Ammonites' citadel is given in some detail (2 S. 10–12). For details on actions against fortified cities, *see* SIEGE.

The more sophisticated armaments and military operations instituted by David saw further development under his successors. Solomon established fortified chariot cities and store-cities at strategic locations in his kingdom (Hazor, Megiddo, Gezer, Lower Beth-horon, Baalath, Tamar and Jerusalem [1 K. 9:15-19]), although he never fought a war. Most of these had been Canaanite chariot cities, so Solomon continued a military tradition. Egyptian chariots carried a driver and a warrior, but Israelite chariots were manned by a crew of three — a driver, a combatant, and a shield-bearer (22:34; 2 K. 9:25). With the division of the kingdom, the bulk of the chariot cities came under the control of Israel and reached their greatest importance under Ahab. At the Battle of Qarqar (853 B.C.) he fielded two thousand chariots against the Assyrians, a number that exceeded the combined total provided by the other members of the coalition in which he participated (cf. *ANET*, p. 279).

Rehoboam strengthened his own defenses with fortified cities (2 Ch. 11:5-11). Although chariot centers are not mentioned, Judah developed that line of defense (2 K. 8:21) so that in Isaiah's time the centers were numerous (Isa. 2:7). Judah continued a decline that began with the

This Greek marble relief shows a warrior with a shield standing over a combatant with a dagger (late 5th cent. B.C.) (The Metropolitan Museum of Art, Fletcher Fund)

conquest of Sennacherib (701 B.C.). When Nebuchadrezzar and his army approached Jerusalem, the Judean military forces were physically weakened and spiritually bankrupt. The Lord had deserted the camp of Israel (2 K. 23:27; 24:3, 20) and even fought against them, contributing to their defeat (Jer. 21:5). The mighty had indeed fallen.

VI. Warfare in the Intertestamental Period.–Warfare in the intertestamental period became the province of the Persians and Greeks and, subsequently, the Greeks and Romans.

The Greek armies were superbly trained and included contingents of chariots, elephants, cavalry, and a navy (1 Macc. 1:17). With them the Greeks defeated the Persian armies. In a revolt against the oppressive policies of Antiochus IV Epiphanes, the Jews took up arms against the Syrians under the leadership of Judas Maccabeus (3:1). Some of the characteristics of the holy war surfaced in this conflict as Mattathias, the patriarch of the Maccabees, called upon "everyone who is zealous for the law and supports the covenant" to follow him (2:27). The Maccabean war was essentially a guerrilla action that reverted back to the ruse, ambush, and similar tactics (cf. 3:23), but the conflict developed into a politically motivated struggle and the organization of a regular fighting force (3:55).

The Maccabean revolt led to the establishment of an independent Jewish kingdom ruled by the Hasmonean dynasty, combining the offices of both high priest and king. The Second Jewish Commonwealth has a bloodstained history with conflicts both within and without as the Jews adopted the war-making techniques and weapons of the Hellenistic Age, which were raised to exceptional heights by Herod the Great with the help of Rome.

The Maccabean revolt also produced a fragmentation of

Judaism into a number of sects. One of these established a community near the northwest corner of the Dead Sea. In 1947 an amazing document popularly known as "The War Scroll" was discovered (*see* DEAD SEA SCROLLS I.A; II.H). The work, one of several scrolls produced by the community, dates to the 1st cent. B.C. and gives rules for the apocalyptic war at the end of time between the Sons of Light and the Sons of Darkness, i.e., between the members of the community on the side of God, and all the pagan nations (including the established priesthood at Jerusalem) on the other. The battle depicted reflects military organization and actions similar to those known from contemporary Roman practices.

VII. War in the NT.–The world of the NT knew the Pax Romana, but Roman military power and prowess was ever present in Roman-occupied Judea. As one of the signs of the last days, Jesus gave the existence of "wars and rumor of wars" (Mt. 24:6). He used an illustration of the total commitment required by a king who would attempt a war as an example of the commitment required of one of His disciples (Lk. 14:31-33). Jesus prophesied the siege and fall of Jerusalem (19:41-44), and He spoke of Himself figuratively as bringing not peace but a sword (Mt. 10:34). Yet He warned that "all who take the sword will perish by the sword" (26:52) the religion of Jesus is essentially a call for peace rather than war.

The NT traces war to the selfishness and greed that dominate people (Jas. 4:1f.). The early Christians were taught that the true warfare takes place within the individual: the base passions of the flesh war against the soul (1 Pet. 2:11). The armor of the Christian is the armor of God, intended to enable one to stand against the forces of wickedness in this present darkness (Eph. 6:10-17). The Bible closes with an apocalyptic book that anticipates the end of war, for "Death and Hades," who have received those slain in war, will be cast into the lake of fire (Rev. 20:14). And the gates of the new Jerusalem will remain open, the threat of siege forever ended (21:25).

Bibliography.–*AWBL*; P. C. Craigie, *Problem of War in the OT* (1978); D. Ussishkin, *Conquest of Lachish by Sennacherib* (1982); R. de Vaux, *Ancient Israel* (Eng. tr. repr. 1965); Q. Wright, *A Study of War* (1965); Y. Yadin, *Art of Warfare in Biblical Lands* (1963).

K. N. SCHOVILLE

WAR, IDEA OF.

I. Theory and Practice of War
  A. Definition
  B. Theory of War
  C. Practice of War
II. Near Eastern Background
  A. Theological Perspectives
  B. Practical Perspectives
III. War in Israel
IV. God and War in the OT
V. Holy War
VI. War and the State
VII. Prophetic Perspectives on War
  A. New Covenant
  B. Apocalyptic Dimension of Warfare
VIII. War and Peace
IX. NT and the Idea of War
  A. Kingdom of God
  B. Spiritualization of the Language of Warfare
  C. War and Political Theology
  D. Apocalyptic Ideas of War

I. Theory and Practice of War.–*A. Definition.* War is a form of hostile conflict between two or more nations, or parties within nations, employing the force of arms. Warfare in various forms has been undertaken throughout the known history of the human race and is not peculiar to any one culture or civilization.

B. Theory of War. In modern times warfare has become a subject of theoretical, even philosophical, reflection; notable modern theorists include Carl von Clausewitz (*On War* [Eng. tr. 1968], published first in German in 1832), and Baron de Jomini, *The Art of War* (Eng. tr. 1832). In the ancient Near East and in OT times the theory of war was generally implicit in religious and historical texts, rather than explicit (see II and V below). In general, war was recognized as a concomitant necessity of the existence of a nation-state; it was also frequently interpreted as an earthly expression of heavenly conflict. For the most part, Near Eastern and biblical texts contain laws of war, historical accounts of war, and religious interpretations of war, rather than strictly theoretical reflections on the causes and nature of warfare.

C. Practice of War. War was practiced by all known nations in the Near Eastern world and by Israel in biblical times. While sometimes war was positively embraced as a means to achieve some stated goal, frequently it was simply accepted regretfully as a necessity of historical existence.

II. Near Eastern Background.–Warfare was practiced by all Israel's neighbors during the biblical period; the ideas of war prevalent in Near Eastern nations can be deduced from religious and historical texts that have been discovered largely as a consequence of archeological exploration and excavation.

A. Theological Perspectives. Many Near Eastern cosmologies employ the notion of warfare to describe the emergence of an ordered and created world out of primeval chaos. Thus in the Babylonian creation myth *Enuma Elish* order is eventually secured by the god Marduk by virtue of his conquest of the deities of chaos. Warfare and victory are thus seen as the means by which an orderly cosmos has been established by the gods; concurrently, the order that was to be preserved in the human world was to be secured and maintained by means of warfare. As the forces of chaos were to be kept at bay by the warrior-king Marduk, so too the human king, Marduk's earthly counterpart, was to employ warfare in the establishment and maintenance of his god's kingdom on earth. This cosmological understanding of warfare, with local variations in expression, is present in various Near Eastern creation texts and provides an ideological and religious background to (and sometimes justification of) the practice of war in the Near Eastern nations. Stemming from this fundamental notion, the chief god of a state was normally also a war-god; numerous minor deities in a pantheon might also serve as war-gods.

B. Practical Perspectives. Thus warfare in the ancient Near East was consistently perceived from a theological or religious perspective. As warfare was an instrument of the state, and as the state in turn was the possession of a god or gods, it follows that religious dimensions thoroughly penetrated the actual practice of warfare. Prior to departing for war a Near Eastern king would consult his gods (through omen-priests) on the appropriateness of going to war and would solicit divine aid for the coming battles. On the battlefield as such the presence of the gods would be symbolized by standards and images and also by the presence of priests (who functioned as military advisors, not chaplains). Following victory in warfare a thanksgiving service was held to honor the gods who had given the victory. Thus a religious perspective influenced every aspect of a state's undertaking of war in the ancient Near Eastern world.

III. War in Israel.–The history of the nation of Israel, as it is expressed in the OT narratives, can be interpreted as a history involving different experiences of warfare. In the narratives describing the emergence of a monarchy in the time of King Saul, warfare was a principal method by which the state was established. By means of invasion and attack, the Hebrew people had settled in the land that was to become Israel, making it their own by expelling or defeating the former residents, the Canaanites. While a detailed study of Israel's early history makes it clear that war was not the only method employed in the settlement of the Promised Land, it is evident that without the use of force the state of Israel would not have come into existence.

With the establishment of the united monarchy (Saul, David, and Solomon), and throughout the history of the separate kingdoms of Israel (922-722 B.C.) and Judah (922-586 B.C.), war continued to be a frequent characteristic of the history of the Hebrew people. War was now principally a means by which the safety and continuity of the state could be secured, though aggressive warfare continued to be employed from time to time in attempts to extend or recapture the territorial possessions of the nation.

Just as warfare had contributed to the emergence and survival of the Hebrew kingdoms, so too the demise of the states of Judah and Israel came about in warfare. The northern state of Israel was defeated by the Assyrian armies in 722 B.C. (2 K. 17:1-6); it never reemerged as an independent Hebrew state. The southern state of Judah survived a little longer; it was defeated eventually by the armies of the Neo-Babylonian empire in the war of 587-586 B.C. and ceased to exist as an independent Hebrew kingdom (2 K. 25; Jer. 52). The states that had begun in wars of aggression and had survived largely through wars of defense finally ended in warfare at the hands of more powerful warrior nations.

IV. God and War in the OT.–The OT narratives consistently identify God with Israel's experience of warfare. In the celebration of the Exodus from Egyptian slavery God is called a "man of war" (Ex. 15:3), through whose victorious acts freedom had been secured. In the later hymnody of the Hebrew monarchy God was celebrated as "the Lord, strong and mighty, the Lord, mighty in battle" (Ps. 24:8). And one of the most common epithets for God in the OT is the "Lord of hosts" (lit. "Lord of armies"), an expression used more than two hundred times in the biblical text.

The association of God with warfare in ancient Israel is integral to the fundamental theology of the Hebrews, namely, that God participated in and through this historical experience. Their liberation from slavery, their possession of the Promised Land, and eventually their loss of independent nationhood were all understood in direct relationship to God, i.e., His will and purpose as expressed in the covenant, and their own obedience and disobedience with respect to the covenant stipulations. Such was the Hebrew conception of divine immanence that inevitably God was perceived in all the experiences of human existence, of which warfare was only one.

V. Holy War.–In much contemporary OT scholarship Israel's wars have been labeled "holy wars" (see esp. G. von Rad). The description "holy wars" emerges not only from the generally religious language in which war is described in the OT, but specifically from the observation that war in ancient Israel was undertaken as a cultic act, the conscious ritual act of a religious community. The expression "holy war" is nevertheless misleading, implying that warfare as such may be considered "holy." Increasingly scholars are coming to recognize that a more appropriate designation for Israel's wars would be "Yahweh War" (cf., e.g., G. H. Jones, R. Smend); such a designation conveys the religious character of Israel's warfare without implying that the conduct of war had moral or religious worth. The purpose of warfare in ancient Israel, including wars that ended in defeat, can be understood within the context of "salvation-history"; while salvation was the goal of human history, warfare as such was evil, yet through both its victories and defeats the goal of salvation would ultimately be achieved within the divine providence.

VI. War and the State.–As with many other Near Eastern nations, the state of Israel was conceived as a theocracy; though the state was ruled by a human king, its ultimate head was God. Thus one of the principal themes of Hebrew thought is the "kingship of God," which is found in both early and late texts. And the kingship of God inevitably has associations with warfare, both in the early texts (Ex. 15:18) and in the texts of the monarchy (e.g., Pss. 47, 93, 96–99, the so-called enthronement psalms). The kingship of God presupposes the notion of the kingdom of God, which in turn was identified in OT times (prior to 586 B.C.) with the nation-state(s) of the chosen people.

The theocratic notion of the state in Israel, and the understanding of the state as the kingdom of God, inevitably led to the further identification of God with warfare (see IV above). No human state, whether in the ancient or modern world, can exist without the contingent possibility of warfare. To oversimplify a complex set of possibilities, states come into existence, survive, and eventually decline and die, in direct relation to the existence and use of force in such activities as warfare. Such was the case with ancient Israel, and thus at each point in Israel's history God as head of state was inevitably associated with Israel's experience of warfare. The God of Israel, however, was conceived to be not only a national God but also a universal God; it was this broader conception that eventually made possible a new understanding of the nature of the kingdom of God and of the kingship of God following the demise of the kingdom of Judah in 586 B.C.

VII. Prophetic Perspectives on War.–The demise of the kingdoms of Israel (722 B.C.) and Judah (586 B.C.) evoked in the Hebrew tradition a radical rethinking of the nature of God, of the relationship between divine kingship and human kingdoms, and indeed of the fundamental nature and role of warfare in human history. Defeat in war precipitated this radical theological revolution; the bitter experience of warfare and defeat secured new perspectives from which new insights emerged that are perpetually relevant to all thinking about warfare. The pioneers in this radical theological revolution were those who lived through the demise of the state of Judah, notably Jeremiah and Ezekiel, and the prophets who succeeded them in subsequent generations.

Two themes are particularly important in the context of these new ideas of the nature of warfare in relation to religion: the notion of a new covenant, and the emergence of apocalyptic thought conveyed in military language and imagery.

A. New Covenant. While earlier prophets anticipated the notion of the new covenant, that which Jeremiah (Jer. 31:31-34) expressed is particularly pertinent to the transformation of the idea of war in ancient Israel. Whereas the original Mosaic covenant, and then the later Davidic covenant, had anticipated the formation of a nation-state of God's chosen people, with the contingent necessity of warfare (see, e.g., the laws of war in Dt. 20:10-18), the new covenant anticipated a different kind of human community. The new covenant would involve an inward transformation of the covenant members and a new knowledge of God. While Jeremiah does not amplify fully his concept of a new covenant community, it appears to be distinct from that of the nation-state and thus does not contain within it the contingent necessity of warfare. From a human perspective, one may say that Jeremiah's perception of the failure, in war, of the kingdom of God as a human state (the failure being a consequence of human evil) led him to perceive the necessity of a kingdom of God not identified with a nation-state. This notion of the state and of warfare was to be influential in the earliest Christian community and indeed central in the teaching of Jesus.

B. Apocalyptic Dimension of Warfare. While apocalyptic thought does not begin with the prophet Ezekiel, his book is particularly pertinent because, as with Jeremiah, it is set against the backdrop of Judah's final defeat in warfare. In Ezekiel's apocalyptic description of the restoration of Israel (Ezk. 38–39), God's final transformation of human history is to be effected by means of warfare. Whether the language of apocalyptic battle is to be interpreted literally or figuratively, it is equally appropriate to the theme. The battle between good and evil has marked all human history; the final conquest of evil is thus set on a field of battle, in which God the warrior destroys the forces of evil. This apocalyptic notion of warfare also influenced early Christianity, not least the book of Revelation, which draws extensively on the imagery of Ezekiel.

VIII. War and Peace.–The notion of peace (*šālôm*) in the OT is a broad one; while the word *šālôm* can imply peace as distinct from warfare it has the fundamental notion of "wholeness, integrity." Thus, while a kind of peace may exist simply in the absence of warfare, complete peace presupposes the full health of a society, the absence of evil and injustice, and the presence of both righteousness and justice. As Jeremiah observed, people may say "peace, peace," when in reality there is no peace (Jer. 6:14).

The ideal of peace is given expression from time to time in the writings of the prophets. The well-known vision of swords being beaten into ploughshares and spears into pruning hooks (Isa. 2:4; Mic. 4:3) is shared by two eighth-century prophets and may antedate both of them. But the prophets were not pacifists; their vision of distant peace was balanced by the contemporary reality of warfare. Both Isaiah and Micah, who shared the ancient vision of peace, affirmed the judgmental role of God in contemporary warfare. In other prophetic writings the notion of peace is more or less absent; the dominant theme is warfare in its instrumental role within the scheme of divine judgment (e.g., Nahum).

Peace is thus recognized in the OT as an ideal, something for which to strive and hope; it would come not only in the absence of war but also in the wholeness and integrity of human society. But this ideal of peace, mellowed by the contemporary realities of violence in the time of the prophets, became eventually a part of the apocalyptic and eschatological traditions in Israel (see VII.B above). Peace was to be a part of God's final work in the transformation of Israel and the nations. In the normal political and daily life of the Hebrew kingdoms, however, a continuing tradition that could be called a peace movement, or any tradition of pacifism, was absent.

IX. NT and the Idea of War.*–A. Kingdom of God.* Fundamental to the teaching of Jesus, and indeed to the meaning of Jesus, His life, death, and resurrection, is the theme of the kingdom of God. It is a principal theme of His preaching (Mk. 1:13f.); by His death and resurrection the kingdom is established. The theology of the kingdom of God in the NT follows principally upon the notion of the new covenant as expressed by Jeremiah, rather than returning to the older notion of the kingdom as a nation-state. Thus the Christian conception of the kingdom of God must be kept separate from the notion of state (though such has not always been the case in Christian history), which in turn means that the kingdom cannot legitimately be engaged in warfare. Indeed, central to the foundation of the kingdom of God is the death of Jesus, which exemplifies the receipt of violence, rather than its exercise. Thus the kingdom of God, identified in a limited sense with the Church, required the rejection of the use of war and violence by its members, and also their willingness to become the recipients of violence.

B. Spiritualization of the Language of Warfare. Christianity's development of the notion of the kingdom of God grew and was nurtured by the OT Scriptures. The appropriation of the OT material concerning war involved the transformation of that language into the account of spiritual warfare, both in the positive sense of "fighting the good fight" and in the negative sense of fighting against the forces of evil. Thus Paul describes his spiritual life in the metaphor of fighting (1 Cor. 9:26), and he encourages Timothy to "fight the good fight of the faith" (1 Tim. 6:12). And Peter writes of the "passions of the flesh that wage war against your soul" (1 Pet. 2:11), and therefore which must be resisted.

C. War and Political Theology. While the NT provides a very complete description of the kingdom of God, it gives a less comprehensive account of Christian political theology, or of the relation of the Christian and the Church to the state. The matter is important since the relation of the Christian to the state determines the relation of the Christian to war, which normally is conducted by the state. On the one hand, the teaching of Jesus concerning the recognition of the authority of Caesar (Mt. 22:21) and Paul's discourse on the divinely ordained authority of the state (Rom. 13:1-7) have sometimes been taken as a basis for permitting Christians to participate in the warfare waged by the state. On the other hand, Jesus' own rejection of force and His receipt of violence in the crucifixion have been taken by others to imply the total rejection of warfare by Christianity. The tension between these two views reflects the difficulty of the dual citizenship to which the Christian is called. Citizenship in the kingdom of God involves the rejection of violence and war; citizenship in a nation-state, as the OT so clearly demonstrates, involves the contingent possibility, if not necessity, of the use of violence and war by the state. The two principal traditions with respect to the idea of war in Christianity reflect the polarity between these two points of tension. The tradition of pacifism has taken as preeminent the principles of the kingdom of God; the tradition of the "just war" has sought to recognize also the responsibilities of citizenship in a nation state, and to live with a certain tension with respect to the two poles of NT teaching. But in both cases, despite how one interprets the biblical data on war, peace is the Christian's primary goal toward which the whole Bible points.

D. Apocalyptic Ideas of War. As in the OT, NT apocalyptic literature (esp. the book of Revelation) employs warfare as one of the principal metaphors for conveying its understanding of the end of human history and the consummation of the kingdom of God. And just as surely as war is the metaphor of apocalyptic vision, so too peace is the principal term to describe the reality lying beyond the conflict that ends all conflicts.

In whatever manner one interprets apocalyptic literature, the language of warfare is clearly appropriate to the subject. Evil, by its very nature, seems to war against good, whether literally or figuratively. And the persistence of evil is such that it does not simply go away; it must be conquered. Thus, lying behind the harsh language of warfare in the apocalyptic account of the Revelation, is a vision of a world in which peace would reign in perpetuity.

Bibliography.–R. H. Bainton, *Christian Attitudes Toward War and Peace: A Historical Survey and Critical Evaluaton* (1960); D. Bergant, *The Bible Today,* 21 (1983), 156-161; P. C. Craigie, *Problem of War in the OT* (1978); V. Eller, *War and Peace from Genesis to Revelation* (1981); J. Ellul, *Violence: Reflections from a Christian Perspective* (Eng. tr. 1969); J. J. Enz, *The Christian and Warfare* (1972); J. Harmand, *La guerre antique de Sumer à Rome* (1973); W. Janzen, *BASOR,* 220 (Dec. 1975), 73-75; *Mennonite Quarterly Review,* 46 (1972), 155-166; G. H. Jones, *VT,* 25 (1975), 642-658; G. Lewy, *Religion and Revolution* (1974); M. C. Lind, *Yahweh Is a Warrior: The Theology of Warfare in Ancient Israel* (1980); P. D. Miller, *Divine Warrior in Early Israel* (1973); *Interp.,* 19 (1965), 39-46; G. von Rad, *Der heilige Krieg im alten Israel* (1951); R. Smend, *Yahweh War and Tribal Confederation* (Eng. tr. 1970); F. Stolz, *Jahwes und Israels Kriege. Kriegstheorien und Kriegserfahrungen* (1972); M. E. Tate, *Review and Expositor,* 79 (1982), 587-596; M. Weippert, *ZAW,* 84 (1972), 460-493; G. E. Wright, *OT and Theology* (1969); J. H. Yoder, *Politics of Jesus* (1972).

P. C. CRAIGIE

WAR, MAN OF. Another designation for a WARRIOR (*see also* SOLDIER). Celebrating Yahweh's victory over Pharaoh's army at the Red Sea, the song of Moses says, "The Lord is a man of war [Heb. *'îš milḥāmâ*]" (Ex. 15:3). The OT frequently depicts Yahweh as a mighty warrior who fights for His people and delivers them from their enemies. *See* WAR, IDEA OF IV.

See P. Miller, *Divine Warrior in Early Israel* (1973).

WARDROBE [Heb. *šōmēr/šōmēr habbᵉgāḏîm*] (2 K. 22:14; 2 Ch. 34:22). The keeper of the wardrobe (e.g., Shallum, husband of the prophetess Huldah, in 2 K. 22:14; 2 Ch. 34:22), employed at the palace or the temple, took care of the costly garments used for important state and religious events. 2 K. 10:22 refers to "him who was in charge of the wardrobe" (Heb. *'ᵃšer ʿal-hammeltāḥâ*; AV "him that was over the vestry"; NEB "the person who had charge of the wardrobe"), i.e., an official who took care of the garments worn by Baal worshipers. In Jer. 38:11 the RSV and NEB emend the MT *taḥaṯ* (AV "under"; NEB mg. "underneath") to read *meltaḥaṯ,* "wardrobe."

G. L. K.

WARES [Heb. *ʿizzāḇôn*] (Ezk. 27:12, 14, 16, 19, 22, 27, 33); AV also FAIRS; NEB also STAPLE WARES; [*maʿᵃrāḇ*] (Ezk. 27:9); AV MERCHANDISE; [*meḵer*] (Neh. 13:16); NEB MERCHANDISE; [*mimkār*] (Neh. 13:20); NEB TRADERS; [*maqqāḥôṯ*] (Neh. 10:31 [MT 32]); NEB MERCHANDISE; [*migdānôṯ*] (Ezr. 1:6); AV PRECIOUS THINGS; NEB GIFTS; [*kᵉlî*] (Jonah 1:5); NEB THINGS; "wares" is supplied contextually by the RSV and NEB in Rev. 18:15. Marketable goods and commodities.

The majority of the RSV's references to "wares" occur in Ezk. 27, which describes the extensive trading enterprises of the city of Tyre. The variety of goods brought to Tyre by caravan and ship indicates the "great wealth of every kind" (v. 12) that was to be found there, e.g., refined metals and vessels made from them, precious stones, grain, spices, animals, and cloth. Geographically, Tyre's trade reached from Tarshish to Asia Minor, and from Damascus to Sheba.

Accustomed to trading with Tyrians (Neh. 13:16) and other foreigners who did not observe the Sabbath, the postexilic Jews of Jerusalem succumbed to the temptation to set aside their covenantal Sabbath obligation (10:31) in favor of the greater prosperity that could be achieved by trading every day (13:15-18). Nehemiah instituted reforms to prohibit trading on the Sabbath (vv. 19-22).

The attitude of the exiles of Ezr. 1:6 contrasts with that of the postexilic Jerusalemites. These exiles generously supported with their gifts their neighbors who were returning to Jerusalem to rebuild the house of Yahweh.

The lament over Babylon (Rome) in Rev. 18 is reminiscent of the lament over Tyre in Ezk. 27. although the saints rejoice over the fall of Babylon (Rev. 18:20), the merchants mourn because of the loss of their profitable trade (v. 15).

See also COMMERCE; MERCHANDISE; MERCHANT.

G. WYPER

WARFARE. *See* WAR, WARFARE.

WARP [Heb. *šᵉṯî*] (Lev. 13:48-59). The long threads extended lengthwise in the loom to form the basis of the web. The threads of the "woof" (Heb. *ʿēreḇ*) are interlaced with the warp at right angles. *See* WEAVING.

WARRIOR [Heb. *gibbôr, gibbôr (ha)ḥayil*] (Jgs. 11:1; 1 Ch. 5:24; 7:2, 5, etc.; 8:40; 12:8; 28:1; 2 Ch. 32:21; Job 16:14; Ps. 33:16; 120:4; 127:4; Cant. 4:4; Jer. 20:11; etc.); AV MIGHTY MAN (OF VALOUR), MIGHTY ONES, GIANT, STRONG, VALIANT MEN (OF MIGHT); NEB also FIGHTING MEN, MEN OF ABILITY, ABLE MEN, VALIANT MEN, TROOPS, BODYGUARD; [*gibbôrê milḥāmâ*] (2 Ch. 13:3); AV VALIANT MEN OF WAR; NEB TROOPS; [*'îš milḥāmâ*] (1 Ch. 28:3); AV (lit.) MAN OF WAR; NEB FIGHTING MAN; [*tōpśê hammilḥāmâ*] (Nu. 31:27); AV (lit.) "them that took the war upon them"; NEB FIGHTING MEN; [*ʿāśâ milḥāmâ*] (1 K. 12:21; 2 Ch. 11:1); [*sō'ēn*–'tramp, tread'] (Isa. 9:5 [MT 4]); NEB SOLDIERS; [qal pass. part. of *qārā'*–'call'] (Ezk. 23:23); AV RENOWNED; NEB STAFF OFFICERS; [*ʿizzûz*] (Isa. 43:17); AV (lit.) POWER; NEB MEN OF VALOUR; [*mišmān*] ("stout warriors," Isa. 10:16); AV (lit.) "fat ones"; NEB "sturdy frame"; [*pārāz*] (Hab. 3:14); AV (lit.) "villages"; [pl. of *qᵉrāḇ*] (Ezk. 23:6, 12); AV "neighbours"; NEB STAFF OFFICERS.

At the beginning of Israel's history every physically fit man could be called upon to fight for the tribe or the nation. As society became more complex under the monarchy, the army developed into a professional one of mercenaries and conscripts. G. E. Wright (*OT and Theology* [1969]) underlined the biblical theme of God as warrior, which he saw as the reverse side of His nature as lover and redeemer; God is a warrior because His redemption is resisted in the sinful world. See also P. Miller, *Divine Warrior in Early Israel* (1973).

Several texts call for comment. In Isa. 10:16 the MT has "fat ones"; the RSV supplies "warriors," apparently on the basis of the context (see E. J. Young, *Book of Isaiah,* I [2nd ed. 1972), 365f. and n. 46). But as commentators have pointed out, such an interpretation is unnecessary, for the prophet may simply be referring to Assyria in general (see, e.g., O. Kaiser, *Isaiah 1–12* [Eng. tr., 2nd ed., *OTL,* 1983], pp. 238f.).

In the difficult text of Hab. 3:14 the RSV follows the versions; the MT *pārāz* is ueally taken to mean "country folk" (see, e.g., W. F. Albright, "Psalm of Habakkuk," in H. H. Rowley, ed., *Studies in OT Prophecy* [*Festschrift* T. H. Robinson, repr. 1957], pp. 13, 17), but such a meaning does not fit the context well. Thus other meanings have been sought on the basis of Arabic cognates (see KoB,

3rd ed., p. 908; *see also* PEASANTRY), or the text has been emended (see comms.).

Finally, two verses in Ezk. 23 are problematic. The RSV takes *qᵉrôḇîm,* the last word of (MT) v. 5, as the first word of v. 6 (see also *BHS*) and derives it from *qᵉrāḇ,* "war" (cf. Akk. *qurbūti,* "guardsmen"; see W. Zimmerli, *Ezekiel,* I [Eng. tr., *Hermeneia,* 1979], p. 472 n. c; see also v. 12). The AV "neighbours" reflects a derivation from *qārôḇ,* "near," following the versions; the problem with this interpretation is, of course, that Assyria was not Israel's neighbor. In v. 23 the RSV reads *qᵉrôḇîm,* as in vv. 5f. and 12, for MT *qᵉrû'îm,* "called" (see RSV mg.), but according to Zimmerli (p. 475 n. c) the MT may be understood as "highly respected men" and need not be emended.

See also SOLDIER; WAR; WAR, IDEA OF.

G. WYPER G. A. L.

WARS OF THE LORD, BOOK OF THE [Heb. *sēper milḥᵃmōṯ YHWH*] (Nu. 21:14). Numbers 21:14f. and possibly vv. 17f.; 27-30 suggest that this document was a collection of popular songs about the early Israelite victories, with the Lord Himself as commander-in-chief (cf. Josh. 24:12f.; Am. 2:9). The LXX omits the reference. References such as this indicate that the present OT documents were partially based on earlier writen documents.

See also JASHAR, BOOK OF.

See D. Christensen, *CBQ,* 36 (1974), 359f.

WASH. Words translated "wash" find their use mainly in connection with the ceremonial cleansings and sacrificial procedures of OT religion, in figurative language having to do with sin and guilt, and in connection with the practice of footwashing.

Hebrew *rāḥaṣ* is broadly used. It can refer to foot washing, which is usually connected with customs of hospitality (Gen. 18:4; 19:2; 24:32; 43:24; Jgs. 19:21; 1 S. 25:41; 2 S. 11:8), but also with religious ceremony (Ex. 30:18-21; 40:30f.; cf. 2 Ch. 4:6), and to bathing one's whole body, usually in preparation for some important event, or, by a woman, in preparation for being with a man (Ex. 2:5; Ruth 3:3; 2 S. 11:2; 12:20; 1 K. 22:38b; Ezk. 23:40). The descendants of Aaron were bathed in preparation for their consecration as priests (Ex. 29:4; 40:12; Lev. 8:6). The high priest and others were also bathed as part of the ceremony on the Day of Atonement (Lev. 16:4, 24, 26, 28). Washing one's hands as a symbol of a claim of innocence had its beginning in sacrificial procedure (Dt. 21:6; Ps. 26:6; 73:13; cf. Ex. 30:18-21; 40:30f.). The legs and internal organs of sacrificial animals intended for the burnt offering were washed before being offered on the altar (Ex. 29:17; Lev. 1:9; 8:21; 9:14).

Rāḥaṣ is also used of cleansing from ceremonial uncleanness brought by "leprosy" (Lev. 14:8f.; 2 K. 5:10-13) or other sources of defilement (Lev. 15; 17:15; 22:6; Nu. 19:7f., 19; Dt. 23:11 [MT 12]). It is found in other literal uses (Job 29:6; Ps. 58:10 [MT 11]), and is used figuratively, e.g., for cleansing of sin (Job 9:30; Isa. 1:16; 4:4; Prov. 30:12; cf. also Cant. 5:12; Ezk. 16:4).

Hebrew *kāḇas* (in the piel) is used of the washing of clothes, whether as part of the ceremonial of worship (Ex. 19:10, 14; Lev. 6:27 [MT 20]), of ordination (Nu. 8:7, 21), or of meeting royalty (2 S. 19:24 [MT 25]), or as part of the ritual for "leprosy" (Lev. 13:6, 34, 54-58; 14:8f., 47) and other forms of uncleanness (Lev. 11:25, 28, 40; 15:8, 11, 13, etc.; 16:26, 28; 17:15f.; Nu. 19:7f., 10, 19, 21; 31:24). A picture of great plenty is provided by a reference to washing garments in wine (Gen. 49:11). The only uses of *kāḇas* for washing anything other than garments are figurative uses for cleansing of sin (Ps. 51:2a, 7b [MT 4b, 9b]; Jer. 2:22; 4:14).

Other less common Hebrew words sometimes translated "wash" are *šāṭap,* "overflow, flood" (1 K. 22:38a; Job 14:19; Ezk. 16:9; NEB also "swilled out," "scours"), *dû(a)ḥ,* "rinse off blood" (Ezk. 40:38), *māhah,* "destroy" (Nu. 5:23; AV "blot out"), and *yāṣaq,* "pour" (Job 22:16; AV "overflown"; NEB "flowing away").

It has been suggested that some or all of the figurative references to washing in the NT (except Gk. *plýnō* in Rev. 7:14; 22:14) are intended to be references to baptism (*apoloúō,* 1 Cor. 6:11; *loúō,* He. 10:22; 2 Pet. 2:22; *loutrón,* "washing," Eph. 5:26; Tit. 3:5). This would appear to be especially likely in Acts 22:16 (*apoloúō*), where "wash away your sins" is parallel to "be baptized." But even there it is likely that "wash away" refers to an inward or spiritual cleansing that is not simply accomplished by the physical act of baptism.

In the NT washing also occurs in reference to rites of Judaism (*níptō,* Mt. 15:2; Mk. 7:3f. [cf. "unwashed," *ániptos,* Mt. 15:20; Mk. 7:2]; a nontechnical use of *baptízō,* Lk. 11:38), part of the action of a healing by Jesus (*níptō,* Jn. 9:7, 11, 15), the preparation of a body for burial (*loúō,* Acts 9:37), the washing of nets by fishermen (*plýnō,* Lk. 5:2), a person's personal washing of the face to appear in public (*níptō,* Mt. 6:17), the cleansing of an injured person's wounds (*loúō,* Acts 16:33), Pilate's washing of his hands as a symbolic claim of innocence (*aponíptō,* Mt. 27:24), and foot washing (*níptō,* Jn. 13:5-14; 1 Tim. 5:10), now partly a symbolic rite within the Church.

See also ABLUTION; BATHE; FOOT WASHING.

G. A. GAY

WASHBASIN [Heb. *sîr raḥaṣ*–'vessel for washing']; AV WASHPOT; NEB WASH-BOWL. A basin used for washing feet. In the oracle cited in Ps. 60:8 (MT 10) and 108:9 (MT 10) Yahweh says, "Moab is my washbasin," i.e., Moab is to be so disgraced that it will be a tub in which the conqueror's feet are washed.

WASHING OF THE FEET. *See* FOOT WASHING.

WASP [Gk. *sphḗx*] (Wisd. 12:8); NEB HORNET. Perhaps a general term denoting both wasp and hornet. The Palestinian hornet is larger than the wasp and in great numbers has caused cattle to stampede. Stinging swarms among an army might be able to change the outcome of battle. *See also* HORNET.

WASTING SICKNESS [Heb. *rāzôn*] (Isa. 10:16; "wasting disease," Ps. 106:15); AV LEANNESS; NEB also DISEASE. Possibly pulmonary tuberculosis in both references. M. Dahood, however, understood Ps. 106:15 as indicating the result of prolonged hunger (*Psalms,* III [*AB,* 1970], 71).

WATCH [nouns: Heb. *'ašmūrâ/'ašmōreṯ* (Ex. 14:24; Jgs. 7:19; 1 S. 11:11; etc.), *mišmār* (1 Ch. 26:16; Neh. 12:24; Jer. 51:12), *šimmurîm* ("watching," Ex. 12:42), *mišmereṯ* ("duty of watching," 1 Ch. 9:27), *niṣṣᵉrâ* (Ps. 141:3), *ṣippîyâ* ("watching," Lam. 4:17); Gk. *phylakḗ* (Mt. 14:25; Mk. 6:48; Lk. 2:8; 12:38), *agrypnía* (2 Cor. 6:5)]; AV also WARD, CHARGE, OBSERVED, etc.; NEB also GUARD, VIGIL, etc.; [verbs: Heb. *šāmar* (Jgs. 7:19; 1 S. 19:11; 26:15f.; Job 14:16; etc.), *ṣāpâ* (Gen. 31:49; 2 S. 13:34; Ps. 37:32; etc.; piel, 1 S. 4:13; Ps. 5:3 [MT 4]; etc.), *rā'â* (Jgs. 21:21; 1 S. 6:9; Ps. 142:4 [MT 5]), *šō'ēr* ("who keep watch," Neh. 11:19), *šāqaḏ* (Job 21:32; Prov. 8:34; Isa. 29:20; etc.), *nāṣar* (Ps. 61:7 [MT 8]; Prov. 2:11; 22:12; 24:12), piel of *pālas* (Prov. 5:21), piel of *nāḥaš* (1 K. 20:33); Gk. *grēgoréō* (Mt. 24:42f.; 25:13; 26:38, 40f.; Mk. 13:34f., 37; etc.), *tēréō* (Mt. 27:36, 54), *paratēréō* (Mk. 3:2; Lk. 6:7; 14:1; 20:20; Acts 9:24), *agrypnéō* (Mk. 13:33; Lk. 21:36; He. 13:17), *theōréō* (Mk. 12:41; Lk. 23:35)]; AV also SEE, BEHOLD, KEEP, PRESERVE, etc.; NEB also BE POSTED, PRESERVE, etc.; **BE WATCHFUL** [Gk. *grēgoréō*] (1 Cor. 16:13; Col. 4:2; 1 Pet. 5:8); AV also BE VIGILANT; NEB BE (ON THE) ALERT, WITH MIND AWAKE; **WATCHER** [Heb. part. of *nāṣar* (Job 7:20); Aram. *ʿîr* (Dnl. 4:13, 17, 23 [MT 10, 14, 20])]; AV also PRESERVER (Job 7:20). In Ezk. 34:16 the MT reads *šāmaḏ* (AV lit. "destroy"); the RSV follows the LXX, Syriac, and Vulgate with "watch." In Ps. 119:82, 123; Lam. 4:17 the RSV supplies "(with) watching."

I. The Noun.–The Hebrew nouns *ʾašmûrâ (ʾašmōreṯ), mišmār, mišmereṯ,* and *šimmurîm* are all derived from the verb *šāmar* (see below). The noun *ʾašmûrâ* denotes a division of the night. In OT times the night was divided into three "watches" (cf. Ps. 63:6 [MT 7]; 90:4; 119:148): the first watch (Lam. 2:19), the midnight watch (Jgs. 7:19), and the morning watch (Ex. 14:24; 1 S. 11:11; cf. Ps. 130:6). By NT times the Jews were following the Roman custom of dividing the night into four watches: evening, midnight, cockcrow, and morning (Mk. 13:35; cf. Gk. *phylakḗ*, Lk. 12:38; Mt. 14:25 par. Mk. 6:48). The "watching" (pl. of *agrypnía*, "wakefulness") mentioned in 2 Cor. 6:5 refers to sleepless nights. *See also* DAY AND NIGHT.

"Watch" can also denote a guard placed on watch (e.g., Heb. *mišmār,* 1 Ch. 26:16 par. Neh. 12:24); in Ps. 141:3 the hapax legomenon *niṣṣᵉrâ* (from vb. *nāṣar*) is used figuratively in parallel with *šomrâ* (RSV "guard"). "Watch" can also refer to a guard post (*mišmār,* Jer. 51:12) or to the duty of guarding (*mišmereṯ,* 1 Ch. 9:27). The meaning of *ṣippîyâ* (from *ṣāpâ*) in Lam. 4:17 is uncertain; some scholars have interpreted it to mean a "watchtower" or "lookout" (see *CHAL,* p. 309; *TWOT,* II, 773), while others have read it as a reference to the act of watching (so AV, RSV; KD, *ad loc.*).

II. The Verb.–The Hebrew verb most frequently rendered "watch" in the RSV OT is *šāmar,* "guard," "keep," "watch," "give heed to." Both *šāmar* and *nāṣar,* a less common synonym of *šāmar,* are often rendered by Gk. *phylássō* in the LXX. Heb. *ṣāpâ* has a more specific meaning; it "conveys the idea of being fully aware of a situation in order to gain some advantage or keep from being surprised by an enemy" (*TWOT,* II, 773). *Rāʾâ* is a common verb meaning "see," "look at," while *šāqaḏ* emphasizes the idea of being alert and watchful.

In the RSV NT the verb "watch" most often represents Gk. *grēgoréō*. This verb and the cognate *agrypnéō* are both derived from the verb *egeírō*, "awaken," "arise," and they mean "be awake," "be alert, vigilant." *Theoréō* ("observe," "perceive") sometimes occurs in its original sense of "watch as a spectator." *Paratēréō,* a compound form of *tēréō* ("guard," "keep"), has a range of meanings, including "observe" (cf. Gal. 4:10), "lie in wait," "keep watch over"; in the NT it usually means "watch maliciously" or "watch lurkingly" (see Bauer, rev., p. 622; *TDNT,* VIII, 147f.).

The verb "watch" is used in various senses in the English versions. It can mean simply to observe closely in order to see what will happen (e.g., 1 S. 4:13; 6:9; Ps. 142:4 [MT 5]; Jer. 48:19), or to watch as a spectator (e.g., Mk. 12:41; Lk. 23:35). To "(keep) watch over" means to "guard," "protect," or "take care of." Thus the king's bodyguard had the responsibility of protecting his master's life (1 S. 26:15f.). To "keep watch over" can also mean keeping someone in custody (e.g., Mt. 27:36, 54).

Some "watching" has malicious intent. Several psalmists complain that their enemies watch them, waiting for an opportunity to ambush them (Ps. 56:6 [MT 7]; 71:10; cf. 10:8; 37:32; Isa. 29:20; Jer. 20:10). Saul sent messengers to watch David's house so that they might kill him (1 S. 19:11). Similarly, some Jews watched the gates of Damascus so that they could kill Saul (Paul) when he left there (Acts 9:24). The scribes and Pharisees watched Jesus for an opportunity to accuse and arrest Him (Lk. 6:7 par. Mk. 3:2; Lk. 14:1; 20:20).

Scripture also speaks of God "watching over" human beings, usually in the positive sense of protecting or guarding them. God "watches over," i.e., protects and cares for, those who trust in Him (Job 29:2; Ps. 127:1; 146:9; Prov. 5:21; 24:12). When Jacob and Laban made their covenant, Laban said, "The Lord watch between you and me, when we are absent one from the other," i.e., the Lord will ensure that both parties keep their agreement (Gen. 31:49f.). At the time of the Exodus the Lord "watched" to bring His people out of Egypt, and the people remembered His watching by thenceforth keeping their own watch on Passover (Ex. 12:42). The psalmist prayed that God would guard his lips to prevent him from speaking evil (Ps. 141:3; cf. also 61:7 [MT 8]; Prov. 2:11; 6:22). (In Ezk. 34:16 the MT has *ʾašmîḏ,* "I will destroy," but most commentators follow the LXX and other versions, which presuppose *ʾešmōr,* "I will watch over" [see RSV mg., *BHS*].)

The implicit threat in God's watching over us, i.e., that He not only will see danger and protect us but that He also will see our sin and could punish us for it, is explicit in a few texts. God can "watch over" people for evil as well as for good (Ps. 66:7; Prov. 15:3; Jer. 31:28; 44:27; cf. 1:12). Job is especially conscious of this (Job 13:27; 14:16; cf. 33:11) and complains directly to God, the "watcher of men" (7:20).

In Gethsemane Jesus asked His disciples to watch with Him (Mt. 26:38), but they fell asleep (vv. 40f.). In these texts "watch" (Gk. *grēgoréō*) connotes "stay awake, be vigilant." Several times Jesus exhorted His disciples to "watch" (Mt. 24:42; 25:13; Mk. 13:33, 35, 37; see also 1 Cor. 16:13; Col. 4:2; He. 13:17; 1 Pet. 5:8; cf. Ps. 119:82, 123; Hab. 2:1), sometimes linking it with "pray" (Mt. 26:41; Mk. 14:38; Lk. 21:36). Following Barth (e.g., *CD,* III/4, 95), J. Ellul asserted that the two actions "watch and pray" are indissolubly united: "Prayer is an act of vigilance and the vigilance is a consequence of prayer" (*Prayer and Modern Man* [Eng. tr. repr. 1979], pp. 134f.; see also pp. 99-137; in commenting on the use of *grēgoréō* in Rev. 3:2f. Ellul stated that the watching or vigilance is "a manifestation of life . . . a matter of not being lulled into security"; *Apocalypse: The Book of Revelation* [Eng. tr. 1977], p. 138).

See also GUARD; HEED; KEEPER; OBSERVE.

N. J. O. G. A. L.

III. Watcher.–The Aram. *ʿîr* occurs in Dnl. 4:13, 17, 23 (Mt. 10, 14, 20). The term has been connected to the Phoen. *ṣpy šmym,* "watcher of heaven" (the *Zōphasēmin* of Philo Byblius preserved in Eusebius *Praep. ev.* i.10), but this inference seems unlikely. Today most commentators assume *ʿîr* is related to the Hebrew root *ʿwr,* "be awake" (cf. Jgs. 5:12; Ps. 7:6 [MT 7]), hence the understanding "watcher." The cognates Ugar. *ʿr* and Akk. *êru* support this meaning.

In the OT these watchers are celestial beings; they descend from heaven and are probably equated with the "holy ones" (Dnl. 4:13). Elsewhere in the OT "holy ones" (*q*^{e}*ḏōšîm*) refers to God's angels (Job 5:1; 15:15; Ps. 89:5, 7 [MT 6, 8]; Dnl. 8:13; Zec. 14:5; *see* ANGEL). The watchers are servants of the Most High, possess a certain joint authority to speak the decrees of God, and apparently form a heavenly council who listen to God's word and then act as divine messengers to bring these commands and revelations to human beings (Dnl. 4:17). Some see the watchers as a special classification of angels who are agents and supervisors employed by God as He controls governments, perhaps even involved in decision making and the execution of decrees that affect world affairs (C. F. Dickason, *Angels: Elect and Evil* [1975], p. 59).

Intertestamental literature describes the watchers with considerably more detail. According to the pseudepigraphic book of 1 Enoch the watchers were angels who fell from heaven and changed the order of their nature by lusting after and fornicating with women, thus corrupting the sons of men and prompting the great flood (1 En. 10:8-10; 12:4; 15:9; cf. T. Naph. 3:5; Gen. 6:1-8). Part of Enoch's ministry was to reprimand and pronounce judgment on the eternal watchers (1 En. 1:5; 10:15; 12:2; 13:10; 14:1, 3; cf. 39:12f.; 40:2). The book of Jubilees affirms this identification of the heavenly watchers (Jub. 4:15, 22), and adds that the watchers violated the law of their ordinances when they lusted after women (7:21), their polygamous relationships with women produced monstrous offspring, and they practiced forms of astrology (8:3; cf. T. Reub. 5:6). The Qumrân literature contains similar accounts of these watchers (cf. CD 2:17-19; 1QapGen, 2:1).

While the precise meaning and exact etymology of Heb. *ʿîr* remain uncertain, the origin of the concept of angels as "watchers" or "wakeful ones" proves even more difficult to trace. According to Gaster (*IDB,* IV, 806) the sleeplessness of celestial beings was a common belief in the ancient world, documented of the Vedic Adityas (Rig Veda II, 27:9), of the Persian Mithra (Yasht 10:7) and Ahuramazda (Videvdat 19.20), and of the Greek Zeus (Sophocles, *Oedipus at Colonus,* 702; although T. F. Glasson, *Greek Influence in Jewish Eschatology* [1961], p. 69, found it in Greek literature as early as Hesiod). Given the acknowledged indebtedness of Jewish angelology to Zoroastrianism, Gaster suggested that the OT here reproduces a yet unidentified Persian expression. Others relate the watchers to the seven Amesha Spentas of Zoroastrianism, a type of guardian angel (see A. Lacocque, *Book of Daniel* [Eng. tr. 1979], pp. 78f.; cf. A. Barnes, *Notes on the OT: Daniel,* [repr. 1950], 1, 251f.).

But one need not go outside Judaism for the origin of the concept since the biblical idea of heavenly beings who watch the earth appears to have originated in Babylon (Ezk. 1:15-20; cf. Midr. *Gen. Rabbah* 48; T.B. *Rosh ha-shanah* 24b, where according to tradition the names of angels were brought to Palestine by Jews from Babylon). The possible influence of Babylonian religious teachings notwithstanding, Ezekiel's vision of a God who has the capacity to see everywhere became a theological necessity for Israelite captives exiled far from the covenant land. Indeed, it is possible these angels may be mere reflectors of Yahweh Himself. He is the keeper of Israel who never slumbers nor sleeps (Ps. 121:4), and the One whose eyes range throughout the whole earth (Zec. 1:10; 3:9; 4:10).

Bibliography.–J. A. Montgomery, comm. on Daniel (*ICC,* 1927), pp. 231-35; *TWOT,* II, 655.

A. E. HILL

WATCHMAN [Heb. part. of *nāṣar*–'keep watch, guard, protect'] (Job 27:18; Jer. 31:6); AV also KEEPER; [part. of *ṣāpâ*–'keep guard, observe intently'] (1 S. 14:16; 2 S. 18:24-27; 2 K. 9:17f., 20; Isa. 21:6; 52:8; 56:10; Jer. 6:17; Ezk. 3:17; 33:2, 6f.; Hos. 9:8; Mic. 7:4); NEB also SENTRY, LIE IN WAIT, etc.; [part. of *šāmar*–'watch, protect, guard'] (Ps. 127:1; 130:6; Isa. 21:11f.; 62:6; Jer. 51:12; Cant. 3:3; 5:7); AV also THEY WHO WATCH; NEB also POST A WATCH; [*p*^{e}*quddâ*–'guard, sentry'] (2 K. 11:18; 2 Ch. 23:18); AV OFFICE, OFFICER; NEB WATCH, DOOR-KEEPER; [Gk. part. of *phylássō*–'watch, guard'] (Jth. 13:11); NEB SENTRY; [*skopós*–'one who watches'] (Sir. 37:14).

In the OT times watchmen protected vineyards and fields during harvest season (Jer. 31:6). They erected huts as shelters from the elements (Job 27:18) and towers to facilitate observation (cf. Sir. 37:14; *see* WATCHTOWER).

Watchmen were also posted on city walls (2 K. 9:17-20; Cant. 5:7) and at city gates (2 S. 18:24-27; Jth. 13:11) to scan the horizon for runners with messages for the king (2 S. 13:34; 18:24). The skilled watchman was able to identify individual runners by their stride (18:27). The watchman also guarded the walls day and night against enemy attack or siege (1 S. 14:16; Isa. 21:6-8; Jer. 51:12); he was responsible for warning the citizens of impending attack by sounding a trumpet (Jer. 6:17); Ezk. 33:2, 6). Watchmen apparently made rounds in Jerusalem during the night watches (Cant. 3:3; 5:7).

Acknowledging the providential hand of God in human affairs, the psalmist recognized the watchman's vigil was useless unless the Lord watched over the city (Ps. 127:1). Another psalm figuratively depicts the righteous as watchmen who expectantly watch for God's mercy and deliverance (130:6).

The OT prophets functioned as God's watchmen over Israel (Jer. 6:17; Hos. 9:8; cf. Isa. 21:6-8, 11f.). Ezekiel, e.g., was commissioned as a "watchman" and charged to warn the nation of threatening judgment because of their sin (Ezk. 3:17; 33:7). While the prophets often signaled certain (and sometimes imminent) disaster because of covenant violations, they also announced the good news of the Lord's return to Israel and His restoration of Zion (Isa. 52:8). Additionally, the prophet carried the heavy burden of accountability to God for the careful execution of His mandates (Ezk. 33:1-9); false prophets are labeled "blind watchmen" (Isa. 56:10). Ironically, the judgment forecasted in Micah's oracle against Israel was to arrive the same day that watchmen were posted (Mic. 7:4).

For interpretations of two difficult passages, Isa. 21:11f. and 62:6, see the commentaries.

Bibliography.–*THAT,* II, *s.v.* נצר (G. Sauer); *TWOT,* II, 594f., 773, 939f.

A. E. HILL

WATCHTOWER [Heb. *migdal* (2 K. 17:9; 18:8; Isa. 5:2), *miṣpeh* (2 Ch. 20:24; Isa. 21:8), *baḥan* (Isa. 32:14); Gk. *skopḗ* (Sir. 37:14)]; AV also (HIGH) TOWER; NEB Apoc. TOWER. A TOWER on which a WATCHMAN can stand in order to gain a better view of the surrounding countryside. Many stone watchtowers have been excavated in Palestine and other ancient Near Eastern countries. Towers constructed in fields and vineyards usually included sleeping quarters, since a watch had to be kept day and night during harvest. Towns and cities also had towers in which watchmen looked for messengers and warned of approaching enemies. *See* FORTIFICATION I.B.

On the use of "watchtower" in Isa. 21:5, AV, *see* RUG.

N. J. O.

WATER [Heb. *mayim*; Gk. *hýdōr*]. Water is the most abundant of all earth's natural resources, covering its surface to about 70 percent. This common, versatile substance alone appears in three different forms, namely, gaseous (water vapor), solid (ice), and liquid (rain). From the beginning of the world water has helped to shape the environment (Gen. 1:2-22), maintaining a proper temperature balance, and through the salt water of the oceans preventing the earth from succumbing to putrefaction. A single drop of water is a miracle of chemical design, consisting of tightly bonded atoms and molecules. Plants, animals, and human beings depend upon water to maintain their fluid balances, and this situation has presented problems throughout history because of the uneven distribution of rainfall.

The earliest Near Eastern cultures lived beside rivers, and used the waters to irrigate the nearby land and make it fertile. While the rivers sustained life, they also brought death with them when polluted. The ancient Hebrews lived predominantly in areas where water was scarce, and the successful excavation of a deep WELL was cause for great rejoicing as the people took possession of it (Nu. 21:17f.). Sometimes the ownership of wells was a matter of vigorous dispute among nomadic peoples, and often resulted in violence (cf. Gen. 26:15-22).

The ancients were well aware of the qualities of water as a life-giving source and as a cleansing agent. These two themes recur constantly in Scripture when water is being alluded to in a figurative or a spiritual sense. This type of imagery enriched the thought of the Hebrews, and consequently furnished such figures of speech as similes and metaphors (potential or implied similes). Examples of this activity include the doubter being tossed like an ocean wave (Jas. 1:6), or death making life as irretrievable as water poured out on the ground (2 S. 14:14). A similar usage is seen in the dying Jacob's assessment of his son Reuben's character (Gen. 49:4) as fundamentally unstable.

These vigorous images grew out of the people's awareness of the basic importance of water for sustaining human life. Thus to speak of "bread and water" (e.g., 1 K. 18:13) was at once to suggest the parameters of diet and also to reduce food to its basic components. Consequently the promise to the Israelites of the wilderness period that they would inherit through God's grace a land in which one could drink water without need of stringent economy and eat bread without scarcity (Dt. 8:7-9) was indeed an assurance of rich and varied provision for their needs.

That God was the provider and sustainer under the covenant agreement was impressed upon the Israelites at all times. Among the promises listed was an open sky that would provide seasonal rains as long as the Israelites obeyed God's commandments scrupulously (Dt. 28:12). By contrast, disobedience on the part of God's covenant people would result in drought, replacing the expected rains with an environment of powder and dust (Dt. 28:24).

This was a particularly sensitive matter for the Israelites when they remembered that, in an earlier age, God had punished the wickedness of the people on the earth by drowning them in a devastating flood (Gen. 6:5, 7, 13). At that time the fury of the outpoured skies had combined with saturating springs from below the water table (Gen. 7:11) to wreak the promised havoc. While God remained true thereafter to His promise never to destroy the earth again (Gen. 8:21), He used periodic droughts and famines to chastise His apostate, idolatrous people (cf. Am. 4:7; Joel 1:10-12; Hag. 1:10f.).

The perils associated with shortages of water were brought home to the twelve tribes during the wilderness wanderings on two distinct occasions (Ex. 17:6; Nu. 20:11). The doubts that the people entertained about God's ability to provide were dispelled when Moses obeyed God's instructions, although on the second occasion not quite so meticulously as required (Nu. 20:12). For failing to hallow God in implicit obedience, Moses forfeited the privilege of leading God's people into the Promised Land.

One of the mighty works that God accomplished for His people, and which is commemorated still in Jewish rituals, was connected with water. This involved the liberating of the Israelites who had been oppressed by the Egyptians in the time of Moses, and who under his leadership passed safely through the waters of the Re(e)d Sea. Once across the marshy area, God allowed the water to return to its normal level, thereby destroying the pursuing Egyptians. The event was celebrated on that occasion by the triumphal "song of the sea" (Ex. 15:1-18) and the song of Miriam (Ex. 15:21), which furnished the impetus for a triumphal dance. In both compositions the miracle of God's power in piling up the waters in a totally unexpected fashion to drown the enemies of Israel formed the focal point of the celebration, expressed in language which has much in common with Amarna-age Ugaritic poetry.

The prophets of the 8th and 7th cents. B.C. used metaphors involving water to lend emphasis to their messages. Isaiah promised punishment upon the nation because the people had spurned God's love and protection, symbolized by the hidden, quietly flowing waters of the underground aqueduct that tapped the spring of Gihon and terminated in the lower pool of Siloam (Isa. 8:6). Instead, they had sought the company of Rezin, the last king of Syria (*ca.* 750-732 B.C.), and also of Pekah of Israel (*ca.* 740-732 B.C.), the son of Remaliah (Isa. 7:1). For this apostasy the Israelites would suffer the fate of the Egyptians by being engulfed in a flood of soldiery from the Euphrates (Isa. 8:7f.). This calamity could be averted, however, if the people would repent of their sins and come to draw water from the wells of salvation (Isa. 12:3; 55:1).

In a passionate plea for his countrymen to return to the covenant ideals of justice and mercy, Amos employed the water imagery of justice and righteousness flowing regularly and consistently, as contrasted with the intermittent watercourses (Am. 5:24). Jeremiah denounced the Judeans for their apostasy in rejecting the One who was the fountain of living (i.e., running) waters and trusting instead in leaking cisterns (Jer. 2:13; 17:13). At the same time the prophet was compelled on one occasion to wonder whether God would Himself prove to be an intermittent stream rather than a continually flowing river (15:18), but was consoled by the Lord's assurance that He would be with him to save and deliver His servant (v. 20).

Water was not merely a life-sustaining agent but a cleansing one. In this regard its use was prescribed in certain purification rituals as part of the legal enactments drawn up with a view to sedentary occupation of the Promised Land. Some of these rituals prescribed small quantities of "living" water, that is, fresh running water from a stream or fountain that would be intrinsically cleaner than water from a stagnant pool or cistern (cf. Lev. 14:5f., 50-52). The ceremonies of cleansing following the healing of a discharge (Lev. 15:1-13) involved the washing of the individual's clothes and bathing in running water which would cleanse the defiled body and also symbolize the complete carrying away of the affliction. By contrast, running water was not prescribed specifically for a woman who was engaging in purification rituals after feminine discharges (Lev. 15:19-33).

A diagnostic ritual for a woman suspected of marital infidelity by a jealous husband (Nu. 5:11-31) involved the "water of bitterness." This consisted of dust from the tabernacle floor dissolved in water, and was administered under oath by a priest to the woman in the Lord's presence. If guilty, the woman would suffer divine execration with concomitant abdominal symptoms, which may have included miscarriage. The water ritual was accompanied by a grain offering of jealousy (Nu.15:25) to complete a ceremony replete with powerful psychological suggestion.

Another rite involving water was associated with the prescriptions for removing ceremonial defilement, whether from a priest through his participation in the sacrifice of a red heifer (Nu. 19:1-10) or from contact with a dead body (19:11-22). The cleansing agent was made of ashes from the sacrifice of an unblemished red cow which were dissolved in clean water from a spring or fountain, and applied through the use of hyssop as an aspergillum to the person and property of the defiled. The "living water" was intended to offset the effects of the impurity occasioned by contact with death. An even more significant use of water as a cleansing agent was promised to Israel through Ezekiel (36:24f.). In the restoration of national life God would sprinkle running water on the people and thereby cleanse them symbolically from their filthiness and sin, a situation for which Isaiah had pleaded in vain (1:16).

While water was frequently depicted as symbolizing divine blessing, redemption, and cleansing, certain narratives of a poetic nature represented water as a foe that God had already vanquished. The passages concerned involve references to a water-dwelling serpent named LEVIATHAN (Job 3:8; 41:1ff. [MT 40:25ff.]; Ps. 74:14; 104:26; Isa. 27:1; Ezk. 29:3ff.) and a dragon-like beast with the title of RAHAB (Job 9:13; 26:12; 38:8ff.; Ps. 87:4; 89:10 [MT 11]; Isa. 30:7; 51:9). When Ugaritic studies began, the similarity of these two creatures to certain mythological figures in Canaanite literature was noted (cf. T. H. Robinson, "Hebrew Myths," in S. H. Hooke, ed., *Myth and Ritual* [1932], pp. 172-196). Scholars who had previously attributed the biblical figures to Mesopotamian origins now began to affirm the direct influence of Canaanite legends upon the corresponding OT narratives. But unlike Babylonian cosmogonic and other materials, the Hebrew narratives transformed references to Leviathan and Rahab from creation to the redemption of Israel from Egypt (cf. Ps. 89:10; Isa. 51:9) to the point where Rahab was used as a synonym for Egypt (Ps. 87:4; Isa. 30:7; cf. Ezk. 29:3). Leviathan has also been interpreted to symbolize the vicious enemies of God's people (Egypt; Ps. 74:13f.; the Assyro-Babylonian empire; Isa. 27:1), but others (e.g., M. Dahood, *Psalms*, III [*AB*, 1970], 45) have seen it as merely a favorite animal of God's, depending upon Him for sustenance.

It would appear that Isaiah, at all events, intended Leviathan to symbolize the eschatological defeat of evil by God (cf. M. G. Kline, *Kingdom Prologue* [1981], pp. 56-59). Without denying the obvious linguistic and literary relationship between Ugaritic materials and the Hebrew Bible, the fact remains, as Gordon stated, that Canaanite mythology furnished little more than a literary background for the poetic images of the Hebrew writers (C. H. Gordon, *Intro. to OT Times* [1953], p. 82).

The assurance that God was lord of the deep and its contents was of great comfort to His people in times of trouble (Ps. 69:1f., 14f., [MT 2f., 15f.]; 124:1-5; Isa. 43:2). In this confidence they could count on Him to engulf arrogant Tyre (Ezk. 26:19-21; cf. 27:26) just as He had destroyed the forces of Egypt at the Exodus. In another eschatological figure, Daniel observed the winds of heaven stirring up the great sea (Dnl. 7:2), from which emerged four beasts. These creatures ultimately succumbed to the judgment of the Ancient of Days, and were described to a perplexed Daniel as representing four kings who would exercise power before the saints ultimately possessed the kingdom forever (Dnl. 5:15-18, 27).

The efficacy of water as a cleansing fluid led to its use by the Jews in the pre-Christian period for initiating proselytes into Judaism. The origin of BAPTISM is at best obscure, however, and while Jesus Himself had been baptized (Mt. 3:13; Mk. 1:9-11; Lk. 3:21-23), He never made baptism a condition of discipleship. At all events, the new birth by water and the Spirit (Jn. 3:5) implied repentance, purification from sin, and a commitment to a way of life under the guidance of the Holy Spirit.

The precise way in which the water was applied is unknown and may not even have been restricted to any particular method, but the symbolism of the act in terms of spiritual renewal and divine sustenance was unmistakable. As against the *ex opere operato* view of baptism, by which the act wrought a work of divine regeneration by being performed, the uniform biblical view was truly sacramental, regarding it as an external sign of inward spiritual grace. Though entire families are said to have been baptized in the primitive church (Acts 16:15; 1 Cor. 1:16; etc.), there is no NT teaching on infant baptism as such.

The OT idea of "living waters" was clearly in Christ's thoughts when He promised the Samaritan woman (Jn. 4:14) such a gift, thereby reaffirming God's gracious promises in Isa. 12:3 to all who believe on Him (cf. Jn. 4:42). The pool of Beth-zatha was credited with possessing healing properties, but Jesus healed a chronically ill man there without recourse to the water (Jn. 5:2-9). On another occasion He used a mixture of clay and saliva on a blind man and instructed him to wash in the pool of Siloam and be healed (Jn. 9:1-11). This event may have reminded some observers of the way in which Naaman had been healed by washing in the Jordan many centuries earlier (2 K. 5:1-14).

In an eschatological discourse, Christ used the illustration of Noah and the Flood to warn His disciples concerning conditions in the end times (Mt. 24:38f.; Mk. 13:32-37; Lk. 21:34-36). In the new heaven (Rev. 21:6) God promised to supply living water freely to the thirsty, because a pure river of crystal-clear water was available to all who desired it (Rev. 22:1, 17).

See also WATERWORKS.

Bibliography.–H. G. May, *JBL*, 74 (1955), 9-21; P. Reymond, *L'Eau, Sa Vie, et Sa Signification dans l'AT* (*SVT*, 6; 1958); *TDNT*, VIII, *s.v.* ὕδωρ (Goppelt); *TWOT*, I, 501-503.

R. K. HARRISON

WATER HEN [Heb. *tinšemeṯ*] (Lev. 11:18; Dt. 14:16); [LXX *porphyríōn, íbis*]; AV SWAN; NEB LITTLE OWL. One of those birds cited as an abomination and not to be eaten by the Israelites. The precise meaning of this Hebrew word is uncertain, a fact vividly illustrated by the wide variety of translations. The AV "swan" follows the Vulgate's *cygnus*, while the RSV reflects the LXX. G. R. Driver's proposal that *tinšemeṯ* is a type of owl (see Driver, p. 15,where he suggests "little owl") has been followed in a number of more recent translations (note also the "horned owl" of the older RV and ASV). *Tinšemeṯ* also appears in the list of unclean "swarming things" in Lev. 11:30 where the context would seem to demand an entirely different animal (so RV, RSV, NEB, NIV "chameleon").

Bibliography.–F. S. Bodenheimer, *Animal Life in Palestine* (1935); G. Cansdale, *Animals of Bible Lands* (1970); G. R. Driver, *PEQ*, 87 (1955), 5-20, 129-140.

J. HUDDLESTUN

WATER OF BITTERNESS [Heb. *mê hammārîm*] (Nu. 5:18f., 23f.); AV BITTER WATER; NEB WATER OF CONTENTION. *See* ADULTERY II; JEALOUS II.A.2.

WATER OF SEPARATION. The AV translation of Heb. *mê niddâ* in Nu. 19:9, 13, 20f.; 31:23 (RSV "water for impurity"; NEB "water of [ritual] purification"). *See* HEIFER, RED.

WATER SHAFT [Heb. *ṣinnôr*] (2 S. 5:8); AV GUTTER; NEB "grappling-iron." The meaning of *ṣinnôr* is uncertain; the LXX renders it "dagger" and Aquila "watercourse" (*see* CATARACT). A water shaft has been discovered that extends from the spring of Gihon into the city of Jerusalem. *See* JERUSALEM III.C.1.a; WATERWORKS.

WATERCOURSE [Heb. *'āpîq*–'water channel'] (Ps. 126:4; Ezk. 31:12; 32:6); AV STREAM, RIVER; NEB also STREAM. A natural or man-made channel through which water flows. In the above passages *'āpîq* denotes a wadi, i.e., a deep valley through which a stream or river flows during rainy seasons. Ps. 126:4 uses the image of a dry wadi that could suddenly become a raging torrent to depict a dramatic change in Israel's fortunes (see *LBHG,* rev., p. 26). The AV uses "watercourse" to render Heb. *yiḇlê mayim* in Isa. 44:4 (RSV, NEB, "flowing stream"), *môṣā' mayim* in 2 Ch. 32:30 (RSV "outlet of the waters"; NEB "outflow of the waters"), and *te'ālâ* in Job 38:25 (RSV, NEB, "channel").

See also RIVER; WATERWORKS. N. J. O.

WATERPOT. The AV translation of Gk. *hydría* in Jn. 2:6f.; 4:28 (RSV "jar," "water jar"). *See* JAR II; POTTER, POTTERY.

WATERS. *See* WATER.

WATERS OF MEROM. *See* MEROM, WATERS OF.

WATERS OF STRIFE. *See* MASSAH AND MERIBAH.

WATERSKIN [Heb. *nēḇel*]; AV BOTTLE; NEB CISTERN. In Job 38:37 a common term for a container of liquids (*see* JAR) is applied to the clouds as sources of rain.

WATERSPOUT. The AV translation of Heb. *ṣinnôr* in Ps. 42:7 (MT 8). *See* CATARACT.

WATERWORKS. Water is the lifeblood of the cultures of the Near East. The river valleys of ancient Mesopotamia and Egypt had a continuous supply of water, but it had to be harnessed through irrigation canals, small dams, and systems of sluice gates to broaden the areas of cultivation. In Syro-Palestine the river systems were of lesser consequence and more difficult to tap for irrigation. Thus much depended upon annual rainfall amounts in this region. The amounts of precipitation varied, however, from one area to the next. Desert and steppe zones like the Negeb averaged only 15-20 cm. (6-8 in.) per year, and this often came in a space of a few days, leaving entire months or even years dry. The more favored green zone of the Galilee region (90-100 cm. or 35-40 in. per year) also faced water shortfall problems. Here, and in the rest of Palestine, rainfall was concentrated into a few wet months from November to March. As a result, water had to be hoarded and channeled to insure a ready supply year round. Hillsides were terraced, springs and wells were tapped, and cisterns were built to catch and store rain runoff. To provide water to the larger, urban population centers and insure a continuous supply during times of siege, water tunnels were constructed from inside the walls to nearby springs. In later periods aqueducts were built to bring water to the cities from sources many miles away.

- I. Irrigation Methods
  - A. Mesopotamia
  - B. Egypt
  - C. Syro-Palestine
- II. Springs and Wells
- III. Water Storage Methods
  - A. Cisterns
  - B. Pools
  - C. *Miqwā'ôṯ*
- IV. Engineered Water Systems
  - A. Water Tunnels
  - B. Water Shafts
  - C. Aqueducts

I. Irrigation Methods.–The history of civilization in the Near East begins with the development of methods for manipulating water and bringing it to where it would be most useful. (*See also* IRRIGATION.)

A. Mesopotamia. An elaborate network of canals to carry water from the Tigris and Euphrates rivers to outlying fields was constructed by the people of Mesopotamia as early as 3000 B.C. Private channels to the fields were then dug; these paralleled and radiated away from the main canals. A lever and counterweight apparatus known as a *šaduf* allowed the farmer to lift water in a skin or basket from the canal into his channel (*see* pictures in IRRIGATION). The development of such a sophisticated irrigation system required organization of labor resources and a strong government. The rulers of the city-states of Sumer, Babylon, and Assyria all set the canal system as one of their major governmental priorities. Royal inscriptions, e.g., those of the Assyrian King Sennacherib (705-681 B.C.), boast of the construction of networks of canals linking fields and cities to the rivers (cf. Isa. 32:2).

Constant maintenance of the irrigation system was made necessary by the sandy soil of the Mesopotamian flood plain, which allowed the canals to become clogged with silt and the channel walls to collapse. The year-name inscriptions of both Hammurabi and Samsu-iluna, rulers of Babylon in the 18th cent. B.C. include statements of their commitment to keep the water flowing. For instance, Hammurabi named both the twenty-fourth and thirty-third years of his reign in honor of his refurbishing of canals. Year thirty-three reads: "He redug the canal (called) 'Hammurabi-(spells)-abundance-for-the-people, the Beloved-of-Anu-and-Enlil,' (thus) he provided Nippur, Eridu, Ur, Larsa, Uruk (and) Isin with a permanent and plentiful water supply" (*ANET,* p. 270).

Many texts from ancient Mesopotamia refer to the importance of constant vigilance over the small dams, sluice gates,and local canals that managed the irrigation network. For instance, in one of the Mari Letters (*ca.* 1750 B.C.) a special overseer (*rabi Amurrim*) is appointed by King Zimri-Lim to conscript laborers to complete work on a dam project (*ARM,* XIV, 22:23-25). Even the Babylonian creation epic, *Enuma Elish,* contains a passage describing irrigation management. The chief god Marduk, after defeating the forces of chaos represented by the salt-water-goddess Tiâmat, placed a "bar" to stem the flow of her waters over the land and appointed several of the gods to guard the operation of the canal (*ANET,* p. 67; cf. Ps. 29:10: "The Lord sits enthroned over the flood").

B. Egypt. Similarly, in Egypt large numbers of workers (generally not slave laborers) were used in the construction and repair of elaborate water systems. Their preparations were designed to take advantage of the regular flooding of the Nile Valley (*see* EGYPT III.D). After the flood waters of the Nile began to recede, large quantities of water and silt were left behind in specially designed storage basins. Canals were dug from these basins to carry the Nile's enriching water and mud to outlying farm areas.

The inundation of Egypt by the Nile River was more predictable than the flooding of the Tigris and Euphrates rivers in Mesopotamia. Despite the Nile's regularity Egypt did experience some dry years (Gen. 41:25-31), and strict control was needed to insure that enough water reached the fields. Egyptian texts speak of officials who were required to "examine water supplies on the first day of every ten-day period" (James, p. 115). An inscription from the tomb of such an official from the First Intermediate period (*ca.* 2100 B.C.) states: "I made the arable lands (well watered?), while everything on both sides (of my territory) was parched" (James, p. 116).

C. Syro-Palestine. There is some evidence of channeling of the rivers of Lebanon, the Jordan, and Transjordanian streams. Since the Jordan is below sea level, however, most areas of Syro-Palestine had to rely upon rainfall and water sources other than rivers for agricultural and personal needs (cf. Dt. 11:11). The two main methods of irrigation were: (1) channels from springs and wadis, and (2) terraced hillsides.

Irrigation canals were built from springs, like those at Jericho (2 K. 2:18-22), to water fields and animals. Archeologists have also uncovered evidence of farm settlements and local forts in the Judean wilderness near Qumrân that channeled water from the wadis to their cisterns and terraced fields during the rainy season.

The pattern of precipitation in Syro-Palestine is seasonal: a wet winter and early spring followed by a dry summer and fall. While some regions received rainfall amounts comparable to well-watered areas of Europe (at both London and Jerusalem the average is 53 cm. [21 in.]), the nearly complete lack of rainfall during several months of the year necessitated a close husbandry of resources. In much of Palestine, therefore, the hillsides were terraced (cf. Isa. 5:1) in strips 3-4.5 m. (10-15 ft.) wide. This provided more arable land for cultivation and also insured a more even distribution of moisture from one level to the next. Some irrigation ditches were also constructed to help carry the rain water between terraces or to pools or cisterns where it could be collected.

II. Springs and Wells.—Human occupation and economic activity centered around natural water sources. Rivers, streams, and lakes were usually choice sites for villages and towns. Along the rivers, fords were jealously guarded to protect against invaders (cf. Jgs. 12:5f.) and to control river traffic (*ARM,* XIII, 58). Where rivers and streams did not exist, settlements could receive a constant supply of water from a spring, such as the Gihon near Jerusalem. A hot spring bubbling from the earth, like that near Tiberias on the Sea of Galilee, drew people to settle and to bathe in its medicinal waters (*Ant.* xviii.2.3 [36]). The combination of a well-watered site with a strategic and defensible location meant generations of occupation despite repeated sieges; e.g., excavations at Megiddo have revealed twenty cities built one on top of the other.

Pastoral nomads and village herdsmen used their knowledge of the locations of perennial streams (cf. Job 6:15) or wells in tending their flocks in semiarid regions (cf. Gen. 26:18-22). Wells were given names (26:22), and the knowledge of their locations was passed on from one generation to the next (v. 18). Since wells were needed for watering flocks and herds, which could not go more than two days without drinking, contention could always arise between herding groups or between nomadic groups and villagers (21:25; 26:15, 19f.).

A stone was sometimes placed as a cap over a well to help prevent evaporation and control the use of the well (Gen. 29:2f.). Deeper wells, like that at Beer-sheba, had sides coursed with stone. Ropes were used to draw up jars or leather buckets (cf. Gen. 21:19) to fill drinking troughs for the animals (24:20; Ex. 2:16). These ropes gradually scored the stones with deep cuts and ridges. The well was visited several times a day by village women (Jn. 4:6f.), herdsman, and travelers. It thus became a natural gathering place for young women, who sometimes met their future husbands in the course of their daily activities there (Gen. 29:2-12; Ex. 2:16-21). *See also* JERUSALEM II.C; WELL.

III. Water Storage Methods.—*A. Cisterns.* Throughout the ancient Near East cisterns were constructed to hold the rainwater and its runoff collected from roofs (cf. Prov. 5:15). The technology required for constructing and plastering cisterns was introduced in Palestine *ca.* 1200 B.C. Prior to this cisterns had been cut into bedrock, since the limestone underlying many of the hill country settlements was too porous to hold water (cf. Jer. 2:13). Plastering allowed for the digging of relatively deep, bell-shaped cistern pits that could be capped to preserve large quantities of water. They were then tapped by lowering a jug or cup on a rope. In some cases (e.g., at Ai and Raddana) a system of interlocking cisterns was constructed, bringing water from a succession of pits into private dwellings. A certain degree of filtration was accomplished by placing small stones in the bottom of each pit to hold some of the sediment. The opening leading into the next cistern was placed slightly above the bottom of the container, again leaving some impurities behind.

The roofs of most houses had channels to direct water

A partially excavated Iron II/Persian reservoir (viewed from the north) at Heshbon. The cut bedrock is visible on the east side (P. J. Bergsma, Heshbon Expedition)

into cisterns or storage pits in the ground (cf. 2 K. 18:31). The Philistine city of Gezer, as well as other excavated sites in the Shephelah and central hill country, was honeycombed with cisterns. In these cities and towns communal cisterns were constructed to hold water for emergencies such as a fire or siege (cf. Jer. 41:9). These large pits often had broader rims than private cisterns, and some had staircases for easier access. They were susceptible to silting (cf. 38:6) and had to be cleaned out periodically.

The wealth and power of kings and their kingdoms were sometimes judged by the defenses of their cities, the size of their herds, and the number of cisterns they constructed (2 Ch. 26:10). This can be seen in the Moabite Stone, an inscription written in honor of a victorious campaign by King Mesha *ca.* 830 B.C. As a way of strengthening the defenses of the newly captured city of Qarḥoh, Mesha ordered each man to carve out "a cistern for himself in his house" (*ANET,* p. 320).

See also CISTERN.

B. Pools. Artificial and natural pools also functioned as water sources, serving the city's needs in peacetime and during prolonged sieges. Conduits were built from springs to carry water into the city and into these holding areas (cf. Isa. 7:3). The pool of Siloam (Jn. 9:7) and several other pools in Jerusalem (2 K. 18:17; Neh. 3:15; Isa. 22:9) were fed with water from the spring GIHON (2). In the Roman period these pools were generally rectangular in shape and they were seldom very deep. Groups of pools were sometimes constructed or appeared naturally because of a nearby spring. For instance, the pool of BETHESDA consists of several linked pools, some of which may have been used for ritual bathing (Jn. 5:2). This pool was said

A *mikvah* or ritual bath at Masada installed during the rebel occupation (The Estate of Yigael Yadin)

(vv. 3f. in some texts) to be a place of miraculous healing for the person who could enter it first after its waters had been disturbed by an angel (perhaps an intermittent spring).

In arid regions like the Judean desert site of Buqei'a near Qumrân, pools were formed by the construction ofsmall dams. In this way the people could take advantage of runoff from nearby wadis (cf. 2 K. 3:16-20) during the occasional rain storm. Water was then easily channeled into the city's reservoirs, pools, and cisterns. The importance of the pool in the city's life also made it a place for community assembly and a site of justice; e.g., David hung the bodies of the murderers of Ishbosheth at the pool of Hebron (2 S. 4:12).

See also POOL.

C. Mikwā'ôṯ. Some of these rain- or spring-fed pools served specifically as places for ritual cleansing (cf. Lev. 16:4, 24). The MIKVAH, or ritual bath, was a small pool or series of pools used for purifying oneself after having sex or coming into contact with a corpse (cf. 15:2-30). Mikwā'ôṯ were also used by worshipers before they entered the temple. The mikvah often had a divided or double staircase, which allowed the ritually unclean person to enter on one side and depart on the other side after being cleansed. (See W. S. LaSor, *Biblical Archaeology Review,* 13/1 [1987], 52-59.)

IV. Engineered Water Systems.–Cities were often constructed on hills or promontories for their defensive advantage. This made it necessary, however, to dig deep wells within the city or to channel rainwater into cisterns or pools. Springs or streams also provided a portion of the city's water supply, but these were usually outside the walls. During the heat of summer, when the cisterns were nearly empty, enterprising merchants carried water-laden jugs from the springs for sale in the city (cf. Isa. 55:1). In some places paved walkways were built to the spring, like that built by Solomon at Megiddo.

In wartime the spring could be easily captured, and the city would then have to rely on its wells and cisterns to survive the siege. To alleviate this problem, many cities in Palestine resorted to complex engineering stratagems.

A. Water Tunnels. One solution was the construction of a water tunnel leading from inside the city walls to a nearby spring. Excellent examples of this type of tunnel have been found at Megiddo and Jerusalem. These cities were often besieged and thus needed a reliable source of water. In each case their principal spring's opening was disguised or covered over, leaving the only access through the tunnel.

The Megiddo tunnel, built by King Ahab in the 9th cent. B.C., consists of two parts: (1) a shaft with a winding staircase driven 35 m. (115 ft.) down to the level of the spring at the bottom of the hill, and (2) a horizontal tunnel 61 m. (200 ft.) long leading from the city to the spring. This tunnel, like the more famous SILOAM tunnel constructed by Hezekiah in the 8th cent. B.C. at Jerusalem, was dug by two teams working from opposite directions toward each other. Hezekiah's tunnel was constructed in preparation for a siege by the Assyrian King Sennacherib (2 K. 18:13–19:37). It used only a small portion of the older Jebusite water system as it wound 533 m. (1749 ft.) from the City of David to the Gihon (2 K. 20:20). The shaft, which in places is 45 m. (150 ft.) below the ground, was graded so that the waters of the spring would be directed to a pool inside the city (2 Ch. 32:30). The length and circuitous route of the tunnel may be due to the difficulties of boring through the rock, or it may have been an attempt to increase the volume of water held in the tunnel. If the spring were stopped up, there would still be about 285 cubic m.

The water tunnel at Megiddo built during Ahab's time (9th cent. B.C.) (L. K. Smith)

(10,200 cubic ft.) of water stored in the channel. *See also* JERUSALEM III.D.2.e-f.

B. Water Shafts. The long water tunnel had a defensive drawback. If the entrance to the spring was discovered, enemy soldiers could use the shaft to enter the city, as David's forces might have done in capturing the Jebusite city of Jerusalem (2 S. 5:8; but *see also* JERUSALEM III.C.1.a). By cutting a water shaft down through the layers of the mound to the water table, this weakness was eliminated. Engineers in the 9th cent. B.C. had learned that groundwater sources could be tapped if the shaft was cut deep enough.

This technology of "stairs-to-water-table" (Cole, p. 21) may have been borrowed by the Canaanites from the Mycenaeans in the Late Bronze period (14th cent. B.C.) and then rediscovered by the Israelites in the 9th century. The skill of these engineers is demonstrated by the sure carving of shafts through the bedrock at Gezer and Hazor, with no false starts or abandoned tunnels. The massive Hazor water system begins with five flights of stairs, which descend 29 m. (95 ft.) as they wind around the walls of the shaft. From this point a tunnel 24 m. (80 ft.) long slopes westward through the rock down to the water table 40 m. (130 ft.) below the ground.

Gezer's shaft is not as monumental in construction as Hazor's. It was first built by the Canaanite inhabitants in the 14th cent. B.C. Gezer was partially destroyed in an Egyptian raid *ca.* 950 B.C., and it became an Israelite fortress city in Solomon's time (1 K. 9:15-17). During this period the shaft may have been filled with debris, but in the 9th cent. it was cleared and put to use once again. The shaft is 11 m. (35 ft.) deep and is connected to a staired ramp 15 m. (48 ft.) long, which slopes down to a groundwater-fed pool.

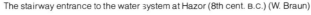

The stairway entrance to the water system at Hazor (8th cent. B.C.) (W. Braun)

Gibeon's water system was constructed during several periods in the city's history. Its earliest engineering project (12th-11th cents. B.C.) was a "pool" (2 S. 2:13), a cylindrical shaft about 11 m. (36 ft.) in diameter and 11 m. (36 ft.) deep with a winding staircase, which served as a large cistern. In the 10th cent. B.C. a staired tunnel was constructed from inside the city to a rock-cut chamber, which in turn was connected by a 12 m. (40 ft.) feeder tunnel to a spring. (*See* pictures in GIBEON.) When defensive considerations prompted further modifications, an attempt was made to connect the cistern shaft with the water tunnel. During this project the engineers struck the water table, thereby providing the city with ample reserves of water without the need to complete the tunnel system. This happy discovery may have provided the impetus for the construction of the similar "shaft-to-groundwater" systems at Hazor and Gezer. In any case, the reliability of the "pool" of Gibeon is evident from its continued use at least until Jeremiah's time, more than four hundred years after the original shaft was dug (Jer. 41:12).

C. Aqueducts. The construction of aqueducts made it possible to channel water from storage areas (such as the spring-fed "Pools of Solomon" near Bethlehem) to major population centers or desert outposts. The technology for these projects, first introduced by the Romans, was utilized by Herod the Great (30-4 B.C.) to funnel water to his Judean wilderness fortress of Herodium (*Ant.* xv.9.4 [323-25]) and, by a series of concrete channels and hollow, arched bridges to his capital at Caesarea. (See picture in SHARON.)

Archeologists have uncovered the remains of two aqueducts that were built to add to Jerusalem's water supply. Both channeled water from sources to the south. The "upper" and more recent channel dates to A.D. 165, when the city had become a Roman outpost known as Aelia Capitolina. Its construction (by Roman legionnaires) can be compared with that of the rock-cut conduits and bridge of the aqueduct built to carry water to Sebaste (Samaria) *ca.* A.D. 200. The "lower" aqueduct is probably the one built by Pontius Pilate (*Ant.* xviii.3.2 [60-62]; *BJ* ii.9.4 [175]). His use of temple funds (*Corbonas*) to pay for the project led to rioting by the Jews. The channel covered a distance of about 37 km. (23 mi.; twice as long in the *BJ* passage). Like other ancient aqueducts, the conduit may have been sealed with a mortar consisting of a mixture of lime and lead (Jeremias, p. 14).

See also JERUSALEM III.G.2.

Bibliography.–J. Callaway, *Biblical Archaeology Review,* 9/5 (1983), 42-53; D. Cole, *Biblical Archaeology Review,* 6/2 (1980), 8-29; M. Drower, "Water-Supply, Irrigation, and Agriculture," in O. Singer *et al.*, eds., *History of Technology,* I (1965), 520-27; Z. Herzog, *Biblical Archaeology Review,* 6/6 (1980), 12-28; T. James, *Pharaoh's People* (1984); J. Jeremias, *Jerusalem in the Time of Jesus* (Eng. tr. 1969); R. Lamon, *Megiddo Water System*

A Roman aqueduct near Perga in Asia Minor (B. K. Condit)

(1935); W. LaSor, *Biblical Archaelogy Review*, 13/1 (1987), 52-59; V. Matthews, *BA*, 49/2 (1986), 118-126; J. Pritchard, *Water System of Gibeon* (1961); N. Shaheen, *PEQ*, 111 (1979), 103-108.

V. H. MATTHEWS

WAVE OFFERING. *See* SACRIFICES AND OFFERINGS IN THE OT.

WAW wou [ו]. The sixth letter of the Hebrew alphabet, transliterated in this encyclopedia as *w* (elsewhere sometimes as *v*). It came also to be used for the number six, and it stands at the head of the sixth section of Ps. 119 (cf. AV). *See* WRITING.

WAX. The noun appears in four RSV OT poetic passages as a translation of Heb. *dônag* (Ps. 22:14 [MT 15]; 68:2 [MT 3]; 97:5; Mic. 1:4). Each passage uses a simile referring to wax's property of melting quickly when exposed to heat. In the Apocrypha it is used similarly in Jth. 16:15 (Gk. *kērós*) and 2 Esd. 13:4 (here the RSV follows the Syr. rather than the Vulg.).

As a verb "wax" appears frequently in the AV in the sense of "grow," "increase," or "become." In the RSV the verb occurs only in Dt. 32:15, where the phrase "wax fat" twice renders Heb. *šāman* (NEB lit. "grow fat").

WAY. This common English word is used by the RSV over 550 times in the singular and about two hundred times in the plural. In the OT it usually represents Heb. *dereḵ*, but occasionally it translates *'ōraḥ* (e.g., Job 16:22; 19:8; Ps. 44:18 [MT 19]; Isa. 26:7). In a few instances "way" represents another term, e.g., Heb. *halîḵâ* (Prov. 31:27; Hab. 3:6), *ma'gāl* (Prov. 5:6), *'ereṣ* (Gen. 48:7). In the NT the primary term is Gk. *hodós*, the term most commonly used by the LXX to render Heb. *dereḵ*. Other Greek terms include *trópos* (Rom. 3:2; Phil. 1:18; 2 Thess. 2:3; 3:16), *propémpō* ("send/speed on one's way," e.g., Acts 15:3; 2 Cor. 1:16; Tit. 3:13), *hoútos* ("in this way," e.g., Mt. 1:18; Jn. 21:1), *hypágō* ("go one's way," Mk. 7:29; 10:52; Lk. 10:3), *poreúomai* ("go [on] one's way," e.g., Mt. 2:9; Lk. 8:14; 10:38), etc.

I. In the OT.–In the OT Heb. *dereḵ* is sometimes used in a literal sense to denote a route of travel such as a path or road (e.g., the *dereḵ* to the Red Sea, Nu. 21:4; the *dereḵ* to Bashan, Dt. 3:1; the *dereḵ* of the sea, Isa. 9:1 [MT 8:23]). In Isa. 40:3 *dereḵ* (RSV "way") occurs in parallel to *mesillâ* ("highway") and refers to a road in the desert by which Yahweh will lead His people home from exile in Babylon.

More broadly, "way" (*dereḵ* or *'ōraḥ*) represents "the course [a person] followed through life, the direction of his going, and the manner of his walking" (Muilenberg, p. 33). This use of "way" — often in parallel with "path" (*see* PATH) — is especially common in the wisdom literature, including the wisdom Psalms. Job complained: "He [God] has walled up my way [*'ōraḥ*], so that I cannot pass" (Job 19:8). Frequently "way" has an ethical dimension; it can be characterized as good or evil, depending on the direction and manner of one's life. The psalmist declared, "I will guard my ways, that I may not sin with my tongue" (Ps. 39:1 [MT 2]). The book of Proverbs advises seeking wisdom, which can deliver one "from the way of evil, from men of perverted speech, who . . . walk in the ways of darkness, . . . men whose paths are crooked, and who are devious in their ways" (Prov. 2:12-15). By pursuing wisdom "you will walk in the way of good men and keep to the paths of the righteous" (v. 20). (*See also* PERVERSE.)

"Way" was also used in this sense by the prophets. Isa. 26:7 confesses: "The way [*'ōraḥ*] of the righteous is level; thou dost make smooth the path of the righteous." Jeremiah proclaimed Yahweh's call to the people to turn from their "evil way" (Jer. 18:11; 23:22; 25:5; 26:3; 35:15; 36:3, 7). *Dereḵ* is especially common in the book of Ezekiel, which warns that God will judge people according to their ways (e.g., 7:3f., 8f.; 18:30; 22:31; 33:20) and calls upon the wicked to turn from their ways and live (e.g., 3:18f.; 13:22; 18:23; 33:8f., 11).

Of special significance are the OT references to the "way(s)" of God. Used in this sense the term often denotes God's deeds (e.g., Ps. 145:17), especially His saving deeds (e.g., Ps. 67:2 [MT 3]; 103:7). Most memorable was God's saving act in leading His people out of Egypt and into the Promised Land: "And you shall remember all the way which the Lord your God has led you these forty years in the wilderness" (Dt. 8:2; cf. Ps. 77:19 [MT 20]; Isa. 43:16; 51:10; Jer. 2:17). Isaiah proclaimed that the Lord would again make a "way" through the wilderness so that His people could return from exile and live in peace (Isa. 40:3; 43:19; 45:13; 57:14; 62:10; cf. 35:8-10). God's way is acknowledged to be holy (Ps. 77:13 [MT 14]), perfect (18:30 [MT 31]), right (Hos. 14:9), and just (cf. Ezk. 18:25, 29; 33:17, 20). His saving ways are beyond human comprehension (Isa. 55:8f.).

In other passages God's "way" is something that is practiced by human beings. Here the term is almost synonymous with God's will as it is revealed in His commandments (see, e.g., 1 K. 2:3; 8:58; Ps. 119:1, 3, 14f., 27, 30, etc.; Jer. 5:4; cf. Gen. 18:19; Ex. 32:8). The Israelites were often exhorted to "walk in" or "keep" the way(s) of the Lord (e.g., Dt. 5:33; 8:6; 10:12; 11:22; 19:9; 26:16f.; 28:9; 30:16; 1 K. 11:38; Jer. 7:23). Sometimes God's people assert that they have kept God's ways (e.g., Job 23:11; Ps. 18:21 [MT 22]; 44:18 [MT 19]; cf. Job 31:7f.; Ps. 17:4f.); at other times they pray that God will teach them His ways (e.g., Ps. 25:4; 27:11; 86:11; 119:33; 143:8).

Human beings are thus confronted with a choice of which course they will follow in their lives: the good way, i.e., the way of the Lord (cf. Gen. 18:19; 1 S. 12:23; 1 K. 8:36; 2 Ch. 6:27; Ps. 18:21 [MT 22]; 25:8f., 12; Prov. 2:20; Jer. 6:16; etc.), or the evil way that rejects God's commands (cf. Gen. 6:12; Nu. 22:32; Jgs. 2:19; 1 K. 13:33; 15:26; Job 22:15; Ps. 36:4 [MT 5]; Prov. 4:14, 19; 8:13; Isa. 53:6; 65:2; 66:3; Jer. 3:21; etc.). The way of God leads to salvation and life (e.g., Dt. 30:15f.); turning from His way leads to destruction (cf. Dt. 30:17f.; Ps. 1:6; 146:9; Prov. 28:18; Ezk. 3:18f.; etc.).

Although the OT does not contain the explicit "two ways" terminology found in later Jewish literature, the idea is present in several passages (e.g., Ps. 1; cf. Dt. 11:26-28; 30:15-19; Ps. 119:29f.; 139:24; Prov. 4:18f.; 12:28; 14:2; 15:19). The earliest known Jewish use of this terminology appears in T. Ash. 1:3 (cf. v. 5). The metaphor also appears in the DSS (e.g., 1QS 3:20f.; 4:15, 17; 5:10f.) and in the rabbinic literature (e.g., Mish. *Aboth* ii.9). The idea of the two ways is clearly present in Mt. 7:13f., where Jesus contrasts the "easy" way that "leads to destruction" with the "hard" way that "leads to life." The theme receives further development in the Apostolic Fathers (see esp. Did. 1:1; Barn. 18:1).

II. In the NT.–In the NT Gk. *hodós* is used in the literal sense primarily in the Synoptic Gospels, which describe various incidents and teachings of Jesus as taking place "on the way," i.e., as He was en route to a destination. Although Jesus traveled from place to place throughout much of His earthly ministry, the roads He used are never mentioned.

In general the NT use of *hodós* is similar to the use of

Heb. *dereḵ* in the OT. Often the NT quotes OT passages. For example, the Gospels (Mt. 3:3 par.; cf. Jn. 1:23) quote Isa. 40:3; by applying the title "Lord" to Jesus, they interpret the work of John the Baptist as a fulfillment of this prophecy. As in the OT, the "way" of God can refer to His saving deeds (e.g., Rom. 11:33; He. 3:10; Rev. 15:3) or to His will as expressed in His commandments (Mt. 22:16; Mk. 12:14; Lk. 20:21).

In addition to Mt. 7:13f., several NT passages use *hodós* to denote a direction or manner of life. In 1 Cor. 4:17 Paul refers to "my ways in Christ," meaning the life of conformity to Christ that he both practiced and taught. In 12:31 the "more excellent way" refers to a life-style governed by love (ch. 13). In Rom. 3:17 Paul quotes Isa. 59:8 ("the way of peace"), referring to a manner of life in which one strives to live at peace with one's neighbors (cf. Lk. 1:79). In Mt. 21:32 Jesus says that John the Baptist "came to you in the way of righteousness," i.e., practicing and teaching a life of obedience to God's will. 2 Peter refers to Christianity as "the way of truth" (2:2), "the right way" (v. 15), and "the way of righteousness" (v. 21) and warns against false teachers who have left this way to follow "the way of Balaam" (v. 15; cf. Jas. 5:19f.). Similarly, Jude 11 warns against heretical teachers who "walk in the way of Cain."

A unique use of *hodós* occurs in Jn. 14:4-6, where Jesus calls Himself "the way" to the Father. Jesus' disciples can enjoy fellowship with the Father only if Jesus takes them to Him.

The author of Hebrews also refers to Jesus as providing believers with access to God. During the age of the old covenant there was no direct access to God, as symbolized by the fact that the "way into the sanctuary" (holy of holies) was not open to worshipers (He. 9:8). But Christ through His sacrifice opened a "new and living way" (10:20) so that believers can now "enter the sanctuary" (v. 19) with confidence.

Another unique NT usage occurs in Acts, where an absolute use of "way" (*hē hodós*) is applied to the Church (9:2; 19:9, 23; 22:4; 24:14, 22). This term was evidently used by the early Christians to denote their movement, since in both its teaching and its manner of life the Christian community expressed the "way of salvation" (16:17; cf. 2:28) and the "way of God" (18:25).

See also ROADS; WALK.

Bibliography.–*DNTT*, III, 935-943; J. Muilenburg, *The Way of Israel* (1961), pp. 33-36; *TDNT*, V, *s.v.* ὁδός (Michaelis); *TDOT*, III, *s.v.* "derekh" (Bergman, Haldar, Ringgren).

V. R GORDON N. J. O.

WAY, COVERED (2 K. 16:18). *See* COVERED WAY.

WAYFARER [Heb. *'ōrē(a)ḥ* (e.g., Jgs. 19:17), *'ōraḥ*–'way' (emended to *'ōrē[a]ḥ*, Job 31:32)]; AV WAYFARING MAN, TRAVELLER; NEB TRAVELLER, "by the wayside" (Jer. 9:2 [MT 1]); **WAYFARING MAN** [*'ōḇēr 'ōraḥ*] (Isa. 33:8); NEB TRAVELLER. One who is "journeying" (*'ōrē[a]ḥ*, part. of *'āraḥ*) or "passing through" (*'ōḇēr*, part. of *'āḇar*) a region. Because there were no inns in OT times (Jer. 9:2 probably refers to a simple shelter without a resident host), the TRAVELER had to depend upon the hospitality of local residents, who were expected to ENTERTAIN him (e.g., 2 S. 12:4; Job 31:32). Those who violated this important obligation to travelers were condemned (cf. the Gibeathites' treatment of the Levite and his concubine, Jgs. 19:13-30). During times of war or enemy occupation travel was not safe (Isa. 33:38; cf. Jgs. 5:6; Jer. 6:25; Zec. 7:14). In Jer. 14:8 the prophet complains that Yahweh shows no more interest in the land than a wayfarer who has merely stopped for the night.

See TRAVEL. N. J. O.

WAYMARK [Heb. *ṣîyûn*] (Jer. 31:21); NEB CAIRN. A sign set up to mark a route. The Israelites were told to mark the road by which they went into exile so that they could return by the same route. The "waymarks" were probably stones; cf. 2 K. 23:17 (RSV "monument") and Ezk. 39:15 (RSV "sign"), where *ṣîyûn* denotes a stone or pile of stones marking a grave.

WEALTH. *See* RICHES.

WEAN [Heb. *gāmal*] (Gen. 21:8; 1 S. 1:22-24; 1 K. 11:20; Isa. 11:8; 28:9; Hos. 1:8); NEB YOUNG CHILD. The completion of the process of nursing a child. The length of time for nursing varied considerably over the ages. The process was apparently lengthy in ancient times. 2 Macc. 7:27 refers to a period of three years. Babylonian practice and 1 S. 1:21-27 seem to suggest that this nursing period was widespread in the ancient Near East. Abraham celebrated Isaac's weaning by preparing a great feast (Gen. 21:8). The young child was then able to leave the immediate care of his mother (Gen. 21:9; cf. 1 S. 1:24-28). Once one child was weaned, the mother was free to bear another (Hos. 1:8; see *TDOT*, III, 26). 1 K. 11:20 attests the use of wet nurses to wean children.

In Isa. 28:9 the term is metaphorically applied to God's rebellious people. G. WYPER

WEAPONS OF WAR.

I. Introduction.–Since the dawn of history human beings have used some sort of weaponry to hunt (*see* HUNTING) and to protect themselves from man and beast alike. The materials from which weapons were made differed according to the technology known at a given period. From the Paleolithic period through the Early Bronze Age (*ca.*

The "Warrior Vase" from Mycenae depicts early Greek soldiers leaving home equipped with helmets, spears, and shields. At far left is a woman in dark clothes with her right hand raised to her head in sorrow (12th cent. B.C.) (National Museum, Athens)

10,000-3000 B.C.) weapons and related implements were made of wood and stone. During this period there was virtually no difference between hunting and battle implements. Even after the introduction of copper and bronze, stone was widely used for weapons. Gradually the weapons became more sophisticated and deadly. As different weapons were invented and used in military situations, defensive counter-measures became necessary. Thus weapons can be divided into two major categories: offensive and defensive. In response to the increased offensive capabilities (esp. the bow), defense systems were constructed around settlements. Jericho's stone walls and defense tower, which date to *ca.* 7000 B.C., are the earliest example of a large-scale defense system (*see* JERICHO). By the E. B. Age most cities in Syria-Palestine and Mesopotamia were encircled by walls. The response to this development was siege warfare, with a range of weapons (*see* SIEGE; WAR) designed to penetrate the city walls by undermining their foundations, smashing through them (or the gates) with the ram, and going over them with scaling ladders.

As early as *ca.* 3000 B.C. the Sumerians used wheeled vehicles in battle. Wider use of the CHARIOT was not known until the second quarter of the 2nd millennium, when chariots became lighter and their mobility was maximized.

The weapons of the Bible must be studied in the wider context of ancient Near Eastern armaments since similarities exist. An abundance of pictorial sources and surviving implements has enhanced our knowledge of ancient weaponry and allows for better visualization of weapons mentioned (though usually not described) in the Bible.

II. Offensive Weapons.–These can be divided into three classes. First, hand-held weapons, used in hand-to-hand combat or for attacking or protecting one's self from wild animals, represent without a doubt the earliest weapons. Second, warriors developed throwing weapons for hunting purposes, enabling them to catch game. Third, warriors created long-range weapons, which virtually allowed an attacker to strike without being seen by the victim.

A. Hand-held Weapons. 1. Club. This instrument is made from a single piece of wood, usually larger at the striking end, and is probably one of the most primitive weapons known. The availability of wood and the simplicity of making a club allowed for a long history of this implement. Early representations of clubs being used in combat come from Egypt in the Late Gerzean Period (3400-3200 B.C.) tomb (no. 100) at Hierakonpolis (see *AWBL,* I, 117) and the Jebel el-ʿAraq knife handle of the same period (see *AWBL,* I, 116). "Club" (so NEB), "war club" (RSV), and "maul" (AV) are translations of Heb. *mēpîṣ* (prob. *mappēṣ*; Prov. 25:18). This word derives from the root *nāpaṣ,* "shatter" (KoB, p. 553). *Tôṯaḥ* in Job 41:29 (MT 21), a hapax legomenon, should probably be rendered "club" (so RSV, NEB; cf. AV "dart"). The word *paṭṭîš,* "hammer," is not usually applied to military con-

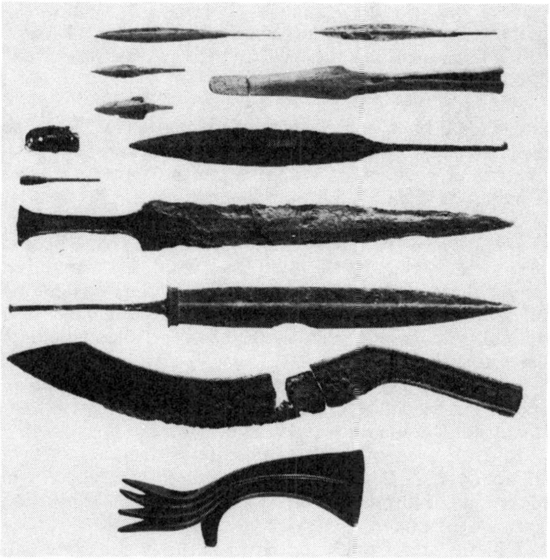

Weapons from Palestine including arrowheads, top and left. Also depicted are a small piece of armor, two spearheads, two daggers, a sword, and (from Beth-shean) a bronze ceremonial axehead in the form of a hand (*ca.* 13th cent. B.C.) (courtesy, Department of Antiquities and Museums, Israel)

texts, except perhaps in Jer. 50:23. The NT includes "clubs" (Gk. *xýlon*; AV "staves") among the weapons used in arresting Christ in Gethsemane (Mt. 26:47, 55, Mk. 14:43).

2. Mace. This weapon is a hand-held stick with a stone attached to the striking end, a small but effective variation of the club. Generally the mace head was made of stone and less often of metal, and shaped as a sphere, pear, or disk. Found both in Egypt and Mesopotamia, the mace is shown in action in the above-mentioned knife handle, in a tomb (no. 100) at Hierokonpolis, and on the hunter's palette (*AWBL,* I, 118f.). These all date to the period before 3000 B.C. The famous Narmer slate palette, from about 3000 B.C., depicts the monarch striking the head of his enemy (*see* picture in ARCHEOLOGY OF EGYPT; Gardiner, plates XXI-XXII). This motif became a standard way of portraying the victorious pharaoh. By the Old Kingdom the mace in Egypt had largely become a ceremonial implement. In Mesopotamia the victory stele of Eannatum shows him striking the head of an enemy (Frankfort, p. 73). It is doubtful that a Hebrew word for mace has survived in the OT. JB renders *mappēṣ* in Jer. 51:20 and *mēpîṣ* in Prov. 25:18 as "mace." This is certainly plausible, but no firm evidence supports it. An allusion to the mace may be found in Hab. 3:13 in the Hebrew expression *māḥaṣ rō'š,* "break the head," and Ps. 68:21 (MT 22) might represent the well-known scenes of pharaoh smiting the head of his foe (see Hoffmeier, "Egyptian Motifs," pp. 55f.). The defensive counterpart to the mace in Egypt was the parrying stick, which has been identified as the *mks* stick. The *mks* is included in ceremonial scenes where the pharaoh holds a mace as well as in some of the head-smashing scenes (cf. J. K. Hoffmeier, *"Sacred" in the Vocabulary of Ancient Egypt* (*Orbis Biblicus et Orientalis,* 59, 1985), pp. 5f., and figures 4-6). (*See* picture in SMITE.)

3. Axe/Battle Axe. The axe is a very old implement that served for both domestic and military purposes. The earliest axes were hand-held stone blades that date to the Paleolithic period throughout the Near East. Precisely when the axe blade was secured to a handle cannot be determined, but with this development the axe became a significantly more lethal weapon. The hunter's palette reveals an early instance of a hunter wielding an axe, the blade of which appears to be shaped like the number 8 on its side (see Emery, p. 113, for a detailed drawing). Thus it likely had a sharpened edge on both sides.

Copper blades have been found from the early part of the 3rd millennium B.C. in Mesopotamia and Egypt. Various shapes of the axeheads are attributable to their function. A broad semicircular blade can be found in the hand of Egyptian warriors during the Old Kingdom (*ca.* 2350 B.C.) while assaulting fortified cities (*AWBL,* I, 146f.). This type of blade would have been sunk into the handle and tied (cf. Wolf, plate 10). The battle axes for the same period in Mesopotamia had socketed blades into which the handle was secured. The blades were longer and narrower. An evolution in the broad circular blade can be detected. By the beginning of the 2nd millennium the shape had been narrowed, looking like a duck bill. Not only was this type known in Egypt, it was used by West Semites as the Beni-hasan relief shows (*AWBL,* I, 166f.). The effectiveness of this type of axe was limited when armor was introduced by the mid-2nd millennium. For this reason, blades became narrower (esp. the Hittite axes) and there was considerable experimentation with shapes to find blades that could penetrate the scale armor.

A socketed axehead with animals molded on the handles. From Tell el-Aḥmar, Syria, 3rd millennium B.C. (Louvre; photo M. Chuzeville)

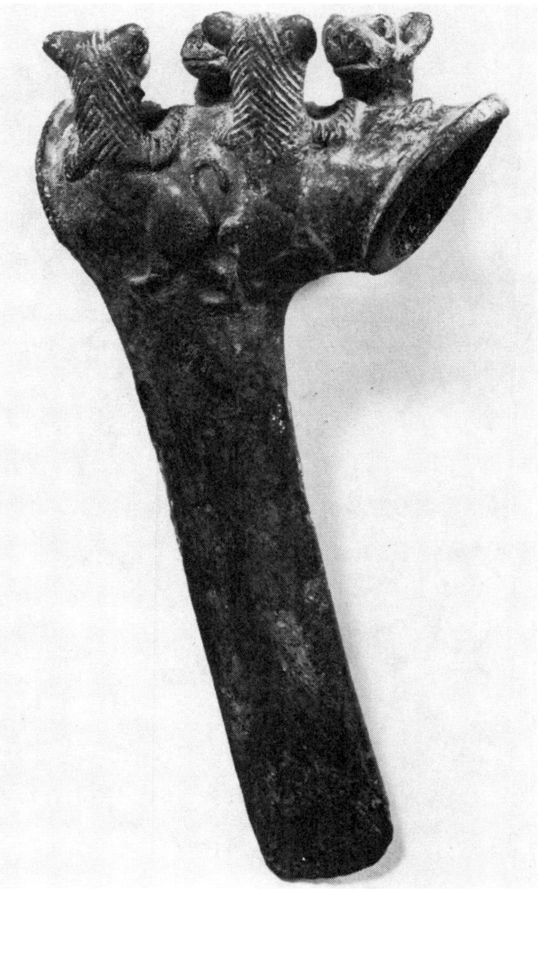

The OT uses numerous Hebrew terms for Axe (e.g., *garzen, ma'aṣār, qardōm, barzel,* etc.). Most of these were used primarily for cutting wood and quarrying and shaping stone. *Mappēṣ* in Jer. 51:20 may be "battle axe" (so AV, NEB; RSV "hammer"). For the range of extant axeheads, see Petrie, plates I-XIII.

4. Spear. The spear, a sharp blade affixed to the end of a stick, is a hand-held stabbing weapon used as early as Paleolithic times. (Only blades have survived). Again the hunter's palette preserves one of the earliest depictions of spears, although European cave art shows what appear to be spears lodged in felled animals. The spear was widely used by the Sumerians, as witnessed by a number of early scenes such as the "Standard of Ur" (*see* picture in Babylonia) and the Eannatum stele (*AWBL,* I, 132-35). The spear (or lance; see II.A.5 below) was used by defenders of besieged cities to keep shock troops at bay when they tried to scale the wall by ladders (*AWBL,* I, 229; II, 346f.).

Spears were still used during the Roman period. Jn. 19:34 records that a Roman soldier took a spear (Gk. *lógchē*) and pierced the side of Christ to ensure that He was dead. Paul received the protection of a unit of spearmen (Gk. *dexiolábos*) who escorted him from Jerusalem to Antipatris (Acts 23:23).

The AV translates such other terms as Heb. *rōmaḥ* and *kîḏôn* as "spear," but they should probably be rendered "lance" and "javelin," respectively (see II.A.5 and II.B.3 below). Petrie's collection contains a variety of spear heads from the ancient Near East and Europe (see plates XXXVII-XL).

5. Lance. The difference between a spear (Heb. *ḥanîṯ*) and lance (*rōmaḥ*) is the length of the shaft (*'ēṣ*). The lance was considerably longer and would have been used by a phalanx of soldiers, as witnessed in the Eannatum stele from *ca.* 2550 B.C. While standing in a chariot Ramses III is shown stabbing a wounded wild bull with a lance. Longer spears would be required by soldiers in the rows behind the shield carriers that formed the front of the array. The longer shaft of the lance would make it ideal for fending off attackers scaling defense walls during a Siege. It is difficult to conclude whether the spear or lance would be used in such situations.

6. Trident. The trident in essence is a three-pronged spear. The evidence, pictorial and linguistic, suggests that it was not a common weapon. Some think that the *ṣinnôr* (2 S. 5:8), used by Joab to take Jerusalem, refers to a trident (*AWBL,* II, 268). *Ṣinnôr* meaning "water shaft" still makes the best sense despite Y. Shiloh's (p. 23) objection to this explanation.

Tridents are virtually unknown in the iconography, although a Hittite weather-god may be holding one (cf. Gurney, plate 28). Generally weather-gods wield lightning bolts or spears. Since these deities are also war-gods, the

The Eannatum Stele from Telloh shows helmeted troops with long spears marching over their dead enemies. In the top and bottom sections they follow their leader Eannatum, who carries a sickle sword and wears a more elaborate helmet. The chariot below is equipped with an axe and a quiver with arrows (mid-3rd millennium B.C.) (CNMHS/ARS, NY/SPADEM)

WEAPONS OF WAR

object held by the above-mentioned Hittite god could be a trident made to look like a thunder bolt. In any event, the trident can hardly have been a very important weapon of war since most battle scenes that have survived do not show it in use. A trident has been found at Lachish (*AWBL,* II, 268), but the use of this implement for military purposes must have been limited indeed.

7. Sword. The primary Hebrew word for "sword" is *ḥereḇ*. It occurs over four hundred times in the OT, attesting its importance as a weapon throughout OT times.

Technically the sword and dagger are the same weapon, but the latter was considerably shorter (40.5 cm. [16 in.] or less). Extant examples and illustrations show that the sword was initially rather small. In Jgs. 3:16 Ehud the judge has a sword that is a cubit (about 44.5 cm. [17.5 in.]) long. This could be regarded as a dagger, and yet it is a *ḥereḇ*. No apparent distinction appears in Hebrew between sword and the sickle sword. The two-edged sword (cf. Ps. 149:6; Prov. 5:4) would be understood as a rapier or thrusting sword, not the sickle type that would be for slashing, since it only had a single sharpened edge.

The sword is usually thought to have developed along with the innovation of metallurgy. The earliest blades were made of copper in the 3rd millennium B.C., but bronze, gold, and even the isolated iron blade are known from *ca.* 2500 B.C. in Mesopotamia and Anatolia (*AWBL,* I, 140-42). In Egypt the small sword or dagger can be traced back to the beginnings of the historical period. An ivory label of Pharaoh Den of the 1st Dynasty (*ca.* 2900) shows the dagger hieroglyph is written for the word "first" (Egyp. *tp*), probably a homonym of the most ancient word for dagger. Its use as a hieroglyph at this early date suggests that the sword or dagger can be traced to an even earlier date. Pharaoh Sekhemkhet (*ca.* 2650) is shown wearing a dagger under his belt in a relief from Wâdī Maghara in the Sinai (A. H. Gardiner and T. E. Peet, *Inscriptions of Sinai* [1955], plate I). This type of dagger was made of copper and had no midrib. The dagger possibly evolved from earlier flint knives of the type used in the battle scene on the Jebel el-ʿAraq knife handle. (For examples of swords and daggers see *AWBL,* I, 140-42, and Petrie, plates XXXII-XXXVI; *see also* pictures in ECBATANA; IRON; KNIFE.)

By the mid-2nd millennium B.C. swords used by peoples of Aegean origin became a heavy and long implement (up to 1 m. [3 ft.] in length). These swords originated in Anatolia and the sea-peoples used them in their ill-fated invasion of Egypt in the early part of the 12th cent. B.C. (see N. K. Sandars, *American Journal of Archaeology,* 65 [1961], 17-28; *Sea Peoples, Warriors of the Ancient Mediterranean* [1978]). Although iron appears in weapons and tools *ca.* 1200 B.C. (the round figure for the beginning of the Iron Age in Syria-Palestine), iron and even steel swords are known much earlier on a limited basis (H. Maryon, *American Journal of Archaeology,* 65 [1961], 173-184). Daggers and swords were generally kept in a sheath or scabbard (Heb. *taʿar*) as in 1 S. 17:51 and Jer. 47:6.

Swords continued to be an important weapon of warfare into Roman times. The Greek terms *máchaira* (Mt. 26:47, 51; Rev. 6:4; etc.) and *romphaía* (Lk. 2:35; Rev. 1:16; etc.) are both translated "sword" in the RSV NT. The former term refers perhaps to a smaller sword than the latter.

8. Sickle Sword. This sword gains its name from its unusual curved shape. The scimitar used by Turks and Arabs in more recent history had the sharpened part on the outside of the C-shaped blade, whereas the ancient sickle sword's cutting edge was on the inside of the C (*AWBL,* I, 10). It was used for striking or hacking a foe rather than for stabbing. It probably functioned like the battle axe, but would have been easier to handle. The sickle sword is attested in Sumer as early as 2500 B.C. (*AWBL,* I, 134-37). The use of this weapon circulated around the Fertile Crescent, arriving in Egypt several centuries later. In the Middle Bronze Age this sword had a rather small blade, but by the Late Bronze period it had a larger striking edge (cf. *AWBL,* I, 172, 206). The Egyptian infantry used it considerably during the New Kingdom, and the Hebrews may have employed it during the conquest. The expression "smiting a person (or a city) with the edge of the sword" (cf. Josh. 10:28, 30, 32, 37) suggests that the sickle sword was in the mind of the biblical writers. Extant specimens of this type of sword have been discovered in Canaanite sites of the L. B. (*AWBL,* I, 10).

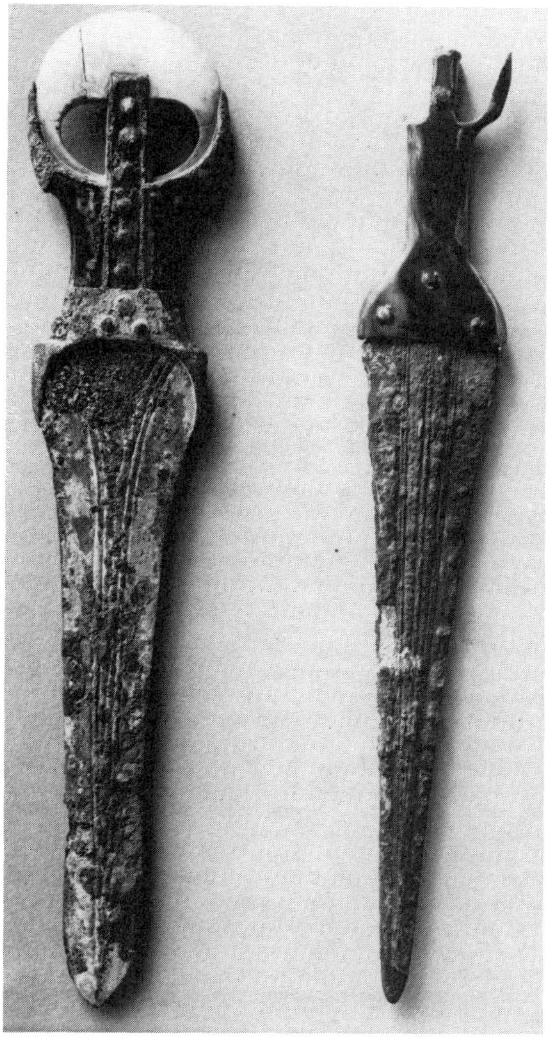

Two bronze swords from Egypt; the sword on the left has an ivory pommel and silver studs (*ca.* 1800 B.C.) (courtesy of the Trustees of the British Museum)

B. Medium-range Weapons. Hand-held weapons were effective only in hand-to-hand combat. A more effective attack on another person or a fortified city required armaments that could travel some distances and still inflict a wound. Medium-range weapons are those that could be

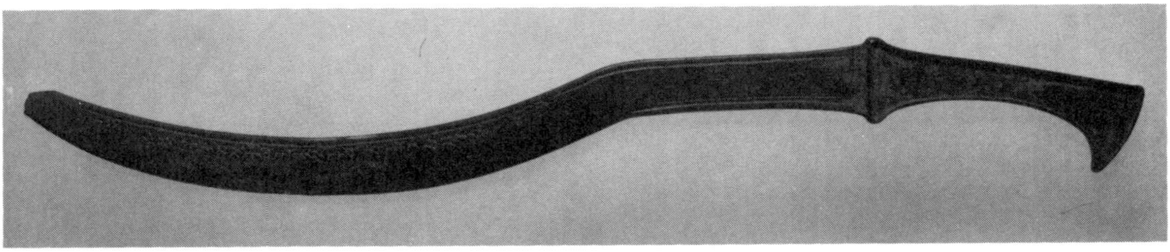

An Assyrian bronze sickle sword with a short handle and a long curved blade. It is inscribed for Adadnirari, king of Assyria (1310-1280 B.C.) (The Metropolitan Museum of Art, Gift of J. Pierpont Morgan)

thrown by the hand and occasionally whipped by a hand-held string.

1. Stone. No doubt the earliest weapon that would have been thrown was the stone, since stones were available nearly everywhere and required no shaping. But the development of the sling and bow rendered the stone alone less effective. In historical times stones proved to be an effective weapon in defending a fortified city. A number of Egyptian siege scenes (11th Dynasty [*ca.* 2100 B.C.]-early 12th Dynasty) show defenders of cities pelting the attackers with rocks (see D. Arnold and J. Settgast, figure 2; *AWBL,* I, 158f.). This practice was well-known in Canaan as evidenced by Egyptian reliefs depicting attacks on cities in Canaan and Syria (*AWBL,* I, 229). Abimelech the son of Gideon was killed while besieging the fortified tower at Thebez when a woman threw the upper part of a millstone from the wall (Jgs. 9:51-53). 2 S. 11:16-21, which recapitulates Jgs. 9:51-53, implies that Uriah the Hittite died in like manner. In Assyrian reliefs of beseiged cities (e.g., Lachish by Sennacherib; see Ussishkin, p. 100), soldiers throw stones at the Assyrian soldiers. 2 Ch. 26:15 indicates that Uzziah's engineers invented a device mounted on the wall that shot arrows and stones. The RSV seemingly suggests that a catapulting machine is in mind, but this seems unlikely in view of the absence of additional evidence for such weaponry until several centuries later (cf. H. G. M. Williamson, *1 and 2 Chronicles* [*NCBC,* 1982], pp. 337f.). Thus the inventions were possibly platforms from which warriors could shoot arrows and throw stones at those attempting to scale the walls (*see* SIEGE IV).

2. Throwing Stick. This wooden implement is usually associated with fowling in the marshy areas of Egypt as a means of recreation (*see* picture in FOWL). Attested as early as the hunter's palette (mentioned above), the throwing stick looks similar to a boomerang. But the throwing stick was used in battle situations as witnessed in the paintings from the Beni-hasan tombs (*ca.* 1900 B.C.), where soldiers wield them as they approach a fortified city (*AWBL,* I, 158f., 169). The celebrated scene of Semitic travelers in the tomb of Khnumhotep III at Beni-hasan shows two men carrying throwing sticks along with their bows and spears (*see* picture in BELLOWS; *AWBL,* I, 166f.). This indicates that the throwing stick was used in military situations, not just for hunting, and that it was used outside the Nile Valley. If flung properly, the throwing stick did apparently return like a boomerang, for Pharaoh Senusert I said of Sinuhe (who had just returned from a self-imposed exile in Palestine), "he has come back like an Asiatic [*ʿ3m*]," which is a wordplay on *ʿm3,* the word for throwing stick (cf. *ANET,* p. 22).

3. Dart/Javelin. Although the dart and javelin look like spears, they were thrown and are generally smaller. A dart is essentially a long arrow and could have feathers to give greater accuracy. The javelin, which did not include feathers, was used at an early date in Mesopotamia (*ca.* 2500 B.C.; cf. *AWBL,* I, 134f.) and probably in Egypt too. Beginning at the end of the 14th cent. B.C. in Egypt, chariots regularly had two long quivers for storing javelins (*AWBL,* I, 231-34, 240).

The RSV usually renders Heb. *kîḏôn* "javelin" (e.g., Josh. 8:18, 26; 1 S. 17:6, 45). The AV and RSV translate *ḥ^{a}nîṯ* as "spear" in the David and Goliath clash (1 S. 17:45), perhaps because it was so much larger than what one would expect for a javelin.

The effective range of the javelin was limited. This can be seen in the story of Sinuhe when he fought with the champion of Retjenu, i.e., Syria (cf. *ANET,* pp. 18-22). Sinuhe kept his distance from the champion and was able to dodge an armful of javelins that were successively thrown at him. Sinuhe drew a single arrow, fired it from the bow and felled the champion. Similarly, David had the advantage of being able to stay out of the effective range of Goliath's javelin (he apparently did not have a bow) and was able to strike him dead with a sling stone (1 S. 17:49).

1 Samuel 17:7 describes the shaft of Goliath's javelin as being like a "weaver's beam." Yadin (*AWBL,* II, 354f.) was probably correct that this refers to a leash that would have been looped on the shaft. When hurled it would increase the distance of the missile and would be more accurate due to the spinning motion caused by the leash. In support of this interpretation Yadin pointed to illustrations of strings attached to Aegean javelins that range in date from the Mycenaean period down to the 5th cent. B.C. (*AWBL,* II, 354f.).

Other Hebrew terms that the RSV translates "javelin" or "dart" include *sēḇeṭ* (2 S. 18:14; Job 41:26 [MT 18]), and *massāʿ* (Job 41:26 [MT 18]).

In the RSV NT "dart" renders Gk. *bélos* (Eph. 6:16).

C. Long-range Weapons. Among ancient weapons the bow and arrow and the sling achieved the greatest effective range. These weapons allowed a warrior a tactical advantage over an enemy's medium-range weapons as seen in Sinuhe's use of the bow and David's skill with the sling (see II.B.3 above).

1. Bow and Arrow. Despite its simplicity, the bow and arrow is a very effective weapon in hunting and warfare. Flint arrowheads have been found that date to Neolithic times (*ca.* 7000 B.C.), demonstrating the antiquity of this weapon. (*See* picture in WAR.)

The Hebrew word for bow is *qešeṯ,* a term that applies to the rainbow (cf. Gen. 9:13f.) as well as to the weapon. This suggests that the term itself may derive from a root that describes the curved shape rather than its function. The bow is not mentioned in the actual conquest narratives in Joshua, but in a retrospective statement Josh. 24:12 indicates that neither the bow nor the sword had been the decisive factor in Israel's victories in Canaan.

WEAPONS OF WAR

Rather it was God's own intervention that gave Israel the land they now possessed. Jonathan used a bow in battle (2 S. 1:22) as well as for sending signals to David (1 S. 20:18-23, 35-37). In 2 S. 22:35 and Ps. 18:34 the bow of bronze does not likely refer to a solid metal bow. Rather, it could refer to the decorative metalwork on composite bows (see W. McLeod, *Composite Bows from the Tomb of Tutankhamūn* [1970], plates III-VII), or the metal handle or tips found on self bows (see W. McLeod, *Self Bows and Other Archery Tackle From the Tomb of Tutankhamūn* [1982], plate I), or it could be symbolic of a powerful bow. The bow was a regular weapon of Israel's army during the monarchy (cf. 1 Ch. 12:2; 2 Ch. 14:8; 17:17; 26:14).

Two distinct types of bows are known from the ancient Near East. The first and earliest type was the self bow which was made of a single piece of wood. The second was the composite bow, a later development and more powerful weapon, which was made of laminated wood, horn, and sinew (W. McLeod, *Journal of the Society of Archer Antiquaries,* 12 [1969], 19-23). The earliest illustrations of bows in use from Mesopotamia and Egypt date to around or just before 3000 B.C. (*AWBL,* I, 118f.). At this early date different shaped bows are found, the arcus (simple curved) and the double convex. A painting from the tomb of Khnumhotep shows that the double convex bow was still in use by the Semites 1000 years later (*AWBL,* I, 167). The self bow continued in use long after the introduction of the composite bow.

The origins of the composite bow are obscure. The earliest representation of a composite bow is incised on a block discovered at Mari that dates to the early dynastic period, *ca.* 2700-2500 (Yadin, *IEJ,* 22 [1972], 89-94). This particular relief is especially significant because the bow is the Scythian or double-curved type, which was previously unknown before the Neo-Assyrian period (9th-8th cents. B.C.). In the period 2300-2000 B.C. numerous examples of the single-curve type of composite bow appear in Mesopotamian reliefs (*see* picture in ARCHER; *AWBL,* I, 150f.). The composite bow gradually made its way to Palestine and then Egypt, with the Hyksos generally being credited for its introduction to Egypt. But no actual evidence supports this view. Since composite bows or representations do not appear until the 18th Dynasty (after 1550 B.C.), it is assumed that the Hyksos must have introduced them. An abundance of self and composite bows have survived from ancient Egypt (W. McLeod, *American Journal of Archaeology,* 62 [1958], 397-401; 66 [1962], 13-19; *Journal of the Society of Archer Antiquaries,* 12 [1969], 19-23), and the tomb of Tutankhamen alone yielded thirty-two composite and fourteen self bows.

The composite bow was a powerful weapon that had an effective range of 160-175 m. (525-575 ft.), and classical sources indicate that an exceptional shot could reach 500 m. (1640 ft.; cf. W. McLeod, *Phoenix,* 19 [1965], 1-14; *Phoenix,* 26 [1972], 78-82). No doubt the deadly force of the composite bow altered the nature of warfare and led to the improvement, if not the introduction, of body armor.

The composite bow was especially sensitive to heat and moisture, which could cause the laminated materials to separate. For this reason, the bow was kept in a case when not in use. Three types of bow cases are attested in antiquity: the hand-held type (*AWBL,* I, 185, 199), the shoulder case that resembled a large Assyrian QUIVER (*AWBL,* II, 430), and the type that was attached to a chariot (*AWBL,* I, 186f., 192-94). A highly decorated bow case was found among the archery trappings in the tomb of Tutankhamen (see W. McLeod, *Self Bows,* plates VI-XVI).

Of course, the arrow propelled by the bow caused the actual damage. It consisted of three parts: arrowhead, shaft, and fletching (feathers). The shaft was usually made of a reed of some sort of wood. The light weight and straightness of the shaft was imperative for accuracy and attaining great distance. The heads varied in style and material, the earliest being made of different stoney materials. The introduction of metals (first copper, then bronze and iron) did not lead to the obsolescence of the flint arrowhead. Metal heads cost more than stone, and because arrows were easily lost, metal tips were not used

Assyrian soldiers with shields and bows and arrows ride in a chariot and on horseback. At far right is a pile of stones for slinging and a slinger (below, fragmented). A relief from the northern palace at Kuyunjik (Nineveh), period of Ashurbanipal, *ca.* 668-633 B.C. (CNMHS/ARS, NY/SPADEM)

Slingers at the siege of Lachish, depicted on a relief from the palace of Sennacherib at Nineveh (704-681 B.C.) (courtesy of the Trustees of the British Museum)

regularly until the metal in question was more readily available and cheaper. The introduction of metal tips appears to parallel the appearance of the composite bow. Since the metal heads would have been heavier than their flint counterparts, a bow with a heavy pull would have been required to deliver the metal-tipped arrow to its target accurately.

Included in the cache of weapons found in Tutankhamen's tomb were over three hundred arrows, each made of a single piece of wood or a reed. Seven different types and shapes were found (see McLeod, *Self Bows,* pp. 58f.). The wooden arrows were usually sharpened to a point. Some had a flared wooden tip and may have been used for hunting fowl. Bronze and lithic blades (chisel-shaped) are also included (for illustrations see McLeod, *Self Bows,* plates IV-VI). Flint blades were widely used in Egypt until the mid-2nd millennium in Egypt. Thereafter it seems that the self bow and flint blade arrows were used in hunting while the composite bow with metal-tip arrows were used in battle. The composite bow and metal-tipped arrow were used throughout the biblical world during the 1st millennium B.C. The numerous Assyrian battle reliefs and scores of iron arrowheads discovered in excavations at Lachish bear this out (see Ussishkin, pp. 54f.).

2. Sling and Stone. The use of the sling complemented the bow as the other long-range weapon used in the ancient Near East. Slingers and archers stand side by side in scenes from the early 2nd millennium in Egypt (*AWBL,* I, 159) as they do in the relief of Sennacherib's attack on Lachish (*AWBL,* II, 434f.; Ussishkin, p. 66).

The OT mentions the use of the sling (Heb. *qela'*) and stone (*'eben*). The David and Goliath story is certainly the most memorable description of the use of a sling in the Bible (1 S. 17:48-50). During the judges period, the militia of Benjamin had seven hundred left-handed slingers who were especially proficient (Jgs. 20:16). When fighting against the Moabites the armies of King Jehoshaphat of Judah and King Jehoram of Israel used slings in besieging Kir-hareseth (2 K. 3:25). 2 Ch. 26:14 says that Uzziah furnished his army with "stones for slinging."

These references make it clear that the sling was a significant part of the arsenal of ancient Israel's armies. Although it did not have the range of the bow and arrow, the sling was an effective and inexpensive long-range weapon. The sling could be made of woven materials, such as wool or palm fiber rope, or of leather. David's example (1 S. 17:40) indicates the availability of smoothed stones from brooks. Excavations in Israel, especially around fortification systems, usually reveal hundreds of sling stones from assaults against a city. Often the stones were worked to make them as round as possible, and they range from about 5 to 7.5 cm. (2 to 3 in.) in diameter. Stones flung from a sling by an accomplished warrior could reach speeds of 160 to 240 km. per hour (100 to 150 mi. per hour), making the stone a lethal force.

III. Defensive Armaments.–As offensive weapons developed, combatants quickly learned that defensive countermeasures had to be taken in order to ensure a degree of security in battle. The types of defensive armaments used depended on the offensive weapon of the attacker, on the weapon that complemented the defensive weapons, on the mobility required, and on the nature of the battle (e.g., siege or open field).

A. Shield. The most common word for shield in the RSV OT is Heb. *māḡēn*. The RSV also gives "shield" for Heb. *šeleṭ* (e.g., 2 S. 8:7; 2 K. 11:10; Jer. 51:11; etc.), which may simply be a synonym for *māḡēn*. The context of some occurrences of *šeleṭ* (e.g., 2 S. 8:7; Ezk. 27:11) suggests that this type of shield may have been ornamental.

Basically warriors employed two types of shield: the small shield, used in hand-to-hand combat, that covered approximately half the body of the defender, and the large shield, used mostly in sieges. The offensive counterparts to the small shield were the sword, battle axe, spear, or similar weapon. The shield had to be light enough to allow for mobility and yet hard enough to ward off blows of an attacker. Leather, wood, and metal were among the materials used to make shields.

Representations of shields over the centuries reveal a variety of shapes, which sometimes are indicative of a particular ethnic group. The Egyptians preferred a shield that was rounded at the top and flat on the bottom. The Hittites used shields shaped like the number 8 (cf. *AWBL,* I, 238f.), while the soldiers in Syria and Palestine in the mid-2nd millennium employed rectangular-shaped shields (*AWBL,* I, 192f.). The round shield was extremely popular, and may have had its origins in the Aegean, for the sea-peoples used them (*AWBL,* II, 336f.), as did the Sheredan mercenaries, who were from the Aegean and were in Egypt during the 13th cent. (Wolf, p. 64). The circular shield continued as the primary defensive weapon of the Assyrians, but the rectangular shield was also used (*AWBL,* II, 390f., 406, 410). The round shield was also used by the neo-Hittites at Carchemish (*AWBL,* II, 368).

The long, full-length shield had a more specialized use. It was most widely employed by besiegers as they approached a city wall so that archers could fire arrows and still be protected (*AWBL,* II, 407, 418f., 434f.; *see* pictures in ARMY, ROMAN; LACHISH; SIEGE). Often a king would be protected by such a shield as he fired arrows at the enemy (*AWBL,* II, 388). The Sumerians utilized large rectangular shields to form the defensive part of their phalanx (*AWBL,* I, 134f.). Some think that Heb. *ṣinnâ* was the word for the large shield (*NBD,* p. 82; Keel, pp. 222-24).

In Eph. 6:16 the "shield of faith" is likely a large shield since the word *thyreós* derives from the word *thýra,* "door." This suggests that the *thyreós* shield was long and rectangular like a door. The Latin *scutum* was a large shield used by Roman soldiers.

B. Buckler. Technically the buckler is a small rounded shield usually worn on the forearm rather than carried in the hand (*see* BUCKLER). The RSV translates Heb. *ṣinnâ* as "buckler" (Ps. 35:2; 91:4; Ezk. 23:24; 38:4). But this

WEAPONS OF WAR

An orthostat from the palace of Kapara at Tell Halâf depicting an Aramean rider with a pointed helmet. He carries a small round shield slung over his shoulder (10th cent. B.C.) (Staatliche Museum zu Berlin, DDR, Vorderasiatisches Museum 8851)

understanding seems unlikely and the large shield is the favored interpretation (BDB, p. 857; *CHAL,* p. 308; *NBD,* p. 82; Keel, pp. 222-24). The AV also renders *māgēn* as "buckler" in 2 S. 22:31; Job 15:26; etc. But there is no proof of this identification, and the association with the small round shield is preferable. In Ps. 91:4 *sōḥērâ* is translated "buckler" in AV, RSV and JB. But "wall" (*CHAL,* p. 255), "rampart" (NEB, NIV), and "bulwark" (NASB) are other suggested meanings for *sōḥērâ*. In 1 Ch. 12:8 (MT 9) the AV translates *rōmaḥ* as "buckler," but "lance" (see II.A.5 above) is more probable.

Close observation of ancient Near Eastern depictions of shields do not indicate that shields had a strap on the forearm (which would make it a buckler), although there is evidence from Greece for such shields (cf. *AWBL,* II, 355). Thus it seems doubtful that the buckler was known in the ancient Near East or used by the Israelites in OT times.

C. Armor. The purpose of body armor is to protect vital parts of the body while still allowing for mobility of a soldier's arms and legs.

1. Coat of Mail. Mail is made either of interlocking rings or small scales that are tied together by thongs. Surviving fragments and artistic representations from the ancient Near East indicate that the latter type was known in OT times. Scaled armor appeared in the ancient Near East during the mid-2nd millennium B.C. (cf. *AWBL,* I, 196f.; Wolf, pp. 96-99). The Hebrew word the RSV translates "coat of mail" is usually *širyôn*/*širyān* (1 S. 17:5, 38; 2 Ch. 26:14; Neh. 4:16 [MT 10]; cf. also *siryôn* in Jer. 46:4; 51:3; AV "brigandine"). These metal coats were heavy, as seen in the case of young David wearing the larger King Saul's *širyôn* (1 S. 17:38). Thus leather jackets were also probably used and would have provided some protection. Such jackets appear to have been worn by soldiers of the invading sea-peoples and the Egyptian defenders in 1186 B.C. (*AWBL,* II, 340f.). Yet a direct hit on scale armor by an arrow could pass between the scales and injure a warrior (cf. *AWBL,* I, 196; Wolf, p. 96). Ahab died as a result of an arrow that had penetrated between his breastplate and his coat of mail (1 K. 22:34; 2 Ch. 18:33). Thus even armor had vulnerable points. In certain instances the AV renders *širyôn* as "habergeon," a medieval term (2 Ch. 26:14; Neh. 4:16; cf. Job 41:26). (*See* picture in SCALE ARMOR.)

In 1 S. 17:38 the RSV and AV render Heb. *maḏ* as "armor," yet this word usually applies to a cloth garment (KoB, p. 495). Perhaps the *maḏ* was a tunic worn under the mail, as suggested by the fact that David was dressed with the *maḏ* and then the coat of mail (1 S. 17:38). The NASB, NEB, and NIV have recognized *maḏ* as a garment of some sort rather than armor. Heb. *taḥra'* (found only in Ex. 28:32; 39:23) is thought to be a "coat of mail" (so NASB, JB) or "habergeon" (AV). The limited usage of this word makes this identification uncertain, but the context suggests that this term applied to a leather garment (*CHAL,* p. 389). Thus it could be a leather counterpart to the *maḏ* or a leather protective jacket.

The Heb. *keli,* "utensil, vessel," also serves as a general term for offensive or defensive weapons (e.g., 1 S. 14:1, 6; 17:54; 20:40 [AV "artillery"]; 31:9f.; 1 Ch. 10:9f.). Presumably one called an "armor-bearer" (Heb. *nōśē' ḵeli*) would carry high-ranking soldier's weapons, as in the case of Jonathan (1 S. 14:7, 12f., 17). The English expression "armor-bearer" conveys the image of a medieval squire carrying the plated armor of a knight, yet the expression *nōśē' ḵeli* should be understood as primarily an "arms-bearer." The tomb of Senbi at Meir in Egypt contains a scene of the tomb owner engaged in a hunt while his retainer or "arms-bearer" stands behind him holding a battle axe, a quiver, and a water bottle (*AWBL,* I, 155).

The RSV NT translates Gk. *hóplon* (Rom. 13:12) and *panoplía* (Lk. 11:22; Eph. 6:11, 13) as "armor." The former word derives from *hoplízō,* which means "to arm." The latter term refers to the full armor of an armed soldier (see IV.D below).

2. Helmet. Helmets, usually made of metal, offered vital protection for the head. The Sumerians utilized them as early as the mid-3rd millennium B.C. (*AWBL,* I, 134f., 137). By the 2nd millennium the helmet was found in Syria-Palestine (cf. *AWBL,* I, 192f.; 222f.). For some reason the Egyptians of pharaonic times never widely adopted the use of the helmet. Egyptian scenes show the helmet in use by non-Egyptian mercenaries (*AWBL,* I, 192f.; II, 340f.). Helmets do appear with greater frequency on Egyptian soldiers in the 13th and 12th cent., but still their use was not widespread. The so-called Blue Crown worn exclusively by pharaohs of the New Kingdom may have originally been a helmet.

Goliath (1 S. 17:5) and King Saul (17:38) are said to have worn a helmet (Heb. *kôḇa'*) made of bronze. 2 Ch. 26:14 and Jer. 46:4 suggest that the helmet was a regular part of the Hebrew soldier's defense (*AWBL,* II, 430-33).

In the RSV NT "helmet" translates Gk. *perikephalaía* (lit. "something around the head") in Eph. 6:17 and 1 Thess. 5:8. Both NT occurrences are allusions to Isa. 59:17. The helmets worn by Roman soldiers would have been made of iron and decked with plumes or hair.

3. Breastplate. Greek *thṓrax* (Eph. 6:14; 1 Thess. 5:8; Rev. 9:9, 17) was a piece of metal armor worn by Greek and Roman soldiers that covered the neck and torso area (a second piece would protect the back area). Paul's use of the word comes from Isa. 59:17, where the LXX has Gk. *thṓrax* for Heb. *širyān,* but the Hebrew term applies to scaled armor, not to the plate armor that would have

Two Persian soldiers carrying shields and spears and wearing undecorated, pointed helmets. A relief from the palace at Persepolis (5th cent. B.C.) (Staatliche Museum zu Berlin, DDR, Vorderasiatisches Museum 2987)

been common when the LXX was translated. But this does not mean that there were no antecedents to the breastplate of Greco-Roman times, for there are a few examples of Egyptian warriors wearing an oval-shaped disk (probably of leather) over the chest area that was held in place by leather straps (E. Naville, *El Bersheh* I [1907], plates 13, 29).

4. Greaves. Practically unknown in the ancient Near East, greaves were shin guards that protected the legs. The OT mentions this protective device only as a part of the giant Goliath's armor (1 S. 17:6). Some representations include greaves as part of the armor of Greek soldiers (*AWBL*, II, 355).

IV. Symbolic Use of Weapons.–Since weapons for offensive and defensive purposes formed a significant part of life in the ancient Near East, the Bible often employs them in symbolic ways. Some of the more common are discussed below.

A. Bow. Because the bow was such a powerful weapon, it symbolized a nation's power. When used in this manner in the OT it generally applies to the power of the nation being broken (e.g., 1 S. 2:4; Ps. 37:15; Jer. 49:35; Hos. 1:5). In ancient thought the bow was closely related to the men of a tribe, and thus corporately to the nation itself (E. Uphill, *Jaarbericht van het vooraziatisch-egyptisch genootschap 'Ex Oriente Lux,'* 19 [1955], 393). To break a nation's bow was to destroy the nation directly (cf. also Hoffmeier, "Egyptian Motifs," 56f.). In Zec. 9:13 Judah is a bow that is about to shoot an arrow (Ephraim) at Greece.

Jeremiah lamented about the verbal abuse he received from his fellow Israelites, pointing out that their tongues were bent like bows (Jer. 9:3), and later he complained that the tongue is a deadly arrow (9:8). The psalmist uses similar imagery in Ps. 64:3-4 (MT 4-5), where he says that evildoers "aim bitter words like arrows."

In Hab. 3:11 and Zec. 9:14 lightning is described as arrows. Depictions of storm-gods (e.g., Baal [Hadad] and Resheph) show them hurling bolts of lightning. In some instances arrows or spears replace the thunderbolt (Keel, pp. 212-221). In Ps. 76:3 (MT 4) the RSV renders Heb. *rišpēy-qāšeṯ* as "flashing arrows," which possibly relates to the mythological storm-god who throws lightning, i.e., flaming arrows.

Psalm 127:4f. compares arrows to sons. Sons were regarded as a sign of God's favor on a man (127:3). Just as arrows defended a man under attack from a foe, so the presence of sons demonstrated God's blessings, and this provided a formidable defense of a man's integrity.

B. Sling and Stone. In Jer. 10:18 the Hebrew verb *qāla'*, "sling," describes the exile of Judah to Babylon. In the same way that one hurls a stone from a sling, so too would the Lord fling Judah into exile.

C. Sword. The sword figures prominently in the OT as a symbol of destruction and judgment (e.g., Ex. 5:3). Like the bow and arrow, the sword is associated with the cutting capability of the tongue (Ps. 57:4 [MT 5]; Prov. 5:4; 12:18). In the NT this meaning takes on a slightly different nuance as it applies to "the word of God" that can penetrate and pierce soul and spirit (He. 4:12). The exalted Christ of Rev. 1:16 and 2:12 has a double-edged sword (Gk. *romphaía*) extending from His mouth. This usage reminds the reader that God's word has a harsh and judgmental aspect to it. This agrees with Jesus' statement in Mt. 10:34 that He came not "to bring peace but a sword [*máchaira*]." The same metaphorical use of "sword" in Rom. 13:4 is extended to human rulers who bear the sword "to execute his [God's] wrath on the wrongdoer." The idea of associating the sword with justice may be associated with this concept.

D. Armor. Paul exhorts the believer to put on the "whole armor [Gk. *panoplía*] of God" in Eph. 6:10 and 13, in order to withstand the attacks of the evil one, the devil. He then systematically describes the various defensive armaments of the Roman soldier (6:14-17). *Panoplía* applies to all of the implements mentioned in this section. Thus the translation "whole armor" (so RSV, AV) is accurate. Paul may have Isa. 11:5 in mind for the imagery of the belt of truth around the waist. He relies on Isaiah for the next piece of equipment, the "breastplate [*thṓrax*] of righteousness" (cf. Isa. 59:17; 1 Thess. 5:8; for futher discussion of this part of the armor see III.C.3 above). Shodding the feet with the gospel of peace (Eph. 6:15) relates to the footgear worn by Roman soldiers. Shoes provided protection for the feet and enhanced mobility; thus the Christian "soldier" would be equipped to go anywhere with the gospel. The "shield [*thyreós*] of faith" (see III.A above) was required to quench the flaming darts (*bélos*) of the evil one (6:16). This shield was a large one that provided ample protection against hostile missiles. The fiery or flaming darts reflect the practice of igniting a projectile before firing it. These particular darts come from the evil one (6:16). The helmet (*perikephalaía*) provides requisite protection for the head and is called the "helmet of salvation," a direct quotation from Isa. 59:17 (cf. 1 Thess. 5:8). In Isa. 59:17 God is the warrior who wears this helmet, but now believers can be equipped with it.

The spiritual warrior also wields offensive armaments that include the "sword [Gk. *máchaira*] of the Spirit," which is identified as the "word of God" (Eph. 6:17). This statement, combined with He. 4:12 and Rev. 1:16 and 2:12, indicates that Scripture is the intended meaning of "word of God" by Paul (so Simpson, pp. 150f.).

E. Shield. In the OT the shield symbolizes God's protection of the nation or individuals. After Abram's victory over the coalition of Mesopotamian kings (Gen. 14:14-17), God says to him, "Fear not, Abram, I am your shield [Heb. *māgēn*]" (Gen. 15:1).

The psalter uses "shield" similarly (e.g., Ps. 3:3; 18:2, 30, 35 [MT 3, 31, 36]; 28:7; 59:11 [MT 12]; etc.). M. Dahood (*Psalms*, I [*AB*, 1966], 16-18) argued that the word should be vocalized *māgān* and thus would mean "suzerain." He applied his argument not only to the occurrences in the psalter, but also to Gen. 15:1. In a suzerainty-vassal relationship, the suzerain was responsible for the protection of his vassal (cf. Ex. 23:22; Josh. 10:6f.). Although *māgēn* and *māgān* are etymologically and semantically related (P. C. Craigie, *Psalms 1-50* [*Word Bible Comm.*, 1983], p. 71), it is difficult to decide emphatically for "shield" or "suzerain." By using *māgān* God implies He is protecting His covenanted party. Perhaps a deliberate wordplay is at work in the choice of *māgēn*.

Bibliography.–D. Arnold, and J. Settgast, *Mitteilungen des deutschen Instituts für ägyptische Altertumskunde in Kairo*, 20 (1965), 49-52 and figure 2; *AWBL*; H. Bonnet, *Die Waffen der Völker des Alten Orients* (1926); T. Dothan, *IEJ*, 26 (1976), 20f.; W. B. Emery, *Archaic Egypt* (1961); H. Frankfort, *Art and Architecture of the Ancient Orient* (1970); A. H. Gardiner, *Egypt of the Pharaohs* (1961); O. R. Gurney, *Hittites* (1954); J. K. Hoffmeier, *Society for the Study of Egyptian Antiquities Newsletter* VI (1975), 8-11; *Journal of the Society for the Study of Egyptian Antiquities*, IX (1980), 195-200; "Some Egyptian Motifs Related to Warfare and Enemies and their OT Counterparts," in J. K. Hoffmeier and E. S. Meltzer, eds., *Egyptological Miscellanies* (*Ancient World*, VI, 1983), 53-70; O. Keel, *Symbolism of the Biblical World* (Eng. tr. 1978); M. Kessler, *VT*, 14 (1964), 494-97; W. M. F. Petrie, *Tools and Weapons* (1971); G. Roux, *Ancient Iraq* (1964); A. R. Schulman, *Journal of the Society for the Study of Egyptian Antiquities*, XII (1982), 165-184; O. R. Sellars, *BA*, 2 (1939), 41-44; Y. Shiloh, *Excavations at the City of David, I, 1978-82* (*Qedem*, 19; 1984); E. K. Simpson, and F. F. Bruce, *Ephesians and Colossians* (*NICNT*, 1957); T. Stech, *American Journal of Archaeology*, 85 (1981), 245-268; D. Ussishkin, *Conquest of Lachish By Sennacherib* (1982); W. Wolf, *Bewaffnung des altägyptischen Heeres* (1929); Y. Yadin, *IEJ*, 22 (1972), 89-94.

J. K. HOFFMEIER

WEASEL [Heb. *ḥōleḏ*] (Lev. 11:29); NEB MOLE-RAT. A member of the family *Mustelidae*, which includes animals such as the badger, otter, mouse, and skunk. In Lev. 11:29 it is listed among the unclean "swarming things" that the Israelites were forbidden to touch. Since Heb. *ḥōleḏ* occurs only here in the OT, it is difficult to define precisely as the variety of English translations illustrates (cf. NJV; NASB, JB "mole"; NAB "rat"). *Ḥoleḏ* may derive from the Semitic root *ḥlḏ*, "to dig, creep" (not attested in Biblical Hebrew, but present in Syriac, Aramaic, and Rabbinic Hebrew; see Jastrow, p. 464). The rendering "weasel" is supported by the versions (including the LXX, Vulg., and Pesh.). More recent translations (excluding NIV, which retains "weasel"), however, have chosen "mole" (*Spalax ehrenbergi*) or "mole-rat" (*Spalax typhlus*) over the traditional "weasel." As with many other hapax legomena, certainty in meaning is impossible without further evidence.

Bibliography.–F. S. Bodenheimer, *Animal Life in Palestine* (1935); G. Cansdale, *Animals of Bible Lands* (1970); *TDOT*, IV, *s.v.* "cheledh" (Beyse). J. HUDDLESTUN

WEATHER [Gk. *eudía*–'fair weather' ("fair weather," Mt. 16:2); Gk. Apoc. *cheimṓn* ("bad weather," 1 Esd. 9:6), *eudía* ("fair weather," Sir. 3:15)]; AV, NEB mg., FAIR WEATHER; AV Apoc. FOUL WEATHER (1 Esd. 9:6), FAIR WARM WEATHER; NEB Apoc. WINTER (1 Esd. 9:6), SUNSHINE. The RSV uses the word "weather" once in the NT (Mt. 16:2) and twice in the Apocrypha (1 Esd. 9:6; Sir. 3:15). In Mt. 16:1-4 (vv. 2f. are textually suspect; cf. Lk. 12:54-56) Jesus contrasts the ability of the Pharisees and Sadducees to predict the weather with their inability to discern the more crucial "signs of the times," a condition that prompts His rebuke. 1 Esd. 9:5f. indicates winter weather that was cool enough to cause "shivering," while the "fair weather" in Sir. 3:15 was warm enough to melt the frost. Sir. 43:11-22 has an impressive list of weather phenomena, all of which reveal the glory and power of God.

See also NATURAL FEATURES VII; SEASONS.

D. BALY

WEAVING. The process of interlacing previously spun lengthwise threads with previously spun crosswise threads to form cloth. Unlike basketweaving or braid, which can be held in the hands while being done, weaving requires a frame, called a loom. The purpose of the loom is to hold the lengthwise threads, called the warp, taut and evenly spaced from each other while the cross-wise threads, called the weft or woof, are being inserted alternately over and under the warp threads. Rather than putting each weft thread over, then under, each warp thread, weavers learned early to lift up all alternate threads at once by tying each odd thread individually to a stick as long as the width of the cloth being woven. When this stick, the heddle, was lifted, all the odd threads at once were pulled up above the level of the even threads, forming a division called the "shed" through which the shuttle, a stick carrying the weft threads, was passed. When the heddle was let down, the odd threads were below the even threads, forming the opposite shed, and the shuttle was passed through in the other direction. After each weft thread was passed through, it was "beaten up," i.e., pressed into the threads already woven with a small slightly pointed and hooked tool. The discovery of the earliest textile remains at Çatal Hüyük attests to weaving in the ancient Near East from *ca.* 6000 B.C. *See* LINEN; WOOL.

Of the two types of looms known to have been used in the biblical period, the horizontal is the earliest and the easiest to set up. The weaver drives four stakes into the ground in the shape of an elongated rectangle, the first pair about a yard apart (a little farther apart than the width of the cloth to be woven) and the second pair the same distance apart, distant from the first pair by the length of the cloth to be woven. A stick is placed on the outside of each pair, and the warp thread is run from the first, over the second, under the first, over the second, and so on until the entire warp is complete. Although the upper and lower warp threads are thus separated by several inches, a stick of wood is run through to hold them apart. Then the lower threads are tied individually with pieces of string to the heddle, which when not in use lies on the top warp threads. When the heddle is lifted and each end set on a rock, it pulls the bottom warp threads up above the top warp threads, forming a shed. After the shuttle is passed through the weft and beaten up, the separating stick is removed, the heddle is lowered, and the opposite shed formed. Then the shuttle can be passed back through, the weft beaten up, and so on.

Since all the parts of this simple loom are of wood, no archeological evidence for its use in the biblical period remains. This type of loom is well known, however, because it is still used by Palestinian village women, and by the bedouin women of the Sinai Peninsula, the Negeb, and southern Jordan. Further, Egyptian tombs from the Middle Kingdom often contain wall paintings or little wooden models of people engaged in daily work, and several such

A model of an Egyptian weaving shop showing a horizontal loom (Middle Kingdom, from northern Egypt) (The Metropolitan Museum of Art)

replicas show the horizontal loom complete in all its parts, with even a little bit of linen cloth in the loom.

This horizontal loom, lying on the ground, is surely the one referred to in Jgs. 16:13f., where Delilah weaves Samson's hair into her cloth as he sleeps; when she cries out that the Philistines are upon him, he jumps up, pulling the loom apart. Textual difficulties here may be due to the fact that approximately from the period of the Hebrew monarchy on (*ca.* 1000 B.C.) the vertical loom gradually replaced the horizontal, at least in cities, so that later scribes and translators would have found this text very hard to understand.

The horizontal loom, which takes up a little more space than the length of the cloth, was too big to set up indoors as a general rule. Therefore weaving on this loom is summer work; no rain at all falls during the dry season from April to October, and the ground is dry. Also, there is less farm work during the dry season, leaving more time for weaving.

The vertical loom is suspended from a crosspiece between two poles. The warp threads are tied at the top to a crossbar, which can be turned in order to roll up the cloth as it is woven. The warp threads at their lower end run around a second crossbar, which can also be turned as the upper one is turned, and tension is provided by a series of weights tied to the warp threads below the crossbar. These clay weights, 7-10 cm. (3-4 in.) in diameter, with a hole through the middle to run the threads through, are the only archeological remains of such looms. They are found at virtually every excavation from the Iron Age and later. The heddle is simply another crossbar to which alternate warp threads have been tied. The crossbars are supported on pegs driven into the uprights.

The vertical loom has significant advantages over the horizontal: (1) Since the cloth can be wound up as weaving progresses, there is virtually no limit to the length that can be woven in one long strip. Long warp threads can be looped up and tied to each loom weight, to be released as needed. (2) This loom takes up little floor space, and thus is well suited to indoor use, so that it can be used all year round. These two features combine to lead to specialization and industrialization.

Excavations have yielded evidence for decorative weaving. Bone tools have been identified as needle shuttles and pattern sticks. These were used to insert colored threads into the warp, independent of the shed formed by the heddle, making possible a variety of colored patterns.

A drawing of an ancient vertical loom, adapted from a Greek vase painting, 5th cent. B.C.

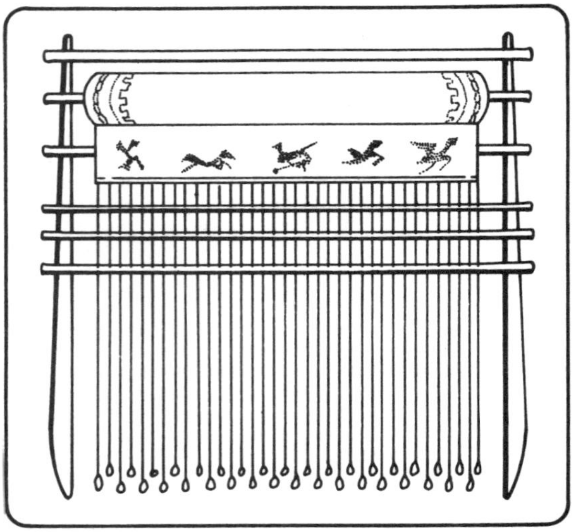

Fortunately, we have wall paintings at two sites that also furnish examples of the earliest textiles, Neolithic Çatal Hüyük, and Chalcolithic Teleilat el-Ghassul in the Jordan Valley. These murals show people dressed in elaborately patterned and very colorful clothing. From the Late Bronze Age we have the colored garments of the nomads in the Beni-hasan tomb paintings (*see* picture in BELLOWS). The weaving tools used to make such cloth have been found at Megiddo, Jericho, Lachish, Hazor, and many other sites. the OT terms for colored weaving and tapestry are *rāqam* (Ex. 26:36; 27:16; 28:39; etc.) *ḥāšaḇ* (Ex. 26:1, 31; 28:6, 15; etc.) It is not possible to know exactly what process each of these terms, or any of the less common terms, referred to.

See also CHECKER WORK; DESIGN; EMBROIDERY.

After being woven, the cloth needed to be washed or bleached, especially if it had been woven on a horizontal loom. This washing procedure was a trade in itself, known as "fulling." Fullers washed the cloth by trampling it with their feet in shallow pools of water, and afterward spreading it out to dry (*see* FULLER). The workplace of Jerusalem fullers is referred to in 2 K. 18:17, Isa. 7:3; 36:2 (*see* FULLER'S FIELD). Fulling became a paradigm for cleanliness and whiteness (Mal. 3:2; Mk. 9:3).

Bibliography.–G. Crowfoot, "Bone Tools from Cave 4067," *Megiddo*, II, (1948), p. 140, plate 165:1; G. Dalman, *Arbeit und Sitte in Palästina*, V (repr. 1964), 94-129; K. Kenyon, *Digging up Jericho* (1958), pp. 57f.; A. Mallon, R. Koeppel, R. Neuville, *Teleilat Ghassul*, I (1934); J. Mellaart, *Çatal-Huyuk: A Neolithic Town in Anatolia* (1967), pp. 119f., plates 116-18. S. Weir, *Spinning and Weaving in Palestine* (1970).

D. IRVIN

Several texts use weaving as imagery. Isa. 59:5 and Mic. 7:3 compare unjust and dishonest plots to natural evils, including the weaving (Heb *'ārag, 'āḇaṯ*, respectively) of a spider's web. Isa. 38:2 compares the abrupt end of a person's life to the weaver's cutting of the cloth from the loom. Similarly, Job likens the swift passing of his life to the rapid movement of a weaver's shuttle (Job 7:6; see comms. on the difficulty of v. 6b).

Three other texts must also be mentioned. In Ex. 35:35 Moses tells the people that God has given Bezalel and Oholiab the ability to do all kinds of craftwork, including weaving. The problematic 2 K. 23:7 apparently refers to ritual garments woven for the cult of Asherah (see NEB; cf. 10:22; on the textual and interpretative problems see comms.). Finally, Jn. 19:23 refers to Jesus' tunic as "without seam, woven [Gk. *hyphantós*] from top to bottom," i.e., it was one piece, hence the soldiers had to cast lots for it. Although some church fathers and commentators have interpreted this seamless garment as symbolizing the unity of Christ's teaching or of the Church, or as referring to Christ as high priest (the high priest's tunic was of one piece; see Josephus *Ant.* iii.7.4 [161]), it is perhaps best to take the text at its face value, for such seamless garments were common under clothing (see R. Brown, comm. on John, II [*AB*, 1970], 903, 920-22).

G. A. L.

WEB. *See* SPIDER'S WEB; WEAVING.

WEDDING. *See* MARRIAGE IV C; WEDDING GARMENT.

WEDDING GARMENT [Gk. *éndyma gámou*] (Mt. 22:11f.). The nature of this garment is unknown. The Greek expression does not occur elsewhere in the NT or the LXX. In the long text of Joseph and Asenath 20:6 (which might have been influenced by the NT) it is used for the clothing of the bride, not of a guest. Some have suggested that it was a special garment — which the host would have had to supply if he expected a guest taken unexpectedly from the street to be wearing it. Others (e.g., J. Jeremias, *Parables of Jesus* [Eng. tr., rev. ed. 1972], p. 187) have maintained that it was merely a garment newly washed for the occasion, not a special garment. While the background might have been better understood by the original hearers of the parable, the general meaning of the garment — something required for the final acceptance of those who respond to the invitation — remains clear. For detailed interpretation see the comms. and studies of the parables.

E. W. S.

WEDGE OF GOLD. The AV rendering of Heb. *lᵉšôn zāhāḇ* ("tongue of gold") in Josh. 7:21, 24. The phrase refers to a bar of gold, one of the forms in which gold was used before the invention of coins for money. In Isa. 13:12 the AV's use of "golden wedge" for Heb. *keṯem* has insufficient grounds; the RSV and NEB have simply "gold."

WEEDS. The translation of several OT and NT terms.

(1) **FOUL WEEDS** [Heb. *bo'šâ* < *bā'aš*–'stink'; Gk. *bátos*] (Job 31:40); AV COCKLE; NEB WEEDS. The Hebrew root seems to indicate foul-smelling weeds rather than the attractive corn cockle; the latter is nonetheless a troublesome, vigorous weed and is Moldenke's choice for this passage (*MPB*, pp. 29f.). Many different weeds have been suggested; perhaps no particular plant is intended.

(2) **POISONOUS WEEDS** [Heb. *rō'š*; Gk. *ágrōstis*] (Hos. 10:4); AV HEMLOCK. The Hebrew word is elsewhere rendered "gall" in the AV; the RSV has "gall" in Lam. 3:19 and "poison" or "poisonous" elsewhere. *See* GALL; POISON.

(3) [Heb. *sûp*] (Jonah 2:5). The context indicates an underwater seaweed. Moldenke (*MPB*, p. 249) identified it as the eelgrass, *Zostere marina* L., which has the required characteristic of tending to become wrapped around a swimmer's body.

(4) [Gk. *zizánia*] (Mt. 13:25-27 etc.); AV TARES; NEB DARNEL. The bearded darnel (*Lolium temulentum* L.) is a vigorous grass closely resembling wheat or rye. The seeds are particularly noxious if infected with the mold ergot, producing vomiting, malaise, and even death. Thus tares have to be separated very carefully from the wheat, but usually only as harvest approaches.

R. K. H.

WEEK [Heb. *šāḇu(a)'*–'unit of seven'] (Gen. 29:27f.; Ex. 34:22; Lev. 12:5; Nu. 28:26; Dt. 16:9f., 16; 2 Ch. 8:13; Jer. 5:24; Dnl. 9:24-27; 10:2f.); NEB also SEVEN DAYS, SEVEN DAYS' FEAST, SEASONS, etc.; [*šabbāṯ*] (Lev. 23:15; 25:8); AV NEB also, SABBATH; [Gk. *sábbata, sábbaton*] (Mt. 28:1; Mk. 16:2, 9; Lk. 18:12; 24:1; Jn. 20:1, 19; Acts 17:2; 20:7; 1 Cor. 16:2); AV also SABBATH DAY; NEB also SABBATH, SUNDAY, SATURDAY NIGHT. A cycle of seven days.

The origin of the seven-day week is disputed. Despite many theories, there is thus far no conclusive evidence that it originated prior to the existence of Israel. It is clear, however, that the seven-day week, culminating in the Sabbath, was an important calendrical unit in Israel from its earliest days. During the period of the Roman empire the use of the seven-day week became widespread, probably through the influence of Jews and Christians.

See CALENDAR II.A.3; SABBATH I, II.

G. WYPER

WEEKS, FEAST OF [Heb. *hag šāḇu'ōṯ*]; NEB PILGRIM-FEAST OF WEEKS. *See* PENTECOST.

WEEKS, SEVENTY. *See* SEVENTY WEEKS.

WEEP; WEEPING [Heb. *bāḵâ* (Gen. 21:16; 23:2; etc.; piel, Jer. 31:15; Ezk. 8:14), *beḵî* (Gen. 45:2; Dt. 34:8; Ezr. 3:13; etc.), *beḵiṯ* (Gen. 50:4), *dāmaʿ*–'shed tears' (Jer. 13:17), *dimʿâ*–'tears' (Ps. 6:6 [MT 7]; Lam. 2:11), piel of *kālâ*–'use up, exhaust' ("weep out," 1 S. 2:33), *sāpaḏ*–'mourn, lament, beat the breast' (Zec. 12:10); Gk. *klaíō* (Mt. 2:18; 26:75; Mk. 5:38f.; etc.), *klauthmós* (Mt. 8:12; 13:42, 50; etc.), *dakrýō*–'shed tears' (Jn. 11:35)]; AV also BEWAIL, MOURN, WAILING, TEARS (Ps. 6:6; Lam. 2:11), CONSUME (2 S. 2:33), etc.; NEB also WAIL-(ING), CRY(ING), GROW DIM (1 S. 2:33), TEARS, STREAM WITH TEARS (Jer. 13:17), etc. To express intense emotion (as sorrow or grief) by shedding tears.

I. In the OT.–Several kinds of circumstances could be occasions for weeping. The loss of a loved one, particularly of a close family member, elicited weeping; cf. Gen. 21:16 (Hagar, for the impending death of Ishmael; here the RSV follows the LXX, in which the child, not Hagar, weeps); 23:2 (Abraham for Sarah); 37:35 (Jacob, on recognizing Joseph's bloody tunic); 50:1 (Joseph at Jacob's death); 2 S. 12:16-21 (David over his infant son); 13:36 (David over Amnon); 18:33 (MT 19:1; David over Absalom).

Intense emotion at reuniting with a close relative or friend could be expressed by weeping as well as by kissing the other's neck, as at Jacob's reunion with Esau (Gen. 33:4) and Joseph's reunions with Benjamin (45:14), his other brothers (v. 15), and his father Jacob (46:29). Weeping and kissing also characterized emotional partings, as at Naomi's dismissal of her daughters-in-law (Ruth 1:9, 14) and David's final meeting with Jonathan (1 S. 20:41).

Weeping could also be a sign of intense personal sorrow. Esau wept after learning that he had been cheated out of his blessing (Gen. 27:38). Hannah likewise wept over her barrenness (1 S.1:7, 10). Saul wept with remorse upon hearing David's voice inside the cave (1 S. 24:16), and Nehemiah cried over the ruined condition of the temple and walls in Jerusalem (Neh. 1:4). Job's three friends wept when they first saw him because his sores had made him unrecognizable (Job 2:12). As in expression of contrition, weeping could be accompanied by fasting (2 S. 1:12; 12:21f.) or by the rending of one's garments (2 K. 22:19 par. 2 Ch. 34:27).

The death of an important leader was an occasion for collective weeping by a tribe or nation. The Egyptians mourned Jacob's death seventy days (Gen. 50:3). The Israelites mourned the deaths of Aaron (Nu. 20:29) and Moses (Dt. 34:8) for thirty days. Similarly, David led the Israelites in national mourning over the fall of Saul and Jonathan (2 S. 1:11f., 24) and the slaying of Abner (3:32-35). Other events could also occasion collective weeping. The Israelites came together to weep after the destruction of the tribe of Benjamin (Jgs. 21:2). Some of the exiles wept together "by the waters of Babylon" when they remembered the destruction of Jerusalem (Ps. 137:1). Communal weeping in response to a disaster (cf. Dt. 1:45; Jgs. 20:23, 26) could also serve as a ritual expression of contrition, which it was hoped, would bring about a return to divine favor (cf. Jer. 3:21). Thus in Esther's time the Jews responded to the news of the coming genocide with "fasting and weeping and lamenting" (Est. 4:3).

The prophets often wept over the coming (or present) sufferings of their people (e.g., Isa. 22:4; Jer. 9:1; 13:17). Rachel's weeping for her children (prob. referring initially to the exiled northern tribes, Jer. 31:15) stands in the same tradition; this text was later applied to Herod's massacre of the children of Bethlehem (Mt. 2:18). Conversely, Isaiah wept mockingly over the fate of Moab (Isa. 16:9; cf. 15:2, 5).

II. In the NT.–The NT refers to weeping in contexts similar to those of the OT. Thus the loss of a loved one is a common occasion for weeping as an expression of grief; e.g., cf. the deaths of the widow of Nain's son (Lk. 7:13), of Jairus's daughter (8:52), of Lazarus (Jn. 11:31, 33; in v. 35 Jesus Himself weeps), of Jesus (Jn. 20:11, 13, 15), and of Dorcas (Acts 9:39). In Rev. 18:9, 11, 15, 19 the kings, merchants, and seamen of the earth weep over the loss of their fortunes as a result of the fall of the allegorical Babylon. Jas. 4:9 advocates weeping and mourning as a proper beginning to repentance, while 5:1 calls on the rich to "weep and howl" over their coming doom. In the prophetic tradition, Jesus wept over the impending destruction of Jerusalem (Lk. 19:41). Peter wept bitterly in remorse for having denied Jesus (Mt. 26:75; Mk. 14:72). The elders of the church at Ephesus wept and kissed Paul when they bade him farewell (Acts 20:37).

Unique to the NT, however, are references to "weeping and gnashing of teeth." According to Matthew and Luke, Jesus warns that those cut off from the Kingdom will find themselves in the "outer darkness" (Mt. 8:12; 22:13; 25:30), in the "furnace of fire" (13:42, 50), among the hypocrites (24:51), or simply being "thrust out" of the Kingdom (Lk. 13:28); and there they will "weep and gnash their teeth" in sorrow over their loss. The Lukan beatitudes promise a reversal of fortunes, however, for those who now weep (— either due to oppression or, possibly, in contrition 6:21); the opposite fate awaits those who now laugh (v. 25).

See also BURIAL II.C; III.D; LAMENT; TEAR.

D. G. SCHLEY

WEIGHT [Heb. *mišqāl,* also *mišqôl* (Ezk. 4:10), part. of *šāqal*–'weigh' ("feel the weight," 2 S. 18:12), *ṭōraḥ* (Dt. 1:12), *sāmaḵ* ("lean [his] weight," Jgs. 16:29), *'eḇen*–'stone,' *kāḇôḏ* (Isa. 22:24); etc.; Gk. *báros* (2 Cor. 4:17), *ónkos* (He. 12:1)]; AV also ENCUMBRANCE (Dt. 1:12), GLORY (Isa. 22:24), etc.; NEB also HEAVY (Dt. 1:12), etc.

The practice of trade by barter led in time to the use of coins, which essentially are guaranteed weights of valuable metals (*see* MONEY). The use of weights in commerce presupposes the invention of the BALANCE, which was used to weigh the goods purchased as well as the metal (silver or gold) used for payment. With no governmentally established standards of weights (but cf. 2 S. 14:26, "king's weight") or regular official inspections, customers in antiquity needed constantly to be concerned with "just" balances and weights (lit. "stones," Lev. 19:36; Dt. 25:13-15; Prov. 11:1; 20:10, 23; Mic. 6:11; etc.). Archeological evidence seem to show that until *ca.* 1500 B.C. balances were useful but not sensitive enough to be wholly accurate. Since the shekel, the basic unit for weighing, was comparatively light, some have suggested that weighing may have originated with jewelers and workers of gold and silver (see Isa. 46:6; Job 28:15).

In figurative usage "beyond weight" (2 K. 25:16; Jer. 52:20; cf. 1 Ch. 22:3, 14) suggests quantity beyond human ability to measure (cf. Eng. "priceless"). A similar phrase occurs in 2 Cor. 4:17, "weight of glory beyond all comparison." In the NT "weighty" (Gk. *barýs,* 2 Cor. 10:10) and "weightier" (*barýteros,* Mt. 23:23) indicate importance. Heb. *neṭel* in Prov. 27:3 and Gk. *ónkos* in He. 12:1 denote an encumbering burden.

See also WEIGHTS AND MEASURES. P. L. GARBER

WEIGHTS AND MEASURES. The use of weights and measures is as old as civilization, since common standards of length, volume, area, and weight must be used in all human cooperative projects, from building a house to sowing a plot of land. The more complex the society and the greater its extent, the more formal are its systems of measurement. "As long as my arm" or "enough seed to fill the pot" will not suffice for complicated architectural or commercial operations. Hence, every society has a more-or-less standardized system of weights and measures. The study of weights and measures is called metrology.

- I. Evidences for Ancient Weights and Measures
  - A. Archeological
  - B. Literary
- II. In the OT
  - A. Linear Measures
    1. Cubit
    2. Span
    3. Handbreadth
    4. Finger
  - B. Measures of Capacity
    1. Homer
    2. Kor
    3. Lethech
    4. Ephah
    5. Bath
    6. Seah
    7. Hin
    8. Omer and Issaron
    9. Kab
    10. Log
    11. System of Measures
    12. Modern Equivalents
  - C. Measures of Area
  - D. Weights
    1. Talent
    2. Mina
    3. Shekel
    4. Beka
    5. Gerah
    6. Other Weights
    7. Modern Equivalents
- III. In the NT
  - A. Linear Measures
  - B. Measures of Capacity
  - C. Weights

I. Evidences for Ancient Weights and Measures.–The study of biblical weights and measures is complicated, partly because metrologies are themselves complicated. Weights and measures change in their values over time without necessarily changing their names, and some become obsolete and fall out of use altogether. Different nations may use the same name for different weights and measures; e.g., British gallons, pints, bushels, etc., are slightly larger than the U.S. measures of the same name. The same term may be used concurrently in the same nation for a different measure; e.g., the U.S. has pounds troy and pounds avoirdupois, long tons and short tons, statute miles and nautical miles, dry quarts and liquid quarts, and so on. The same practices were in use in ancient times and must be taken into account when reconstructing their systems of weights and measures.

Two kinds of evidence are available for reconstructing ancient systems of weights and measures: archeological and literary.

A. Archeological. Archeological excavations sometimes turn up artifacts — either the measuring instruments themselves or objects made according to a standard — that cast light on the metrological standards of the society. Ancient weights in particular, since they were made of stone or metal, are often well preserved. If they are inscribed with the weight standard used, the value of the ancient standard can be determined in terms of modern systems. The same is true of capacity measures, but since the vessels were made of more fragile materials such as pottery or woven reeds, they are rarely found intact. Standards of length can sometimes be inferred or estimated from the dimensions of excavated buildings, or measured exactly from artifacts such as the cubit rod. Inscriptions found on the ancient remains, such as the Siloam tunnel inscription (see II.A. 1 below), can provide valuable information.

B. Literary. Ancient literature sometimes contains explicit formulations of a metrological system or uses expressions from which a system can be inferred. Of course, modern equivalents cannot be determined in this way. There is no single verse or chapter in the Bible that describes the metrological system of ancient Israel. By comparing occasional statements of equivalence (e.g., Ex. 38:26, where a beka is said to be half a shekel) with others, one may construct at least a partial system of biblical metrology. Where the Bible itself does not give information, the ancient translations (e.g., the LXX, Vulg., Pesh., or Tgs.) sometimes throw light on certain words or expressions. Later Jewish tradition preserved in the writings of Josephus or the Mishnah can be helpful as well.

When all is said and done, we are still in the dark about several aspects of biblical metrology — partly because the archeological evidence is insufficient or ambiguous at certain points, or because it does not agree with inferences made from the biblical text, or because the text is itself

Weights shaped like a cow and a goat reclining, 14th-13th cent. B.C., found at Ugarit (Louvre; photo M. Chuzeville)

hard to interpret. Keeping these reservations in mind, however, we have a tolerably clear picture of the weights and measures of the Bible.

II. In the OT.–A. Linear Measures. The basic unit of length was the cubit or "forearm." In the absence of a measuring instrument the forearm or parts of the arm itself might have been used, but normally a cane or rod (Heb. *qᵉnēh middâ,* "reed of measure," Ezk. 40:5) one or several cubits long was employed. It is highly improbable that "the architects, masons and craftsmen measured with their own arms" (de Vaux, p. 197). A number of cubit rods made of wood or stone have been found in Egypt. In Mesopotamia, too, cubit rods were sometimes kept in a central place for public use. A tablet from Nuzi says, "they have taken the copper cubit which is (kept) at the city gate of Nuzi, and they have measured the orchard according to the copper cubit" (*CAD,* I/2, 74).

Lengths sometimes came to be described in "rods" or "canes," as if the instrument itself were the unit of measure (e.g., Ezk. 40:5-7). Larger multiples of cubits were measured by rope (Heb. *ḥeḇel middâ,* "measuring rope," Zec. 2:1 [MT 5]), twine or string (*qaw hammiddâ,* "measuring line," Jer. 31:39), thread (*ḥûṭ,* Jer. 52:21), or the like. Such flexible instruments were particularly useful for measuring round objects like pillars (Zec. 2:1 [MT 5]) or square areas such as a parcel of land (Am. 7:17).

The following paragraphs describe the standard measures in use in the OT, from the largest to smallest.

1. Cubit. The cubit (Heb. and Aram. *'ammâ*; Akk. *ammatu*; Ugar. *'mt*) was the basic measure of length in Israel and the ancient Near East. The word denoted originally the length from the elbow to the tip of the middle finger. The word is found 247 times in the OT, giving the measures of, e.g., the height of a man (1 S. 17:4) or of a statue (Dnl. 3:1), the depth of the flood (Gen. 7:20) or of a pile of quail (Nu. 11:31), the length of a bed (Dt. 3:11) or of a scroll (Zec. 5:2). Most of the references, however, are to the dimensions of buildings, particularly the tabernacle or temple (Ex. 25–27, 36–38; 1 K. 6–7; 2 Ch. 3–4; Ezk. 40–48).

Two kinds of cubit were in use in ancient Israel, the ordinary cubit and a longer cubit. Ezekiel mentions a measuring reed six cubits long, "each being a cubit and a handbreadth" (Ezk. 40:5; cf. 43:13), i.e., the longer cubit. This practice was common in ancient times. The ancient Egyptians also had two cubits, the royal cubit of seven handbreadths and the ordinary one of six handbreadths. In Mesopotamia, too, there were two cubits, the "great cubit" (*ammatu rabîtu*) and the ordinary cubit (*CAD,* I/2, 74; Scott, *JBL,* 77 [1958], 207f.). The Mishnah knows of different sizes of cubit: a five-handbreadth cubit and a six-handbreadth cubit (Mish. *Kelim* xvii.10), but it is likely that the OT cubits were of six and seven handbreadths, like the Egyptian cubits.

The OT terminology for its cubits is obscure. The bed of Og was said to have been nine cubits long and four cubits wide, "according to the *'ammaṯ 'îš*" (Dt. 3:11). This "cubit of a man" is generally thought to be the ordinary shorter cubit of six handbreaths. This is possible; but the word *'îš,* "man," can also mean "an important man," and so Tgs. Onkelos and Neofiti translate the phrase "by the royal cubit" (cf. Pesh. "by the hero's cubit"; Tg. Pseudo-Jonathan "by his own cubit," i.e., as measured by Og's own larger-than-normal forearm). The LXX translates literally, as does the AV. The RSV has "by the common cubit," while the NEB leaves out the phrase altogether.

2 Chronicles 3:3 gives the dimensions of the temple as sixty by twenty cubits "by the former measure" (*bammiddâ hāri'šônâ*; AV "after the first measure"; RSV "by the old standard"). It is uncertain whether this refers to the longer or shorter cubit.

Ezekiel 41:8 notes that the foundations of the side chambers of the temple measured "a full reed of six long cubits [*'aṣṣîlâ*]." The word *'aṣṣîl* means "upper arm." Ezekiel's "cubit and a handbreadth," then, might be understood here as "the cubit to the upper arm," i.e., its measure extended from the middle finger to the upper arm rather than to the elbow (cf. AV "six great cubits"; RSV "six long cubits"; NEB "six cubits high").

A different word, Heb. *gōmeḏ,* is used to measure the length of Ehud's sword (Jgs. 3:16; AV, RSV, "cubit"; NEB "only fifteen inches long"). The Aramaic cognate *garmîḏâ'* is sometimes used as an equivalent to a cubit (see Tg. Pseudo-Jonathan on Ex. 16:29); but the context clearly indicates a weapon small enough to be hidden under clothing, hence probably shorter than a cubit as defined below. The LXX translates it with Gk. *spithamḗ,* "span" (see 2 below); the Vulgate interprets it as meaning "palm."

The length of the shorter cubit in today's measures is generally accepted to be about 4.4 cm. (17.5 in.). This measure is based on information from the Siloam tunnel inscription; this tunnel was built in Jerusalem in the time of King Hezekiah (2 K. 20:20). The inscription gives the tunnel's length as 1200 cubits. Since the tunnel is about 533 m. (1749 ft.) long, this yields a cubit of 44.4 cm. (17.49 in.) long, about equal to the Egyptian common cubit of 44.2–45.0 cm. (17.4–17.7 in.); *see* CUBIT. The long Israelite cubit, then, was presumably equal to the long Egyptian cubit (about 52.3–542.6 cm., 20.6–20.7 in.) as well.

Scott (*JBL,* 77 [1958], 212-14) has interpreted the dimensions of excavated buildings in Palestine in terms of the shorter cubit. Barkay (*Biblical Archeology Review*) has found that the dimensions of two preexilic burial complexes near Jerusalem divide evenly into the cubits of the lengths stated above — one according to the common cubit, and the other according to the longer cubit.

2. Span. The span (Heb. *zereṯ*) is mentioned seven times in the OT. The priest's breastplate was to be a span square (Ex. 28:16; 39:9). The rim of the altar in Ezekiel's vision was a span thick (Ezk. 43:13). Goliath's height was "six cubits and a span" (1 S. 17:4). Isa. 40:12 says that God has "marked off the heavens with a span."

In anatomical terms the span is the distance from the thumb to the little finger with the fingers outspread. In later Hebrew *zereṯ* refers to the little finger itself; a popular but implausible etymology derives it from *zᵉ'ereṯ,* "little."

The span was half a cubit long, about 22.2 cm. (8.75 in.). It seems to have been little used as a measurement, since the OT mentions "half a cubit" three times as often as the "span." *See* SPAN.

3. Handbreadth. The handbreadth or palm (Heb. *ṭepaḥ, ṭōp̄aḥ*) was considered the breadth of the four fingers of the hand excluding the thumb and was one-sixth of a common cubit, thus about 7.4 cm. (2.9 in.). It is mentioned eight times in the OT. The framework of the table for the bread of the presence (Ex. 25:25; 37:12) was one handbreadth wide (Vulg. "four fingers"). The thickness of the bronze sea was one handbreadth (1 K. 7:26; 2 Ch. 4:5). The stone tables for sacrifices in the temple were to be supplied with hooks a handbreadth in length (Ezk. 40:43). The shortness of the handbreadth is indicated by the psalmist: "Behold, thou hast made my days a few handbreadths, and my lifetime is as nothing in thy sight" (Ps. 39:5 [MT 6]).

4. Finger. The finger (Heb. *'eṣba'*) is used as a measure of width in Jer. 52:21, where the hollow pillars of the temple are said to be "four fingers" thick, i.e., one handbreadth. There would be twenty-four fingers in a cubit at 1.85 cm. (0.73 in.) per finger.

The following system emerges from the above measures:

	cubit(s)	span(s)	handbreadth(s)	finger(s)
1 cubit (44.4 cm., 17.5 in.)	1	2	6	24
1 span (22.2 cm., 8.75 in.)	1/2	1	3	12
1 handbreadth (7.4 cm., 2.9 in.)	1/6	1/3	1	4
1 finger (1.85 cm., 0.73 in.)	1/24	1/12	1/4	1

The larger cubit of Ezekiel probably did not imply correspondingly larger sub-units.

B. Measures of Capacity. Dry and liquid measures were measured by containers holding the specified unit of measure. Thus, for instance, an ephah was not only a dry measure of capacity but also a kind of basket. Such containers were used in measuring out grain and other materials for buying and selling, and to tamper with them was a crime. The Egyptian "Instruction of Amenemope" admonishes the hearer, "Beware of robbing the grain measure/To falsify its fractions/ . . . May you have it measure exactly as to its size,/your hand stretching out with precision./Make not for yourself a measure of two capacities, /For then it is toward the depths that you will go" (Simpson, p. 257). Likewise an Akkadian text condemns a "merchant who lends barley or silver, and when lending it he uses a small weight for the silver, and a small *sūtu* for the barley, but on taking receipt he uses a large weight for the silver, and a large *sūtu* for the barley" (*CAD,* XV, 421). Dt. 25:14 condemns the practice of using "two different measures [lit. ephah-baskets], a large and a small," and Prov. 20:10 says, literally, "Two different weights, two different ephah-baskets — both of them are an abomination before the Lord" (*see* DIVERSE).

It is possible that ancient Israel distinguished between units of dry measure and units of liquid measure, but such a distinction is not always clear in our sources. It may be a matter of chance that certain measures are associated with only one kind of material. It is also possible that some dry and liquid measures with the same name differed in their capacity. The discussion below will make no attempt to differentiate systematically between dry and liquid measures.

The following are the measures of volume mentioned in the OT, from the smallest to the largest.

A man weighing gold rings against an ox-head-shaped weight. A plummet hangs from a tongue attached to a beam. From a wall painting in the tomb of Nebamun and Ipuky at Thebes, 1411-1375 B.C. (courtesy of the Oriental Institute, University of Chicago)

1. Homer. Hebrew *ḥōmer* (Akk. *imēru*; Ugar. *ḥmr*) is apparently related to *ḥ^a^môr,* "ass," and so originally meant "ass-load." It is, with the kor, the largest unit of measure for volume mentioned in the OT. The homer is mentioned only in connection with measuring barley (Lev. 27:16; Ezk. 45:13; Hos. 3:2) and wheat (Ezk. 45:13); but one of the Arad ostraca from the monarchical period mentions "a full homer of wine" (Arad Letter 2, line 5), and Ezk. 45:14 states that there are ten baths — a liquid measure — in a homer. The equivalent measure in Assyria, the *imēru,* was both a liquid and a dry measure (*CAD,* VII, 114). Therefore, although the homer is generally considered a dry measure, it probably served to measure both dry and liquid materials.

Ezekiel 45:11, 14 prescribes the proper proportions of the principal volume measurements, but unfortunately these verses are rather obscure. Literally, they say, "The ephah and bath shall be one measure, the bath containing a tenth of a homer, and the tenth of a homer being an ephah. The homer shall be the standard. . . . Now the proper portion of oil — the bath of oil — is a tenth of a bath from the kor, ten baths a homer, for [*kî*] ten baths are a homer." It seems clear that v. 11 means to say that the ephah equals the bath, and both are one-tenth of a homer. All the versions have trouble with v. 14. Tg. Jonathan has, "And that which is proper to take of oil in the liquid measure is a tenth of a bath from the kor, the bath being a tenth of the kor, for ten baths are a kor." The Peshitta has, "And as for the oil, from ten measures which are a kor they shall take a tenth, one measure." The LXX reads, "A bath [Gk. *kotýlē*] of oil from ten baths, for ten baths are a homer." None of these ancient translations preserves a better text; they are all attempts to interpret the Hebrew. Probably the first *ḥōmer* in the text should read *hakkōr* ("the kor"), and *kî* should be interpreted as "just as," so that the text reads: "The proper portion of oil, the bath of oil, shall be a tenth of a bath from the kor; the ten baths are the kor just as ten baths are a homer." This makes explicit the implied equation of homer and kor taken for granted in the ancient versions, many of which translate *ḥōmer* as *kōr*.

2. Kor. The Heb. *kōr* (< Akk. *kurru* < Sum. GUR; AV "cor," Ezk. 45:14; elsewhere "measure"), as noted above, was equal to the homer in its volume. The word occurs nine times in the OT, as a measure for flour (1 K. 4:22 [MT 5:2]), wheat (5:11 [MT 25]; 2 Ch. 2:10 [MT 9]; 27:5; Ezr. 7:22), oil (1 K. 5:11 [MT 25]), and barley (2 Ch. 2:10 [MT 9]; 27:5). Hence it was used, like the homer, for measuring both dry and liquid material. Trinquet (*DBSup.*, V, col. 1222) theorized that the kor was not a liquid measure until Ezekiel's time (see Ezk. 45:14), citing the LXX reading of 1 K. 5:11 ("twenty *baths* of oil" instead of "kors"), but this hypothesis is not necessary.

3. Lethech. Hosea 3:2 says that the prophet bought his wife back for "fifteen shekels of silver and a homer and a lethech of barley." The lethech (Heb. *leṯeḵ*; cf. Ugar. *lth*) is translated by the Vulgate and later Greek versions as half a kor/homer (thus AV "half a homer"). The LXX reads Gk. *nebel oínou,* "a skin of wine," apparently reflecting a different text (followed by the NEB). Due to the lethech's obscure relation to the metrological system, it will not be included in the reconstructions below.

4. Ephah. The ephah (Heb. *'êpâ, 'ēpâ* < Egyp. *'pt*) was equal to the bath (Ezk. 45:11), one-tenth of the homer/kor. It is the most frequently mentioned measure of capacity in the Bible. It was used to measure flour (1 S. 1:24), barley (Ruth 2:17), and roasted grain (1 S. 17:17), and so is generally considered a dry measure. "Ephah" also denotes the container holding an ephah's worth of material; the ancient and modern versions have often translated it "measure" in texts referring to the container rather than the unit of measure (e.g., Dt. 25:14f.; Prov. 20:10; Mic. 6:10).

The ephah ceased to be used in the postbiblical period, and the ancient versions vary greatly in their translations of it. Tg. Onkelos usually translates it simply as "three seahs," and so does the LXX in Isa. 5:10; Ex. 16:36 and the Vulgate in Isa. 5:10; Ruth 2:17. The Peshitta often translates simply (and erroneously) as "seah." In Ezk. 45:24; 46:5, 11 the LXX translates it as Gk. *pémma,* "cake," wrongly assuming an etymology from the verb *ʾph,* "bake." The Mishnah considered it necessary to explain that the ephah is three seahs (Mish. *Menahoth* vii.1).

5. Bath. Although the form of Heb. *baṯ,* "bath," is identical to *baṯ,* "daughter," Scott's suggestion that the bath "was about the capacity of the water jars carried from the well by the daughters of the household" (*BA,* 22 [1959], 29) is farfetched. It is probably true that *baṯ,* like *ʾēpâ,* was originally the name of a vessel such as a jar. Ezekiel demanded "an honest bath" (Ezk. 45:10), meaning (like the "ephah" in the same passage) not the volume in the abstract but the container, perhaps the large type of jug found in archeological excavations (see II.B.12 below).

The bath was unambiguously a liquid measure and is mentioned as a measure of oil (Ezr. 7:22; Ezk. 45:14), wine (2 Ch. 2:10 [MT 9]), and water (1 K. 7:26). As noted above, the bath was one-tenth of a homer/kor (Ezk. 45:14).

The LXX translators did not render Heb. *baṯ* consistently. In 1 K. 7:26, 38 it is translated *choús,* an ancient Greek measure comprising twelve *kotýlai* (one *kotýlē* holding about half a pint). Within four verses in Ezk. 45, the LXX translates *baṯ* by Gk. *métron* ("measure," v. 10), *choínix* (v. 11, a Greek measure of three or four *kotýlai*), and *kotýlē* itself (v. 14). In Isa. 5:10 it is rendered *kerámion,* "jar." Hence it appears that the Greek translators had no very clear idea of what the bath was. The Peshitta is similarly inconsistent.

6. Seah. The seah (Heb. *s^{e}ʾâ*) is mentioned as measuring a quantity of fine meal (Gen. 18:6), of barley (2 K. 7:1, 16, 18), and of roasted grain (1 S. 25:18); thus it is generally considered a dry measure. But the equivalent measure in Mesopotamia, the *sūtu,* is both a liquid and a dry measure (*CAD,* XV, 420), and in the Mishnah the seah serves as a liquid measure (e.g., Mish. *Mikwaoth* i.7). Probably in ancient Israel it was a liquid as well as a dry measure. The LXX normally translates it *métron,* "measure," which is followed by the English versions (AV, RSV, NEB). As mentioned above (II.B.4), the ancients considered the seah to be a third of an ephah. In 1 S. 25:18 the LXX uses Gk. *oiphi,* "ephah," perhaps implying that its text was different from the MT.

The text of Isa. 27:8 reads, literally, "you will contend with them by sending them off *b^{e}sass^{e}ʾâ.*" The Peshitta, Tg. Jonathan, and Vulgate interpret this word as *bisʾâ s^{e}ʾâ,* "seah by seah" (AV "in measure"; RSV "measure by measure"). The seah may also be referred to in Isa. 40:12, where God is said to have "enclosed the dust of the earth in a *šālîš* [lit. "third"]." Since the seah was one-third of an ephah, the prophet may have been referring to a vessel holding one seah.

7. Hin. The hin (Heb. *hîn* < Egyp. *hn, hnw*) is mentioned primarily in texts prescribing the proper amount of a liquid to be used in ritual. The hin was used to measure olive oil (Ex. 30:24) and wine (29:40). The Egyptian measure from which the hin takes its name was both a dry and liquid measure. The ancient versions and modern translations generally use the transliteration "hin."

8. Omer and Issaron. Hebrew *ʿōmer* appears in the OT only in Ex. 16:16, 18, 22, 32f., and 36 in the story of the gift of manna; it is defined there as a tenth of an ephah (v. 36). McCarter (pp. 281, 393) has suggested that *ʿōmer* originally stood in the Hebrew text in 1 S. 16:20 (MT *ḥ^{a}môr,* "ass") and 25:18, on the basis of the LXX reading *gomor* in those verses; it is equally as likely, however, that Heb. *ḥōmer* is to be read, since the LXX transliterates both words by the same term (cf. NEB "a homer of bread," 1 S. 16:20). The term *ʿōmer* evidently was not in general use in the Bible, since *ʾ^{a}śîriṯ hāʾēpâ* ("a tenth of an ephah," Lev. 5:11; 6:20 [MT 13]; Nu. 28:5) occurs where *ʿōmer* might have served just as well.

The term *ʿiśśārôn* (< the root *ʿśr,* "ten"), which occurs over thirty times in the Pentateuch as a measure of flour (e.g., Lev. 14:10, 21; Nu. 15:4, 6, 9), is very likely a tenth of an ephah, hence equivalent to an omer. The AV always translates it "tenth deal"; the RSV and NEB usually have "tenth of an ephah."

9. Kab. The kab (Heb. *qaḇ*; AV "cab"; RSV, NEB, "kab") is mentioned only in 2 K. 6:25, which states that during a famine in Samaria a quarter-kab of dove's dung sold for five shekels of silver. Despite its solitary mention in the Bible, the kab was known in postbiblical Judaism as a dry and liquid measure (cf. Mish. *Eduyoth* i.3) equivalent to one-sixth of a seah (see Jastrow, II, 1307). The word is evidently related to the Akk. *qa,* used as both a dry and liquid measure.

10. Log. The log (Heb. *lōg*; Ugar. *lg*) is mentioned five times in Lev. 14 (vv. 10, 12, 15, 21, 24) as a measure of oil (cf. Mish. *Menahoth* ix.2f.); the Ugaritic cognate also is used as a measure of ointment.

11. System of Measures. The Hebrew measures of volume are difficult to make into a system. We know that the ephah and the bath were equal and that each of these was a tenth of a homer, the homer itself being equivalent to a kor (Ezk. 45:11, 14). Ex. 16:36 states that the omer was a tenth of an ephah; in all probability it was identical to an *ʿiśśārôn.* The unanimous witness of the ancient versions and Jewish tradition is that the seah was a third of an ephah. Set out in chart form, these data appear as follows:

	homer(s)/ kor(s)	**ephah(s)/ bath(s)**	**seah(s)**	**omer(s)/ ʿissaron(s)**
1 homer = kor	1	10	30	100
1 ephah = bath	1/10	1	3	10
1 seah	1/30	1/3	1	3 1/3
1 omer = ʿissaron	1/100	1/10	3/10	1

This is as much as can be inferred from the biblical data and ancient translations alone. For the relative values of the hin, kab, and log the only sources are ancient extra-biblical works and the various inconsistent translations of the LXX and Vulgate.

The following chart gives the prevailing Greco-Roman metrology of dry capacity measures:

	metrētḗs	**choús**	**xéstēs**	**kotýlē**
1 *metrētḗs*	1	12	72	144
1 *choús*	1/12	1	6	12
1 *xéstēs*	1/72	1/6	1	2
1 *kotýlē*	1/144	1/12	1/2	1

The first-century historian Josephus stated that the bath was equal to seventy-two *xéstai* (*Ant.* viii.2.9 [57]). If this is accurate, then the bath corresponded to the *metrētḗs*; in fact, Josephus stated elsewhere (xv.9.2 [314], following a commonly accepted emendation) that the kor was equivalent to ten *metrētaí* (baths). The LXX does translate the bath as *metrētḗs* in 2 Ch. 2:9 (although, as noted above, it also uses *kotýlē, choús,* and *choínix* in other passages). Josephus also said that the hin was equal to two *chóes* (iii.8.3 [197]). Such a hin would be a sixth of a *metrētḗs*/bath/ephah.

Two other data allow us to round out the picture. The Vulgate always translates Heb. *lōg* as Lat. *sextarius* (= Gk. *xéstēs*). Josephus equated the *xéstēs* with the one-fourth kab mentioned in 2 K. 6:25 (*Ant.* ix.4.4 [62]). The equation would then be that one *xéstēs* equaled one log, and four logs equaled one qab. Josephus indirectly confirmed this equation by giving the measure of a seah (Gk. *sáton*; twenty-four log) as one and a half *módios,* i.e., twenty-four *xéstai* (ix.4.5 [85]).

The Hebrew chart, filled out with inferences from these data, appears below.

Further indirect confirmation of this reconstruction can be derived from the Neo-Babylonian metrology. Its units of *kur, sūtu,* and *qa* are philologically cognate to the Hebrew measures *kōr, seʾâ,* and *qaḇ,* and their proportions of one *kur* = thirty *sūtu* = 180 *qa* are the same as the Hebrew system.

This reconstruction should not be regarded as absolutely certain. Many of the relative proportions are derived by inference from works of different dates and backgrounds, and the biblical data are often of uncertain interpretaton. It is certainly not clear that this particular system prevailed at all times and in all places in ancient Israel, but it is a plausible reconstruction.

12. Modern Equivalents.–Determination of the modern values of the ancient Israelite measures of capacity is even more uncertain than a reconstruction of their relative proportions. Archeology has uncovered no easily measurable inscribed artifact from ancient times to serve as an equivalent to the Siloam tunnel inscription.

Some scholars have begun from the evidence of Josephus. His writings imply that the ephah/bath equaled one Greco-Roman *metrētḗs,* which we know contained about 39 liters (41 U.S. liquid, 35 dry quarts). That would produce a homer/kor of 390 l. (412 liquid, 354 dry quarts), a seah of 13 l. (13.7 liquid, 11.8 dry quarts), a hin of 6.5 l. (6.9 liquid, 5.9 dry quarts), an omer/ʿissaron of 3.9 l. (4.1 liquid, 3.5 dry quarts), a kab of 2.2 l. (2.3 liquid, 1.9 dry quarts), and a log of a little more than half a liter (0.57 liquid, 0.49 dry quarts). An intact jar found at Qumrân was marked to contain "two seah and seven log" (Milik); the ephah/bath inferred from the jar's volume would be 43-45 l. (45-48 liquid, 39-41 dry quarts) — too large for the *metrētḗs,* but close enough to support the kind of vague equivalence that Josephus might have intended.

On the other hand, jars from the 1st cent. A.D. found near Jerusalem, although unmarked, support a bath of 21 l. (22 liquid, 19 dry quarts) (Segrè, p. 357 n.2), roughly half of the bath according to the Josephan evidence. W. F. Albright also estimated the bath to be around 22 l. (23 liquid, 20 dry quarts), based on the estimated capacity of fragmentary jars marked *bt* ("bath") and *bt lmlk* ("royal bath") in the Lachish and Tell Beit Mirsim excavations. The jars date from the 8th cent. B.C.

A 22-liter bath would yield a homer/kor of 220 l. (232 liquid, 199 dry quarts), a seah of 7.3 l. (7.7 liquid, 6.6 dry quarts), a hin of 3.6 l. (3.8 liquid, 3.3 dry quarts), an omer/*ʿiśśārôn* of 2.2 l. (2.3 liquid, 2.0 dry quarts), a kab of 1.2 l. (1.3 liquid, 1.1 dry quarts), and a log of 0.30 l. (0.32 liquid, 0.27 dry quarts). On the other hand, jars marked simply *lmlk* ("for the king" or "royal") were found at Lachish with a 44-liter capacity (46 liquid, 40 dry quarts), falling more into line with the "Josephan" bath described above.

Although most authorities today tend to favor the 22-liter ephah/bath, the presently available evidence does not make a final decision possible. Possibly some sort of bath, at least at some times and places, was twice as big as the 22-liter bath. An analogous situation prevailed in Egypt during the Old Kingdom, which had a *ḥq3t,* and a double-*ḥq3t,* ten of which made, respectively, a "sack" (*ẖ3r*) and a "double-sack" (*Lexicon der Ägyptologie,* III, col. 1207). Thus Israel may have had both a bath and a double-bath.

C. Measures of Area. In biblical times areas were often measured as they are measured today, in terms of length and breadth in linear measures (e.g., 1 K. 6:2-6, 20; Ex. 40:25, 29f., etc.).

Another method was to estimate the extent of an area in terms of how much a yoked pair (*ṣemeḏ*) of oxen could plow in a given amount of time. Thus Isa. 5:10 says that a vineyard of ten yoked pairs (RSV "ten acres") will produce only one bath of wine. According to the traditional interpretation of 1 S. 14:14, Jonathan and his armor-bearer killed twenty men "within as it were half a furrow's length in an acre [*ṣemeḏ*] of land" (RSV); the verse is generally deemed corrupt, however, and McCarter (p. 236), following the LXX, reads "with darts and crude flint weapons." In any case, the translation "acre" is purely conventional; there is no reliable method of determining how large the *ṣemeḏ* was in Israel.

Yet another method was to describe an area in terms of how much seed it took to sow it. Ample attestations are found in Mesopotamian literature as well as in postbiblical Jewish tradition, which speaks, e.g., of a "four-kab area" or a "one-kor area" (Krauss, II, 392). A trace of this practice is found in 1 K. 18:32, where Elijah makes a trench enclosing a two-seah area (*teʿālâ keḇêṯ sāʾtayim zeraʿ*) around the altar (the English versions imply that the trench itself would hold two seahs of seed, but this is incorrect). A late Jewish tradition makes a two-seah area equal to 5000 sq. cubits (T.B. *Erubin* 96a), but this equivalence cannot be verified for the biblical period.

D. Weights. Weights were measured on balances (*see* picture in BALANCE). The material to be weighed was placed into one of the pans of the scale, and the weights, often marked with weight-units as well as the owner's name, were placed in the other. The Hebrew word for "stone" (*ʾeḇen*) also means "weight," and in fact most weights found in Palestine are made of stone (usually pink

	homer(s)/kor(s)	ephah(s)/bath(s)	seah(s)	hin(s)	omer(s)/ʿissaron(s)	kab(s)	log(s)
1 homer/kor	1	10	30	60	100	180	720
1 ephah/bath	1/10	1	3	6	10	18	72
1 seah	1/30	1/3	1	2	3 1/3	6	24
1 hin	1/60	1/6	1/2	1	1 2/3	3	12
1 omer/ʿissaron	1/100	1/10	3/10	3/5	1	1 4/5	7 1/5
1 kab	1/180	1/18	1/6	1/3	5/9	1	4
1 log	1/720	1/72	1/24	1/12	5/36	1/4	1

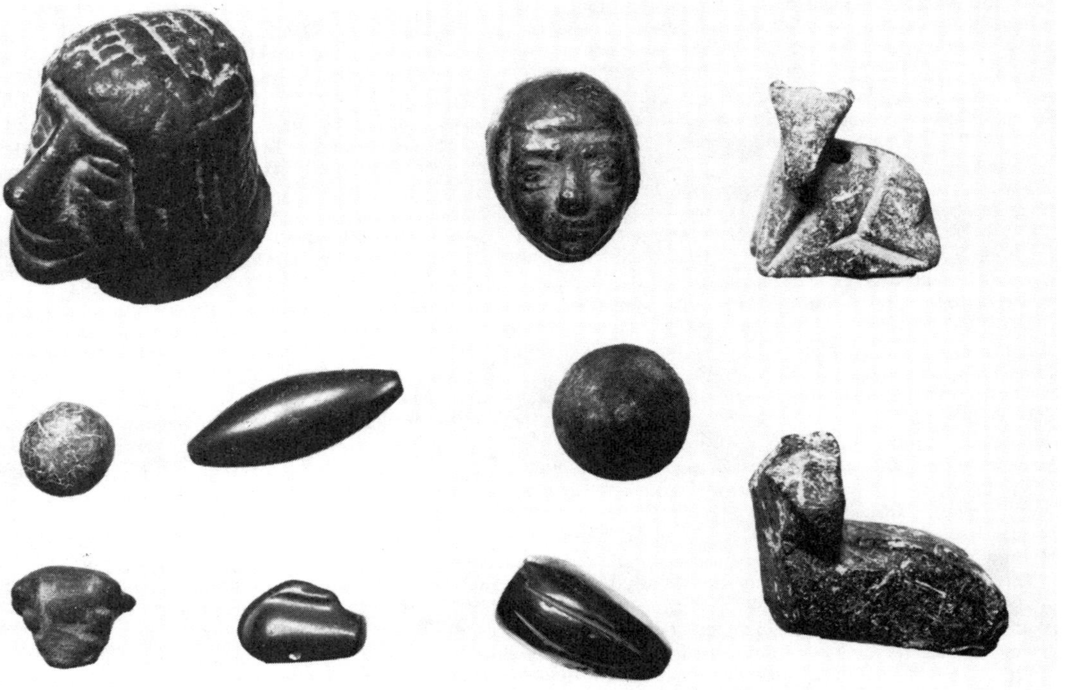

Hematite weights of distinctive shapes (Ugarit, Late Bronze Age) (Louvre; photo M. Chuzeville)

or white limestone, more rarely basalt or hematite), although a number of iron weights have also been discovered. Palestinian scale weights are usually dome-shaped, but occasionally they are rectangular, spindle-shaped, or carved into the likeness of animals (Barkay, *IEJ,* 28 [1978], 216).

It must have been difficult to make such stones exactly the same. Many stones of the same putative weight vary widely in their actual weight. This could be the fault of the stonecutter or the result of abrasion and wear from constant use, but fraud must have been both easy and tempting. The Bible contains numerous exhortations to fair dealing: "You shall have honest scales, honest-weight stones, an honest ephah basket, and an honest hin jar, says the Lord" (Lev. 19:36, author's translation; cf. Ezk. 45:10). Prov. 16:11 states: "A just balance and scales are the Lord's; all the weights in the bag are his work" (Prov. 16:11; cf. 11:1; 20:23). The prophets denounced merchants who "make the ephah-basket small and the shekel-stone large and deal corruptly with deceitful balances" (Am. 8:5, author's translation; cf. Mic. 6:11).

Because of these variations, the parties in a commercial transaction had to agree as to whose weights were to be used — the buyer's, the seller's, or some third party's. Perhaps this is what is meant in Gen. 23:16, which states that Abraham weighed out to Ephron the Hittite four hundred shekels of silver "according to the weights current among the merchants" (Heb. *'ōḇēr lassōḥēr*), i.e., using the merchant's weight-stones (*see* MONEY, CURRENT).

2 Samuel 14:26 speaks of "the king's weight-stone," referring not to a weight standard different from the ordinary standard, but simply to the weight-stones used by the king and palace officials (Rainey). Certain Aramaic contracts from the fifth-century B.C. Jewish community at Elephantine in Egypt refer to items weighed with the "king's weight-stone" (*'bny mlk'*), indicating that royal weights were available to the public (Porten, p. 63). The Bible also refers to the "shekel of the sanctuary" (*šeqel haqqōḏeš,* Ex. 30:24), probably referring to the shekel weights kept at the temple or other sanctuary for weighing offerings. It is possible, however, that the shekel of the sanctuary was heavier than the ordinary shekel, since it was fitting to give more for sacred purposes.

The weight units of ancient Israel, from largest to smallest, are as follows.

1. Talent. The talent (Heb. *kikkār*; Aram. *kakkār*; Ugar. *kkr*) was the largest unit of weight. The Hebrew word denotes something round and is used to describe loaves of bread (e.g., in Jer. 37:21) and the flat alluvial plain in which Sodom or Gomorrah were located (RSV "valley," Gen. 13:12), as well as the large flat ovals used for weighing. Eng. "talent" is derived from Gk. *tálanton* and Lat. *talentum,* the LXX and Vulgate renderings of *kikkār*. The *tálanton* in the Greco-Roman world was roughly equivalent to the Heb. *kikkār*.

The talent was used particularly for weighing out gold (Ex. 37:24) and silver (1 K. 20:39) to be used in building (Ex. 38:27), as a gift (1 K. 10:10), as tribute (2 K. 23:33), and in commercial transactions (1 K. 16:24).

The relation of the talent to the shekel, the basic Israelite weight unit, can be calculated from Ex. 38:25f. The half-shekel (beka) brought by each of 603,550 men amounted to one hundred talents and 1775 shekels; hence it may be inferred that the talent was equivalent to three thousand shekels. Such a proportion might be due to Canaanite contact, since the Ugaritic talent was also composed of three thousand shekels, unlike the Akkadian talent (*biltu*), which was divided into 3600 shekels.

2. Mina. The mina (Heb. *māneh*; AV usually "pound," but "maneh" in Ezk. 45:12; RSV, NEB, "mina") is mentioned five times in the OT, in references to measuring the amount of gold in some shields Solomon had made (1 K.

A man walking with open balance scales in one hand and folded scales in the other. A Hittite funerary stele, 9th cent. B.C. (RMN/ARS, NY/SPADEM)

10:17) and measuring the amount of silver given by the elders and people for the reconstruction of the temple (Ezr. 2:69; Neh. 7:71f.), as well as in the metrological passage of Ezk. 45:12. Since most of the occurrences are in undoubtedly exilic or postexilic passages, some have concluded that the mina was not used in Israelite metrology until this period. There is not enough evidence to prove this theory, but it is possible. In the Ugaritic texts the mina (*mn*) is occasonally mentioned, but almost all weights are given in terms of shekels and talents.

Ezekiel 45:12b gives the value of the mina in shekels. The Hebrew reads, "twenty shekels, twenty-five shekels, fifteen shekels the mina shall be for you" (cf. RSV mg.). The total is sixty shekels. The Babylonian mina (*manû*) also consisted of sixty shekels (*see* picture in MINA). It has been argued that Ezekiel introduced an innovation in the division of the mina, since, on the analogy of the 6:5 proportion between the Mesopotamian talent and the Israelite talent, we would have expected an Israelite mina of fifty shekels, as at Ugarit and in the Greek world (where the talent consisted of three thousand didrachms and the mina of fifty didrachms). LXX A in fact reads, "five shekels are five, and ten shekels are ten, and fifty shekels the mina shall be for you" (cf. RSV; LXX B, though differing from the Hebrew, affirms the sixty-shekel mina). The whole question may be irrelevant if, as mentioned above, the mina was not in regular use before the Exile. Ezekiel may have been defining the mina rather than redefining it. In any case, there is no direct evidence for or against a fifty-shekel mina; it remains a possibility. Scott (*BA*, 22 [1959], 32) argued for a fifty-shekel mina because, he said, "sums of 50 shekels and upwards . . . always are divisible by 50 and not by 60." His examples of multiples of supposed fifty-shekel units (e.g., four hundred in Gen. 23:15 [= eight minas]; five hundred in Ex. 30:24 [= ten minas]) are tendentious, since counterexamples in sixty-shekel units can be found (e.g., 2400 in Ex. 38:29 [= forty minas]; thirty in Lev. 27:4 [= one-half mina]; six hundred in 1 S. 17:7 [= ten minas]).

Assuming a sixty-shekel mina and a three-thousand-shekel talent, the mina must have been one-fiftieth of a talent. This, too, is in tension with the surrounding metrologies, which had sixty-mina talents.

3. Shekel. The shekel (Heb. *šeqel*; Aram. *t*^{e}*qēl*; Akk. *šiqlu*; Ugar. *ṯql*) is derived from the root *šql,* "weight," and thus it is "the weight" par excellence. At times the word "shekel" must be supplied in translation, since in the Hebrew text it is often taken for granted. "Shekel" appears explicitly in the MT eighty-eight times, compared to over 130 times in the AV.

In commercial transactions the shekel was used to weigh out silver (Gen. 23:15f.; Jgs. 17:10) or gold (1 Ch. 21:25) for payment. It was also used to assess the weight of other objects, e.g., utensils (Nu. 7:13f., 19f., etc.), spices (Ex. 30:23f.), armor and weapons (1 S. 17:5, 7; 2 S. 21:16), hair (2 S. 14:26), and nails (2 Ch. 3:9).

4. Beka. The beka (Heb. *beqaʿ,* from the root *bqʿ,* "split, break," hence "piece, fraction") is explicitly defined in Ex. 38:26 as "half a shekel." It is also mentioned in Gen. 24:22 as the weight of a gold nose ring (AV, RSV, NEB, "half [a] shekel"). Beka weights have been found in excavations of ancient sites (see 7.b below).

5. Gerah. The gerah (Heb. *gērâ*; Akk. *girû*) is mentioned five times in the OT, always defined as one-twentieth of a shekel (Ex. 30:13; Lev. 27:25; Nu. 3:47; 18:16; Ezk. 45:12).

The following chart shows the relative values of the weights discussed above:

	talent(s)	**mina(s)**	**shekel(s)**	**beka(s)**	**gerah(s)**
1 talent	1	50(60?)	3,000	6,000	60,000
1 mina	1/50 (1/60?)	1	60 (50?)	120	1,200 (1,000?)
1 shekel	1/3000	1/60 (1/50?)	1	2	20
1 beka	1/6000	1/120 (1/100?)	1/2	1	10
1 gerah	1/60,000	1/1200 (1/1000?)	1/20	1/10	1

6. Other Weights. Two additional weights, the pim (Heb. *pîm*) and the *q*^{e}*śîṭâ* should be discussed here. The pim is mentioned in 1 S. 13:21. The Israelites, when they went to the Philistines to have their implements sharpened, had to pay "a pim for the plowshares and for the mattocks" (so RSV; AV "file," based on Tg. Jonathan; NEB "two-thirds of a shekel"). A number of pim weights have been found in Israel, but, as will be seen, their place in the ancient metrological system is obscure (see 7.d [2] below).

Jacob had to pay a hundred *q*^{e}*śîṭâ* for a piece of land near Shechem (Gen. 33:19; Josh. 24:32); when the Lord restored Job's fortunes, Job received as a present from each person who visited him a gold ring and a *q*^{e}*śîṭâ* (Job 42:11). The ancient versions (including the very old Job Targum from Qumrân) uniformly translate this word as "lamb," contrary to the modern versions' interpretation as "money," and this ancient translation seems likely. If *q*^{e}*śîṭâ* designated "a weight of unknown value" (de Vaux, p. 207), one would expect to find mention of the material weighed.

7. Modern Equivalents. The difficulty in assessing the absolute values of OT weights in modern metrologies is

WEIGHTS AND MEASURES

not that there is a paucity of evidence, as with the measures of capacity, but that there is so much evidence. Scores of ancient weights have been found in Israel; some are inscribed, some are not, and some have markings difficult to interpret. Although many details remain obscure, the general values of the principal Israelite weights are clear.

a. Shekel. The starting point is the value of the shekel. Many weights found in Israel have a peculiar sign on them (ɣ), which has been variously interpreted, e.g., as a stylized scarab (Yadin) or as a sketch of the bag in which weights were kept (Scott, *BA*, 22 [1959], 36). Whatever its origin, it unquestionably signifies the shekel. Shekel weights in denominations of one, two, four, and eight — signified by Egyptian hieratic numerals (Aharoni) inscribed next to the shekel sign — are the most common. From them, experts have determined the weight of the shekel to be in the neighborhood of 11.4 gm. (0.4 oz.).

b. Beka. A number of beka weights have been discovered. Their average weight is 6.1 gm. (0.22 oz.), a little heavier than would be expected for a shekel of 11.4 gm. (0.40 oz.), but it was difficult in ancient times to make weights conform precisely to an absolute standard. Ancient weighing instruments were not as exact as modern ones; probably a weight needed to be only generally correct. The important thing was not that all weights of the same type be exactly equal, but that the same weight-stones be used for buying and selling, for lending and paying back.

c. Gerah. This range of allowable variation is illustrated in the case of gerah weights as well. Barkay (*Eretz-Israel*) published a study of small weights marked only with numbers, in denominations of two, three, four, five, six, seven, eight, ten, and eleven. Their size makes it probable that they are gerahs. The average gerah implied by these weights is a little smaller than the expected gerah of 0.57 gm. (0.02 oz.), but not so small as to invalidate the equation of the gerah with one-twentieth of a shekel.

In all probability, instead of giving a particular weight as the "ideal" for a shekel and its subdivisions, we should speak of an ideal range. The ideal range for a shekel would be 11-12 gm. (0.38-0.42 oz.), for a beka 5.5-6.0 gm. (0.19-0.21 oz.), for a gerah 0.55-0.60 gm. (0.019-0.021 oz.). Even these ideal ranges have been violated in some cases by some grams or tenths or hundredths of a gram, but not enough to cast doubt on the general picture.

The approximate values of the weights, then, would be as follows: talent: 33-36 kg. (73-79 lbs.), mina: 550-600 gm. (19-21 oz.) (50 shekels), or 660-720 gm. (23-25 oz.) (60 shekels), shekel: 11-12 gm. (0.4 oz.), beka: 5.5-6 gm. (0.2 oz.), gerah: 0.5-0.6 gm. (0.02 oz.).

d. Other Weights. Two additional kinds of inscribed weights have been found in archeological excavations in Israel: the pim, mentioned above, and the *nṣp,* not mentioned in the OT. The pim stones average 7.8 grams (0.27 oz., about two-thirds of an average shekel), and the *nṣp*s average 9.8 grams (0.35 oz., about five-sixths of an average shekel). Scholars have had great difficulty fitting these standards into the Israelite metrological system described above.

(1) *Nṣp.* The word *nṣp* is mentioned in Ugaritic texts in association with the Ugaritic shekel. The Arabic cognate means "half," so Ugar. *nṣp* may be half an Ugaritic shekel. Since in Ugarit there was evidently a heavy shekel twice as heavy as the light shekel, Scott (*BASOR,* 200 [Dec. 1970]) plausibly proposed that the *nṣp* was the Syrian light shekel. This identification is supported by a weight found in Samaria bearing the inscription *rbʿ nṣp,* "quarter *nṣp,*" and on the other side *rbʿ š[q]l,* "quarter shekel."

Scott went on to suggest that the *nṣp* was the standard shekel in Judah and Israel before a reform in Josiah's reign increased the shekel's weight. Later on, Ezekiel reintroduced the *nṣp*-shekel (Ezk. 45:12) as the sanctuary standard, reducing the shekel by one-sixth as well as increasing the gerah to one-twentieth of a shekel from one-twenty-fourth of a shekel. This complicated theory founders on a number of facts: (a) There is no evidence for the posited Josianic weight reform; (b) the preexilic gerah weights examined by Barkay (see c above) confirm that the gerah was one-twentieth of a shekel even before Ezekiel; and (c) it is unlikely that Ezekiel would have made the sanctuary shekel *lighter* than the standard shekel.

Ben-David suggested that the *nṣp* was a Philistine weight, since *nṣp* stones have not been found outside of the Philistine sphere of influence. The above-mentioned Samarian weight tells against this idea. It is probably true, however, that the *nṣp* is an intruder from an alien metrology (Phoenician?) with no systematic relationship to the Israelite weights, although it was recognized to correspond to the shekel in some way. These weights have been found at Israelite sites because the Israelites used them to conduct business with outsiders.

(2) Pim. The stones marked *pym* have been vocalized *payim* (= *pî-šᵉnayim,* "two-thirds," Zec. 13:8, therefore two-thirds of a shekel) by some scholars on the grounds that internal consonants used as vowel letters were unknown in the preexilic period; this is now known to be inaccurate (Sarfatti, pp. 59, 73). The MT vocalization *pîm* is more likely. Probably the word is non-Hebrew, and the weight, like the *nṣp,* belongs to a non-Israelite metrology — perhaps, as Ben-David has argued, to the Philistines, which would suit the context in 1 S. 13:21.

III. In the NT. –The NT contains few passages of metrological significance. It is sometimes difficult to reconstruct the systems used by the writers, since they used not only Semitic terms but also Greco-Roman terms that themselves have complicated histories and provenances.

A. Linear Measures. The Roman cubit used in first-century A.D. Palestine was about the same size (44.4 cm., 17.5 in.) as the Israelite cubit. The cubit (Gk. *pḗchys*) is used in Jn. 21:8 to indicate the distance of the disciples' fishing boat from the shore (AV "as it were two hundred cubits"; RSV, NEB, "about a hundred yards"). In Rev. 21:17 the walls of the new Jerusalem are to be 144 cubits high "by a man's measure [lit. "cubit"], that is, an angel's." The cubit is also used in Mt. 6:27 par. Lk. 12:25 in a metaphorical sense.

In Acts 27:28, as the sailors approach the land they take soundings of twenty Gk. *orguiaí,* then of fifteen *orguiaí.* In Greco-Roman metrology the *orguiá* was composed of four cubits; therefore it was equal to about 1.8 m. (5.8 ft.). The English translation "fathom" (AV, RSV, NEB), i.e., 6 ft., is therefore quite appropriate.

The *stádion* is the most frequently used measure of distance in the NT. It was composed of 600 ft., and, since the foot of Hellenistic times varied from place to place, the stadion had different values; we know of the Olympic *stádion* (192 m., 630 ft.), the Alexandrian or Ptolemaic *stádion* (185 m., 607 ft.), the Epidauran *stádion* (181 m., 594 ft.), and the Delphic *stádion* (177.6 m., 583 ft.).

Many favor the Alexandrian *stádion* as the one used by the writers of the NT (*see* FURLONG). Segrè (p. 369) has proposed a stadion of 205-213 m. (673-699 ft.), but this is clearly too long. If the Roman foot of 29.6 cm. (11.7 in.) was used as a standard in first-century A.D. Palestine, then the Delphic *stádion* is more likely. The Delphic measure also has the advantage of being exactly equivalent to four hundred Palestinian cubits of 44.4 cm. (17.5 in.). In Lk. 24:13 Emmaus is said to be sixty stadia from Jerusalem (AV "threescore furlongs"; RSV, NEB, "about seven miles"). According to Jn. 6:19 Jesus came walking on the sea to the disciples' boat over a distance of twenty-five or thirty stadia (AV "five and twenty or thirty furlongs"; RSV, NEB, "about three or four miles"). Bethany was about fifteen stadia from Jerusalem (Jn. 11:18; AV "about fifteen furlongs"; RSV "two miles"; NEB "just under two miles"). In the book of Revelation the flow of blood from the winepress extends 1600 stadia (14:20; AV "a thousand and six hundred furlongs"; NEB "two hundred miles"), while the sides of the new Jerusalem are twelve thousand stadia each (21:16; AV, NEB, "twelve thousand furlongs"), about 2220 km. (1380 mi.) according to the Alexandrian standard, 2131 km. (1324 mi.) according to the Delphic.

The Roman mile or *mílion* (Mt. 15:41, AV, RSV, NEB, "mile") had a standard length (1479 m., 4854 ft.); the local variations of the smaller measures did not affect it. It was about 9 percent shorter than the English mile of 5280 feet.

A "sabbath day's journey" — the maximum distance one was permitted to travel on a sabbath (Acts 1:12) — was, based on Jewish interpretation of Nu. 35:5, two thousand cubits (Mish. *Sotah* v.3), i.e., about 888 m. or a little over half an English mile.

B. Measures of Capacity. Some of the volume measures in the NT are the same as those encountered in the OT, while others are derived from Greco-Roman measures.

The *bátos* (AV, RSV, NEB, "measure") of oil and the *kóros* (AV, RSV, NEB, "measure") of wheat in Lk. 16:6f. are the bath and kor of Semitic metrology, just as the three *sáta* of Mt. 13:33 par. Lk. 13:21 are three seahs. (See II.B.2, 5f. above.)

The water jars of Jn. 2:6 contained "two or three *metrētai*" (AV "firkins"; RSV, NEB, "twenty or [to] thirty gallons") apiece; this is the same *metrētḗs* (about 39 l., 10.3 gals.) encountered in the LXX (see II.B.11f. above).

The *choínix* was one-thirty-sixth of a *metrētḗs*, therefore about 1.08 l. or a little more than a quart. It is mentioned in Rev. 6:6, where the writer hears the voice of famine calling, "A *choínix* [AV "measure"; RSV, NEB, "quart"] of wheat for a denarius, and three *choínikes* of barley for a denarius." since a DENARIUS was a laborer's daily wage, the price is extremely high.

In Mt. 5:15 Jesus says that people do not place a lighted lamp under a *módios* (AV, RSV, "bushel"; NEB "meal-tub"), i.e., a container holding one *módios* (from Lat. *modius*), a measure of about 6.4 l. (1.7 gal.). According to Mk. 7:4 (cf. v. 8 in some witnesses) the Jews had many rules governing the washing of *xéstai* (AV, RSV, "pots"; NEB "jugs"), i.e., vessels holding one *xéstēs* apiece, about 546 ml. or just over a pint.

C. Weights. By the NT period coins were used for money in Israel instead of the ingots that had earlier been weighed out by the shekel and its subdivisions. Weights were still used, of course, for large quantities of coins, metal, and other materials.

The talent (Gk. *tálanton*) holds a central place in the parable of the talents (Mt. 25:15-30) and is mentioned in 18:24 to quantify a huge monetary debt. The weight of the Greco-Roman talent — if in this passage it is not simply the Israelite *kikkār* (see II.D.1, 7.c above) — ranged from 26.4 kg. (58 lbs.) to 37.8 kg. (83 lbs.) in different periods. It is not known what standards prevailed in NT Palestine.

The mina (Gk. *mná*; AV, RSV, NEB, "pound") appears in the parable of Lk. 19:12-27, which is similar to the parable of the talents. The Greco-Roman mina weighed from 420 to 630 g. (14.8 to 22.2 oz.).

In Jn. 19:39 Mary brings a *lítra* of nard to anoint Jesus' feet, and Nicodemus brings a mixture of spices weighing about a hundred *lítra*. The *lítra* (AV, RSV, "pound") weighed 340 gm. (12 oz.).

Bibliography.–*General:* A. Barrois, *RB*, 40 (1931), 185-213; 41 (1032), 50-76; *DBSup.*, V, *s.v.* "Metrologie Biblique" (J. Trinquet); *Encyclopedia Judaica* (1971), XVI, *s.v.* "Weights and Measures" (E. Stern); *Harper's Dictionary of Classical Literature and Antiquities* (1897, repr. 1962), Appendix, pp. 1696-1701; S. Krauss, *Talmudische Archäologie*, II (1911), 382-416; *Lexicon der Ägyptologie*, III (1980), *s.v.* "Masse und Gewichte" (Helck); P. K. McCarter, Jr., *I Samuel* (*AB*, 1980); B. Porten, *Archives from Elephantine* (1968), pp. 62-72; A. Rainey, *BASOR*, 179 (Oct. 1965), 34-36; R. B. Y. Scott, *BA*, 22 (1959), 22-40; A. Segrè, *JBL*, 64 (1945), 357-375; R. de Vaux, *Ancient Israel*, I (Eng. tr. repr. 1965), 195-209.

Linear Measures: G. Barkay, *Biblical Archeology Review*, 12 (1986), 37; Pauly-Wissowa, III A.2, 1930-1966 (Jüthner); R. B. Y. Scott, *JBL*, 77 (1958), 205-214.

Capacity: W. Albright, *BASOR*, 31 (Oct. 1928), 10; J. Milik, *Bibl.*, 40 (1959), 985-991; W. Simpson, ed., *Literature of Ancient Egypt* (1972), pp. 241-265.

Weights: Y. Aharoni, *BASOR*, 184 (Dec. 1966), 13-19; G. Barkay, *IEJ*, 28 (1978), 209-217; *Eretz-Israel*, 15 (1981), 288-296; A. Ben-David, *Ugarit-Forschungen*, 11 (1979), 29-65; G. Sarfatti, *Maarav*, 3 (1982), 59, 73f.; R. B. Y. Scott, *BASOR*, 200 (Dec. 1970), 62-66; Y. Yadin, *Scripta Hierosolymitana*, 8 (1960), 1-17.

E. M. COOK

WELL [Heb. *b^{e}'ēr*] (e.g., Gen. 16:14; 21:19, 25, 30; 2 S. 17:18, 21; Cant. 4:15); AV also PIT, FOUNTAIN; NEB also SPRING, WATER-HOLE etc.; [*bôr*] (1 S. 19:22; 2 S. 23:15f.; 1 Ch. 11:17f.); NEB also CISTERN; [*'ayin*] (Neh. 2:13); NEB SPRING; [*ma'yān*] (Isa. 12:3); NEB SPRING; [*qûr*] ("dig wells," 2 K. 19:24; Isa. 37:25); AV DIG; [Gk. *pēgḗ*] (Jn. 4:6); [*phréar*] (Lk. 14:5; Jn. 4:11f.; AV also PIT. A deep hole or shaft dug into the earth to tap the water table.

By far the most common word translated "well" is Heb. *b^{e}'ēr*. Although it most frequently means a shaft to reach the water table (e.g., Gen. 21:30; 26:15-18; Nu. 21:16), it can also refer to a cistern (cf. 2 S. 17:18, where David hides in a cistern dug beneath a house) or an open mine pit (Gen. 14:10). Several passages use this term together with *'ayin* ("spring") to refer to the same feature (e.g., Gen. 24:13, 16), possibly indicating a well that opened a spring. Because the *b^{e}'ēr* tapped the water table far beneath the surface of the earth and thus produced "living water" (i.e., flowing water; cf. Cant. 4:15), it was sometimes depicted as providing access to the cosmic underworld river (RSV "pit," Ps. 55:23 [MT 24]; 69:15 [MT 16]). The word was used in many place names: Beer in Moab (Nu. 21:16), Beer in Israel (Jgs. 9:21), Beer-elim (Isa. 15:8), Beer Lahai-roi (Gen. 16:14), Beeroth in Sinai (Dt. 10:6), Beeroth in Benjamin (e.g., Josh. 9:17), and Beer-sheba (e.g., Gen. 26:15). In addition, Beera (1 Ch. 7:37), Beerah (5:6), and Beeri (Gen. 26:34) are said to be names of persons but probably were place names.

b Hebrew *bôr*, usually translated "cistern" or "pit," was probably a cistern which, when dry, could be viewed as a pit. It could be large enough to be regionally famous (1 S. 19:22) or publicly owned (2 S. 23:15f.). Both *'ayin* and *ma'yān* should be translated "spring," although the former appears in a place name that was probably translated "well" by the RSV because of the traditional rendering ("Jackal's Well," Neh. 2:13).

Greek *pēgḗ* is usually translated "spring." Again, it probably was translated "well" twice in Jn. 6:4 because of the traditional rendering of the name "Jacob's Well" (but cf. v. 14, where it is translated "spring"). The meaning of *phréar* is ambiguous. Although it is deep and water can come from it (Jn. 4:11f.), an ox can fall into it (Lk. 14:5), and it can refer to a bottomless pit with smoke spewing from it (Rev. 9:1f.).

A well at Beer-sheba from the biblical period (L. K. Smith)

As in modern villages of the Middle East, most wells were covered with stones to protect people and animals from falling into them and to keep out dust and debris (Gen. 29:10). Their favored location was in wadi beds, where underground pools could gather (26:19); they could be constructed with a wheel for a windlass above. Although the limestone topography of the hill country is not conducive to wells and cisterns are thus much more common, shafts could nonetheless be sunk to the water table. Examples are the wells at Hazor and Gezer, which were probably dug during the Iron Age (the water shafts at Megiddo, Jerusalem, and Gibeon went to springs and were thus not "wells"). Deep wells have been excavated at Beer-sheba and Arad in the Negeb; both of these date from the biblical period, but it is difficult to date the construction of such features specifically.

See also CISTERN; PIT; WATERWORKS.

See D. Cole, *Biblical Archaeologist Review,* 6 (1980), 8-29.

L. G. HERR

WELL, JACOB'S. *See* JACOB'S WELL.

WELLSPRING. A spring that is the source of a continual supply of water. The AV uses this term to render Heb. *māqôr* in Prov. 16:22; 18:4. *See* FOUNTAIN.

WEN. The AV's mistranslation of Heb. *yabbāl,* "running," i.e., a suppurating sore, in Lev. 22:22 (cf. NEB "running sore"; RSV "discharge").

WENCH. The AV translation of Heb. *šipḥâ* in 2 S. 17:17 (RSV "maidservant"). "Wench" was formerly a common term for a female servant. *See* MAID.

WEST. ***I. OT Usage.***–In the OT three methods are used for designating the direction west. (1) Most common is the geographical reference to Heb. *yam,* "sea" (i.e., Mediterranean Sea), for the obvious western boundary of Israel. *Yam* is often coupled with the terms for the other three compass points (e.g., Gen. 13:14; 28:14; Nu. 35:5; 1 K. 7:25). It is found with the *hê directive* to indicate direction or movement "toward" the west and with the preposition *min* to indicate motion "from" the west. (2) Solar terms for west are also used, though less frequently. Heb. *māḇô'* (lit. "entrance, place of entry") is coupled with *šemeš,* "sun" (Dt. 11:30; Josh. 1:4; 23:4; Ps. 50:1; 113:3; Zec. 8:7; Mal. 1:11), to designate west as the place in which the sun sets. The similar term *ma'ᵃrāḇ,* "place of [the sun's] going in" (cf. *'ereḇ,* "evening"), is also connected at least implicitly with *šemeš* (Isa. 45:6; 59:19), although it sometimes appears entirely alone (Isa. 43:5; 1 Ch. 7:28; 12:15 [MT 16]; 26:18, 30; 2 Ch. 32:30; 33:14; Dnl. 8:5). (3) Relative to the position of the speaker, *'āḥôr* ("back, behind") can also assume the meaning "west," especially in opposition to *qeḏem,* "in front of," "east" (Isa. 9:12 [MT 11]).

II. NT Usage.–The NT knows a single term to designate west. Gk. *dysmḗ* (lit. "setting," from *dýnō,* "sink, set"), like Heb. *māḇô'* and *ma'ᵃrāḇ,* relates to solar movements and is used antithetically to Gk. *anatolḗ* ("rising"; cf. Mt. 8:11; 24:27; Lk. 13:29; Rev. 21:13, where both terms occur).

See also ORIENTATION.

G. H. WILSON

WESTERN SEA. *See* MEDITERRANEAN SEA.

WHEAT [Heb. *bar* (Jer. 23:28; Am. 5:11; 8:5f.), *ḥiṭṭâ*; Aram. *ḥinṭîn* (Ezr. 6:9; 7:22); Gk. *sítos, pyrós* (Jth. 3:3; Sir. 39:26)]; NEB also GRAIN.

Hebrew *ḥiṭṭâ* is the specific term for wheat, *Triticum aestivum* L. (Gen. 30:14; Ex. 34:22; etc.). It was the chief grain of patriarchal times (Gen. 30:14). Five varieties of wheat are native to Palestine; probably abundant in antiquity were *Triticum monococcum* L., *T. thaoudar* Reut., and *T. hermonis* Cook. The "wheat harvest" was one of the regular divisions of the ancient calendar (Ex. 34:22; Jgs. 15:1; 1 S. 12:17), following the barley harvest (Ex. 9:31f.), and occurring between April and June, depending upon the altitude. During the winter months, in November and December, the wheat sowing took place, the grain being scattered by hand and pressed down or trodden in lightly (cf. Isa. 32:20). The sowing of wheat in fairly straight rows (Isa. 28:25) was not very common.

Wheat was used from the settlement period onward as an item of Israelite commerce, some of it being exported to Tyre (Am. 8:5) and other areas of the Levant. Under Jotham the local production was supplemented by a tribute of 100,000 bushels of wheat demanded from the Ammonites. Wheat exports were still flourishing in NT times (Acts 27:38).

Wheat formed an important part of the sacrificial offerings (Lev. 2:1; 24:5-7), being ground as required into fine flour. A cereal offering to the Lord consisted of flour mixed with oil and frankincense, part of which was burned as a memorial portion upon the sacrificial altar, and the remainder allocated to Aaron and his sons. Even if the offering had been baked in an oven or cooked in a pan, finely ground flour was still required. Such grain offerings were regarded as a most holy part of the Lord's fire offerings.

The twelve cakes of shewbread (so AV; RSV, NEB, NIV, "bread of the Presence") placed on the golden table in the tabernacle and dusted with pure frankincense were also made of fine flour and became a priestly perquisite. When the offerings for the dedication of the tabernacle in the wilderness were made, they included cereal offerings of fine flour mixed with oil (e.g., Nu. 7:13).

Wheat was used in Christ's parables to signify something of a choice nature, reflecting the OT sacrificial prescriptions. In Mt. 3:12 the time of the final harvest will witness a separation of the wheat from the chaff, the former being stored for useful purposes but the latter burned as refuse. The kingdom of heaven was compared to a farmer sowing good wheat in his field (Mt. 13:24-31), only to have it contaminated deliberately by tares, a poisonous grass resembling wheat but bearing much smaller seeds. Once the contamination had been discovered it was more prudent to wait for the harvest before separating the two grains. On this basis the farmer instructed his workers to burn the tares, having once isolated them, but to store the wheat in his barn.

The imagery of threshing wheat at harvest was applied by Jesus to Simon Peter (Lk. 22:31f.), who was to be sifted as wheat by Satan. Jesus promised him spiritual support in that critical hour of trial, and urged Peter to strengthen his associates once he had become regenerated. Christ also employed a familiar agricultural concept of gestation to explain to His disciples how His forthcoming death would in the end produce an abundant harvest (Jn.12:24). This same thought of growth through death was applied by Paul to the idea of the resurrection body (1 Cor. 15:35-43). This glorious configuration is to the earthly body what the stalk of ripe wheat was to the grain kernel that was sown.

In Rev. 6:6 wheat was part of the vision of the third seal, in which an apocalyptic voice demanded of a mounted rider a quart of wheat for a denarius, but three quarts of barley for the same sum, thereby demonstrating the relative value of wheat as a choice grain. Fine flour and wheat were also included in the wares of the "merchants of the earth" (Rev. 18:13), who were bewailing their loss of business transactions because mighty Babylon, the dwelling place of demons (18:3), had fallen under God's judgment owing to her wickedness.

R. K. HARRISON

WHEEL [Heb. *'ôpān* (Ex.14:25; 1 K. 7:30, 32f.; Prov. 20:26; Isa. 28:27; Ezk. 1:15f.; etc.), *galgal* (Eccl. 12:6; Isa. 5:28; Jer. 47:3; "whirling wheel," Ezk. 10:2, 6, 13, [*gilgāl*] (Isa. 28:28), *'oḇnayim* (Jer. 18:3); Aram. *galgal* (Dnl. 7:9)].

Hebrew *'ôpān* could represent wheels of various types: chariot wheels (Ex. 14:25; Nah. 3:2), wheels for the bronze lavers of the temple (1 K. 7:30, 32f.; these included axles, rims, spokes, and hubs), wheels on threshing carts (Isa. 28:27), and wheels giving mobility to the cherubim in Ezekiel's vision (Ezk.1:15-21; 10:6, 9-19). Many suggestions have been made about how to visualize the latter wheels ("their construction being as it were a wheel within a wheel," 1:16; cf. 10:10), ranging from a set of double wheels to wheels at right angles in a kind of gyroscopic design that would allow them to move in four directions (1:17; 10:11). Some scholars have interpreted these wheels as forming a chariot (see W. Zimmerli, *Ezekiel 1* [Eng. tr. *Hermeneia,* 1979], pp. 128-130).

Hebrew *galgal* could also be used of chariot wheels (Isa. 5:28), the wheels of the cherubim (Ezk. 10:2, 6, 13), and cart wheels (cognate *gilgāl,* Isa. 28:28); but in Eccl. 12:6 it appears to indicate the windlass of a well. It is frequently used to describe a "whirlwind" and may thus emphasize the rolling or moving aspect of a wheel (cf. Ezk. 10:2, 6, 13). In a usage reminiscent of that in Ezekiel, the Aramaic cognate appears in Daniel's description of a visionary fiery throne supported by wheels (Dnl. 9:7; cf. also En. 14:18). *'Oḇnayim* (lit. "two stones") denotes a potter's wheel in Jer. 18:3 (see below).

The wheel was apparently invented in Sumer; it spread abroad rapidly because of its many uses. The earliest pictured wheels from Mesopotamia (mid-3rd millennium B.C.) were made of solid wooden planks (usually three) pegged together and were used on chariots. Lighter spoked wheels (six or eight spokes) were used for chariots at least by the 15th cent. B.C. in Egypt, where they were perhaps brought by the Hyksos. These wheels may have been invented *ca.* 2000 B.C.

The earliest potter's wheel was a single disk (*tournette*) and seems to have been invented in the 3rd millennium B.C., when pottery first shows signs of wheel manufacture. One of these wheels is depicted on the famous Egyptian relief of itinerant Asiatics from a tomb at Beni-hasan, which dates to *ca.* 2000 B.C. The potter's wheel with a flywheel (two stones), suggested by the dual form in Jer. 18:3, is pictured on an Egyptian relief that shows the god Khnum fashioning a man as a potter would form a vessel; this representation is strikingly similar to the message of Jer. 18, namely, that God fashions what He wills. A few potter's wheels have been found at Megiddo, Tell el-'Ajjûl, Lachish, and Hazor, but they are generally quite rare.

See also POTTERY V.

L. G. HERR

WHELP [Heb. *gûr*] (Gen. 49:9; Dt. 33:22; Ezk. 19:2f., 5); NEB also CUB; [*gôr*] (Jer. 51:38; Nah. 2:12 [MT 13]); [*bēn*–'son'] (Job 4:11). One of the young of a carnivorous animal; in the Bible it always refers to a lion cub.

All biblical references to lions' whelps are figurative. Judah is pictured as a lion's whelp because of his strength (Gen. 49:9). Similarly, in Ezk. 19:1-9 Judah is depicted as a lioness and its princes (particularly Jehoahaz and Jehoiachin) as whelps that became powerful lions (kings) but were taken captive. In Dt. 33:22 the tribe of Dan is apparently compared to a young lion leaping forth from Bashan; some, however, have suggested that *bāšan* should be understood as a cognate of Ugar. *bṯn* ("snake"), in

A votive chariot with solid wheels. From Tell Kheweyrat, 4th-3rd millennium B.C. (courtesy of the University Museum, University of Pennsylvania; photo W. S. LaSor)

which case the metaphor may signify not aggression but timidity: Dan "shies away from the viper" (see F. M. Cross and D. N. Freedman, *JBL,* 67 [1948], 191-201).

Conversely, the imagery of lions and lions' whelps is used to depict the rapacious nations of Assyria (Nah. 2:11-13) and Babylon (Jer. 51:38-40), which had destroyed and devoured other peoples but were now about to be slaughtered by Yahweh. Eliphaz uses a similar metaphor to portray the fate of the wicked (Job 4:10f.).

See also LION. G. WYPER

WHIP [Heb. piel of *yāsar*–'chastise, discipline'] (Dt. 22:18); AV CHASTISE; NEB PUNISH; [*šôṭ*–'whip'] (1 K. 12:11, 14; 2 Ch. 10:11, 14; Prov. 26:3; Nah. 3:2); [niphal of *nāḵā'*–'be whipped, beaten'] (Job 30:8); AV "viler"; NEB "hounded"; [Gk. *phragéllion*] (Jn. 2:15); AV SCOURGE. *See* SCOURGE.

WHIRLWIND [Heb. *s^eʿārâ* (2 K. 2:1, 11; Job 38:1; 40:6; plural, Zec. 9:14), *sûpâ* (Job 27:20; 37:9; Prov. 1:27; Isa. 5:28; 29:6; Jer. 4:13; Am. 1:14; Nah. 1:3; plural, Isa. 21:1; var. *sûpāṯâ,* Hos. 8:7), *galgal*–'wheel' (Ps. 77:18 [MT 19]), *sāʿar* ("come like a whirlwind," Hab. 3:14; "scatter like a whirlwind," Zec. 7:14), hithpael of *śāʿar* ("rush like a whirlwind," Dnl. 11:40)]; AV also TEMPEST, STORM, "heaven"; NEB also STORM, HURRICANE, TEMPEST, STORM-WIND, "drove out."

When two air currents from opposite directions meet, the resulting circular motion is called a whirlwind. But most of the biblical references do not imply a circular motion, and most of the terms translated "whirlwind" are the general terms for "storm, tempest" (note the use of synonymous terms in, e.g., Isa. 29:6 — "tempest," *s^eʿārâ;* Am. 1:14 — "tempest," *sāʿar;* Nah. 1:3 — "storm," *ś^eʿārâ*). According to D. Baly (*GB,* p. 64) *sûpâ* in Job 37:9 refers to "the bitter southwest wind of a winter cyclone" (see also Prov. 1:27), but the same term in Isa. 21:1 "suggests the grim fury of a sandstorm"; and *s^eʿārâ* in 2 K. 2:1, 11; Job 38:1; 40:6 describes "the devastating onslaught of a thunderstorm."

Most of the biblical references are figurative. Several texts compare chariots (or chariot wheels) to a whirlwind (Isa. 5:28; Jer. 4:13; Dnl. 11:40; cf. Hab. 3:14). Frequently God's coming in judgment is compared to a whirlwind (Isa. 29:6; Hos. 8:7; Am. 1:14; Nah. 1:3; Zec. 7:14; 9:14).

Two texts are problematic. The difficult text of Job 27:20-23 apparently describes the fate of the rich man: he is blown about by a strong wind (cf. N. H. Tur-Sinai, *Book of Job* [Eng. tr., rev. ed. 1981], pp. 392-94, who offered the sensible interpretation that the rich man's possessions were blown about by the wind). In Ps. 77:18 (MT 19) Heb. *baggalgal* (lit. "in [or with] the wheel") seems to make no sense (cf. *CHAL,* p. 60), and scholars have made various suggestions. Many modern versions translate it as "whirlwind" (e.g., RSV, NEB, NIV), apparently on the basis of the stormy context and the connection with the root *gll,* "roll." But nowhere else does *galgal* mean "whirlwind," and other suggestions seem more cogent. The AV "heaven," which at first seems improbable, has some support from postbiblical Hebrew, in which *galgal* can mean "globe, celestial sphere" (Jastrow, I, 245; see also M. Dahood, *Psalms,* II [*AB,* 2nd ed. 1973], 232, who offered an interesting analysis of the parallelism). Another suggestion is that *galgal* means "rolling," i.e., the thunder rolled (so JB; J. Perowne, *Book of Psalms* [3rd ed. 1882], II, 53, 56).

See also STORM; WIND. G. A. L.

WHISPER; WHISPERING [Heb. hithpael of *lāḥaš* (2 S. 12:19; Ps. 41:7 [MT 8]), pilpel of *ṣāpap* (Isa. 29:4), *dibbâ*–'rumor,' 'slander' (Ps. 31:13 [MT 14]; Jer. 20:10), *šēmeṣ* (Job 4:12; 26:14); Gk. *eis to oús*–'to the ear' (Mt. 10:27), *laléō prós to oús*–'speak to the ear' (Lk. 12:3)]; AV also SLANDER, DEFAMING, LITTLE (*šēmeṣ*), IN THE EAR (NT); NEB also SQUEAK (Isa. 29:4); **WHISPERER** [Heb. niphal part. of *rāgan*–'slander, backbite'] (Prov. 16:28; 18:8; 26:20, 22); AV also TALEBEARER; NEB TALE-BEARING, GOSSIP, TALE-BEARER.

Whispering is usually associated with the telling of secrets that one does not wish to have overheard (e.g., 2 S. 12:19; Ps. 31:13 [MT 14]; Mt. 10:27 par. Lk. 12:3). Sometimes it refers specifically to gossip (e.g., Ps. 41:7 [MT 8]; Jer. 20:10). Several proverbs warn about the destructiveness of malicious GOSSIP, which is eagerly devoured by those who hear it (Prov. 18:8; 26:22) and has great power to create strife and alienate friends (16:28; 26:20).

Hebrew *šēmeṣ* occurs in the OT only at Job 4:12; 26:14; although most translate it "whisper," some prefer "a little" based on its use in the Talmud (cf. AV). In each instance it refers to hearing only a fragment of what has been said. In Isa. 29:4 the pilpel of *ṣāpap* refers to the unnatural voice used by necromancers to represent the voice of a ghost (*see* DIVINATION III.G.; MEDIUM).

N. J. O.

WHITE. *See* COLOR V.I.

WHITE HORSE. *See* HORSE, WHITE; REVELATION, BOOK OF II.

WHITEWASH [Heb. *tāpal*] (Job 13:4); AV FORGER; NEB SMEAR; [*tāpel*] (Ezk. 13:10f., 14f., 22:28); AV UNTEMPERED MORTAR; [Gk. *koniáō*] (Mt. 23:27; Acts 23:3); AV WHITED. A solution of lime in water used for whitening walls.

Both the verb *tāpal* and its derived noun *tāpel* are used to illustrate hypocrisy. Ezk. 13:10-16 states that the false presentations of some prophets are whitewashed to look more attractive than they really are. In the NT, likewise, Gk. *koniáō* refers figuratively to the pretenses that hide evil and lies.

Most lower-class houses were not whitewashed in antiquity; instead the normal brown, streaked, and patchy mud daubing was visible. A coating of whitewash tended to indicate a higher-class occupant. Tombs were often white-washed to make them appear conspicuous. Thus whitewash was a natural metaphor for hypocrisy. In Acts 23:3 the high priest sported a posture of piety that lent an appearance of sanctity to an evil heart.

Because whitewash is so ephemeral, being quickly washed off by rain, signs of its use are discovered only rarely by archeology.

See also LIME. L. G. HERR

WHOLE; WHOLESOME. "Whole," originally "hale," had at first the meaning now expressed by its derivative "healthy." In this sense "whole" and "make whole" are fairly common in the AV, but the RSV usually changes the translation to "heal," "healed," or "well" (cf. Josh. 5:8; Job 5:18; Mt. 9:12, 21f.; 14:36; 15:28; Mk. 5:34; Jn. 5:6, 9, 11, 14f.; etc.). From this meaning of "whole" developed the modern meaning "complete, entire," which is the most common sense of the term in the RSV (but cf. the original meaning in RSV Mt. 12:13; 15:31) and also appears frequently in the AV. "Wholesome," however, is derived from the earlier meaning of "whole." It is used by the RSV in 2 K. 2:21f. (Heb. niphal and piel of *rāpā'*; AV "heal") and Prov. 15:31 (*marpē'*).

B. S. EASTON N. J. O.

WHORE. *See* HARLOT; FORNICATION.

WICK [Heb. *pištâ* (Isa. 42:3; 43:17); Gk. *línon* (Mt. 12:20)]. The twisted fibers that provide a steady supply of oil for the flame in a LAMP. Both *pištâ* and *línon* usually mean FLAX.

WICKED; WICKEDLY; WICKEDNESS [Heb. *rāšā'*–'wicked, guilty,' qal and hiphil of *rāša'*–'be guilty, unjust,' 'act wickedly,' *reša'*–'wrong, injustice,' *riš'â*–'guilt, wickedness,' *mirša'aṯ* ("wicked woman," 2 Ch. 24:7), *ra'*–'bad, evil,' hiphil of *rā'a'*–'do evil,' *rā'â*–'perverseness, wickedness,' *rō(a)'*–'badness, evil' (Hos. 9:15), *'āwen* (Job 22:15; etc.), *'awlâ*–'perversity' (e.g., Job 11:14; 24:20; Ps. 89:22 [MT 23]), *bᵉlîya'al*–'worthlessness, wickedness' (Job 34:18; Nah. 1:15 [MT 2:1]), *zimmâ* (e.g., Lev. 18:17), *'āšām*–'guilt' (Prov. 14:9), *hawwâ*–'(cause of) calamity,' 'wickedness' (Ps. 94:20), hiphil of *'āwâ*–'do wrong' (2 S. 24:17), *'ōṣeḇ*–'pain' (Ps. 139:24; AV and RSV follow LXX); Aram. *bi'yš*–'evil' (Ezr. 4:12); Gk. *ponērós* (e.g., Acts 17:5; 1 Cor. 5:13; 2 Jn. 11), *ponēría* (e.g., Lk. 11:39), *adikía* (e.g., Acts 1:18), *kakós* (Mt. 24:48), *kakía* (Acts 8:22; Jas. 1:21), *áthesmos* (2 Pet. 2:7), *átopos*–'out of place, improper' (2 Thess. 3:2), *anomía* (Mt. 24:12)]; AV also EVIL, UNGODLY, EVILDOER, INIQUITY, VANITY, UNRIGHTEOUSNESS, etc.; NEB also BAD, GUILTY, WRONG, WORTHLESS, RUFFIAN, LEWDNESS, INJUSTICE, etc.

The Hebrew adjective *rāšā'* is the most common OT term used to designate wicked persons. Occasionally the RSV supplies a noun such as "man" in translating *rāšā'* (e.g., Ps. 109:6; 112:10), but usually it simply has "the wicked." The frequent antithetic parallelisms contrasting the "wicked" with the "righteous" (e.g., Gen. 18:23, 25; Ps. 1:6; 11:5; 37:16, 21; 68:2f. [MT 3f.]; 75:10 [MT 11]; Prov. 3:33; 4:18f.; 10:3, 6f., 11, 16, 20, 24f., 28) indicate that *rāšā'* is an exact antonym of *ṣaddîq* (*see* RIGHTEOUSNESS I). The wicked are consistently characterized in terms of their actions: they give evil counsel (Ps. 1:1), pursue the poor (10:2), renounce the Lord (vv. 3f., 13), curse and lie (v. 7), murder the innocent (v. 8; 11:2; 37:14, 32), despoil others (17:9), plot against the righteous (37:12), and are often overbearing (v. 35). The AV sometimes translates *rāšā'* as "ungodly" (e.g., Ps. 1:1, 4-6); while this word may be archaic, it correctly emphasizes that the action of the wicked is against God and His covenant. The wicked are also frequently contrasted with the poor who are their victims (e.g., Ps. 37:14, 16; 82:4; 94:3-6; 146:9). While this contrast obviously does not mean that there was an exact correlation between the poor and the righteous or between the wealthy and the wicked, it does suggest that many of the wealthy were wealthy because they wickedly oppressed the vulnerable members of their society, and many of the poor were poor because they refused to follow wicked ways. Although the OT writers were sometimes disturbed by the present prosperity of the wicked (e.g., Job 9:24; 10:3; 21:7-34; Ps. 73:3-14; Eccl. 7:15; 8:14; Jer. 12:1), the OT consistently expresses the faith that God will eventually vindicate the righteous and destroy the wicked (e.g., Job 20:4-29; 27:7-23; Ps. 1:4-6; 11:5f.; 37:1f., 9f., 12-17; 73:18-20; Ps. 92:7 [MT 8]; Prov. 2:21f.; 10:24-30; Eccl. 8:12f.; Isa. 3:11; 13:11; Jer. 23:19). The prophet's task was to call upon the wicked to forsake their evil ways and turn to the Lord that they might find salvation (e.g., Isa. 55:7; Ezk. 3:17-19; 18:20-23, 27; 33:7-19).

The OT clearly makes no simple identification of Israelites with the righteous and non-Israelites with the wicked. The examples of wicked Israelites are too numerous to mention, and many non-Israelites receive approval (e.g., Melchizedek, Jethro, Rahab, Ruth, the widow of Zarephath). The Qumrân literature shows a clear tendency to identify the wicked with one group and the righteous with another, for the followers of the Wicked Priest (*hakkōhēn hārāšā'*) are set against the followers of the Teacher of Righteousness (cf. 1QpHab 8:8; 9:9). The OT, however, restricts the identification *rāšā'* to those who act wickedly, and these can be found in any nation or class; therefore the message is that all must repent and turn to the Lord.

Also occurring frequently are the cognates of *rāša'*: the verb *rāša'* and nouns *reša'* and *riš'â* (cf. also the fem. noun *mirša'aṯ*, occurring only in 2 Ch. 24:7). In 1 S. 24:13 (MT 14) David quotes an ancient proverb: "Out of the wicked [*rāšā'*] comes forth wickedness [*reša'*]," i.e., wicked deeds are performed by wicked people (and this is why David did not commit the wicked deed of slaying King Saul). Other proverbs warn of the self-destructive consequences of wickedness, e.g., "the wicked [*rāšā'*] falls by his own wickedness [*riš'â*]" (Prov. 11:5; cf. 10:2; 12:3; 18:3; 26:26). Several texts show the close association of "wickedness" (*reša'*) with social injustice (e.g., Eccl. 3:16; Ezk. 7:10f.; Mic. 6:10f.). The OT writers affirm that wickedness is totally opposed to God's character (e.g., Job 34:10; Ps. 5:4 [MT 5]; 45:7 [MT 8]).

Hebrew *ra'* and the cognate noun *rā'â* are rendered by the RSV as "evil" more frequently than as "wicked(ness)." There appears to be no clear reason for this choice; frequently the RSV has changed the AV translation "wicked" to "evil," and vice versa. This illustrates how closely synonymous "evil" and "wicked" are in the English language (*see* EVIL). At times *ra'* or *rā'â* indicates an unacceptable condition, at other times unacceptable actions (cf. the cognate verb *rā'a'*, which in the qal means "be bad, displeasing," and in the hiphil means "do evil, act wickedly"). That which is *ra'* is contrary to God's will and is injurious to His creation; thus it damages the relationship between God and human beings and relationships among human beings. Frequently *ra'* and *rā'â* denote harmful and unjust actions against other persons (e.g., Gen. 38:7; 1 S. 30:22; Est. 7:6; Jer. 15:21). One who persistently chooses the pathway of *ra'* will be destroyed, and only divine power can redeem such a person (2 Ch. 7:14). In the time of Noah human wickedness had reached such massive proportions that God decided to destroy most of the human race with the Flood (Gen. 6:5). *See also* VIOLENCE.

According to Bernhardt (*TDOT,* I, 141), the bas of *'āwen* is "power used in relation to a community or an individual with a negative effect or intention." Often it refers to social injustice (e.g., Job 22:15 [cf. vv. 6-11]; 34:36 [cf. v. 28]; Mic. 2:1).

Hebrew *'awlâ* denotes an act that is wrong, contrary to what is right (cf. the frequent RSV translation "wrong," e.g., Job 6:29f.; 36:23; Ps. 119:3; 125:3; Mic. 3:10; Zeph. 3:5, 13; Mal. 2:6). It is frequently used for violent and unjust deeds such as murder (2 S. 3:34), oppression (Ps. 107:42), and false testimony (Isa. 59:3); cf. the RSV translations "injustice" (Prov. 22:8; Hos. 10:13) and "perversion of justice" (2 Ch. 19:7).

The noun *zimmâ* appears to have two different meanings in the OT: sometimes it denotes a "plan" or "device" (cf. vb. *zāmam*; see RSV Job 17:11; Ps. 26:10; Prov. 24:9; Isa. 32:7); more often, however, it denotes "disgraceful or infamous behavior" (cf. "wicked devices," Isa. 32:7). The term occurs three times in Leviticus (18:17; 19:29; 20:14), each time referring to a sexual offense (*see also* LEWD). (See KoB, 3rd ed., p. 261; *TDOT,* IV, 89f.)

In the NT the RSV renders Gk. *adikía* by "wickedness" seven times and by "wicked" once. The AV never translates *adikía* by these terms but commonly uses "unrighteousness" — an appropriate translation (in old English, at least), since *adikía* is the opposite of *dikaiosýnē* ("righteousness," "justice") and denotes opposition to God's just order. Elsewhere the RSV translates it by "iniquity" (Lk. 13:27; Acts 8:23; etc.), "unrighteous(ness)" (Lk. 16:9; 18:6; 2 Thess. 2:12; etc.), "wrong(doing)" (1 Cor. 13:6; 2 Pet. 2:13, 15; etc.), "injustice" (Rom. 9:14), etc. In Acts 1:18 *misthós tḗs adikías* (RSV "reward of wickedness") refers to the thirty pieces of silver that Judas received for betraying Jesus. In Rom. 1:18 *adikía* (paired with *asébeia,* "ungodliness") is used to characterize heathen humanity in its rebellion against God. In v. 29 it stands at the head of a list of vices as a comprehensive term for all forms of immorality. In 2:8 obedience to *hē adikía* is contrasted with obedience to *hē alḗtheia* ("the truth"; cf. 2 Thess. 2:10), and in Rom. 3:5 and 6:13 *adikía* is contrasted with the *dikaiosýne* of God (*see* RIGHTEOUSNESS III.B).

In six instances the RSV uses "wicked" to render *ponērós* — a term it usually renders "evil" (cf. the AV, which uses "wicked" nineteen times). *Ponērós* is synonymous with *kakós,* which the RSV renders by "wicked" only once, usually preferring "evil." Both *ponērós* and *kakós* are common LXX translations of Heb. *raʿ,* and both terms are rendered "wicked" in references to worthless servants (*kakós* in Mt. 24:48; *ponērós* in 18:32; 25:26; Lk. 19:22) and other depraved persons (Acts 17:5; 1 Cor. 5:13; cf. also 2 Jn. 11). The nouns *ponēría* and *kakía* (the two common translations of Heb. *rāʿâ* in the LXX) are also synonymous, both being general terms for depravity or moral deficiency (cf. *ponēría* in Acts 3:26; Eph. 6:12 and *kakía* in Acts 8:22; Jas. 1:21). Both terms appear in NT lists of vices: *ponēría* in Mk. 7:22; Rom. 1:29 (RSV "evil") and *kakía* (RSV usually "malice"; *see* MALICE) in Rom. 1:29; Eph. 4:31; Col. 3:8; 1 Pet. 2:1.

The adjective *áthesmos* (lit. "apart from or contrary to statute," thus "lawless" or "unlawful") is used as a substantive in 2 Pet. 2:7, where it is applied to the people of Sodom and Gomorrah (cf. 3:17 [RSV "lawless"], where it is applied to heretics). Similarly, the noun *anomía* means literally "apart from or contrary to (the) law," thus "lawlessness" (cf. RSV 2 Thess. 2:3, 7; etc.). In Mt. 24:12 the term denotes a general state of rebellion against God's reign. *See* LAWLESS.

See also EVIL; INIQUITY; SIN.

Bibliography.–Bauer, rev.; *DNTT,* I, 561-67; III, 573-76; *TDNT,* I, *s.v.* ἄδικος κτλ.: ἀδικία (Schrenk), ἄθεσμος (Oepke); III, *s.v.* κακός κτλ.: κακός, κακία (Grundmann); IV, *s.v.* νόμος κτλ.: ἀνομία (Gutbrod); VI, *s.v.* πονηρός, πονηρία (Harder); *TDOT,* I, *s.v.* "'āven" (Bernhardt); IV, *s.v.* "zmm" (Steingrimson); *TWOT,* II, 652f., 854-56, 863f.

C. J. VOS N. J. O.

WIDOW [Heb. *'almānâ,* also *'almānûṯ*–'widowhood' (Gen. 38:14), *'iššâ*–'woman,' 'wife' (Ruth 4:5, 10; 1 S. 27:3; 30:5; 2 S. 2:2; 3:3); Gk. *chḗra,* also *gynḗ*–'woman,' 'wife' (Mt. 22:24), *neṓtera*–'younger' ("younger widow," 1 Tim. 5:14)]; AV also WIFE (Heb. *'iššâ*; Gk. *gynḗ*), YOUNGER WOMAN (*neṓtera*); NEB also WIFE.

I. In the OT.–Hebrew *'almānâ* denotes a woman whose husband has died and who has no adult male relative (e.g., husband's brother, grown son) to serve as her legal protector (*TDOT,* I, 288f.). The term thus connotes not only the death of a woman's husband but also her abandonment and helplessness.

There were four ways in which a woman whose husband had died might find economic security: (1) if she had no sons, by the law of levirate marriage her HUSBAND'S BROTHER (or another relative) was expected to marry her, although he could refuse to perform this duty (Dt. 25:5-10; Ruth 3–4; *see also* MARRIAGE IV.A.2); (2) she could return to her father's house (Gen. 38:11; cf. Ruth 1:8); (3) she might marry again, especially if she was young or wealthy (e.g., 1 S. 25:39-42; 2 S. 11:26f.; cf. Ruth 1:9, 13); (4) either by necessity or by her own choice she might remain unmarried and attempt to support herself and any children she might have.

Without a legal protector, the position of the widow in Israelite society was precarious; she was often neglected or exploited. Part of the reason for the harsh treatment of widows may have been the common view that widowhood was a reproach from God Himself (Ruth 1:13, 20f.; Isa. 54:4). The high priest could not marry a widow (Lev. 21:14), and in Ezekiel's ideal cult no priest could marry a widow unless she was the widow of another priest (Ezk. 44:22).

If a woman's husband died when her children were young, she became a "widow" and her children became "orphans" (*see* ORPHAN). Although the widow without grown sons inherited the property of her deceased husband, and in rare instances the widow could be quite wealthy (cf. Jth. 8:4, 7), she was almost always very poor, since she was vulnerable to being defrauded of whatever property she did possess (e.g., Job 22:8f.; 24:2f., 21; Isa. 10:1f.; cf. Mt. 23:14 par.). If she had a son, however, her lot was not as hopeless, for as soon as her son reached manhood he would inherit his father's property and assume the responsibility of caring for his mother. Thus the death of a widow's only son was a calamity indeed (1 K. 17:20; cf. 2 S. 14:5-7).

In the ancient Near East widows, orphans, and other disadvantaged groups were given special consideration. Thus Hammurabi boasted that his laws provided justice for widows (see *ANET,* p. 178), and the Ugaritic texts mention "judging the cause of the widow" as a mark of a good ruler (see *ANET,* pp. 149, 151, 153; see also Fensham).

In the OT, widows, along with other disadvantaged groups such as orphans and aliens, are an object of special concern to God and to the righteous. God is said to be their protector (Ps. 68:5 [MT 6]; 146:9). He maintains the widow's boundaries (Prov. 15:25) and executes justice for her (Dt. 10:18). OT law forbids exploiting the widow (Ex. 22:22 [MT 21]) or taking her garment in pledge (Dt. 24:17). Other laws are designed to provide her with a minimal level of support. The widow is to receive a share of the tithe every third year (Dt.14:28f.; 26:12f.), and she is among those for whom gleanings are to be left in the field during harvest season (Dt. 24:19-21; cf. Ruth 2:1f.).

Despite these protective laws, widows were the victims of harsh oppression (Ps. 94:6; Ezk. 22:7), and their cause was seldom heard in court (Isa. 1:23). In fact, the exploitation of widows was so common that this sin could be used to typify the general wickedness of mankind (Job 22:9; 24:3, 21; 31:16). In addition, the term "widow" was applied symbolically to cities and nations to describe their desolation and oppression (Babylon, Isa. 47:9; Jerusalem, 54:4; Lam. 1:1; 5:3f.; cf. Rev. 18:7 [Babylon/Rome]).

The prophets strongly condemned oppression of the widow, the orphan, and the alien and warned that Israel faced exile unless it returned to the ways of justice (Jer. 7:6f.; 22:3-5; Zec. 7:8-14). Because God had rescued His people from oppression in Egypt, they were now required to help the helpless or be returned to foreign oppression themselves. Malachi warned that on the Day of the Lord, God Himself would come in judgment against those who oppressed the widow and orphan (Mal. 3:5).

II. In the NT.–The social and legal position of the widow in NT times was no different. Widows were typically poor (Lk. 21:2-4 par. Mk. 12:42-44; Acts 6:1). they were victims of exploitation even by religious leaders (Mk. 12:40 par.) and were unable to secure justice (cf. the parable in Lk. 18:1-5). They were representative of oppressed people; thus James, continuing OT teaching, defined true religion as aiding "widows and orphans" i.e., the helpless and oppressed (Jas. 1:27). Jesus demonstrated this concern in a unique way by raising the only son of the widow of Nain (Lk. 7:11-15), thereby restoring her protector and provider.

Widows sometimes served as examples of the righteous POOR who looked to God for their deliverance. One such widow, Anna the prophetess, was an early witness to Jesus as the fulfillment of Israel's hope (Lk. 2:36-38). Jesus pointed out the poor widow who gave as an offering her last two copper coins as an example of true devotion to God (Mk. 12:41-44 par. Lk. 21:1-4).

Care for the widows became an important priority in the NT Church (Acts 6:1; *see* SEVEN, THE). Dorcas is an example of an individual who devoted herself to this type of ministry (9:39). By the time that the Pastoral Epistles were written an official order of widows had been established, which was supported by the Church and probably assigned a particular ministry in the Church (1 Tim. 5:3-16). Although the nature of the widows' task is uncertain, the qualifications for enrollment in the order (v. 10) suggest a ministry of hospitality and service to others. It is specified that only "real" widows, i.e., widows with no relatives to provide for them, are to be enrolled (vv. 3-8, 16). Moreover, whereas Paul in 1 Cor. 7:8f. had advised widows, if possible, not to remarry, the younger widows are here urged to remarry (1 Tim. 5:14). To be enrolled, a widow was to be at least sixty years old and was to have demonstrated a commitment to remain unmarried and give herself to the service of God (vv. 5f., 9-15). Thus in the NT Church the widow was cared for and placed in a position of responsibility.

Bibliography.–*DNTT*, III, 1073-75; J. N. D. Kelly, Comm. on the Pastoral Epistles (*HNTC*, 1963), pp. 111-121; F. C. Fensham, *JNES*, 21 (1962), 129-139; *TDNT*, IX, *s.v.* χήρα (G. Stählin); *TDOT*, I, *s.v.* "'almānāh" (H. A. Hoffner).

D. E. HOLWERDA
N. J. O.

WIFE. *See* FAMILY; MARRIAGE; RELATIONSHIPS, FAMILY; WOMAN.

WIFE, BROTHER'S. *See* BROTHER'S WIFE.

WILD BEAST [Heb. *ḥayyâ*] (Ps. 74:19; Zeph. 2:15); AV "multitude of the wicked," BEAST; NEB also BEAST; [*ḥayyaṯ haśśāḏeh*] (Ex. 23:11, 29; Lev. 26:22; Dt. 7:22; 2 K. 14:9 par. 2 Ch. 25:18; Job 39:15; 40:20; etc.); AV also BEAST OF THE FIELD; NEB also WILD ANIMAL; [*ḥayyâ rā'â*] (Gen. 37:20, 33; Ezk. 5:17; 14:15; 34:25); AV EVIL BEAST, NOISOME BEAST; NEB also BEAST OF PREY; [*ḥayyaṯ hā'āreṣ*] (1 S. 17:46); [*bahamôṯ śāḏeh*] (Joel 1:20); AV BEAST OF THE FIELD; NEB CATTLE IN THE FIELD; [*ṣî*] (Isa. 13:21; 23:13; 34 14; Jer. 50:39); AV also "them that dwell in the wilderness" (23:13); NEB MARMOT, "ship" (23:13; cf. mg.); [*ṭerēpâ*–'animal torn by predators'] ("that which was torn by wild beasts," Gen. 31:39); AV ". . . of beasts"; [Gk. *thēríon*] (Mk. 1:13; Rev. 6:8); AV BEAST.

Although Heb. *ḥayyâ* is a general term for "animal," it sometimes designates a wild animal as distinguished from a domesticated animal (*behēmâ*), especially when it is qualified by *haśśāḏeh* or *hā'āreṣ*. These terms all refer to the ancient population of non-domesticated Palestinian fauna. The heavy settlement of Palestine in modern times, coupled with the gradual deforestation of the Palestinian hills, has driven out many of the species native to the area in earlier times. The ancient Palestinian fauna, however, resembled a blend of East African, Mediterranean, and Eurasian types. Predators included lions, leopards, cheetahs (not distinguished in the Bible from leopards), bears, wolves, jackals, hyenas, and foxes. Among the herbivores were the wild ass (Syrian onager), various kinds of deer, gazelles, antelopes, the ibex, and the wild ox. Wild boar, the Syrian coney (hyrax), and several kinds of rodents also deserve mention.

The humanitarian concern of the Mosaic law extended to herbivorous wildlife as well as to the poor: every seventh year the fields were to lie fallow, and whatever grew in them was to be for the poor and the "wild beasts" (Ex. 23:11). Conversely, Yahweh's threat "to let loose the wild beasts among you, which shall rob you of your children, and destroy your cattle, and make you few in number" (Lev. 26:22) refers to predators (cf. Dt. 7:22), which posed a limited threat to human life (cf. 2 S. 23:20; 1 K. 13:24f.). 2 K. 17:25 relates how Yahweh sent lions to ravage those whom the Assyrians settled in Samaria in place of the Israelites. Rev. 6:8 similarly envisions the loosing of "the wild beasts of the earth" upon the human population as one of the scourges during the last days. Predators and scavengers of the open country are referred to in 1 S. 17:46, which speaks of leaving the bodies of those slain in battle to "the birds of the air and the wild beasts of the field" (an ancient form of desecration). *Ḥayyâ rā'â* (lit. "evil beast") is a general term for predator.

The term *ṣî* (pl. *ṣiyyim*) may designate an actual species, but it is obscure. It receives diverse renderings in the LXX and other versions, and scholars have likewise offered various interpretations, e.g., "demons" (cf. LXX Isa. 34:14), "desert animals" (cf. Arabic *ḍayūna*, perhaps a form of wildcat), or "inhabitants of the desert." The RSV reflects the LXX usage at Isa. 13:21 (*thēría*, "animals") and Jer. 50:39 (LXX 27:39; *indálmata*, "species").

See also BEAST; ZOOLOGY.

Bibliography.–F. S. Bodenheimer, *Animal and Man in Bible Lands* (Eng. tr. 1960); R. Pinney, *Animals in the Bible* (1965).

D. G. SCHLEY

WILD OLIVE. *See* OLIVE, WILD; OLEASTER.

WILD OX [Heb. *re'ēm, rêm*] (Nu. 23:22; 24:8; Dt. 33:17; Job 39:9; Ps. 22:21 [MT 22]; 29:6; 92:10 [MT 11]; Isa. 34:7); AV UNICORN. Hebrew *re'ēm* is thought to refer to the wild bovine mammal known to the Europeans as aurochs, of the species *Bos primigenius* Bojanus. A magnificent wild animal with a dark brown or blackish coat and long curved horns, the aurochs was widely distributed in Europe, central Asia, and areas of North Africa. In Assyria it was known as Akk. *rimu*; hunting the *rimu* was a favorite sport of the Assyrian monarchs. The aurochs is generally regarded as the progenitor of modern domesticated cattle.

Although bones of aurochs have been found in Palestine from earlier periods (see Bodenheimer, p. 22), there is some question as to whether the animal still existed in Palestine in the Middle Bronze Age. Biblical allusions to it may have derived from the lore attached to wild oxen in Egypt, where the aurochs was hunted as late as the 12th cent. B.C. In the OT the wild ox is a symbol of strength and vigor (Nu. 23:22; 24:8; Ps. 29:6). Its powerful, dangerous horns (cf. Ps. 22:21 [MT 22] are attributed poetically to Joseph, who had the majesty and strength of a firstborn bull (Dt. 33:17). Job 39:9-12 describes the contrast between wild and domesticated oxen. Isaiah, in prophesying divine vengeance upon Edom, classes the wild ox with the ceremonially clean animals that will fall victim to the sword (34:7). The psalmist rejoices that God has endowed him with power as fearsome as the horns of the wild ox (Ps. 92:10 [MT 11]).

The AV rendering "unicorn" is unfortunate in that it associates a purely mythical beast with the real prehistoric wild bull. *See* UNICORN.

See F. S. Bodenheimer, *Animal and Man in Bible Lands* (1960), pp. 22, 51, 102-104, 108, 123. R. K. H.

WILDERNESS [Heb. *midbār*] (Gen. 14:6; 16:7; 21:14, 20f.; etc.); AV also DESERT (e.g., Ex. 3:1), SOUTH (Ps. 75:6); NEB also DESERT (e.g., Nu. 21:5), PASTURES, OPEN PASTURES (e.g., Ezk. 34:25), OPEN (Joel 1:19f.), WASTE (e.g., Joel 3:19 [MT 4:19]), WILD (Jer. 23:10), "inhospitable" (Jer. 2:31); [*yešîmôn*] (Dt. 32:10; Ps. 68:7 [MT 8]); NEB VOID; [*ṣîyâ*] (Ps. 74:14); NEB "sharks" (conjecturing that *leʿām leṣîyîm* should read *leʿamleṣê yam*; see *BHS*); [Gk. *érēmos*] (Mt. 3:1, 3; 4:1; 11:7; etc.); AV also DESERT; NEB also WILDS (e.g., Lk. 1:80), OPEN PASTURE (Lk. 15:4), LONELY PLACES (Lk. 5:16), DESERT (e.g., Jn. 6:31); [*erēmía*] (2 Cor. 11:26); NEB COUNTRY. Land of varying degrees of aridity, not suitable for permanent dwelling.

I. Geographical Designation
II. Biblical Motifs
  A. In the OT
  B. In the NT

I. Geographical Designation. The Israelite concept of "wilderness" (primarily Heb. *midbār* and Gk. *érēmos*) included several types of terrain. It included the arid regions surrounding Palestine on the east and south (e.g., the ARABAH, the Transjordan plateau, and the Sinai peninsula). These were not vast sandy deserts like the Sahara, but desolate areas where rainfall was minimal. The wildernesses of ZIN in the Negeb, of PARAN farther south, of Sin in Sinai, and of SHUR toward Egypt were also examples of the this type of terrain (*see also* WANDERINGS OF ISRAEL). (Dt. 32:10 [Heb. *yešîmôn*] probably refers to Israel's wilderness experience at Sinai.) The term also included the steppeland where sheep and goats might be pastured.

Several passages refer "pastures in the wilderness" (e.g., Jer. 9:10; Joel 1:19f.; 2:22; cf. also 1 S. 17:28; Lk. 15:4). It was through this steppeland that the nomads and caravans passed. Even areas of arable land were classified as wilderness. Bezer, one of the cities of refuge, is described as being in the *midbār* on the Transjordan tableland, even though it was within the bounds of cultivable land (Dt. 4:43; Josh. 20:8). From year to year the boundaries of arable land probably advanced or receded as the quantity of rainfall increased or diminished.

The term *midbār* was especially applied to rugged areas — whether or not they had minimal rainfall. Joab and Abishai pursued Abner toward the wilderness of Gibeon, i.e., the rough, uncultivated countryside N of Jerusalem (2 S. 2:24). "Wilderness" is linked with "forest" in contrast to "fruitful field" in Isa. 32:15f. (cf. 29:17, which has "Lebanon" — famous for its forests — in place of "wilderness"). The association of "wilderness" with forest or woods (Ezk. 34:25) suggests that the term connotes not just a desolate or lonely place but also a place where

The wilderness in the Valley of Jericho with the Jordan River in the foreground (Philip Gendreau, NY)

people may become disoriented (see *GB*, rev., pp. 103, 108).

II. Biblical Motifs.–A. *In the OT.* The wilderness is regarded both positively and negatively in the OT. Negatively, the wilderness through which Israel journeyed to Canaan was "great and terrible" (Dt. 1:19), a place of "flinty rock" and "no water" populated by "fiery serpents and scorpions" (8:15), a "howling waste" (32:10). In the wilderness Israel rebelled against Yahweh. The murmuring motif that runs through the Exodus narratives describes open rebellion, not merely disgruntlement (see Coats). Frequently complaining that God had brought them into the wilderness to die (e.g., Ex. 14:11f.), the generation that left Egypt brought upon themselves the destruction that they feared. Because of their disobedience, Yahweh condemned them to wander in the wilderness for forty years (Nu. 14:33) and to perish there. The memory of that experience was kept alive throughout Israel's history. Both psalmist and prophet returned to that theme (e.g., Ps. 78:40; Ezk. 20:13).

The wilderness experience also had its positive side. Not only was it "great and terrible": it was where the mountain of God was located (Ex. 4:27). The desert was the route by which the Israelites escaped their bondage in Egypt; here Yahweh guided them (Dt. 1:31; Ps. 78:52), fed them (Ex. 16:32), and established his covenant with them (Ex. 19:1-6; cf. Acts 7:36, 44). Moreover, God promised through the prophets that in the future He would make the wilderness to be so well watered that forest and cultivated trees would grow there, and it would be a place where justice and righteousness would dwell (Isa. 32:15f.; 41:18f.).

A pass through the wilderness of Sinai (A. H. Tolhurst)

Because of the extensiveness of the wilderness theme, some biblical scholars have perceived a desert ideal in the OT. In 1895 K. Budde coined the phrase "nomadic ideal" and used it to refer to the style of life reminiscent of the journey from Egypt to Canaan; this lifestyle was practiced by the Rechabites (Jer. 35) and was pointed to by Jeremiah, Hosea, and Isaiah as a solution to the social and religious ills of their times. In 1923 J. Flight expanded the thesis of Budde and others so that the "essential element" of the prophets' earlier and later messages was that Israel be brought back to "the simple and uncorrupted faith of their fathers" that had been exemplified by God's people during the golden age of its nomadic existence (p. 223). Jesus Himself was viewed as elevating the ideal to its highest point by His proclamation of the "simplicities" of faith and love. More recently, in 1974, M. Seale proposed that nomadic culture be viewed not so much as an ideal to which to return, but as the interpretative key to the OT. In his opinion the failure to understand the Hebrews as a nomadic people has continued to cause problems in translation and interpretation.

The presence of such an ideal has been disputed by other scholars. First, some have cast doubt on the thesis that Jehonadab the son of Rechab and his followers represent the historical beginning of the ideal in its concrete form. The Rechabites' living in tents, abstinence from wine, and refusal to engage in agriculture, which are usually set forth as indicators of their nomadic life-style, need not be interpreted as such. An alternate explanation is that they were permanently mobilized for holy war (see Frick, p. 214). In any case, Jeremiah's approbation of the sect (Jer. 35:14-16) concerned their loyalty to their spiritual forebear's command and not their living patterns as such. Scripture merely describes the Rechabite way of life; it does not present it as a model.

Again, the prophets' purpose as they attacked the degeneration of the covenantal relationship between Israel and its God was not to urge a return to the desert way of life. Although Am. 2:10 and 5:25 may seem, at first glance, to be longing for such a return, further examination reveals that they describe Yahweh's care for Israel and Israel's departure from that care. Similarly, Jer. 2:2, often a touchstone of the nomadic ideal thesis, has been analyzed as pointing to God's love for Israel during the wilderness period rather than to Israel's devotion to God (see Fox). Israel must return not to the wilderness but to the God who led them through the wilderness to the Promised Land.

B. In the NT. Several NT passages allude to the wilderness wanderings of Israel. Some compare God's care for His people during that period with His greater provision in Christ (Jn. 3:14; 6:49f.; cf. Acts 7:30-44). Others note the hardening of the Israelites' hearts and God's testing of them in the wilderness (He. 3:8) in order to warn Christians against giving themselves over to the same unbelieving disposition.

Like Israel, Jesus also was tested in the wilderness (Mt. 4:1) — in His case by the devil; the Spirit drove Jesus there for that very purpose (Mk. 1:12). There, like Moses and Elijah before Him (Ex. 34:18; 1 K. 19:4-8), He fasted forty days, although His circumstances were very different. Occasionally He withdrew from the crowds in order to pray in a LONELY place (e.g., Mk. 1:35; cf. Lk. 5;16). Once it became dangerous for Him to go about openly because of the opposition against Him, He withdrew to a town overlooking the *érēmos* to the east (Jn. 11:54).

John the Baptist, the forerunner of Christ, was in the wilderness until the beginning of his public ministry (Lk. 1:80). Some have suggested that John was raised in the sectarian desert community of Qumrân, but the evidence for this is inconclusive. Clearly, though, John's ministry as the one who prepared "the way of the Lord" (Mk. 1:3; cf. Isa. 40:3) took place at various wilderness locations.

Acts 21:38 mentions an Egyptian who "stirred up a revolt and led the four thousand men of the Assassins out into the wilderness." Josephus referred to this Egyptian (*Ant.* xx.8.6 [169-172] and to other impostors who led their followers to the wilderness with promises of performing marvels and signs for them (xx.8.6 [167f.]). The magician Theudas claimed that the Jordan would separate at his command and his people would cross on dry ground, but cavalry sent by the procurator Cuspius Fadus crushed his revolt (xx.5.1 [97-99]). Acts 5:36f. mentions an earlier Theudas and a Judas the Galilean whose insurrections were likewise crushed. Jesus warned His disciples against such false Christs and prophets: "If they say to you, 'Lo, he is in the wilderness,' do not go out" (Mt. 24:26; cf. vv. 23-25). Jesus seems, therefore, to have roundly rejected any expectation of messianic salvation coming from the wilderness.

It might appear, however, that Rev. 12:6, 14 supports just such a wilderness eschatology. The woman who bears the male child "who is to rule all the nations with a rod of iron" (v. 5) flees into the wilderness to a place God has prepared, in order to be nourished by Him. But the point of this passage is to present an Exodus typology rather than a wilderness eschatology (cf., e.g., R. Mounce, *Book of Revelation* [*NICNT*, 1977], p. 245). The motif of God's care during Israel's wilderness journey is expressed, e.g., in His provision of the manna for nourishment (cf. v. 6) and in His leading, which is described as bearing Israel "on eagles' wings" (cf. Ex. 19:4; Rev. 12:14). God's judgment displayed in the earth's swallowing the Korahites, who had opposed His purposes (Nu. 16:31-33), parallels the earth's swallowing the river that the dragon had sent forth to sweep away the woman (Rev. 12:16). The reverse side of the Exodus symbolism is seen in Rev. 17, in which John from the wilderness (v. 3) sees a vision of the destruction of "Babylon the great, the mother of harlots" (v. 5). The two strands of wilderness experience are brought together: God's protection and sustenance of His people and His relentless judgment of those who oppose His purposes.

See also DESERT.

Bibliography.–N.-E. Andreasen, *Encounter,* 42 (1981), 259-275; K. Budde, *New World,* 4 (1895), 726-745; G. W. Coats, *Rebellion in the Wilderness* (1968); J. W. Flight, *JBL,* 42 (1923), 158-226; M. V. Fox, *CBQ,* 35 (1973), 441-450; F. S. Frick, *The City in Ancient Israel* (1977); R. W. Funk, *JBL,* 78 (1959), 205-214; *GB,* rev., pp. 101-111; *LBHG,* rev., pp. 8-11; M. S. Seale, *The Desert*

Bible (1974); S. Talmon, "The 'Desert Motif' in the Bible and Qumran Literature," in A. Altmann, ed., *Biblical Motifs* (1966), pp. 31-63. G. WYPER

WILDGOATS' ROCKS [Heb. *ṣûrê hayy*^{e}*ʿēlîm*] (1 S. 24:2 [MT 3]); AV, NEB, ROCKS OF THE WILD GOATS. Ledges near En-gedi on the western shore of the Dead Sea, favored as vantage points by the ibexes of the region. Here David cut off the skirt of Saul's robe to show Saul that he wished him no harm.

WILFUL; WILLFULLY [Heb. *zîḏ*] (Ex. 21:14); AV PRESUMPTUOUSLY; [Gk. *authádēs*] (2 Pet. 2:10); AV SELFWILLED. The RSV usually translates Heb. *zîḏ* by "presumptuous(ly)," as does the AV at Ex. 21:14. "Willfully" better expresses the idea of "with malice aforethought" in "premeditated" murder, distinguished from the killing that occurs in the heat of passion, described in v. 13. The concept of self (Gk. *aut-*) is integral to the term in 2 Pet. 2:10, which is translated "arrogant" in Tit. 1:7.

WILL (TESTAMENT) [Gk. *diathḗkē*] (He. 9:16f.); AV, NEB, TESTAMENT. A legal expression of a person's wishes for disposition of his or her property after death. The Greek word, which is regularly used in the LXX for Heb. *b*^{e}*rîṯ*, "covenant," is elsewhere in the RSV NT translated "covenant." The argument in He. 9:15-22 uses the term in both senses, which the RSV expresses by changing the translation to "will" in vv. 16f. and using a footnote to indicate the identity of the underlying Greek word with the word translated "covenant" in vv. 15, 18, 20. The NEB uses "covenant, or testament," at the first appearance of the term in v. 15a, "testament" in vv. 16f., and "covenant" in vv. 15b, 18, 20. E. W. S.

WILL OF GOD. The biblical understanding of God as a person who created human persons in "His" image recognizes in God the characteristic of desiring, or delighting in, certain things or people, as well as the capacity to choose and initiate one course of action in preference to another. Psychology has traditionally grouped these capacities under the heading of "the will."

I. Terminology
II. In the OT
III. In the Gospels
IV. In Early Christianity
V. God's Will and Human Will

I. Terminology.–It is significant that there is no one Hebrew word for "will." The principal expressions used are the nouns *ḥēpeṣ* ("delight" or "pleasure," e.g., 1 S. 15:22; Jer. 22:28) and *rāṣôn* ("favor," e.g., Prov. 10:32; 14:35), with their corresponding verbs *ḥāpēṣ* ("desire" or "take pleasure in," Gen. 34:19; Isa. 1:11) and *rāṣâ* ("be pleased with," e.g., Gen. 33:10). Related ideas are occasionally conveyed by the verbs *ʾāḇâ* ("consent," "be willing," e.g., 1 K. 22:50 [MT 51]), the hiphil of *yā'al* ("begin," "intend," e.g., Hos. 5:11), *bāḥar* ("choose," e.g., Ps. 135:4), *ʾāhaḇ* ("love," e.g., Hos. 3:1), and *ḥāšaq* ("love," or "desire," 1 K. 9:19), among others.

Greek terminology is more uniform. By far the most common Greek noun for "will" in the LXX and NT is *thélēma* ("will" or "desire") from the verb *thélō*. *Thélēma* can be used objectively for what is willed or desired (e.g., Mt. 6:10) or subjectively for the act of willing or desiring (e.g., 1 Pet. 3:17; cf. also *thélēsis* in He. 2:4). *Thélēma* in the sense of "desire" must be carefully distinguished from *epithymía*. Both terms can refer to either good or evil desires, but *epithymía* is never used in the NT for the will of God (although in Lk. 22:15 it does refer to Jesus' desire for the Passover meal).

Other Greek terms for "will" are *boulḗ* (e.g., Acts 2:23; 4:28) and *boúlēma* (e.g., Rom. 9:19), both in the sense of "plan" or "intention," with the corresponding verb *boúlomai* ("wish," "want," or "decide"; e.g., 1 Cor. 12:11); also *eudokía* ("good will" or "favor"; e.g., Mt. 11:26) with its verb *eudokéō* ("be pleased," "delight in"; e.g., Gal. 1:16), *próthesis* ("purpose," e.g., Rom. 8:28), *arestós* (e.g., "what pleases," 1 Jn. 3:22) with its compound *euárestos* (e.g., "pleasing," Eph. 5:10), and *euprósdektos* (e.g., "acceptable," 1 Pet. 2:5). Some NT passages accentuate the divine sovereignty by combining two or more of these roughly equivalent words into a single expression (e.g., Rom. 12:1f.; Eph. 1:5, 11; He. 13:21; see IV below).

II. In the OT.–The terminology of complying with someone else's wishes is used in the OT both of human relationships and of relationships between human beings and God. In the former sense, Hiram of Tyre agrees to do all that Solomon desires (Heb. *ḥēpeṣ*; LXX *thélēma*) with regard to "cedar and cypress timber" in return for Solomon carrying out Hiram's wishes (Heb. *ḥēpeṣ*; LXX *thélēma*) with regard to food supplies (1 K. 5:8f. [MT 23f.]; cf. Solomon and the Queen of Sheba in 2 Ch. 9:12).

Similarly, the OT expects God's people to do the will of God (e.g., Heb. *rāṣôn* in Ps. 40:8 [MT 9]; 143:10; cf. Gk. *thélēma* in 1 Esd. 9:9; 2 Macc. 1:3; 4 Macc. 18:16). This is also expected of God's angelic hosts (Ps. 103:21). Even foreign kings acknowledge that the Jews live "according to the will of your God" (1 Esd. 8:16). The psalmist praises God because He "fulfils the desire [i.e., does the will] of all who fear him" (Ps. 145:19; cf. Mish. *Aboth* ii.4, attributed to Rabban Gamaliel: "Do his will as if it was thy will that he may do thy will as if it was his will").

Above all, however, the OT states that God does His own will. God fulfils His covenant with His people because it pleases Him to do so. In human affairs only fools (Eccl. 8:3) and kings (Dnl. 11:3, 16, 36; cf. 8:4) do whatever they please; but "whatever the Lord pleases [Heb. *ḥāpēṣ*; LXX *thélō*] he does, in heaven and on earth, in the seas and all deeps" (Ps. 135:6; cf. 115:3). The same idea (with Gk. *thélēma*) appears in 1 Macc. 3:60 ("But as his will in heaven may be, so will he do") and in Theodotion's version of Dnl. 4:35 ("he does according to his will"). The God of Israel "performs his purpose [Heb. *ḥēpeṣ*; LXX *thélēma*]" even on Israel's enemies (Isa. 48:14). Thus God's will initiates creation, redemption, and all that happens in heaven and on earth; and the people with whom God has made His covenant are called to live according to His will as this has been revealed to them in the law,

Part of a will from Mesopotamia stating which property belongs to a certain man after the paternal property has been divided among him and his brothers (courtesy of the University Museum, University of Pennsylvania)

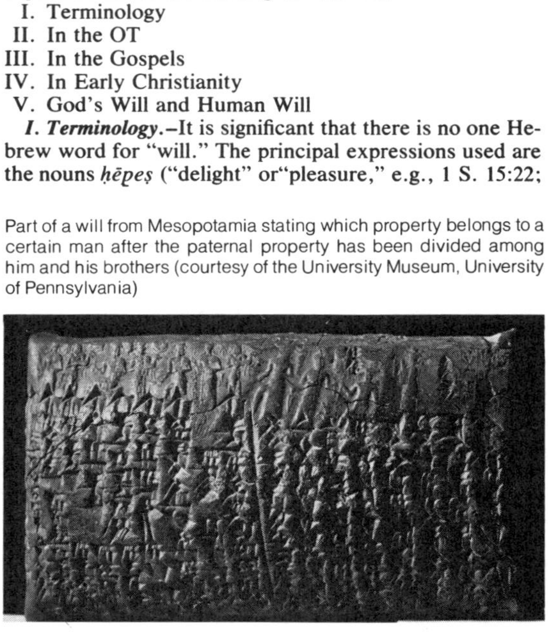

wisdom teaching, and prophetic utterances. In the last analysis, to "delight" (Heb. *ḥāpēṣ*) in doing God's will (*rāṣôn*; LXX *thélēma*) is the same as having God's law written in one's heart (Ps. 40:8 [MT 9]; cf. Jer. 31:31-34), and such willing obedience takes precedence even over the sacrifices and burnt offerings prescribed in the tradition (cf. Ps. 40:6 [MT 7]).

III. In the Gospels.—The theme of the will (Gk. *thélēma*) of God is almost as central to the teaching of Jesus as that of the kingdom of God. In the Matthaean form of the Lord's Prayer the third petition ("Thy will be done, on earth as it is in heaven," Mt. 6:10) explains and virtually defines the first two ("Hallowed be thy name," and "Thy kingdom come"). The idea of the universality of heaven and earth as the sphere where God's will is realized was not new to the Judaism of Jesus' day (cf. Ps. 135:5f.; 1 Macc. 3:60). But rabbinic Judaism more often assumed that God's will would inevitably be done, and therefore simply prayed, "May it be Thy will . . ." (cf., e.g., the series of prayers appended by different Rabbis to the *Amidah* or *Eighteen Benedictions* in T. B. *Berakoth* 16b-17a).

In Matthew, Jesus' prayer in Gethsemane echoes the prayer that He taught His disciples: "My Father, . . . not as I will, but as thou wilt. . . . thy will be done" (Mt. 26:39, 42). In Mark's Gospel, which does not record the Lord's Prayer, Jesus prays at Gethsemane, "not what I will, but what thou wilt" (Mk. 14:36), but does not use the specific phrase "Thy will be done." Luke preserves this petition in a slightly different form: "Father, if thou art willing [Gk. *boúlomai*], . . . nevertheless, not my will, but thine, be done" (Lk. 22:42). Although Luke's version of the Lord's Prayer lacks the petition about God's will (11:2), Luke's awareness of the "will of God" terminology in prayer (particularly in times of crisis) can be seen not only in his Gethsemane account but also in Acts 21:14, where Paul, on being warned of the danger of death if he goes to Jerusalem, says, "The will of the Lord be done" (cf. also M. Polyc. 7:1).

Matthew's version of the Lord's Prayer accents a link between the theme of God's will and that of God as Father — whether of Jesus or of His disciples. The Sermon on the Mount closes with the warning that "Not everyone who says to me, 'Lord, Lord,' shall enter the kingdom of heaven, but he who does the will of my Father who is in heaven" (Mt. 7:21). The context suggests that the one who does God's will is the same as the one "who hears these words of mine and does them . . . like a wise man who built his house upon the rock" (v. 24). Jesus' teaching is the decisive embodiment of God's will for His hearers precisely because God is His Father. In Mark, Jesus says, "Whoever does the will of God is my brother, and sister, and mother" (Mk. 3:35), but in Matthew the phrase becomes "whoever does the will of my Father in heaven" (Mt. 12:50). The same idea is expressed in a parable (21:31) in which Jesus asks which of two sons "did the will of his father" (referring in the parable to their own father, but in Jesus' application to God the Father; cf. Luke's play on the phrase, "the will of his lord" [RSV "his master's will"], in a different parable, Lk. 12:47).

These examples show that the distinctly Matthaean form of the Lord's Prayer (particularly the words "Our Father who art in heaven. . . . Thy will be done, on earth as it is in heaven") stands close to the heart of that Gospel's understanding of Jesus as the one who both teaches and does the will of God. Surprisingly, the Gospel that most nearly approaches Matthew's perspective on this point is John. The principal difference is that John roots the "will of God" more emphatically in the mission of Jesus. If the keynote of Matthew's Gospel is the "will of the Father" (i.e., of God as Father to both Jesus and the disciples), the keynote of John's is "the will of him who sent me" (i.e., God in relation to Jesus in particular). In Samaria, Jesus tells His disciples, "my food is to do the will of him who sent me," i.e., "to accomplish his work" (Jn. 4:34). Later, in language reminiscent of the Synoptic Gethsemane accounts, Jesus defends His judgment as being just, "because I seek not my own will but the will of him who sent me" (5:30). He presents Himself to the crowds as the bread of life who has "come down from heaven not to do my own will, but the will of him who sent me" (6:38); He then concretely defines the "will of him who sent me" (v. 39), or "the will of the Father" (v. 40), as the realization of corporate and individual salvation for all who believe in Him: "that I should lose nothing of all that he has given me, but raise it up at the last day" (v. 39; cf. v. 40). In John's Gospel the will of God is nothing less than the entire work of Jesus, the Son of God sent from heaven to secure eternal life for all whom the Father has given Him (cf. the summary of how Jesus "accomplished the work" of the Father in 17:1-8; see esp. v. 3).

Only twice in John's Gospel (7:17; 9:31) is the will of God understood as a more generally applicable ethical standard; but even in these two passages Jesus' mission is not far from the author's mind. The formerly blind man simply voices conventional Jewish wisdom when he reminds the Jewish authorities questioning him about his healing that "if anyone is a worshiper of God and does his will, God listens to him" (9:31); it is clear from what immediately follows (vv. 32f.), however, that he is referring specifically to Jesus. Earlier, Jesus Himself had reminded a similar group of authorities that "if any man's will is to do [God's] will, he shall know whether the teaching is from God or whether I am speaking on my own authority" (7:17). There the context, quite characteristically, was Jesus' claim that "my teaching is not mine, but his who sent me" (v. 16). Although John's Gospel is often remembered as the one that particularly stresses "knowing" God, this passage demonstrates that to this author (like the author of Matthew) "doing" is just as important as "knowing," both for Jesus and for His disciples (cf. 13:15, 17).

IV. In Early Christianity.—Paul introduces himself in several of his letters as an apostle of Jesus Christ "by [*diá*] the will of God" (1 Cor. 1:1; 2 Cor. 1:1; Eph. 1:1; Col. 1:1; 2 Tim. 1:1; cf. Gal. 1:1, "by Jesus Christ and God the Father"; 1 Tim. 1:1, "by the command of God our Savior and Christ Jesus our hope"). Because an "apostle" is one who is sent, the formula recalls Jesus' reference to "the will of him who sent me" in the gospel of John. Paul's use of it suggests that he viewed his apostolic calling as an extension of the mission of his Lord. More specifically, he viewed the prospect of his visiting the church at Rome (Rom. 15:32), and also the Macedonian Christians' full participation in the collection for poor believers in Jerusalem (2 Cor. 8:4f.), as possible only "by [*diá*] the will of God." The same preposition occurs in Rev. 4:11, the only NT passage that links God's will to creation: "for thou didst create all things, and by [*diá*] thy will they existed and were created" (cf. 1 Cor. 8:6b: "Jesus Christ, through whom are all things and through whom we exist").

Other prepositions are also used with *thélēma*. Paul's hope of visiting Rome "by the will of God" can be expressed with the preposition *en* (lit. "in") as well as *diá* (Rom. 1:10). Epaphras prays that the Colossians may stand mature "in all the will of God" (i.e., in every single thing that God wants for them, Col. 4:12; cf. Paul's description of David in Acts 13:22). Gal. 1:4 states that the redemptive plan by which Jesus Christ "gave himself for our sins to deliver us from the present evil age" is "according to [*katá*] the will of our God and Father" (cf. Ign. Smyrn. 1:1). More elaborately, redemption is described as "according to the purpose [*eudokía*] of his will [*thélēma*]" (Eph. 1:5) and "according to the purpose [*próthesis*] of him who accomplishes all things according to the counsel [*boulḗ*] of his will [*thélēma*]" (Eph. 1:11). He. 2:4 refers to God's testimony through "signs and wonders and . . . gifts of the Holy Spirit distributed according to his will [*thélēsis*]."

The nouns *boúlēma* and *boulḗ* are also used for God's redemptive plan as a whole. "For who can resist his will [*boúlēma*]?" Paul asks in Rom. 9:19 in connection with God's sovereign choice of Jacob over Esau. In Acts *boulḗ* is used twice of God's plan with regard to the crucifixion of Jesus by Jewish and gentile authorities (2:23; 4:28), once in connection with David as the instrument of God's plan in his own generation (13:36), and once to describe the message ("the whole counsel of God") that Paul proclaimed at Ephesus (20:27). Elsewhere *boulḗ* is used of God's purpose implicit in His promise to Abraham (He. 6:17) and of God's intent that people should accept the baptism of John the Baptist (Lk. 7:30). In Jas. 1:18 the Christian experience of new birth by the "word of truth" is explicitly connected with the purpose or initiative of God (vb. *boúlomai*; cf. Jn. 1:13, which contrasts being born "of the will of the flesh [*thélēma*]," or "the will of the male," with being "born of God").

Several of these passages suggest that God's plan is a mystery, or something contrary to human expectations. Nowhere is this point more clearly made than in Mt. 11:25f. par. Lk. 10:21, where Jesus gives thanks to God for having "hidden these things [i.e., the kingdom of God at work in His ministry] from the wise and understanding and revealed them to babes; yea, Father, for such was thy gracious will" (*eudokía,* lit. "well pleasing before thee").

Twice in 1 Thessalonians Paul defines God's will concretely. In 4:3 he states, "For this is the will of God, your sanctification: that you abstain from immorality"; in 5:18 he identifies the "will of God" with the command to "Rejoice always, pray constantly, give thanks in all circumstances" (vv. 17f.). Similarly, in 1 Pet. 2:15 God's will is defined concretely as "doing right," so as to "put to silence the ignorance of foolish men." The precise definition of God's will depends on the specific situation. To some extent, however, it seems to be related to the ancient concept of sacrifice, i.e., the offering to God of something holy: the "sanctification" of oneself rather than ceremonial offerings in 1 Thess. 4:3, "thanksgiving" (perhaps already regarded as a bloodless Christian sacrifice) in 5:18, and good deeds (possibly regarded in a similar way) in 1 Pet. 2:15 (cf. the sacrificial imagery in vv. 5, 9). In any case, the notion that praise to God and good deeds to fellow human beings are "sacrifices . . . pleasing [*euarestéō*] to God" is explicit in He. 13:15f.

Paul himself explicitly connects God's will with sacrifice in Rom. 12:1f. with its decisive appeal "to present your bodies as a living sacrifice, holy and acceptable [*euárestos*] to God, which is your spiritual worship. . . . be transformed by the renewing of your mind, that you may prove what is the will [*thélēma*] of God, what is good and acceptable [*euárestos*] and perfect." As in 1 Thessalonians, Paul is attempting to define God's will, but here he is referring to God's general will in all circumstances, and therefore it is defined less concretely. God's will for His servants is always obedience, the giving of oneself to Him as an instrument for righteousness (cf. Rom. 6:13, 19). What that means concretely must be discovered in the situation, but for Paul this is the only appropriate "sacrifice" for those who have accepted the gospel. He. 10:5-10 draws out the contrast between offering sacrifices and doing the will of God. After quoting Ps. 40:6-8, the author highlights two statements: "Thou hast neither desired nor taken pleasure in sacrifices and offerings . . ." (Heb. 10:8), and "Lo, I have come to do thy will" (v. 9). He then concludes, "He [Christ] abolishes the first [sacrifices] in order to establish the second [doing God's will] (v. 9b), with the observation that "by [*en*] that will we have been sanctified through the offering of the body of Jesus Christ once for all" (v. 10). Sacrificial language appears even in the closing benediction of Hebrews: "Now may the God of peace . . . equip you with everything good that you may do his will [*thélēma*], working in you that which is pleasing [*euárestos*] in his sight . . ." (13:20f.).

In early Christianity *thélēma* was so closely identified with God's will that the term was sometimes used without modifiers for "what is acceptable" or "what is required," with the understanding that the will of God was meant. Paul, e.g., rebukes those in Judaism who "know the will [*tó thélēma*] and approve what is excellent" (Rom. 2:18). In explaining why Apollos has not come to Corinth, Paul states that "it was not at all *thélēma* [i.e., acceptable or fitting] for him to go now. He will come when he has opportunity" (1 Cor. 16:12). Jesus' pronouncement in Mt. 18:14, "So it is not *thélēma* [i.e., acceptable] before your Father in heaven that one of these little ones should perish," probably belongs in this category as well. The expression "if it be *thélēma* [God's will] . . ." is common in the letters of Ignatius of Antioch (Ign. Eph. 20:1; Ign. Rom. 1:1; Ign. Smyrn. 11:1; Ign. Polyc. 1:1; cf. Jas. 4:15 with the vb. *thélō*). But more often the whole phrase, "will of God," was used because Christians were aware of other wills and other forces in their world. It was possible to be caught in the devil's trap and to do his will (*thélēma,* 2 Tim. 2:26), and there was a time when gentile Christians followed the "desires [*tá thelḗmata*] of the flesh and of the senses" (Eph. 2:3). Jesus Himself was "delivered up to the will [*thélēma*]" of those who demanded his death (Lk. 23:25).

As a characterization of Christian believers, expressions like "doing the will of God" are as common in the rest of early Christian literature as in the teaching ascribed to Jesus. Eph. 6:6 urges servants to "do the will of God from the heart." He. 10:36 reminds readers that "you have need of endurance, so that you may do the will of God and receive what is promised" and 1 Jn. 2:17 assures its readers that though "the world passes away, and the lust of it, yet whoever does the will of God remains forever." Prayer offered to God "according to his will" is not only heard but answered (5:14). 1 Pet. 4:17 assures those who "suffer according to God's will" that their "faithful Creator" will protect and vindicate them in the end (cf. 3:17).

In order to do the will of God one must first know it, and most NT writers assume that the knowledge of God's will, once the prerogative of the Jews (Rom. 2:18), has now been made available to the Gentiles. Ananias reminded Paul before his baptism that he had been appointed by God "to know his will" (Acts 22:14). Paul in turn prays for the gentile believers at Colossae that they "may be filled with the knowledge of his will in all spiritual wisdom and understanding" (Col. 1:9), and he commands other Christians, "do not be foolish, but understand what the will of the Lord is" (Eph. 5:17). 1 Pet. 4:2f. sums up the aspiration of the earliest gentile Christians: they tried (not always successfully) to stop doing "what the Gentiles want" (the *boúlēma* of the Gentiles, v. 3) and to "live for the rest of the time in the flesh no longer by human passions [*epithymíai*] but by the will [*thélēma*] of God" (v. 2). It was indeed the "will of God," a concept long familiar to the Jews and now revealed to the Gentiles through Jesus Christ, that had transformed their lives and made of them a new community with a new religion.

V. God's Will and Human Will.–The Jewish and Christian notion of "the will of God" has implicatons for the philosophical issue of human "free will." A common approach has been to place human freedom in tension with forces outside or beyond humanity, whether these forces are attributed to nature (i.e., determinism) or to a personal deity (i.e., predestination or "the will of God"). Though Jewish and Christian philosophers have struggled with this tension as much as anyone, the Bible provides little basis for even posing the question in terms of "tension," as if human freedom and divine freedom mutually limited each other. Instead, human freedom is viewed as a corollary of divine freedom. Human beings are free — or, rather, are set free — precisely by the freedom of God. The NT writers viewed the "free" choices of their pagan contemporaries as choices leading to "slavery." They saw the world around them as locked in bondage to sin and death, a bondage from which they believed themselves delivered through God's free intervention in the person of Jesus Christ. A person might have all kinds of choices, but never the choice not to die. Only redemption through Jesus Christ for the Christian, and for the Jew obedience to the will of God revealed to Moses, made that choice possible.

When Jews and Christians reflected back on creation, they concluded that human free will was the result of humanity's creation in the image of God. To the extent that God's image had been obscured or damaged by sin, human freedom was limited. Only in obedience to a personal God who was free and who had freely provided salvation could the image be restored and freedom regained. Free will is therefore defined not as the freedom to move in whatever direction one's impulses might lead, but as the realization — partial though it be — of God's purpose for one's life. The first is the freedom of fools (cf. Eccl. 8:3), while the second is the freedom of kings — or at least of those who inherit a Kingdom!

From the standpoint of philosophical thought, the "tension" admittedly still stands. It will not go away at the bidding of faith or theology. But to Christians and Jews the tension is there because twice — in creation and in redemption — God ventured to share with human creation the freedom that first belonged to God alone.

Bibliography.–Aquinas *Summa Theol.* i.72-102; Augustine *De spiritu et littera; DNTT,* III, 1015-1023 (D. Müller); J. Edwards, *Freedom of the Will* (1754); Erasmus, *Diatribe Concerning Free Choice* (1524); *HDB,* IV, *s.v.* "will" (V. H. Stanton); E. Lohmeyer, *The Lord's Prayer* (Eng. tr. 1965), pp. 111-133; M. Luther, *Bondage of the Will* (1525); H. Riesenfeld, *Zum Gebrauch von thelō im NT* (1936); G. Segalla, *Rivista Biblica,* 13 (1965), 121-143; E. Stauffer, *NT Theology* (Eng. tr. 1955), pp. 180-84; *TDNT,* III, *s.v.* θέλω κτλ. (G. Schrenk); *TDOT,* V, *s.v.* "ḥāpēṣ" (G. J. Botterweck).

J. E. MICHAELS

WILL WORSHIP (Col. 2:23, AV). A literal rendering of Gk. *ethelothrēskía,* translated "rigor of devotion" in the RSV. *See* RIGOR OF DEVOTION.

WILLOW [Heb. *ṣapṣapâ*; cf. Arab. *ṣafṣāf*] **WILLOWS** [Heb. *ᵃrāḇim*; Gk. *itéa*–'willow'] (Lev. 23:40; Job 40:22; Ps. 137:2; Isa. 15:7; 44:4); NEB also POPLARS (Job 40:22; Isa. 44:4), ARABIM (Isa. 15:7). Leviticus 23:40 and Ps. 137:2 probably refer to the Euphrates aspen (*Populus euphratica* Oliv.), a tall tree with spreading branches that is common along river banks from Syria to southern Arabia. This tree was probably also the "balsam" of 2 S. 5:23f. par. 1 Ch. 14:14f. The remaining references are to some species of *Salix* or true willow, either *S. fragilis* L., *S. safsaf* Forsk., *S. alba* L., or *S. acmophylla* Boiss. These are shrubs or small trees, with reddish branches and oblong-elliptic or lanceolate leaves. They grow by watercourses (Job 40:22; Isa. 15:7) and flourish in the Jordan Valley. Of the approximately twenty-one species of willows that grow in Palestine, the most common is the Palestine willow (*S. safsaf*). This is probably the "willow" of Ezk. 17:5. The "weeping willow" (*S. babylonica* L.) was introduced into Palestine from the Orient long after the Exile and cannot be the species referred to in Ps. 137:2.

See MPB, pp. 183, 216-18. R. K. H.

WILLOWS, BROOK OF THE [Heb. *naḥal hāᵃrāḇîm*]; NEB GORGE OF THE ARABIM. A name mentioned only in Isa. 15:7, obviously as one of Moab's boundaries; thus it may be the brook ZERED. The RSV rendering has been questioned, and the NEB is probably wise in transliterating the name. H. L. ELLISON

WIMPLE. A cloth that is worn over the head and around the neck. The AV uses this term to translate Heb. *miṭpaḥaṯ* in Isa. 3:22 (RSV, NEB, "cloak"). *See* GARMENTS IV.

WIND [Heb. *rû(a)ḥ*; Gk. *ánemos,* also *pneúma* (Jn. 3:8), *pnoḗ* (Acts 2:2), *pnéousa* (Acts 27:40)].

I. Wind in Palestine.–Wind is caused when heated air rises and air from around moves in to take its place. The conjunction of land and sea in Palestine and close juxtaposition of highlands and lowlands cause great differences of temperature and consequently an almost constant movement of air. Periods of stagnant air are short.

Wind is most regular in the summer when the general movement of air over the eastern Mediterranean is from west to east, bringing with it no rain, but often heavy dew to the coastal areas and seaward slopes. The day begins with complete calm, but as the sun heats the land a strong sea breeze develops. It tops the central ridge at about midday and pours into the central rift in a torrent, heated by descent. At about 3 P.M. it surmounts the eastern plateau, once more cool and refreshing. The farmer depends upon this very regular wind for winnowing the grain (Isa. 41:16). The contrary land breeze at night is decidedly weaker.

In winter the atmosphere is much less stable and powerful cyclones move eastward across the Mediterranean bringing with them strong winds, sometimes of gale force, and often torrential rain or even snow. Intervening periods are relatively calm with brilliantly clear air. In the two transitional seasons comes the *ḥamsîn,* an intensely hot and dry east wind, filling the air with a haze of yellow dust, and lasting for about three to five days, though occasionally longer. It is exceedingly exhausting and destructive to vegetation (e.g., Isa. 27:8; Jer. 4:11; Jonah 4:8), and pouring down the slopes of the Lebanon mountains could destroy the ships of Tarshish in Tyre harbor (Ezk. 27:26).

II. The Symbolism of Wind.–In Israelite understanding only God could control the wind (Job 28:25; Ps. 147:8; 148:8), which comes from His storehouse (Ps. 135:7; Jer. 10:13; Am. 4:13) and upon which He rides (2 S. 22:11). Men and animals are helpless before it (Jer. 49:32). But it is symbolic also of emptiness and folly (e.g., Job 6:26; Prov. 11:29; Eccl. 1:6; Isa. 26:18), of false prophets (Jer. 5:13), of useless foreign policy (Hos. 12:1), and especially of idols and idolatry (e.g., Isa. 41:29; 57:13; Jer. 5:13). The uncertainty of human life is sometimes compared to wind (Ps. 78:39; 103:16).

III. Wind and Spirit.–The Heb. *rû(a)ḥ* and the Gk. *pneúma* can both mean "spirit" as well as "wind." This double meaning is contained in the description of primeval chaos at creation (Gen. 1:2; AV and RSV "Spirit of God"; NEB "mighty wind"), the account of Ezekiel prophesying to the "wind" (AV and NEB; RSV less suitably "breath"), and in the conversation between Jesus and Nicodemus (Jn. 3:5-8).

See also RAIN; STORM; NATURAL FEATURES VI, VII.

D. BALY

WINDOW [Heb. *ḥallôn*] (Gen. 8:6; Josh. 2:15; 2 S. 6:16; Prov. 7:6; Ezk. 40:16; etc.); NEB also EMBRASURE, OPENING, TRAP-DOOR; [*'ᵃrubbâ*] (Gen. 7:11; Eccl. 12:3; Isa. 60:8; Hos. 13:3; etc.); AV also CHIMNEY; NEB also CHIMNEY, DOVECOTE; [*meḥᵉzâ*] (1 K. 7:4, 5); [*ṣōhar*] (Gen. 6:16); RSV footnote; [Aram. *kawwâ*] (Dnl. 6:10 [MT 11]); [Gk. *thyrís*] (Acts 20:9; 2 Cor. 11:33). An opening in a building, vehicle, ship, etc., usually for admitting light and air.

Ancient houses probably contained windows much like the small rectangles in old stone houses of the region today. Those on the ground floor would have been high on the wall and may have been barred to keep out thieves (Joel 2:9). The *ḥallôn* was large enough to allow a man to pass (Josh. 2:15; 1 S. 19:12). Some windows were closable by a lattice shutter (Prob. 7:6; Cant. 2:9) and others, especially in temple architecture, were set into recessed frames (1 K. 6:4; Ezk. 41:16). The latter is illustrated by ivories found at Nimrûd but possibly from Samaria. The term *'ᵃrubbâ* is used primarily for the openings in heaven through which heavy rain is seen to fall (Gen. 7:11; etc.). Both Hebrew words are associated with birds (Zeph. 2:14; Isa. 60:8), probably reflecting the habit of birds to use window sills as perches (there is no reason to extend the meaning to "dovecote" with NEB).

An ivory carving from Nimrûd showing a woman (possibly the goddess Astarte or a harlot) in a window. The frame is recessed with four decorative columns underneath for support (first half of the 8th cent. B.C.) (courtesy of the Trustees of the British Museum)

The RSV translates *ṣōhar* "ROOF" but footnotes "window" as a possible alternative. The term *meḥᵉzâ* is used only with Solomon's palace. The Aram. *kawwâ* appears only once, but seems to be a shuttered window that was openable.

The Gk. *thyrís* is the standard term for window corresponding to Heb. *ḥallôn*.

L. G. HERR

WINDOWS OF HEAVEN. *See* HEAVEN, WINDOWS OF.

WINE. The fermented juice of grapes or another plant product.

- I. Terminology and Types
  - A. Wine
  - B. Red Wine
  - C. New Wine
  - D. Sweet Wine
  - E. Sour Wine
  - F. Mixed and Spiced Wine
  - G. Locale
- II. Use
  - A. Personal
  - B. Religious
    - 1. Offerings and Libations
    - 2. OT Feasts
    - 3. Lord's Supper
  - C. Medicinal
  - D. Commercial
- III. In Biblical Imagery
  - A. Blessing
  - B. Judgment

I. Terminology and Types.–Wine can be named and classified according to certain varietal characteristics, including type of grape, color, and place of origin. The type is also dependent on the time allowed for fermentation and the age of the wine.

A. Wine. The common terms for wine are Heb. *yayin* (141 times), Aram. *ḥᵃmar* (six times, Ezr. 6:9; 7:22; Dnl. 5:1f., 4, 23), and Gk. *oínos* (thirty-four times). Additional terms are *soḇe'* in Isa. 1:22 and *ḥemer* in Dt. 32:14 and Isa. 27:2 (RSV "pleasant vineyard," but lit. "wine vineyard"). The origin of Heb. *yayin* is uncertain. Most scholars posit a non-Semitic base (possibly Hittite) underlying the Semitic root *wyn* or *yyn*. They believe that this gave rise to Heb. *yayin* and to Gk. *oínos* and other Indo-European cognates (Lat. *vinum*; German *Wein*; Eng. "wine") derive. In the minority, van Selms has suggested a Semitic root *yānâ,* "to press," deriving from the method of production.

Wine was generally made from juice of the common *Vitus vinifera* L. grape, but other types of wine are also attested. The Talmud mentions a wine made from raisins (T.B. *Baba Bathra* 97b), and wine could also be made from dates, figs, and pomegranates. A drink called "mead" (Gk. *méthy*) was made from fermented honey mixed with water and herbs.

Wine is frequently mentioned with other foodstuffs. It appears in the Chronicler's tribute lists, royal storehouse lists, and temple commodity lists alongside oil, grain, honey, incense, oxen, and sheep (1 Ch. 12:40; 2 Ch. 31:5; Neh. 10:37; cf. Rev. 18:13). The phrase "bread and wine" is found in Gen. 14:18; Dt. 29:6; Jgs 19:19; Neh. 5:15; cf. Lk. 7:33.

Wine is paired with "strong drink" thirteen times in the OT (Heb. *šēḵār*) and once in the NT (Lk. 1:15; Gk. *síkera,* from Sem. *šēḵār*; cf. Akk. *šikaru,* "barley beer").

The phrase "wine and strong drink" is usually found in contexts warning against or forbidding the use of alcoholic beverages (cf. Lev 10:9; Nu. 6:3; Dt. 29:6; Jgs 13:4; 1 S. 1:15; Isa. 5:11, 22; 24:9). Strong drink is probably beer rather than a distilled liquor (but *see* DRINK, STRONG). Synonyms for wine are "new wine (see I.C below), "blood of grapes" (Gen. 49:11; Dt. 32:14), and "fruit of the vine" (Lk. 22:18; cf. Isa. 32:12). "Wine on the lees" (Heb. *šᵉmārîm,* Isa. 25:6; cf. Ps. 75:8 [MT 9]; Jer. 48:11) is wine that has been matured in one vessel, resting undisturbed on the dregs or solid particles of the wine-making process that have settled out of suspension.

B. Red Wine. The color of wine depends in part on the color of the grape skin. Red wine gets its color from being fermented in contact with the crushed grape skins. But white wine can also be made from red grapes, if the macerated skins are removed quickly before fermentation takes place.

Several passages suggest that wine was typically red. Prov. 23:31 attests a red wine. The poetic parallel "blood of grapes" (Heb. *dam ʿᵃnāḇîm*) occurs in Gen. 49:11 (cf. *dam ʿēnāḇ,* Dt. 32:14 [MT 15]; Gk. *haíma staphylḗs,* Sir. 39:26; 50:15; Ugar. *dm ʿṣm,* "blood of trees/grapevines"). In Isa. 63:2 the garments of the treaders turned red from their work. An inscription on a wine decanter removed from a burial tomb in the Hebron area reads *lyḥzyhw yyn kḥl,* translated by Demsky "Belonging to Yaḥzeyahu dark wine." Citing similar words in Gen. 49:12 (RSV "his eyes shall be red with wine") and Prov. 23:29f., Demsky has suggested that "dark" here designates a dark-colored wine produced in the Judean hills. Such wine is mentioned in Mishnaic sources (*Berakoth* vii.5; *Niddah* ix.11), and "dark-colored wine" (Akk. *karānu daʾmu*) is mentioned in cuneiform documents from the time of Darius (see S. M. Paul). The analogy of bread and body, wine and blood in the Lord's Supper (Mk. 14:22-25 par.; 1 Cor. 11:23-26) also suggests that wine was typically red. White wine is not mentioned in the biblical sources, although rabbinic sources refer to "white wine" and "clear wine" (T.B. *Yoma* 18a; *Zebahim* 78b; *Kerithoth* 6a; *Baba Bathra* 97b; *Shabbath* 109a, 139b; *Gittin* 69a). The "choice vine" (Heb. *śōrēq*) of Gen. 49:11; Isa. 5:2; and Jer. 2:21 produces a red variety of grape.

C. New Wine. The biblical terms for "new wine" are Heb. *tîrôš* (Hos. 9:2; Hag. 1:11; Zec. 9:17), Gk. *oínos néos* (Mt. 9:17; Mk. 2:22; Lk. 5:37f.), *gleúkos* Acts 2:13). New wine was wine from the most recent harvest, while old wine was wine from the previous year. The AV and RSV render Heb. *tîrôš* simply by "wine" or by "new wine." This OT term for wine is frequently paired with "grain" (Heb. *dāgān,* Gen. 27:28, 37; Ps. 4:7 [MT 8]) and/or "oil" (Heb. *yiṣhār,* Dt. 7:13; 11:14; 12:17; Jer. 31:12) in contexts extolling productivity and abundance. Both *yayin* and *tîrôš* are fermented grape juice with alcoholic content; hence both are able to cause intoxication (cf. Hos. 4:11) and are to be distinguished from "must" or unfermented grape juice. In the saying about new wine in old wineskins (Mt. 9:17 par.) the new wine is the recent product of the harvest, which should not be placed in brittle, unpliant wineskins because it may burst them. In the process of fermentation carbon dioxide gas is released, creating pressure within the container (cf. Job 32:19). The "new wine" (Gk. *gleúkos*) of the Pentecost account (Acts 2:13) was the vintage of the recent harvest; the thrust of the taunt requires that it refer to wine that can cause intoxication.

D. Sweet Wine. Biblical terms for sweet wine are Heb. *yayin haṭṭôḇ* (AV, RSV, lit. "best wine," Cant. 7:9 [MT 10]; cf. Ugar. *yn ṭb, UT,* 1084:1, 4, 6, 9), Heb. *ʿāsîs* (Joel 1:5; 3:18 [MT 4:18]; Am. 9:13; cf. *ʿᵃsîs rimmōn,* "juice of pomegranate," Cant. 8:2), and *mamtāqqîm* (Neh. 8:10). Rabbinic sources (T.B. *Baba Bathra* 97b; Mish. *Menahoth* viii.6) mention a sweet wine produced by exposing the grapes in the sun for three days and then treading them in the midday heat.

A Persian official carrying a wineskin on his shoulder. From a relief on a staircase at Persepolis, 485-465 B.C. (courtesy of the Detroit Institute of Arts, Gift of Mrs. Lillian Henkel Haas)

E. Sour Wine. Wine that has turned sour was called VINEGAR. Vinegar was used for seasoning foods (Ruth 2:14) and pickling vegetables, as an inferior drink and as a medicine (Jn. 19:29f.). The "wine" mentioned in Ruth 2:14, RSV, is vinegar (Heb. *ḥōmeṣ*; cf. *ḥōmeṣ yayin,* Nu. 6:3 [RSV "vinegar made from wine"]; Gk. *óxos,* "vinegar," Mt. 27:48; Mk. 15:36; Lk. 23:36; Jn. 19:29f.). Vinegar could be deliberately produced by encouraging extra fermentation of new wine in the open air. Or wine would simply turn into vinegar, since acetic bacteria in wine turn wine sour when it is exposed to the air for any great length of time. Because impermeable containers with tight stoppers were nonexistent, wine frequently turned sour. The

Greeks first solved the problem by using large clay vessels called amphorae, sometimes lined with pitch and stoppered with wax, to store wine and keep its taste intact.

F. Mixed and Spiced Wine. The terms for mixed wine are Heb. *meseḵ* (Ps. 75:8), *mezeg* (Cant. 7:2 [MT 3]), and the vb. *māsaḵ* (Prov. 9:2, 5; 23:30, Isa. 65:11; wine mixed with milk, Cant. 5:1; wine mixed with water, Isa. 1:22; cf. 2 Macc. 15:39). The most common mixture was wine diluted with water. The ratio of water to wine varied, but the quantity of water was almost always greater than that of wine. The favored mixture for the Greeks was one part wine and three parts water. The normal drink at meals at Qumrân was wine (*tîrôš*) after it was blessed (1QS 6:4ff.; 1QSa 2:17f., 20; 1QH 10:24). During Roman times the ordinary table beverage was wine mixed with water (see Ferguson). Since the water was not always completely safe to drink, mixing wine with water had a purifying effect on the water (cf. 1 Tim. 5:23). Wine mixed with myrrh was offered to Jesus as He hung from the cross (Mk. 15:23), but He refused to drink it. Did. 13:6 mentions wine mixed with oil.

Spices could be added to wine to improve its aroma and taste (cf. "spiced wine," Heb. *yayin hāreqaḥ*, Cant. 8:2). Sometimes wine was given increased aroma by rubbing the wine press with wood resin. The Talmud mentions various kinds of mixed wine: old wine mixed with clean water and balsam, wine mixed with honey and pepper, wine added to oil and garum, and wine mixed with spices (T.B. *Abodah Zarah* 30a; Mish. *Shabbath* xx.2).

G. Locale. The "wine of Helbon" mentioned in Ezk. 27:18 (RSV "wine from Uzah," following the LXX) is attested also in Mesopotamian and classical sources. The village of Helbon NW of Damascus is still today a wine-producing center. "Wine of Lebanon" (Hos. 14:7 [MT 8]) was renowned for its bouquet. Other wine producing areas were Jezreel (1 K. 21:1), Samaria (Jer. 31:5), the Valley of Eshcol (Nu. 13:23f.; Heb. *'eškôl* denotes a cluster of grapes), and Sibmah (Isa. 16:8; Jer. 48:32). The *s^emāḏar* of Cant. 2:13, 15; 7:13 is apparently a type of wine or vine. Samaria ostraca 53f. mention "wine of Kerem-hattel," and the Talmudic sources refer to "wine of Sharon" (Mish. *Niddah* v. 7) and "wine of Carmel" (T.B. *Niddah* 21a). Seal impressions marking the place of origin or the owner of the vineyard are widely attested on wine storage jar handles.

II. Uses.–A. Personal. Wine is not attested as the normal table beverage of OT times. It seems generally to have been reserved for special occasions, such as the meal when Isaac was to transfer the patriarchal blessing to Esau (Gen. 27:25). Wine is associated with times of joy and feasting (e.g., the feasting of Job's children, Job 1; Ahasuerus's banquet, Est. 1; Belshazzar's feast in Babylon, Dnl. 5; cf. also Isa. 22:13). Wine was served at coronations (1 Ch. 12:39f.) and at weddings (Jn. 2). A banquet hall is called a *bêṯ mišteh hayyayin* (lit. "house for drinking wine," Est. 7:8), and a "feast" is literally a "drinking" (Heb. *mišteh*, Gen. 21:8; Jgs. 14:10; 1 S. 25:36; 2 S. 3:20); *see also* BANQUET. Wine was viewed as a blessing from God "that gladdens the heart of man" (Ps. 104:15; cf. also Eccl. 2:3; 9:7; 10:19; Zec. 10:7). It is mentioned along with grain and oil as a gift of God and a sign of His blessing (Gen. 27:28; Dt. 7:13; Ps. 104:15).

But drunkenness was a potential problem against which especially the writer of Proverbs warned (20:1; 21:17; 23:30f.; see also Isa. 5:11f.; Hab. 2:5; Sir. 19:1f.). The episode of Noah's drunkenness (Gen. 9:20-27) showed that sin was still present after the Deluge, and it became the occasion for the cursing of the progenitor of the Canaanites. According to 1 Pet. 4:3 "drunkenness" (Gk. *oinophlygía*) is one of the characteristic vices of the Gentiles. Leaders are counseled not to drink wine (Prov. 31:4f.; 1 Tim. 3:3, 8). Overindulgence leads to reeling and vomiting (Isa. 28:7f.), hallucinations, and ultimately addiction (Prov. 23:28-35). Some of the Rabbis held that the "tree of knowledge" from which Adam and Eve partook was a vine (Midr. *Gen. Rabbah* XV.7).

According to pagan belief, wine was especially appreciated by the gods (cf. Jgs. 9:13: "wine which cheers gods and men"; cf. also Dt. 32:37f.). Consequently it was a frequent component of offerings to the gods. In the Ugaritic text RS 24.258 (see J. Nougayrol, ed., *Ugaritica, V* [1968], text 1) the god 'El arranges a banquet at which he himself drinks too much wine (*yn* and *trṯ*) and becomes drunk; eventually he loses control of his bodily functions and begins hallucinating (see Pope).

Wine was forbidden to priests when they ministered in the central sanctuary (Lev. 10:9; Ezk. 44:21); and those under a Nazirite vow (Nu. 6:1-4; cf. Samson, Jgs. 13:4f.; cf. also Am. 2:11f.) were not allowed to have wine, strong drink, or any produce of the vine, including grapes or raisins. They were to be animated instead by the Spirit of the Lord. The Rechabites (Jer. 35) practiced total abstinence as part of a countercultural desert-nomad life-style that set them apart from the urbanized Judeans. Planting vineyards, sowing fields, and building houses were viewed as a betrayal of their traditional life-style. Daniel and his three friends abstained from the king's wine (Dnl. 1) either because it was not kosher or because it was associated with the pagan cult. John the Baptist was also distinguished by his abstinence from wine (Mt. 11:18 par. Lk. 7:33). On the day of Pentecost the empowerment of the Spirit of God was mistaken for the effects of alcoholic spirits (Acts 2:1-13). Eph. 5:18 contrasts inebriation by wine with animation by the Holy Spirit. Although total abstinence from wine is not required in the age of Christ, since everything is redeemed, Paul suggested that it may be right at times to abstain in order to keep a brother or sister from stumbling (Rom. 14:20f.; cf. 1 Tim. 3:8). Jesus Himself did not disapprove of or abstain from wine, as evidenced by the miracle of abundant wine at the Cana wedding (Jn. 2; cf also Mt. 11:19 par. Lk. 7:34).

Wine, like other liquids, was measured by the bath (2 Ch. 2:9), equivalent to about 22 liters (23 quarts), and the hin (Ex. 29:40, Lev. 23:13), equivalent to about 3.6 l. (3.8 quarts). Wine was stored in jars or wineskins (1 S. 1:24; 10:3; Mt. 9:17). Normally it was drunk from a cup (Heb. *kôs*, Gen. 40:11; Prov. 23:31; Gk. *potḗrion*) made out of pottery. Only royalty, the rich, and the divine would have vessels made of precious metals (Dnl. 5:1-4).

B. Religious. 1. Offerings and Libations. In sacrifices of petition, thanksgiving, and expiation (Ex. 29:38-41; Nu. 15:2-15) wine was poured out as a LIBATION or "drink offering" (Heb. *nāsaḵ yayin*, Lev. 23:13; Dt. 32:38; Hos. 9:4; cf. Gen. 35:14; Nu. 28:7, 14). The drink offering could be an act in its own right or could accompany a burnt offering. Wine was also one of the firstfruits brought to the sanctuary as a tithe (Neh. 10:36-39).

2. OT Feasts. The Feast of Tabernacles (or Ingathering) was celebrated in the autumn at the end of the grain and vine harvest (Dt. 16:13; Lev. 23:39). (The Canaanites celebrated the season with eating and drinking in the temple of their pagan god; see Jgs. 9:27). The first evidence for the use of wine at PASSOVER comes from the Hellenistic period (Jub. 49:6). According to Jewish tradition the Passover feast was celebrated with four cups of wine (Mish. *Pesahim* x), symbolizing the four expressions of redemp-

An Egyptian wall painting showing a banquet scene. At left are tables laden with fruits, meats, and poultry with flasks of beer and wine underneath. Above, a servant girl serves wine in a shallow bowl. Below, she carries a pitcher for refilling and a napkin, as does the servant boy at right (from the tomb of Nedjannu at Thebes, late 15th cent. B.C.) (courtesy of the Trustees of the British Museum)

tion found in Ex. 6:6f. It also became a tradition to set aside one cup of wine for Elijah in anticipation of his coming, which would precede the final redemption. In accordance with a tradition derived from Prov. 31:6 (cf. the "cup of consolation" for mourners in Jer. 16:7), wine was also offered to the bereaved after a funeral at the meal of comforting. *See also* FEASTS.

3. Lord's Supper. The Synoptic Gospels present the Last Supper within the context of the Jewish Passover (cf. Mk. 14:12-16). When Jesus hosted the Last Supper He appropriated the elements of the Jewish Passover, which by this time included the use of wine. The use of bread at the Passover derived from the feast of unleavened bread (*ḥag hammaṣṣôṯ*, Ex. 12:17-20; Lev. 23:5-8; Nu. 28:16-25). The wine of Passover, as Jesus appropriated it, symbolized the blood of the slaughtered paschal lamb (although it is not clear that this was the case in the Jewish Passover). In the Gospel and Pauline accounts of the Last Supper "the cup" stands for wine, which in turn symbolizes the shed blood of Jesus (Mk. 14:22f. par.; 1 Cor. 11:25).

Wine functions in three significant ways in the Lord's Supper. Insofar as the Lord's Supper is a memorial to Jesus' death, the wine symbolizes His blood poured out ("proclaiming the Lord's death"). The Lord's Supper is also the fellowship meal of the early Church, affirming Jesus' continuing presence among the believers and confirming God's covenant with them; in this mode wine functions as a traditional table drink. Finally, the Lord's Supper looks toward the future. It is the anticipation of the messianic banquet that is to come. At the Last Supper Jesus says, "from now on I shall not drink of the fruit of the vine until the kingdom of God comes" (Lk. 22:18). Eschatological salvation in the kingdom of God is pictured as a banquet or feast (cf. Mt. 8:11; Lk. 13:29f.), and wine is shared with the guests in jubilation. The parables of the marriage feast (Mt. 22:1-14; Lk. 14:7-14) and the great banquet (Lk. 14:15-24) anticipate the festivity of eschatological salvation. Expectations of an eschatological feast celebrated in the Lord's presence (undoubtedly including wine, which was an essential part of feasting in the biblical tradition) appear abundantly in the OT and in later Judaism (Ex. 24:8-11; Isa. 25:6; 65:13; 1 En. 62:14; 2 En. 42:5; 2 Bar. 29:8).

C. Medicinal. Wine was apparently used to revive those who were fainting, for when David was fleeing Absalom, Ziba brought him wine "for those faint in the wilderness" (2 S. 16:1f.). Both oil and wine served as dressings on open wounds (cf. the parable of the good Samaritan, Lk. 10:34). Paul urged Timothy to "use a little wine for the sake of your stomach and your frequent ailments" (1 Tim. 5:23), apparently suggesting that he mix wine with his water to purify it (see I. F above). Jesus was offered wine mixed with myrrh (Mk. 15:23; cf. Mt. 27:34, which changes this to *cholḗ*, "gall," to demonstrate the literal fulfillment of LXX Ps. 68:22 [MT 69:22]) but He refused it, choosing instead to bear the full pain of the cross. The Talmud states that "wine is the greatest of all medicines: where wine is lacking, drugs are necessary" (T.B. *Baba Bathra* 58b).

D. Commercial. Israel's wine became a significant commercial product. As partial payment for Hiram of Tyre's manpower and material assistance in building the temple, Solomon provided twenty thousand baths of wine (2 Ch. 2:10, 15). Wine served as a notable gift (e.g., Melchizedek gave bread and wine to Abram, Gen. 14:18; cf. also 1 S.

25:18) and as tribute to a king (1 Ch. 12:40). According to Rev. 6:5f. the plague of the third seal would destroy all the foodstuffs except wine and oil; but on the day of Babylon's fall wine, along with all the other merchant goods, will go unsold (18:13).

III. In Biblical Imagery.–*A. Blessing.* The Bible uses an abundance of wine as a symbol of blessing from God (Gen. 27:28, 37). The grape harvest and wine making were times of joyous celebration (cf. Isa. 16:10; Jer. 48:33), and the filling and overflowing of the wine vats represented the epitome of rich blessing (Joel 2:24). The fulness of blessing connected with the return from the Babylonian exile was symbolized by the possibility for everyone to "buy wine and milk without money and without price" (Isa. 55:1). In Canticles the sweetness of love is said to be better than wine (1:2, 4; 4:10; 7:9).

B. Judgment. In several passages the images of wine-making jubilation are turned into an expression of judgment. The Lord will roar in judgment from heaven and shout like those who tread the grapes (Jer. 25:30). God's judgment on the wicked will be like the treading of grapes in a winepress (Isa. 63:1-6; Lam. 1:15; Joel 3:13; Rev. 14:18-20; 19:15). The cup of wine in God's hand is a frequent expression of His wrath against Israel and other nations; He forces them to drink from the cup filled with the wine of His wrath, which causes them to stagger (Jer. 25:15f.; cf. Ps. 75:8; Isa. 51:17, 22; Jer. 25:27f.; 49:12; Ezk. 23:31-34; Hab. 2:16; Rev. 14:10; 16:19). The book of Revelation depicts the nations that have entered into illicit relations with Rome as having drunk the "wine of [Babylon's] impure passion" (14:8; 18:3) and the "wine of [Babylon's] fornication" (17:2), which has corrupted them and made them ready for destruction.

See also VINE.

Bibliography.–J. P. Brown, *VT*, 19 (1969), 146-170; A. Demsky, *IEJ*, 22 (1972), 233f.; W. Dommershausen, *Trierer Theologische Zeitschrift*, 84 (1975), 253-260; E. Ferguson, *Restoration Quarterly*, 13 (1970), 141-153; R. J. Forbes, *Studies in Ancient Technology*, III (1955), 70-77; M. Jastrow, *JAOS*, 33 (1913), 180-192; M. H. Pope, "A Divine Banquet at Ugarit," in J. M. Efird, ed., *Use of the OT in the New and Other Essays* (1972), pp. 170-203; S. M. Paul, *IEJ*, 25 (1975), 42-44; A. van Selms, *Journal of North West Semitic Languages*, 3 (1973), 76-84; C. Seltman, *Wine in the Ancient World* (1957).

B. L. BANDSTRA

WINE FAT. *See* WINE PRESS.

WINE PRESS; WINEVAT. Wine presses and winevats were used in the process of wine making. Grapes were harvested in August and September and were spread out for up to fourteen days in the sun to increase their sugar content. The grapes were then placed in a wine press, where they were trodden with bare feet (Isa. 16:10; Jer. 48:33). The time of grape harvest was a time of rejoicing, and grapes were pressed to songs and cries of jubilation (Isa. 16:9f.; Jer. 48:33).

The process of making WINE required at least two vessels, one larger and higher than the other. Archeologists have discovered many of these square or circular pits, which were either hewn out of rock or dug out of the ground and then lined with rocks and sealed with plaster. The upper vessel was the wine press (Heb. *gaṯ*, Neh. 13:15; Isa. 63:2 [AV "wine fat"] Lam. 1:15; Joel 3:13 [MT 4:13], Gk. *lēnós*, Mt. 21:33; Rev. 14:19f.; 19:15; Gk. *hypolḗnion*, Mk. 12:1 [AV "wine fat"]) in which the grapes were placed and trampled. The juice then flowed through a channel or conduit into the lower vessel, the winevat (*yeqeḇ*; the Hebrew term first designates the lower vat, but it can also designate the wine press; cf. Job 24:11; Isa. 16:10). The winevat functioned as a collecting and fermenting container for the must (grape juice). The terms "wine press" and "winevat" are frequently found in association with "threshing floor" (Heb. *gōren*; Nu. 18:27, 30; Dt. 15:14; 16:13; 2 K. 6:27; Hos. 9:2; Joel 2:24); wine and wheat represented two of the chief agricultural products of Palestine. Gideon threshed out his wheat underground in a wine press (*gaṯ*) to hide his activity from marauding Midianites (Jgs. 6:11). Wine presses may also have been used for the production of beaten olive oil (see *WBA*, p. 185).

In the warm climate of Palestine fermentation began almost immediately after the grapes were pressed. The first stage of fermentation took place in the winevat. Then the wine was separated from the LEES (i.e., deposits of dead yeast, tartar crystals, small fragments of grape skins, and other solids that had fallen out of suspension; cf. Ps. 75:8; Isa. 25:6; Jer. 48:11). The wine was strained through a sieve or piece of cloth (cf. Mt. 23:24) before it was put into clay jars (Heb. *neḇel*, Jer. 13:12 or animal skins (*nō'ḏ*, Josh. 9:4, 13; 1 S. 16:20; Gk. *askós*, Mt. 9:17 par.; *see* SKIN) for storage and further fermentation.

Bibliography.–G. Dalman, *Arbeit und Sitte in Palästina*, IV (1935), 291-413; H. F. Lutz, *Viticulture and Brewing in the Ancient Orient* (1922).

B. L. BANDSTRA

WINEVAT. *See* WINE PRESS; VAT.

WINEBIBBER [Heb. *sōḇē' yayyin*] (Prov. 23:20); NEB DRUNKARD. One who is addicted to wine. The proverb warns that excessive drinking leads one to poverty (v. 21). Jesus was falsely accused of being a glutton and a "winebibber" (AV Mt. 11:19 par. Lk. 7:34 [Gk. *oinopótēs*]; RSV "drunkard"; NEB "drinker") because, unlike John the Baptist, He ate and drank with others.

See DRUNKENNESS.

WINESKIN. *See* SKIN.

WING [Heb. *kānāp*]; AV also OVERSPREADING (Dnl. 9:27); NEB also WING-TIP, PINION, TRAIN (Dnl. 9:27), etc.; [*'ēḇer*] (Ps. 55:6 [MT 7]; Isa. 40:31); [*ṣîṣ*] (Jer. 48:9); NEB "warning"; [*pāšaṭ*] ("spread wings," Nah. 3:16); AV "spoil"; NEB SPREAD OUT; [Aram. *gap*] (Dnl. 7:4, 6); [Gk. *ptéryx*] (Mt. 23:37; Lk. 13:34; Rev. 4:8; 9:9; 12:14); supplied by the RSV in 1 Ch. 28:18 and Ezk. 1:11. One of a pair of movable feathered or membranous appendages by means of which a creature (e.g., a bird or insect) may fly.

The term is used frequently in descriptions of symbolic winged creatures such as the CHERUBIM (Ex. 25:20; 37:9; 1 K. 6:24, 27; 2 Ch. 3:11-13; 5:7f.; Ezk. 1:5-25; 10:5, 8, 16, 19, 21; etc.), the SERAPHIM (Isa. 6:2), the "four beasts" of Dnl. 7:3-6, and the "four living creatures" of Rev. 4:6b-8 (*see* CREATURE, LIVING II). Such winged creatures appear frequently in the mythology and monuments of the ancient Near East (*see* Vol. I, Plate 4; picture in CHERUBIM).

The remaining references to wings are also primarily figurative. The wings of the eagle, untiring in flight and capable of carrying heavy burdens, were a favorite symbol of strength, endurance, and speed (e.g., Prov. 23:5; Isa. 40:31; Rev. 12:14; cf. Dt. 28:49; 2 S. 1:23; Job 9:26f.; Ps. 103:5; Jer. 4:13; Ob. 4). The eagle was also renowned for its devotion to its young and its method of teaching them to fly: it will drop one of the young birds from a great height, then swoop underneath to catch the fledgling and carry it on its strong wings. This imagery provided the metaphor of Yahweh carrying the Israelites out of Egypt on eagles' wings (Ex. 19:4; Dt. 32:11). But the eagle's wings can also symbolize destruction: Jer. 48:40 and 49:22

An ivory furniture ornament showing a winged female figure next to a sacred tree. From Arslan Tash, Syria, 9th cent. B.C. (The Metropolitan Museum of Art, Fletcher Fund)

prophesy that an enemy will "spread his wings against" Moab and Edom as an eagle swoops down to seize its prey.

The Psalms speak frequently of finding protection under the "wings" of Yahweh (Ps. 17:8; 36:7 [MT 8]; 57:1 [MT 2]; 61:4 [MT 5]; 63:7 [MT 8]; 91:4; cf. Ruth 2:12). Although a few scholars have sought to relate this image to the wings of the cherubim above the ark of the covenant (e.g., see A. Weiser, *Psalms* [Eng. tr. *OTL*, 1962], pp. 41, 309), the psalmists were more likely comparing God to a mother bird who gathers her chicks under her wings to protect them from danger; cf. Jesus' use of this simile in Mt. 23:37 par. Lk. 13:34.

In Ps. 55:6 (MT 7) the psalmist expresses his wish to escape like a dove, which finds safety in inaccessible precipices. The reference in Ps. 68:13 (MT 14) to "the wings of a dove covered with silver, its pinions with green gold," is enigmatic, and widely divergent interpretations have been suggested (see comms.). The MT of Job 39:13 is obscure; possibly the point is that the ostrich can flap its wings but cannot fly (see comms.).

Several passages poetically refer to Yahweh riding on the "wings of the wind" (2 S. 22:11; Ps. 18:10 [MT 11]; 104:3). Hos. 4:19 uses the metaphor of a wind that has caught the Israelites in its "wings" (i.e., currents) and drives them toward their doom. In Zechariah's vision of the ephah, two women with wings like a stork's are borne along by the wind, Yahweh's agency of movement (Zec. 5:9; see D. L. Petersen, *Haggai and Zechariah 1–8* [*OTL*, 1984], p. 259).

In two passages "wings" seems to refer to the rays of the sun. Ps. 139:9 speaks of "the wings of the morning"—probably a reference to the sun's first rays at dawn (*see* MORNING, WINGS OF THE). Mal. 4:2 (MT 3:20) prophesies that on the day of judgment, "for you who fear my name the sun of righteousness shall arise, with healing in its wings." Many scholars have suggested that the imagery in this verse derives from the winged sun disk that appears on many monuments throughout the ancient Near East as a symbol of the deity's protection (see comms., e.g., *IB*, VI, 1142f.; see also *ANEP*, nos. 355, 653, 705f., 855, etc.).

The expression "upon the wing of abominations" in Dnl. 9:27 is enigmatic. Some scholars, following the LXX and Vulgate, have interpreted "wing" as a wing of the temple; others have understood it as referring to a winged idol; still others have emended the text to read "and instead thereof" or "in their place" rather than "on the wing" (see comms., e.g., *IB*, VI, 498f.).

The description of Cush as a "land of whirring wings" in Isa. 18:1 has also occasioned various interpretations. According to some the expression describes Cush as a land notable for its insects. Another prominent interpretation follows the LXX and Targum in reading "wings" as a reference to ships (cf. the common reference to sails as "wings" by sailors); this view fits well with the context in vv. 1f. (see J. N. Oswalt, *Book of Isaiah: Chapters 1–39* [*NICOT*, 1986], pp. 359f.).

Scholars have disagreed on both the translation and the interpretation of Jer. 48:9. Although *ṣîṣ* came to mean "wing" in later Hebrew, it means "blossom" in biblical Hebrew (KoB, p. 802); moreover, the translation "fly away" in the next line is also dubious. Some scholars have suggested reading *ṣîyûn*, "signpost," in place of *ṣîṣ*, following the LXX (*sēmeía*; see *BHS*; KoB). Others have followed W. L. Moran's suggestion (*Bibl.*, 39 [1958], 69-71), based on Ugaritic evidence, that *ṣîṣ* means "salt"; the verse would then refer to the ancient practice of sowing cities with salt as a sign of their destruction (cf. Jgs. 9:45; see J. Bright, *Jeremiah* [*AB*, 2nd ed. 1984], p. 320; J. A. Thompson, *Book of Jeremiah* [*NICOT*, 1980], pp. 700, 704).

See *TWOT*, I, 446f.

N. J. O.

WINK. *See* GESTURE V.B.

WINNOWING [Heb. *zārâ*] (Ruth 3:2; Isa. 30:24; 41:16; Jer. 4:11; 15:7); AV also FAN; [piel of *zārâ*] (Prov. 20:8, 26; Jer. 51:2); AV SCATTER (AWAY), FAN; NEB also SIFT; [*ben-gōren*–'son of the threshing floor'] (Isa. 21:10); AV "corn of (the) floor'; [Gk. *diaskorpízō*] (Mt. 25:24, 26); NEB SCATTER; **WINNOWER** [Heb. part. of *zārâ*] (Jer. 51:2); AV FANNER; **WINNOWING FORK** [Heb. *mizreh*] (Jer. 15:7); AV FAN; NEB SCATTER; [Gk. *ptýon*] (Mt. 3:12; Lk. 3:17); AV FAN; NEB SHOVEL. The separation of CHAFF and straw from the grain, usually by means of tossing it into the wind. *See* Color Plate 21.

Hebrew *zārâ* could apparently be used for any activity involving scattering to the wind, including the scattering of chaff and straw during the winnowing process. The various contexts suggest that after the grain stalks were threshed, the resulting mixture was winnowed (Isa. 41:15f.). A fork and then a shovel (Isa. 30:24) were used to throw the chaff and grain into the wind, which usually blew strongest in the late afternoon and evening (Ruth 3:2). A time of plenty is described in terms of the cattle being fed winnowed grain (Isa. 30:24). The winnowing process was also used figuratively to picture the judicial function of discriminating between good and evil and destroying what is evil (e.g., Prov. 20:8, 26, Jer. 15:7; 51:2; cf. Mt. 3:12 par.).

Greek *diaskorpízō*, should be translated "scatter" (its usual meaning) in Mt. 25:24, 26, where it refers to the scattering of seed (so NEB).

Modern Arab villagers and bedouin still practice this ancient manner of winnowing at their threshing floors.

See also AGRICULTURE III.A.3; THRESH.

L. G. HERR

WINTER. *See* SEASON.

WINTER HOUSE [Heb. *bêṯ haḥōrep*]; NEB also WINTER APARTMENTS. Either a separate residence used during the cold season, or a heatable room or apartment within a larger building (so KoB, p. 122). Some houses are known to have had two stories, with a heatable lower floor and a cooler roof chamber (cf. Jgs. 3:20). The *bêṯ haḥōrep* used by King Jehoiakim (Jer. 36:22) was located in the palace precinct of Jerusalem and was equipped with a brazier. Very likely the royal palace had an apartment that was specially built and furnished for the cold season (see NEB; Thompson). In Am. 3:15, however, the context suggests separate dwellings for the summer and winter seasons. King Ahab had a second palace in the warmer plain of Jezreel as well as his palace in Samaria (1 K. 21:1), and quite possibly by Amos's time the upper class was also able to enjoy the luxury of two residences.

Bibliography.–J. A. Thompson, *Book of Jeremiah* (*NICOT*, 1980), pp. 626f.; H. W. Wolff, *Joel and Amos* (Eng. tr., *Hermeneia*, 1977), pp. 201f.

N. J. O.

WISDOM. In the Bible the most common, technical terms for wisdom are Heb. *ḥoḵmâ* in the OT and Gk. *sophía* in the NT. Alongside these expressions exists a wide variety of other words and phrases that express the same or related ideas. Because the understanding of these terms changed over time and differed in various sociocultural settings, the semantic field of these terms is not historically constant. For that reason, synonyms and related "wisdom" vocabulary vary throughout the biblical traditions. A full appreciation of the significance of "wisdom" in the Bible depends on a recognition of this historical complexity. At the same time, comprehension of "biblical wisdom" must not lose its peculiar focus on "wisdom" as an essential idiom and as a particular literary manifestation within the composition of Jewish and Christian Scriptures.

I. Wisdom in the Ancient Near East.–Ancient Israelites often borrowed forms of wisdom from non-Israelite sources, through oral and literary interactions with Edom, Egypt, Mesopotamia, and other nations. At present, the only extensive extrabiblical examples of wisdom literature are texts from Egypt and Mesopotamia. Tablets from Ebla may change this picture, but these are not yet available for our consideration (*see* TELL MARDIKH). With large fertile river valleys and prime geographic locations, Egypt and Mesopotamia had numerous economic advantages over Israel. In prosperous times they exercised tremendous political influence, and their cultural standards undoubtedly spread throughout the lesser nations in the Near East. International reputations for wisdom expertise could be attained both by individuals (see Solomon below) and by whole nations, suggesting that despite many variations in what each culture might value as particular manifestations of wisdom, some degree of consensus existed among nations. At a minimum, this internationally recognized wisdom would have comprised technical skills, a general knowledge of the world, and a great facility in the use of proverbs and riddles (*see* PROVERB; RIDDLE).

Despite some conceptual consensus internationally about the nature of wisdom, there is no common linguistic term for "wisdom" throughout the ancient Near East. Substantial differences occur from nation to nation regarding its conception, its social provenance, and its literary manifestation. In Egyptian texts the verbs *š33* and *šbk* parallel the Hebrew conception of wisdom, though *maʿat* most closely resembles *ḥoḵmâ* but with a much wider religious view of truth, order, and justice than in the OT sense of wisdom. In Mesopotamia the stative verb *emequ(m)* and its cognates include the idea of "being wise," like *ḥoḵmâ*, and the term *nemequ(m)* describes a kind of wisdom familiar to gods and humanity. But these terms can also denote the religious inspection of omens and participation in cultic ritual. The voluminous Egyptian wisdom texts reflect only a limited number of genres; conversely, Mesopotamian "wisdom" is associated with a smaller group of extant examples, though they exhibit a much greater variety of literary types. Canaanite-Phoenician wisdom is no longer accessible as part of a specific wisdom literature, though epigraphic survivals demonstrate the use of proverbs and other wisdom types familiar in the biblical tradition.

The most common, extensive literary form of wisdom shared among the nations consisted of "instructions" addressed to "my son" or to "children" from a "father," occasionally including references to the teaching of a mother. The author of this instruction is usually a high political official or the king himself, so that one might conceive the purpose of these lessons to be the formal training of courtiers or administrative advisors. While instructional literature seems to derive from the official schools in both Egypt and Mesopotamia, its lofty prologues present the proverbs as an ideal for the training of children generally, regardless of social status.

A. Egyptian Wisdom. Though we do not have from Egypt a corpus explicitly labeled "wisdom literature," scholars have taken note of several types of school literature that conform generally to the pragmatic, utilitarian character of wisdom. Among this literature we find texts designated as *sebayit* or "teaching." The most prominent examples of this "teaching" are didactic texts that sustained popularity from 2300 to 100 B.C. Intended to provide training in *maʿat* ("order, justice, truth"), these earliest texts of didactic prose and learned sayings, which in later periods contained an increasing number of aphorisms, are usually presented in the form of advice from a prominent official to his son. This pattern corresponded conveniently to the teacher-student relationship in Egyptian scribal schools. Accordingly, the school setting became a surrogate for common education in the home. Some texts, such as *The Instruction of a Man for His Son*, portray vividly the classroom setting of scribes to whom these "teachings" belong as part of their educational resources.

Similarities between Egyptian and biblical wisdom became obvious in the modern period with the discovery of the instructional text of a minor official, Amenemope (probably belonging to the 18th Dynasty). This text, or an oral counterpart, appears to have been the source for

A section of Papyrus Anastasi I: a satirical letter from the scribe Amenemope to the royal official Hori, used as instruction for apprentice scribes (end of the 13th cent. B.C.) (courtesy of the Trustees of the British Museum)

much of Prov. 22:17–23:14 (*ANET,* pp. 421-25). Derived originally from the 13th or 12th cent. B.C., if not earlier, the style corresponds to the father-son pattern of instruction found in Proverbs. The close resonance of a part of Proverbs with this Egyptian text confirms that Israel freely borrowed and adapted wise sayings from other nations in the composition of a distinctly Israelite "wisdom" literature.

Other Egyptian literature designated as "teaching" includes advice specifically directed to scribes. These compositions incorporate essays based on various carefully structured genres, "onomastica" (encyclopedia-like lists of items belonging to the same general class), and polemical texts such as the so-called Satire on the Trades (*ANET,* pp. 432-34). A number of parallels can be found to Israelite wisdom. The partial lists in Prov. 30:15f., 18-20, 24-31 may show familiarity with specific Egyptian onomastica or, at least, with that genre within international wisdom circles. Other "teachings" in the Egyptian schools were of a didactic sort, including sarcastic texts in the form of letters. These texts explored the limits and ironies of life itself. Their tough-minded, even bitter, scrutiny corresponds in many ways to the "skeptical wisdom" of the biblical books Ecclesiastes and Job.

Outside of "teaching" literature, a number of rhetorical exercises, pessimistic treatises, and eloquent discourses have been found that derive from scribal sages. These may reflect a personal or general political despondency, or, as in *The Protests of the Eloquent Peasant* (*ANET,* pp. 407-410), they may contain a critique of social injustices. Whether or not these texts are technically "wisdom" literature, scholars have found in them thematic and stylistic resemblances to Job or Ecclesiastes. The scribal schools seem to have been open to a wide range of genres familiar to Israelite wisdom, though correspondences between these texts and the biblical wisdom traditions remain, at most, partial and sporadic.

B. Mesopotamian Wisdom. Scribal schools in Mesopotamia provided a formal setting for wisdom training, as they did in Egypt; however, an even wider variety of genres might be considered candidates for "wisdom" literature. Instructional literature, like that found in Egyptian and biblical texts, appears from the earliest period until the latest. The oldest known text contains the teaching of a father, Shuruppak, to his son, Ziusudra, the hero of the Sumerian flood epic (*ANET,* pp. 594-96). The most famous example of Mesopotamian wisdom literature is the instructional treatise attributed to a certain AHIKAR, later mentioned in Tobit (1:22; 14:10). His work, allegedly dating from the 8th cent. B.C., circulated widely and in various languages throughout the Near East until well into the Christian period. The famous Ahikar served as a royal adviser under the Assyrian administrations of Sennacherib (704-681) and Esarhaddon (680-669). Proverbs and aphoristic advice in Ahikar's instruction appears to have been a resource for Prov. 23:13f. and 27:3 (*ANET,* pp. 427-430).

Alongside this specific type of literature, there exist numerous collections of proverbs analogous to the biblical Proverbs and a wide variety of religious texts, such as *I Will Praise the Lord of Wisdom* (*ANET,* pp. 434-37), that offer advice to those who suffer. The latter text reminds us that the scribal schools were attached to temples and that wisdom in Mesopotamia was overtly related to worship. Leo Purdue has pursued similar associations between Israelite wisdom and religious observance in the temple. At the very least, a description of Israelite wisdom as "secular" is neither required according to the international evidence nor accurate according to a careful treatment of the book of Proverbs itself.

C. Canaanite-Phoenician Wisdom. Besides the evident contribution of the major southern and northern neighbors to the cultural milieu of Israelite wisdom, we would expect similar exchanges among the nations with Syria-Palestine. Our extant resources for observing this phenomenon are quite limited. Despite the large number of texts from UGARIT (14th-13th cent.), a city located beside the coast of Syria on the Mediterranean Sea, no specifically didactic literature has been found. Nevertheless, a significant number of distinctive words, pairs of words, and formulaic language in Proverbs can be found in the Ugaritic mythological and legendary materials. In the cuneiform AMARNA TABLETS, exchanged in the same period between Egypt and cities in Syria-Palestine, proverbs occur occasionally. Furthermore, scholars have repeatedly pointed to the similarities of ideas and expressions between biblical wisdom and these extant materials. Thus W. F. Albright asserted, "Proverbs teems with isolated Canaanitisms" (p. 9); and H. L. Ginsburg argued that the term *ḥoḵmôṯ*, for personified Wisdom in Prov. 8, is Phoenician, analogous to the title for a deity, *millôṯ* (instead of **milkaṯ*), "Queen." It is likely that much of wisdom was orally borrowed or shared among nations, and that the bulk of the sayings in Proverbs could go back to a time before Solomon. Some of their original aesthetic features and semantic import may well have been forgotten over

An Akkadian tablet inscribed with various proverbs, e.g., "The strong man is fed through the price of his hire, the weak man through the price of his child" (translation from *ANET,* p. 425) (courtesy of the Trustees of the British Museum)

time, only to be revised or "upgraded" later in association with Solomon and his successors.

II. Wisdom in Ancient Israel.–A description of wisdom in Israel during the preexilic period must inevitably rely on critical reconstructions of prebiblical traditions that have been preserved as part of a much later Hebrew Scripture (OT). Through them one can seek to envision life in ancient Israelite society and ponder the changing circumstances through which different understandings of wisdom evolved. For this purpose a convenient distinction can be made among general conceptions of wisdom, wisdom as a learned discipline, and the influence of wisdom upon non-wisdom traditions preserved in the Bible.

A. Essential Characteristics and Historical Development. The most common term for wisdom in the OT, *ḥoḵmâ*, predominately refers to an educated discipline or skillful performance in the world. This term occurs commonly throughout the OT traditions to denote almost any acquired skill or learned craft. It includes an ability in waging war (Isa. 10:13), tailoring (Ex. 28:3), cloth making (Ex. 35:26), metalwork and carpentry (Ex. 31:1-5), navigation at sea (Ps. 107:27), and political administration (Dt. 34:9). *Ḥoḵmâ* may also concern one's level of intelligence; the absence of it explains why the ostrich lacks the common sense expected of other animals (Job 39:17). Conversely, certain prophets and magicians are led astray because of poor judgment (Jer. 47:10; Dnl. 1:4, 17, 20). "Wisdom" is designated as an attribute of God (Job 38:36), the acquisition of some famous persons, and a distinguished asset of some nations. A mundane, practical wisdom (cf. Prov. 10ff.) within Israelite understanding may have preceded in time a more articulate expression of its religious nature (Prov. 1–9). Undoubtedly, some substantial changes in the religious interpretation of wisdom occurred within the history of Israel. Certainly in the exilic and postexilic periods a transformation took place in the relationship of wisdom to the Torah, and eventually in the perception of its relation to other biblical traditions. Occasionally this way of seeking to derive biblical wisdom from scriptural traditions that were not "wisdom" according to either genre or designation is invited by late editorial additions (e.g., Hos. 14:9; Ps. 1; 2 S. 23:1-7). These historical modifications in the understanding of "wisdom" are difficult to recover solely from the book of Proverbs because the sayings in it lack historical references and accentuate their gnomic, universal nature.

At least by the postexilic period, Wisdom became personified both as a preexistent companion of God at creation (cf. Prov. 8:22-31) and as an itinerant female teacher who searches out humanity at the gate and in the city streets with the offer of knowledge, discipline, long life, happiness, success, and wealth (cf. 1:20-33; 8:1ff.; 9:1ff.). Scholars have long debated whether the preexistence of Wisdom implies a true personification, a hypostatic expression of God Himself, or a restructuring in monotheistic terms of an older tradition of Wisdom as a Hebrew goddess. Whatever may be the prehistory behind this presentation in Proverbs, the counterpoint with "a foolish woman" (8:13-18) now suggests the role of a personification. The exact relation of Wisdom to creation in Proverbs remains uncertain. In Prov. 8:29 Wisdom, whom God "created at the beginning of his work" (v. 22), is portrayed either as a "child" or a "craftsman," depending on how one translates the word *'āmôn* (v. 30a). Again, the context, as well as a parallel element in Egyptian goddess speeches, makes the image of a playful child more likely, for she is God's "delight" and "rejoices" before Him (cf. v. 30b). In this portrayal, Wisdom does not appear to help God with the activity of creation, and there is no explicit term for "order," as in the Egyptian or later Hellenistic sense, to explain Wisdom's relation to what God has made. Elsewhere, however, Wisdom is described more explicitly as a participant in creation itself (cf. Job 28:23-28; Prov. 3:19). Wisdom, then, constitutes knowledge and practical expertise that corresponds to the world God has made and, much as the Torah, provides a guide to the obedient life.

A specialized "wisdom" knowledge in Scripture is more than just a naturalistic or humanistic appraisal, for it presumes an awareness of the limits to wisdom in relation to what is revealed elsewhere and the freedom of God to intervene in ordinary affairs (e.g., Prov. 21:30f.). Therefore, the domain within which wisdom finds its crucial place and efficacy in Scripture is circumscribed by an awareness of its own distinctive contribution and its point of departure in "the fear of the Lord" (e.g., Prov. 1:7; 1:27).

B. A Learned Discipline. In various degrees, Israel and Judah thought that they shared a common understanding of "wisdom" with the other nations and that they could compete with their neighbors for recognition in this area. Riddles provided one acceptable test for evaluating a person's sapiential expertise. Solomon's fame as a sage allegedly induced the Queen of Sheba to journey from Egypt for the purpose of verifying his reputation by testing him with riddles (1 K. 10; cf. Prov. 1:6). Similarly, Israelites acknowledged certain specific wise men and women among the Egyptians and the nations to the east (cf. Gen. 41:8; Ex. 7:11; 2 K. 4:30 [MT 5:9f.]; Isa. 19:11-15; Dnl. 2:12ff.). From Israel's perspective, Phoenicia (cf. Zec. 9:2) and Edom (cf. Jer. 49:7; Ob. 8) were centers of wisdom. While fully accepting the international nature of wisdom, Israel retained an awareness of the indigenous religious and political limits to its usefulness. The prophets warn against depending on wisdom alone (cf. Isa. 47:10; Jer. 8:9), acquiescing in foreign wisdom when it leads to apostasy (cf. Jer. 8:9), and trusting in advice apart from a reliance on God's own guarantee of national security (Isa. 31:1-3).

Within Israel itself, regions and persons achieved national reputations according to Israel's own standards of wisdom. The area around Tekoa may have gained such notoriety. It was the home of the "wise woman" whom Joab employed to speak with King David on behalf of Absalom (2 S. 14:2). Perhaps the indication of Amos's home (Am. 1:1) as Tekoa reflects an association of him with a territory known for its expertise in folk wisdom. The outstanding number of sayings or rhetorical expressions typical of wisdom in the book of Amos would support this assumption. Some scholars have speculated that Amos's background in wisdom is an essential component of his prophetic message. (*See* PROPHET III.C.)

Individuals could be elevated in public status nationally because of their demonstrated sagacity. Solomon, the most famous of "the wise" in the Bible, can be compared to "Ethan the Ezrahite, and Heman, Calcol, and Darda, the sons of Mahol" (1 K. 4:31; cf. 1 Ch. 2:6f.). David's adviser Ahithophel had a comparable reputation, for his counsel could be trusted "as if one consulted the oracle of God" (2 S. 16:23). Daniel is presented as one trained in wisdom (Dnl. 1:17), which included an ability to interpret dreams and visions. Elsewhere, Jeremiah seems to describe a distinct social class of "wisemen," alongside "prophets" and "priests" (Jer. 18:18). In the OT, however, no social group of "sages" appears consistently or vividly in connection with formal schools. Throughout the Bible "scribes" are frequently mentioned in a variety of public roles without the necessity that they all belong to a particular official class of "the wise," in contrast to other functionaries.

A major factor in discussing wisdom in ancient Israel turns precisely on how one assesses the existence and activity of scribal or sage schools. The biblical traditions say nothing specific about such schools, in sharp contrast to the many textual references to official education and examples of discursive school texts in the literature from ancient Egypt and Mesopotamia. While limited epigraphic evidence of crude Israelite abecedaries suggests that some kind of formal education may have been pervasive, no archeological attestation of schools or scriptoriums has been discovered from the Israelite period. Proverbs depicts the provenance of wisdom instruction to be the home. Both "mother" and "father" teach their children; we have no reason to assume that references to "father" and "mother" are exclusively employed only as metaphors for professional "teachers" conducting schools outside the home under official sanctions of priest, prince, or king.

Some impressions of official "teachers" outside the home do belong to the later levels of biblical tradition. According to 2 Ch. 17:7-9, five princes, nine Levites, and two priests who were appointed by King Jehoshaphat took the law through various cities and "taught the people." Similarly, the epilogue to Ecclesiastes, though itself probably postexilic, notes that "besides being wise, the Preacher taught the people" (12:9). These instances convey a general public instruction having little or no connection with an official "school." The first unambiguous reference to such a school occurs in a second-century B.C. description of Ben Sira's "house of instruction" (*bêṯ miḏraš;* cf. Sir. 51:23). Here wisdom is recommended as a principal means by which one can engage in a devout "study of the law of the Most High" (39:1ff.). Ben Sira's "house" may be thought of as a "wisdom school" only in the sense that he exploits in a sapiential direction the identification of the written Torah with Wisdom. In other words, wisdom is used hermeneutically as a biblical idiom through which all of Scripture can be interpreted. The result is instruction in the Torah cast in wisdom forms.

In Ben Sira's school most of the present OT was recognized as authoritative Scripture that could be interpreted by means of combining citations and allusions to biblical texts in the style of an anthological midrash. A motivation for its wisdom orientation may have been the need for a religious response to the cultural impact in Palestine of hellenization. Just as ancient wisdom had borrowed from the wisdom of the nations, this hermeneutical form of wisdom exegesis did not hesitate to learn and borrow from extrabiblical resources, ancient and contemporary (19:2-4).

Evidence of the presence of aesthetic rules governing the editing of biblical traditions points to the existence of long-established literary conventions typical of a professional guild of writers/editors. Various titles attached both to whole biblical books and to various internal subsections, topical organization of materials, inner-biblical dislocations and plays upon key motifs, as well as fixed patterns for organizing diverse traditions, all betray self-conscious conformity to laws of beauty and competence among the anonymous editors of biblical traditions. In Prov. 25:1 the phrase "the men of Hezekiah" probably refers to such a professional group. Nevertheless, little information survives about particular scribal guilds, much less any assurance that they were directly related to any formal training in "wisdom."

We can readily imagine a wide variety of formal and informal settings in which people may have learned to read and to write. The imagery of "Wisdom" wandering the streets and calling out at the city gates for disciples may well reflect how itinerant teachers could have summoned children to study with them. Perhaps parents would have paid for such instruction of the young on their behalf, though we have no account of that situation — only the assurance that one should seek to acquire wisdom with money (e.g., Prov. 23:23, 17:16). We might imagine that classes could have been conducted under the shade of a tree or in rooms of a house. Such instruction might have been viewed as an extension of education in the home that is superintended by the father and mother. Hence teachers may have, in fact, gained reputations on an *ad hoc* basis and been recognized loosely as an elite group performing a social service, without maintaining any relation to "official" schools. *See* EDUCATION.

C. Wisdom Influences. Since the 1930's biblical scholars have carried out a programmatic search for wisdom sayings discernible by form-critical methods as well as wisdom themes, elements, features, or orientations in traditionally non-wisdom OT books. Particularly if one relies on the evidence of the practice of wisdom in the ancient Near East and attempts a strictly historical reconstruction of the role of wisdom in Israelite society, then the perception of wisdom's influence outside the corpus of Solomonic books increases. For example, Job appears to be intentionally composed as wisdom literature at many places (esp. Job 28), and wisdom themes seem constitutive of the Joseph story (Gen. 37–50), the Succession Narrative (2 S. 9–1 K. 2), and the book of Esther. Some of the prophets, especially Isaiah and Amos, employ numerous wisdom sayings and what might be called sapiential rhetoric (Isa. 10:15; Am. 3:3-6, 8; 5:13). Conversely, Canticles, though Solomonic in ascription, shows few of these characteristic wisdom features.

Such evidence raises questions about the provenance of wisdom in Israel before the promulgation of "scripture" in the postexilic period. R. N. Whybray, for example, has suggested that "wisdom" in ancient Israel really is the entire intellectual tradition that arises from various places in society. Other scholars, e.g., W. McKane, have sought to define it more narrowly as a learned discipline with a social history, from a preexilic "old wisdom" — empirical, mundane advice in association with state advisers — during the Exile to a later, postexilic "theological wisdom." At times wisdom has been viewed as deriving from groups disillusioned with the failure of prophecy and committed to an alternative "creation humanism," but this view remains highly speculative, suspiciously modern, and, in any case, is without warrant in the present place of wisdom in Jewish and Christian Scripture. In sum, while there is consensus on some basic wisdom forms, scholars lack agreement regarding the definition and role of wisdom in ancient Israelite society. Not every tradition in the Solomonic books (e.g., Canticles) can be considered to be wisdom literature historically; conversely, many non-Solomonic traditions prove historically to be the product of sages or, at least, strongly influenced by them.

III. Wisdom in the OT.–In the earliest period of Jewish interpretation, "wisdom" — as a term derived from Scripture — came to signify a religious construct or idiom comparable to the Torah and the Prophets. Though the Torah is not confined to a religious assessment of the first five books of Scripture, its association with Moses provided a fundamental contextual indication regarding both the nature of the Torah and how other books potentially related to it. Since Moses is portrayed as the prophet par excellence who cannot be superseded by any future prophet (Dt. 34:10), no other prophetic books could threaten the essential content of the Torah. The biblical prophetic books placed after the Torah were subordinated as commentary upon it. As Moses came to be associated with the literary locus of the Torah, so Solomon became linked with a set of "wisdom" books: Proverbs, Ecclesiastes, and Canticles. According to the narrative traditions, Solomon is given an exceptional, divine gift (1 K. 3:12f.) and is presented as the sage par excellence (1 K. 4:29-34; 10:23). This wisdom is not self-sufficient, for it must be accompanied by obedience to the revealed Torah (1 K. 3:14).

The biographical dimension in these two instances cannot be reduced simply to a modern notion of authorship; modern critics have properly questioned whether a historical Moses or Solomon could have actually written all the literature associated with their names. Regardless of how one decides this latter issue, the biographical dimension concerning Moses and Solomon belongs integrally to the canonical context in order to express the form and function of these ancient traditions as part of a larger Scripture. This dimension helps to delimit how diverse ancient traditions came to be read biblically, and, apart from that context, one may legitimately ask whether they should be called "biblical" at all. Hence "biblical wisdom" is not to be uncritically identified with the historical development of wisdom in ancient Israel, for within Scripture it finds its own special, semantically differentiated place in its relation to the Torah and the Prophets. In Scripture the five "books of Moses" now circumscribe the principal witness to the revealed Torah, and the Solomonic books provide the specific locus of "biblical wisdom."

In pre-modern Jewish and Christian interpretation this contextual nature of wisdom in Scripture was recognized in a variety of ways. The Solomonic books were repeatedly called the "didactic books" and interpreted for, among other concerns, their distinctive contribution to "wisdom" in the context of the Torah or the gospel. Rabbinic tradition called each of the three Solomonic books *ḥoḵmâ* and occasionally labeled them collectively as *ḥoḵmâ*, in a tripartite division of Scripture into Torah, Prophets, and Wisdom (cf. *Yalkut Shimeoni Tehillim* 702). Later rabbinic tradition speculated that Solomon wrote Canticles in his youth, Proverbs in his maturity, and Ecclesiastes as a cynical old man (Midr. *Cant. Rabbah* i.1.10). Christianity inherited this contextual orientation toward the Solomonic books. Only in the modern period, when the historical connections between these books and their "authors" came under criticism, did this biblical context of wisdom become lost or depreciated. One need not return to pre-modern interpretations of authorship in order to value these key hermeneutical clues regarding the context of wisdom within the larger claims of Jewish and Christian Scripture.

A. Proverbs. The superscription in Prov. 1:1 is only one of many that attribute parts of the book to various known and unknown authors (30:1; 31:1; 22:17; 31:10ff.). In addition, the notation in 25:1 regarding Solomonic proverbs collected during the time of Hezekiah indicates a complicated tradition history. Prov. 1:1 significantly now introduces the book by highlighting Solomon's historical identity as "the son of David," recalling the narrative traditions in the Deuteronomistic History and attesting to the antiquity of wisdom from the beginning of the monarchy. The international character of wisdom mentioned in 1 Kings is here confirmed by titles assigning portions to sources outside Israel (Prov. 30:1; 31:1). Again, the narrative tradition about wisdom, being complementary but different from obedience to the Torah (1 K. 3:10-14), appears confirmed by the prologue to the book and its description of a goal different from that typical of the Torah (Prov. 1:1-6). Both the Torah and these Solomonic traditions "teach" things integral to the life of the believer. Lest these two guides to the obedient life, Torah and Wisdom, be construed either as alternatives or opposing paths or norms, a biblical editor placed, after the initial prologue and before the first polemical appeal to the readers/hearers, a summarizing statement: "The fear of the Lord is the beginning of knowledge; fools despise wisdom and instruction" (1:7).

According to this orientation of Proverbs, all the wisdom that follows is presented as part of a larger scripture that participates in a common understanding of the "fear of the Lord" (cf. Ex. 20:20; Dt. 31:12f.). Mirroring the narrative about Solomon, the wisdom literature is presented as instruction self-conscious of a distinction between territory belonging essentially to the revealed Torah and the domain more appropriate to wisdom like that shared with the other nations. In the Solomonic books basic features of salvation-history are omitted, while other topics, not directly touched upon by the Mosaic Torah, come into view. At some points there are overlaps, such as the judgment against those who falsify weights and measures (e.g., Prov. 11:1; 16:11; 20:10; cf. Lev. 19:36). Though both the Torah and the Solomonic Proverbs distinguish between the actions of the righteous and the wicked, the wisdom texts treated this pair virtually as a dualism corresponding to the wise and the foolish. Both the wisdom of the teacher and the revealed Law delivered by Moses require obedience, which is a matter of life and death (Prov. 3:1f.; 8:36; cf. Dt. 5:33; 32:47). Traditions in Prov. 1–9 derive from the exilic period or, at least, have been edited in that period to form a religiously explicit prologue to the collections of proverbs in the probably older traditions of Prov. 10ff. The effect is to incorporate fully even proverbs that have been borrowed from international resources into the specific context of a Jewish scripture and into the religious quest of postexilic Judaism.

This transformation of older traditions is registered in Prov. 30:5f., which gives an editorial response to the fundamental question of international wisdom. A sage expresses despair regarding his lack of wisdom and inability to know what only "the Holy One" could comprehend. He asks rhetorically if anyone knows a sage or the son of a sage who really can claim to have grasped wisdom: "Who has ascended to heaven and come down?" (v. 4). Prov. 30:5 responds with quotes from other parts of Scripture, in v. 5 from 2 S. 22:31 (= Ps. 18:30 [MT 31]) and in v. 6a from Dt. 4:2. This answer confirms what is known already about the Torah in Dt. 30:12, "It is not in heaven, that you should say, 'Who will go up for us to heaven, and bring it to us, that we may hear and do it?'" By citing Scripture in affirmation of the revealed "word of God" and its accessible presence among an elect people ("Do not add to his words," v. 6a), the editor answers the question by referring to the Torah and the Prophets. Wisdom is neither something entirely independent of the Torah nor, because God's word has been made available in the Torah and in the Prophets, is it a heavenly object too distant for humanity to affirm and to obey. The same implication is entailed in the song of wisdom in Prov. 8 that relates wisdom to the Genesis traditions solely by claiming that wisdom was preeminent to creation. This contextual ambiguity over exactly how wisdom relates to God's activity at creation, and to the events that follow, naturally became a matter of interest within the later history of Jewish and Christian interpretation.

Consequently, Proverbs shows signs of an intentional

distinction between wisdom and other books of the Torah and the Prophets, combined with a certain acquiescence in the Torah through an acknowledgment of wisdom's limits. Nevertheless, this scriptural context of Proverbs leaves remarkably unharmonized and uninterpreted precisely *how* these different perspectives in Scripture are to be related to each other. If, as some scholars have argued, there are a considerable number of very subtle plays upon other biblical books in Prov. 1–9, then those responsible for such inner-biblical interpretation must have self-consciously sought to avoid any overt and easily recognizable connection between this "wisdom" book and the other biblical traditions. Later conflicts over the interpretation of wisdom within Judaism and Christianity illustrate the options generated, but not simply resolved, by this contextual relationship of understated complementarity within Scripture.

See also PROVERBS, BOOK OF.

B. Ecclesiastes. The voice of this collection is identified by an unusual epithet, a participial form based on the root *qhl* ("call an assembly, gather"). Transliterated "Qohelet(h)," the terminal morpheme *-et(h)* suggests that this term denoted some kind of office. The LXX rendered it *Ekklēsiastēs*, "the one calling an assembly," while in more recent times it has popularly been translated "the Preacher" (Luther). In any case, the superscription ("the son of David") makes an identification with Solomon unequivocal, as do the other internal references in the opening section regarding this person as "surpassing [in wisdom] all who were over Jerusalem before me" (1:16; cf. 1 K. 4:26ff). The formula at the beginning and end of the poetic core — "Vanity of vanities, says the Preacher, all is vanity" — elevates the despair unrelentingly (cf. 1:2 and 12:8). Only in the epilogue do we find a description of the teacher (12:9-11) reminiscent of 1 K. 4:32-34. Just as in Prov. 1:7, a summary is offered that locates this wisdom in the context of the Torah: "The end of the matter. . . . Fear God, and keep his commandments; for this is the whole duty of man" (Eccl. 12:13).

In the talmudic literature this dimension in the prologue and the epilogue of the book proved instrumental in support of its canonicity. Rabbi Judah (A.D. 260-300) argued in the name of Rab (220-250) that it should not be withdrawn from Scripture despite its allegedly contradictory character because "it begins with the words of Torah and it ends with words of Torah" (T.B. *Shabbath* 30b). As with Proverbs, this link between parts of Scripture remains only suggestive and leaves to the history of interpretation any detailed explication. The apparent cynicism within Ecclesiastes, in contrast to the optimistic thrust of Proverbs and the assurances of the Torah, continues to be a matter of debate for scriptural interpretation. At a minimum, a stark vision of daily life blunts the driving edge of optimism based on belief, fantasy, or revelation.

See also ECCLESIASTES.

C. Canticles. The opening title of the book marks it as Solomon's (cf. 8:11). The phrase "Song of Songs" attributes to this song a superlative quality, as the best of Solomon's song compositions. According to the description of his work in 1 K. 3, Solomon's songs "were a thousand and five" (v. 32). Unlike Ecclesiastes, Canticles contains several explicit references to Solomon (e.g., 3:7). At numerous places the song seems to entail the words of both Solomon and his lover, who is described only vaguely as "my bride" (e.g., 4:8) and as a Shulammite woman (6:13). Likewise, the prose description of Solomon in 1 Kings corresponds well with the claim here that "love is strong as death" (8:6). It helps to explain the apostasy of someone so wise. According to 1 K. 11:2, he "clung to these [foreign wives] in love" and idolatry followed. Certainly in the Torah and the Prophets restrictions and prohibitions can be found that presume the strong, irrational powers of erotic love. But only in Canticles do we find a celebration of it as territory not condemned per se and outside the direct address of either the Torah or the Prophets. Just as Dame Wisdom seductively calls to men in Prov. 8, it is left to wisdom to contemplate areas of sexuality that are pertinent to an international appreciation of human love.

In the context of a Solomonic book, the mystery and irrational dimension of love belong positively to the riddle of life that the wise seek to understand and to affirm. The tenacity of erotic human love became within Jewish and Christian interpretation a paradigmatic analogy to explain God's clinging to Israel and Christ's showing undiminished love for the Church. Hence a sapiential knowledge and appreciation of erotic love as a this-worldly gift of creation came to provide by a figural correspondence a source of hope that God's love will not depart from a wayward elect. Once again, the relationship between the prohibitions and restrictions of the Torah and the unbridled celebration of erotic love in Canticles remains a subject provoking much interpretation later. No ethic of sexuality can be found here alone; at the same time, the issues it raises now belong to a larger arena in which wisdom, law, and gospel accompany the interpretation of it as Scripture. The lack of a facile harmonization of this book with others deepens the demand for interpretation of its subject matter, away from a shallow moralistic reading.

See also CANTICLES.

D. Outside the Solomonic Books. The context of Scripture marked out a special place for wisdom in the Solomonic books and, as we have seen, some editorial indicators within these compositions show that the traditions contained in them were read in connection with other parts of Scripture. The implications, from the standpoint of subsequent scriptural interpretation, are threefold. First, in the formation and fixation of a scripture, older, once independent, traditions were put into a specific context with each other and therefore were read in a new and decisive way. A fresh set of criteria arose among religious believers to determine when the sense of a tradition *as part of scripture* is considered explicit, vague, ambiguous, unharmonized, or contradictory.

Second, the context of Hebrew Scripture at a minimum elevated certain idioms — Torah, Prophecy, and Wisdom — as principal expressions for how Scripture could be pragmatically appropriated as a testimony or oracle of God's revelation. Though the definitive locus of each of these idioms pertains most closely to certain sub-collections within Scripture — the Mosaic Pentateuch, the prophetic books, and the Solomonic books — the assumption that the parts of Scripture complemented each other allowed for the possibility of reading all of Scripture through any one of these idioms. Therefore, within Judaism and early Christianity these categories or "hermeneutical constructs" allowed one to read the extra-pentateuchal parts of Scripture as commentary on the Torah (cf. Ps. 1), or to read the Torah (cf. Dt. 4:6) and prophetic texts as sources of wisdom, or to read the Solomonic books as complementary guides to the explication of the legal portions of the Torah or as a source of prophetic hope.

Third, books such as Job, Psalms, or Esther contextually maintained a multivalent character. They could be fully appreciated for their wisdom orientation or interpreted in direct connection with the Torah and the Prophets. Evidence here and there of standard wisdom forms (e.g., proverbs) outside the Solomonic books only confirmed the ability to interpret Scripture through other Scripture in service to the totality of revelation, in terms of Wisdom, Law, and Word of the self-same God. Of course, literature that is form-critically of an ancient Near Eastern wisdom type can often be found in books associated primarily with the Torah or the Prophets, while traditions of originally non-wisdom genres (e.g., the love songs of Canticles) may form part of a biblical "wisdom" book. The semantic import of "Scripture" depends less on this evidence of a retention of pristine forms than on the compositional transformation of them into a new canonical context, in which they attain a new authority and significance for the religious communities that treasure and interpret them as Scripture.

IV. Wisdom Between the Testaments.–The religious understandings regarding wisdom in early Christianity and rabbinic Judaism find rootage in the period prior to the NT. The identification of Wisdom and Torah became a common theme. Most Jewish interpretation viewed the wisdom books as commentary on the Torah. Thus *Pirke Aboth* vi.10 answers the question, How do we know that Torah is one possession? "Because it is written, The Lord possessed me in the beginning of his way, before his works of old" (cf. Prov. 8:22). In the opposite direction, the Torah could be read as commentary on wisdom. For example, the wisdom song of Sir. 24 interprets Dt. 33:4 as support for the claim that "all this is the book of the covenant of the Most High God, the law which Moses commanded" (v. 23). This wisdom song is modeled on Prov. 8, but unlike the latter it interprets the narrative traditions of the Torah so that wisdom is present in the various symbols of the numinous (e.g., the misty cloud at creation, the pillar of cloud, incense in the temple). Interpretation could move in both directions or emphasize one over the other.

Whole books could be modeled after biblical wisdom or directly identified as additional Solomonic books. Both Sirach and the Wisdom of Solomon are based generally on the style of Proverbs. Bar. 3:9–4:4 concentrates on the signficance of wisdom analogous to Sir. 24. 4 Maccabees and Judith are self-consciously "biblical" reflections on wisdom themes or the human dilemma. The Letter of Aristeas, in support of the LXX, contains answers to questions addressed to the seventy sages that suggest sapiential principles. While the conception of wisdom in some of this literature departs from biblical depictions by reflecting a very different Hellenistic, philosophical milieu (e.g., the Wisdom of Solomon), the biblical context of Solomonic wisdom still exercises strong influence on these later attempts to continue or to interpret the biblical tradition under new circumstances. Much of their identity as "wisdom" tradition depended on overt imitation of the Solomonic books in form, style, or content.

V. Wisdom in the NT.–As with the discussion of wisdom in the OT, a consideration of wisdom in the NT involves attention both to the historical understandings of "wisdom" within various periods and to the crystallization of canonical, religious views of wisdom within a Scripture that evokes its own unique postbiblical history of interpretation. In the Greco-Roman world, wisdom as *sophía* occurs as a synonym for "philosophy" generally, or for reasoned rhetoric, occasionally viewed in a pejorative sense by Paul. Among the Stoics the goal of being a *sophós* often reflected an ideal, including skill in divine matters that not every philosopher could attain. Any attempt to describe wisdom in the NT traditions confronts these newer conceptions of wisdom, in addition to the older inheritance of the competing Jewish interpretations of biblical wisdom. "Wisdom" common to the predominate Hellenistic culture could be wedded to indigenous Jewish understandings in a great variety of ways.

A. In the Formation of the NT. Investigations since the 1960's make an impressive case for viewing a "Q" tradition shared by Matthew and Luke, though not Mark, as cast in the genre of the "Words of the Wise" (Prov. 30:1; 31:1). With J. M. Robinson, one might speculate on a long history for this genre that runs from sub-collections within the book of Proverbs, to *Pirke Aboth,* to Q, and finally to the Gnostic Gospel of Thomas, and other orthodox traditions among the rabbis and early Christian fathers. Without giving attention to the passion of Jesus, Q could be viewed as a collection of sayings that stresses Jesus' role as someone, at last, wiser than Solomon (cf. Mt. 12:42; Lk. 11:31). One might contrast this wisdom view of Jesus with the prophetic interpretation in the book of Hebrews that emphasizes Jesus as one greater than Moses, therefore, a bearer of new Torah. If this description of Q is correct, it is significant that this view of Jesus has now been complicated by its incorporation into a presentation of His teaching in connection with His passion, though the ascription of wisdom to Jesus has not been diminished.

Moreover, the Jewish background of debate over the relationship between the Torah and Wisdom in Scripture seems fully reflected in the teachings of Jesus. The Sermon on the Mount, for example, is strongly reminiscent in style and content to sayings in Sirach. At least one major area of conflict between Jesus and the Pharisees may be best understood as a difference in how each related Torah to Wisdom. The Pharisees are portrayed as using wisdom to help in the interpretation of the legal portions of the Torah, while Jesus appears to assess the essence of the Torah in terms of wisdomic revelation rather than Halakic or legal deliberation. In other words, if Pharisees read wisdom as commentary on the Torah, Jesus seems to do the reverse. Of course, Jesus' teaching also exceeds the normal bounds of the usual biblical interpretation since He speaks as one claiming direct and special revelation from God.

From the standpoint of the OT, numerous motifs and forms of wisdom can be detected in the NT. The parables and sayings of Jesus might be viewed in this light. Aphorisms found in collections occur at various places (e.g., Mt. 5–7; Rom. 12; James), as well as succinct treatises on the obedient life (e.g., He. 3:12-19; 4:11-13; 6:1-12b; Jas. 2–3). Though neither the Gospel of John nor the Johannine Epistles employ the term "wisdom," many scholars have suggested that a Jewish wisdom understanding may lie behind the Johannine prologue (Jn. 1:1-5). In both cases "Wisdom" and "the Word" are described as preexistent and, consequently, able to be related to the first acts of God at creation.

In the Pauline and "Deutero-Pauline" Epistles wisdom constitutes a key motif. Among these texts, 1 Cor. 1:10–4:21 represents the only systematic treatment on the subject of wisdom in the Pauline corpus, providing part of Paul's polemical defense of himself as the Corinthians' true teacher. While many scholars agree that a key matter of dispute turns on the nature of wisdom and its relationship to the cross, H. Conzelmann proposed that Paul was the founder of a "wisdom school" from which the subsequent "Deutero-Pauline" traditions derive. Reminiscent of the "father-son" metaphor for the teacher-student relationship in OT wisdom literature, Paul addresses the Corinthians as "my beloved children." While acknowledging that they have "countless guides," he argues that these are not "many fathers" because: "I became your father in

Christ Jesus through the gospel" (1 Cor. 4:14f.). The pattern of the argument parallels in a number of respects the Jewish wisdom homily of Bar. 3:9–4:4 with wisdom no longer manifested by the Torah but by the crucified Christ (1 Cor. 1:23f., 30). Paul's disputations seem to view Hellenistic "worldly wisdom" as ineffective because it either lacks or assumes an inadequate place for the cross. Nevertheless, by advocating a hidden "divine wisdom" revealed in the cross, Paul appears to share a Jewish-Hellenistic tradition that thinks of wisdom as once belonging to creation, and later removed from the world to become inaccessible due to humanity's rejection of it (Sir. 1:20-32; 1 En. 42:1-3; 84:3). For some Jewish interpreters this hidden wisdom remains accessible only through the revealed Torah (Sir. 24; Bar. 3:9; 4:2) or becomes available again only when the righteous and the elect diligently seek it (Wisd. 7:24-27f.; cf. also Sir. 1:10, 15; 6:20-22).

Clearly, for Paul this hidden wisdom of God is revealed in Jesus Christ "whom God made our wisdom" (1 Cor. 1:30). Due to the rejection of divinely given wisdom by humanity (cf. 1:19f.) wisdom had disappeared only to reemerge in the world through the "foolishness" of Jesus' death on the cross (1:27). A contrast is established between the wisdom of the present world and that of a hidden wisdom revealed through Christ (2 Cor. 2:6-8). For the structure of his argument Paul depends on a familiar Jewish debate concerning the accessibility of law and wisdom (cf. Dt. 30:12-14; Bar. 3:9ff.; Rom. 10:6-13; 2 Esd. 4:7-12). Similarly, 1 Cor. 13 might be called a "wisdom discourse," which mentions neither God nor Christ. As Canticles focuses on erotic love, so 1 Cor. 13 propounds an eloquent, didactic statement about "love." Many other cases of wisdom orientation, motifs, or traces have been suggested. The problem in critically judging such evidence is analogous to similar concerns in the investigations of wisdom influence familiar in OT studies.

B. "Wisdom" Books in the NT. Conzelmann has also suggested that Colossians and Ephesians "could almost be characterized as Christian wisdom literature" because of how wisdom is presented as an alternative to misleading "philosophy" (Col. 2:8). This judgment turns more on the topical preoccupation of these letters with wisdom themes than on evidence of distinctive wisdom genres. By far the best candidate for an NT wisdom book remains that of James. It seems to stand conspicuously within the tradition of Jewish wisdom instruction, only twice referring to Christ and composed of a series of independent sayings and short treatises. More than any other NT book, James conforms to the restraints familiar in Jewish wisdom instruction. Like Sirach, James interprets various parts of Scripture in order to explicate biblical wisdom, while avoiding topics more peculiarly central to the Torah, Prophets, or the Christian gospel. This attempt to maintain a place for revealed wisdom informed by but distinct from either law or gospel conforms to the pattern of the Solomonic books in the context of Hebrew Scripture. Like Paul, James distinguishes between a wisdom "from above" and "wisdom" in pagan society that is "earthly, unspiritual, devilish" (3:15). As with the Solomonic books, the absence of "revelatory" claims within this book contributed to some ambiguity about its reception by the Christian Church as a full part of an inspired NT.

VI. Wisdom in the Rabbinic Tradition.–After the destruction of the second temple in A.D. 70 and the events leading to the sharp separation between Judaism and Christianity by the mid-2nd cent., rabbinic Judaism arose with its own distinctive conceptions and forms of wisdom. Without altering the biblical heritage, two new factors played a special role. First, the Pharisees, who had been a minority group in the time of Jesus, emerged as the chief architects of indigenous Judaism. Among the literature attributed to them, there is a surprising lack of proverbial collections reminiscent of biblical wisdom. In their place came midrashic commentary and a talmudic style of religious deliberation. In midrashic commentary and in the early editions of the oral Torah (Mishnah and Talmud), Solomon took on a less celebrated role as a model of wisdom than that of the sages among the Tannaim and their predecessors: Hillel the Elder, Eliezer ben Hyrcanus, Joshua ben Hananiah, Rabbi Meir, and Rabbi Akiba. An antiapocalyptic tendency, perhaps partly in reaction to Christianity, was accompanied by a more practical emphasis on the "Tradition of the Elders." This chain of authoritative instruction allegedly extended back to the time of Ezra and the so-called Council of the Great Synagogue and, according to Jewish beliefs, found its true origin in the passing of oral tradition by Moses to his appointed seventy elders. Precedent for this way of interpreting can be found in pre-Christian Jewish texts, such as *Pirke Aboth*. The importance of this oral tradition diminished the importance of appeals made solely to Scripture and put the weight of Jewish interpretation on the Mosaic Torah, oral and written.

The other factor stems from the enormous impact on the Near East of Greco-Roman culture. The "rabbis" or "sages" in Judaism after the formation of Christianity often sought to emulate famous Greco-Roman thinkers from Socrates to Aristippus. Philo's view that the Solomonic literature lacked divine authority helps to explain his endeavor to find in Abraham and Moses, rather than in Solomon, the primary resources for wisdom rivaling those of the Hellenists. Building on the earlier, postexilic identification of wisdom and Torah, Moses came to be viewed as a sage par excellence. Philo, among others, attributed to the oral teaching of Moses some of the ideas of Plato and Aristotle. While acknowledging the value of international wisdom, the rabbinic sages retained the special relation of the Torah to wisdom. Without the Torah a complete grasp of wisdom was impossible. Just as Christianity linked true wisdom to the gospel revealed only through the crucified Christ, so Judaism believed the ultimate locus of all wisdom to be found only in the revealed Torah.

Prior to the medieval period, rabbinic literature included no large collections of wisdom sayings analogous to Proverbs. In the rabbinic tradition, "wisdom" included knowledge of the oral Torah, biblical interpretations, as well as skills valued commonly in the world. Proverbs, fables, riddles, and other biblical forms of wisdom continued to be used primarily for rhetorical purposes in rabbinic argumentation and homily. In this respect, wisdom's definition had been enlarged to embrace the whole encyclopedia of religious and non-religious knowledge, skill, and diplomacy. Members of the Sanhedrin were considered "sages" — equally versed in Jewish religious lore and in foreign languages, mathematics, zoology, and the philosophical heritage recognized by the contemporary culture. Only in the Middle Ages would the biblical wisdom books of Solomon reassert themselves forcefully as models of divinely given wisdom, though inevitably in close association with the center of Jewish Scripture, the Torah of Moses.

VII. Wisdom in Early Christian Interpretation.–Like Judaism, Christianity valued the Solomonic books as didactic books in Scripture and found in them guidance for an obedient life. When Christianity turned away from the ritual observance of the Torah, biblical wisdom provided an alternative discipline for believers. The content of the gospel, described as secret or hidden wisdom now revealed, was often mediated in the form of collected "sayings" of Jesus or in later collections of wisdom sayings that might include words of Jesus. The Didache (end of the 1st cent.) takes up a Jewish document on the "Two Ways" and gives it a Christian slant. The result is the oldest known proposal for church order, one that is cast in a wisdom framework rather than a legal orientation like that familiar later in canon law. The importance of the role of wisdom in Christianity, again, shows up clearly in the Gnostic interpretations of the Gospel of Thomas and the Dialogue of the Savior. Core traditions in these works may go back to the end of the 1st century. The Dialogue, for instance, includes sayings that seek to detect a deeper, esoteric wisdom resident in some of the words of Jesus. Even when Irenaeus first appropriated from Marcion the idea of a "New Testament" in the 2nd cent., he proposed in addition to the Gospels and the Pauline Epistles a subdivision entitled "the Sayings of the Lord." Undoubtedly the importance of collections of wisdom-like sayings of Jesus early in the history of Christianity helped stimulate later forms of Christian sapiential tradition.

Hellenistic cultural and philosophical traditions strongly colored the development of Christian thought, as they had in Judaism. In the various expressions of Christian wisdom, older biblical conceptions and the newer Greco-Roman philosophical views intermingled. Some church fathers, e.g., Origen and Gregory of Nyssa, were heavily indebted to the Greco-Roman philosophical traditions, while others, e.g., Clement of Alexandria, seemed more constrained to cast their wisdom in familiar biblical forms.

Among the outstanding examples of early Christian wisdom literature is a collection of wise sayings written in Greek from the end of the 2nd cent. known as "The Sentences of Sextus." As with the biblical Proverbs many of these sayings are borrowed verbatim from non-Christian Hellenistic sources, although frequently reworked by a Christian editor. While some of the sayings derive from the NT itself, the name of Jesus is not mentioned. Again, just as the Solomonic books lack key vocabulary indicative of the Torah, despite signs of accommodation to the same, so "The Sentences" lack overt Christian terminology peculiar to the gospel. This type of literature may have met certain apologetic needs, besides offering a selection and orientation of approved wisdom in an awareness of the limits imposed on it by the crucial revelation of the gospel itself. The early debate over the relation of the gospel to Wisdom and Law in Christian traditions and in the context of Scripture provided the specific milieu out of which a later concern with "ethics," "practical" or "pastoral theology," "philosophical theology," and other disciplines arose within the churches.

Bibliography.–W. F. Albright, "Some Canaanite-Phoenician Sources of Hebrew Wisdom," in M. Noth and D. W. Thomas, eds., *Wisdom in Israel and in the Ancient Near East* (*SVT*, 3; 1955), pp. 1-15; W. A. Beardslee, *JAAR*, 35 (1967), 231-240; P. E. Bonnard, *La sagesse en Personne annoncée et venue* (1966); H. Conzelmann, "The Mother of Wisdom," in J. M. Robinson, ed., *The Future of Our Religious Past* (1971), pp. 230-243; *NTS*, 12 (1965/66), 231-244; J. Crenshaw, *OT Wisdom: An Intro.* (1981); J. Crenshaw, ed., *Studies in Ancient Israelite Wisdom* (1976); J. G. Gammie, *et al.*, eds., *Israelite Wisdom: Theological and Literary Essays in Honor of S. Terrien* (1978); K. Hruby, *Bible et Vie Chrétienne*, 76 (1967), 65-78; W. G. Lambert, *Babylonian Wisdom Literature* (1960); B. Lang, *Wisdom and the Book of Proverbs: An Israelite Goddess Redefined* (1986); B. L. Mack, *Logos und Sophia: Untersuchungen zur Weisheittheologie im hellenistischen Judentum* (1973); W. McKane, *Prophets and Wise Men* (*SBT*, 1/44; 1965); D. F. Morgan, *Wisdom in the OT Traditions* (1981); R. E. Murphy, *Wisdom Literature: Job, Proverbs, Ruth, Canticles, Ecclesiastes, Esther* (*FOTL*, 13; 1981); M. Noth and D. W. Thomas, eds., *Wisdom in Israel and in the Ancient Near East* (*SVT*, 3; 1955); L. G. Perdue, *Wisdom and Cult* (1977); G. von Rad, *Wisdom in Israel* (Eng. tr. 1972); H. Ringgren, *Word and Wisdom* (1947); J. M. Robinson and H. Koester, *Trajectories through Early Christianity* (1971); J. C. Rylaarsdam, *Revelation in Jewish Wisdom Literature* (1946); H. H. Schmid, *Wesen und Geschichte der Weisheit: Eine Untersuchung zur Altorientalischen und Israelitischen Weisheitsliteratur* (1966); G. T. Sheppard, *Wisdom as a Hermeneutical Construct: A Study in the Sapientializing of the OT* (*BZAW*, 151; 1980); P. W. Skehan, *Studies in Israelite Poetry and Wisdom* (1971); M. J. Suggs, *Wisdom, Christology, and Law in Matthew's Gospel* (1970); *TDNT*, VII, *s.v.* σοφία κτλ. (Wilckens, Fohrer); R. N. Whybray, *Intellectual Tradition in the OT* (*BZAW*, 135; 1974); U. Wilckens, *Weisheit und Torheit: Eine exegetisch-religionsgeschichtliche Untersuchung zu 1 Kor. 1 und 2* (*Beiträge zur historischen Theologie*, 26; 1959); R. L. Wilken, ed., *Aspects of Wisdom in Judaism and Early Christianity* (1975).

G. T. SHEPPARD

WISDOM, BOOK OF. *See* WISDOM OF SOLOMON.

WISDOM LITERATURE. *See* WISDOM.

WISDOM OF SOLOMON.

I. Name
II. Authorship and Language
III. Provenance and Date
IV. Literary Characteristics and Genre
V. Structure
VI. Message
VII. History of Interpretation and Canonicity
VIII. Text

I. Name.–Due to a long and varied history of interpretation, this book has many different titles. It is known as the "Wisdom of Solomon" in the Greek MSS (*Sophía Salōmōnos* in B; *Sophía Solomōntos* in A and V; *Sophía Salomōntos* in א). It is known in the Syriac Peshitta as the "Book of the Great Wisdom of Solomon, son of David," in Arabic as the "Book of the Wisdom of Solomon, son of King David, who ruled over the children of Israel," and in the *Vetus Latina* as the "Book of Wisdom" (*Liber Sapientiae*). Patristic sources refer to it as "Solomon" or the "Wisdom of Solomon" (Cyprian), or as the "Divine Wisdom" (Clement and Origen).

II. Authorship and Language.–The author is unknown, but he was surely steeped in both the Jewish biblical tradition and Greek philosophical teachings. Pseudonymity was a common characteristic of late postexilic Jewish writing, and this book's central concern with wisdom made Solomon an ideal choice for authorship. It is not clear whether the final author was a member of a wisdom school (as, e.g., Jesus ben Sira); but the book's intentional identification with Solomon, the wisest of kings, would surely have functioned to legitimate its teaching and to secure its place in such wisdom settings.

The uneven character of its content and style has led to much debate about whether the book is the work of a single author or a composite creation. The earlier chapters have often been seen as a translation of a Hebrew original, while the latter chapters have almost always been viewed as an original Greek composition. In the 20th cent. there has been a growing consensus for a single Greek author, with the divisions within the book attributed to the sources and particular concerns of this author. The pervading influence of Greek philosophical teaching and the presence of Greek literary devices throughout the book confirm the premise that it was composed by a Greek writer.

III. Provenance and Date.–Despite the presence of Hebraisms in the text, virtually all commentators locate the place of final composition as Alexandria. The book is, therefore, a sterling example of Hellenistic Jewish writing. An important characteristic of such writing is its mixture of Greek literary style and philosophical teaching with the Jewish biblical tradition.

The book's date is subject to debate. It was surely not written before the 3rd cent. B.C. (cf. the use of the LXX of Isaiah in 2:12 and 15:10) or later than A.D. 50. The two most significant criteria for determining its date are the nature and extent of the Greek thought found within it and the situation of Jewish strife that it presupposes. Given the Alexandrian provenance, Winston has argued persuasively for an early 1st cent. A.D. date; the author is then seen as dependent upon Philo's teaching and as speaking to Jews suffering persecution under Gaius "Caligula" (A.D. 37-41).

IV. Literary Characteristics and Genre.–The Wisdom of Solomon contains many different literary conventions and styles common to both Hebrew and Greek writing of the period. Some of the early poetry uses parallelism (*see* POETRY, HEBREW III) as well as a few Hebraisms (e.g., 1:1; 2:9, 15). On the Greek side there are compound words, iambic or hexameter rhythms, epithets, alliteration, assonance, homoioteleuton, paranomasia, anaphora, and much philosophical terminology (e.g., 6:24; 7:17). Chiasm (e.g., 1:1; 3:15), inclusio (e.g., 1:1-15), antithesis (e.g., 3:5; 4:16), and various forms of exhortation are found throughout the work and are common to both Greek and Hebrew literary traditions. Larger literary forms include comparisons (*synkrisis*; e.g., 11–19), ode (e.g., 10:1-21), diatribe (e.g., 1:4-6; 18:15), and speeches (e.g., 7:1-22a).

Many have characterized the entire work as an exhortatory discourse. While surely such a designation adequately characterizes the book's intention (i.e., to exhort), it does not define its form, which sometimes includes speech forms (e.g., chs. 6–9) as well as extended historical comparisons (e.g., 11:1–12:2). It is difficult, and perhaps unwise, to place the entire work under the rubric of one genre.

V. Structure.–The book is divided into three major sections: (1) wisdom and immortality (1:1–5:23), (2) Solomon's quest for wisdom (6:1–9:18), and (3) wisdom and history (10:1–19:22). This threefold structure reflects the author's general concerns, although commentators have made several subdivisions.

The first major section (1:1–5:23) commends wisdom and its attributes to the righteous. It is characterized by the wisdom tradition's fundamental distinction between the righteous and the wicked and is colored by an eschatological hope for immortality in the light of present oppression.

The second major section (6:1–9:18) highlights the figure of Solomon as a seeker after and obtainer of wisdom. It is characterized by speech forms that exhort others to follow his lead and learn from him.

The structure and intention of the final section (10:1–19:22) are debated by the commentators. This section focuses on the role of wisdom in the history of Israel, giving special attention to the Egyptian experience and drawing contrasts and comparisons between the fortunes of the Egyptians and those of the Israelites. Idolatry receives extended treatment (13:1–15:19).

Although the book's larger divisions and their internal structure are subject to interpretation, its threefold concern to commend wisdom, to see Solomon as a paradigm of the wise, and to emphasize the role of wisdom in history (esp. in Egypt) is compatible with the provenance of the work. The overall intention is clearly to provide for Alexandrian Judaism a historical, philosophical, and theological guide that is firmly grounded in the biblical traditions.

VI. Message.–Any attempt to set forth the major concerns and teachings of this book must keep in mind the interrelationships between the Hebrew and Greek thought contained within it. On the one hand, the author is heir to biblical teaching, especially as mediated through the wisdom traditions (Job, Ecclesiastes, Proverbs, Sirach; *see* WISDOM). The centrality of Torah (even its equation with wisdom; cf. Sir. 24:23-29) and the emphases on the Exodus event, Solomon, and a retributional theological system are all a part of the author's biblical heritage. On the other hand, concerns with the hope for immortality (also present in some late portions of the OT), the soul's relationship to the body, and free will and determinism are all part of the author's Hellenistic heritage. The writer has drawn on both traditions to address a particular people in its own historical situation. The resulting message is a peculiar mixture of past and present, Greek thought and Hebrew thought. While certain characteristics and sources point toward one tradition or the other, the two traditions are often incapable of being separated.

The most central theme in the entire book is the concept of wisdom. Wisdom is portrayed as something separable from human beings but capable of dwelling in the righteous (e.g., 6:12-16). Under the influence of Greek thought, wisdom is seen as emanating from — but not equated with — God. As in both Hebrew and Egyptian wisdom traditions, wisdom is found in and is responsible for the rhyme and reason of the created order. Although wisdom is not explicitly equated with the teachings and Scriptures of Jewish tradition, the biblical writings are compatible with and reflective of wisdom's teaching (cf. 6:4, 9; 11:1). Study and careful attention to Scripture are surely one way to attain wisdom, but the ability to reason and understand is no more important than prayer and the recognition of wisdom's source. For this writer wisdom is the source of understanding but also an elusive, unattainable characteristic of God.

Combined with this focus is an eschatological hope that those who trust in wisdom will receive immortality despite the suffering of the present age (e.g., 4:16–5:23). Such a teaching reflects the influence of the Greek hope for an afterlife as well as that of the Hebraic apocalyptic visions current in other Hellenistic Jewish literature (cf., e.g., Enoch). For the Jewish wisdom tradition in which this author stood, such an eschatological emphasis was new. Most earlier sages had emphasized the present rewards of following wisdom; Ecclesiastes had even disparaged any hope of future reward for being righteous or wise. In his desperate situation the author of this work developed new ways of understanding the character of wisdom, thereby creating an appeal to the righteous that goes beyond the traditions of the past while still affirming their basic ethical teachings.

While the righteous may have to wait for their ultimate reward, the history of Israel provides a clear perspective on their present plight and their appropriate response to it. The emphasis on the Egyptian experience is explainable not only in terms of the author's Alexandrian setting but also because it is the saving event par excellence in the Torah, central to all Jews. This wisdom teacher makes no radical separation between this age and the next; in spite of his eschatology, the past and present remain primary in ascertaining the will and action of God, who has "not neglected to help [the Israelites] at all times and in all places" (19:22).

The author continues in the mainstream of the Jewish wisdom tradition by affirming a long-standing "two ways" retributional theology. Despite appearances, God rewards the righteous and punishes the evil; the history of the Jews confirms this judgment. For those who gain wisdom, the actions of personified wisdom in the created order assure the right results. While the author is surely not nationalistic or chauvinistic, the teachings of the Jewish tradition are a primary source for such a conception of God. Although he sometimes uses Greek philosophical teaching to complement the message of books such as Ecclesiastes or Job, which raise radical questions about God's justice and mercy, this author finally stands within the mainstream of the sages as found in Proverbs and Sirach.

VII. History of Interpretation and Canonicity.–As a Jew steeped in the biblical tradition and in Greek thought, the author of the Wisdom of Solomon sought to present a picture of wisdom and Jewish history that would provide both comfort in present trials and direction for the future. The resultant message was ultimately not acceptable to mainstream Palestinian Judaism, but the way that it relates past teaching to present need is characteristic of all Jewish and Christian teaching to the present day.

The book was used extensively by the early Church, although its formal place in the Roman Catholic and Orthodox canon was not official until the Council of Trent (1545-1563) and the synod of Jerusalem (1672). Because it characterizes wisdom as emanation and closely connects it with the *lógos* concept, the book lends itself easily to christological readings.

Although the Reformers excluded it from the canon, the book continues to have an important status in some Protestant Churches, as witnessed by its presence in the lectionary cycle. Whether "inspired" in the fullest sense or not, the Wisdom of Solomon contains an interpretation of wisdom and the biblical tradition that repays careful study with important insights into contemporary issues and the nature of God.

VIII. Text.–The basic critical text of the Wisdom of Solomon is found in the Göttingen version of the LXX (1962). The most important Greek MSS are A B C א and V. Several other Greek MSS contain fragments of the text, and Syriac, Arabic, and Latin versions are also valuable for textual criticism.

Bibliography.–Comms. on the Wisdom of Solomon, including A. Calmet, *Comm. littéral sur le livre de la Sagesse* (1713); C. L. W. Grimm, *Das Buch der Weisheit* (1860); J. Fichtner, *Weisheit Salomos* (1938); J. Reider, *Book of Wisdom* (1957); E. G. Clarke, *Wisdom of Solomon* (*CBC*, 1973); D. Winston, *Wisdom of Solomon* (*AB*, 1979); J. M. Reese, *Book of Wisdom, Song of Songs* (1983). See also the standard introductions.

D. F. MORGAN

WISE. *See* WISDOM.

WISE MEN (OT). The international character of wisdom is well established. Much of Israel's own wisdom literature could easily cross national boundaries and find close parallels in the literatures of Egypt and Mesopotamia. The biblical corpus itself gives evidence that Israel knew of foreign wise men and valued their insights. Job of Uz is generally considered non-Israelite, as are Agur and Lemuel, whose wisdom is recorded in Prov. 30–31. It has long been noted that Prov. 22:17–23:18 owes considerable debt to the Teaching of Amenemope of Egypt (*see* PROVERBS I.C). It was therefore possible for an Israelite to be initiated into the intricacies of foreign wisdom and to excel in its practice without condemnation (e.g., Daniel and his friends in the book of Daniel, and Moses according to Acts 7:22). Where foreign wisdom and wise men failed according to biblical critique was in their refusal to recognize or to acknowledge YHWH as the source of true knowledge. "[Foreign wise men] are both stupid and foolish; the instruction of idols is but wood!" (Jer. 10:8). "I am the Lord . . . who frustrates the omens of liars, and makes fools of diviners; who turns wise men back, and makes their knowledge foolish" (Isa. 44:24f.). Foreign wise men most often appear in contexts of competition in which this negative critique is clearly expressed through their inability to compete with the Israelite wise man who is aware of the source of his knowledge (Gen. 41:8; Ex. 7:11; Dnl. 2:27; 5:15). Lack of knowledge of YHWH leads these wise men into association with magic, divination, and astrology, practices condemned by Israel and God (Dt. 18:9-14).

For the wise men of Mt. 2, *see* WISE MEN (NT).

G. H. W.

WISE MEN (NT) [Gk. *mágoi*] (Mt. 2:1, 7, 16); NEB ASTROLOGERS. An indeterminate number of individuals who saw an unusual astronomical phenomenon, and journeyed from the east to Jerusalem to worship the newborn king of the Jews (Mt. 2:1f.).

I. Greek and Persian Background.–According to Herodotus, *mágoi* were members of a Persian priestly caste who specialized in astrology, interpretation of dreams, and magic (i.101, 107, 120; iii.65, 73, 79; vii.19, 37, 113). In a more general sense, a *mágos* in the Hellenistic world had supernatural knowledge and ability and was sometimes a practitioner of magic (Philo *De specialibus legibus* iii.101) or an interpreter of dreams (Josephus *Ant.* x.10.2 [195]; x.10.6 [216]).

II. Jewish and OT Background.–In rabbinic literature a *mágos* is usually a magician (*SB,* I, 76). In the LXX the "enchanters" or "necromancers" (Heb. *'aššāp*/Aram. *'ašāp*) of Dnl. 2:2, 10 are called *mágoi.* Of special significance is the second-century A.D. translation of Theodotion, which uses *mágos* to translate *'aššāp/'ašāp* in Dnl. 1:20; 2:2, 10, 27; 4:7; 5:7, 11, 15.

Astrology was prevalent throughout the ancient world and, despite the OT condemnation of its practice, affected Judaism to some degree. Josephus mentioned stars on the veil of the temple (*BJ* v.5.4 [214]), and numerous synagogue excavations have turned up the sign of the zodiac (*see* picture in ASTROLOGY). Aramaic fragments of an astrological treatise have been found in Qumrân Cave 4. Thus the wise men and their experience would have been tremendously significant to Matthew and his readers, especially because Nu. 24:17, ". . . a star shall come forth out of Jacob," was being interpreted messianically by the rabbis (cf. Tgs.).

The name chosen by the leader of the Jewish uprising in A.D. 130-135 also illustrates this interest. Bar Kosba (which probably means "son of a young ram") changed his name to Bar Cochba, "son of the star" (cf. W. F. Albright and C. F. Mann, *Matthew* [*AB,* 1971], p. 15). When his "messianic" mission failed, the rabbis called him Bar Kosiba ("son of the lie").

III. In the NT.–Apart from Mt. 2 *mágoi* are mentioned only twice in the NT; a man named Simon amazed the Samaritans with his works (*mágeia;* Acts, 8:9-11); and on Cyprus Paul confronted Elymas (Bar-Jesus) the *mágos* (13:6). Both of these men are pictured as deceivers and charlatans.

In contrast to the *mágoi* in Acts, the visitors in Mt. 2 are presented with approval. They understood the implications of the star and acted appropriately, coming with gifts and worshiping the child. Two details seem to suggest that as much as two years had passed since the birth of Jesus. First, Herod questioned the wise men about when the star had appeared (v. 7) and then ordered the

A fresco in one of the rock churches in Göreme in Cappodocia (Turkey) depicting the three wise men, late 5th-7th cent. A.D. (B. Van Elderen)

slaughter of all the children in the Bethlehem region who were two years and under, "according to the time which he had ascertained from the wise men" (v. 16). Second, at the time of the visit the family of Joseph was living in a house (vv. 10f.). Herod may only have been giving himself a margin of safety, but certainly the visitors from the east arrived appreciably after Jesus' birth (cf. the wording of v. 2). *See also* INNOCENTS, MASSACRE OF THE.

The wise men's interest in the Messiah may well have arisen from contact with the Jewish exiles in the east and from knowledge of the OT. Several OT passages foreshadow these events, although Matthew does not mention them. The Messiah is a star who will come forth out of Jacob (Nu. 24:17); the nations shall come to His light and kings to the brightness of His rising (Isa. 60:3). Kings are to come worshiping and bearing gifts (Ps. 68:29 [MT 30]; 72:10-15; Isa. 60:6). The notion that the wise men were kings rests upon an inference from these passages, and that there were three of them rests upon the number of gifts — gold, frankincense, and myrrh. There is no unanimity in the tradition about their number, however; it has been represented as anywhere from two to twelve. By "from the east" (2:1) Matthew probably meant that they came from Persia or Mesopotamia, although Arabia is also a possiblity. It is not explicitly stated that they were Gentiles, and attempts to name them (e.g., Gaspar, MELCHIOR, and Balthasar) rest upon legends.

W. W. BUEHLER

WISH. In only a few instances in the RSV OT does "wish" translate a specific Hebrew term of that meaning. "Wish" represents the verb *ḥāpēṣ* ("want, desire") in Dt. 25:7f.; Job 9:3, and the cognate noun *ḥēpeṣ* in 1 K. 5:9 (MT 24). The noun *nepeš* ("breath," "life," "desire") carries a similar force in Dt. 23:24 (MT 25), where *kᵉnapšᵉḵā* (lit. "according to your desire") is rendered "as you wish." In 1 S. 2:16 "you wish" represents *napšeḵā* ("your soul," "your desire") with the piel of *ʾāwâ* ("crave"). In Job 37:20 the RSV translates *ʾāmar* ("say") by "wish."

Elsewhere in the RSV OT "wish" represents no particular Hebrew term. Sometimes it is used in translating idiomatic expressions: Heb. *lû*, a particle expressing a wish or prayer, is rendered "I wish" in Nu. 22:29, and *mah-llāḵ* (lit. "what to you?") is translated "what do you wish?" in Josh. 15:18 par. Jgs. 1:14. More often "wish to" is supplied to convey the sense of certain verbal forms. In Lev. 27:13, 19, 31 the infinitive absolute of *gāʾal* ("redeem") together with the imperfect is rendered "wish to redeem." In vv. 15 and 20 this phrase is used simply to convey the sense of continuing action indicated by the imperfect tense of *gāʾal;* since the process of redeeming involves negotiation and an uncertain outcome, it is natural in English to say that one "wishes" to redeem it. Similarly, the context indicates that "wish to offer" is an appropriate translation of *ʿāśâ* ("make," "prepare") in Nu. 15:14, and that "wish to become" is the intended meaning of the part. of *hāwâ* ("become") in Neh. 6:6.

The situation is quite different in the NT. Here the Greek verb *thélō* ("will, wish") lies behind nineteen of the thirty-two occurrences of "wish" (Mt. 7:12 par. Lk. 6:31; Mk. 6:22; Jn. 12:21; Acts 25:9; 1 Cor. 7:7, 36, 39; etc.), and the nearly synonymous verb *boúlomai* (which in older Greek meant to "plan") accounts for nine more occurrences (Mk. 15:15; Acts 17:20; 18:27; 19:30; Jas. 4:4; 2 Pet. 3:9; etc.). The verb *zētéō* ("seek," "desire") is rendered "wish" once (Jn. 4:27).

In Rom. 9:3 the RSV uses "wish" to render *eúchomai,* which is better translated in its usual sense of "pray" (so NEB). Precisely when Paul is making profoundly clear his concern for his fellow Jews and his willingness to give up his own salvation on their behalf, the strength of *eúchomai* needs to be retained (for a discussion of the problems of translating this phrase, see C. E. B. Cranfield, *ICC* on Romans [1979, repr. 1983], II, 454-57). The form *óphelon* functions as a particle expressing a wish ("would that"). Used with the imperfect indicative, as in 2 Cor. 11:1, it expresses an unattainable wish (BDF §359). When used with the future indicative it expresses an attainable wish (BDF §384); so strong were Paul's feelings against those who were preaching the necessity of circumcision that he expressed the sarcastic wish that they would mutilate themselves (Gal. 5:12).

See also DESIRE.

Bibliography.–TDOT, V, *s.v.* "ḥāpaṣ" (F. Maas, G. J. Botterweck); *TDNT,* I, *s.v.* βούλομαι (G. Schrenk); III, *s.v.* θέλω (G. Schrenk).

G. CHAMBERLAIN N. J. O.

WIST. *See* WIT.

WIT; WITTY; UNWITTINGLY. The verb "to wit" in the AV is interchangeable with "to know" and is conjugated with a present "wot" and a past "wist." This inflection is derived from more complicated forms in the older English, and in post-Elizabethan times it has become quite obsolete (but cf. the roots in "wisdom," "witness"). The noun "wit," then, means simply "knowledge," and "witty" is "having knowledge," although the noun and the adjective have acquired more narrowly specialized uses in modern English. Even in Elizabethan English, however, the indicative of "to wit" was becoming displaced by "know," and "wot" and "wist" together occur only twenty-four times in the AV (not at all in the AV Apocrypha). The infinitive "to wit" is still in use (chiefly in legal formulas) before an apposition, and the AV has supplied it rather frequently to clarify a construction (e.g., Josh. 17:1; 1 K. 2:32); the RSV has not retained it. In the two instances where the AV uses this infinitive to translate Heb. *yāḏaʿ* the RSV has replaced it with "to learn" (Gen. 24:21) and "to know" (Ex. 2:4). The very obsolete expression in 2 Cor. 8:1, AV, "We do you to wit" (i.e., "We cause you to know"), has become in the RSV "We want you to know."

The noun "wit" occurs in the RSV only at Ps. 107:27 in the phrase "at their wits' end," translating Heb. *ḥoḵmâ,* "wisdom," "technical skill." The phrase means "their skilled seamanship cannot cope with the danger." The AV also uses "wit" in 1 Esd. 4:26 (Gk. *diánoia,* "mind");

2 Esd. 5:9 (Lat. *sensus,* here "intelligence"); Sir. 31:20 (Gk. *psyché,* "soul," with the force of "reason").

"Witty" does not occur in the RSV, but the AV uses it in three passages: in Prov. 8:12 it uses "witty inventions" to translate Heb. *meẓimmâ,* "discretion" (so RSV); in Jth. 11:23 it has the phrase "witty [Gk. *agathós,* "good"] in thy words," probably meaning "you have spoken sound sense"; and in Wisd. 8:19 it has "witty child" (RSV "a child . . . well endowed"; Gk. *euphuḗs,* "well grown," "of a good disposition," "clever"). The AV uses the adverb "wittingly" in Gen. 48:14, interpreting Heb. *śāḵal* as belonging to a root meaning "act intelligently"; the RSV ("cross") interprets it as belonging to a different root meaning "exchange," "cross."

The RSV uses the adverb "unwittingly" to translate Heb. *šegāgâ* ("sin of inadvertance") in Lev. 4:2, 22, 27; 5:15, 18; Nu. 15:24-29 (AV usually "through ignorance"), the piel of *šāgâ* in Lev. 4:13 (RSV "commit sin unwittingly"; AV "sin through ignorance"), and *biḇlî ḏaʿaṯ* (lit. "without knowledge") in Josh. 20:3, 5. All these passages refer to sins or crimes committed inadvertently. Although OT law viewed inadvertent wrongdoings as less serious than those committed deliberately (cf. Josh. 20:2-6), it did not exuse them. Inadvertent sins were seen as incurring guilt, and a sacrifice was required before they could be forgiven (Lev. 4–5; Nu. 15:22-29). They were clearly distinguished, however, from sins committed "with a high hand" (v. 30), i.e., deliberately; for such sins there was no sacrifice and no atonement. *See also* IGNORANCE.

B. S. EASTON
N. J. O.

WITCHCRAFT, PRACTICE (Lev. 19:26). *See* MAGIC II.A.(5).

WITHER; WITHERED (AWAY) [Heb. *yāḇēš*] (Job 8:12; Ps. 90:6; 102:4, 11 [MT 5, 12]; 129:6; Isa. 15:6; 40:7f., 24; Jer. 12:4; Ezk. 17:9, 10; 19:12; Joel 1:12; Am. 1:2; 4:7; Jonah 4:7; Zec. 11:17); AV also CLEAN DRIED UP; NEB also PARCHED, SHRIVELLED, BLIGHTED, IS DESPERATE, IS DRIED UP; [Heb. *nāḇēl*] (Ps. 1:3; 37:2; Isa. 1:30; 24:4; Jer. 8:13; Ezk. 47:12); AV also FADE (AWAY); NEB also FADE; [Heb. *šāḵaḥ*] (Ps. 137:5); AV FORGET; [Heb. *nāpal*–'fall'] (Prov. 11:28); AV FALL; NEB "is riding for a fall"; [Heb. *nāmal*] (Job 14:2; 18:16; 24:24); AV BE CUT DOWN/OFF; NEB also BE LAID LOW; [Heb. hithpolel of *mûl*] (Ps. 58:7 [MT 8]); AV CUT IN PIECES; [Heb. *ṣānam*] (Gen. 41:23); NEB SHRIVELLED; [Heb. *qāmal*] (Isa. 33:9); AV HEWN DOWN; NEB CRUMBLING; [Gk. *xēraínō*] (Mt. 13:6; 21:19, 20; Mk. 3:1, 3; 4:6; 11:20f.; Lk. 8:6; Jn. 15:6; Jas. 1:11; 1 Pet. 1:24); AV also DRIED UP; [Gk. *xērós*] (Mt. 12:10; Lk. 6:6, 8).

The principal words translated "wither" or "wither away," Heb. *yāḇēš* and Gk. *xēraínō,* refer to both the wilting of plants which have not received enough water and to the paralysis of human limbs resulting from various conditions (including 1 K. 13:4; RSV, AV "dried up"; NEB "paralysed"). The former is most often mentioned as a figure of speech for the expected result of wickedness (Job 8:12; Ps. 129:6; Ezk. 17:9f.; 19:12; Am. 1:2; Jn. 15:6; cf. Mt. 13:6 par.), for human suffering in general (Ps. 90:6; 102:4, 11 [MT 5, 12]), or for what is temporary in contrast to what is permanent (Isa. 40:8, 24; Jas. 1:11; 1 Pet. 1:24). It is also mentioned as a literal result of wickedness (Jer. 12:4; Am. 4:7). *Yāḇēš* appears three times in Joel 1:12 (RSV has "fails" for the third; NEB paraphrases "none make merry"). The curse in Zec. 11:17 mentions paralysis together with blindness in one eye, which might suggest posterior spinal sclerosis (*see* DISEASE III.C). The hand of the man healed by Jesus in a synagogue (Mt. 12:9-14 par. Mk. 3:1-6; Lk. 6:6-11) may have been shrunken by an affliction such as anterior poliomyelitis (*see* DISEASE IV.B).

Because Nah. 1:4b must begin with *d* in order to take its place in the incomplete acrostic poem that begins with v. 2, suggested replacements for *'umlal,* "fade" (which may be duplicated from the end of the verse in place of an original word which has dropped out), include *dā'aḇ,* "mourn," *duḵ'û,* "are crushed," and *dallû,* "are dried up," "are brought low" (so *BH*). The last of these may be the basis of RSV "wither." AV follows MT with "languisheth" in both the third and fourth clauses of the verse (NEB "languish" and "wither" in these two clauses). LXX *ōligṓthē* can be considered evidence for the correctness of *'umal.*

R. K. HARRISON
J. W. S.

WITHS (Jgs. 16:7-9, AV). *See* BOWSTRINGS, FRESH.

WITNESS. A noun and verb used by the RSV almost two hundred times in reference to attestation of a fact or event by a human or divine being or by an inanimate object. Heb. *ʿēḏ* and cognates (e.g., *ʿûḏ, ʿēḏûṯ, ʿēḏâ*) and Gk. *mártys* and cognates (e.g., *martyréō, martyría, martýrion*) underlie most of the uses.

The Pentateuch contains the greatest number of OT references to witnesses or testimony in forensic matters. False witness is forbidden (Ex. 20:16; 23:1; Dt. 5:20; cf. Prov. 6:19; 19:5, 9; 21:28; 25:18); it is to be punished according to the law of retaliation (Dt. 19:16-21). A flagrant instance of false witness is Jezebel's action against Naboth (1 K. 21:10-13). Those who are witnesses but refuse, after an official summons, to testify are culpable (Lev. 5:1; cf. Prov. 29:24). The practice of requiring two or three witnesses to establish evidence is enjoined in Dt. 19:15 (cf. 17:6; Mt. 18:16; Jn. 8:17; 2 Cor. 13:1; 1 Tim. 5:19; He. 10:28). In the absence of human witnesses, God might be called upon to attest an agreement (Gen. 31:50; cf. 1 S. 20:12; *see* COVENANT [OT]). The witnesses against persons indicted of capital crimes were required to take the leading role in the execution (Dt. 17:7; cf. Jn. 8:7; Acts 7:58), thereby demonstrating their confidence in their own testimony. Ex. 23:7 voices a strong warning against false charges in capital cases. When a person was condemned to be stoned, all the witnesses were first required to lay their hands on the head of the condemned (Lev. 24:14). Mark's account of Jesus' trial (Mk. 14:56-60) suggests that the tribunal disregarded the principle of invalidating contradictory evidence. Other NT references to witness in judicial matters include Mt. 18:16; 26:60, 65 par.; Acts 6:13; 7:58; 2 Cor. 13:1; 1 Tim. 5:19.

Biblical terms for witness are also used in a variety of contexts outside the public legal forum. A tone of uncommon solemnity pervades the narrative when God is invoked as witness. The divine witness may be either affirmative (1 S. 12:5; cf. He. 11:4) or negative (Jer. 29:23; 42:5; Mic. 1:2). Paul frequently called on God to attest his deportment and attitudes (Rom. 1:9; 2 Cor. 1:23; Phil. 1:8; 1 Thess. 2:5). God (or the Holy Spirit) authenticates the mission of Jesus (Jn. 5:37, etc.; 1 Jn. 5:7-9) and affirms the people of God (Acts 15:8 [referring to the Gentiles]; Rom. 8:16; He. 2:4; 10:15; 11:4). Jesus also attested Himself (Jn. 3:11, 32; 8:13f.) and His own word of grace (Acts 14:3). He testified about what He knew and had seen (Jn. 3:11), i.e., the Father's character and purpose (cf. Rev. 1:5, 9). John the Baptist bore witness to the messianic "light" (Jn. 1:7) and to the "truth" (5:33). The people could testify that

John did not lay claim to messianic credentials (3:28). The crowd attested Jesus' raising of Lazarus (12:17), and the disciples witnessed His entire ministry (15:27). An eyewitness testified that blood and water came out of Jesus' side (19:35; cf. 21:24). Many witnessed Timothy's instruction by Paul, according to 2 Tim. 2:2. Perhaps on the same occasion Timothy made a "good confession in the presence of many witnesses" (1 Tim. 6:12). Tit. 1:12f. cites a Cretan author who indicts his own islanders.

Benefactors and administrators in the Greco-Roman world sometimes received commendation for their services. Permission to honor them might come in answer to testimonials by a grateful public. Similarly, in the NT God, Jesus, and leading figures in the Christian communities receive adulation for their character and performance (cf. 3 Jn. 12). The apostles proclaimed the gospel on the basis of Jesus' words and deeds, with special reference to His death and resurrection (Lk. 24:48; Acts 1:22; 3:15; 5:32; 10:39; 26:16; cf. 1 Pet. 5:1). According to He. 12:1 the saints are a "cloud of witnesses" who attest God's faithfulness in the face of a variety of perils. Paul calls on his readers for a character reference in 1 Thess. 2:10 (cf. Acts 26:5); in turn, he commends his readers in Gal. 4:15, and Epaphras in Col. 4:13.

Inanimate things can also serve as witnesses, especially in cultures that do not depend primarily on written documents as evidence for a transaction. A heap of stones serves Laban and Jacob (Gen. 31:48, 52; cf. Abraham's seven ewe-lambs, 21:30). Other impersonal witnesses include a song (Dt. 31:19, 21), an altar (Josh. 22:27f., 34), a pillar (Isa. 19:19f.), Jesus' works (Jn. 5:36), the Scriptures (Dt. 31:26; Jn. 5:39), and the "tent of witness" (Acts 7:44; Rev. 15:5).

The use of Gk. *mártys* (RSV "witness") in Acts 22:20 (of Stephen) and Rev. 2:13 (of Antipas; cf. 11:3) in connection with testimony that imperils a witness prepares the way for the more specific denotation of the transliterated term "martyr" (so AV; cf. Rev. 17:6). *See* MARTYR.

See also TESTIMONY.

Bibliography.–F. W. Danker, *Benefactor: Epigraphic Study of a Graeco-Roman and NT Semantic Field* (1982), pp. 442-47; *DNTT,* III, 1038-1051; *TDNT,* III, *s.v.* μάρτυς κτλ. (H. Strathmann); A. A. Trites, *NT Concept of Witness* (1977). F. W. DANKER

WITNESS OF THE SPIRIT. ***I. Biblical Usage.***–The phrase "witness of the Spirit" does not occur in Scripture, but three NT passages speak of the Spirit bearing witness. Jn. 15:26 states that the Counselor, as the Spirit of truth, has the function of testifying to Jesus in the sense of speaking about Him (cf. 16:14). The following verse then associates the disciples' witness with that of the Spirit. Acts 1:8 is a parallel, for although this does not refer to the Spirit's witness, it is when the disciples receive the Spirit's power that they are to become witnesses to Christ, so that the force of their testimony depends on the operation of the Spirit.

The statements in 1 Jn. 5:7ff. are similar to those in Jn. 15:26f. After referring to Christ, who came by water and blood (v. 6), the author describes the Spirit as a witness, a reliable witness because the Spirit is truth (v. 7). To meet the demand for more than one witness, three are mentioned: the Spirit, the water, and the blood (v. 8). This threefold witness, being divine, surpasses human testimony: "this is the testimony of God that he has borne witness to his Son" (v. 9). The faith that responds to this witness of the Spirit, or of God, carries with it an inner testimony, an assurance that the witness is indeed true (v. 10), for in faith God's people have eternal life in Christ, the giving of which is the content of the testimony (v. 11).

Paul's thinking runs along similar lines when he makes perhaps the most familiar reference to the witness of the Spirit in Rom. 8:16. He is arguing that Christians are no longer slaves. Led by the Spirit, they are the children of God, crying "Abba, Father" (v. 15). The Spirit bears witness with our spirit to this new status (v. 16). Exactly what Paul meant has given rise to much discussion, reflected in the different renderings. He certainly cannot have taught that the Spirit confirms a general impression of the human spirit that all people are God's children. But does the Spirit merely corroborate what the believer's spirit already knows, or does He bear the witness that is the basis of that knowledge, making possible the crying to God as Father? The comms. of both Cranfield (*ICC,* 1975) and Murray (*NICNT,* repr. 1973) insist with some cogency that the real force of the verb is "witness to," the believer being enabled to address God as Father only because the Spirit bears witness to this truth in the gospel and its promises. Translations like the RSV which closely link the cry to the Spirit's witness tend in this direction inasmuch as it is only in and by the Spirit that the believer can make the cry, just as it is only by the Spirit that he or she can say "Jesus is Lord" (1 Cor. 12:3). Both Barrett (*HNTC,* 1957) and Käsemann (*Comm. on Romans* [Eng. tr., 1980]) find here a liturgical context, suggested by the word "cry." Impelled by the Spirit, and possibly in response to the reading and preaching of the Word, the believer invokes or acclaims God as Father, possibly in the Lord's Prayer, but possibly in Spirit-directed prayer (Barrett) or in a shout of acclamation (Käsemann). True worship of the Father is worship in the Spirit (Jn. 4:24), so that a link between liturgical expression and the Spirit's witness has much to commend it, avoiding as it does the danger of misleading subjectivism.

In sum, the Spirit's witness in the NT is witness to Christ, in whom God grants believers eternal life as His children. Accepting this witness, and therefore knowing the truth of God's promises, believers have inner assurance of their acceptance by God. They are thus bold to call upon Him or to acclaim Him as Father in an outward expression of their inner confidence. In the gospel of Christ the Spirit says to the believer: "Thou art God's child," and in faith the believer confidently replies to God in the Spirit, both inwardly in the heart and outwardly with the lips: "Thou art my Father."

II. Historical.–A special use of the phrase "witness of the Spirit" developed in Reformation and post-Reformation theology. It related specifically to the authenticity of canonical Scripture, the reliability of its promises, and the unique authority of its teaching. Zwingli prepared the way with his stress on the illuminating ministry of the Spirit (*LCC,* XXV, 75, 82). Calvin worked out the thought with a more direct reference to the Spirit's witness, sometimes described as "inward," as the only sure basis of confidence that Scripture is God's Word. Human arguments, for Calvin, could serve as "useful aids," but the Word would find acceptance only as "sealed by the inward testimony of the Spirit" (*Inst.* i.7.4). Naturally Calvin had in view not merely intellectual acceptance but a "saving knowledge" which could rest only on the "inward persuasion of the Holy Spirit," who gives "the chief and highest testimony" (i.8.13).

Reformed confessions quickly followed Calvin's lead, the Gallican referring to the Spirit's "testimony and inward illumination" (Art. IV) and the Belgic to the Spirit's witness in the heart (Art. V). Later theologians, both Lutheran and

Reformed, maintained this stress on the Spirit's witness as the ultimate basis of confidence in Scripture and its promises, though attaching more weight to indications or criteria in reply to objections. The Westminster Confession gave a fine summary of the doctrine when it spoke of the "inward work of the Holy Spirit bearing witness in and with the Word in our hearts" (I, v).

In later centuries rationalist attacks tended to push the appeal to the Spirit's witness into the background, especially as it came to be equated increasingly with an unsubstantiated feeling or experience, but Barth revitalized the Reformation teaching in the 20th cent., boldly claiming that he found here, not the Achilles' heel of the Protestant system as D. F. Strauss had alleged, but "its indestructible strength" (*CD,* I/2, 537).

The charge of subjectivism gains force from the fact that the modern stress on religious experience tends to merge the Spirit's witness into an inner feeling or intuition. The biblical texts are sometimes taken in this way, and the Reformation use of the word "inward" can also lend itself to this understanding. In Scripture, however, the Spirit's witness clearly differs from the believer's self-witness, and the Reformers saw plainly that although the Spirit does an inward work by bringing God's Word and its truth home to believers, both He and His witness are external to believers. Far from being the same thing as the believers' persuasion, the Spirit's witness is the basis of this persuasion, inward insofar as it involves personal application, outward insofar as it is a work of God Himself in and through His Word.

A second problem that became acute with the literary and historical criticism of Scripture is that this witness provides no obvious protection against the undermining of the Bible's authority by the discovery of apparent mistakes, contradictions, and dubious authorships. If the claim is to hold up that the Bible is God's Word, are not convincing explanations needed? Can the Spirit's witness be anything more than confirmation after solid evidence is produced or a temporary prop until it is? The Reformers, of course, had no doubt that Scripture demonstrates its unique character even at the human level, and they could appreciate the need to respond to critical objections. They also saw, however, that considerations of this kind, though they might demonstrate the uniqueness of the Bible, do not alone establish it as God's Word. Furthermore, they believed firmly that to receive the Spirit's witness is to know beyond question that Scripture is God's Word, so that difficulties at the human level will not cause undue alarm. First and last the authenticity of the Bible rests, not on the ability of believers to resolve difficulties, but on the Spirit's own attestation of the truth of its message.

A final and more radical objection to the Reformation doctrine is that it has itself no obvious biblical basis. Neither John, 1 John, nor Romans refers to the authenticating of Scripture by the Spirit's witness. The Reformers might advocate Scripture as a norm, but they offered little biblical support for their specialized use of the phrase "witness of the Spirit." They did not do so, however, because they regarded the matter as self-evident. Commenting on Jn. 15:26, Calvin found a reference to "the inward and secret testimony of the Spirit," and added that "he retains and settles our faith in Him [Christ] alone," and "wherever He speaks, He frees men's minds from all doubt and fear of deception" (Comm. on John, Eng. tr., *ad loc.*). But how does the Spirit speak? He speaks in and by the written Word which He Himself inspired, and in the spoken Word for which He empowered the disciples. This Word carries the promises on which the self-witness of believers rests, along with the assurance with which they can call upon God as Father. Giving this divine witness by the Word, the Spirit does not merely speak words. He gives the weight of divine authority to the words, so that, taught by Him, believers know them to be the Word of the living God who fulfilled His promises in the incarnate, crucified, and risen Son. Thus the witness of the Spirit, with which the apostolic witness is associated and which underlies the self-witness spoken of in 1 John and the assurance of adoption spoken of in Romans, has as such the irrefutable force of testimony to Scripture as God's Word, definitively establishing for believers its authenticity and authority. The Spirit's witness is naturally and necessarily a witness to Scripture inasmuch as it provides it with the supreme proof, "that God in person speaks in it" (*Inst.* i.7.4), God being Himself "the sole and proper witness of himself" (i.11.1; cf. Hilary *De trinitate* i.18).

G. W. BROMILEY

WITTY. *See* WIT.

WIZARD. *See* MEDIUM.

WOE [Heb. *ʾôy* (Nu. 21:29; 1 S. 4:7f.; Prov. 23:29; etc.), *ʾôyâ* (Ps. 120:5), *hôy* (Isa. 5:8, 11, 18, 20-22; 10:1; 28:1; etc.; Jer. 22:13; 23:1; etc.), *hî* (Ezk. 2:10), *ʾalᵉlay* (Job 10:15; Mic. 7:1); Gk. *ouaí* (Mt. 11:21 par.; 18:7 par.; 23:13-16, 23-29 par.; 26:24 par.; Lk. 6:24-26; 1 Cor. 9:16; Jude 11; Rev. 8:13; 9:12; etc.)]; NEB also ALAS, TOO LATE!, SHAME, OH, AH, TROUBLE, etc. An interjection expressing great distress or sorrow; or a noun signifying a condition of deep suffering due to a calamity that has befallen or will befall a person or community.

The term is used frequently by the prophets in oracles of judgment against cities (e.g., Jer. 13:27; Ezk. 24:6, 9; Zeph. 3:1; Nah. 3:1; cf. Mt. 11:21 par. Lk. 10:13), nations (e.g., Jer. 48:46; Zeph. 2:5; cf. Nu. 21:29), erring spiritual leaders (e.g., Jer. 23:1; Ezk. 13:3; cf. Mt. 23:13-30 par. Lk. 11:42-52), and other classes of people who have forsaken God and His law (e.g., Isa. 3:11; 5:8, 11, 18, 20-22; 10:1; 29:15; 30:1; 45:9f.; Jer. 22:13; Ezk. 13:18; 16:23; Hos. 7:13; Am. 6:1, 4; Mic. 2:1; Hab. 2:9, 12, 15, 19; cf. Lk. 6:24-26). Sometimes the interjection is used to express one's own grief or despair (e.g., 1 S. 4:7f.; Ps. 120:5; Isa. 6:5; Jer. 4:13, 31; 6:4; 10:19; 15:10; Lam. 5:16; cf. 1 Cor. 9:16).

In Rev. 8:13; 9:12; 11:14 the term is a classification of punishments that will be inflicted upon the earth's inhabitants (*see* REVELATION, BOOK OF IV.C). Similar end-time catastrophes, commonly called "messianic woes," are mentioned frequently in Jewish apocalyptic literature (e.g., 2 Esd. 4:51–5:13, 18, etc.; 2 Bar. 24; 27:1–29:8; 1 En. 80:2, etc.; 94:6, etc.; 95:4, etc.; 99:11, etc.).

G. WYPER
N. J. O.

WOLF [Heb. *zᵉʾēḇ* (e.g., Gen. 49:27; Isa. 11:6); Gk. *lýkos* (e.g., Sir. 13:17; Mt. 7:15)]; cf. also Heb. *zᵉʾēḇ* as the proper name of a Midianite chieftain ("Zeeb," Jgs. 7:25; 8:3; Ps. 83:11 [MT 12]). A member of the family of predatory mammals known as *Canidae*, larger than the related JACKAL and all but a few breeds of dogs. Known for their savagery and voracity, wolves hunt either singly or in packs.

The European wolf (*Canis lupus lupus*) was native to ancient Palestine and was a scourge to the flocks that pastured in the hill country. Although the Bible recounts no incidents directly involving wolves, it makes ample use of the imagery of wolves falling upon flocks or devouring their prey. Thus, Jacob's blessing likens the tribe of Ben-

A gold and electrum wolf's head from Tepe Gawra, *ca.* 3200 B.C. (courtesy of the University Museum, University of Pennsylvania)

jamin to "a ravenous wolf, in the morning devouring the prey, and at even dividing the spoil" (Gen. 49:27). Jeremiah prophesied that because of Judah's unfaithfulness and immorality, "a lion from the forest shall slay them, a wolf from the desert shall destroy them" (Jer. 5:6). Ezekiel likened the rulers in Jerusalem to "wolves tearing the prey, shedding blood, destroying lives to get dishonest gain" (Ezk. 22:27). Similarly, Zephaniah wrote of Jerusalem that "her judges are evening wolves that leave nothing till the morning" (Zeph. 3:3), referring to the wolf's habit of lying low until dusk, when it begins its prowl (cf. also Hab. 1:8), as well as to its tendency to gorge itself.

2 Esdras 5:18 introduces the motif of the irresponsible leader described as a "shepherd who leaves his flock in the power of cruel wolves." Jesus also used this metaphor, contrasting Himself, the "good shepherd [who] lays down his life for the sheep" (Jn. 10:11), with the hireling, who "sees the wolf coming and leaves the sheep and flees; and the wolf snatches them and scatters them" (v. 12). Jesus also described false prophets (probably the messianic pretenders who arose in first-century Judea) as "ravenous wolves" who came to believers in sheep's clothing (Mt. 7:15). Paul likewise referred to the false teachers who would descend upon his churches after his departure as "fierce wolves [that] will come in among you, not sparing the flock" (Acts 20:29). Both Mt. 10:16 and Lk. 10:3 preserve the tradition of Jesus sending forth His apostles "as sheep/lambs in the midst of wolves" — a figure that suggests the perils they could expect to encounter on their mission.

Finally, as a sign of the peace and security of the messianic age, Isa. 11:6 reverses the image of the wolf devouring the sheep: "The wolf shall dwell with the lamb." This theme is echoed in 65:25: "The wolf and the lamb shall feed together, the lion shall eat straw like the ox." Both passages look forward to an end of the predation of stronger animals on the weaker and a return to the vegetarian order of creation (cf. Gen. 1:30).

D. G. SCHLEY

WOMAN.

- I. Terminology
- II. Background
  - A. Israel's Neighbors until 323 B.C.
  - B. Hellenistic Age
- III. In the OT and Apocrypha
  - A. General Attitudes
  - B. Marriage, Divorce, and Sexual Role
  - C. Women in the Religious Life of Israel
  - D. Women as Leaders in Society
  - E. Woman as a Theological Symbol
- IV. In Later Judaism
- V. In the NT
  - A. Attitudes toward Women and Their Religious Role
    1. Evangelists
    2. Jesus
    3. Acts
    4. Pauline Epistles
    5. Other NT Writings
  - B. Marriage and Divorce
  - C. Woman as a Theological Symbol
- VI. Later Developments
- VII. Conclusion

***I. Terminology.**–A. Hebrew.* The most common term is *ʾiššâ* (occurring about 775 times), which is used for (a) "woman" without regard to age or marital status; (b) "wife" or "bride"; (c) female animals. Its meaning can be made specific by an accompanying noun in apposition (e.g., *ʾiššâ zônâ,* "harlot" [Josh. 2:1; Jgs. 11:1; etc.], *ʾiššâ ʾalmānâ,* "widow" [2 S. 14:5; 1 K. 17:9; etc.], *ʾiššâ pîlegeš,* "concubine" [Jgs. 19:1], *ʾiššâ neḇîʾâ,* "prophetess" [Jgs. 4:4]) or by a qualifying adjective or participle (e.g., *ʾiššâ zārâ,* "strange [i.e., loose] woman" [Prov. 2:16; etc.], *ʾiššâ menāʾāpeṯ,* "adulteress" [Prov. 30:20], *ʾiššâ mêneqeṯ,* "wet nurse" [Ex. 2:7]). The noun *neqēḇâ,* "female," occurs where contrast with "male" is specially required (e.g., Gen. 1:27; 5:2).

Hebrew also has many specific terms for women of different ages and functions, notably *beṯûlâ, naʿarâ,* and *ʿalmâ* ("young woman," "virgin"), *ʾēm* ("mother"), *malkâ* ("queen"), *ʾāmâ* and *šipḥâ* ("female slave"). *Baṯ* ("daughter") is used as a term of kindly address (e.g., Ruth 3:10), for women of a particular city or people (e.g., Isa. 3:16, "daughters of Zion"), and for women more generally (e.g., Isa. 32:9). Heb. *ʾāḥôṯ* ("sister") may be a term of endearment (Cant. 4:9; etc.).

B. Greek. In the LXX *gynḗ* regularly translates *ʾiššâ.* In the NT it occurs about 225 times for "woman" or "wife," sometimes ambiguously (e.g., 1 Cor. 9:5; 1 Tim. 3:11). Lk. 4:26 uses *gynḗ* with *chḗra* ("widow") Hebraistically; usually distinct terms are used for women of different ages and marital status, e.g., *parthénos* ("virgin"), *doúlē* and *paidískē* ("female slave"), *nýmphē* ("bride"), *thygátēr* ("daughter"), *mḗtēr* ("mother"), *pórnē* ("prostitute"), *mathḗtria* ("woman disciple," Acts 9:36), *prophḗtis* ("prophetess," Lk. 2:36; Rev. 2:20). For many functions one term serves for both sexes, e.g., *país* ("child"), *diákonos* ("servant," "deacon"). *Adelphoí* ("brothers"), when used of Christian believers, may include women, although *adelphḗ* ("sister") occurs occasionally for a woman believer. Where both male and female persons are involved, Greek grammatical usage demands the masculine form. In 2 Tim. 3:6 the diminutive *gynaikárion* occurs with the sense "foolish woman."

See also DAUGHTER; FEMALE; MAID; MOTHER; RELATIONSHIPS, FAMILY; VIRGIN; WIDOW.

***II. Background.**–A. Israel's Neighbors until 323 B.C.* Nowhere in the ancient Mediterranean or Near East were women accorded the freedom that they enjoy in modern Western society. The general pattern was one of subordination of women to men, just as slaves were subordinate to the free, and young to old. Women's life centered on marriage, children, and the home. Domestic tasks were time-consuming, involving spinning, weaving, fetch-

A Phoenician pottery figurine of a pregnant woman, from Akhzir, 8th cent. B.C. (courtesy, Israel Department of Antiquities and Museums)

ing water, grinding corn, baking bread, washing clothes, care of children, etc. Women also worked in the fields or produced goods for sale in the home; in wealthy families they supervised female slaves.

Male children were more highly esteemed than female, and baby girls were sometimes left to die by exposure. Boys received a better education than their sisters. Marriages were generally arranged, with girls being betrothed to husbands older than themselves, thus perpetuating the pattern of subordination. Various forms of dowry were used. Polyandry (plurality of husbands) is attested in early Sumer; polygyny (plurality of wives) occurred in some classes in the Old Assyrian and Old Babylonian periods, and in Middle Kingdom Egypt. Assyrian and Persian kings regularly had harems. Where monogamy prevailed, the husband had much greater sexual freedom than the wife: in the code of Hammurabi: (*see* HAMMURABI V.C) and the Middle Assyrian Laws he could keep a concubine or resort to prostitutes, but the wife was expected to remain faithful (*ANET,* pp. 171, 181f.); his children by female slaves could be made legal heirs (*ANET,* pp. 173, 183; cf. Gen. 16). At Athens a wife might have to compete for her husband's affection with a *hetaíra* ("companion") and a concubine. In his speech *Katá Neaíras* (122) Demosthenes argued that *hetaírai* were kept for pleasure, concubines (*pallakaí*) for personal service, and wives for the production of legitimate children. In most societies divorce was widespread, operating in favor of the husband. The Middle Assyrian Laws state: "If a seignior wishes to divorce his wife, if it is his will he may give her something; if it is not his will, he need not give her anything; she shall go out empty" (*ANET,* p. 183).

Not all societies permitted women to own property: sometimes women engaged directly in trade, but sometimes they operated only under male "guardianship." The economic rights of women were particularly limited in Classical Athens (see Schaps, *passim*). Descent was reckoned in the male line (Lycia was an exception); frequently women inherited only when male heirs were lacking, and then with restrictions (cf. Nu. 27:7f.). Women had few political rights: in the Athenian democracy they had no vote; in Athens and elsewhere they were excluded from councils of elders and similar bodies. Wives of kings and leading officials sometimes exercised political influence from behind the scenes, however. Hatshepsut, who ruled Egypt in her own right from 1503 to 1482 B.C., was an exception to the general pattern. Other unusually powerful figures include Siptu of Mari, the Hittite queen Puduhepa, Semiramis of Assyria, and Artemisia of Caria.

All of Israel's neighbors were polytheistic, worshiping female as well as male deities. Some cults, especially Egyptian, had only male priests; others had priestesses. Sacred prostitution was common in fertility cults (*see* ASHERAH), but sacral virginity was also known. Religious festivals provided opportunities for women to partake in activities outside the home.

Attitudes toward women varied. The Egyptian *Instruction of Ani* (before 1100 B.C.) urges kindness to both mother and wife (*ANET,* pp. 420f.). Egyptian artistic representations show connubial affection, but women often appear on a smaller scale than men, indicating their lower status. In Attic tragedy women sometimes act with initiative and freedom, but silence and discretion are held up as ideals for them (Sophocles *Ajax* 293; Euripides *Heracleidae* 476). Other sources suggest a low social status for Athenian women: Pericles is reported to have said that the greatest glory for a woman is to be talked of as little as possible (Thucydides ii.45). Aristotle stated that man is by nature superior to woman and more fitted to command (*Pol.* i.2.12f., 5.2). See further *TDNT,* I, 777f.; *IDB* Supp., p. 963.

B. Hellenistic Age. During this period the condition of women seems to have improved. Papyri from Egypt attest marriage contracts where husband and wife are treated equally (see Pomeroy, pp. 127f.). The wives of the Ptolemies were politically powerful (cf. Arsinoe II and Cleopatra VII). Occasionally there were even women magistrates. Women's rights to own and dispose of property increased. At Rome, where women traditionally enjoyed a higher status than at Athens, they were sometimes well educated; satirists lampooned learned women (Juvenal vi.434-456). Some philosophical schools admitted female pupils. A few women acquired great wealth and became public benefactors. But inequalities continued: under Augustan law adultery was a public offense for a woman but not for a man; a father could make his daughter divorce her husband against her will; for many purposes a woman remained under male "guardianship" (see Pomeroy, pp. 149-204, esp. p. 159; Balsdon, esp. pp. 77f.).

III. In the OT and Apocrypha.–*A. General Attitudes.* In the creation narrative of Gen. 1 (ascribed to "P"), man and woman are created equal, both made in God's image and as the crown of creation (note the generic use of "man" [Heb. *hā 'āḏām*] and the plural "them" in 1:26f.). In the narrative of Gen. 2–3 (ascribed to "J") woman is created after man; she first takes the forbidden

A carved ebony head of the consort of Amenophis III, Queen Tiy, a common woman who rose to power (Medinet Habu, *ca.* 1360 B.C.) (Preussischer Kulturbesitz, Ägyptisches Museum)

fruit; both she and the man are cursed — he to toil and she to pain in child-bearing and subjection to her husband. Scholarship has shown that woman's designation as "helper" does not denote inferiority, but rather man's incompleteness without woman; the making of Eve from Adam's rib symbolizes their essential unity. The woman's subjection *describes* rather than *prescribes* the role of women after the fall (cf. J. C. L. Gibson, *Genesis,* I [1981], esp. 118). Nevertheless, the second creation account was used in later Judaism to support the principle of female subjection to men and to condemn woman as the first sinner (Sir. 25:24; Life of Adam and Eve; see IV and V.A.4 below; but cf. 1 Cor. 15:22, where Paul wrote: "in Adam all die").

The OT documents were composed over many hundred years, and attitudes naturally changed and developed. They were all, apparently, written by men, and all (except parts of Canticles) from a male viewpoint, as can be seen, e.g., in the wording of the Decalogue (Ex. 20:17; Dt. 5:21) and of certain Psalms (e.g., 1:1; 127:5; 128:3). It should be remembered that the OT books were written for a specific theological purpose and were not designed to give future generations a complete picture of the role of women. Their evidence is therefore both complex and partial; they suggest, however, that women faced increasing restrictions on their public and religious roles as the law became codified and as the Jerusalem temple cult evolved.

At all periods of Israel's history women were legally subject to men, as they were in the ancient world generally. They were valued chiefly as wives and mothers. Prov. 31:10-31 paints a vivid picture of the ideal wife (AV "virtuous woman"): while her wisdom, charm, kindness, and fear of the Lord are all mentioned, prime emphasis is on her industriousness and on the credit and profit she brings to her husband (see also Prov. 18:22; 19:14; Sir. 7:19; 26:1-4). Apart from industriousness, the qualities most frequently admired in women are beauty, quietness ("a silent wife is a gift of the Lord," Sir. 26:14), modesty, shrewdness, marital fidelity, and fecundity. Abigail is praised for her intelligence and good sense (1 S. 25:3, 32; contrast her husband's behavior), and Judith for her wisdom and piety (Jth. 8:8, 28-31). Women are prominent in the patriarchal narratives, in some of the early historical books, and in writings named after them (Ruth, Esther, Judith, Susanna). They are least sympathetically portrayed in the Prophets, which compare weak men to women (e.g., Isa. 19:16; Jer. 51:30; Nah. 3:13) and strongly condemn extravagant, drunken, and wanton women (e.g., Am. 4:1; Isa. 3:16ff.), and in wisdom literature, both canonical (e.g., Prov. 9:13; 21:9, 19; 27:15; Eccl. 7:26) and apocryphal. Negative sentiments are particularly common in Ben Sirach (e.g., 25:16-26; 26:6-12; 42:9-14). (See also Nunally-Cox; J. G. Williams.)

B. Marriage, Divorce, and Sexual Role. Israelite society was strongly patriarchal. A woman was always under the authority of a man, initially her father and later her husband, who was known as her *baʿal* or "lord." A young woman's father could sell her into a form of slavery (Ex. 21:7), although not into prostitution (Lev. 19:29). Her father or husband could annul her vows (Nu. 30:3-15). Jephthah acted legally when he sacrificed his own daughter to fulfil a vow (Jgs. 11). To protect his male guests, Lot offered his unmarried daughters for the sexual pleasure of strangers (Gen. 19:8); a Levite's concubine died after continual sexual abuse in similar circumstances (Jgs. 19:1-26). Abraham drove Hagar out into the desert, and she was saved from death only by divine intervention (Gen. 21).

Throughout OT times polygyny and concubinage were legal. Solomon reputedly had seven hundred wives and three hundred concubines. Bigamy was practiced by ordinary people and frequently caused tension (1 S. 1:6; Dt. 21:15-17; cf. Gen. 30). Marriages were arranged, the groom's father paying a bride price or marriage present (Heb. *mōhar*) to the bride's father (e.g., Gen. 34:12); occasionally it is mentioned that a parting-gift or dowry (*šillûḥîm*) was given by the bride's father (e.g., 1 K. 9:16). Tob. 7:14 refers to a written contract (Gk. *syngraphē*; cf. the Heb. *keṯûḇâ* of rabbinic Judaism).

Women captured in war could be treated as wives and were protected from subsequent sale as slaves (Dt. 21:10-14). But intermarriage with foreign women was discouraged because it might lead to idolatry (e.g., Ezr. 9:14); Ruth the Moabitess provided an exceptional example of fidelity. Levirate marriage (known also among Assyrians, Hittites, Hurrians, and in parts of Greece) provided for widows (*see* MARRIAGE IV.A.2); the woman had no right to refuse her brother-in-law, but he could reject her. Judith was exceptional in that she refrained from remarriage and was able to retain her own property (Jth. 16:21-23).

Deuteronomic legislation permitted a man to divorce his wife if he found something "indecent" in her (Dt. 24:1); she could not, however, divorce him. In cases of adultery both partners were liable to death by stoning (Lev. 20:10; Dt. 22:22). A husband who suspected his wife of adultery could subject her to a humiliating ordeal (Nu. 5:11-31; cf. *ANET,* pp. 171, 181); but no reciprocal right existed for her, and she received no compensation if proved innocent. The apocryphal story of Susanna is remarkable for relating the vindication of an innocent woman. The penalty for raping an unbetrothed virgin was that the man had to marry the woman and pay a fine to her father (Dt. 22:28f.). A betrothed virgin who was raped was presumed innocent only if the attack occurred in the country where she could not summon help (Dt. 22:23-27). Prostitution was condemned for Israelite women (Lev. 19:29), but harlotry is frequently mentioned, suggesting that it was fairly common. Tamar, the daughter-in-law of Jacob, may have disguised herself as a cult-prostitute (Gen. 38:14f.). *See* HARLOT.

The OT never denigrates the physical aspect of marriage, nor does it extol the ideal of perpetual virginity; it warmly appreciates married love (Prov. 5:18f.; Eccl. 9:9). Isaac's love for Rebekah and Jacob's love for Rachel are sympathetically portrayed (Gen. 24:67; 29:20, 30); Michal's love for David is also mentioned (1 S. 18:20f.). Canticles bears eloquent witness to the joy of heterosexual love; the woman's part is depicted with special understanding.

See also MARRIAGE; DIVORCE: IN THE OT; SEX.

C. Women in the Religious Life of Israel. Women and children formed an integral part of the community; like the men they were called upon to hear and obey the law and were liable to punishment for transgression (Dt. 17:2-7; 31:12; Neh. 8:2). But there were far-reaching restrictions on women's public religious role. Circumcision, symbolizing Yahweh's covenant relationship with His people (Gen. 17:11), was exclusively for men; no special ceremony marked a woman's membership in the religious community. Only males had to appear three times a year before the Lord (Ex. 23:17), although women were also bidden to keep feasts (Dt. 16:9-15). In the special vows of persons, a woman was valued at half the price of a man (Lev. 27:1-8).

Women were restricted by laws concerning ritual purity. Bodily functions such as menstruation and childbirth rendered a woman ceremonially "unclean," and everyone and everything she touched became "unclean" (Lev. 15:19-33). This ritual impurity had no moral connotations and may have originated in a sense of awe at woman's mysterious biological functions, since blood, for a Jew, stood for life. Comparable purity laws applied to men with regard to seminal emissions (cf. Lev. 15:16-18), but the laws much more seriously restricted the active life of women, especially their part in public worship: "Thus you shall keep the people of Israel separate from their uncleanness; lest they die in their uncleanness, by defiling my tabernacle that is in their midst" (Lev. 15:31).

The extent to which women participated in public cult is not fully clear. Miriam played the timbrel and sang to the Lord (Ex. 15:20f.). Two hundred male and female singers are mentioned in Ezr. 2:65 (cf. Neh. 7:67). They may have formed part of the temple choir, although some think that they were employed only at banquets and funerals (cf. 2 S. 19:35; 2 Ch. 35:25). Certain texts refer to "women who ministered at the door of the tent of meeting" (Ex. 38:8; 1 S. 2:22). Their function has been much debated: roles as diverse as singing and dancing, sweeping and cleaning, and even sacred prostitution, have been suggested. It should be noted that these women served (or assembled) *at the door.* Eli was sitting by the doorpost when he observed Hannah praying at the Shiloh temple (1 S. 1:9, 12); it is not clear whether she actually entered the temple precincts. Later she personally brought a sacrifice when she dedicated Samuel (vv. 24-28). Many sacrifices were offered only by men, on behalf of their families, but women brought their own offerings for their "purification" to the door of the tent of meeting (Lev. 12:6; 15:29). (Men also brought purificatory offerings to the door, 14:11; 15:14). The priesthood was restricted to men. Most of the prophets were also men, but Miriam (Ex. 15:20), Deborah (Jgs. 4:4), Huldah (2 K. 22:14), and Isaiah's wife (Isa. 8:3) are all described as prophetesses. Several early narratives attest that women regularly approached God in private prayer; sometimes they received revelations and angelophanies (Gen. 16:7-14; 25:22f.; Jgs. 13:2-7).

A statue of the Egyptian Queen Hatshepsut, who ruled as pharaoh in the 15th cent. B.C. (from the temple to Hatshepsut, Thebes) (The Metropolitan Museum of Art, Rogers Fund and Edward S. Harkness Gift)

D. Women as Leaders in Society. Israel's social organization presupposed male leadership; yet exceptions occurred at all periods. Miriam was remembered along with Moses and Aaron as a national leader (Mic. 6:4); she publicly rebuked Moses for marrying a Kushite woman (but she was stricken with leprosy, Nu. 12:1-15). Deborah was a judge as well as a prophet (Jgs. 4:4f.). She took the initiative in rousing her people against the Canaanites, and Barak agreed to go to war only if she accompanied him; her leadership is celebrated in a victory song (ch. 5). A decisive part in that struggle was played by another woman, Jael the wife of Heber, who killed Sisera with a tent peg (4:17-22; 5:25-27).

Some queens and queen mothers were particularly influential, e.g., Bathsheba (1 K. 1:11-40), Ahab's wife Jezebel, famous for extending the cult of her own Phoenician gods (18:4, 13, 19; 19:1f.; 21:25f.; 2 K. 9:22), and the bloodthirsty Athaliah, who reigned both as Jehoram's consort and as queen regnant (2 K. 8:18; 11:1-16). Notable among foreign queens was the Queen of Sheba, who visited Solomon, exchanging gifts with him and testing him with "hard questions" (1 K. 10:1-13). *See also* QUEEN; QUEEN MOTHER.

Huldah the prophetess was a woman of high standing who was consulted by Josiah's chief men (2 K. 22:14-20). Her outspoken words to the king may have influenced him to initiate his reforms. Esther used her influence to save her people from the Persians, and the Feast of Purim was established to commemorate her courageous actions (Est. 9). Similarly Judith became a national heroine for her assassination of Holofernes; she is depicted as a model of prayer, fasting, piety, and trust, as well as of bravery (Jth. 8–16). 2 Macc. 7 vividly describes the "manly" courage (Gk. *ársēn thýmos*) and faith of a Jewish mother who was martyred with her seven sons. Such women were the subject of story because of the exceptional character of their reputed deeds. One can only surmise what personal or political influence may have been exercised by women from behind the scenes.

E. Woman as a Theological Symbol. The OT frequently personifies the community of Israel as a woman. Israel's sufferings are compared to labor at childbirth (Isa. 26:17f.; 66:7; Jer. 4:31; Mic. 4:9f.). Yahweh is often pictured as Israel's husband, and Israel's unfaithfulness to the covenant relationship is described as adultery or prostitution (e.g., Jer. 3:1-3). Hosea represents God as repudiating Israel because of her adultery, but then accepting her back into a new relationship (ch. 2) in which she no longer calls Him *baʿal,* "master," but *ʾîš,* "husband" (2:16 [MT 18]. Isaiah similarly depicts God's enduring love in terms of the marital relationship: "'Your Maker is your husband . . . [He] will call you back, as if you were a wife deserted and distressed in spirit — a wife who married young, only to be rejected,' says your God. 'For a brief moment I abandoned you, but with deep compassion I will bring you back'" (Isa. 54:5-8, NIV). Ezekiel uses sexual imagery with exceptional boldness, picturing Israel as a baby girl who is abandoned by her mother in a field, her umbilical cord still uncut (ch. 16). But God sees her and says, "Live." He washes the blood from her, provides her with clothes, and she grows to womanhood. When she turns to prostitution, God threatens punishment, but He promises that He will not abandon His covenant (16:59-63). Another passage (ch. 23) speaks of Yahweh marrying two sisters, both prostitutes, who bear Him children. According to Jewish exegesis, the book of Canticles is an allegory of God's love for Israel.

In some passages feminine imagery is applied to God. Isaiah describes God's love as greater than that of a woman for the child she has breast-fed (49:15) and compares God's care to that of a woman comforting her son (66:13); the prophet also applies the image of the travailing woman to God (Isa. 42:14; cf. Nu. 11:12). Several passages speak of God's care for Israel from the moment of birth, possibly using the metaphor of a midwife (e.g., Ps. 22:9 [MT 10]; 71:6; Isa. 46:3). Hos. 11:3 depicts God as teaching Ephraim to walk (an image that could represent either parent). A tender passage in Baruch speaks of God suckling His sons and daughters (4:8, 11; in v. 8 Gk. *tropheúō* may refer to a wet nurse). Wisdom literature regularly personifies divine wisdom as a woman (Prov. 1:20-33; 8:1–9:6). Such passages show that, even coming from a patriarchal society, the biblical imagery applied to God is not exclusively masculine; for many women they have a special significance today (cf. Mollenkott, pp. 56f.).

IV. Later Judaism.–In the intertestamental and Roman periods, perhaps as a reaction against the growing freedom of women in Hellenism, Jewish attitudes tended to become more negative and women's everyday life more restricted. The women of the Hasmonean and Herodian court circles, including SALOME Alexandra (who herself reigned 76-67 B.C.), Bernice, and Herodias, are exceptions to this rule. The Pseudepigrapha express some strongly misogynistic sentiments: women are "rash . . . prone to change their minds suddenly through false reasoning, and by nature weak" (Letter of Aristeas 250; cf. Vergil *Aen.* iv.568f.); "women are evil" (T. Reub. 5); they entice men by their beauty and stratagems. Eve, not Adam, was corrupted by the serpent, and she was therefore the primary sinner (2 En. 31:6; see also Swidler, *Women in Judaism,* pp. 47f.).

According to Philo the Essenes rejected marriage because woman is "a selfish creature, immoderately jealous, and skilled at seducing the morals of her husband" (*Hypothetica* xi.14). Nevertheless, some married in order to propagate the human race: Josephus explained that they had no intercourse with their wives during pregnancy, "demonstrating that their motive in marrying was not pleasure but the procreation of children" (*BJ* ii.8.13 [161]; contrast Canticles, where the woman is loved for her own sake). The Dead Sea Scrolls denounce harlots in strong language, reject polygamy, and apply strictly the Levitical laws on uncleanness and incest (4QWiles [4Q184]; CD 4–5). Among the Therapeutae at Alexandria men and women lived apart. Philo reported that they were separated in their regular worship by a screen some five feet high, but every seventh week men and women sang and danced together at a special service (*De vita contemplativa* 32f., 83-89).

In orthodox Judaism the Mosaic laws on women were applied in elaborate detail. Women continued to experience inequalities in betrothal, polygamy, levirate marriage, suspected adultery, earnings, and ownership of property, but a written contract (*k^eṯûḇâ*) fixed the sum for a woman's support if she was divorced or widowed (Mish. *Ketuboth*). Rabbis debated whether a woman might be divorced for trivial offenses, such as burning her husband's dinner, or only for sexual misconduct (Mish. *Gittin* ix.10). In public and in private life a woman remained under male tutelage and control.

Women's participation in public worship was limited. In Herod's temple they were confined to an outer court fifteen steps below the men's. It is generally believed that they were separated also in synagogue worship, though the evidence for this is not fully conclusive (no specific regulation prescribes segregation; the remains of some early synagogues lack evidence of galleries or separate halls, while in others the archeological evidence is ambiguous; see Brooten, pp. 103-138; Swidler, *Women in Judaism,* pp. 88-91). Perhaps custom varied at first; but eventually separation became normal, as it is in orthodox Judaism today.

Rabbinic writings attest other restrictions. Women did not count as part of the *minyan* (quorum for a congregation); by custom they were not called upon to read lessons at worship; they could not act as legal witnesses; they could not pronounce the blessing at meals; they were discouraged from studying the law, the special privilege and delight of a Jew. Rabbi Eliezer is reported to have said, "If a man gives his daughter a knowledge of the Law it is as though he taught her lechery" (Mish. *Sotah* iii.4). A woman's first obligation was to enable her husband and sons to study, even if this involved abstaining from sexual relationships (the Talmud permitted men to leave their wives, without their permission, for up to three years to study Torah; longer periods are attested where the wife consented). Every day a Jewish male thanked

God that he had not been created a gentile, slave, or woman. Women received little education; Beruria, the wife of Rabbi Meir (2nd cent. A.D.), was remembered as a rare example of a learned woman.

Women were restricted in their social as well as their religious life. Philo believed that they should stay indoors as much as possible, "not meddling in affairs outside the household management" (*De specialibus legibus,* iii.169-171). In public they were expected to be veiled; an uncovered head in public could make a woman liable for divorce. Their social relationships were mostly confined to other women. Women did not eat with male guests, and men were discouraged from talking with women. Jose ben Johanan (1st cent. B.C.) advised, "Talk not much with womankind"; such talk, even with one's wife, could lead to Gehenna (Mish. *Aboth* i.5). Conversation with a woman in a public place was particularly scandalous, even if she were a member of one's own family. These restrictions led to the isolation of women and made any kind of religious leadership exceedingly difficult. Nevertheless, a good wife was appreciated (see III.A above). Rabbi Jacob said, "He who has no wife lives without good, or help, or joy, or blessing, or atonement" (Midr. *Gen. Rabbah* xvii.2); similar sayings are recorded of other rabbis (see Swidler, *Women in Judaism,* pp. 72f.; Montefiore and Loewe, pp. 507-515). Many rabbis were monogamous and deprecated divorce. But the more positive affirmations of women remain in the context of their relationship to husband and children.

In some parts of the Hellenistic world Jewish women may have had slightly greater freedom than what is implied by Philo and the rabbinic texts. Inscriptions from the 1st to 6th cents. A.D.refer to women as synagogue leaders (Gk. *archisynágōgos, archḗgissa, presbytéra*; Lat. *mater synagogae, pateressa*). B. Brooten has recently argued that such titles were not merely honorific but implied active religious roles. Certainly at Elephantine in Egypt women had greater equality in marriage and property ownership (5th cent. B.C.), but this exceptional situation seems not to have influenced mainstream Judaism.

V. In the NT.–A. Attitudes toward Women and Their Religious Role. 1. Evangelists. There are no striking differences in the attitudes of the four Evangelists: all preserve many stories about women and relate them sympathetically. Whereas Jewish genealogies normally included only males, Matthew's genealogy of Jesus mentions four women: Tamar, Rahab, Ruth, Bathsheba (Mt. 1:3, 5f.). Matthew tells the birth narrative primarily from Joseph's viewpoint, while Luke tells it from Mary's. Luke portrays both Mary and her relative Elizabeth with understanding, highlighting Mary's positive and ready acceptance of God's will in contrast to Zechariah's skepticism (Lk. 1:18-20, 38, 45). He relates that Elizabeth was filled with the Holy Spirit upon seeing Mary (vv. 41-45), and he records Mary's prophetic song of praise (vv. 46-55). Luke alone tells of the aged prophetess Anna (2:36-38). John's sympathetic portraits of women (see V.A.2 below) have been interpreted as evidence for women's equality in the Johannine Church (see Brown, Appendix II), but most likely they also represent Jesus' own attitudes.

2. Jesus. All the Gospels portray Jesus as one who fully accepted women. Regardless of their social or marital status, He was unfailingly courteous and compassionate towards them. When a woman, ritually unclean with a hemorrhage, touched Him on the way to the house of a synagogue leader, He stopped to heal her and commended her faith, addressing her affectionately as "Daughter" (Mk. 5:34 par.). He affirmed the dignity of a crippled woman, calling her "daughter of Abraham" (Lk. 13:16). He repeatedly responded to women's needs no less than to men's: He healed Peter's mother-in-law (Mk. 1:29-31 par.), Jairus's daughter (5:35-43 par.), Mary Magdalene (said to have been possessed by seven devils, Lk. 8:2), and the Syro-Phoenician woman's daughter (even though she was a Gentile, Mk. 7:24-30 par.). Moved with compassion for the widow at Nain, He told her not to weep and restored her son to life (Lk. 7:11-15). He commended a poor widow as an example of generous giving (Mk. 12:41-44).

Jesus used women's activities to illustrate the character of the Kingdom, mentioning the baking of bread (Lk. 13:20f.), grinding of corn (17:35), wedding festivities (Mt. 25:1-13), and sweeping of a house to find a lost coin (Lk. 15:8-10; this parable, paralleling that of the lost sheep, uses a woman's activity to illustrate God's character). No saying of Jesus ever denigrates or belittles women; in the parable of the unjust judge the widow stands for the faithful who persist in prayer (Lk. 18:1-8).

In a society in which women were not counted as full members of a congregation and were discouraged from studying the law, Jesus taught women alongside men (Mt. 14:21; 15:38; etc.). Whereas some rabbis laid down that a man should not even speak to a woman in a public place, Jesus shared a drinking vessel with the Samaritan woman and spoke to her of the deepest spiritual things (Jn. 4:1-30). He similarly revealed Himself to Martha, who declared her faith with the words, "I believe that you are the Christ, the Son of God" (11:27; cf. Peter's confession in Mt. 16:16 par.). While it is likely that John exercised some literary freedom in relating these episodes, one cannot doubt that they represent Jesus' own attitude, which contrasted with contemporary Jewish teaching and even with some later Christian teaching.

Though not originally part of John's Gospel, the story of the woman taken in adultery (Jn. 7:53–8:11) may also preserve an authentic memory. Jesus shows characteristic compassion, understanding, and astuteness as He silences the woman's accusers, then assures her of forgiveness: "Neither do I condemn you; go, and do not sin again." Luke similarly records Jesus' acceptance of sinful women. When a woman who was a sinner (prostitute ?) lavishly anointed His feet and wiped them with her hair, He accepted her service and commended her love (Lk. 7:47; cf. Mk. 14:3-9; Mt. 26:6-13; Jn. 12:1-8). He encouraged Mary to sit at His feet and listen to His teaching, and He declined Martha's request that He bid her sister help her with the serving, saying: "It is Mary who has chosen the better part; it is not to be taken from her" (Lk. 10:41, JB). He thus affirmed a woman's right to be a disciple and not to be concerned solely with domestic affairs.

In the Gospels Jesus nowhere stresses the importance of motherhood. When a woman in a crowd called out, "Blessed is the womb that bore you and the breasts that you sucked," He replied, "Blessed rather are those who hear the word of God and keep it" (Lk. 11:27f.). He taught that the family of the Church is of even greater importance than the nuclear family: when His mother and brothers asked for Him, He turned to those around Him saying, "Here are my mother and my brothers! Whoever does the will of God is my brother, and sister, and mother" (Mk. 3:31-35; note the inclusion of "sister").

The twelve apostles were all men, and there is no evidence that any of the Seventy were female; this is hardly surprising in the prevailing social conditions. Nevertheless, some women did leave their homes to follow Jesus: Lk. 8:1-3 records how Mary Magdalene, Joanna the wife of Herod's steward, Susanna, and others ministered to His material needs. Women stood by Jesus at the crucifixion (Mt. 27:55f.; Lk. 23:49, 55; Jn. 19:25; contrast Jesus' male disciples, who "all forsook him and fled," Mk. 14:50). Women were the first witnesses of the Resurrection, though some of the men were skeptical (Mk. 16; Mt. 28:1-10; Lk. 24:1-11, 22-25; Jn. 20). This Gospel testimony is all the more significant, because in Jewish law the witness of women was not admissible (cf. 1 Cor. 15:4-8, where no women are mentioned).

Jesus not only accepted the service of women, but He also used them to spread the gospel: Mary Magdalene was sent as the *apostola apostolorum* (Jn. 20:17f.; cf. Mt. 28:10); the Samaritan woman spread the news of Jesus in her village, so that "many Samaritans believed in him because of the woman's testimony" (Jn. 4:39).

3. Acts. In Acts the pattern continues: women are full members of the Church. Luke specifically records that both women and men were baptized (Acts 8:12; cf. 16:15). Women, including Jesus' mother, joined with the men in prayer (1:14). They were present at Pentecost (2:1). Quoting from Joel, Peter referred to "daughters" and "maidservants" prophesying (2:17f.); the Holy Spirit is said to fall on all (2:4). Saul persecuted both men and women (8:3; 9:2; 22:4). Acts frequently mentions women converts, including Timothy's mother (16:1; cf. 2 Tim. 1:5); Lydia, a wealthy woman who gave Paul hospitality (Acts 16:13-15); Damaris at Athens (17:34); and women of high social standing at Philippi (v. 4) and Beroea (v. 12). Women were miraculously healed (9:36-42; 16:16-18). The Church cared for its widows (6:1-6); Dorcas herself dispensed charity (9:36, 39, 41). The Church met for prayer at the house of Mary, the mother of John Mark (12:12); Luke provides a graphic description of Rhoda's joy at Peter's release (12:13-16). Sapphira was held responsible for sharing in her husband's deception (5:1-11). Philip had four daughters who prophesied (21 9).

In spite of the frequent references to women, the early Church's leadership, as depicted in Acts, was mostly male. (Luke wrote selectively, focusing on the spread of the Church through its great leaders, esp. Peter and Paul.) An exceptional figure is Priscilla, who with her husband instructed the learned Apollos (Acts 18:2, 18, 26; cf. Rom. 16:3f.; 1 Cor. 16:19; 2 Tim. 4:19).

4. Pauline Epistles. The attitude of Paul in the Epistles is more difficult to determine because of the variety of teaching found there, given in response to specific situations. The key to his teaching is Gal. 3:25-29, the "Magna Carta of humanity" (Jewett, p. 142), which states: "There is neither Jew nor Greek, there is neither bond nor free, there is neither male nor female; for you are all one in Christ Jesus" (v. 28). The context shows that Paul was speaking of the new relationship that comes through faith and Christian baptism. His use of "male" and "female" echoes Gen. 1:27, where both man and woman are made in God's image. The threefold affirmation recalls — and utterly transforms — the traditional Jewish prayer in which a man thanks God that he has not been created a gentile, slave, or woman (see IV above). Here we have the abolition not of sexual differences between men and women but of their religious inequality (F. F. Bruce, *Epistle to the Galatians* [*NIGTC,* 1982], pp. 187-191).

Paul's recognition of women as full members of the Christian community is further illustrated by his affectionate greetings to them — e.g., "the beloved Persis" (Rom. 16:12), "Apphia our sister" (Philem. 2), Rufus's mother, "a mother to me too" (Rom. 16:13, NIV) — and his references to them as fellow workers. Phoebe (Rom. 16:1f.) is described as *diákonos,* a "deacon" or "minister," "servant" of the church at Cenchreae (cf. 1 Tim. 3:8; Phil. 1:1; Eph. 6:21; Col. 1:7; etc.), and as Paul's "patron" (Gk. *prostátis*; cf. masc. *prostátēs,* "leader," "chief," "patron," and the related verb *proístēmi*; see Prohl, pp. 70f.). Priscilla, Mary, Tryphaena, Tryphosa, Euodia, and Syntyche are all described as fellow workers or laborers in the gospel (Rom. 16:3, 6, 12; Phil. 4:3; the term *synergós* is used of both men and women). Junia (Rom. 16:7) is said to be "outstanding among the apostles." (The evidence that this name should be read as feminine is overwhelming; see Chrysostom *Hom. 31 in Rom.*; C. E. B. Cranfield, *ICC* on Romans (1979, repr. 1983), II, 788f.; Brooten, "Junia . . . Outstanding among the Apostles," in Swidler, *Women Priests,* pp. 141-44; no example of this name in the masculine has ever been attested.)

Nevertheless, some passages suggest limitations on women's freedom and religious role. (a) In 1 Cor. 11:2-16 Paul argues that a man should pray with his head uncovered, a woman with hers covered. It is not clear whether he is prescribing the wearing of veils (so RSV and many comms.) or requiring that women arrange their long hair decorously on top of their heads (so Hurley and O'Connor). His essential point is that the customary distinctions in the outward appearance of men and women should be observed. (Paul may have been concerned about sexual license or possible homosexual tendencies at Corinth.) The reasons he adduces to support his view, namely, that woman is the glory of man, having been created from him (vv. 7-9; cf. the rabbinic exegesis of Gen. 2, on which see Jewett, pp. 119-128), and that by nature and custom women universally wear their hair long (vv. 13-15), have posed difficulties for interpreters. To some commentators it is clear that Paul's arguments are designed for a particular audience in a particular situation and cannot be applied as a general principle, while others think it unlikely that Paul would invoke such arguments in support of purely local customs. It is important to note that Paul assumes that women will be praying aloud and prophesying in the congregation (v. 5); their head covering (whether long hair or veil) is a sign of their authority to do so (cf. M. D. Hooker, *NTS,* 10 [1963/64], 410-16, and O'Connor, defending the authenticity and logic of the passage).

(b) 1 Corinthians 14:33b-35 enjoins women to keep silence in the churches and be subordinate: "If there is anything they desire to know, let them ask their husbands at home." It is not clear whether women are here prohibited from all public speaking or only from chattering. The passage presupposes that all are married (but cf. 1 Cor. 7) and contains an uncharacteristic appeal to the Jewish law. Many commentators suspect it of being non-Pauline on textual and other grounds. If it is genuine, and if Paul is not contradicting what he said in 1 Cor. 11:5, it must be assumed that he is here permitting women to pray and prophesy, but not to disturb the congregation with unnecessary questions.

(c) The author of 1 Tim. 2:8-15 states categorically: "I permit no woman to teach or to have authority over men; she is to keep silent." The reason given is that Adam was formed first and that Eve, not Adam, was deceived (note again the dependence on late Jewish exegesis of Gen. 2–3). The Pauline authorship of the Pastorals has been widely questioned. If this passage is deutero-Pauline, it may be a restatement of traditional Jewish limitations on female religious leadership; if it is Pauline, it may be a reaction against license caused by the declaration of Gal. 3, or it may be a strongly worded limitation for a particular context (cf. D. Williams, pp. 112-14). 1 Timothy elsewhere presupposes a ministry of women (see 3:11, where *gynaíkas* probably refers to female deacons rather than to women in general or the wives of ministers; see *DNTT,* III, 1065; Daniélou, p. 14).

Though both 1 Cor. 14:33b-35 and 1 Tim. 2:8-15 were later used by the Church to discourage women's public ministry, these passages must be understood in the light of Paul's fundamental teaching in Galatians and of his clear recognition of women as ministerial colleagues, as evidenced in both the Epistles and Acts.

For further discussion of these passages, *see* WOMEN IN CHURCH LEADERSHIP.

5. Other NT Writings. The author of Hebrews used two OT women (Sarah and Rahab) as examples of faith (11:11, 31). 1 Pet. 3:7 cites Sarah as an example of wifely obedience and speaks of husband and wife as "joint heirs of grace" (see also V.B.below). James cites Rahab along with Abraham as an example of faith completed by works (2:25) and urges loving care toward widows (1:27) and other Christian sisters in need (2:15). 1 John gives the impression of being addressed primarily to men (cf. 2:12-14), but terms such as "beloved" and "little children" might well include sisters (see I.B above). 2 John is addressed to "the elect lady and her children" (v. 1; cf. vv. 4f., 13). Though frequently interpreted today as the personification of a church, there is much to be said for the older view that the "elect lady" is an individual (cf. 3 Jn. 1) who was in a position of leadership within a Christian group (cf. other references to churches meeting in the houses of individual women, e.g., Acts 12:12). For references to women in Revelation, see V.C below.

B. Teaching on Marriage and Divorce. In contrast to the OT, which permitted polygamy, Jesus upheld strict monogamy, emphasizing the oneness of the married couple with His citation of Gen. 2:24: "The two shall become one flesh" (Mk. 10:8 par. Mt. 19:5f.). Mark records that He added: "Whoever divorces his wife and marries another, commits adultery against her; and if she divorces her husband and marries another, she commits adultery" (Mk. 10:11f.). This statement is problematic, since in Jewish law only a man could initiate divorce, and adultery was an offense against the husband. Either the Markan formulation is an adaptation of Jesus' words to a gentile, possibly Roman, setting, or Jesus is here radically differing from the Jewish position by placing the woman on an equal footing with the man. According to Matthew (5:32; 19:9) Jesus permitted divorce in case of *porneía* (usually "fornication," here perhaps "adultery"), but many interpreters view this as a softening of Jesus' teaching to meet a pastoral situation. Paul in 1 Cor. 7:10-16 presupposes a dominical teaching of no divorce; he permits separation only when an unbelieving partner takes the initiative. *See also* DIVORCE: IN THE NT.

Some have held that Paul teaches a low view of marriage in 1 Cor. 7, where he writes, "It is well [*kalón*] for a man not to touch a woman" (7:1), and wishes that all were single like himself (vv. 7f.), implying that he is either unmarried or widowed. It is important to see Paul's words in their context: he is responding to specific questions raised by the Corinthians, not giving a full theology of marriage. In 7:1 (where *kalón* means "advantageous," "profitable," rather than "morally good") he may be quoting the Corinthians' own words. He wrote probably in the expectation that the Parousia would occur soon (for how could the human race continue if all remained celibate?), and to encourage Christian harmony, devotion, and sexual morality. He also believed that an unmarried person experiences less distraction from "the affairs of the Lord" (vv. 32-35), but he did not enforce celibacy.

Concerning marriage the Pauline Epistles teach the need for the subordination of the wife to the husband within a relationship of love and respect (cf. Eph. 5:21). Paul explicitly discourages sexual abstinence within marriage for ascetic reasons, except by mutual agreement for short periods as an aid to prayer (1 Cor. 7:3f.). Teaching on subordination appears in the so-called *Haustafeln* or Household Codes, which follow a definite pattern illustrated by Eph. 5:21–6:9: (1) wives be subject to husbands . . . husbands love wives; (2) children obey parents . . . fathers do not anger children; (3) slaves obey masters . . . masters treat slaves justly. Other examples are Col. 3:18–4:1; Tit. 2:1-10; and 1 Pet. 2:13–3:7 (where obedience to civil authorities is also enjoined); cf. also 1 Tim. 2:8-15; 5:1f.; 6:1f.

Such codes teach conformity to existing patterns of social behavior and are closely paralleled in Stoic and other Greek philosophical sources, as well as in Hellenistic Judaism. D. L. Balch has brought out clearly the missionary and apologetic purpose of these codes: the hope is that unbelieving husbands may be converted by the chaste and modest behavior of their wives (1 Pet. 3:1f.) and that opponents may be silenced by the sobriety and conscientious work of Christians (Tit. 2:7f.). The codes also enshrine the basic Christian principles of putting others first: they stress *mutual* care and respect in the Lord (Eph. 5:21; cf. Rom. 12:10).

C. Woman as a Theological Symbol. Ephesians compares a husband's love for his wife to that of Christ for the Church (5:23-33; cf. the OT image of Yahweh as Israel's husband; see III.E above). In 1 Cor. 11:2 he speaks of betrothing the Corinthian church to Christ "as a pure bride to her one husband." In Gal. 4:26 he refers to "the Jerusalem above" as "our mother" (cf. the allegorical use of Hagar and Sarah for the two covenants in vv. 22-31).

Woman appears frequently as a theological symbol in Revelation. The great harlot, "arrayed in purple and scarlet" and "drunk with the blood of the saints" (Rev. 17), represents the Roman empire; in contrast the woman "clothed with the sun" (ch. 12) is the mother of the Messiah and a figure for the messianic community. Her flight to the desert and conflict with the dragon represent both Christ's victory over Satan and the continuing struggle of the Church (possible symbolic use of the figure of the Virgin Mary is explored further by R. Brown, *Gospel According to John* [*AB*, 1966], I, 107-109; II, 924-27). Rev. 19:7f. uses the image of the marriage feast of the Lamb, the Church being the bride who is clothed in pure linen, i.e., "the righteous deeds of the saints." The climax is in 21:2, where John sees the new Jerusalem "coming down out of heaven . . . prepared as a bride adorned for her husband."

VI. Later Developments.–Among Gnostic thinkers negative attitudes toward women prevailed; even within marriage sexual intercourse was often seen as evil (see Pagels, p. 66). In the apocryphal Gospel of Thomas (logion 114) Peter asks that Mary be sent away, "For women are not worthy of Life"; Jesus replies that He will make her male, "so that she too may become a living spirit, resembling you males." On the other hand, some Gnostics prayed to a divine Mother, identified with the Holy Spirit, Grace, or Thought (Pagels, pp. 48-57). Tertullian attested that some Gnostic women taught, exorcized, and baptized (*De praescriptione haereticorum* 41, etc.)

Thecla, Marcellina, and Maximilla were famous female leaders in the early Church; Blandina and other women gained renown as martyrs. In some groups women became priests and bishops (for some relevant archeological evidence, see Nunally-Cox, pp. 128f.). Various inscriptions refer to women as deacon, subdeacon, teacher, and *presbytis* (see Horsley, p. 121; Gryson, pp. 90f.). Prominent women like Helena and Theodora also played an important part in church affairs, less happily in the case of the empress Eudoxia.

It is clear, however, that in mainstream Christianity the comparative freedom of NT times was followed by a period of some restriction with regard to women's leadership, with more attention paid to the scriptural injunctions to female silence than to Jesus' recognition of women or Paul's proclamation of equality in Gal. 3:28. Old social customs and stratification continued: husbands were urged to direct their wives to what is good, women to be silent and modest and to see to their proper tasks of child-bearing and house-keeping. Chrysostom asserted that affairs of state and outdoor activities belong to men, while domestic activities like cooking and spinning belong to women; but he also affirmed a woman's right to teach privately and to serve as deacon (*Quales ducendae sint uxores* 3; *Hom. 31 in Rom.*; *Hom. 1 in Prisc. et Aq.* 3).

Other texts reaffirm the prohibition on women's teaching and even forbid women to bear witness or administer justice. Jerome considered it "against nature" for a woman to speak in an assembly of men (*Comm. in 1 Cor.* 14). Virginity became more prized than marriage. The work of deaconesses became limited to minor liturgical roles and to ministry to women (see Gryson, *passim*).

There appear to have been several reasons behind these limitations: a growing tendency to interpret Christian ministry in terms of the Jewish priesthood, an overly literal or one-sided understanding of Paul's teaching (including 1 Cor. 7), a strongly culturally conditioned sense of what is appropriate, and a reaction against the excesses of some heretical sects. Some of the church fathers were openly misogynistic: Tertullian called women "the devil's gateway"; Epiphanius castigated them as "a feeble race, untrustworthy, and of mediocre intelligence" (see Daniélou, p. 25). This is a far cry from Jesus' attitude in the Gospels and the role of women in the first-century Church.

VII. Conclusion.–However high a view is taken of the Bible's inspiration, it is clear that its teaching must be understood in its social setting. While some Christian leaders and scholars (e.g., Clark, Hurley) believe that the OT and NT references to wifely subjection were intended as permanent instructions for posterity, other Christians today would see male headship as a culturally orientated teaching, and a loving partnership of equals as the ideal for Christian marriage (e.g., Jewett, Pape) — especially in a society where men and women are legally recognized as equals. Similarly, while some exegetes argue that passages on women's subordination presuppose restricted active religious leadership for women, others have drawn attention to passages indicating that they did in fact fulfil leadership roles in both social and religious contexts. The important point is not, e.g., the precise circumstances in which Paul permitted a woman to speak, but the general principles underlying the biblical message as a whole. Increasing emphasis is being put on the fundamental biblical teaching that both men and women are made in God's image; that Jesus Christ died for all humanity; that both women and men are called to be full members of the Church; and that both are endowed with spiritual gifts equipping them for ministry. In the modern context this is seen by many scholars and church members as entailing the eligibility of women for ordination beyond the rank of deacon. (See further Howe, Langley, Mollenkott, Nunally-Cox, and D. Williams.)

Bibliography.–D. L. Balch, *Let Wives be Submissive* (1981); J. P. V. D. Balsdon, *Roman Women* (1962); B. J. Brooten, *Women Leaders in the Ancient Synagogue* (1982); R. E. Brown, *Community of the Beloved Disciple* (1979), Appendix II; S. B. Clark, *Man and Woman in Christ* (1980); J. Daniélou, *Ministry of Women in the Early Church* (2nd ed. 1974); *DNTT*, III, 1055-1078; R. Gryson, *Ministry of Women in the Early Church* (1976); G. H. R. Horsley, *New Documents Illustrating Early Christianity* (1981); E. M. Howe, *Women and Church Leadership* (1982); J. B. Hurley, *Man and Woman in Biblical Perspective* (1981); J. Jeremias, *Jerusalem in the Time of Jesus* (Eng. tr. 1969); P. K. Jewett, *Man as Male and Female* (1975); M. Langley, *Equal Woman* (1983); V. Mollenkott, *Women, Men, and the Bible* (1977); F. J. Moloney, *Woman: First Among the Faithful* (1985); C. G. Montefiore and H. Loewe, *Rabbinic Anthology* (1938); J. Nunally-Cox, *Foremothers* (1981); J. M. O'Connor, *CBQ*, 42 (1980), 482-500; E. Pagels, *Gnostic Gospels* (1979); D. Pape, *God and Women* (1977); S. B. Pomeroy, *Goddesses, Whores, Wives, and Slaves* (1975); R. C. Prohl, *Woman in the Church* (1957); D. M. Schaps, *Economic Rights of Women in Ancient Greece* (1979); A. B. Spencer, *Beyond the Curse* (1985); E. and F. Stagg, *Woman in the World of Jesus* (1978); L. Swidler, *Women in Judaism* (1976); L. and A. Swidler, eds., *Women Priests* (1977); *TDNT*, I, *s.v.* γυνή (A. Oepke); *TDOT*, I, *s.v.* "'îsh" (N. P. Bratsiotis); D. Williams, *The Apostle Paul and Women in the Church* (1977); J. G. Williams, *Women Recounted* (1982); B. Witherington, III, *Women in the Ministry of Jesus* (1984).

R. B. EDWARDS

WOMB [Heb. *beṭen* (Gen. 25:23f.; 30:2; 38:27; Jgs. 16:17; Job 1:21; 3:10; etc.), *reḥem* (Gen. 20:18; 29:31; 30:22; Ex. 13:2, 12, 15; 34:19; Nu. 3:12; 8:16; 12:12; 18:15; etc.), *raḥam* (Gen. 49:25; Prov. 30:16; Isa. 46:3), *mēʿeh* (Ruth 1:11), *ʿāṣar* ("shut the womb," Isa. 66:9), *mašbēr bānîm* ("mouth of the womb," Hos. 13:13); Gk. *koilía* (Lk. 1:15, 41f., 44; 2:21; 11:27; 23:29; Jn. 3:4), *mḗtra* (Lk. 2:23; Rom. 4:19), *gastḗr* (Lk. 1:31)]; AV also MATRIX (Ex. 13:12, 15; 34:19; etc.). BREAKING FORTH OF CHILDREN (Hos. 13:13); NEB also paraphrases (e.g., "birth"), omits.

The most specific OT term for "womb" is Heb. *reḥem/raḥam,* which is related to the root *rḥm,* "love deeply," "be compassionate," and is rendered "womb" by the RSV twenty-seven times. The other common term, *beṭen* (rendered "womb" twenty-five times), seems to have the basic meaning "interior" (see KoB, p. 119). It can denote the belly or stomach as well as the womb; thus it has a much broader range of meaning than *reḥem/raḥam. Beṭen* and *reḥem* often appear in parallelism (e.g., Job 10:18f.; 31:15; Ps. 58:3 [MT 4]; Isa. 46:3). *Mēʿeh* generally refers to the "inward parts," e.g., the intestines (*see* BOWELS) or the belly; in Ruth 1:11, however, it clearly refers to the female reproductive organs. The verb *ʿāṣar* means to "restrain" or "shut"; the English versions have supplied "womb" as the verb's object in Isa. 66:9. *Mašbēr* is derived from the root *šbr,* "break," and denotes the "place of the breach" (Hos. 13:13; cf. AV lit. "breaking forth of children [*bānîm*]"), thus the "mouth of the womb" (so RSV, NEB). To depict the desperate situation of Ephraim, the prophet used the image of a fetus that is in the wrong position and thus fails to emerge from the womb despite the mother's labor pains.

Greek *koilía* and *gastḗr* (both lit. "hollow") are the two terms used almost exclusively by the LXX to render Heb. *beṭen.* Both terms can refer to the belly or stomach as well as the womb. Gk. *mḗtra,* derived from the term for "mother" (*mḗtēr*), refers more specifically to the womb.

In Scripture it is clearly God who controls conception and birth. It is God who opens (e.g., Gen. 29:31; 30:22) or closes (e.g., Gen. 20:18; 1 S. 1:5f.) the womb. In recognition of this fact and also of God's deliverance when He "passed over" their firstborn in Egypt, the Israelites were instructed to set apart to God every animal or child that "opens the womb [*reḥem*]," i.e., the firstborn. The animals were to be sacrificed and the human children were to be redeemed (Ex. 13:2, 12, 15; 34:19; etc.; cf. Lk. 2:23).

The writers of Scripture confessed that God's people are the objects of His care from their conception until their death (e.g., Isa. 44:2, 24; 46:3). One psalmist confessed, "Thou didst knit me together in my mother's womb [*beṭen*]" (Ps. 139:13); and Ps. 22:9 (MT 10) states, "Yet thou art he who took me from the womb [*beṭen*]." Some persons were chosen for a special calling while they were yet in the womb. When Jeremiah was called to be a prophet, Yahweh told him: "Before I formed you in the womb [*beṭen*] I knew you, and before you were born [*yāṣā' mēreḥem*] I consecrated you" (Jer. 1:5; cf. Isa. 49:1; Lk. 1:15).

In biblical times the woman's most important role was the bearing of children, and to be BARREN was the worst fate a woman could suffer. Jesus, however, rejected the reduction of women to the reproductive role. When a woman called out, "Blessed is the womb that bore you and the breast that you sucked!" Jesus responded, "Blessed rather are those who hear the word of God and keep it" (Lk. 11:27f.). *See* SEX III.D; IV.C.

See also BELLY; SEX II.B.5.

Bibliography.–*TDNT*, III, *s.v.* κοιλία (J. Behm); *TDOT*, II, *s.v.* "beṭen" (D. N. Freedman, J. Lundbom); *TWOT*, I, 102f.; II, 842.

N. J. O.

WOMEN IN CHURCH LEADERSHIP. The question of whether it is proper for women to preach or exercise leadership in the church has received much attention in recent decades. Some denominations permit and even encourage the unrestricted use of women's gifts in all the offices of the church, while others, based on passages such as 1 Tim. 2:9-15, 1 Cor. 11:2-16, and 14:33-36, consider it unbiblical for a woman to preach or exercise authority over an ecclesiastical body that includes men.

Several passages figure prominently in the debate. The passages cited above seem to imply a subordination of women in the church; others, it is argued (esp. Gal. 3:28), seem to point in the direction of equality of the sexes. Moreover, the Bible contains a number of impressive examples of women exercising political and spiritual leadership over men. This article will summarize some of the chief arguments on both sides of the issue as they relate to these often-cited passages.

I. Galatians 3:28.–Many scholars have interpreted this passage and others (e.g., 1 Cor. 11:11f.; 1 Pet. 3:7) as teaching the abolition of all inequality between the sexes within the church (e.g., see Stendahl, pp. 32-35; Scanzoni and Hardesty, pp. 106-111, 204f.; Jewett, pp. 142-49). Scholars who maintain that the Scriptures prohibit women from holding a teaching or ruling office within the church have argued that these passages, if they even bear on the issue, at most support an ontological or salvific equality of men and women and do not contradict the functional subordination of women in the domestic and ecclesiastical spheres as required by other texts. S. Clark (pp. 137-163) has pointed out that Gal. 3:28, while certainly having social implications, nevertheless is concerned to insist not on the *equality* of the sexes but on the *unity* of all believers in Christ (so also Boucher, p. 56; Davis [1976], p. 202; Knight, p. 39).

II. Biblical Examples of Women in Authority.–Scholars who defend the subordination of women in the church often urge that the biblical examples of women exercising authority over men (e.g., Deborah, Abigail, the Queen of Sheba, the prophetess Huldah, Queen Esther, the four prophesying daughters of Philip, Priscilla, Phoebe, Junia, etc.) need to be interpreted in the light of relevant didactic passages.

For example, some scholars dismiss Deborah the wife of Lappidoth, who was a prophetess and judge (presiding elder over Israel), as a regrettable exception to a preferred male leadership by appealing to Isa. 3:12: "My people — children are their oppressors, and women rule over them." This passage appears to concede female leadership but interprets it as a rebuke to Israel. These scholars also point to Barak's reluctance to go to war against Sisera without Deborah in Jgs. 4:8f. (cf. LXX). The MT of Isa. 3:12, however, in addition to its problematic vocabulary, appears to be textually corrupt (see *BHS*). The NEB offers a preferable rendering: "Money lenders strip my people bare, and usurers lord it over them." Moreover, it should be noted that Deborah is introduced as judging Israel before Barak's failure to take leadership (Jgs. 4:4-7).

Another approach to the striking example of Deborah has been offered by J. H. Gerstner, *et al.*, who view Deborah's authority as the result of "God's exceptional appointment" but warn against setting aside biblical norms to build a church polity on such an exception. Still other scholars point out that even if women governed in the OT and prophesied in both Testaments, this is not the same as their leading in worship.

Scholars who maintain that the Scriptures support women in ruling and teaching offices do not so readily dismiss these and other biblical examples. In the NT they call attention especially to three of the ten women commended by Paul in Rom. 16:1-23: (1) Phoebe (vv. 1f.), who can plausibly be identified as a "deacon" (Gk. *diákonos*; RSV "deaconess," so also Ford, pp. 670-72, 676f.; but cf. Cranfield, pp. 781; Hurley, p. 124; cf. also E. E. Ellis, pp. 441-45); (2) the remarkable Priscilla (vv. 3-5), who is listed before her husband here as well as in Acts 18:18, 26, possibly indicating that she had the more prominent role in teaching Apollos (but cf. Knight, p. 52); and (3) Junia(s) (v. 7), who may well have been a female apostle (so Cranfield, pp. 788-790; Scholer [1980], pp. 5f.; for the opposing view *see* JUNIAS).

III. 1 Timothy 2:9-15.–Four major approaches to 1 Tim. 2 and the other "subordination texts" may be discerned among scholars supportive of women exercising authority in the church. (For a discussion of the relevant hermeneutical issues raised by these approaches, see also Swartley, pp. 183-191, and esp. Foh, pp. 5-49.)

(1) Some scholars simply deny Pauline authorship to 1 Timothy (so Scroggs; but cf. Spencer, p. 221; *see also* PASTORAL EPISTLES) and assume that this undermines the authority of this text. With similar intent, some scholars identify as a post-Pauline interpolation both 1 Cor. 11:2-16 (so Walker and Cope; but cf. O'Connor) and 14:34-35 (so Bittlinger, and Schweizer; but cf. Grudem, pp. 240-255). But even apart from the question of whether these passages are actually Pauline, such an approach lacks conviction in that it appears to confuse issues of authorship with canonicity.

(2) A second approach, like the first, begins by agreeing that these texts do in fact plainly forbid women in church leadership, but it argues that they are not so much un-Pauline as unchristian — i.e., that they are superseded by the fuller insight set forth in the equality texts. K. Stendahl (pp. 32-37; cf. Jewett, pp. 111-147, and Mollenkott, pp. 20-25) has taken such an approach. He concluded that the texts that speak of subordination merely reflect Paul's rabbinic training and deeply ingrained cultural bias, analogous to the prevailing attitude toward slavery, whereas those that speak of equality, beginning with the breakthrough of Gal. 3:28, reflect a more authentically Christian reversal of the order of creation.

This approach commits a kind of "genetic" fallacy, assuming that the derivation of a NT teaching from earlier Jewish convictions would be grounds for rejecting its authority (cf. Cowling, p. 27; Clark, pp. 356f.). Moreover, there appears to be a growing scholarly consensus that Paul's insight in Gal. 3:28 may not constitute after all so radical a departure from the Judaism of his day (see Boucher; Barth, pp. 655-662; Brooten). Brooten has offered a provocative reassessment of the inscriptional evidence for female leadership, including elders, among Jews during the Roman and Byzantine periods.

(3) A third approach asserts that 1 Cor. 11 and 14 and 1 Tim. 2 record culturally relative applications of what may well be abidingly valid principles (hence Paul's appeal to creational norms), but that in any case these injunctions ought not be applied uncritically to the often radically dissimilar situation of the modern church. A. Spencer, e.g., has suggested that 1 Tim. 2 actually marks a radical and liberating departure from the repressive Jewish practice of the time, which discouraged teaching women the Scriptures, since women are here encouraged to study the Word ("learn in silence, v. 11"). As for Paul's prohibition of women teaching, Spencer argued that this is based solely on the regrettable similarity between the women of Ephesus and Eve, in that the Ephesian women had been deceived (cf. 2 Tim. 3:6f.) and were promoting false doctrine. After the women received further instruction, however, such a parallel would happily break down and so the prohibition would be made void. Similar interpretations have been offered by Olthuis (p. 142f.), Scholer (1975), Williams (p. 111), and Davis (1979); cf. also N. Hommes. Arguments have been brought against this view by S. Foh (pp. 122-29). In addition, R. Forsyth (p. 237) has warned against the overly simplistic picture of the Jewish or Greek cultural background that is often assumed by scholars following this approach (so also Boucher, pp. 50-58; Barth, pp. 655-662); e.g., certainly Eunice and Lois (2 Tim. 1:5; 3:15) knew the Scriptures better than might be inferred from the Jewish practice adduced by Spencer.

(4) A fourth approach differs from the other three in that it begins by contesting the exegesis of these subordination passages. Thus M. Griffiths (p. 196) has appealed for a closer study of these passages, convinced that they admit of a "more positive exegesis." For example, when Paul insists in 1 Cor. 14:33-36 that "the women should keep silent in the churches," the context of this requirement may well limit its scope to the particular kind of disturbing or self-serving questions Paul considered to be best asked by wives when they got home (v. 35; but cf. Hurley, pp. 188-193). Certainly a similar contextual limitation on the command to remain silent is demanded in vv. 28, 30. Interpreted in this manner, Paul's statement does not contradict his earlier comments about women praying and prophesying publicly (11:5).

Similarly, as Griffiths has suggested, while 1 Tim. 2:8-15 possibly intends to exclude women from church office (since ch. 3 is concerned with church polity), this may not be its intention. The terms rendered "man" and "woman" in the RSV (Gk. *anḗr* and *gynḗ*) can as easily be rendered "husband" and "wife" throughout these verses, and such renderings are entirely suited to the present passage (cf. H. C. Oswald, ed., *Luther's Works,* XXVIII [Eng. tr. 1915], 276; Prohl, p. 80; Hommes, p. 13; Zerbst p. 51). The RSV appears to exclude this possibility by its unwarranted plural translation of *anḗr* in v. 12: "I permit no woman to teach or to have authority over men." A better translation would be: "I permit no wife to teach or to have authority over her husband."

Favoring this suggestion, it may be noted that elsewhere in Paul's writings *anḗr* occurs fifty times and *gynḗ* occurs fifty-four times in close proximity within eleven distinct contexts, and in each case these terms bear the meanings "husband" and "wife" rather than "man" and "woman" (so G. K. Beale, oral communication). Indeed, it may be argued that, if Paul had intended to speak about man in relation to woman in 1 Tim. 2, rather than about husband in relation to wife, he would have used *ánthrōpos,* "man," rather than *anḗr,* in contrast to *gynḗ,* as he did in 1 Cor. 7:1. Alternatively, Paul could have used the very terms that most stress gender, *ársēn,* "man," in contrast to *thḗlys,* "woman," as he did in Rom. 1:26f.

B. W. Powers has recently argued that the widely held assumption that 1 Tim. 2:8-15 concerns behavior in public worship is far from self-evident, and he has suggested instead a reference specifically to the home. Elsewhere in the NT (Eph. 5) Adam and Eve are paradigmatic for marriage, not for male-female relations in general. Against those who would disparage marriage and the homemaking role as unspiritual (1 Tim. 4:3; 5:14), Paul in 2:15 urges that childbearing — clearly an activity outside the worship service — need be no detriment to salvation (Powers [pp. 57f.] prefers instead to interpret *sṓzō,* "save," as a reference to physical safety in childbirth), provided that such a woman "continues in faith and love and holiness, with modesty." Certainly Powers is correct in pointing out that the prayer with uplifted hands "in every place" (v. 8) need not be restricted to formal church gatherings, for nowhere else in the NT does this expression require such a restrictive definition.

Guthrie (p. 77), finding it impossible that Paul would command silence for wives in the home, has insisted that 1 Tim. 2:12 must be concerned with public worship. But such an objection strangely overlooks a passage such as 2 Thess. 3:12, where Paul enjoins men to "silence" (RSV "quietness") without implying a total ban on speech; cf. also 1 Tim. 2:2.

Interpreting 1 Tim. 2:8-15 in terms of the home is especially attractive in light of the often overlooked but extensive verbal parallels that this passage has with 1 Pet. 3:1-7 (so Powers, p. 58), where the sphere for submission is clearly domestic. These parallels are so impressive that Selwyn (pp. 432-35), among others, assumed "dependence of both on a common source." It is noteworthy that both passages include not only a concern for wifely submission but also a warning that husbands avoid domestic strife that would undermine their prayer life.

For a more general discussion of the roles of women in biblical times, *see* WOMAN.

Bibliography.–M. Barth, *Ephesians* (*AB,* 1974); A. Bittlinger, *Gift and Graces: A Comm. on 1 Corinthians 12-14* (Eng. tr. 1967); M. Boucher, *CBQ,* 31 (1969) 50-58; B. J. Brooten, *Women Leaders in the Ancient Synagogue* (1982); S. B. Clark, *Man and Woman in Christ* (1980); L. Cope, *JBL,* 97 (1978), 435f.; G. Cowling, *Interchange,* 21 (1977), 23-47; C. E. B. Cranfield, *ICC* on Romans, II (1979); J. J. Davis, *JETS,* 19 (1976), 201-208; *Presbyterian Communique,* 12 (1979), 1, 10f., 15; E. E. Ellis, *NTS,* 17 (1971), 437-452; M. Evans, *Woman in the Bible* (1984); S. Foh, *Women and the Word of God* (1979); J. M. Ford, *Journal of Ecumenical Studies,* 10 (1973), 669-694; R. Forsyth, *Interchange,* 20 (1976); J. H. Gerstner, *et al.,* "Ordination and Subordination," in R. Hestenes, ed., *Women and Men in Ministry* (1980), pp. 81-88; M. Griffiths, *The Church and World Mission* (1980); W. Grudem, *Gift of Prophecy in 1 Corinthians* (1982); D. Guthrie, *Pastoral Epistles* (*Tyndale NT Comms.,* 1957); N. J. Hommes, *Calvin Theological Journal,* 4 (1969), 5-22; J. B. Hurley, *Man and Woman in Biblical Perspective* (1981); P. K. Jewett, *Man as Male and Female* (1975); G. W. Knight, *NT Teaching on the Role Relationship of Men and Women* (1977); V. Mollenkott, *Women, Men, and the Bible* (1977); J. M. O'Connor, *JBL,* 95 (1976), 615-621; J. H. Olthuis, *I Pledge You My Troth* (1975); B. W. Powers, *Inter-*

change, 17 (1975), 55-59; R. Prohl, *Woman in the Church* (1957); L. Scanzoni and N. Hardesty, *All We're Meant to Be* (1974); *Soundings*, 53 (1970), 374-78; D. M. Scholer, *Daughters of Sarah*, 1 (1975), 7f.; 6 (1980), 3-6; E. Schweizer, *Interp.*, 13 (1959), 400-408; R. Scroggs, *Christian Century*, 89 (1972), 307-309; E. G. Selwyn, *First Epistle of Peter* (2nd ed. 1947); A. Spencer, *JETS*, 17 (1974), 215-222; *Beyond the Curse* (1985); K. Stendahl, *The Bible and the Role of Women* (Eng. tr. 1966); W. M. Swartley, *Slavery, Sabbath, War, and Women* (1983); W. O. Walker, Jr., *JBL*, 94 (1975), 94-110; D. Williams, *The Apostle Paul and Women in the Church* (1977); F. Zerbst, *Office of Woman in the Church* (Eng. tr. 1955).
G. P. HUGENBERGER

WONDER; WONDERFUL; WONDROUS(LY) [Heb. *môpēṯ*, niphal, hiphil, and hithpael of *pālā'* (esp. niphal pl. part. *niplā'ôṯ*), *pele'*, *pelî* (Jgs. 13:18; Ps. 139:6), *miplā'â* (Job 37:16), niphal of *pālâ* (Ps. 139:14), hithpolel of *šāmēm* (Isa. 59:16), hithpael of *tāmah* (Hab. 1:5); Aram. $t^{e}mah$ (Dnl. 4:2f. [MT 3:32f.]; 6:27 [MT 28]); Gk. *téras, thaumázō, thaumastós* (Rev. 15:1, 3), *thaumásios* (Mt. 21:15), *thaúma* (2 Cor. 11:14), *thámbos*–'astonishment' (Acts 3:10), *aretḗ*–'excellence' ("wonderful deed," 1 Pet. 2:9), *potapós*–'of what sort' ("what wonderful," Mk. 13:1); supplied in Acts 5:24]; AV also MARVEL, MARVELLOUS(LY), MIRACLE, SECRET (Jgs. 13:18), WHAT MANNER (Mk. 13:1); NEB also PORTENT, MIRACLE, etc.

I. In the OT.–In the OT "wonder," etc., usually represent Heb. *môpēṯ* or a form of the word-group *plʿ*. *Môpēṯ* (also rendered "miracle" or "portent" by the RSV, e.g., Ps. 78:43; 105:5, 27; Joel 2:30 [MT 3:2]) occurs frequently in combination with *'ôṯ*, "sign" (as in the expression "signs and wonders," Ex. 7:3; Dt. 6:22; 26:8; etc.). It generally refers to a miraculous event through which Yahweh reveals His power in history. Frequently it denotes the extraordinary events associated with Israel's exodus from Egypt (Ex. 7:3; 11:9f.; Dt. 4:34; 6:22; 7:19; 26:8; 29:3 [MT 2]; 34:11; Neh. 9:10; Ps. 135:9; Jer. 32:20f.; cf. also 1 Ch. 16:12). In Dt. 13:1f. (MT 2f.), however, it refers to a miraculous act performed by a false prophet or dreamer. In 28:46 the reference is to the curses that will come upon the Israelites if they are disobedient, causing them to become a spectacle illustrating the rewards of disobedience. *See* MIRACLE I.A; SIGN III, IV.

The stem *pl'* refers to things or events that are extraordinary and beyond human capabilities and thus evoke a response of astonishment (*TWOT*, II, 723). The reference is "not to the subjective experience of wonder, but to the objective fact" (*TDNT*, III, 31). Both the verb and the substantives are applied primarily to the mighty acts of God, either in creation or in history. The verb does not occur in the qal; the basic meaning of the hiphil is "cause a wonderful thing to happen" (Jgs. 13:19; 2 Ch. 2:9 [MT 8]; Ps. 17:7; 31:21 [MT 22]; Isa. 28:29; 29:14; Joel 2:26), while the hithpael means "show oneself marvelous" (Job 10:16) and the niphal connotes "be wonderful," "be too marvelous for" (e.g., 2 S. 1:26; Job 42:3). Most common is the niphal plural participle *niplā'ôṯ*, "wonderful works, miraculous deeds" (Ex. 3:20; Josh. 3:5; Jgs. 6:13; Ps. 9:1 [MT 2]; 26:7; 40:5 [MT 6]; 71:17; 72:18; 75:1 [MT 2]; 78:4, 32; etc.), which is used synonymously with *pele'* (pl. p^{e}*lā'îm*; e.g., Ex. 15:11; Ps. 77:11, 14 [MT 12, 15]; 88:10, 12 [MT 11, 13]; 89:5 [MT 6]; 119:129; Isa. 9:6 [MT 5]; 25:1).

The basic meaning of Heb. *tāmah* is "be astounded." In Hab. 1:5 the use of both the hithpael (RSV "wonder") and the qal (RSV "be astounded") of *tāmah* "serves to strengthen [the verb], so as to express the highest degree of amazement" (KD, *in loc.*) — i.e., amazement at the terrible work that Yahweh is about to perform. In Dnl. 4:2f. (MT 3:32f.) and 6:27 (MT 28) the cognate Aramaic noun $t^{e}mah$ is linked with Aram. *'āṯ* (in the phrase "signs and wonders") in the same way that Heb. *môpēṯ* is linked with *'ôṯ*. The references are to Yahweh's miraculous deliverances from the fiery furnace and the lion's den.

The root idea of *šāmēm* is to be appalled and DESOLATE due to a great disaster (*see also* HORROR). In Isa. 59:16 the hithpolel of this verb describes Yahweh's dismay at finding no leader who could set things right for His people.

In general, the OT uses of "wonder," etc., point to the unique activity of God. The psalmists call forth the memory of God's mighty acts in exhortations to joyous faith and obedience (e.g., Ps. 9:1 [MT 2]; 40:5 [MT 6]; 77:11 [MT 12]; 78:4; 105:5; 107:8, 15, 21, 31; 145:5). This theme appears also in the historical and prophetic literature (e.g., 1 Ch. 16:9, 12; Neh. 9:10, 17; Isa. 25:1; Dnl. 4:2f. [MT 3:32f.]; 6:27 [MT 28]). More frequently in the prophetic literature "wonder" expresses anticipation of God's future action — whether that be judgment (e.g., Hab. 1:5) or redemption (e.g., Isa. 29:14; cf. 9:6). The wisdom literature employs the concept of wonder in the sense of things beyond human comprehension. A proverb states: "Three things are too wonderful for me; four I do not understand: the way of an eagle in the sky, the way of a serpent on a rock, the way of a ship on the high seas, and the way of a man with a maiden" (Prov. 30:18f.). In Job 37:14, 16 the young Elihu challenges Job: "Hear this, O Job; stop and consider the wondrous works of God. . . . Do you know the balancings of the clouds, the wondrous works of him who is perfect in knowledge?" And in 42:3 Job at last says, "I have uttered what I did not understand, things too wonderful for me, which I did not know."

II. In the NT.–In the NT "wonder," etc., represent predominantly the Greek noun *téras* or a form from the *thaumázō* word-group. *Téras* occurs sixteen times in the NT (nine times in Acts), exclusively in the plural and always linked with Gk. *sēmeía* ("signs"); in a few instances it is additionally linked with *dynámeis* ("mighty works," Acts 2:22; 2 Cor. 12:12; "miracles," He. 2:4). Its meaning in the NT is governed by its use in the LXX as a translation of Heb. *môpēṯ* (which is frequently linked with *'ôṯ*, "sign"). As with *môpēṯ*, Gk. *téras* always includes the idea of God's self-revelation. Although the Synoptics consistently refer to Jesus' miracles simply as *dynámeis* and John refers to them as *sēmeía*, Acts 2:22 uses all three terms, emphasizing the divine source of these acts: "Jesus of Nazareth, a man attested to you by God with mighty works and wonders and signs which God did through him in your midst" (cf. v. 19). "Signs and wonders" performed "through the apostles" also served to accredit their ministry as being from God (2:43; 5:12; 6:8; 14:3; 15:12; cf. 4:30; Rom. 15:19; 2 Cor. 12:12; He. 2:4). Jesus warned His followers not to be deceived, however, by false messiahs and prophets who will attempt to validate their claims through performing "signs and wonders" (Mt. 24:24 par. Mk. 13:22). Paul also warned that "the coming of the lawless one by the activity of Satan will be with all power and with pretended signs and wonders" (2 Thess. 2:9).

The Greek verb *thaumázō* is translated "wonder" about fifteen times in the RSV NT; elsewhere it is rendered "marvel" (twenty-four times) and "be astonished" (two times). It is most common in the Gospels, where it is used to describe the spectators' reaction to the surprising and unexpected events in Jesus' birth, ministry, and resurrection. Often such wonder is accompanied by fear; but the reaction is not entirely negative, for the persons affected are not driven away.

According to the Lukan Infancy narrative, wonder

attended the events surrounding Jesus' birth. The people were surprised at Zechariah's delay in coming out of the temple to give them the priestly blessing (Lk. 1:21). Astonishment was the response of all who heard the shepherds' Christmas story (2:18). (Cf. also the use of *thaumázō* [RSV "marvel"] in 1:63; 2:33.)

The element of surprised wonder is frequent in accounts of Jesus' ministry. When through His miraculous deeds He fulfilled the great signs of the messianic age, the crowds "wondered" and glorified God (Mt. 15:31; cf. 9:33 [RSV "marvel"]). Jesus' words also evoked a response of wonder, e.g., His words of grace in the synagogue at Nazareth (Lk. 4:22; cf. Mt. 22:22 par.; Jn. 3:7 [RSV "marvel"]). Pilate was greatly amazed at Jesus' silence in response to his questioning (Mt. 27:14; Mk. 15:5); he was also astonished at how quickly Jesus died (15:44). When Jesus appeared to the disciples after His resurrection, they were unable to believe for joy and amazement (Lk. 24:41; cf. the uncertain text of v. 12).

The supernatural signs that marked the Spirit's presence in the young Church likewise met with wonder (*thaumázō,* Acts 2:7; 3:12; cf. v. 10, where "wonder" represents *thámbos* and "amazement" represents *ékstasis; see also* AMAZE). Similarly, the extraordinary boldness of the apostles Peter and John, who were otherwise very ordinary men, evoked the amazement of the members of the Sanhedrin (4:13). The recipients of 1 John were told that they should not be surprised if the world hates them (3:13).

The related noun *thaúma* can describe a response of amazement (cf. Rev. 17:6), but in 2 Cor. 11:14 it denotes an object of wonder. In vv. 13-15 Paul says that it should come as no surpise to the Corinthians that his opponents disguise themselves as apostles of Christ, since they are servants of Satan, the master deceiver. The adjective *thaumásios* occurs only in Mt. 21:15, where the substantive form *tá thaumásia* refers to the "wonderful things" (i.e., miracles of healing) accomplished by Jesus in the temple. The synonymous adjective *thaumastós* is rendered "wonderful" in Rev. 15:1, 3 (elsewhere it is rendered "marvelous"). In v. 1 it is used to describe John's vision of seven angels with seven plagues — awe-inspiring symbols of God's wrath; in v. 3 it describes God's redemptive deeds, which excite wonder not only because of their greatness but also because of their righteousness. (Cf. the reaction of the people of the world in 13:3, who follow the beast "with wonder" [*thaumázō*].)

See also ASTONISHMENT; MARVEL; MIRACLE; SIGN.

Bibliography.–*DNTT,* II, 620-26, 633f.; *TDNT,* III, *s.v.* θάμβος (Bertram), θαύμα κτλ. (Bertram); VIII, *s.v.* τέρας (Rengstorf); *TWOT,* II, 723, 936f., 972, 1085. C. N. DILLMAN N. J. O.

WOOD. *See* FLORA; FOREST; TREE.

WOOL [Heb. *ṣemer*; Gk. *érion*]. Wool and linen were the most common fibers woven into cloth for garments (Lev. 13:47f., 59; Prov. 31:13; Hos. 2:5), although any blending of the two was expressly forbidden (Dt. 22:11). The priests were required to wear linen rather than woolen clothing in the inner temple court to prevent perspiration. (Ezk. 44:17f.).

Wool was of considerable commercial value and was accepted as tribute from Moab by the king of Israel (2 K. 3:4; Isa. 16:1). The "white wool" of Damascus was valuable merchandise (Ezk. 27:18 — a wool of tawny color, Heb. *ṣaḥar*; cf. BDB).

Wool provided clothing for the rich (Jas. 5:2, by implication), in contrast to the rough sheepskin clothing of the destitute (He. 11:37). The skins were useful material for tents, and the tabernacle had a covering of rams' skins dyed red (Ex. 26:14). Scarlet wool, together with hyssop, was used in ritual sprinkling of blood (He. 9:19f.; cf. Lev. 14:1-7; Nu. 19:5f.).

Since wool was commonly used in Israel, similes were naturally derived from it. The earth and unbelieving men will be consumed, as a woolen garment is by moths, but God's salvation is everlasting (Isa. 51:6-8). The whiteness of wool makes it a suitable comparison for snow (Ps. 147:16), for forgiven sins (Isa. 1:18), and for the hair of the ancient of days (Dnl. 7:9) and son of man (Rev. 1:14).

G. I. EMMERSON

WORD [Heb. *dāḇār, ʾēmer, ʾōmer, ʾimrâ, nᵉʾum, millâ*; Aram. *mēʾmar, millâ*; Gk. *lógos, rhḗma*]. The words, speech, sayings, or message of human beings; the message, command, or revelation of God; also, the Christian gospel; title of Christ.

- I. Terminology
  - A. Hebrew
  - B. Aramaic
  - C. Greek
  - D. English Versions
- II. In the OT
  - A. Human Words
  - B. God's Word as Prophetic Revelation
  - C. Creative and Effective Word of God
  - D. God's Word as Law
- III. Intertestamental Developments: Later Jewish and Hellenistic Thought
  - A. Greek Philosophy
  - B. LXX, Apocrypha, and Pseudepigrapha
  - C. Philo
  - D. DSS and Rabbinical Literature
  - E. Gnosis and Similar Thought
- IV. In the NT
  - A. Human Words
  - B. OT Word in the NT
  - C. Divine Revelation through Voice and Vision
  - D. Words of Jesus
  - E. Word as Christian Message
  - F. Word as a Title of Christ
- V. Later Developments
  - A. Developed Gnostic Thought
  - B. Patristic Doctrines

I. Terminology.–"Word" is used in the English versions of the Bible to translate a substantial number of different words, some of which have a wide range of meaning.

A. Hebrew. Most frequent is *dāḇār* (about 1430 times), which generally means "matter," or "thing," but also applies to the spoken word, or written communication. Other Hebrew words are *ʾēmer, ʾōmer,* and *ʾimrâ* (< *ʾmr,* "say"), which occur mostly in poetic passages, *nᵉʾum,* "ecstatic or divine utterance" (361 times, mostly in the Prophets), and *millâ* (< *mll,* "speak"), largely in poetic passages.

B. Aramaic. The word *millâ* in Daniel has the sense of both "word" and "thing," and *mēʾmar* in Dnl. 4:17 (MT 14) and Ezr. 6:9 has the sense of "word."

C. Greek. The two chief nouns are *rhḗma* (cf. Lat. *verbum*), used for the spoken word (sometimes in LXX and NT to render *dāḇār,* "thing"), and *lógos,* (< *leg-*; cf. the common verb *légō,* meaning originally "pick up," and hence "count," "tell," "speak"). *Lógos* embraces an exceptionally wide semantic field, including the ideas of account, proportion, explanation, principle, reason, thought, as well as continuous statement (e.g., narrative, story, speech, history), individual utterance (e.g., proverb, maxim, command), discussion, debate, and, as a grammatical term, phrase or sentence. It is not normally used in the sense of a single word; it is sometimes set in antithesis to *érgon* (deed, fact) or to *mýthos* (story, fiction). In the LXX no special distinction exists in the theological uses of *rhḗma* and *lógos*; *rhḗma* is more common in the Pentateuch, *lógos* is more frequent in the Prophets and Writings. In the NT *rhḗma* is used mostly for individual spoken utterances, and in OT citations and echoes; *lógos,* occurring more frequently (331 times, in all NT writings except Jude and Philemon), is used for God's word in all its senses, for Christ's words, for ordinary human words, and with other non-theological meanings. The diminutive *lógion* occurs in both the LXX and NT, usually in the sense of God's words.

D. English Versions. All translations, but especially more recent versions, render these same Hebrew, Aramaic, and Greek words by a great variety of expressions. According to context they may appear as SPEECH, COMMAND, PROMISE, PROPHECY (IV.B), etc.; sometimes they are rendered by a verbal phrase, such as "what you say," or "thus says the Lord." This article focuses on special theological uses of "word," though brief mention will be made of other uses.

II. In the OT.–A. *Human Words.* "Word" is used regularly and frequently for ordinary human communication, whether written (e.g., a letter [Est. 9:26], scroll [Isa. 29:11, 18], or historical acts [2 Ch. 12:15; etc.), or oral, such as the words of poems and songs (e.g., Dt. 31:30), the sayings of wise men (e.g., Prov. 1:6; 22:17), and the ordinary spoken utterances of men and women. Sometimes it is difficult to distinguish between the two senses of *dāḇār,* "word" and "matter" (e.g., Dt. 22:20). In Ex. 4:10 Moses protests that he is "not eloquent" (lit. "no man of words"), but God replies that He will be with Moses' mouth (v. 12).

B. God's Word as Prophetic Revelation. The Word of God (*d^{e}ḇar YHWH, d^{e}ḇar ’ĕlōhîm*) is one of the key OT concepts. God's direct revelation comes to mankind either orally or visually — "word" and "vision" respectively, with the idea of oral or verbal communication predominating. The sense of having heard God actually speak is so strong that when the child Samuel was called, he thought that Eli was speaking to him (1 S. 3:2-14). The prophet's own words are thus readily identified with God's words: the prophet may preface his message with the phrase "Thus says the Lord," or he may conclude it with "oracle of Yahweh" (*n^{e}’um YHWH*; NEB "This is the word of the Lord"). A frequent expression (over 120 times) is the so-called word-event formula — "The word of the Lord/God came to. . . ." This may be used of an individual message to a prophet (e.g., 1 K. 12:22), or it may be adapted to preface a whole prophetic book (e.g., Hos. 1:1; Joel 1:1). Sometimes word is combined with the idea of vision: "the word (*dāḇār*) which Isaiah the son of Amoz saw" (Isa. 2:1). God's communication of the word to the prophet may also be symbolized by the touching of his mouth (Jer. 1:9; cf. Isa. 6:7), or it may be considered so much a part of his being that he is actually described as eating it (Jer. 15:16; Ezk. 2:8–3:3).

The word that comes with such clarity is never simply a piece of information, but rather the will of God in a particular situation. It may come as a message of salvation, exemplified par excellence in the words of Isa. 40:1: "Comfort, comfort my people, says your God." It may be, and often is, a sober message of warning or judgment, as when Amos denounced the transgressions of the nations and of Israel, and pronounced God's judgment on them: "Hear this word which I take up over you in lamentation, O house of Israel" (Am. 5:1). We are told that Amaziah the priest of Bethel complained to the king that the land was not able to bear Amos's words (7:10); yet a prophet felt compelled to deliver his divine message, no matter how unpopular he or it might be. As Balaam says in Nu. 22:38, "The word that God puts in my mouth, that must I speak" (cf. Ezk. 12:25; 33:7f.). Although God's word to the prophet might be a joy and delight (Jer. 15:16), it could also be a torturous burden. Jeremiah complains: "For the word of the Lord has become for me a reproach and derision all day long. If I say, 'I will not mention him, or speak any more in his name,' there is in my heart as it were a burning fire shut up in my bones, and I am weary with holding it in, and I cannot" (Jer. 20:8f.).

Although false prophets may speak lying words, the word of the Lord that comes to His true prophets is utterly dependable. When Elijah told the widow of Zarephath that the jar of meal and cruse of oil would not fail until the Lord sent rain, then that was precisely what happened "according to the word of the Lord which he spoke by Elijah" (1 K. 17:16).

C. Creative and Effective Word of God. Closely related to the concept of the word as God's will or command revealed to His spokesman the prophet in a particular situation is the concept of the dynamic word by which creation is effected. Ps. 33:6 expresses the idea vividly: "By the word of the Lord the heavens were made, and all their host by the breath of his mouth" (cf. Gen. 1:3; Ps. 148:5, etc.).

Not only is the initial act of creation effected through God's word, but He regularly "speaks" through the forces of nature. In Ps. 29 the voice (Heb. *qôl*) of the Lord is described as "powerful" and "full of majesty"; it is heard in the thunder; it breaks the cedars and shakes the wilderness. In Ps. 147:16-18 God's word is again associated with meteorological phenomena: "He gives snow like wool . . . He casts forth his ice like morsels . . . He sends forth his word, and melts them." The concept is slightly different in Ps. 19:1-4 where the whole created order "tells" the glory of God, and their "words" go out to the ends of the earth.

It is a small step from this concept of the word effective in creation and nature to that of God's word effective in history. In what has been called "the most profound statement about God's word to be found in the OT" (Whybray, p. 194), God says: "For as the rain and the snow come down from heaven, and return not thither but water the earth, making it bring forth and sprout, giving seed to the sower and bread to the eater, *so shall my word be that goes forth from my mouth; it shall not return to me empty, but it shall accomplish that which I purpose,* and prosper in the thing for which I sent it" (Isa. 55:10f.). As the context makes clear, the word is God's message of salvation. Cf. the powerful statement about the permanence of God's word in Isa. 40:6-8.

Much has been written about the origins of this concept of the creative and effective word of God. Von Rad, Procksch, and others have stressed that, in contrast to the "abstract" understanding of the modern Western world, ancient peoples thought of words as concrete and powerful entities, almost material forces (von Rad, II, 81-85; cf. *TDNT,* IV, 93). It is true that in many civilizations certain utterances, especially blessings and curses, are thought of as having a power of their own, so that once spoken they cannot be revoked (cf. Gen. 27:32-38), and striking parallels to the OT idea of the creative word are found in Mesopotamian and Egyptian sources (see *TDOT,* III, 84-94). The idea of the supposed power of words in Hebrew thought has nevertheless been challenged, notably by James Barr and A. C. Thiselton (see Bibliography), who argue that it rests upon a mistaken view of the linguistic evidence (esp. the double meaning of *dāḇār* as "word" and "thing"; cf. I.A above). The dynamic and effective word of God may be more closely related to the "performative utterances" of modern language study (phrases like "I hereby bequeath," or "I will" of the Marriage Service) than to primitive magic. Only in special cases in biblical thought are human utterances conceived as automatically effective; while the effectiveness of God's word depends ultimately on the biblical concept of His character rather than anything intrinsic to words themselves. *See also* NAME I.

D. God's Word as Law. A further important way in which the terms "word(s)," and "God's word" are used in the OT is with reference to His commands to His people about their behavior, especially in the context of the covenant relationship. The Ten Commandments, given to Moses on Mt. Sinai, are called simply the "ten words" (Ex. 34:28; Dt. 4:13; 10:4). The "word" has indeed a special part to play in the message of Deuteronomy where it is used both for the individual commandments of God, and for the law as a whole. This "word" is the people's life (32:47); they are continually urged to obey it, warned of the penalties for disobedience, and reminded of the blessings of obedience. Nor is this "word" to be thought of as something inaccessible or difficult: "For this commandment which I command you this day is not too hard for you, neither is it far off. . . . But the word is very near you; it is in your mouth and in your heart, so that you can do it" (Dt. 30:11, 14; cf. Rom. 10:8).

In many poetic passages of the OT "law" and "word" occur in synonymous parallelism (e.g., Isa. 2:3 par. Mic. 4:2). The identification of the word with the law is particularly striking in Ps. 119, where "word" (*dāḇār* or *'imrâ*) appears continually in parallel with various words for law (e.g., "precept," "command," "statute"). For the psalmist God's word is a lantern to his feet; His words are sweeter than honey in his mouth; His word is true, firmly fixed in the heaven; it brings him hope and strength in affliction. This Psalm, a lengthy and elaborate acrostic poem, is more than a literary tour de force; it is a spiritual classic, an eloquent testimony to the inspiration which God's word as law provided to a devout Jew.

III. Intertestamental Developments: Later Jewish and Hellenistic Thought.–*A. Greek Philosophy. 1. The Classical Background.* In Greek philosophical writing *lógos* takes on a special significance as early as the pre-Socratic philosopher Heraclitus, "the obscure" (*ca.* 500 B.C.), who seems to have used the term for an underlying coherence or principle of the universe. Heraclitus's works survive only in short fragments, and it is doubtful what he intended precisely by his *lógos* (see Kirk, Raven, and Schofield, pp. 186-88; Barrett, *NT Background,* pp. 54f.), but Stoic philosophers of the Hellenistic Age looked back to his enigmatic words as the source of their *lógos* doctrines.

In the mid-5th cent. B.C. the Sophists (influential teachers of rhetoric) used *lógos* in a broad sense to include both the rational faculty, which makes cultural and political life possible, and the art of public speaking or presenting arguments. Gorgias in particular stressed the power of the *lógos,* describing it in quasi-personal terms as a great ruler (*dynástēs mégas*), capable of effecting the most divine deeds in the smallest body (see *TDNT,* IV, 82).

Neither Socrates nor Plato made any major direct contribution to a doctrine of the *lógos,* but Plato's theory of "ideas" (belief in the existence of an eternal world, absolute, changeless and perfect, which contrasts with the visible, changing world of the senses) was to influence later philosophical *lógos* doctrines. Aristotle's contribution here was likewise small: he used *lógos* (among other things) for the mental faculty of reason, possessed by human beings alone as opposed to the animals, enabling them to express themselves in speech (*Pol.* i.1.1253a). Also in the 4th cent. B.C. Antisthenes, founder of the Cynic school of philosophy, defined *lógos* as "that which sets forth what a thing was or is" (see Guthrie, III, 210).

2. Hellenistic Developments. More important developments occurred among the Stoics, whose school of philosophy was founded at Athens by Zeno (*ca.* 300 B.C.). Recalling Heraclitus, Stoic philosophers regularly used *lógos* as a technical term for the underlying principle of natural order pervading the universe. Zeno, Cleanthes, and others identified this with Zeus, the supreme god of the Greeks, and interpreted *lógos* as a pantheistic world soul (see texts in Barrett, *NT Background,* pp. 61-65). Sometimes *lógos* was also identified with Hermes the messenger god.

In developed Stoic thought, various types of *lógos* were distinguished, namely, *lógos orthós* (true reason), the principle of cosmic order which gives human beings the power of knowledge, *lógos spermatikós* (seminal reason), being the creative principle and source of ideas and growth, *lógos prophorikós* (expressed reason), used especially for ideas in general, and *lógos endiáthetos* (immanent reason), used for unexpressed thought.

B. LXX, Apocrypha, and Pseudepigrapha. As already noted, *lógos* occurs frequently in the LXX to translate Heb. *dāḇār.* J. N. Sanders has suggested (see *IDB,* IV, 870) that, for Jews familiar with Greek philosophy, this would in itself bring with it connotations of the Stoic doctrine of the *lógos,* particularly in the accounts of creation.

A significant development in this literature is the vivid personification of *Sophía* or Wisdom (cf. Prov. 8–9), described as the "breath of the power of God" and the "reflection (or "effulgence") of eternal light" (Wisd. 7:25f.); she is said to be with God, knowing His works (9:9), and to have come from the Most High to make her dwelling in Israel (Sir. 24:7-12). Since Wisdom was closely associated with creation and is used in synonymous parallelism with Word (e.g., Wisd. 9:1f.), it is easy to see how *lógos* also became personified. This occurs most strikingly at Wisd. 18:15f.: "Thy all-powerful word leaped from heaven, from the royal throne, into the midst of the land that was doomed, a stern warrior carrying the sharp sword of thy authentic command, and stood and filled all things with death. . . ." It should, however, be noted that here *lógos* is the destructive agent of judgment, not the creative word.

The pseudepigraphic Odes of Solomon describe the word as existing in God before time, as the means of creation, as powerful and active in the universe, as a source of light and truth, and as revealing God's thought (see esp. Odes 12:1-3; 16:19; 41:11-14). An important verse states, "For the dwelling-place [tabernacle] of the Word is man [or a son of man], and his [or its] truth is love (12:12). The background of the Odes (1st or 2nd cent. A.D. [?]) has been much debated; Jewish, Gnostic, and even Christian origins have been postulated. It seems clear that at some stage they were used in the Christian church, and direct Johannine influence on them cannot be excluded.

Other Pseudepigrapha do not greatly extend our picture, "word" being used mostly in senses already discussed.

C. Philo. An important figure for the development of later Logos doctrines is the Alexandrian Jew Philo Judaeus (*ca.* 20 B.C.-A.D. 50), who uses the term *lógos* over thirteen hundred times in his extensive writings. Sometimes it is used simply for the spoken word, or for "reason," or in some other non-technical sense; but it is also used with the epithets *theíos* ("divine") and *hierós* ("holy"), or with dependent genitive *theoú* ("of God"), in a special religious sense for the manifestation or expression of God's activity in the world. This *lógos* is said to be God's image (*eikṓn*), and is sometimes described metaphorically in personal terms as His first-born son (*De agricultura* 51) or High Priest (*De gigantibus* 52). Sometimes *lógos* seems to be equated with the whole world of Platonic "ideas"; elsewhere it seems to be used more in a Stoic sense for the ordered principle of the universe. We also see it used for the mind of God with which every human being has a kinship, being a copy, fragment, or ray (*apaúgasma*) of His nature (*De opificio mundi* 145f.). In the plural it is used for God's guidance, which directs the searching soul in the path of goodness (e.g., *De somniis* i.69). By a process of allegorization *lógos* is identified with the fiery sword of the cherubim, guarding the entrance to Eden (*De cherubim* 21-39).

Philo's writings were composed on a wide variety of subjects, over a period of time, resulting in no coherent doctrine of the *lógos*. But his flexible and imaginative use of the term to express Jewish and Greek philosophical ideas undoubtedly influenced early Christian fathers, and his influence has also been postulated on Hebrews and John (see IV.E and F.1 below; *see also* PHILO JUDAEUS III).

D. DSS and Rabbinical Literature. There are no significant developments in the DSS. Heb. *dāḇār* is used, as in the OT, with reference to God's word as His command or promise; human speech is seen as a special gift from Him (1QH 1:28f.).

In the Aramaic Targums of the OT, *mēmrâ* (cf. biblical Aram. *mēʾmar*) occurs very frequently in the phrase "word of the Lord." This has sometimes been interpreted as referring to a divine hypostasis or intermediary, but probably represents no more than a reverential periphrasis for God in His dealings with humankind ('so Barrett, comm. on John, p. 153). Possibly more important for understanding the development of Johannine doctrine is rabbinical Torah theology, by which the OT "word" became increasingly interpreted as the Law, described in elevated terms as pre-existent and the life of the world; sometimes Torah is personified as the daughter of Yahweh (see Hoskyns and Davey, p. 155; Schnackenburg, I, 484f.).

E. Gnosis and Similar Thought. 1. Corpus Hermeticum. The Hermetic Texts from Egypt, written in Greek and dating mostly to the 2nd-3rd cent. A.D., contain a complex amalgam of Greek and oriental (including Jewish) ideas, in which *lógos* appears fairly frequently. It is used both for the rational human faculty (and as such intimately associated with *noús*, "mind"), and for the agent of creation, imagined as a divine intermediary. The tract *Poimandres* describes how the "holy word" falls on a sea of darkness and fire, and creation follows (*Corpus Hermeticum* I.5). The language here and in the dialogue *The Bowl* is reminiscent of Gen. 1, which appears to have been interpreted in the light of Stoic and Platonic philosophy.

2. Mandean Texts. These religious texts, which date from a period much later than the NT, belong to an unusual Baptist sect with strong gnostic affinities. "Word" appears frequently in many senses, most notably for the means of creation: "The sublime King of Light pronounced his word, and everything came into being by his word." "True words" are said to come from the "place of light"; the "word of life" comes with power to rule and command (Foerster and Wilson, *Gnosis*, II, 157, 183, 212, 223; see further Schnackenburg, I, 138-143, 489). (For the Odes of Solomon see III.B above; for the Nag Hammadi Texts see V.A below.)

***IV. In the NT.**–A. Human Words.* Both *lógos* and *rhḗma* are used for ordinary human utterances, which may take the form of question, warning, rumor, command, discourse, teaching, etc.; occasionally they are used for the written word (e.g., Acts 1:1, where *lógos* refers to Luke's earlier book, i.e., his Gospel). Although "word" normally implies a rational utterance, it is also used for ecstatic speech "in tongues": in 1 Cor. 14:19 Paul says that he would rather speak five intelligible words that instruct others in the church than ten thousand words in a tongue. Sometimes words are seen as complementary to actions, or the two are contrasted, as in 1 Jn. 3:18, where we find the classical antithesis between word and deed.

Specific NT teaching about the use of words includes Jesus' warning that at the Last Judgment people will be held responsible for every idle word they have spoken: "For by your words you will be justified, and by your words you will be condemned" (Mt. 12:37). He taught in the Sermon on the Mount that the Christian's word should be so reliable that oaths are unnecessary (5:37). Various warnings in the Epistles indicate the danger of using corrupt or lying words (e.g., Eph. 4:29; 2 Pet. 2:3). James stresses the importance of controlling the tongue (Jas. 1:26; 3:5f.). 2 Tim. 2:14-17 warns not to dispute about words (*logomachéō*), contrasting the "word of truth" with the godless chatter of those who have gone astray, whose "talk" (*lógos*) is compared to a "gangrene." In 1 Cor. 1–4 Paul contrasts the word of the gospel with the empty words of human wisdom.

A specific use of *lógos* in the sense of "account" is found in set phrases (e.g., *lógon [apo]dídonai*, "render account"), used particularly in connexion with the doctrine of final judgment (see Rom. 14:12; He. 13:17; 1 Pet. 4:5).

B. OT Word in the NT. In a number of passages "the word" or "the word of God" is used with the same theological connotations as in the OT. The "word-event" formula (see II.B above) appears as such only in Lk. 3:2 where the word of God (*rhḗma theoú*) comes to John the Baptist. Elsewhere in the NT the idea of direct divine revelation is expressed in other ways (see IV.C, D below). The concept of the dynamic word creating and sustaining the universe (cf. II.C above) appears most strikingly at He. 1:3 and 11:3, 1 Pet. 1:23-25 (citing Isa. 40:6-9), and 2 Pet. 3:5 (note that in this context *lógos* and *rhḗma* appear interchangeable). Quite frequently God is said to have spoken through David or the Prophets; sometimes individual OT passages are referred to as God's word (e.g., Mk. 7:13; Jn. 10:34f.; Rom. 9:6); but sometimes they are attributed to named individuals, such as Isaiah (e.g., Lk. 3:4; Jn. 12:38). Study of the relevant passages shows that, whatever the formula, God is regarded as the one speaking in OT Scripture (cf. *TDNT*, IV, 109-113). A classic passage on biblical inspiration (2 Pet. 1:19-21) refers to the "prophetic word made more sure," which is compared to a lamp shining in the dark.

C. Divine Revelation through Voice and Vision. At times the NT portrays God as communicating to humanity through a heavenly voice and through the medium of angels. The Gospels tell of a voice from heaven (cf. Dnl. 4:31) on three occasions, all major turning points in Jesus' ministry — His baptism (Mk. 1:11 par.), His transfiguration (Mk. 9:7 par.; cf. 2 Pet. 1:17), and before His passion (Jn. 12:28) (*see* BATH KOL). Other significant events — Christ's birth and resurrection — are marked by the appearance of angels, who convey their message through ordinary human words. The book of Acts regularly portrays God as communicating to individuals through dreams and visions, e.g., in Acts 26:14 Paul hears the voice of the risen Jesus speaking in the Hebrew language. In the book of Revelation divine communication comes by means of a heavenly voice (e.g., 1:10; 21:3), through angelic intermediaries (e.g., 5:2), and through the words of the glorified Christ (e.g., 22:16). Although the terms *lógos* and *rhēma* are used only incidentally in these accounts (e.g., Lk. 1:29, 38), the divine communication performs the same function as the "word" which came to the prophets or the words which God spoke to Abraham, Moses, etc. God's supreme communication in the NT, however, is expressed in the person of Jesus Christ Himself, who speaks God's word and makes Him known (cf. Jn. 1:18; He. 1:2).

D. Words of Jesus. The entire NT lays stress on the need for the spoken word as the means of proclaiming the Good News. The "word-event" formula of the OT prophets is never used of Jesus or of the apostolic preaching (see IV.B, C above). This is probably because Jesus' teaching is seen as something new, going far beyond the prophetic revelation. The NT often notes that Jesus spoke with remarkable authority (Mk. 1:22; cf. Mt. 5:21-48; etc.); He assures His hearers of the reliability of His words by the "Amen formula" — "Truly, I say to you . . ." (Mk. 3:28; etc.); He explicitly claims that His words provide a firm foundation for faith (Mt. 7:24) and will not pass away (Mk. 13:31; Lk. 21:33). They call people to a point of decision, so that they either accept or reject them (Mt. 15:12; Mk. 10:22; cf. 8:38). Their effect on the believer is particularly emphasized in the Fourth Gospel, where "word" is associated with eternal life: "Truly, truly, I say to you, he who hears my word and believes him who sent me, has eternal life" (Jn. 5:24); Jesus' disciples are urged to abide in His word, and to let His words abide in them (8:31; 15:7).

Jesus' words are identified with God's word in the Synoptic Gospels (Lk. 5:1), in Acts (11:16), and especially in John (3:34; 14:24; 17:14, 17). A particularly interesting usage in Mark's Gospel is that of "word" used absolutely for Jesus' teaching (Mk. 2:2; 4:33).

Jesus' proclamation of the kingdom of God, which is central to His mission, includes not only teaching and preaching, but also healing: His word alone is sufficient to cast out evil spirits (Mt. 8:16) and heal from a distance (e.g., 8:8).

E. Word as Christian Message. It is a short step from describing Jesus' own preaching as the word of God to describing the early Christian preaching about Him as the Word of God. This usage is already implied in the Synoptic explanations of the parable of the Sower (Mk. 4:14-20 par.); it is commonly found in Acts and the Pauline Epistles where the apostolic preaching is called "the word of God" (e.g., Acts 6:2; 1 Cor. 14:36), "the word of the Lord" (e.g., Acts 8:25; 1 Thess. 1:8), or simply "the word" (e.g., Acts 17:11; Gal. 6:6) (full statistics in *TDNT,* IV, 115).

Preaching this word is a matter of urgency (2 Tim. 4:2), not to be prevented by threats or imprisonment (Acts 4:13-31; 2 Tim. 2:9); people cannot hear without a preacher (Rom. 10:14). OT passages about the word of God are freely applied to Christian preaching (10:15; 1 Pet. 1:23-25).

The content and effect of the proclaimed word are indicated by descriptive genitives, such as "word of life" (Phil. 2:16; cf. 1 Jn. 1:1), "word of his grace" (Acts 14:3; 20:32), "message [*lógos*] of reconciliation" (2 Cor. 5:19). Emphasis is placed on the death of Jesus — "the word of the cross" — "folly to those who are perishing, but to us who are being saved . . . the power of God" (1 Cor. 1:18).

An interesting usage is that found three times in Acts (6:7; 12:24; 19:20), where the word is said to "grow" or "increase." J. Kodell has shown that here "word" means more than just the Christian message: it is somehow the whole Christian community. Even more important is the way in which the word is almost identified at times with Christ Himself: Paul talks equally freely about preaching the word (or gospel) and preaching Jesus or Christ (cf. 1 Cor. 1:23; 2 Cor. 11:4; Gal. 2:2; 6:6). "The word of Christ" (Col. 3:16) is used in parallel with "Christ" (Eph. 3:17). Such usages may well have facilitated the development of the Johannine doctrine of the word as Christ Himself.

In Hebrews the author warns his readers not to be like the Israelites in the wilderness, who failed to avail themselves of the word; he urges them rather to strive to enter into God's rest: "For the word of God is living and active, sharper than any two-edged sword, piercing to the division of soul and spirit . . ." (4:12). The precise significance of "word" here has been much discussed: it is probably a mistake to see, along with certain early church fathers, a direct allusion to the Johannine doctrine of the Logos; but "word" here is clearly more than OT Scripture or merely the Christian message. The writer may have been influenced by Philonic language, but probably the vivid imagery derives directly from the OT doctrine of the effective word of God applied in a new context (for the sword imagery cf. Isa. 49:2; Philo, *De cherubim* 30; Eph. 6:17; Rev. 1:16).

F. Word as a Title of Christ. In the NT this seems to be confined to the Johannine writings.

1. Jn. 1:1-18. The prologue introduces and encapsulates the Gospel itself. It presents the person of Christ *sub specie aeternitatis* as the incarnate Word (*lógos*), who makes God known to the world. The Word is described as preexistent, as the agent of creation, source of grace and truth. He is fully God (1:1), yet He also became flesh (*sárx*; 1:14).

The background of this momentous concept has been very fully explored (*see* JOHANNINE THEOLOGY). While scholars earlier this century made much of the affinities with Stoic thought (see III.A.2 above), in later decades more emphasis has been laid on the OT and Jewish background. The Johannine doctrine would seem to relate closely to the OT concepts of the creative word of God (II.C above) and the Word as God's revelation and law for the world (II.B, D above). The author may well have been influenced also by developments in later Jewish thought, especially the personification or hypostatization of *Sophia* (Wisdom) and *Torah* (Law) (see III.B, D above). Early Christian usage of "the word" as a technical term for the gospel (see IV.E above) may also have facilitated the identification of Christ as the *lógos*.

It is perhaps wrong to dismiss completely the possibility that the Fourth Evangelist might also have been influenced by Stoic doctrines. These were widely known in popular religious thought, and if he had lived at Alexandria, Antioch, or, as is widely believed, at Ephesus, he could hardly have failed to be aware of them. Such Stoic influence might well have been derived from Hellenistic Judaism rather than through any direct knowledge of actual Stoic writings. Dependence on Philo (see III.C above) has sometimes been suggested, but close examination of the parallels shows that the differences between John's *lógos* and that of Philo are substantial, and most scholars today think direct Philonic influence unlikely (so Dodd, *Interpretation,* pp. 73, 276f.; Schnackenburg, I, 485-87).

Another possibility that has been explored in detail, especially in German scholarship, is that the Fourth Evangelist was influenced by gnostic thought. Drawing on the Odes of Solomon (see III.B above), the Mandean Texts (see III.E above), and other writings, R. Bultmann argued that John's prologue incorporates a gnostic Baptist hymn on the *lógos* as heavenly revealer and redeemer (see his comm. on John, pp. 14-18). The hypothesis of a gnostic hymn has been sharply criticized (though the idea of a Christian hymn has been fairly widely accepted: so Schnackenburg and Brown; contra Barrett). The question remains whether the prologue incorporates any gnostic thought. A major problem here is chronology: the gnostic or semi-gnostic writings that have been compared to the Fourth Gospel are all to be dated later than it, some of them much later. It is a matter of speculation which of their ideas might have been current in the 1st cent. A.D. R. Schnackenburg has argued that there is a good case for accepting the existence of a pre-Christian gnostic myth that used the term "word" for an envoy sent from the heavenly world and that influenced both Jewish Wisdom speculation and John's prologue (comm. on John, I, 488-493). Others hold that the case for any dependence of John on postulated early oriental Gnosticism is extremely tenuous (so Brown, I, lvi). The differences between John's *lógos* and that of the Gnostics should certainly not be underestimated; in view of the late date of the texts in question, it seems most likely that the similarities that exist are due to parallel development of thought, or, in some cases, to Johannine influence (see further Dodd, *Interpretation,* pp. 34f., 50f., 53 on John and the Hermetic Texts).

The most reasonable conclusion in our present state of knowledge is that the Fourth Evangelist was influenced primarily by his OT, Jewish, and Christian background. But he could have been aware of the wider connotations of *lógos* for both Jews and pagans in the Hellenistic world, so that he might have deliberately chosen this term (in preference to *sophía,* which in any case presented problems, being a feminine noun) for the purpose of conveying additional meaning to those familiar with Greek philosophy and the syncretistic religious thought of his contemporaries.

2. 1 Jn. 1:1-4. These verses contain a reference to "the word of life" (*ho lógos tḗs zōḗs,* v. 1) which has been interpreted either as referring simply to the gospel message (so most recently R. Brown, *Epistles,* pp. 164f., comparing Phil. 2:16) or to Christ Himself as the personal Word. The distinction between these two meanings is not so great as might be supposed (cf. IV.E above); the affinities of thought between the Johannine Gospel and Epistles are strong, so that it would seem plausible (especially in view of the verbs of seeing and touching) to assume that the author intended both meanings (cf. I. H. Marshall, pp. 102f.).

3. Rev. 19:11-16. In an apocalyptic vision the prophet John sees a rider on a white horse, who judges and makes war, leading out the heavenly armies to smite the nations. He is called Faithful and True, and his name is said to be "the Word of God" (*ho lógos toú theoú,* v. 13). The passage describes the glorified Christ in judgment. He is identified both by His epithets and His personal description ("eyes . . . like a flame of fire," v. 12) with the heavenly Son of Man of the author's letters to the churches (1:14; 2:18; etc.). The vivid description combines the OT picture of God as a warrior and vintager (cf. Isa. 63:1-6; Joel 3:9-13) with the OT concept of the Davidic Messiah, crushing the nations in judgment (Ps. 2:9; Isa. 11:4).

The relationship of the passage to Jn. 1:1-18 is uncertain. If Revelation could be dated earlier than John, it might be seen as a partial anticipation of the *lógos* doctrine there; if later, then it serves as an echo of it. But the function of Christ as *lógos* in Revelation is really very different from that in the Gospel prologue. It seems more plausible, especially if we accept separate authorship, to assume that its concept is derived directly from OT tradition as developed in the intertestamental period. (Cf. the image of the all-powerful Word [*lógos*] of Wisd. 18:15 and the thought of He. 4:12.) Certainly Revelation's picture of Christ as the Word of God coming in eschatological judgment at the consummation of all things fittingly complements the Gospel's picture of Him as the creative Word that existed from the beginning.

V. Later Developments.*–*A. Developed Gnostic Thought. In the elaborate gnostic systems of the 2nd cent. A.D. Logos appears as one of a number of aeons or emanations, which together make up the *plḗrōma* (*see* GNOSTICISM). According to Ptolemaeus, Logos emanated from Nous and united with Life to emit Man and the Church. In the *Gospel of Truth,* recovered from Nag Hammadi and probably also from Valentinian circles (*see* NAG HAMMADI LITERATURE), the Word appears as a savior who is in the mind and thought of the Father, and who brings redemption and the gift of knowledge to the ignorant; in one passage (26.8) he is said to have "become a body." The role of the Word is further developed in the *Tripartite Tractate.* It is possible that such texts incorporate elements from earlier pre-Christian oriental Gnosticism (see Schnackenburg, I, 194), but as they stand they clearly postdate the Gospel of John and show signs of dependence on it.

B. Patristic Doctrines. The early church fathers took up the concept of the Logos, which they interpreted and developed in the light of Greek philosophy and their own theological insights. Ignatius (Magn. 8:12) spoke of Jesus Christ as the Logos proceeding from silence; Justin understood it as the rational power of God generated for the work of creation and active in both the OT and in pagan thinkers. Clement of Alexandria made much of the Logos concept, while Theophilus used Stoic terminology to distinguish between *lógos endiáthetos,* reason immanent in God before creation, and *lógos prophorikós,* the expressed word (see III.A.2 above). Irenaeus sharply criticized gnostic speculations; Origen wrestled with the relationship of the Logos to the Father; Athanasius castigated Arius for believing that "there was when the Logos was not." Although the word *lógos* does not occur in it, the Nicene Creed (*see* CREEDS AND CONFESSIONS IV.B) owes much to the doctrine of the Logos as shaped by Athanasius and other orthodox fathers.

It may be noted that a trinitarian reference to the Logos as one of the three heavenly witnesses became at some time incorporated into some Latin versions of 1 Jn. (i.e., 5:7), and was for a period accepted as an authentic part of the text. Though appearing in the AV, this verse is now rightly omitted on textual grounds.

Bibliography.–In addition to the standard commentaries and lexicons (BDB, KoB, LSJ, Bauer) see J. Barr, *Semantics of Biblical Langauge* (1961); C. K. Barrett, *NT Background: Selected Documents* (1956); *Gospel according to St. John* (2nd ed. 1978); R. Brown, *Gospel according to John,* I (*AB,* 1966); *Epistles of John* (*AB,* 1982); R. Bultmann, *Faith and Understanding,* I (Eng. tr. 1969), 286-312; *Gospel of John* (Eng. tr. 1971); J. H. Charlesworth, *Odes of Solomon* (1973); *DNTT,* III, 1078-1146; C. H. Dodd, *Interpretation of the Fourth Gospel* (1953); W. Foerster and R. McL. Wilson, *Gnosis* (2 vols., 1972-1974); W. K. C. Guthrie, *History of Greek Philosophy* (6 vols., 1962-1968); E. C. Hoskyns and F. N. Davey, *The Fourth Gospel* (2nd ed. 1947); *ISBE* (1929), *s.v.* "Logos" (Alexander); G. S. Kirk, J. E. Raven, and M. Schofield, *Presocratic Philosophers* (2nd ed. 1983); J. Kodell, *Bibl.,* 55 (1974), 505-519; I. H. Marshall, *Epistles of John* (*NICNT,* 1978); L. Morris, *Gospel according to John* (*NICNT,* 1971); G. von Rad, *OT Theology* (2 vols., Eng. tr. 1962-1965); A. Richardson, *Intro. to the Theology of the NT* (1958), pp. 155-168; J. M. Robinson, ed., *Nag Hammadi Library* *in English* (1977); R. Schnackenburg, *Gospel according to St. John,* I (Eng. tr. 1968); *TDNT,* IV, *s.v.* λέγω κτλ. (Debrunner, Kleinknecht, Procksch, Kittel); *TDOT,* III, *s.v.* "dābhar" (Bergman, Lutzmann, Schmidt); A. C. Thiselton, *JTS,* N.S. 25 (1974), 283-299; R. N. Whybray, *Isaiah 40–66* (*NCBC,* 1975); E. Yamauchi, *Pre-Christian Gnosticism* (1973).

R. B. EDWARDS

WORK.

I. Terminology
  A. In the OT
  B. In the NT
II. Work(s) of God
  A. In the OT
  B. In the Gospel of John
  C. Through the Church
III. Works of the Law and Good Works
IV. Daily Work and Occupations

I. Terminology–A. In the OT. The Hebrew words most commonly translated "work" in the RSV are the verb *ʿāśâ* and the nouns *maʿᵃśeh* (related to *ʿāśâ*) and *mᵉlāʾḵâ.*

ʿĀśâ is a very common word in the OT, usually translated "do" or "make" and usually referring to the production or preparation of some tangible object. When context requires it is given a more specific translation, such as "sacrifice" (Ex. 10:25) or "deal (kindly)" (Jgs. 1:24; AV "show [mercy]"; NEB "see that you come to no harm"). Where *ʿāśâ* is translated "work," it usually refers to the work of people in projects such as the tabernacle, the temple, the furnishings of the tabernacle or temple, or the walls of Jerusalem (e.g., Ex. 31:4; 36:1; 1 K. 9:23; Neh. 2:16). It is also used of God's activities as these are perceived by human beings (see II below).

Maʿᵃśeh is used for "work" both as activity (e.g., Ex. 5:4; 23:24) and, more often, as what is produced by activity (Ex. 39:8 [twice]; Ps. 135:15). It is often used for the work of God, again both as activity (e.g., Eccl. 8:17), in which case it is often translated "deed(s)" (e.g., Dt. 11:3; AV "acts"), and as what is produced (e.g., Ps. 138:8). In a few contexts, *maʿᵃśeh* represents the style in which an artifact is fashioned (Ex. 28:8; 39:5; Nu. 8:4; 1 K. 7:8; RSV "workmanship").

Mᵉlāʾḵâ, like *maʿᵃśeh,* refers both to the activity of working (e.g., Ex. 35:29) and to the products of that activity (e.g., Ex. 39:43). The "work" from which God rested on the seventh day is called *mᵉlāʾḵâ* (Gen. 2:2f.), and the work from which the Israelites were to rest on the sabbath and on feast days subject to the sabbath regulations is usually called *mᵉlāʾḵâ* (e.g., Ex. 12:16; 20:9f; 31:14f.; Jer. 17:22) or *mᵉleʾḵeṯ ʿᵃḇōḏâ* (RSV "laborious work"; AV "servile work"; e.g., Lev. 23:7; Nu. 28:18; *maʿᵃśeh* in Ex. 23:12). *Mᵉlāʾḵâ* often represents skilled and artistic labor (e.g., Ex. 31:5; 35:24; 1 K. 7:22), though, as with the sabbath regulations, it could be used quite generally and could include the most menial labor (so also in 1 S. 8:16; 1 Ch. 27:26) and great building projects (e.g., Ezr. 6:22; Neh. 4:15). When a project was done by a large number of people for a ruler, it could be referred to as the ruler's *mᵉlāʾḵâ* (e.g., 1 K. 7:51; 2 Ch. 16:5); the same manner of speaking is used of "the work of the Lord" in Jer. 48:10.

The Hebrew verb *ʿāḇaḏ* and the noun *ʿᵃḇôḏâ* are related to *ʿeḇeḏ,* "servant, slave," and generally carry the same idea of service rendered for one of superior status. They are, therefore, most commonly translated "serve" and "service." This focus is also reflected where these words are translated "work" (*ʿāḇaḏ:* Ex. 5:15; 2 Ch. 2:18; *ʿᵃḇôḏâ:* Ex. 5:9, 11; Neh. 3:5; AV sometimes "service"), which may be in mind where *ʿᵃḇôḏâ* is used of the work of the Levites (Ex. 38:21; Nu. 4:23-47) and temple musicians (1 Ch. 25:1) and the work of the people of Israel in providing for the tabernacle (Ex. 39:32, 42). They are also used of laborious agricultural work (*ʿāḇaḏ:* Ex. 34:21; Dt. 15:19; 21:3; *ʿᵃḇôḏâ:* Ex. 1:14). The related noun *maʿᵃḇāḏ* is found in Job 34:25, where it refers to human activity in general, and (in Aramaic) in Dnl. 4:37 (MT 34), where it refers to the works of God. The related Aramaic noun *ʿᵃḇîḏâ* is used of the construction of the second temple in Jerusalem (Ezr. 4:24; 5:8; 6:7).

The Hebrew verb *pāʿal* is used almost exclusively in poetic contexts and bears a broad range of meaning similar to that of *ʿāśâ.* Its participle is commonly used in phrases such as "workers of iniquity" (*pōʿᵃlê ʾāwen,* variously translated in, e.g., Job 31:3; Ps. 141:4 [and seventeen other times in the Psalms]; Prov. 10:29; Isa. 31:2). This use reflects the verb's concentration on abstract objects of positive or negative value that is also seen in the designation of God as the one who is "working salvation" (Ps. 74:12). *Pāʿal* is also used of the work of the ironsmith making an idol in Isa. 44:12.

Nouns related to *pāʿal* are *pōʿal, pᵉʿullâ,* and *mip̄ʿāl(â). Mip̄ʿāl(â)* refers in all of its OT appearances to the actions of God (Ps. 46:8 [MT 9]; 66:5 [RSV "what God has done"]; Prov. 8:22b [RSV "acts"]), as does the much more common *pōʿal* in about one-third of its appearances (e.g., Dt. 32:4; Ps. 92:4a [MT 5a]; Isa. 45:11). Otherwise, *pōʿal* is used broadly of human work and deeds (e.g., Dt. 33:11; Ps. 9:16 [MT 17]; Isa. 41:24). *Pᵉʿullâ* most often represents the recompense from God for work done by humans, but in some cases represents the work itself (2 Ch. 15:7; Ps. 17:4; Jer. 31:16). It is used of God's works in Ps. 28:5a.

Among other Hebrew words translated "work" in the RSV are *yāḏ* (usually "hand" or "power"; Ex. 14:31), *ṣāḇāʾ* (usually "host" or "army"; Nu. 8:25; AV "waiting"; NEB "regular"), and *yᵉgîaʿ* (usually "labor"; Job 10:3; NEB "fruit").

A number of Hebrew terms are represented by Eng. "work" in the sense of a type of product of the craftsman's

A wall painting of harvest workers, from the Tomb of Menna, *ca.* 1420 B.C. (The Metropolitan Museum of Art)

skills. *Miqšâ* is metalwork shaped by hammering (e.g., Ex. 25:18; Nu. 10:2). It is not clear what *śᵉḇāḵâ* is or even that it represents the same kind of product in all its OT appearances (*see* CHECKER WORK). Other examples are *riqmâ,* "dyed work" (Jgs. 5:30; AV "needlework"; NEB "striped stuff") or "embroidered work" (Ezk. 27:16, 24; AV "broidered work"; NEB "brocade"), the pual part. of *ḥāqâ,* "carved work" (1 K. 6:35), *maʿᵃśēh šaršᵉrôṯ,* "chain work" (7:17), *maʿᵃśēh môrād,* for which the RSV has "beveled work" (v. 29; *see* BEVELED WORK), and *maʿᵃśēh šûšan,* "lily-work" (vv. 19, 22; *see* LILY-WORK).

B. In the NT. Most often "work" and derivatives of "work" in the NT represent Greek words of the *erg-* group. The most common of these are the noun *érgon,* which represents "work" both as activity and as the products of activity, and the verb *ergázomai,* "work, do." Others are the verbs *energéō, katergázomai* ("work"), and *synergéō* ("work [together] with") and the nouns *enérgeia* ("working," Eph. 1:19; 3:7; 4:16; Col. 2:12; AV also "effectual working," "operation"), *energḗs* ("effective work," 1 Cor. 16:9; AV "effectual"), and *enérgēma* ("working," 1 Cor. 12:6, 10; AV also "operation").

Words translated "work" by the RSV only in particular contexts are the noun *cháris* (usually "grace"; translated "gracious work" in 2 Cor. 8:6f., 19) and the verbs *heurískō* (usually "find"; passive translated "work" in 2 Cor. 11:12), *kopiáō* ("labor, become weary"; translated "work hard" in Rom. 16:6, 12; 1 Cor. 15:10), and *poiéō* ("do"; translated "work" six times). RSV "workmanship" represents *érgon* (1 Cor. 9:1) and *poíēma* (Eph. 2:10). For "mighty work" (*dýnamis* thirteen times; *megaleíos* only in Acts 2:11), *see* POWER II.

II. Work(s) of God.–A. *In the OT.* The Hebrew words most often used for the work(s) of God are *maʿᵃśeh* and the related verb *ʿāśâ.* God is known as the one who works first of all in His work of creation. The creation and maintenance of all that exists are the "works" of God (Job 36:24 [Heb. *pōʿal*]; 37:7, 14, 16 [*pālāʾ*]; Ps. 86:8; 96:3 [*pālāʾ*]; 104:13, 24, 31; 139:14).

It was by His word of commandment that God created (Ps. 33:6, 9; 148:5); God is one who speaks, not one who brings things into being by physical labor like that of human beings. In this way the sovereignty of God in the work of creation is communicated. But the image of the Creator as a potter (Isa. 45:9; 64:8) and the portrayal of creation as work (Heb. *mᵉlāʾḵâ*), after which God rested (Gen. 2:2f.), set forth another aspect of the event of creation, the close involvement of the Creator with what He creates. A common anthropomorphic figure refers to what God has created as the work of His hands (e.g., Job 10:3 [*yᵉgîʿ(a)*]; 14:15; 34:19; Ps. 8:6 [MT 7]; 28:5 [*pᵉʿullâ*]; 102:25 [MT 26]; 138:8; Isa. 19:25; 29:23; 45:11; cf. Ps. 8:3 [MT 4]; Isa. 45:12). When personified Wisdom speaks of God's work of creation (Prov. 8:22-31), it speaks of itself as a "master workman" by God's side (v. 30 [*ʾāmôn*]; AV "one brought up"). *See* CREATOR.

That God does His work is the presupposition of human beings' reception of revelation and salvation. Just as creation brought the human race into being, so also its experience of God's redemption does not begin with human seeking or working, but with the work of God on its behalf. "The works of God" are, therefore, the works of redemption as well as the works of creation, and include the deliverance of the people of Israel from Egypt (Ex. 14:13, 31 [*yāḏ*]; Dt. 11:7; Josh. 24:31; Jgs. 2:7, 10; Ps. 74:12 [*pāʿal*]; 77:14 [MT 15]; 95:9 [*pōʿal*]; 106:7 [*pālāʾ*], 13), the giving of the law (Ex. 32:16), His driving out the inhabitants of Canaan before Israel (34:10), and His other acts done for deliverance of Israel (e.g., 1 S. 14:6; Jer. 51:10). The work of God the Redeemer in general, without reference to any particular actions, is often referred to (Dt. 32:4 [*pōʿal*]; 1 Ch. 16:9 [*pālāʾ*]; Ps. 33:4; 46:8 [MT 9, *pāʿal*]; 73:28 [*mᵉlāʾḵâ*]; 77:12 [MT 13, *pōʿal*]; 78:7 [*maʿᵃlāl*]; Isa. 43:13 [*pāʿal*]).

Since it is often by miraculous or extraordinary events that God's actions on behalf of His people are recognized, God is known as one who does mighty works and works wonders (Dt. 3:24; Jgs. 13:19; 1 Ch. 16:12, 24 [*pālāʾ*]; *see* MIRACLE; SIGN; WONDER). When individuals ask for God's intervention in their own troubles, they ask for God to work (Ps. 90:16 [*pōʿal*]; cf. 88:10 [MT 11]); when they have been helped they are grateful for His work(s) (Ps. 92:4f. [MT 5f., *pōʿal, maʿᵃśeh*]). In Hab. 3:2 the prophet expresses his awe of God's redemptive work (*pōʿal*) and asks God to renew it. Ps. 111 is a litany of praise to God for His works (*maʿᵃśeh, pōʿal, niplāʾâ*) of providence and redemption (cf. Pss. 107 [*pālāʾ*], 145).

Judgment as well as redemption can be called the work of God (Isa. 5:19; 10:12; Jer. 48:10 [*mᵉlāʾḵâ*]; 50:25 [*mᵉlāʾḵâ*]), but Isa. 28:21 shows that for those who believed in God's salvation of His people, judgment of Judah could only be understood as God's "strange deed" (*zār maʿᵃśeh*) and "alien work" (*nāḵrîyâ ʿᵃḇōḏâ*; cf. Hab. 1:5 [*pōʿal*]).

According to Prov. 16:11 honest weights are God's "work"; standard weights were often authorized by a king, but the effort to maintain honesty in the matter of weights gives to them the authorization of God Himself. Qoheleth speaks of the work of God as that which is irresistible because it comes from the sovereign one (Eccl. 7:13; cf. Isa. 43:13) and as that which cannot be understood by human beings (Eccl. 8:17; 11:5).

B. In the Gospel of John. A matter of significant concern in the Gospel of John is the interconnection between the works of God and the works of Jesus (terms used are Gk. *érgon* and *ergázomai*). Jesus' presence in the world is the particular occasion for the works of God to be made manifest (Jn. 9:3); when Jesus is no longer present, that occasion will be gone (v. 4). Jesus' life has no other purpose than to do the work God has given Him to do (4:34; cf. 17:4). Because "the Father" works on the sabbath, Jesus works on the sabbath (5:16f.; cf. Lk. 13:14-16).

A fundamental reason for this concern for the interconnection between God's works and Jesus' works is the idea that miraculous works should give attestation to anyone who seeks to be heard as a spokesman for God (cf. Jn. 5:36; 6:30; 7:3; 10:37f.). Jesus takes this further: the works He does should attest to the mutual indwelling of Jesus and the Father (14:10f.) and to the very nature of the Father (15:24). But this proves to be ineffective with many, those who do not believe (10:25f.) and who seek to do away with Jesus (vv. 32f.).

There is also concern in the Gospel of John for the relationship between the works of God and the person who has been exposed to the message of Jesus. The response that is called for by the message — that which means that a person's works are done "in God" (Jn. 3:21) or that he does the works of God (6:28) — is a response of belief in Jesus (6:29). The works of healing done through Jesus point beyond themselves; "greater works" will be done, first of all, in that Jesus will give life to those who believe, (5:20f.) and second, in that those who believe will themselves do even greater works than Jesus has done (14:12).

For the "mighty works" of Jesus in the Synoptic Gospels and in Acts (e.g., Mt. 11:20; Acts 2:22) *see* POWER II.

C. Through the Church. Because God's redemption is present in the spread of the gospel and in the Church, the writers of some of the NT epistles speak quite freely of their own missionary activity and the activity of the churches as products or evidences of God's working (*energéō, érgon, synergéō, synergós, kopiáō*). Thus God works through Peter and Paul in their preaching of the gospel (Gal. 2:8; cf. 1 Cor. 16:10; Phil. 2:30); preachers of the gospel can be called God's co-workers (1 Cor. 3:9; 2 Cor. 6:1; cf. 1 Cor. 16:16); God works miracles among the Galatian Christians (Gal. 3:5); God or His Spirit or His word is at work in believers to accomplish His purposes (Eph. 3:20; Phil. 1:6; 2:13; 1 Thess. 2:13; He. 13:21); service for the Church can be called work "in the Lord" (Rom. 16:12 [cf. v. 6]; 1 Cor. 9:1); and the peace and growth together of the Christian community is the work of God (Rom. 14:20). In a generalized closing exhortation Paul refers to the work of the Church as "the work of the Lord" (1 Cor. 15:58).

III. Works of the Law and Good Works. Basic to Paul's understanding of the state of affairs brought about by the coming of the eschatological age of salvation is that faith in Jesus Christ is the one condition for the reception of the justification that God has effected. Because of the circumstances that arose among Gentile Christians (partly, at least, as a result of the activity of Jewish Christian missionaries who attempted to bring Gentile Christians more completely into the Jewish fold), Paul set up an opposition between God's calling and faith in Christ, on the one hand, and "works of the law" (sometimes just "works"; Gk. *érga [nómou]*), on the other hand (Rom. 3:20, 27–4:6; 9:11, 32; Gal. 2:16; 3:2-12; Eph. 2:8f.; 2 Tim. 1:9). The problem with works of the law is that they can bring into a person a sense that what he or she receives from God is due as payment, in effect, for the person's working (Rom. 4:4f., *ergázomai*).

This opposition between justification and works seems to be consciously broken down in Jas. 2:14-26. While the most important aspect of the solution to this apparent conflict between Paul and James is the recognition that "faith" bears a different meaning for James than it does for Paul, it should also be said that "works" are not for James "works of the law" by which one vainly hopes to win God's favor, as they are in Paul's exposition of justification by faith. They are, rather, the works of charity that Paul and every NT writer expect as the outcome of faith in Christ. *See* JAMES, EPISTLE OF I.B.3; JUSTIFICATION.

"Works" is, indeed, a characteristic term in the activist view of the life of the Christian and of the Christian community found in the NT. There are "works of darkness" (Rom. 13:12; Eph. 5:11), "works of the flesh" (Gal. 5:19), "dead works" (He. 9:14), "works of the devil" (1 Jn. 3:8), and "wicked work" (2 Jn. 11). But there are also "good works" (Acts 9:36; 2 Cor. 9:8; Eph. 2:10; Col. 1:10; 2 Thess. 2:17; 1 Tim. 2:10; 5:10, 25; 6:18; 2 Tim. 2:21; 3:17; Tit. 1:16; 2:7, 14; 3:8, 14; He. 10:24; 1 Pet. 2:12; RSV sometimes "good deeds"), the "work of the Lord" (1 Cor. 15:58; 16:10), the "work of ministry" (Eph. 4:12), the "work of faith" (1 Thess. 1:3; 2 Thess. 1:11), and "any honest work" (Tit. 3:1).

This distinction between good and evil works comes to have eschatological significance with the assumption of Paul and other NT writers that the final judgment will be a judgment of human "works" (Rom. 2:6; 1 Cor. 3:13-15; cf. Mt. 16:27; Gal. 6:4f.; Rev. 2:23, 26; *see* JUDGMENT, LAST VI). Jesus criticized those who would make an osten-

A wall painting from Egypt depicting brickmakers (facsimile from the tomb of Rekhmira, 18th Dynasty, Thebes) (The Metropolitan Museum of Art)

tatious show of good works (Mt. 23:5; RSV "deeds"), but He also regarded the visibility of His disciples' good works among people as a positive thing (5:16; cf. 1 Pet. 2:12).

IV. Daily Work and Occupations.–God is a worker, and He established people on earth to work (Gen. 2:5-8, 15, 18). The Bible maintains a positive view of people at work (*see* LABOR), while recognizing the results of the fall (3:19).

In urban settings persons of a particular craft would often be gathered into one neighborhood (Isa. 7:3; Jer. 37:21; cf. Neh. 11:35). But many forms of work were done in each household by nonprofessionals. The great majority of the population, especially those living outside cities, performed many tasks that might in other situations be identified with professionals. The life of the ordinary rural person might often be filled with a number of different tasks.

AGRICULTURE was, of course, basic to the economy of the biblical peoples. The growing of grain, vegetables, and herbs involved plowing (*see* PLOW), sowing (*see* SOW), cultivating, IRRIGATION, harvesting (*see* HARVEST), and, with grain, threshing (*see* THRESH; WINNOWING). Some of the tasks of viticulture are described in Isa. 5:1-6 (*see* VINE). Care for trees, such as Amos's work with sycamores (Am. 7:14), was also important. Of particular importance was the OLIVE TREE. Care of livestock was the occupation of many of the people of Israel, both when they were seminomadic (Gen. 46:34; 47:3) and after they had settled in Palestine, much of which is not suitable for crops. A wealthy man's riches could be measured in the number of his livestock, and he might have large numbers of herders working for him (Job 1:3; *see* CATTLE; GOAT; HERDSMAN; SHEEP). Food was also provided by fishermen (*see* FISH; FISHING) and hunters (*see* FOWLER; HUNTING).

A terra-cotta tablet depicting a miner at work. From Corinth, 6th cent. B.C. (Staatliche Museen zu Berlin, Antiken-Sammlung)

Preparing food — grinding grain, baking BREAD, butchering meat, and cooking (*see* COOK) — might be specialized occupations in wealthy households or, in the case of baking and butchering, also in cities. But for most people, these tasks were performed within the household. Much the same can be said with regard to winemaking (*see* WINE) and brewing of beer.

Like food preparation, the manufacturing of some items used in all or nearly all households was often done by each household for itself but in some circumstances by persons specializing in particular crafts. This includes the manufacture of cloth of plant and animal fibers (*see* SPINDLE; WEAVING), dyeing (*see* DYE; FULLER), and the making of GARMENTS. EMBROIDERY was used to decorate fine fabrics. Other work involving the use of plant and animal

A stevedore loading an amphora onto a Roman vessel. From a mosaic on a trading company floor at Ostia (1st cent. A.D.) (Superintendent of Ostia Archaeology)

fibers included carpet making and rope making (*see* ROPE). Pottery making (*see* POTTER) was another type of work that could be done by individuals for their own household but was quite often done by full-time potters (cf. Jer. 18:2-4). There were specialized potters, such as lamp makers. Basketry (*see* BASKET) was another such field of work.

Some branches of manufacturing were, by the time of the biblical narrative, done almost invariably by persons specializing in those fields. These included perfumery (*see* PERFUME), leather working (*see* LEATHER; TANNER; TENTMAKER), and GLASS manufacture and working. Metallurgy (*see* METAL) called for a number of specialized workers, including mining engineers, miners (*see* MINE), refiners (*see* REFINE; SMELTING), smiths to work the different metals (*see* SMITH), and jewelers (*see* JEWEL, JEWELER). Woodworking also involved a number of specialized workers from forest to finished product, including the carpenter, the carver (ivory was also carved), the furniture maker, and the boat builder.

Carpenters were also engaged in building, which involved a number of specialized workers and unskilled laborers (*see* BUILD). Among these were engineers and designers, brickmakers (*see* BRICK), stone quarriers, masons (*see* MASON), sculptors, and plasterers (*see* PLASTER). Some of the same occupations were also involved in building waterworks.

Goods produced and sold locally were generally sold by those who produced them; the potter sold pots, the silversmith sold objects of silver, etc. But when products were moved over great distances, another group of occupations comes into view, those involved with shipping and trade. In addition to the traders, shippers, and merchants themselves (*see* COMMERCE; MERCHANT) were those who worked for them, such as sailors and camel drivers. Trade over borders and other circumstances of a money economy necessitated the services of money changers and banks (*see* BANK, BANKING). Travelers were also served by innkeepers (*see* INN).

The services of magicians, diviners, and the like might be sought for a number of reasons (*see* DIVINATION; MAGIC), often for the same reasons as a PHYSICIAN (*see also* DISEASE) or an apothecary (*see* PERFUME) might be sought. There were full-time barbers (*see* BARBER). Midwives were called on at the time of birth, and the embalmer and the professional mourner when a person had died (*see* BURIAL). Writing was a professional skill that supported SCRIBES in most communities. Though much teaching might occur in the home, teaching was practiced as a full-time occupation by some (*see* EDUCATION; TEACH).

Many people were employed by rulers to contribute their skills to the task of governing and to serve the normally elaborate and wealthy households of rulers (*see* GOVERNMENT). A KING and subordinate rulers (*see* PRINCE; RULER) would normally have a number of advisors, including prophets (*see* PROPHET), diviners, and astrologers (*see* ASTROLOGY). Emissaries and interpreters aided communication among governments. Scribes were significant at all levels of government, as were judges (*see* JUDGE) and other local officials. Servants and slaves of widely varying status and duties, including court musicians (*see* MUSIC), dancers (*see* DANCE), cooks, servers, guards, and attendants, were a normal part of the households of rulers. Some of these servants might have authority in the functioning of the government. Tax collectors were either employed directly by the government or served contractually (*see* TAX; TAX COLLECTOR). A constant function of government was military defense and conquest, which involved people in a number of professional and nonprofessional occupations (*see* ARCHER; ARMOR-BEARER; ARMY; OFFICER; SOLDIER; WAR).

The corporate practice of religion in most communities involved full-time workers. This was particularly so since worship was almost invariably sacrificial. These included priests (*see* PRIESTS AND LEVITES), the various classes of those who assisted the priests, including the Levites and NETHINIM, cult prostitutes (*see* HARLOT), and prophets attached to the cult.

Wet-nursing (*see* NURSE) and prostitution were occupations filled, of course, only by women (though there were male cult prostitutes). Midwifery and mourning were also exclusively female occupations. In the normally patriarchal societies of the ancient Near East, most non-slave women filled the roles of wife and mother, which involved many of the tasks that have been named above, some of which were, indeed, usually done by women. If there were slaves or servants in the household, such a woman might bear much of the task of directing the work of the household. Few occupations were absolutely closed to women, but the woman who carried on an activity normally that of a man or who had the prominence attainable by men was rare (*see* WOMAN).

Begging and gleaning are distinguishable as occupations specifically of the non-slave poor (*see* POVERTY). Lastly, crime should be mentioned as a category of work.

See also CRAFTS; SERVANT; TOOLS.

Bibliography.–*DNTT*, III, 1147-59; R. J. Forbes, *Studies in Ancient Technology* (9 vols., 2nd ed., 1964-72); C. Singer, E. J. Holmyard, and A. R. Hall, eds., *History of Technology*, I-II (1954, 1956); *TDNT*, II, *s.v.* ἔργον (Bertram).

J. W. SIMPSON, JR.

WORKER; WORKMAN [participles of Hebrew vbs. *ʿāśâ* (often followed by *m^e lā'ḵâ*–'work'), *ḥāraš*, *ʿāḇaḏ*, *pāʿal*, and *yāṣar*; Hebrew nouns *ʿāmēl*, *ḥārāš*, *ʿ^a ḇōḏâ*, *ḥāḵām*, *ʿeṣeḇ*, *'āmôn*; Gk. *ergátēs*, part. of *kopiō*]; AV also HE THAT WORKETH, HE THAT LABOURETH, CUNNING MAN, "them that wrought," "them that do the work"; NEB also ONE WHO WORKS, CRAFTSMAN, etc.; **FELLOW WORKER** [Gk. *synergós*, part. of *synergéō*]; AV also HELPER, WORKFELLOW, LABOURERS TOGETHER, FELLOWHELPER, COMPANION IN LABOUR, FELLOWLABOURER, ONE THAT HELPETH; NEB also FRIEND IN THE FELLOWSHIP, COLLEAGUE, ASSOCIATE, etc. RSV supplies "workers" in 1 Cor. 12:28.

Literal references to workers include those who made the tabernacle and its furnishings (Ex. 35:35; 36:8), those involved in the construction and repair of the temple (1 K. 7:14; 2 K. 12:14f. [MT 15f.]; 2 Ch. 34:10, 17; Ezr. 3:9), and craftsmen who made idols (Isa. 40:19; Hos. 8:6; Hab. 2:18). Typical figurative uses are "worker of treachery" (Ps. 52:2 [MT 4]), "workers of iniquity" (Job 31:3; Lk. 13:27), and "workers of evil" (Ps. 6:8 [MT 9]; 28:3). While Gk. *ergátēs* was commonly used of agricultural laborers and vine tenders (as in Mt. 9:37; 20:1), the NT uses it also for those who proclaim the gospel (Mt. 10:10; RSV "laborer"; 2 Tim. 2:15). Paul's opponents may have used this term of themselves; he refers to them as "deceitful workers" (2 Cor. 11:13). Paul spoke often of his co-workers, usually persons who were, like him, involved in itinerant ministry at least some of the time (Rom. 16:3, 9, 21; 1 Cor. 16:16; 2 Cor. 8:23; Phil. 2:25; 4:3; Col. 4:11; Philem. 1, 24; cf. 3 Jn. 8). It is possible but not certain that with "God's fellow workers" in 1 Cor. 3:9 Paul is referring to himself

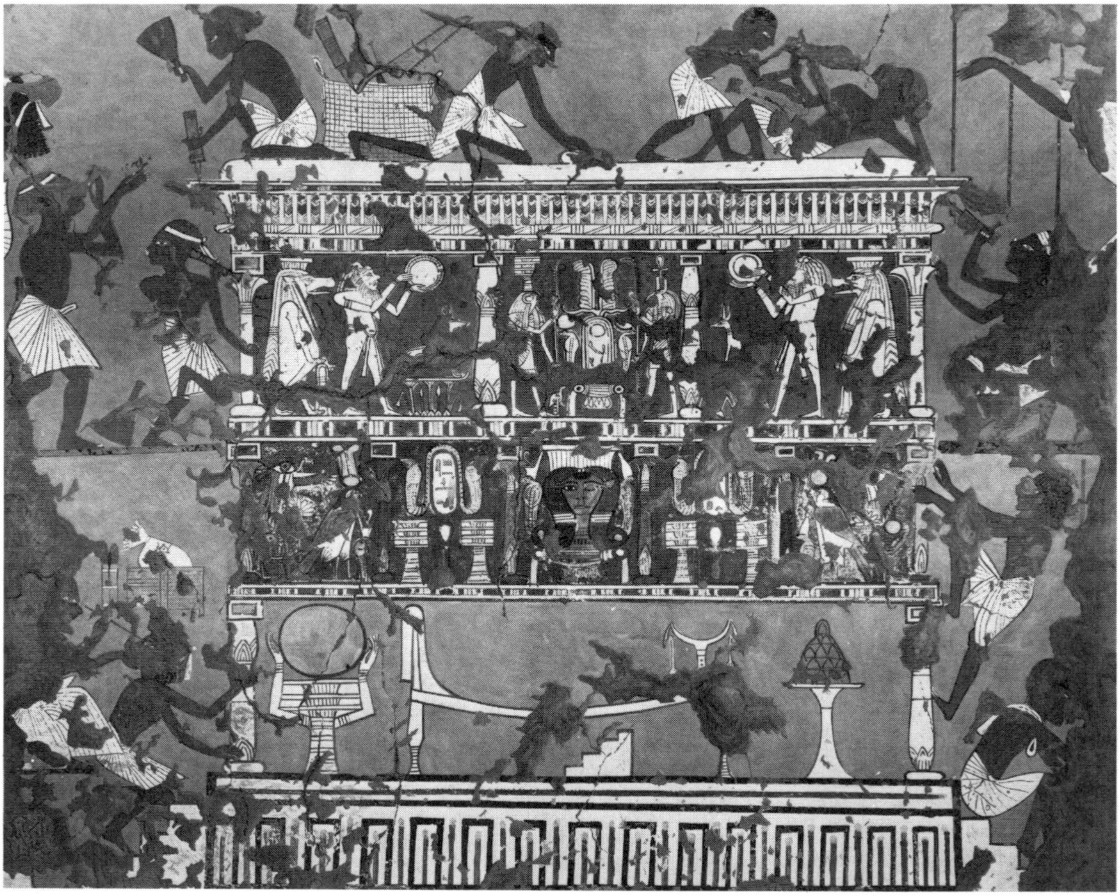

Carpenters making a catafalque for the deified Amenhotep I. At upper right a comrade wakes up a sleeping fellow worker; and at lower left, a worker has his eyes made up. Facsimile of a wall painting from the tomb of Ipuy, 19th Dynasty (The Metropolitan Museum of Art)

and Apollos as those who, figuratively speaking, work alongside God in their preaching and teaching.

See also WORK. L. D. HAWK

WORKMANSHIP. *See* WORK I.

WORLD.

I. In the OT
  A. Terms and General Meaning
  B. Creation and Cosmogony
II. In the Apocrypha
III. In the NT
  A. Terms and General Meaning
  B. In the Pauline Epistles
  C. In the Johannine Writings
IV. In the Early Church

I. In the OT.–*A. Terms and General Meaning.* The concept of world or cosmos in ancient Israelite religion stands, with the concepts of history and covenant, as an integral part of the framework within which His people understood the relationship with Yahweh. Unlike the Greek NT, where *kósmos* can indicate the entire created universe, the OT has no single Hebrew word for the "universe," but links *šāmayim* ("heavens") with *ʾereṣ* ("earth") in what amounts to a technical term for the entire created order: *haššāmayim* w^{e}*hāʾāreṣ*. This phrase designates the entire created order in both Creation accounts (Gen. 1:1; 2:1, 4), in passages referring to God as ruler and possessor of all things (Gen. 14:19, 22; Ps. 89:11 [MT 12]), in subsequent references to the creative work of God (2 K. 19:15; Ps. 121:2; 124:8; 134:3; 146:6; Isa. 37:16; Jer. 32:17) and to the absolute power of God over His creation (Isa. 65:17; 66:1; Joel 2:30 [MT 3:3]; 3:16 [MT 4:16]; Hag. 2:6, 21), and also in oaths, commands, and prayers representing Yahweh as exclusive sovereign (Dt. 3:24; 4:26, 39; 5:8; 30:19; 31:28; 1 K. 8:23; Neh. 9:6). These uses of "the heavens and the earth" manifest the theological underpinnings of biblical cosmology. Scripture does not simply describe the world for its own sake, but it describes the world as belonging and as related to God.

In the concrete imagery characteristic of the OT, the universe was described as having three levels: the heavens, the earth, and the regions under the earth. On the one hand, this imagery was grounded in the ancient world view that Israel held in common with its neighbors. On the other hand, it was a vehicle for the expression of divine transcendence and immanence, a description of the theater of divine and human activity. This dual implication must be kept in mind by the reader of Scripture. First, the basic world view ought not to be juxtaposed to its disadvantage with that of modern science, but seen functionally and practically as a description of the world simply as it appears to the eye and relates to the individual. The language of the three levels belongs not only to simple observation, but also to a profound feeling for the way the world is arranged around humanity and to poetic and religious insight. Second, since the language is frequently the expression of poetic and religious impressions of the world order, it ought not to be understood rigidly, as if all biblical descriptions of heaven and earth and the lower parts of the earth could be harmonized into a single structural portrait of the universe. This point will become clear in the following discussion of the three levels and the terms used to describe them.

The term "heavens," *šāmayim,* refers to all that is above the earth; the air and the clouds, the firmament, and the spaces above the firmament. In the Creation account (Gen. 1:6-8) the "firmament" (*rāqî[a]'*) is called, by extension, "heaven" (v. 8), and is described as a vault that divides waters above from water below. On a theological level, this is a clear statement of the power of God over impending chaos, the power to create a stable world and to isolate the forces that would impinge destructively upon it. In the story of the Flood (Gen. 7–9) and in the Isaiah apocalypse (Isa. 24:18) the destruction of the sinful world is accomplished by God breaking the firmament, opening "the windows of (the) heavens," and allowing the waters above to inundate the earth in a resumption of chaos. On a purely physical and descriptive level, the OT writers are quite aware that rain comes from the clouds in the air under the firmament (Jgs. 5:4; Ps. 77:17), and they can even describe the water cycle of evaporation, cloud formation, and rain (Job 36:27f.). The FIRMAMENT itself is variously described as a solid vault (37:18) upon which the heavenly luminaries are fixed (Gen. 1:14-18) or as a tent or a curtain (Ps. 104:2; Isa. 40:22). Nor are the heavenly bodies always said to be "set" or fixed; they can be described as coursing through the heavens (Jgs. 5:20; Job 31:26; Ps. 19:5f.). In addition, the firmament may be described as resting on pillars (Job 26:11), perhaps signifying the strength and stability of its construction, or as resting upon the earth at the circle of the horizon (Prov. 8:27f.; cf. Job 26:10), implying a more visual picture of its structure.

The heavens are also the dwelling place of God (Ps. 11:4; 14:2; Eccl. 5:2; Lam. 3:50), and the imagery of pillars in the heavens may indicate the palace of God built in the "upper chambers" of the sky (Am. 9:6; cf. Ps. 104:3). Stadelmann (e.g., pp. 41f.) noted that Hebrew thought, as distinct from Babylonian, did not speculate concerning structures or levels in the heavens, although poetry could speak of "the highest heaven" (Ps. 148:4; Eccl. 16:16). Instead, references to God in the heavens point to the divine transcendence and to the demythologization process within the OT. HEAVEN is part of creation and its phenomena are under the control of Yahweh. He rages in anger and shakes the pillars of heaven. He transcends even the heavens: the "highest heaven" cannot contain Him (1 K. 8:27 par. 2 Ch. 6:18; Neh. 9:6). The very heavens can pass away, can "wear out like a garment," but God endures forever (Ps. 102:26f.). Despite the continuing language of a "heavenly court" (Job 1:6; 2:1; Ps. 82:1), heavenly beings such as gods of the sun and moon, rain and thunder are excluded. Ps. 82 actually describes the summoning of deities to the heavenly dwelling for their judgment and undoing at the hands of Yahweh.

The idea of an ordered, habitable world is conveyed by *'ereṣ* and *tēḇēl*. The former term has several usages. It can occasionally be equivalent to *'adāmâ,* "ground"; it is a technical term for the land of the promise or for the territories of other nations and is used in such phrases as "the people of the land"; finally, as considered here, it indicates the habitable world, the sphere of divine and human activity (cf. Gen. 11:1, 4, 8f.; Ex. 9:14-16; Ps. 19:4 [MT 5]; 24:1; Isa. 18:3; etc.). Heb. *'ereṣ* (e.g., Isa. 10:14; 11:4; 24:4-6; Jer. 23:5; 33:25; Am. 5:7; 8:9), with *tēḇēl* (e.g., Ps. 9:8 [MT 9]; Isa. 13:11), is that portion of "the heavens and the earth" in which God and humanity relate under categories such as dominion, stewardship, covenant, and promise. Typical of ancient peoples, Israel could speak of the earth as a flat disk with the temple of God at its center (Jgs. 9:37; Ex. 38:12) or resting upon pillars sunk deep into the primeval sea below (Job 9:6; Ps. 24:1f.; 104:5-9). The expanse of the earth could be described as circular (Isa. 40:22) and as "dry land" encompassed by the ocean (Gen. 1:9f.) or, figuratively, as having "ends" or "corners" relating to the points of the compass (Isa. 11:12; Dt. 33:17; Job 37:3; Ps. 19:6 [MT 7]). *See also* EARTH.

More important than any physical description of *'ereṣ,* or *tēḇēl,* is the sense of "world" as an orderly creation distinct from but always dependent upon Yahweh. Not only does the entire creation rest upon the will of Yahweh, but it also manifests His presence: "faithfulness will spring up from the ground, and righteousness will look down from the sky" (Ps. 85:11 [MT 12]). God, the creator and sustainer of the order, stands against chaos and for His creatures. He creates a world, a dry expanse of earth upon which humanity can flourish. His creation is also, as Knierim points out, a paradigm against which history and present-day humanity can be evaluated, indeed, the larger reality to which both humanity and its history belong. This theology of the created order in turn explains the sense of the world, found in the Prophets, as a sphere of existence tainted by human disobedience and either tending toward destruction or dramatic, apocalyptic redemption (Isa. 24; 65:17-25; Joel 2:10; 3:16-18 [MT 4:16-18]).

The final component in the structure of the world order is the underworld, which consists of the place of the dead (Heb. *še'ôl*), the waters under the earth and, in the graphic language of ancient cosmology, the pillars upon which the earth itself is founded (cf. Job 38:4; Ps. 104:5; Prov. 8:29). In general terms, the underworld is called "the depths of the earth" (Ps. 63:10 [MT 11]; 139:15; Isa. 44:23; cf. Ezk. 26:20; 31:14, 16). This is a place of shadow, desolation, emptiness, distance, and even alienation from God. Heb. *še'ôl,* the common grave of all the departed in which there is no praise and from which there is no escape, describes precisely this sense of alienation and half-existence. The waters under the earth, the *tehôm,* also represent desolation, even the threat of chaos, for this is the primeval sea, the "deep" of Gen. 1:2 over which the Spirit moved before the formation of the dry land. Yet even this underworld cannot ultimately shut out the divine presence, for even in *še'ôl* God's hand is felt (Job 11:7-9; 26:5f.; Ps. 139:8; Prov. 15:11). *See also* NETHER WORLD; SHEOL.

Other terms, occasionally translated as "world," such as *ḥeleḏ* (Ps. 17:14; 49:1 [MT 2]; Isa. 38:11) and *'ôlām,* "indefinite time" (Eccl. 3:11 and Ps. 73:12, AV only), have some interest insofar as they indicate the transitory character of worldly life and approximate the meaning of Gk. *aiṓn*. They do not contribute greatly to the OT conception of "world."

B. Creation and Cosmogony. The OT contains two cosmogonies or CREATION accounts (Gen. 1:1–2:4a and 2:4b-7) and numerous other cosmogonic passages (e.g., Job 38; Ps. 104; Prov. 8:22-31; Isa. 45:18). All maintain the distinction between God and His creation and the absolute dependence of the created order upon God. The cosmogony in Gen. 1:1–2:4a can be elucidated in its relation to the cosmogony of the Babylonian epic *Enuma Elish.* In the Babylonian account the lineage and descent of the gods (theogony) precedes the cosmogony as a prologue, setting the stage for the idea of a world. Genesis knows only the one God. Commentators differ over the punctuation of Gen. 1:1, but if it is taken as a separate sentence, summarizing and defining the work of creation, it stands in agreement with the general perspective of Israelite religion on the sole sovereignty of Yahweh insofar as it will allow no preexistent materials over against God. Genesis, in contrast to *Enuma Elish,* presents no cosmic battle and no production of the material order from the bodies of defeated deities. The structure of the universe is much the same in both documents — the heavens and the firmament, the earth and the lower regions — but the interpretation is entirely different. Genesis refers to the "deep" (*t^e^hôm*) as a chaotic waste upon which God acts creatively, whereas the Babylonian cosmogony refers to the defeat of the goddess Tiamat and the rise in power of the Babylonian pantheon. The philological relation between Heb. *t^e^hôm* and Tiamat alone remains — and that may be part of a purposeful demythologization underlying the biblical narrative. Israel's neighbors viewed the heavenly bodies, the great sea-creatures, and the animal life of air and earth mentioned in the narrative as gods. Here they are all manifest as creatures dependent upon God. The narrative stands as an anti-theogony. Creation comes into being by divine fiat. God is not part of the world process.

The second Creation narrative, assigned by higher criticism to the older, "Yahwistic" source, states briefly the fact of God's creative act (2:4b) and passes on immediately to discuss the place of humanity in the created order. Whereas the first narrative introduces man (male and female) as the apex of creation, given dominion in God's image, this account presents man as a steward or caretaker whose tilling of the soil parallels and supplements the divine gift of rain. If the first narrative argues human power with responsibility to God, this narrative argues responsibility coupled with partnership.

Also worthy of independent mention is the cosmogony included in the great theophany of Job 38. The underlying theme of the passage is the omnipotence and transcendence of God. The cosmos itself appears to Job as an impenetrable mystery: he did not exist when the foundations of the world were laid and lacks understanding (38:4). But the God who announces the mystery was there as creator and orderer; He is beyond the mystery of origins: transcendent, incomprehensible.

II. In the Apocrypha.–In 2 Maccabees and Wisdom, the term *kósmos* first appears as a reference to the material world, the place of human life (2 Macc. 7:23; 13:14; Wisd. 1:14; 5:20; 7:17; 9:3). Following the Genesis narrative, God is termed "creator of the world" (2 Macc. 13:14) and man is denominated the delegated ruler whose task is to superintend the world "in holiness and righteousness" (Wisd. 9:3). We see here on the one hand a philosophical conception of a world order, *kósmos,* which crystallizes in Hebrew thought with the adoption of the Greek language (Wisd. 11:17; cf. 9:1ff.), and on the other, a norm of created goodness, an expectation of righteousness. The latter idea develops into a sense of world-corruption because of human sin (14:13, 21). Here, too, we encounter explicit reference to the devil and his envy as the beginning of death in the world (2:24).

Two important developments in cosmology also occur in the Apocrypha. Wisd. 11:17 states that the "all-powerful hand" of God created the world out of "formless matter" (*amórphou hýlēs*). 2 Macc. 7:28 is also an explicit reference to creation *ex nihilo.* Both passages ought to be viewed as doctrinal extrapolations within the bounds of the Creation account in Gen. 1. Eichrodt (II, 102) argues that creation *ex nihilo* is the correct conclusion to be drawn from the text. Wisdom's conception of the creative informing of formless matter may have affinities with Platonic philosophy, but it also fairly represents the biblical view of God ordering the primeval chaos. Rather than seeing here a clash of Hebrew and Greek world views, we should set aside the inaccurate dichotomy and think in terms of a natural affinity of thought forms resting on the common oriental background of Hebrew and Greek cultures and on the profound interpretation of ancient cultures that took place at least as early as the 8th cent. B.C.

III. In the NT.–A. *Terms and General Meaning.* The term most frequently translated as "world" in the RSV NT is Gk. *kósmos.* This is significant in view of the preference of the LXX for *gḗ* (the usual equivalent for Heb. *'ereṣ*) and *oikouménē* (generally rendering Heb. *ṯēḇēl*). In the first place, *kósmos* has a broader meaning than *gḗ* and can more easily refer to the entire material universe; second, *oilouménē* functioned in NT times as a term for the Greco-Roman world and was restricted in its use. This restriction is clearly seen in Luke (2:1; 4:5) and Acts (17:6; 19:27; 24:5). In the frequent Pauline references to "world," *oikouménē* occurs only in Rom. 10:18, which is a quotation from the LXX. Third, a shift in usage had already occurred in between the LXX (*ca.* 280 B.C.) and Wisdom (*ca.* 50 B.C.), with *kósmos* replacing *oikouménē* as the favored term. This shift can be explained by the above reasons, compounded with the preference of Greek philosophy for *kósmos* in passages signifying the material universe. In addition to these terms, the NT also occasionally uses *aiṓn,* "age," in a sense that can be rendered "world."

The NT uses the term *kósmos* in three distinct ways. First, it can denote the universe or world order that God created according to His purposes; it is, therefore, the place where His eternal plan is put into operation (cf. Mt. 24:21; 25:34; Lk. 11:50; Rom. 1:20). The fullest cosmological reference and most positive use of *kósmos* as the material universe is surely Paul's Areopagus speech, "the God who made the world and everything in it, being Lord of heaven and earth . . ." (Acts 17:24). The passage draws on ideas familiar to the Greek mind — Paul cites the poet Aratus (v. 28) — but it also echoes the language of the OT cosmology in the equation of *kósmos* with "heaven and earth." This use of *kósmos* also frequently includes reference to the work of Christ as part of the underlying pattern and meaning of the created order (Lk. 11:50; Eph. 1:4; Heb. 4:3; 9:26; 1 Pet. 1:20), thereby associating the work of creation with the work of redemption.

Second, *kósmos* can be used in the sense of *oikouménē,* in reference to the habitable world. This usage appears in the Synoptic Gospels, e.g., "all the kingdoms of the world" in Mt. 4:8 (*kósmos*) and its parallel in Lk. 4:5 (*oikouménē*). There is also some relation between this usage and an ethical usage (see below). Jn. 16:28 says that Jesus is "come into the world" and is "leaving the world." And children are "born into the world" (16:21; cf. 1:9; 3:19; 1 Cor. 5:10). These references may simply indicate the world of humanity, but they may also have overtones of a world in need of redemption.

Third, *kósmos* indicates the ethical order in which human responsibility and human sinfulness stand in relationship to God. Thus "world" can have a highly negative connotation, indicating a place of corruption, a place antagonistic and antipathetic to God, a place in the grip of the demonic "powers." It is, nevertheless, the very place that God has chosen as the theater of redemptive activity, an activity that takes place in the midst of human history. This third meaning is the principal theological usage in the Pauline and Johannine writings.

The noun *oikouménē* translated in the RSV as "world" appears only fifteen times in the NT, eight times in Luke-Acts. The whole *oikouménē* is taxed (Lk. 2:1). When Satan offers political power to Christ, he offers the kingdoms of the *oikouménē* (4:5), and the apostles are viewed as radicals who disturb the political status quo in the *oikouménē* (Acts 17:6; 19:27; 24:5). The word points in two directions: first, the Greco-Roman world and the realms of political powers, and second, by extension, a realm of satanic dominion. By way of exception, Mt. 24:14 refers to the preaching of the gospel throughout the whole *oikouménē,* and He. 2:5 refers to the coming *oikouménē* as subject to Jesus. Matthew refers simply to the inhabited world, and if Hebrews gives the word a political connotation, that connotation is not negative. Three other references (Rev. 3:10; 12:9; 16:14) use the term to denote the political world as perverted by Satan and the demons.

By way of contrast with the two preceding terms, *aiṓn,* refers not to the spatial world but to the world viewed from the perspective of time. The sphere of human activity and of bondage to sin is the present "age." An important theological connection between *aiṓn* and the third meaning of *kósmos* appears in the phrase, "the age of this world," *tón aiṓna toú kósmou toútou* (Eph. 2:2; cf. 1 Cor. 1:20), during which disobedience rules. Whereas the *kósmos,* God's creation, will be redeemed from its sins, this *aiṓn,* in which sin, death, and devil rule, will pass away. In language of great contrasts, the NT juxtaposes the rulers, wisdom, and evils of this age with the godliness, blessing, and divine rule of the age to come (Mt. 12:32; Mk. 10:30; Lk. 18:30; 2 Cor. 4:4; Gal. 1:4). *Aiṓn* tends to have a more fully ethical connotation than *kósmos,* since "this age" can be totally identified as the antithesis of the coming kingdom.

B. In the Pauline Epistles. Paul is so certain of the sovereignty of God in His creation that, despite the presence of sin and the demonic "powers," he can view the entire created order as given to humanity for its use. Nothing is ultimately forbidden as unclean (1 Cor. 10:23-31; Rom. 14:14, 20). In accord with this principle Paul can speak positively of the *kósmos* as the place where the gospel bears fruit (Col. 1:6) and as the object of the divine work of reconciliation (Rom. 11:15; 2 Cor. 5:19; 1 Tim. 1:15). Nevertheless, the *kósmos* is so tainted that it lies under judgment (Rom. 3:6; 19; 1 Cor. 6:2). The whole creation (*ktísis*) groans "in travail" awaiting redemption (Rom. 8:21f.), but this new cosmic birth, under judgment, is so radical that Paul can also state that "the form of this world is passing away" (1 Cor. 7:31). It may be a sign of the depth of sin that Paul does not speak of a new or renewed *kósmos.*

This problematic nature of the *kósmos* as presently experienced accounts for the majority of Pauline references to *kósmos.* The world, given to the human race for its use, has been perverted through its fall and sin (Rom. 5:12-21). The *kósmos* now is the place of sin, sorrow, and bondage to the powers (4:15; 5:11; 1 Cor. 2:12; 5:10; 6:2; 7:31; Gal. 4:3). Its very patterns of thought contrast radically with the truth and wisdom of God (1 Cor. 1:20, 21, 27; 4:9, 13). A "spirit of the world" exists (2:12) that is not from God. In view of this dichotomy, Christians must not be of the world even though they dwell in it. Christians belong to Christ (3:21-23) and are conquerors of the powers (Rom. 8:31-39; Col. 2:8-15). They therefore live in a paradoxical relation to the world: they "mourn as though they were not mourning" and "deal with the world as though they had no dealings with it" (1 Cor. 7:30f.).

C. In the Johannine Writings. Much like Paul, John describes Christians as present in the world (Jn. 17:11) but liberated from its darkness by the Son, who is the "light" sent into the world (12:46). Neither the world nor the things of the world ought to be loved by Christians. The *kósmos* and its lusts are not of the Father, but will pass away (1 Jn. 2:15-17). Bultmann (II, 17) explains this antithesis as resting on a pre-Christian Gnostic dualism; and it is undeniable that John's Gospel contains profound contrasts of God and world, divine truth and worldly falsehood, God's light and cosmic darkness. Nevertheless, the dualism is not absolute and does not rest upon a cosmogonic myth like those of the Gnostics. If the *kósmos* stands apart from God in darkness and ignorance (Jn. 1:5; 3:19; 12:35; 1 Jn. 2:8), it exists because of God and His word (Jn. 1:3, 10), and the Word incarnate has been sent into the *kósmos* to redeem it (1:29; 3:16-19; 12:46f.; 17:21, 23; 18:37). "This world" (*ho kósmos hoútos*), the present condition of things (8:23; 9:39; 11:9), lies under the rule of the devil (12:31; 14:30; 16:11), but he and his rule are presently under judgment and are being "cast out" (12:31). No power of the world can overcome the love of God for the world and for those in the world that He has chosen (3:16; 17:6-26). In John, as in Paul, we see an ambivalence toward the world, a sense of its evil, its rebellion from God, but also a reluctance, which stops short of dualism, to pronounce the *kósmos* as essentially evil. Judgment comes upon the unredeemable, but redemption is also available (cf. Rev. 3:10f.).

Implicit in the foregoing discussion of the NT view of "world" has been the absence from the NT of a fully stated cosmology or cosmogony. This fact ought never to obscure the concern of the NT for a positive view of the creation as God's handiwork and as the sphere of divine activity in which all things tend toward God despite the evils of the present age (Col. 1:15-20). Steck argued (*World and Environment*) that the saving work of Christ, the goal and climax of God's work, must be viewed within the framework and as the fulfillment of OT faith. The concentration of the NT upon the work of redemption does not exclude the cosmology of the OT but rather presupposes it.

IV. In the Early Church.–The negative sense of *kósmos* found in both John and Paul carries over into the writings of the Apostolic Fathers. In the Didache we find a radical dichotomy between the worldly "way of death" and the godly "way of life" (chs. 1–6). The same views appear in the Epistle of Barnabas (chs. 18–20). Life under the imminent threat of persecution and death was conducive to the equation of world, the Greco-Roman *oikouménē,* with the domain of the powers. In the early 3rd cent. A.D., Tertullian (*De spectaculis* viii.9) could state the case simply: Satan and his angels filled the entire world (*totum saeculum*). But this negative view must be balanced against a positive concept of the divinely created world order, found as early as 1 Clement (ch. 20), *ca.* A.D. 95. Clement combined a sense of the harmony of the world order, possibly of Stoic origin, with a sense of the divine governance of the world and the relation of that benevolent governance to the greatest divine gift of peace and mercy in Christ Jesus.

The Apologists of the 2nd cent. provide more insight into early Christian cosmology than do the Apostolic Fathers. The biblical theme of divine transcendence is supplemented by Platonic and Stoic philosophy, with the result that the creation can be defined as a mediated work of God performed by the Logos. The Apologists thus confront the problem of interpreting biblical and philosophical cosmologies in relation to one another. Justin Martyr (*ca.* 150 A.D.) manifested the opinion that the creation myth of Plato's *Timaeus* represents a contact between Greek and Hebrew culture and, indeed, a borrowing from the Mosaic account (*Apol.* i). Justin accepted Plato's teaching but modified it by denying the eternity of the world and identifying God as the sole ingenerate being. He accepted the philosophical premise that the divine work is the informing and ordering of matter without answering the implied question of a creation *ex nihilo* (chs. 59–60). Justin strongly represented the world as an order governed by the *Logos*. While these doctrines follow the more positive and philosophical pattern of Clement, Justin also taught the NT view of the *kósmos* as troubled and tainted, as ruled in this *aiṓn* by the powers or demons. The redemptive work of the Logos is of cosmic significance in that it is a victory over the powers and the reestablishment of the true wisdom of the world principle, the Logos (cf. chs. 14, 23, 46, 56).

From this period, Tatian's *Discourse to the Greeks* (A.D. 172) and Athenagoras's *A Plea for Christians* (A.D. 177) are noteworthy for their cosmological discussions. Tatian defined God as "alone without beginning" and "the beginning of things." He is the maker of all material things and of the forms of the material world. Tatian explicitly affirmed the creation *ex nihilo* by means of the Logos (cf. chs. 4–5). Athenagoras's cosmology stands in substantial agreement with Tatian, insisting that God is transcendent, beyond the world order, but sustaining it by His providential care. Athenagoras also added — a point of common knowledge in the classical world — that the world is spherical and "confined with the circles of heaven" (ch. 8). Athenagoras viewed this cosmology as proof of the oneness and sole rulership of God.

It is significant, and a sign of better grasp of meaning than often encountered in our age, that the fathers who held to a Ptolemaic theory of the spherical universe accepted also the bibical narrative of creation and its socalled three-level universe without worry over "scientific" problems. The fathers also accepted, as biblical, the doctrine of creation *ex nihilo,* quite against the philosophical tendencies of their day. Thus no matter how strong the influence of philosophy, the biblical doctrine of divine transcendence and of the priority of God over world was maintained. In general, the fathers of the 2nd cent. A.D. represented well the balance of the biblical teaching, while avoiding on the one side a Gnostic dualism, and on the other any loss of the NT sense of the sinfulness of the present age.

Bibliography.–R. Bultmann, *Theology of the NT* (2 vols., Eng. tr. 1951-1955); C. N. Cochrane, *Christianity and Classical Culture* (1940); *DNTT*, I, 517-526; W. Eichrodt, *Theology of the OT*, II (Eng. tr. 1967); R. Knierim, *Horizons in Biblical Theology*, 3 (1981), 59-123; R. A. Norris, *God and World in Early Christian Theology* (1965); H. Ringgren, *Israelite Religion* (Eng. tr. 1966); L. I. J. Stadelmann, *Hebrew Conception of the World* (*Analecta Biblica*, 39, 1970); O. H. Steck, *World and Environment* (Eng. tr. 1981); *TDNT*, III, *s.v.* κοπμέω κτλ.: κόσμος (Sasse); *TDOT*, I, *s.v.* "'erets" (Bergman, Ottossan); W. Zimmerli, *OT and the World* (Eng. tr. 1976).

R. A. MULLER

WORLD, END OF THE. *See* ESCHATOLOGY.

WORLDLY [Gk. *kosmikós* (Tit. 2:12), *sarkikós* (2 Cor. 10:4), *psychikós* (Jude 19), elsewhere rendering variants of three whole phrases, *katá (tén) sárka*–'according to the flesh' (1 Cor. 1:26; 2 Cor. 1:17; 10:2f.; 11:18), *tḗ sarkí*–'in the flesh' (1 Cor. 7:28), *(tá) toú kósmou*–'(the things) of the world' (1 Cor. 7:33f.; 2 Cor. 7:10)]; AV also CARNAL, SENSUAL, ACCORDING TO THE FLESH, OF THE WORLD, etc.; NEB also EARTHLY, UNSPIRITUAL, BODILY, etc. The RSV here groups ideas expressed by a variety of words in the Greek, whereas the AV and (in part) the NEB preserve more of the verbal distinctions.

Both world and flesh (Gk. *kósmos, sárx*) are used in the NT in a variety of nuances ranging from neutral to negative, i.e., indicative of opposition to God. Thus in the *kósmos* word-group the "worldly" is opposed to the "godly" (*katá theón*) (2 Cor. 7:10), and to the things "of the Lord" (1 Cor. 7:34). The "world" in this sense denotes the whole human system of things as organized apart from the factor of God.

The derivatives of "flesh" are contrasted in varying ways with those of "spirit" (*pneúma*). "Flesh" sometimes stands for earthly life neutrally (Rom. 15:27; 1 Cor. 9:11; etc.), but its use in Rom. 7:14; 1 Cor. 3:1-3; etc. speaks of sinful humanity, separated from God. Similar contrasts are made between the "natural" (*psychikós*) and the "spiritual" (1 Cor. 2:14; 15:44, 46; Jude 19). In fact, the NT, and especially the Pauline Epistles, contains a series of overlapping expressions of the fundamental contrast between the divine and human orders (cf. also 1 Cor. 15:48f.; Gal. 5:16-26; Col. 3:2).

Thus the NT expressions of the idea of "worldliness" are fluid. Pagan or LXX usage provides no clear precedent; e.g., *kosmikós* is absent from the LXX, and *kósmos* itself figures mainly in later books. *Kósmios* always retains a favorable sense, "seemly," "dignified" (as in 1 Tim. 2:9; 3:2). In the fathers, however, *kosmikós* is more particularly "worldly," "secular."

The rendering "worldly" is appropriate where the stress is upon the practical outworking of standards unrelated to the fact of God. Thus believers may be worldly in this sense if their conduct is motivated by fallen human nature (1 Cor. 3:3).

See FLESH; WORLD.

See *TDNT,* III, *s.v.* κοσμικός (Sasse); IX, *s.v.* ψυχικός (Schweizer).

C. J. HEMER

WORM [Heb. *tôlēʿâ* (Ex. 16:20; Dt. 28:39; Ps. 22:6 [MT 7]; Job 25:6b; Isa. 14:11d; 41:14; 66:24; Jonah 4:7), *rimmâ* (Ex. 16:24; Isa. 14:11c; Job 7:5; 17:14; 21:26; 25:6a), *sās* (Isa. 51:8); Gk. *skṓlēx* (Mk. 9:44, 46, 48), *skōlēkóbrōtos*–'eaten by worms' (Acts 12:23)]; RSV, NEB also MAGGOT (Job 25:6a; Isa. 14:11c); NEB also GRUB (Dt. 28:39; Isa. 51:8). The Hebrew words translated "worm(s)" do not refer to worms, properly speaking (e.g., earthworms, *Oligochaeta*), but to the larvae of various insects, especially flies (*Diptera*), beetles (*Coleoptera*), and butterfly-moths (*Lepidoptera;* the Hebrews did not regard butterflies and moths as separate types).

These "worms" fell into two categories: those which fed upon vegetation or non-animal matter (Ex. 16:20, 24; Dt. 28:39; Isa. 51:8; Jonah 4:7), and those which devoured decaying flesh (Job 7:5; 17:14; 21:26; 25:6; Ps. 22:6; Isa. 14:11; 41:14; 66:24; Mk. 9:44, 46, 48; Acts 12:23). With regard to the "worms" which infested old manna, MT uses both *tôlāʿîm* (Ex. 16:20) and *rimmâ* (v. 24). The use of these two terms in parallel in reference to maggots (i.e., the larvae of flies) in Isa. 14:11 and Job 25:6 justifies the NEB translation "maggots" in Ex. 16:20, 24. Nevertheless, there is no indication that the manna in the wilderness was flesh, so that meal worms or the like might also have been meant. In either case, both the plural *tôlāʿîm* and the collective noun *rimmâ* refer to the mass of moving larvae upon decaying matter and evoke a profound sense of revulsion. This sense is a recurring element in the book of Job, and results in the use of these terms as expressions of deprecation. Thus Isa. 41:14 and Ps. 22:6 compare humanity, the highest form of created life, with the worm, which the Hebrews seem to have viewed as the lowest. Similarly, 1 Macc. 2:62 speaks of the sinner's wealth as turning into "dung and worms."

It is in the book of Isaiah, however, that one finds the most graphic allusions to the worm-infested end of those upon whom God's judgment falls. Thus it is said of the king of Babylon, brought down to Sheol, "maggots are beneath you, and worms are your covering" (14:11). Isa. 66:24 describes the eternal death of those who have rebelled against Yahweh: "Their worm shall not die, their fire shall not be quenched, and they shall be an abhorrence to all flesh."

This refrain is taken up in Mk. 9:48 (vv. 44, 46 are textually suspect, and accordingly have been dropped from the RSV, NEB, NIV, NASB, etc., though they are retained in the AV), where it also serves as a figure for eternal death. In both cases, "their worm" refers to the twitching, teeming mass of maggots, eternally gorging themselves upon the corpse. Herod Agrippa, who died suddenly in A.D. 44, is described in Acts 12:23 as having been "eaten by worms" (*skōlēkóbrōtos*). While this fate has not yet been medically determined, other Hellenistic authors mention men being eaten by worms (*skṓlēkes;* Lucian *Alexander the False Prophet* 59; Josephus *Ant.* xviii.6.5 [169]; 2 Macc. 9:9). *See* DISEASE IV.E.

For Mic. 7:17 (AV "worms") *see* CRAWLING THINGS.

See F. S. Bodenheimer, *Animal and Man in Bible Lands* (1960), pp. 73, 78.

D. G. SCHLEY

WORMWOOD [Heb. *laʿanâ* (Prov. 5:4; Jer. 9:15 [MT 14]; 23:15; Lam. 3:15, 19; Am. 5:7; 6:12); Gk. *apsínthion/ápsinthos* (Rev. 8:11)]; AV also HEMLOCK (Am. 6:12); NEB also UPSIDE DOWN (Am. 5:7), POISON (6:12). Several plants in Palestine within the genus *Artemisia,* all of which are bitter in taste. Several species and varieties grow in Palestine, but those mentioned in the Bible are most likely *Artemisia herba alba* Asso, *A. Judaica* L., or *A. absinthium.* Used figuratively of bitter things, the term denotes the result of illicit sexual relations (Prov. 5:4), God's punishment due to sin (Jer. 9:15; 23:15; Lam. 3:15, 19), and perverted justice (Am. 5:7; 6:12). In Dt. 29:18 (MT 17) the AV translates Heb. *laʿanâ* as "wormwood" (RSV "bitter") in a description of the bitter results of practicing idolatry. Also, Heb. *laʿanâ* often parallels Heb. *rō'š,* a term that frequently refers to a bitter and poisonous herb (Dt. 29:18 [MT 17]; Jer. 9:15 [MT 14]; 23:15; Lam. 3:19; *see* GALL). In Rev. 8:11 "wormwood" describes the resultant quality of water into which the star named "wormwood" fell. R. H. Mounce said that "although wormwood itself is not poisonous, its bitter taste suggests death" (*Book of Revelation* [*NICNT,* 1977], p. 188).

See *DNTT,* II, 27-29; *MPB,* pp. 48f.

G. L. K.

WORSHIP.

Worship as traced in both the OT and NT originates in salvation-history (*Heilsgeschichte*); i.e., worship begins with God. God the creator, the rescuer, and the redeemer initiates our human approach to Him. The remembered events of the Exodus, the Passover, the crucifixion, and the Resurrection evoke a response from God's people. The response is worship. Hence, worship originates with God in its theological roots as opposed to anthropological initiation from the human side.

I. Definition and Word Usage.–The origins of the word "worship" aid in defining its meaning and usage. "Worship" is from the Saxon/Old English word "weorthscipe" or "weordhscipe," which means "worthship" or worthiness. This connotes actions motivated by an attitude that reveres, honors, or describes the worth of another person or object. In the context of the OT and NT worship refers specifically to worship of the divine. Worship is seen as reverent devotion and service to God motivated by God's saving acts in history.

A. Hebrew. While no one Hebrew term is an equivalent for worship, many Hebraic ideas define the activity of worship in the OT. The verb *'āḇaḏ* means "serve"; the corresponding noun means "service, adoration." *Hištaḥ^awâ* is another verb in the liturgical vocabulary that means "prostrate oneself" (cf. *TDOT,* IV, 248-256). The Hebrew terms that are used synonymously for the word worship are verbs that indicate some type of activity. *See* OBEISANCE.

B. Greek. The Greek word *proskynéō* is probably the term most closely related to the English word "worship." This word depicts the posture of kissing the ground, a reverent act used mainly in reference to worship of a deity. The NT seldom uses this word, perhaps because of its close connection with pagan worship. The word demands a visible act, a concrete gesture of reverence to a visible deity. The image is used in the Synoptic Gospels and in the eschatological references of Revelation. Since apostolic worship is a joyous experience, the key here is one of glad access to God rather than an uncertainty and dread in His presence.

The *góny* ("knee")/*gonypetéō* ("bend the knee") word-group reflects a GESTURE of worship. From the Latin form of this word we get the English word "genuflect," meaning the bending of the knee or even full prostration. This gesture of worship expresses an inner attitude of humility and self-abasement. OT usage illustrates a broader context than the cultic setting of worship. 2 K. 1:13 and 1 Ch. 29:20 respectively record men falling on their knees before holy men and the king. 1 K. 8:54 and Dnl. 6:10 describe this position as a worship position before Yahweh. The NT uses *góny* and *gonypetéō* to depict the act of bowing the knee in prayer to God (Lk. 22:41), making petitions to the Lord (Mt. 17:14), greeting a teacher (Mk. 10:17), and paying homage to the pagan deity Baal (Rom. 11:4), and to Jesus (Lk. 5:8). The word connotes an inner attitude of adoration, respect, and humility spontaneously expressed in a physical manner.

The *latreúō* ("serve")/*latreía* ("service") word-group refers to the offering of sacrifice or service with no thought of reward. Generally this term refers to specific cultic preparations. Dt. 10:12, however, roots this service in a deep commitment of the heart. The OT view reflects the holistic nature of service and sacrifice to Yahweh. The lack of this commitment in later cultic worship was the major complaint of the prophets (esp. Hosea and Jeremiah). In its best sense, service to Yahweh has a cultic and ethical expression that involves the whole of the worshiper's life. The OT uses this word in reference to specific acts of service: the service of prayer and fasting, the service of work, and the specific service ministries of the temple priests (Nu. 16:9; Josh. 22:27). The NT also emphasizes the demand from God for service in a totally committed way. The apostle Paul insisted on the need of dedication of one's whole life, which includes both the inward motivational aspect and the outward expression of cultic devotion (Rom. 12:1f.). True service must include both.

The definition of service also can be applied to the *leitourgía* ("service")/*leitourgéō* ("serve") word-group. This term generally refers to service rendered on behalf of a people or a nation. It has a technical meaning in the Greek mystery cults. Liturgies were performed to the gods. The word had an official governmental aspect when it spoke of compulsory service rendered in state or community. This general or classical aspect of the word is not used in the LXX. By this time the word referred to God, His temple, tabernacle, or altar as the object of the liturgy. A liturgy was rendered to God in the form of a public service on behalf of the whole people. Owing to the sacrificial connotations associated with this word it was not used much in NT description. Most of the NT examples (Lk. 1:23; He. 9:21; 10:11) pick up the OT usage.

Worship, then, is the dramatic celebration of God in His supreme worth in such a manner that His "worthiness" becomes the norm and inspiration of human living. Defined in this way worship (1) places God at the center because of His worthiness; (2) avoids the tyranny of subjectivism; (3) allows for the reexamination of the self in the light of God's knowledge of us. From the beginning Israel's worship is a response to Yahweh for the acts He has performed in its history. Israel's whole history is a life of "co-existence with God," a partnership in a historical drama. The emphasis is on Yahweh as the initiator, but Israel responds. The people address Yahweh in a personal way. They offer praise, ask questions, complain about suffering, and converse with Him about all the issues of life. This conversation of worship is recorded throughout the Scriptures, binding Jewish history together in celebration of this relationship with the Creator God. In the NT church the emphasis falls on the historical acts of the triune God, with the central focus on the incarnation, the cross, and exaltation of Jesus Christ the Lord, made real by the Holy Spirit (Eph. 1:3-14; 2:18).

II. Patriarchal Period.–The book of Genesis records the history of Israel's ancestors from their nomadic beginnings. Abraham was called by Yahweh to leave his country and travel to a new land. A promise was given to Abraham that his name would be great and his family would become a mighty nation (Gen. 12). These themes originate in Genesis and weave throughout the whole of Israel's history. The fulfillment of these promises became the impetus for the people's response of worship and thanksgiving.

At Hebron, Abraham built the first altar to Yahweh in thanksgiving for the promise of the land (Gen. 13:18). Worship was offered to Yahweh after Abraham defeated the four kings (14:17-24). The worship was "led" by Melchizedek, "the priest of God Most High." Bread and wine were part of the worship. Melchizedek pronounced a blessing on Abraham (cf. He. 7:1-3). Abraham responded by giving the high priest a tithe of everything he had. At this early offering of thankful worship to Yahweh, the basic elements of Israel's worship form were present. From its nomadic beginnings Israel's worship included theophanies, promises of the land, the practice of marking important places with an altar, the figure of a high priest, and a cultic celebration using bread and wine. The following chapter (Gen. 15) and the sacrifice of Isaac (Gen. 22) rooted the cultic practice of sacrifice in Israel's tradition, though as a protest against human sacrifice.

III. Mosaic Worship and the Exodus.–Worship forms became more formalized in the book of Exodus. Yahweh's active intervention into Israel's history is characterized in the contest with Pharaoh. The deliverance from Egypt embodied the essence of Yahweh's relationship with His people; the "Song of Moses" (Ex. 15) enshrined deep-seated truths. One of Israel's great festivals looks back to this experience of liberation. The remembrance of the Passover incorporates Jews of every generation as actual participants in the Mosaic Exodus (Mish. *Pesahim* x.1-9).

Despite their murmurings through the desert wanderings the Israelites learned to know Yahweh as He provided food for them and called them His own. The desert experience became in later worship symbolic of God's

Gold leaf covers this bronze statue of a man kneeling in worship (2nd millennium B.C.) (CNMHS/ARS, NY/SPADEM)

provision and care (Dt. 8:1-20). God's instructions for the building and arrangement of His dwelling in the tabernacle, and the details pertaining to the priesthood, the sacrifices, and the worship service were very specific. Many chapters of the Pentateuch are dedicated to the details of the tabernacle's construction (Ex. 25–31). Worship and the manner in which worship was offered were evidently extremely important to Yahweh.

The tent of meeting illustrated the mobility of Yahweh. Unlike the pagan gods who were deities of limited geographical areas, Yahweh went with His people as an ever-present reality through their wanderings. In the desert wanderings Yahweh led Moses and the people to Mt. Sinai. Here an encounter with Yahweh grounded Jewish worship in an event that would profoundly affect the rest of Judeo-Christian history. The covenant of the Sinai bound the whole nation of Israel to Yahweh. The nation received the law, i.e., the decalogue, and the book of the covenant, which would direct its future. The covenantal relationship and the commitment to the law of Yahweh became the stamp of Judaism. Ironically, what is one of the historic highpoints of Yahweh's relationship with His people also revealed the sin and the alien worship that God's people were tempted to embrace later (Ex. 32). The golden calf became a reminder of the syncretistic nature of God's people. From this point forward "false" versus "true" worship would be a theme for the worshipers of Yahweh.

The event of the Exodus was a fulfillment of God's promise to Abraham (Gen. 12:1-3). The book of Exodus is pivotal in describing the central experience of the Jewish people. This story records the celebrations and ritual acts of Israel that arose in response to the liberation event that gave freedom to a nation. Exodus records the transformation of the old pagan notions into new forms, such as covenant and law, that brand Israel as unique among nations, with the Passover rite (Ex. 12) at the heart of all.

IV. Settlement in Canaan.–Syncretism, the mixture of foreign elements with the Yahwism of Israelite worship, became an increasing problem as the people of God moved from the wilderness to the promised land of Canaan. The religious procession to the land can also be seen as a military movement that collided with the cultures already existing in the area (see *BHI* [3rd ed.], ch. 3). Among other peoples, the Israelites encountered and settled near a Semitic people called the Canaanites. The Canaanite culture is thought to have existed in this area from perhaps as early as 3000 B.C. The Canaanite gods quickly became competitors for the loyalty and worship of the Israelites. The desert incident of the golden calf only foreshadowed the problem of idolatry that would intensify during this period of settlement.

For the OT writers the word "idolatry" meant veneration of an object other than the God of Abraham, Isaac, and Jacob. Since Scripture records Canaanite cultic centers at all the major cities and towns, including Dan, Gilgal, Shechem, Bethel, Shiloh, and Jerusalem, the temptation of idolatry for the Israelites was great (see, e.g., Am. 4:4f.). The difficulty for God's people was identifying what idolatry was. Syncretistic practices crept into the worship of the Israelites almost without their awareness. Scripture records examples of this pervasive and subtle cultural lure (see esp. Hos. 2:1-23).

One of the Canaanite deities was a god designated as BAAL (see 1 K. 18:21). The Heb. *baʿal* can mean "owner," "master," "lord," or "husband." Baal's power was over a particular locality. Thus Baal was the deity of a settled people. As the Israelites moved into a more settled lifestyle, they confronted the beliefs of Baal worship. The domain of the local baals lay in the fertility cycles of human beings, animals, and agriculture. Baal power was closely linked with nature, particularly the bringing of rain to Palestine's parched landscape. The influence of the Baal cult led to extreme forms of worship such as child sacrifice (Jer. 19:5) and ritual prostitution (Jgs. 2:17; Jer. 7:9; Am. 2:7).

The origins of Baal worship are uncertain but evidence indicates that the Amorites brought their gods with them on their migration into Canaan in the 2nd millennium B.C. Another Canaanite god, El, is mentioned as the original head of the Canaanite gods in the Râs Shamrah texts. El, however, was the distant source, the "Father of years" in the pantheon description. Baal symbolized the vigor and power behind the natural cycles of life-giving powers. ASHERAH became the feminine counterpart to Baal by the time of Judges (Jgs. 3:7).

Baal was often depicted with some characteristics of a bull, which was the ancient symbol of strength and fertility. Baal statues exhibit helmets with horns of a bull or picture the god as riding a bull. The statues show Baal with a club in one hand, most likely representing thunder, and a spear with leaves in the other depicting lightning and fertility (*see* picture in BAAL).

Israelite worship was constantly threatened by the foreign aspects of Baal worship that conflicted with Yahweh's prescribed law. Syncretism was a serious issue for two major reasons. First, the Israelites settled in the land with the Canaanites and often intermarried with the Baal worshipers. This brought the seductive elements of the cult closer, even into the Israelites' homes. Second, the way in which Yahweh was viewed as the god of the wanderings posed a threat. Owing to Baal worhsipers' polytheistic background, it was a natural tendency to view the gods as having power along geographical lines. Since the Israelites were dependent on the land once they settled in

Canaan, it might have seemed wise to pay homage to the god of that land, a feature recognized in David's confession (1 S. 26:19) and Naaman's request (2 K. 5:17f.).

These syncretistic tendencies can be seen in Scripture itself (Jgs. 3:5-7; 6:25f.). Many of the names in Scripture have elements of the Canaanite gods: Esh-baal, Merib-baal (1 Ch. 8:33f.), and Beeliada (14:7). It is difficult to know whether these references directly refer to the Canaanite deity or whether the term was used in reference to the lord Yahweh as owner and master. In time the syncretistic tendency became so blurred that the Israelites banned the use of *ba'al* in reference to the lordship of Yahweh.

The syncretistic tendency was particularly prominent in the northern kingdom according to the scriptural authors. This area was more exposed to pagan elements and more agricultural than the south. The north was therefore more susceptible to elements of the Baal worship. In the northern kingdom the golden calves at Dan and Bethel horrified those who were seeking true worship of Yahweh. Even the southern kingdom eventually experienced the influence of the Canaanite worship despite the reforms of Hezekiah and Josiah. Scripture indicates that even Jerusalem itself was influenced (2 K. 21:7). One of the most blatant attempts of syncretism was a deliberate ploy by Queen Jezebel to make Baal the official god of the land. Scripture states that only seven thousand Israelites resisted her to follow the true religion of Yahweh (1 K. 19:18). Throughout the 8th cent. the prophets constantly reminded the people of the syncretistic danger that was on all sides. It seems that the people of Yahweh did not recognize the apostasy in which they were involved (Jer. 2:23; Hos. 2:16f.).

Although syncretism posed a threat and led to a struggle throughout Israel's history, periods existed in which Yahweh's place of centrality in the life of His people and their worship was stronger and clearer. One of these periods was that of the Davidic monarchy. David had been blessed by Yahweh from a young age and had been ordained to be Israel's king after a unstable period when it was administered by the judges and then by Saul. David united the kingdom under one central government headquartered in Jerusalem in place of Hebron. King David linked this political move to the center of cultic worship by bringing the ark of the covenant to Zion.

V. Davidic Period.–This period focused primarily on King David during a politically stable period in Israel's life. David is credited primarily as the one who organized Israel as a worshiping community. While the biblical narratives do not spare David's sinful side, they show a man who is willing to confess and be forgiven for his sin. In later literature this then became the biblical example of a true worshiper of Yahweh. Perfection of ethical and moral character was thus not indispensable for faith. Rather Yahweh desired an honest worshiper who could confess and praise Him in sincerity and truth (Mic. 6:6-8). David becomes the example par excellence of a true worshiper, the traditional author of "the psalms of David" (e.g., 24, 150) that express cultic acts of worship.

David's political strategies established a monarchy with its cultic center in Jerusalem. David brought revival to a people and a faith that had experienced a low period lacking unity and strength. The ark of the covenant had disappeared in the Aphek disaster (Ps. 78:60) where the Israelites were defeated by the Philistines. David recovered the ark and purchased Araunah's threshing floor in Jerusalem (2 S. 24) for its new home. The ark reminded the people that Yahweh was not represented in wood or stone, but that He is a living presence with His people. The basis of the whole practice of worship in Israel looked back to the covenantal relationship established in the Exodus and celebrated in the tabernacle that had been the ark's previous dwelling place. The ark was also a reminder that worship alone is not enough. A broad requirement of service to Yahweh involves ethical implications of justice and mercy. In the reestablishment of the ark in a cultic center of worship, David laid a foundation for the royal ideology and the theme of a unique covenant established with David's lineage.

From the Chronicler's viewpoint David made a central contribution to Israel's worship. Jerusalem became the holy city, the religious capital of the tribes of Israel. The temple began to take form and structure under David. This temple was completed and embellished in *ca.* 950 B.C. by the king's successor and son, Solomon. David assigned to the Levites the official duties of leading the community in praise and prayer. The priesthood began to take on a stratified hierarchy of functions. The priesthood would eventually be represented by the Zadokites (functioning in the sacrificial capacity), the high priests, the priests, and the Levites. While the major components of worship remained constant, according to the tradition, David instituted some changes, especially the addition of instrumental worship (1 Ch. 23–27).

David is said to have been skilled on the lyre. He is considered the composer of many songs and laments that were incorporated into the temple worship. From allusive indications, music guilds may have been established during this period (1 Ch. 25:6f.) and given a special role in the service. The collection of these Davidic compositions and other songs is known as the Psalter, with David as the traditional author.

VI. Psalms.–*A. Their Collection and Function.* The Hebrew word *tᵉhillîm,* "songs of praise," is used to describe this collection. It is part of the Hebrew Scripture known as Kethubhim, or "writings." *Mizmôr,* a Hebrew term which precedes fifty-seven of the Psalms, refers to a musical accompaniment of the hymns (*see* MUSIC III.B.1). The term "songs" seems to be a special reference to the "Songs of Ascent" used as the worshiping community approached the temple (Pss. 120–134). Gk. *psaltḗrion* refers to the string instrument used for the accompaniment of these songs or psalms, utilizing the Greek verb *psállō,* "pluck the strings" (*see* MUSIC II.B.2).

The collection is from a broad historical period, some of it even dating from the conquest period (1250 B.C.). The final collection was not made until postexilic times. King David quite probably authored many of the Psalms. Because the content of the Psalms conveys the whole of Israel's history the Psalter was used as the devotional guide for Israel in many situations, and became the hymn book of the second temple. Worship was one natural setting for using the Psalms, for the Psalms represent the entire range of emotion; from anguish to hope, from fear to joy, from national pride to anger at Yahweh. The Psalms embrace adoration, thanksgiving, and supplication, all focused on glorifying the Creator in worship. The Psalms were Israel's response to Yahweh's active presence.

The Psalms brought a new meaning to the cultus. Incorporated into the Psalms is an eschatological element that bridges the significant events and periods of Israel's history, concentrating the range of history into a single cultic act. In the Psalms, past, present, and future are brought together to witness Yahweh's presence and power to the world. The great themes of the history of Israel, creation, the kingship of Yahweh, the promise of the land, and the future promise of salvation are attested in the Psalms. All these themes are bound together by the Israelite notion of "remembrance" by which the past is made to come to life in the present and to anticipate the future (see B. S. Childs, *Memory and Tradition in Israel* [*SBT*, 1/37; 1962]).

Music had a place within Israel's worship from the beginning. The festivals of Yahweh were celebrated with song and dance (Jgs. 21:19-21; 2 S. 6:5, 15). Temple worship had cantors as part of worship. Through all social and historical changes Israel's primary identity was that of a worshiping community. The Psalms epitomized this. The covenant community's primary bond as an identifiable group was in the worship of Yahweh as expressed in the Psalms.

B. Types and Styles of Psalms. The Psalms are fluid and expressive and as such cannot be neatly labeled into categories. But some general characteristics shared by many of the Psalms summarize common elements.

1. Liturgical Hymns. Hymns are used as an imperative call to worship as in Ps. 117. The Heb. *kî*, "for," indicates a ground for praise (e.g., 117:2), a reason that Yahweh's people should come together and worship in song. Hymns are also used to renew a summons of praise.

2. Sacred History Hymns. This type of hymn expresses *Heilsgeschichte,* "the salvation-history" of Yahweh's actions throughout Israel's history (Pss. 7, 8, 105, 106, 135, 136). These songs depicted the liturgical act of recitation at festivals and temple worship. Israel's remembrances were built into the cultic worship so that the past became the present and Yahweh's saving acts were not only celebrated but actually experienced afresh in the lives of the people as if they were contemporary with the events (as in the Passover Haggadah). The nature of this continuity is expressed by the present tense of the verbs used in many of the historic Psalms. The cultic use of the Psalms indicates that these were not private prayers to Yahweh as modern individualism might view them, for only as the Israelite entered into the commnity of worship, did he/she share the promises and obligations of the covenant with Yahweh. Thus the *Sitz im Leben* of many of the songs is the worshiping community, the cultic celebration of the people together, even when the language form is the singular "I". H. Wheeler Robinson found here a good illustration of what he called "corporate personality" or social solidarity where one voice speaks for the group (*The Cross in the OT* [1955], pp. 76-78, 83).

3. Laments. These Psalms call out to Yahweh in times of trouble. They include an invocation to God in difficult situations. Ps. 44 illustrates a typical pattern for a Psalm of lament. It begins with a complaint to Yahweh. Following the complaint the writer confesses trust in Yahweh because He has shown His faithfulness in the past. The worshiper offers supplication for help and forgiveness and concludes with a vow to praise Yahweh in spite of trouble or abandonment (see Pss. 3, 13, 22, 31, 54, 56, 102).

4. Thanksgiving Psalms. Although other types of Psalms have thanksgiving in them, this type of Psalm has thanksgiving as its main theme (Pss. 18, 21, 20, 33, 34, 40, 65–68, 92, 116, 118, 124, 138, 144). Some of these Psalms are group laments, while others are individual. Thanksgiving is offered for danger that Yahweh has averted, for answered prayers, for the gift of harvest, for divine favor shown to the king. This genre would play an important role in the Hymn Scroll of the Qumrân community.

5. Royal Psalms. These are Psalms or prayers on behalf of the king. The king of the Israelites was divinely anointed (Ps. 2). The king was seen as one who is blessed by Yahweh to rule His chosen people. The dynasty of David and the promises made to his lineage foreshadow the Messiah (esp. 2 S. 7), the One without equal. Therefore the royal Psalms after the fall of the monarchy were adapted only slightly and used as messianic Psalms that pointed to the eschatological King of kings that Yahweh would send to His people (Pss. 2, 20, 21, 45, 72, 110).

VII. From Solomon to the Exile.–David's son and successor to the throne was Solomon. During his reign Solomon continued to focus on the cultic worship of the temple, adding ornamentation to the building of such glory and splendor that all who visited Israel marveled at its beauty. Solomon's emphasis on beautifying the temple was not only because he was dedicated to the worship of Yahweh and desired to show his gratitude, but because he had also begun to be influenced by surrounding foreign powers. The temple and its ornamentation were a sign to foreigners of the wealth and cultural elements of Solomon's court. Scripture attests to these foreign influences during the reign of Solomon. This accentuated the syncretistic tendency that the Israelites had been dealing with since they had first covenanted to be the people of Yahweh. Solomon often allowed civil policy to dictate ecclesiastical practices. He married foreign wives in order to establish alliances. These wives brought their alien gods into court (1 K. 11:1-8).

The foreign influences from within the country cumulatively resulted in disaster. The northern kingdom's destruction (722 B.C.) and the demise of the southern kingdom, including Jerusalem and the temple (587 B.C.), were viewed by the postexilic writers in the light of the corrupt worship practice that had infiltrated the practices ordained by Yahweh. The religion of Israel before the Exile is depicted as a headlong spiraling decline leading to disaster. Ahab had allowed Jezebel's Sidonian influences to foster idolatry and despotism (1 K. 16:32). Intermarriages between Jezebel's family and the southern kingdom continued to spread the destructive influences. The situation, viewed in hindsight, was so severe and irreversible that it necessitated the destruction of both kingdoms, the temple, and the city of Jerusalem to reestablish the pure remnant of Yahweh's chosen. The essentials of worship had been lost. The word of God, prayer, praise, confession, and forgiveness had become empty rituals that had lost the inner meaning and therefore impeded access to Yahweh.

VIII. Exile and Restoration.–*A. Developments in Worship.* The nature of worship in the exilic period is much debated. One theory postulates that the absence of the temple and the deportation to a new land forced the faithful to restructure worship to accommodate the new situation. The Psalms speak to the discouragement of those in exile and their longing for the land of Zion (e.g., Ps. 137:3-6). Historically it seems that not all Jews desired to return as earnestly as the author of Ps. 137, for not all Jews did return to Jerusalem when they were eventually allowed to do so by an edict of Cyrus (538 B.C.). It also appears that not all Jews were deported from the land in the Exile. Tension developed between the returning Babylonian Jews and those who had remained behind and intermarried with other peoples.

The Persian armies under Cyrus swept across the eastern frontier of the Babylonian empire in 539 B.C. and reached as far as the Egyptian frontier. He was one of the most truly enlightened rulers of ancient times. His aim, as far as it was possible, was to allow subject nations to enjoy cultural autonomy within the framework of his empire. His successors tended to follow in his steps. By means of a complex civil and military bureaucracy a firm control was established over the empire, but within this framework local customs were respected, established cults were fostered and protected, and responsibility was entrusted to native rulers. In the first year of his reign Cyrus issued a proclamation permitting the Israelites to return to their homeland, ordering the rebuilding of the temple and inviting Jews remaining in Babylon to assist with contributions. Although this edict would seem to have been received with overwhelming gratitude, and a mass exodus back to Israel was expected, this did not happen.

Many of the Jews had become well established in Babylon and had no wish to leave, particularly on a long journey with uncertain goals. The initial wave of returnees was not large, and though they were reinforced by later immigrations, Jerusalem was still thinly populated and in a state of ruin seventy-five years after the edict. The inhabitants of the land, Judeans who had been left behind in the Exile, plus Edomites who had moved to fill the vacant land, were not happy to have these returnees move back. The Samaritans to the north were antagonistic, claiming that they had held fast to true worship while their exiled kin had become polluted with Babylonian influences. The Samaritans and the Judeans, who had remained in the land, had absorbed pagan customs into their worship and in these ways began to infect some of the returnees. The leadership feared for the integrity of the community and sought to end all contact with the native population.

With the return of the exiles came a renewed interest in temple worship. The building of the second temple commenced *ca.* 520 B.C. and was completed in 515 B.C., overseen by the high commissioner Zerubbabel and the high priest Joshua. Nehemiah and Ezra the priest played important roles in the gradual return of the exiles and the rebuilding of the community of faith. Although the temple was rebuilt and worship, priestly sacrifices, and pilgrimages were reestablished at the cultic center, the enthusiasm was never to be of the same intensity. The frailty of a faith focused on one central location had been demonstrated in the fall and destruction of the temple a half-century earlier. The noncultic aspect of this faith, particularly as expressed through emerging synagogue worship developed greater importance during the Exile; and Ezekiel and the prophet of Isa. 40–55 had known God's presence in a strange land, without the use of the temple.

Synagogue worship had a distinctive pattern. Wisdom and the study of Torah became the goal and focus of the synagogue. A crisis existed in the faith of the Jews who had been without a temple for the greater part of a century. A new form was needed to adapt to the new circumstances. The synagogue became the *ekklēsía,* i.e., the assembly, congregation. The worship in the synagogue stressed reading and exposition of the Torah, prayer, recitation of the *Shema* (based on Dt. 6:4), and reciting of Psalms. *See* SYNAGOGUE.

Ezra's reorganization brought a fundamental change to Israel. No longer was Israel's identity centered on a national cult. Rather its identity from this point forward would be seen as that of a religious remnant who rallied around the Torah. Judaism did not change the basic elements of worship during the Exile and return; the focus and stress, however, were simply heightened to accent one feature of the tradition. Law/Torah became the organizing principle.

B. Place of Law. For the Israelite the giving of the law was a cause for joyous celebration. The Torah was seen as a source of joy and life. The law was Yahweh's way of expressing His love for His people. The boundaries and limits provided by the law were a gift from God to prevent destruction and harm from coming to the lives of the Israelites. The importance of Torah interpretation was highly valued throughout Israel's history. The later midrashim, or commentaries and lengthy rabbinic debates over legal situations, illustrate the centrality of the law. God's commands were examined and applied to life in a dynamic process of discovery. The Torah fenced the life of a Jew but it was not seen as a static, rigidly set boundary. Rather, the Jew viewed the Torah as the living word, the pulse and heartbeat of life. The idea of "dancing with the law" embodies the celebration and the joyous guidance that adherence to Torah could bring. It was a gift from Yahweh, a gift of love. Jews rejoiced over the law in a celebration that they still practice each fall. The reading and exposition of the Torah became increasingly an important focus for worship. Neh. 9 illustrates the ceremony of covenant renewal that wed the remnant to Yahweh through His word.

In time legalism did develop. The rituals of worship tended to become empty forms that stifled the spirit of prophecy. Preoccupation with the letter of the law robbed the Torah of its beauty and grace (cf. 2 Cor. 3:6). The externalism of worship that emphasized performance versus the examination of the inner spirit was an abomination to Yahweh. The prophets saw this tendency and confronted the discrepancy between word and action, inner and outer commitment (1 S. 15:22; Am. 5:21). This critique is powerfully expressed in postexilic Judaism (e.g., in Malachi).

The empty formalism, coupled with syncretism, was the major theme of these prophetic complaints. This hypocrisy was sin to the Israelites because it destroyed the covenantal relationship with Yahweh. The call was for joyful admission to the cult, not requirements of a ritual nature.

***IX. Early Judaism* (200 B.C.–A.D. 100).**–During this period Palestine came under the rule of Alexander the Great. Following the Exile, Cyrus had opened the way for the reestablishment of the Jews in Judah. The Persian rule under Cyrus had been positive for the Jews. Under imperial order Ezra and Nehemiah had reestablished the people in Jerusalem and made the "law of Moses" the civil law of the Jews. Even though many Jews did not live in Judah, those in the Diaspora accepted the "law of Moses" as their law. The land continued to be an important part of Jewish identity and worship.

Jerusalem became the center for Jewish ritual life, in spite of the fact that a large number of writings were written outside of Israel. Jerusalem was the authoritative center for the Jews. The legal tradition developed under Ezra and Nehemiah, and the court of the law known as the Sanhedrin with its priests, elders, and scribes had their roots in Jerusalem centered on the temple.

As a result of renewed interest in and tremendous value placed on the law of Moses, the art of translation, interpretation, and study was developed. The language of the Persian empire, Aramaic, was used to translate the Pentateuch into Aramaic (*see* TARGUM). During this period the seeds were planted for the emergence of Beth ha-Midrash "house of interpretation," later to be schools for the study of Scripture and the debating of the traditions of the fathers. The synagogue, as previously mentioned, was also taking structural shape during this period.

A. Hellenism. The Persians began to lose control of their empire during the latter part of the 4th cent. B.C. The great warrior from Macedonia, Alexander the Great, conquered the whole of the Persian empire. Alexander did not change the situation that the conquered peoples had experienced under Cyrus. What he did bring to the empire was a new way of thinking. Alexander was a student of Aristotle and as such had been steeped in Greek thought. Alexander not only wanted to conquer the whole world, but he also wanted to hellenize it and bring all the known world under a single ethos.

Hellenization influenced the Hebrew culture in many ways. Education, especially in science and anthropology, strongly influenced the formation of Jewish thought after Alexander. The Greek language became the lingua franca, replacing Aramaic as the language of trade and education in the empire. *Koine,* or spoken Greek, emerged as a language used throughout the ancient world. Along with language came Greek literature. Schools developed and were probably related to synagogues. Some suggest that many similarities existed between the method of teaching and even the pattern of argument within the synagogues and the institutions of Greek learning. The most important result of Greek impact on Palestinian Judaism was the formation of a Jewish intelligentsia, different from the priesthood and not dependent on the sanctuary. The new class was known as "scribes."

The movement toward a literate public was strong in the Greek polis, or city, and even though the Jews had already been a literate people as early as the Babylonian Exile, the Greek ways of education, logic, and organizing left their mark. The Greek forms were accepted and allowed Judaism a vehicle for the expression of its ideas.

The process of hellenization placed Israel in the position of determining the difference between survival within a culture and syncretistic adoption of the culture, which threatened the true worship of Yahweh. This struggle between faith and culture can be seen in the divisions that emerged within this period. The Hasidim ("loyal" or "pious ones") emerged as a group determined to keep the Jewish faith pure from the negative impact of the Greek world.

Acculturation might have occurred gradually if not for Antiochus IV and his outlawing of Jewish worship in 167 B.C. This instigated the Maccabean revolt. After a period of years the Jews regained control of the land, securing the freedom to worship in their own ways. But hellenization had affected the Hasmonean dynasty and Judaism was represented by a new order. The Sanhedrin became the governing body. Internal tensions developed during this period among the Sadducees, who sought tolerance and compromise, the Pharisees, who originated from the Hasidim and stood for legalism and separatism, and the Zealots, who were revolutionaries attempting to overthrow the politically oppressive structures. Into this arena a child was born in Bethlehem who would bring into being a new system of worship.

Jewish worship had been influenced by Persian customs, laws, purification rites, mythology, cosmology, angelology, and eschatology. The Greek influence, especially in education and thought forms, can be seen in the life of the synagogues. Although the cultures surrounding the Israelites had changed drastically, the central motif of the worship of Yahweh had allowed flexibility in a faith that sustained itself through crisis and domination by numerous foreign powers. Elements within the worship pattern grew to have more or less emphasis in differing situations, yet the praise and continuing echo of corporate and private worship express the soul of the people of Israel.

B. Worship in NT Times. The lines between Jewish worship and Christian worship are not clearly distinguishable until late into the 2nd cent. A.D. Because the first Christians were Jewish, Christian worship had many similar elements to temple and synagogue worship. The Gospels presuppose forms of worship that were native to Palestinian Judaism in the 1st cent. A.D. The temple was still important (cf. Zachariah in Lk. 1:5; Joseph and Mary in 2:21; and Jesus, who is said to have gone to the temple when He came of age at bar mitzvah time). Throughout the Gospels Jesus is shown as a Jew who participated in the feasts and lived within the framework of the life and practice of Israel (Lk. 4:16-31). Jesus prophetically criticized aspects of the legalism and external show that prohibited true worship. But His goal was to fulfil the law, not to destroy it (Mt. 5:17; Jn. 1:17). Yet His attitude to the temple was ambivalent. He reverenced it, but foretold its destruction (Jn. 2:19).

In order to examine worship in the NT one must see the intimate connection between Judaism and the early worship forms of the church. Acts 2:46 records that the earliest Christians attended the temple together and broke bread in their homes. The difference might have been expressed first in the communal meal. The sacrificial element of the temple was also eventually rejected by the Christians, for they viewed Jesus' self-offering as a once-for-all sacrifice for all sins.

The synagogue, the local center of worship in postexilic Judaism, gave Christianity much of its worship form in the inheritance of Scripture reading, preaching, singing, and prayer. The service of the synagogue consisted of a service of the word that proclaimed the creedal Shema (6:4). This service included Scripture reading and exposition, prayer, and benedictions, which we shall now investigate.

X. Jewish Inheritance in the Temple and Synagogue.–Jewish scholars have helped to form a picture of the essential pattern of synagogue worship; some details, however, are debatable. For the period before the destruction of the temple in A.D. 70 a most valuable source of information is found in the NT (esp. Lk. 4:15-21). Even if very few precise details are given in any contemporary document, the general picture is tolerably clear. Three main elements stand: praise, prayer, and instruction. (Two straightforward accounts are G. Dalman, *Jesus-Jeshua* [Eng. tr. 1929], and P. P. Levertoff, "Synagogue Worship in the First Century," in W. K. L. Clarke, ed., *Liturgy and Worship* [1932]).

A. Praise. Corporate praise is the note that opens the service; and this accords with the principle laid down in the Talmud: "Man should always first utter praises, and then pray." It is illustrated in the synagogue liturgy for morning prayer, called *Alenu*: "It is our duty to praise the Lord of all things."

The "ruler" summons the "minister" (see Lk. 4:20) to invite someone from the congregation to commence the service with this "call to worship." He begins with the cry: "Bless ye the Lord, the One who is to be blessed;" and the people respond with the benediction: "Blessed be the Lord . . . for ever," in the spirit of Neh. 9:5.

B. Prayers. Prayers in Jewish worship fall into two parts. The first group comprise two lovely utterances (the *Yotzer,* which means "He who forms" and takes up the theme of God as Creator of all things; and the *Ahabah,* which means "love" and is concerned both to recall God's love for His people and to pledge their obligation to love Him in return. It ends: "Blessed art Thou, O Lord, who hast chosen Thy people Israel in love"). Immediately following these prayers comes the Shema, which is both a confession of faith and a glad benediction. The title for the Shema derives from the opening word in Dt. 6:4: "Hear [*šᵉma'*], O Israel: The Lord our God is one Lord." The term "one" emphasizing the unity of God has always been the central Jewish confession. It receives, therefore, a special prominence in the liturgy.

The second division of united prayer comes next. The way for it is prepared by the reciting of the prayer known as "True and firm", with its reminder that God's promises

A 15th-century MS page showing a rabbi sounding the shofar for the day of prayer at the Jewish New Year (Rothschild MS from Italy) (Israel Museum)

are sure and dependable to His people. At this point the "minister" summons a member of the assembly to lead in "Prayer proper," i.e., the Eighteen Benedictions. These cover a wide range of themes. They are partly an expression of praise, partly supplication for those in need (exiles, judges and counselors, and the chosen people). We may catch the tone of these prayers by considering the last one: "Grant peace upon Israel Thy people and upon Thy city, and upon Thy inheritance, bless us all together [lit. "as one"]. Blessed art Thou O Lord, the Maker of peace."

C. Instruction. Once the prayers were said, the service assumed a form that has given the synagogue its distinctive ethos. Indeed, the Jews themselves called it "the house of instruction," for nothing is more in keeping with Jewish worship than the emphasis that is placed upon Scripture reading and exposition. Instruction was given by two means. First, the Law and the Prophets were read by members of the congregation who came up and shared the task (according to the length of the portion involved). As the ancient language of Hebrew was not understood by all persons present, a translator would turn the Scripture lessons into the vernacular, usually Aramaic. Second, a homily followed that was based on the passages read. Any person in the assembly who was considered suitable was invited to deliver this "sermon" — as proved the case both at Nazareth (Lk. 4:21-29) and at Antioch (Acts 13:15-41). The service concluded with a blessing and the congregational "Amen."

Seasons and the day of the week sometimes altered this basic pattern (market days, Monday and Thursday, had shorter Scripture lections). But the ingredients that provided the staple diet of synagogue worship — praise, prayer, and instruction — are found in every case.

XI. Prayers and Praises of the NT.–Two types of prayer are known in the teaching and example of the NT Church. First, the NT includes private prayer in the secret place of personal communion between the believer and his or her Lord. Included here are the prayers of Jesus Himself, which are eloquent testimony to the reality and power of prayer, and equally a guide and inspiration to us today in our prayer life. Second, the NT records the Church's corporate prayer as the united assembly of believers voices its praise and supplication.

The book of Acts describes the prayer fellowship of the earliest believers. Acts 2:42 refers to the practice of their corporate assembly, whether at home (2:46; 4:23-31; 5:42) or in the temple (3:1, 11; 5:12, 42). It is interesting to observe the circumstances that drew Christians together, and the thoughts that found expression in articulate prayer and praise. They needed and sought guidance (1:14, 24). They came together under the duress of persecution and hostility (4:23-31), and requested the strengthening grace of their Lord to continue their witness for Him. They took the arrest and imprisonment of Peter (12:5) as a challenge to earnest intercession. They gathered at Antioch to worship the Lord, seeking the guidance that came in the Spirit's summons, "Set apart for me Barnabas and Saul" (13:2); and with further united prayer these men, who later hazarded their lives for the name of the Lord Jesus (15:26), were sent forth to the work of the gospel in Asia Minor and the Christian mission was launched on its epoch-making way (13:1-3). Other allusions to the united praying of the people of God are in 20:36 and 21:5 — both touching scenes of tender pathos.

A. Contents of Prayers and Praises. The historical records contain little to guide us when we try to discover the contents of the prayers in the early Church. The prayers of the Church in Acts are *ad hoc* utterances, heartfelt praises and petitions called forth by the demands of the hour.

The use of the Psalter was important to the early Christians, who, like their Lord (Lk. 24:56), turned to the Psalms for language in which to express their deepest emotions. Perhaps in both cases the synagogue liturgy was the abiding influence. Acts 13:1f. indicates that the church at Antioch offered worship to the Lord. It is tempting to relate this to the worship of Jesus, a calling upon Him in devotion and supplication, as did both Stephen (Acts 7:59) and Paul (2 Cor. 12:8). Many scholars find Christ-hymns (e.g., Phil. 2:6-11; 1 Tim. 3:16) in which Jesus is praised with a worship that belongs properly to God Himself. The phrase "call upon the name of the Lord" (see Acts 2:21; 9:14; 22:16; Rom. 10:13f.) points in the same direction, for it seems to show that Jesus was hailed in worship as One worthy of adoration and surrender. The phrase likely comes from the OT Scripture, where it denoted to "practice the cult of Yahweh," "to be a worshiper of . . . the true God" (Gen. 4:26; 21:33; etc.).

One piece of evidence that occurs in 1 Cor. 16:22 is of considerable interest and value. There we read the strange-sounding transliterated Aramaic term *maranathá* (*see* MARANATHA), which our English translations render as either "our Lord cometh" (RV mg.) or "our Lord, come!" (RSV). It seems fairly certain that the second alternative is to be preferred and that this phrase is a prayer of invocation addressed to Jesus. Similar language is found in Rev. 22:20: "Come, Lord Jesus," and the Didache uses the formula for a service preparatory to the Lord's table (10:6). The use of an Aramaic phrase can be satisfactorily explained only on the assumption that *maranathá* is an ancient watchword which takes us back to the earliest days of the Church in Palestine where Aramaic was the spoken language, for we can hardly imagine why Paul would trouble to include a foreign Aramaic term in a letter written to those who spoke and understood Greek; perhaps, in fact, *maranathá* had become accepted as a liturgical term from the earliest days of the Church.

The evidence of this ancient Christian invocation to Christ throws a flood of light on the way in which the Jewish Christians worshiped their Lord. Not only is *maranathá* the oldest recorded Christian prayer, but it also indicates that those who had previously invoked the name of their covenant God as "Lord" in the synagogue liturgy now came to apply the same divine title to Jesus the Messiah.

B. Corporate Prayer in the Epistles. We are assured that the first communities of Christian people called upon the name of their risen Lord as they met to worship. In 1 Cor. 1:2 Paul reminds the church that they are united with all the other assemblies in the world who "call on the name of" a common Lord. The phrase used in this verse implies a public invocation of Jesus and a profession of faith in Him as the exalted Head of His people. But have we any examples of the sort of prayer and praise that was offered to Him?

It is true that no objective description of an early Christian service of worship exists. Perhaps the nearest we get to that is the account of Paul's visit to Troas (Acts 20:7-12). Yet it seems clear that Paul had before his mind's eye, as he wrote or dictated his letters, a picture of the Church assembled for public worship. The introductory greetings and opening prayers of thanksgiving are couched in no commonplace language but reflect the liturgical life of the churches by their fulness of expression and unusual vocabulary. The passage in Eph. 1:3-14 well illustrates this.

Yet another line of evidence exists. From 1 Cor. 5 we learn that Paul regards himself as no detached and impartial observer of the life of his converts. In a solemn mood he enjoins what must be done at Corinth as though he himself were personally present in the congregation. Indeed he is present in the midst (v. 4) as he shares with them in spiritual communion. This is no isolated incident occasioned by the seriousness of the situation at Corinth, as Col. 2:5 shows: "For though I am absent in body, yet I am with you in spirit, rejoicing to see your good order." Thus his reported prayers may be the shared possession of all his churches.

C. Special Words for Prayer. 1. Abba. This term suggests our Lord's Gethsemane prayer (Mk. 14:32-39): "Abba, Father, all things are possible to thee." As was the case with *maranathá* in 1 Cor. 16:22, this Aramaic word recurs in transliterated form in Paul's Greek letters (Rom. 8:15; Gal. 4:6). *See* ABBA.

Our Lord's favorite designation for God is "Abba," and it has been the subject of much scholarly research (for the discussion on its meaning, see *TDNT*, I, 5f.). While Abba was the child's word for its earthly father, no evidence shows that pious Jews ever used precisely this form (meaning "dear father," "daddy") of God. Instead, they used a variant form, and avoided "Abba" because it was thought to be too daring and familiar an expression. The so-called Lord's Prayer (Mt. 6:9-13; Lk. 11:2-4), which we should notice is more the disciples' prayer than the Lord's, became accepted very early in the Church's history as a pattern prayer and was backed by dominical authority. As early as the Didache, compiled as a manual of church order and practice (early 2nd cent. A.D.), this prayer had become an integral part of Christian worship: "As the Lord commanded in his Gospel . . . pray thus three times a day" (Did. 8:2f.). It was intended to be said corporately, "when ye pray, say," as Cyprian pointed out in a later century (*De Dominica Oratione*; discussed in Bradshaw, ch. 3); and Tertullian (*ca.* A.D. 150-225) speaks of "common prayers and united supplications," probably with the Lord's Prayer in mind (*De Oratione* 10).

2. Amen. This familiar Christian term means literally "be firm, true," and is connected with the verb "believe." It occurs most obviously at the close of the NT doxologies that ascribe praise to God and His Christ (Rom. 1:25; 9:5; 11:36; 16:27; Gal. 1:5; Eph. 3:21; Phil. 4:20; 1 Tim. 1:17; 6:16; 2 Tim. 4:18; He. 13:21; 1 Pet. 4:11; 5:11; Jude 25; Rev. 5:14). Rev. 5 portrays a dramatic scene and probably reflects the worship of the Church militant as well as the Church triumphant in heaven.

2 Corinthians 1:20f. pictures a scene that most likely takes us back to early worship. "That is why, when we give glory to God, it is through Christ Jesus that we say 'Amen' . . . it is God also who has set his seal upon us, and as a pledge of what is to come has given the Spirit to dwell in our hearts" (NEB). The liturgical terminology of the whole passage is especially rich, and quite possibly Paul is alluding to the rite of Christian baptism under the figure of the "seal."

In 1 Cor. 14:16 Paul rebukes the church for their unbridled indulgence in the more exotic "gifts of the Spirit" in public assembly: "How will the plain man who is present be able to say 'Amen' to your thanksgiving when he does not know what you are saying?" This clearly shows that worshipers commonly used "Amen" to give assent to what they heard from the lips of their fellow believers.

3. *Thanksgiving*. 1 Cor. 14:16 also contains a reference to the prayer of "thanksgiving." The presence of the definite article in "*the* thanksgiving" seems to suggest that a particular type of praying is envisaged, as distinct from the general use of the term "give thanks" (e.g., 2 Cor. 1:11; 9:12; 1 Thess. 5:18). Little is said about the content of such a prayer of thanksgiving, but the prayer at the Lord's table is possibly in mind, for 1 Cor. 14:17 employs the verb Gk. *eucharistéō*, "give thanks," a term that has given the name Eucharist to the Lord's Supper as an occasion when, in a preeminent way, the Christian Church offers praise and thankful acknowledgment of the blessings of redemption in Christ (see XVIII.C.3 below).

XII. Hymns and Spiritual Songs.–Christian song did not break forth upon a world that had been hitherto dumb and in which hymns were unknown. The Church was cradled in Judaism and borrowed many of its forms of worship from the temple and synagogue. Antiphonal singing goes back to the preexilic period of Jewish history (Ex. 15:21; Nu. 21:17; 1 S. 18:7). Many of the Psalms were intended to be sung in the congregational worship of the temple (e.g., Pss. 24, 118, 134, 145). Postexilic writings indicate a well-ordered arrangement for responsive singing between two choirs of musicians: "and they sang responsively, praising and giving thanks to the Lord" (Ezr. 3:11; cf. Neh. 12:24, 31). Also, in the 1st cent. B.C. the sect of the Therapeutae developed hymnic worship (Philo *De vita contemplativa* 80–85).

The community that produced the Dead Sea Scrolls also had musical features in their worship. One scribe wrote, "I will sing with knowledge and all my music shall be for the glory of God. (My) lyre (and) my harp shall sound for His holy order and I will tune the pipe of my lips to His right measure" (1QS 10:9).

Some doubt exists, however, about the extent to which the singing of divine praises had developed in first-century A.D. Palestinian synagogues. The synagogues of the Dispersion — the exiled Jews who lived and worked outside the Holy Land — were probably more advanced in the use of psalmody than their more conservative Palestinian counterparts. But no doubt exists that the early believers in Jesus inherited the desire to express their gratitude to God in the offering of vocal praises.

A. Nativity Hymns. A section of NT literature that evidences the influence of OT lyrical writing is the Nativity and Infancy preface to Luke's Gospel. Four canticles in Lk. 1–2 have a distinct poetic form and may be arranged in strophes as a species of early Christian hymnody that takes us back to the Jewish-Christian Church.

Luke 1:46-55 contains the hymn known to Christian worship as the MAGNIFICAT, a designation that comes from the opening word of the Vulgate translation in v. 46. The Psalm of Zachariah in 1:68-79 is called the Benedictus, also from the opening Latin word of the Vulgate text. Two shorter hymnic tributes occur in ch. 2. The Gloria in Excelsis (2:14) is a memorable statement of angelic jubilation at the coming of the Redeemer. This paean of praise quickly found a place in the Church's corporate worship, and became a regular feature of its morning worship, according to the fourth-century Apostolic Constitutions, which was an early church order. The Nunc Dimittis ("Lord, now lettest thou thy servant depart in peace") of the venerable Simeon in Lk. 2:29-32 is also given in the Apostolic Constitutions as an evening hymn of the Church's liturgy.

B. Distinctive Christian Compositions. 1 Corinthians 14:26 gives the injunction for the assembly at Corinth: "When you come together [for public worship], each one has a hymn, a lesson, a revelation, a tongue or an interpretation." Col. 3:16 and Eph. 5:19f. go together, and show the existence of "psalms and hymns and spiritual songs."

Scholars have looked for passages that have a lyrical quality and rhythmical style, an unusual vocabulary that differs from the surrounding context of the letter in which the passage appears, some distinctive piece of Christian doctrine, and hints that the passage in question finds its natural setting in a baptismal or communion service. From these features it is possible to identify and classify with a reasonable degree of accuracy and certainty the following NT hymns.

1. Ephesians 5:14. This verse is usually regarded as the most cogent example of early Christian hymnology. Good grounds support this confidence. The introductory words, "therefore it is said," read as though they were added expressly to prepare for the citation of a familiar passage, well known to Paul's readers. The verse naturally falls into three lines on the grounds of style, with a swinging trochaic rhythm in the Greek and the employment of a rhetorical device by which the first two lines end with the same sound. As a whole the verse contains an invocational appeal addressed to Christians and summoning them to action. At the same time it offers them the promise of divine favor and aid. The first two lines are a rousing summons to moral activity, and the third line an accompanying promise of God. The lines would then be the concomitant chant to the actions of the baptismal service when the believers were buried in the water with Christ and raised again to newness of life (Rom. 6:4; Col. 2:12); and this leads several biblical commentators to submit that such a verse as Eph. 5:14 would be fixed indelibly upon the heart and mind of the converts as they emerged from the baptismal water. Paul recalls it in his appeal to the Ephesian Christians.

2. 1 Timothy 3:16. After the introductory sentence, "Great indeed, we confess, is the mystery of our religion," the verse falls into six lines of rich truth concerning the person and action of Jesus Christ. By a series of antithetical couplets in which a second line complements the thought of the first line, the gospel message of the Church's Lord is set forth. It treats of two world orders, the divine and the human; and shows how Christ has brought together the two spheres by His coming from the glory of the Father's presence into this world ("manifested in the flesh"; cf. Jn. 1:14; Rom. 8:3) and by His lifting up of humanity back again into the divine realm. Thus heaven and earth are joined, and God and humanity reconciled. His victory is acknowledged in the heavenly regions as the angelic powers confess Him, and upon earth as the gospel is proclaimed to the nations and accepted in faith.

3. Philippians 2:6-11. A similar idea of the binding together of the divine realm from which the preexistent

Christ comes and the human domain into which He enters at His birth runs through Phil. 2:6-11. This is one of the finest christological portions in the NT, and powerfully portrays the drama of Christ's pretemporal glory with the Father, His abasement and obedience upon earth, even to the death of the cross, and His exaltation to God's presence and cosmic triumph and lordship, which all the spiritual powers confess. In its original form the Philippians hymn possibly consisted of a series of couplets and belonged to an early tribute to Christ's divine person. Paul incorporated it into his letter and drew out the important teaching by the insertion of certain interpreting words and phrases.

4. Colossians 1:15-20. As early as 1913 the German scholar E. Norden (*Agnostos Theos* [repr. 1956], p. 252) had arranged these verses into a hymnic form and detected certain liturgical traits. His analysis produced the following arrangement: Strophe A (vv. 15-18a); Strophe B (vv. 18b-20). This division shows that these two stanzas cover two subjects: Christ and creation (A), and Christ and the Church (B). Moreover, the two parts are comparable in a number of ways and certain stylistic peculiarities are present that cannot be there by chance. We may note, e.g., the repetition of words and phrases in the two halves, and in some cases the words are repeated in exactly the same position in each stanza.

5. Hebrews 1:3. As a final example of what may be adduced as NT odes to Christ, we may cite He. 1:3. Again the telltale marks of style are evident, such as the use of the relative pronoun ("Who," AV) and participles ("being," "upholding," "had . . . purged," AV), and the elevated, ceremonial style on which Norden writes, "It is instructive to notice how this style is the best among NT authors" (Norden, p. 386). The vocabulary, too, is rare, and the sonorous ending of v. 3 contains a splendid climax. By the threefold test of theological content, stylistic construction, and unusual vocabulary we may confidently classify this passage as a "hymn to Christ."

It is just as important to notice that these hymns to Christ have a common pattern of thought that makes their presence in the NT of highest value (to the passages above may be added: Jn. 1:1-14; 1 Pet. 1:18-21; 2:21-25; 3:18-22; Rev. 5:9f., 12; 12:10-12; 19:1-3, 6-8). These hymns relate to the person and mission of Christ Jesus and tell how He existed in the preexistent glory of His Father and was the agent in creation. He became man and accomplished redemption for the world through His suffering and death. At length He is exalted and enthroned and in a solemn acclamation receives from God the supreme name. This celestial enthronement as Lord of the universe and of all the cosmic spheres, which according to the thought of the 1st cent. controlled human destiny by means of the stars, receives universal acknowledgment in heaven, on earth and in the realm of evil spirits. Thus the cosmic dominion of the Church's Lord is hailed as the answer to the deep need of the human beings who were held in the iron grip of "Fate" and whose nerve had failed. If one motif pervades the NT hymns, it is the ringing assurance that Christ is victor over all our enemies, and is rightly worshiped as the image of the God who is over all.

In the 2nd cent. A.D. the Roman governor Pliny told of Christians in Bithynia who sang a hymn to Christ as God (*Ep.* x.96). That practice, we may believe, goes back to the NT Church (see H. H. Rowden, ed., *Christ the Lord: Studies in Christology Presented to Donald Guthrie* [1981], chs. 3 [R. P. Martin], 4 [R. T. France], 14 [D. R. Carnegie]).

XIII. Early Creeds and Confessions of Faith.–We turn to consider what evidence the NT Scriptures contain for other credal and confessional forms. The Church in the NT is already a believing, preaching, and confessing community of men and women; and this fact implies the existence and influence of a body of authoritative doctrine (although in an embryonic form in certain matters, such as the belief in the trinity) that was the given and shared possession of those who formed the nascent Christian communities in the world of the Roman empire.

In NT times, a corpus of distinctive doctrines was held as a sacred deposit from God. The references to such a web of saving truth are set forth with a fulness of description and variety of detail, although the evidence must not be pressed to suggest that there was anything approaching the later creeds that are couched in a style and language different from the NT. The following shows the diversity of credal terminology used by the early Christians: "the apostles' teaching" (Acts 2:42); "the standard of teaching" (Rom. 6:17); "the word of life" (Phil. 2:16); "the words of the faith and of the good doctrine" (1 Tim. 4:16); "the pattern of the sound words" (2 Tim. 1:13); "sound teaching" (2 Tim. 4:3); "sound doctrine" (Tit. 1:9).

The body of doctrine is referred to in certain contexts as material that is to be utilized in the public proclamation of the Christian message (e.g., Phil. 2:16; 2 Tim. 2:15). The most celebrated credal passage that contains the crystallization of apostolic teaching on the basic elements of the gospel is 1 Cor. 15:3-5.

Vernon H. Neufeld has subjected all the NT confessions of faith to a close inspection (*Earliest Christian Confessions* [1963]) and has concluded that the earliest form of Christian witness may be taken back into the period of the Gospel record to the utterance, "Jesus is the Christ" (see Mk. 8:29). The question of Jesus' messiahship was a live issue in the period covered by the book of Acts and the Christian mission to the Jews of the Dispersion, and it is not surprising that the confession "Jesus is the Messiah" is found as a major theme in the early parts of the NT (e.g., Acts 9:22).

As the Church moved out into a gentile environment the debate concerning messiahship became an irrelevant issue; therefore, in Paul's dealings with the gentile churches of the Roman empire the messianic status of Jesus was a secondary concern. The confession "Jesus Christ is Lord" may be placed in the setting of the Church's worshiping life.

In Phil. 2:11 Paul quotes the confessional acclamation: "Jesus Christ is Lord." As already noted, this cry comes as the climax of the hymnic adoration of the cosmic Christ as all creatures throughout the universe bow down and submit to His dominion. A study of the passage by the Scandinavian scholar J. Jervell (*Imago Dei. Gen. 1.26s im Spätjudentum, in der Gnosis und in den paulinischen Briefen* [1960], pp. 206-209) has sought to place this hymn and its closing acclamation in a baptismal context. The line of reasoning runs as follows. The confession of Jesus Christ as Lord by converts may well have betokened for them the passing from the domain of the spirit-powers by which their old life was controlled (cf. 1 Cor. 12:2; Gal. 4:3-9) into the liberty and joy of the gospel (see Rom. 8:15, 21, 38f.; Gal. 5:1-26; Col. 1:21f.; 2:8-15). If this attempt to place the Phil. 2 hymn in such a setting is correct, it would provide yet one more endorsement of the general view that the affirmation "Jesus Christ is Lord" belongs to the cultic life of the early Christians as they engaged in their worship of the sovereign Master of their lives and of the universe.

The NT confessions extend from the simple "Jesus is Lord" to the detailed summaries of 1 Cor. 15:3-5; Rom. 1:3f.; 4:24f.; 8:34; Phil. 2:6-11; 1 Tim. 3:16 and 1 Pet.

3:18-22. As confessions of Christ, they comprehend the various aspects of His person (both preexistent and incarnate), His mission (His death, burial, descent into Hades), and His victory and exalted status and role as Intercessor and Lord of all. Extant binitarian creeds also unite the Father and the Son (1 Cor. 8:6; 1 Tim. 2:5f.). Nor should we overlook the implicit trinitarian fragments such as Mt. 28:19; 1 Cor. 6:11; 12:4-6; 2 Cor. 1:21f.; 13:14. Also, a triadic scheme in several verses set out the "division of work" of the trinity — the Father who sends, the Son who is sent, and the Spirit who applies the work of salvation (see Gal. 3:11-14; 4:4-6; He. 10:29; 1 Pet. 1:2). These constitute the raw materials of the later fully developed trinitarian creeds, which bid us praise the name of God, Father, Son, and Holy Spirit (see Wainwright, chs. 2, 6).

XIV. Baptism in Jesus' Teaching.–Our immediate concern is with the worship of the NT Church. This delimiting of our interest means that we may pass over the meaning of the term "sacrament" and the significance of the sacraments in present-day discussion and ecumenical debate. Our task is much simpler. We have to inquire into the NT teaching in as impartial a way as possible.

The use of water in religious ceremonial is age-old. Ritual ablutions are very prominent in the OT, both in the cases of religious impurity (in Leviticus *passim*; Nu. 19), and in those instances when a ritual washing was part of the ceremony that a person practiced in approaching God (e.g., the high priest in Ex. 40:12-15; Lev. 8; Nu. 8). But, in addition to these ceremonial acts, a number of graphically worded texts bring out the need for moral cleansing (e.g., Ps. 51:7; Isa. 1:16; Ezk. 36:25; Zec. 13:1). And other verses look forward to the day when God will renew His people (Isa. 4:2-6; Jer. 33:8; Ezk. 36:25-33; 37:23).

The more spiritually sensitive among Israel's people looked for a time of national renewal and hope. It is therefore not surprising that some "sectarian" groups (the Essenes are the best-known examples; see 1QS 3:4-9; 4:21; 5:13) made much use of the baptismal lustrations in order to secure a holy people. The documents of the covenanters of Qumrân give some vivid instances of this fervent hope and of the serious preparations that they made to fit themselves for the part they would play in God's new order. But the sectaries of Qumrân knew that water alone could not cleanse the soul; the Holy Spirit working within the community must bring about the essential purification.

Another line of development that also prepared the Jews of the 1st cent. B.C. and A.D. for the advent of the gospel and its accompanying ceremonial acts was the practice of proselyte baptism. This ceremony made it possible for a Gentile to enter the fold of Judaism. The candidate was required to accept the demands of the law, to receive circumcision (if he were a male), and later to be baptized in the presence of witnesses as a prelude to the offering of sacrifice. The entire procedure was a means of entry into the new religion; but the "point of no return" came in the moment when the proselytes emerged from the water. Thenceforth they were regarded as newly born children of Abraham's family. (Cf. W. S. LaSor, *Biblical Archaeology Review*, 13/1 [Jan.-Feb. 1987], pp. 52-59.)

Both sectarian and proselyte baptism are important for an understanding of John's baptismal practices. No single baptism is more significant than his receiving and baptizing his cousin, Jesus of Nazareth (Mt. 3:13-17; Mk. 1:9-11; Lk. 3:21f.; Jn. 1:29-34). This event provides us — as it provided the first generations of Christian believers — with a fixed starting-point in regard to the full import of the Christian ordinance.

A. He Submitted to Baptism. The account in Mt. 3:13-17 is not easy to interpret; some evidence from the apocryphal gospels shows that the early Church was puzzled by the fact that the sinless Lord should submit to a baptism "for the remission of sins" (Mk. 1:4f.). The difficulty is eased if, with T. W. Manson (*Servant-Messiah* [1956], pp. 46f.), we recall that the people who came to John's baptism did so with a great variety of motives. John's most illustrious candidate saw in the revival movement on Jordan's banks the sign that His public ministry was about to begin. He came, therefore, to identify Himself openly with John as "a man sent from God" (Jn. 1:6), the predestined herald of Messiah's coming (Mt. 11:6-15; Lk. 7:24-30; Mk. 9:9-13), and also with the people whom He came to save (Jn. 1:11).

B. He Sanctioned Baptism. The Synoptic Gospels have no record that our Lord or His disciples actually baptized. But Jn. 3:22-26; 4:1f. clearly indicate it. Above all, this Johannine tradition confirms the importance of a practice of baptism in this initial stage of the ministry, about which W. F. Flemington has written, "If baptism were practiced (in this early stage of the public ministry of Jesus) with the approval of Jesus, it becomes easier to explain why, immediately after Pentecost, baptism took its place as the normal rite of entry into the Christian community" (*NT Doctrine of Baptism* [1948], p. 31).

C. He Interpreted Baptism. Although the first three Gospels do not record the practice of baptism as an integral part of the public mission of Jesus, the word (used in a figurative sense) is found twice upon the lips of the Master. Both sayings are significant, for both are explanations of His Passion (Mk. 10:38f.; Lk. 12:50).

The saying of Lk. 12:50 ("I have a baptism to undergo. What tension I suffer, till it is all over!" [Moff.]) shows us how the Lord in His true humanity reacted, as at Gethsemane, to the horror of sin-bearing which loomed before Him. But another meaning may be present. Since the OT looked forward to God's renewal of His people in terms of a baptismal renewing, Jesus may have foreseen that His death and victory would usher in the kingdom of God and inaugurate the final chapter of God's dealing with humanity. At all events, He clearly interpreted His death as a baptismal action, full of deep significance both for Himself and His Church. It cannot be without an intended connection that Paul uses exactly the same two terms, baptism and death, in reverse order, as he interprets Christian baptism as a sharing of Christ's death and resurrection (Rom. 6:3-11; Col. 2:12).

D. He Commanded Baptism. Matthew 28:19f. contain what are among the most important — and the most controverted — words of Jesus Christ. All sorts of objections have been brought against this text — literary, textual, historical, and theological; and no consensus of agreement prevails among the commentators. James Denney makes an important point when he comments on the congruity of the Lord's command to baptize both with what has gone before in the Gospels and with what will follow in the other NT literature and the practice of the apostolic Church (*Death of Christ* [1959], p. 74). Flemington agrees with this reasoning (although he is more skeptical about the veracity of the actual words of Jesus in the text), and finds the key in the authority of Jesus that the early Church claimed as they, following the pentecostal preaching, began immediately to baptize the converts. Such an authority must go back to some dominical word, and this word, we may hold, lies in Mt. 28. Thus we may continue to see in these words at the end of Matthew "a supreme expression of the Christian belief that baptism is no human rite, but rests upon an authority no other than that of Jesus himself" (Flemington, p. 129).

XV. Apostolic Practice of Baptism.–*A. Baptism in Acts.*

The following are the salient points of the baptismal practice in the Acts.

1. In the Name of Jesus. Baptism was administered "in the name of Jesus Christ" (Acts 2:38; 10:48), or "into the name of the Lord Jesus" (8:16; 19:5). Much discussion has been evoked by the reference to the "name" in these contexts and in Mt. 28:19.

Acts 22:16 suggests that the name of Jesus was invoked by the baptizands in the act of their baptism, or even that the name of Jesus Christ was called over the candidates as they made their baptismal profession.

2. Coming of the Spirit. Baptism is connected with repentance (Acts 2:38), the offer of forgiveness (2:38; cf. 22;16), and the gift of the Spirit (2:38; cf. 10:44-48), although there is no strict order of sequence. Sometimes the Holy Spirit is given with baptism; at other times baptism follows the descent of the Spirit (10:44-48). The laying on of hands marked the coming of the Spirit in Samaria (8:14-17) and Ephesus (19:5f.) after baptism, and in Damascus (9:17f.) before baptism.

3. Spiritual Effects. The blessings of the new age that baptism makes real — forgiveness, entry into the Church, the fellowship of believers, and that conquering newborn joy that is denoted by the words "exultation" (Gk. *agallíasis*) and "boldness of speech" (Gk. *parrhēsía*) — were offered by the apostolic preaching as people "heard the word" and "believed."

The sequence of "hearing," "believing," and "being baptized" is preserved throughout the book of Acts; and the frequency of mention gives an impressive continuity to the apostolic practice (2:37f., 41; 8:12f., 35f.; 10:44; 11:14f.; 16:14f., 32f.; 18:8; 19:5).

4. Summary. All in all, allowing for certain deviations from this regular pattern, the witness of Acts is straightforward. Baptism (with or without the laying on of hands — a practice recorded in 8:15-17, which some scholars describe as a rudimentary "confirmation" of believers) is the rite of initiation into the visible Church, if this term is allowable. Its mode follows that of Jewish proselyte baptism, namely, immersion (8:38f.). The Greek terms for "baptize" and "baptism" mean strictly "douse" or "saturating"; yet from the use of the language employed a lack of decisiveness persists as to the mode of baptism.

Other studies, however, have paid more attention to the meanings that underlie the baptismal actions. While the thought of baptism (= "washing") from the defilement of sin is attested (e.g., Acts 22:16; see also 1 Cor. 6:11; Eph. 5:26; Tit. 3:5f. and possibly Rev. 1:5 [AV]; 7:14), the more important emphasis for the theology of baptism falls on the idea of baptism (= "immersion in the sea of death") as typifying a death to the old life and a new creation, as J. Ysebaert phrases it (*Greek Baptismal Terminology* [1962], p. 53). The metaphor is linked with the removal of clothes before entering the baptismal bath, and the putting on of fresh garments upon emergence from the water. Paul often pictures such a divestiture and reclothing (Gal. 3:27; Col. 3:9f., 12) in a context of death and new life (cf. Rom. 13:14; Col. 3:3, 9f., 12); and the entire thought is related to Christ's death and baptism (Eph. 4:22-24; Col. 2:11f.).

The households mentioned in regard to baptism in Acts are those of Lydia (16:15) and the Philippian jailer (16:33). The texts (esp. 16:31-34) seem to presuppose that entire "families" (used in the wide sense to include servants and kinsfolk) became committed to the faith.

No countenance is given to any magical or superstitious notions of baptismal efficacy (see, e.g., 8:13, 21f.). Moreover, we should observe that baptism is never presented as an option to Christian discipleship. It follows directly upon the initial act of faith, and may be said to be complementary to it. The call "Why do you wait? Rise and be baptized" (22:16) is the order that early Christians accepted with alacrity. Prebaptismal instruction and the catechumenate came later — although some scholars find an allusion to the preparation of candidates in He. 6:2 and even traces of a baptismal service in 1 Peter and 1 John.

B. Paul's Doctrine of Baptism. The chief contribution of Paul was to enlarge the understanding of his converts and fellow believers as to the deeper significance of what they already knew and experienced. He assumes that baptism is "in" or "into" the name of Christ, and is a symbol of cleansing (1 Cor. 1:13; 6:11; Eph. 5:26). As Acts also depicts the rite, the Pauline literature regards baptism as the outward sign of admittance into the fellowship of the Church. The positive and negative contributions of Paul, however, are made in terms of the drawing out of some latent implications, and the stating of some drastic basic truths in relation to an accepted Christian practice. Three points call for comment.

First, a negative, though important, consideration is that Paul recoils from any superstitious use of the sacraments. The Corinthians imagined that to have been baptized by some important person (like Peter, Apollos, Paul himself) was an occasion of great benefit to them. They seem to have had a strange practice of baptizing Church members for their deceased relatives and friends (1 Cor. 15:29; on this verse see R. P. Martin, *The Spirit and the Congregation* [1984], pp. 118-121). Paul dissociates himself from the implied superstition of the first idea. No magical bond is set up between the baptizer and his convert — a notion that continued in the pagan religious customs of his day (1:13-17).

Second, two passages demonstrate the meaning of baptism as a means of entry into the community of the Church, Christ's body (12:13; Gal. 3:27; on these verses see R. P. Martin, pp. 19-25).

Third, the clarion call to live as those who are dead to self and alive to God is sounded in Rom. 6:1-4 in a baptismal context. Baptism clearly means this as the snatch of baptismal hymnody in Eph. 5:14 makes plain. The convert is plunged into the water — this means a dying with Christ. He or she remains for a moment under the surface — this means that one is buried with Him. The Christian emerges from the water — this means that he or she is raised with Him.

Paul describes in Rom. 6:1-4 what really happens in baptism, which (in the early Church) followed so closely upon conversion that the two experiences could be spoken of in the same breath and as virtual synonyms. Baptism is no empty symbol or "bare sign," but a genuine sacramental action in which God works, applies the saving efficacy of the death and resurrection of Christ in which we died and rose again, and places us in that sphere of divine life in which sin is conquered (6:7, 9-11).

In summary, two sides to Paul's baptismal teaching issue forth from the above texts. The ordinance "re-presents" the saving acts and events of the gospel, portraying in a dramatic way the death and rising of Jesus. In so far as conversion and baptism are two sides of the same coin, the sacrament brings to the participant the reality it signifies. But this is done not in any mechanical fashion, as though the mere performance of the rite guaranteed its inevitable efficacy. The subjective side is always needed. What God has done (in the gospel) and does (in the baptism) requires a personal appropriation; and this means, on the human side, the indispensability of faith (Col. 2:12; Eph. 2:8).

XVI. Background and Significance of the Upper Room Supper.—Although many precedents for a meal occurred between Jesus and His own followers in the course of the Galilean ministry, this meal was unique. The Lord's own words reveal His attitude to it: "How I have longed to eat this Passover with you before my death!" (Lk. 22:15, NEB). The special significance of this Passover, which stamped it with an unforgettable importance (1 Cor. 11:23), was not in what He did, but in what He said. At certain places in the customary service He interjected His words of interpretation and thereby illuminated three topics.

A. Words of Institution. With the bread on the table before Him and the disciples, they heard Him say, "This is my body which is for you"; and after the meal, over a closing cup of wine, "This cup is the new covenant in my blood" (1 Cor. 11:23; cf. Mt. 26:26-28; Mk. 14:22-24; Lk. 22:19f.).

The key to His words lies in the Passover interpretation of Dt. 16:3. While Jewish tradition says that the bread and the wine in the various paschal cups stand for the past redemption that is thereby brought into the present and made to relive, Jesus declares that the bread in His hands represents His body, shortly to be yielded up in the service of God's redeeming purpose (He. 10:5-10); and that the cup of blessing on the table represents His blood, poured out in death, recalling the sacrificial rites of the OT. Both dishes are invested with a new significance — a parabolic one — as they speak of (and bring into the present for personal appropriation by the Church, as often as the Lord's table is spread) the new Exodus that He effected for His people.

B. New Covenant. The cup is associated with the covenant (Ex. 24:3-11) that God made with the nation of Israel. But this compact failed because of Israel's defection (Jer. 3:20; 31:32) and rebellion (Isa. 1:2; Hos. 6:7f.). Jeremiah spoke, therefore, of a new covenant that the Lord would make (Jer. 31:31-34); and Jesus announced the fulfillment of this hope in the upper room, with the emphasis falling on those elements that Jeremiah had predicted: the inwardness of faith, personal responsibility, and the pledge of full forgiveness.

With many nuances to be understood from the use of the cup, it is not possible to say exactly what was in the Lord's mind as He pointed to red wine on the Passover table and exclaimed, "This cup means My covenant-blood." Certainly, we should see in this allusion an interpretation of His death as inaugurating the new covenant of Jeremiah. But while His work is solitary and unique, He calls His followers to share the benefits and avail themselves of the fruits of His Passion; for in drinking the cup (as in eating the bread) they will be appropriating His life laid down in sacrifice and taken up in newness of power. Jn. 6:32-35 preserves this teaching that His work does not avail unless it is received, even as food does not nourish until it is assimilated.

C. Command to Repeat. Because Jesus attached such significance to His death and its parabolic enactment in the bread and the cup, it is natural that He should go on to command that His actions at the table be perpetuated. Lk. 22:19 (AV) contains the words: "This do in remembrance of me," an instruction renewed in Paul's account of 1 Cor. 11:24f. At the table of remembrance, the Church does not simply reflect (as a mental exercise) upon the cross of Calvary, but relives the accomplished redemption, returns to the upper room and the hill, and shares in that saving work that it knows as a present reality — because its Author is the living One in the midst of His ransomed people.

XVII. Paul's Doctrine of the Lord's Supper.—In this subject Paul was no innovator. He did not introduce a teaching that his contemporaries suspected as newfangled and foreign to the gospel they had known. Theologians in the early part of the 20th cent. cherished the notion that Paul was such a novel teacher. But the evidence is against it, and the theory that the apostle was a Hellenist who foisted on the Church a sacramental doctrine that was modeled on the Greek Mystery practice of a meal in honor of a cult deity is rightly discredited.

The clearest proof we have of Paul's faithful exposition of the doctrine is the way in which he unfolds all that is implicit in the Lord's own teaching in the upper room. Three features marked this dominical teaching, as we noted: (1) there was a common meal and table-fellowship; (2) as bread and wine were taken, the Lord's presence was to be recalled "in remembrance of Me"; (3) the simple rite pointed beyond itself to a future hope in the kingdom of God. Paul's contribution lies in an application of these basic ideas.

A. Fellowship. Nothing is more characteristic of the apostle's sacramental teaching than his use of the term "fellowship" (Gk. *koinōnía*). In baptism we are united with Christ in His death and risen life; in the Lord's Supper we share in His body and blood. This is the plain sense of 1 Cor. 10:16. By reception of the bread and wine and in response to faith — for the elements have no inherent efficacy or magical power to produce the blessing they signify — the believer is united to the sacrifice of Christ. Paul seems to view the bread and wine as signifying to the Christian what the Passover dishes mean to the Jew. Ex. 13:8 is a confession of "what the Lord did for me," even though the participant of later Passover feasts had never personally set foot in Egypt, and had never known the wonder of the Red Sea miracle. The Corinthian believers had never been to the Palestine of Jesus' earthly ministry, had never seen Him in His human form in the days of His flesh (He. 5:7), and had never sat at His table nor stood at His Cross. Yet by taking into their hands the things that He handled and hearing the words that He spoke, and realizing that He is present by the Holy Spirit, they were united with Him in His atoning sacrifice and its potent benefits.

But the fellowship has a horizontal as well as a vertical reference. As we are knit with an unseen yet present Lord at His table, so we are united with His people. This is the meaning of 1 Cor. 10:17: "Because there is one bread, we who are many are one body, for we all partake of the one bread."

In 1 Cor. 10:14-22 Paul relates the teaching of the Supper to some pressing needs of his readers. The most obvious is the glaring disunity of the Church (1 Cor. 1:10-13; 3:3; 4:6f.; 6:1-8; etc.). He meets this need by pointing out how fellowship at a common table, and eating from a single loaf, are both meaningless practices unless the Church realizes that its unity should be expressed in tangible ways.

B. Remembrance. The tradition that Paul received contained the words: "Do this in remembrance of me" (1 Cor. 11:24f.). His account goes on to interpret this command: "you proclaim the Lord's death until he comes" (v. 26). Both sentences are of consequence for our understanding of the ordinance; and both are to be seen on a Passover backcloth.

"To recall," in biblical thought, means to transport into the present an action that is buried in the past, and to do it in such a way that its original potency and vitality are not lost. "In remembrance of me," then, is no bare historical reflection upon the cross, but a recalling of the crucified and living Christ in such a way that He is personally present in all the fulness and reality of His saving power and is appropriated by the believers' faith. The question now presses, how is this done?

The apostolic answer lies in the words: "you proclaim the Lord's death." The verb Gk. *katangéllō* is the same as in 1 Cor. 2:1, and indeed the verb is a usual one for the proclaiming of an event, the announcement of the gospel. It is the death that is preached at the table, not the dying of Jesus that is reenacted. This emphasis has obvious links with the Passover liturgy.

Provided we insist on the importance of a living communion by faith, we may agree (in the light of the strong realism of 1 Cor. 10:16) with Hauck's interpretation: "For Paul the bread and wine are vehicles of the presence of Christ" (*TDNT,* III, 805).

C. Future Hope. "Until he comes" (1 Cor. 11:26) points to the future. The gospel ordinance belongs to the Church age that will run its course until the inbreaking of the final kingdom. The table bids the Church look to that day when the kingdom will be fully consummated; and our invocation of "Maranatha" ("Our Lord, come!") as a prayer for the end and the establishment of the kingdom naturally found a place in the communion services of the early Church (see Did. 10:6). The double thought of the Lord's presence at the table and at the end of the age runs through this primitive watchword.

Past, present, and future are thus gathered up in one sacred and joyful festival of the Lord's table in the apostolic practice and teaching. "Indeed, in this Sacrament the whole of what our religion means is expressed" (C. H. Dodd, *Christian Worship* [1936], p. 82); for one Lord Jesus Christ, incarnate, atoning, and triumphant, is the sum and substance of it all.

XVIII. Some Theological Aspects of Christian Worship.– At the close of our study, we revert to the meaning of Christian worship. At its most elemental level, worship may be defined (as by E. Underhill, *Worship* [3rd ed. 1937], ch. 1) as "the response of the creature to the eternal" or "an acknowledgment of Transcendence." That response or acknowledgment is best interpreted and expressed in terms of adoration as the worshiper, conscious of his or her creatureliness and finiteness, bows before the transcendent and wholly other being who is God.

It is true that this definition of worship as "response to transcendence" has been assailed in recent times. The so-called crisis of worship, which was discussed at the Uppsala sessions of the World Council of Churches in 1968, has arisen partly because the secular version of the gospel calls in question the relevance of worship in its traditional form (see *Studia Liturgica* 7 [1970], for collected essays on this theme) and partly because the concept of transcendence and the "numinous" has been challenged (as by J. G. Davies, *Every Day God* [1973]). To discuss these issues here would take us too far afield, and it must be sufficient to say that a modernizing of worship forms has so far failed to gain acceptance among Christians generally, and that the critique of transcendence leaves an empty space in our understanding of the divine that no updated version of immanence or idea of God as the "ground of being" can fill. (See further R. P. Martin, *Worship of God* [1982], pp. 2-6.)

We may return to the accepted definition of worship as the creature's response to the Creator who is at once above and yet graciously near. Two important aspects of worship are already implicit in this opening statement. One is the *theocentric* nature of Christian worship. It is an exercise of the human spirit that is directed primarily to God; it is an enterprise undertaken not simply to satisfy our need or to make us feel better or to minister to our aesthetic taste or social well-being, but to express the worthiness of God Himself. And this observation corresponds with the derivation of the very word we use, which has, incidentally, no semantic equivalent in Hebrew, Greek, Latin, or any modern European language. As noted, "worship" means by its Anglo-Saxon etymology "worth-ship." We may recall that in the Marriage Service of Cranmer's *Book of Common Prayer,* the prospective husband's promise is, "With my body I thee worship." This is a pledge of utter loyalty and devotion to his bride who is worthy of this, at least in his eyes. Now if we elevate this thought to the realm of divine-human relationships, we have a working definition of "worship" ready-made for us. To worship God is to ascribe to Him supreme worth, for He is uniquely worthy to be honored in this way. For confirmation of this proposal we need only glance at the hymnbook of the second temple: "Ascribe to the Lord the glory due his name" (Ps. 96:8). Because the Lord is great, He is "greatly to be praised" (v. 4). "Extol the Lord our God, and worship at his holy mountain" is the call of Ps. 99:9, with the reason for this invitation to worship supplied as "for the Lord our God is holy!"

The other side of worship is derivative and secondary, but nonetheless important in its place. Because God is eminently praiseworthy and worshipful, those who address worship to God in an act of acclamation and devotion will want to offer their very best and to demonstrate, by that offering of praise, prayer, and giving, the seriousness with which this religious exercise is regarded. If the theocentric aspect of worship heads the list of priorities, a second element will be that Christians intend by what they do in worship to make *a thoughtful, costly, and worthy offering,* appropriate to the high occasion and in line with the serious intent of their coming into the presence of the all-holy, all-gracious God. (The character of God determines the nature of worship, as the present writer has tried to show in *Worship in the Early Church* [rev. ed. 1974], pp. 12ff.) The OT rituals and ceremonies heavily accent this need for the worshiper's preparation for and participation in the various prescriptions and requirements that have to be met. Consider David: "I will not offer burnt offerings to the Lord my God which cost me nothing" (2 S. 24:24). "You cannot serve the Lord" was Joshua's admonition (Josh. 24:19) to a people who in their easygoing, idolatrous ways had forgotten that "he is a holy God; he is a jealous God," who requires a wholehearted and unshared dedication to His name and a commitment to His cause in terms of a full allegiance and avowal. Put into modern terms, these biblical verses stress the seriousness of our worship and the imperious claim it lays upon us. A flippant attitude to worship is obviously out of place and shows only that we have not yet even begun to understand what the worship of God is intended to be and do. Conversely, a deep sense of privilege in our approach to God will mean that our worship will be ordered with careful thought and thus will be acceptable to Him.

With this introduction we may turn to see how the Holy Spirit plays His role in promoting just these two heartfelt desires within the worshiping body of Christ. He leads the Church to think on God as central and to direct its thought from self-centered ways and works to a God-oriented perspective. Furthermore, it is a mark of His leading that we are disposed to worship at all, and to do so in a manner that is worthy of the enterprise to which we set ourselves. Both these ministries of the Spirit may be covered by Paul's general rubric, stated with clarity and force in Phil. 3:3 (RSV mg.): "We . . . worship by the Spirit of God," and read out from the familiar verse of Jn. 4:24: "God is spirit, and those who worship him must worship in spirit and truth."

The NT teaching on the offices of the Holy Spirit is organized only in a loose fashion. No systematic statement is present, and our task is to draw together the various threads that hang down from a number of passages in the hope of weaving them into a pattern. The overall impression we gain is that the first Christians had a vivid awareness of the Spirit's presence and power, and their worship stood within the "magnetic field of the Holy Spirit" (W. C. van Unnik, "*Dominus Vobiscum,*" in A. J. B. Higgins, ed., *NT Essays,* [1959], p. 294). To justify this notable description we may note the following features of the Spirit's activity.

A. The Holy Spirit and Jesus' Lordship. "No one can say 'Jesus is Lord' except by the Holy Spirit" (1 Cor. 12:3) is usually taken to mean that it is the Spirit's gracious work to lead a person by way of conviction of sin (Jn. 16:8) and apprehension of the truth of the gospel to the place of faith in Christ and confession of His name. But the context of Paul's writing is that of the exercise of spiritual gifts in the Church and it is more likely that the cry "Jesus is Lord" echoed in a meeting for congregational worship when also the heretical ejaculation "Jesus is damned" was heard. Paul's reply is to indicate that no influence of the Spirit of God in the Corinthian assembly would ever lead to this blasphemy, which probably reflects an attempt to tear apart the Jesus of the Gospel tradition from a heavenly Christ-figure whom the Corinthian Gnostics exaggerated at the expense of the former. "Jesus is Lord" is Paul's counterstatement of apostolic confession; and such a tribute, he remarks, can be made only as the Holy Spirit works in the Church at worship. Alternative possibilities of the meaning of this text do exist. But whether it is the danger of uncontrolled enthusiasm expressed in speaking in ecstatic language (cf. 1 Cor. 14), or the specific temptation of being enticed to deny the faith under cross examination, it seems clear that Paul's rebuttal of any suggestion that he regards as blasphemous is to be found in the invocation of the lordship of Jesus that the Spirit alone can make possible.

B. Role of the Spirit. According to Pauline teaching the Holy Spirit pervades Christian worship. He inspires the Church to pray, helping believers in their weakness (Rom. 8:26f.), and, in a mysterious way that Paul does not explain, interceding for Christians by apparently interpreting before God the hidden secrets and unspoken requests that we find hard to articulate in words. "Praying in the Spirit" (Eph. 6:18; cf. 1 Cor. 14:15) carries this sense of calling upon His assistance in prayer and allowing Him to express through our spirits the desires that accord with God's will for our lives and the well-being of His people. Our entire access to God through Christ the Son depends upon the vivifying ministry of the Spirit who makes the nearness of the Father real and vital in our experience as we plead the intercessory work of the Redeemer. So, in a summarizing statement, "Through him [Christ the Lord] we both [Jews and Gentiles, now one in the new man] have access in one Spirit to the Father" (Eph. 2:18). "The Spirit gives life" (2 Cor. 3:6) is a well-attested Pauline conviction (Rom. 8:2, 11; Gal. 5:25).

C. Aspects of NT Worship. 1. Charismatic. This element is prominent in the Corinthian correspondence. By this term we understand the offering of enthusiastic praise and prayer under the direct afflatus of the Holy Spirit, whether in intelligible speech — what Paul calls "speaking . . . with my mind" (1 Cor. 14:19) — or in ecstatic speech — what he refers to as the gift of tongues (14:2, 6ff.). While Paul does not condemn the latter practice, he is sensitive to its apparent dangers of exhibitionism and meaninglessness (14:20-23); he knows how easily such an exuberance can get out of hand (14:32f.); and how in this way the motif of worship on its human side can be defeated, as a selfish lust for spiritual experience cancels the believer's concern for the upbuilding of the whole community (14:12). Paul, in fact, sets some controls by his channeling of glossolalia into the realm of the Christian's private devotion (clearly 14:2, 18); and whenever the gift is practiced "in church" (14:19, 28), where worship is a public affair as Christians come together (vv. 23, 26), Paul insists that there shall be a corresponding interpretation to explicate the tongue and make its message plain and meaningful, so that in this way the body of Christ may be edified (14:5). "Interpreting" the esoteric message of a tongue is itself a gift of the Spirit (12:10). This is part and parcel of the apostle's basic interest: "To each is given the manifestation of the Spirit for the common good" (12:7). (On the situation that called forth this Pauline statement see R. P. Martin, *The Spirit and the Congregation* [1984], ch. 2.)

2. Didactic. Congregational worship in the Pauline churches has its didactic side. This term covers all ministry by the spoken word that aimed at clarifying the will of God for His people. Various verbs show how seriously Paul took this ministry of instruction and Christian education: teaching (1 Cor. 12:8; 14:26; Eph. 4:11; 1 Tim. 3:2; 4:13; 5:17), instructing (1 Cor. 2:13), prophesying (which, from 1 Cor. 11:4, 5; 14:3, 31, looks as though it meant what we today call preaching), and discerning the truth and testing the content of prophetic utterances (1 Cor. 14:29; 1 Thess. 5:21). This ability to speak the word of wisdom and knowledge, to prophesy, and to distinguish the genuine oracle from the spurious utterance (see 1 Jn. 4:1) is made possible as those who engage in it "are inspired by one and the same Spirit" (1 Cor. 12:11). He is Christ's gift to the church (Eph. 4:7) and He makes Christ's bestowal of ministry (4:11f.) effectual. And once more Paul's insistence stands, "Let all things be done for edification" (1 Cor. 14:26).

3. Eucharistic. This feature of corporate worship strikes the note of praise, for which the term eucharistic conveys the exact sense. From the Greek verb *eucharistéō,* "thank" or "praise," this description applies equally to prayers of thanksgiving (referred to as "blessing [God] in the Spirit"; 1 Cor. 14:16), to hymns of praise inspired by the Spirit (Eph. 5:19f.; Col. 3:16f.), and to the occasion par excellence when believers met to celebrate with thankful spirits the festival of redemption at the Lord's table. At Corinth, party rivalries and selfish behavior marred the assembling for the Lord's Supper (1 Cor. 11:20), and the very objective that the eucharistic gathering should have achieved, namely, a true fellowship between believers, was never attained. The purpose of edification and mutual enrichment within the body of the Lord was frustrated. To that extent the desire of the Spirit to achieve a unity within the body (1 Cor 12:13; Eph. 4:3f.) failed of its purpose because of this massive breakdown of fellowship and concord. Not "discerning the body" (1 Cor. 11:29) sums up the tragic denial of the Spirit's work to create *koinōnía* at Corinth (see R. P. Martin, "Spiritual Gifts," *Anchor Bible Dictionary* [forthcoming]).

D. Conclusion. Our conclusion seems an inevitable one. Whatever the outward forms or expressions of worship, the work of the Holy Spirit was to promote the well-being of all participating members of the one body in Christ and to build up that body in its true oneness. The thought that the church at worship is an accidental convergence in one place of a number of isolated individuals who practice their own private devotional exercises, is alien to the NT picture.

Two consequences can be drawn from Paul's insistence that worship on its "human" side is to be understood as upbuilding. First, Christian worship is a truly corporate experience. It is not a case of the individual seeking his or her own ends. That person must remember that he or she worships as an individual who is a member within the body of Christ. This rule puts a check upon selfishness and the gratification of personal taste. Second, we all have a part to play. Eduard Schweizer has shown that most of modern worship is defective at this point. "It is completely foreign to the NT to split the Christian community into one speaker and a silent body of listeners" (E. Schweizer, *Reformed and Presbyterian World,* 24 [1957], 295), when we have regard to Paul's full exposition of the Spirit-in-the-community-at-worship in 1 Cor. 12 and 14:26-33. The opposite extreme is hinted at in 14:33-40, on which J. Moffatt comments, "Worship is not to be turned into a discussion-group, he insists" (*First Corinthians* [*MNTC,* 1938], p. 233).

In the final section we may deduce some practical considerations that may be stated categorically as summarizing conclusions.

(1) The centrality of God-in-Christ in the pattern of NT worship emphasizes the function of the Spirit's ministry to enable us to emerge from the straitjacket of our oversensitive preoccupation with our "feelings" at any given time, and rise into the presence of God through a contemplation of Him in His goodness, beauty, and truth, and especially in His redeeming acts. The Johannine Paraclete helps us to achieve this goal (Jn. 16:13f.).

(2) Our reliance upon the Spirit to arouse in us a desire to worship God will mean that we will then want to offer our best, and to turn away from an indifferent, casual, or mechanical observance of our holy offices of praise.

(3) The gifts of the Spirit are all personal, and this reminds us that the Holy Spirit acts upon the worshiping company as persons. He respects us as personalities made by God and for God. True worship, therefore, will disown any practice that suggests a manipulation of people, a cajoling of them to accept what the preacher says or what the priest offers, or an unhealthy play upon the emotions.

(4) The polarization of "liberty" versus "liturgy" (see the balanced discussion in S. F. Winward's *Reformation of Our Worship* [1964], ch. 5) is really a false one, since the Spirit is greater than all our forms and can work both through them and apart from them. The Pauline emphasis on upbuilding is more important, and the use (or nonuse) of service books, set prayers, sung responses and ceremonial acts needs to be decided in the light of the prior question: What is the pattern of worship that best conveys the richness of divine grace, faithfully interprets the gospel in our modern world, and helpfully consolidates the body of Christ?

(5) Congregational participation follows directly from the teaching on the gifts of the Spirit, for the gifts are imparted not to a spiritual elite or a ministerial caste but to the entire body. This gives a dignity to the worshiping company in the exercise of its priestly function (1 Pet. 2:1-10) and makes real in our modern church life the fulfillment of that ancient promise that God will pour out His Spirit upon all flesh (Joel 2:28-32 [MT 3:1-5]; Acts 2:16-21).

Bibliography.–J. J. von Allmen, *Worship: Its Theology and Practice* (1965); P. F. Bradshaw, *Daily Prayer in the Early Church* (1981); O. Cullmann, *Early Christian Worship* (Eng. tr., *SBT,* 1/10; 1953); R. Deichgräber, *Gotteshymnus und Christushymnus in der frühen Christenheit* (1967); G. Delling, *Worship in the NT Church* (Eng. tr. 1962); C. W. Dugmore, *Influence of the Synagogue on the Divine Office* (1944); A. R. George, *Communion with God in the NT* (1953); F. C. Grant, *Ancient Judaism and the NT* (1960); F. Hahn, *Worship of the Early Church* (Eng. tr. 1973); J. Jeremias, *Prayers of Jesus* (Eng. tr. 1967); H. J. Kraus, *Worship in Ancient Israel* (Eng. tr. 1966); E. Lohmeyer, *Lord's Prayer* (Eng. tr. 1965); J. Lowe, *Lord's Prayer* (1962); R. P. Martin, *Carmen Christi* (repr. 1983); G. F. Moore, *Judaism,* II (1927), 212-238; C. F. D. Moule, *Worship in the NT* (1961); P. T. O'Brien, *Introductory Thanksgivings in the Letters of Paul* (1977); W. O. E. Oesterley and G. H. Box, *Religion and Worship of the Synagogue* (1907); H. H. Rowley, *Worship in Ancient Israel* (1967); J. T. Sanders, *NT Christological Hymns* (1971); J. G. S. S. Thomson, *The Praying Christ* (1959); G. Wainwright, *Doxology* (1980); C. Westermann, *Praise of God in the Psalms* (Eng. tr. 1965); G. P. Wiles, *Paul's Intercessory Prayers* (1974).

R. P. MARTIN

WORSHIPER [Heb. part. of *ʿāḇaḏ*–'serve,' 'worship' (2 K. 10:19-23; Ps. 97:7); Gk. part. of *latreúō*–'serve,' 'worship' (He. 9:9; 10:2), part. of *proskynéō*–'prostrate oneself before' (Rev. 14:11), *proskynētḗs* (Jn. 4:23)]; AV also SERVE, DO SERVICE; NEB also MINISTER; **WORSHIPER OF GOD** [Gk. *theosebḗs*–'God-fearing' (Jn. 9:31), *sebómenos tón theón*–'one who fears God' (Acts 16:14; 18:7); NEB also DEVOUT.

See DEVOUT; FEAR IV.B.1; WORSHIP.

WORTH [Heb. *ḥayil*–'power, wealth' (Ruth 3:11), *k*^{e}*mô*–'like, as' (2 S. 18:3), *(ki)m*^{e}*ʿaṭ*–'a little, few' ("little worth," Prov. 10:20), pual part. of *sālāʾ*–'be paid' ("worth their weight," Lam. 4:2); Gk. *áxios* ("worth comparing," Rom. 8:18), *dokimḗ*–'test, proof' (Phil. 2:22), part. of *hyperéchō*–'rise above, surpass, excel' ("surpassing worth," Phil. 3:8)]; AV also VIRTUOUS, COMPARABLE, PROOF, EXCELLENCY, etc.; NEB also CAPABLE, TRASH (Prov. 10:20), RECORD, etc.; **WORTHLESS** [Heb. *(ʾîš/b*^{e}*nê) (hab)b*^{e}*lîyaʿal*–'(man/son of) uselessness' (1 S. 2:12; 10:27; 2 S. 16:7; 20:1; Job 34:18; Prov. 6:12; 16:27; 19:28), *rêq*–'empty, unsteady' (Jgs. 9:4; 11:3; "worthless pursuits," Prov. 12:11; 28:19), *heḇel*–'vanity' (Isa. 30:7; Jer. 10:15; 16:19; 51:18), *ʾělîl*–'nought, vain' (Job 13:4; Ps. 97:7), *q*^{e}*lōqēl*–'contemptible' (Nu. 21:5), *šāwʾ*–'vain, unfounded' (Job 11:11), *ʾěwilî*–'useless' (Zec. 11:15); Gk. *achreíos*–'useless' (Mt. 25:30), *adókimos*–'counterfeit, worthless' (He. 6:8); (vbs.) Heb. *hāḇal*–'be vain, empty' (Jer. 2:5), part. of *zālal* (Jer. 15:19)]; AV also VANITY, VAIN, REFUSE, SONS/CHILDREN/MAN OF BELIAL, UNGODLY, etc.; NEB also SCOUNDREL, IDLE, WORTH NOTHING, "of no value," etc.; **WORTHLESSNESS** [Heb. *heḇel*–'vanity' (Jer. 2:5)]; AV VANITY; NEB EMPTY PHANTOM; **WORTHY** [Heb. *qāṭōn*–'be small' (Gen. 32:10 [MT 11]), *ḥayil* (1 K. 1:42, 52); Gk. *áxios* (Mt. 10:11, 13, 37f.; Lk. 15:19, 21; Jn. 1:27; Acts 13:25; 1 Tim. 1:15; He. 11:38; Rev. 3:4; etc.), *hikanós*–'sufficient, adequate, large enough', *axíōs*–'worthily' (Eph. 4:1; Phil. 1:27; Col. 1:10; 1 Thess. 2:12), (vbs.) *axióō*–'consider worthy, deserving, suitable, fitting' (2 Thess. 1:11; 1 Tim. 5:17; He. 3:3), *kataxióō*–'consider worthy' (pass., Lk. 20:35; Acts 5:41; 2 Thess. 1:5)]; AV also VALIANT, MEET (Acts 26:20), etc.; NEB also FIT, HONOURABLE, DESERVE, etc.; **UNWORTHY** [Gk. *achreíos*–'useless, worthless' (Lk. 17:10), *ouk* + *áxios*–'not worthy' (Acts 13:46), *anaxíōs* (1 Cor. 11:27)]; AV also UNPROFITABLE, UNWORTHILY (1 Cor. 11:27); NEB also "deserve no credit" (Lk. 17:10), UNWORTHILY (1 Cor. 11:27). The words "worth" and "worthy" are derived from their respective contexts in Gen. 23:15; Ezr. 8:26f.; Mk. 6:37; and Phil. 4:8. In Isa. 7:23 the Hebrew preposition *b*^{e}- (RSV, NEB, "worth"; AV "at") implies price or exchange (see R. J. Williams, *Hebrew Syntax*

[2nd ed. 1976], § 246, p. 45). In Jer. 14:14 Heb. *'ĕlûl* should probably read *'ĕlîl*, "nought, vain." In Zec. 11:17 the RSV emends *'ĕlîl*, "idol" (so AV), to *'ĕwîlî*, "useless" (see *BHS*). See the comms. for "worthy" in 2 S. 22:4 par. Ps. 18:3 (MT 4), and "worthless" in 1 S. 15:9.

In the RSV OT a significant term translated "worth" is Heb. *ḥayil*. In Ruth 3:11 Boaz uses this term to describe Ruth's sterling character, which was known by all of Boaz's fellow townsmen (for similar uses of *ḥayil*, see "good" in Prov. 12:4; 31:10). In 1 K. 1:42, 52 the RSV translates *ḥayil* as "worthy"; in v. 42 it refers to one who possesses social and economic status, but in v. 52 it seems to refer to one who is trustworthy (see S. J. DeVries, *1 Kings* [*Word Biblical Comm.*, 1985], p. 20; *TDOT*, IV, 350).

The most significant term translated "worthless" in the RSV OT is Heb. *heḇel*. Jeremiah frequently uses it in reference to idols (e.g., Jer. 10:15; 51:18; "worthless things," 16:19; cf. "false," 10:3; "idols," 8:19; 10:8). Also, "worthlessness" (cf. "Lord Delusion" in J. Bright, *Jeremiah* [*AB*, 2nd ed. 1984], p. 15) translates *haheḇel* in Jer. 2:5, which may function as a pun on "Baal" (Heb. *habbaʿal*) in v. 8 (see W. L. Holladay, *Jeremiah 1* [*Hermeneia*, 1986], pp. 86, 89; also Bright, p. 15).

The RSV OT also translates Heb. *rêq* as "worthless." In Jgs. 9:4 and 11:3 it refers to individuals who perhaps were "without visible evidence of material success" (J. Gray, *Joshua, Judges, Ruth* [*NCBC*, rev. ed. 1986], p. 302; cf. 1 S. 22:2). Prov. 12:11 and 28:19 use it in reference to ventures that lack serious accomplishment or profit.

In the RSV NT thirty-six of the forty-eight words translated "worthy," etc., derive from the *áxios* word-group. "Worthy" (*áxios*) usually applies to people, e.g., a house (i.e., people) that is not "deserving" (Mt. 10:13), uncommitted people who do not deserve to be disciples of Jesus (10:37f.), guests who are not "worthy" or deserving of the host's graciousness (22:8), the prodigal who no longer deserved to be called a son (Lk. 15:19, 21), people who view themselves as unsuitable to perform a task (Jn. 1:27; Acts 13:25; cf. Gk. *hikanós* in Mt. 3:11 par.), masters who deserve honor from their servants (1 Tim. 6:1), the Lamb and the Lord who are in a position to receive glory, honor, and power (Rev. 4:11; esp. 5:12), the Lamb who alone deserves to open the scroll (Rev. 5:2, 4, 9), etc.

The cognate verb *axióō* occurs three times. In 2 Thess. 1:11 Paul prays that God may make the Thessalonians deserving of His call. In 1 Tim. 5:17 the author states that Timothy should regard elders who rule well as "worthy" and act accordingly toward them. Also, Jesus' superiority to Moses means that He deserves more glory than Moses (He. 3:3).

"Worthy" also translates the related adverb *axíōs*. Paul implores his readers to lead lives that correspond to their calling (Eph. 4:1) and to the gospel of Jesus Christ (Phil. 1:27), and to live in a way deserving of the Lord (Col. 1:10; 1 Thess. 2:12).

Greek *anaxíōs*, translated "unworthy" in 1 Cor. 11:27, is significant. It does not refer to a moral quality but to an attitude determined by the gospel (*TDNT*, I, 380). The self-examination encouraged by Paul as a corrective to eating and drinking in an "unworthy manner" is not a plea for personal introspection; rather it is a call to remember the true nature and purpose of Christ's sacrificial death on the cross and the meaning of this for the community of the Church. The AV rendering "unworthily" is unfortunate in that it can shift the focus of the Supper onto the communicant and fosters a highly individualistic and pietistic response to the Lord's Supper. See G. Fee, *First Epistle to the Corinthians* (*NICNT*, 1987), pp. 559-561.

The RSV NT translates Gk. *hikanós* as "worthy" five times (Mt. 3:11; 8:8; Mk. 1:7; Lk. 3:16; 7:6). It functions as a confession of the supreme authority and messiahship of Jesus (*TDNT*, III, 294).

The Greek term *achreíos* basically means "useless." The RSV NT translates it as "worthless" (Mt. 25:30) and "unworthy" (Lk. 17:10); in both instances it refers to servants but with significant differences. In Matthew it appears in a dominical saying of judgment, whereas in Luke it reflects the disciples' humility.

Bibliography.–*DNTT*, III, 728-730; *TDNT*, I, *s.v.* ἄξιος κτλ. (Foerster); III, *s.v.* ἱκανός (Rengstorf).

G. L. KNAPP

WORTHIES. AV term meaning "prominent persons," used to translate Heb. *'addîrîm* (RSV "officers"; NEB "leaders") in Nah. 2:5 (MT 6). *See* OFFICER.

WOT. *See* WIT.

WRATH; ANGER [Heb. *'ap, 'ānap, ḥēmâ, ʿeḇrâ, qeṣep, zāʿam, zaʿap, ḥārôn, rōgez*; Gk. *orgḗ, thymós*]; AV also FURY, INDIGNATION, HOT DISPLEASURE, etc. *See also* SLOW.

I. Human Anger.–The OT contains numerous examples of human anger, generally without comment on the abstract rightness or wrongness of anger apart from specific situations in which it arises. Moses is notable in often being spoken of as angry (e.g., Ex. 11:8; 16:20; 32:19-22; Lev. 10:16). His anger, though it was motivated by concern for the people's allegiance to the God of Israel and was often simply a reflection of the divine wrath (as in Nu. 16:15-49 [MT 16:15–17:14]), did not unvaryingly accomplish God's purposes (Ps. 106:32f.; cf. Nu. 20:10-12).

The NT shows a desire to deal with human anger as a problem of ethics and behavior, regarding it entirely negatively. Jesus regarded anger and insults as of serious eschatological consequence, even though they are less serious than murder, and He extended the Law to them (Mt. 5:21-22). Eph. 4:26f. appears to support a milder attitude by recognizing the inevitability of human anger, but calling for vigilance against its dangers and for it not to be nursed beyond the end of one day. But the same pericope goes on to say forcefully that anger should be "put away" (v. 31). According to James, anger must be carefully controlled, because it does not accomplish God's righteous purposes (Jas. 1:19f.). A similar insistence on control of anger appears in the OT wisdom literature (e.g., Prov. 15:18; 19:11; 29:11). The NT message of love for enemies includes the abandonment of human vengeance (Rom. 12:19-21).

II. God's Wrath.–God's wrath is such an essential aspect of the biblical message that biblical writers can speak of "(the) wrath," meaning God's wrath, without specifying that His wrath is in view (e.g., 2 Ch. 28:13; Mt. 3:7; Lk. 21:23; Rom. 12:19; 13:4). It has been thought that this usage indicates that "wrath" is considered an impersonal force, "merely an inevitable process of cause and effect in a moral universe" (Dodd, p. 23). But because the terms for God's response to sin are terms used for human emotions and behavior (esp. in a graphic description of emotion such as Isa. 30:27f.), His judgments are not portrayed as impersonal; a personality like that of human persons is behind the judgment of sin. Furthermore, God's wrath is not pictured as a constant without variation; the revelation that God's wrath is, in the final analysis, far outweighed by His love does not wait for the NT, but is already a fundamental part of the OT message, most clearly in the Prophets (Isa. 54:8; Hos. 11:8-11; Mic. 7:18; cf. also Ps. 103:8-12).

A. OT. God's wrath is most simply His displeasure, understood as the basis of every kind of human misfortune, such as leprosy (Nu. 12:9f.), plague (2 S. 24:1f. 10-25), drought (Dt. 11:17), the desolation brought by war (Isa. 13:13-18), exile (2 K. 23:26f.), the destruction of an established social and cultural order (Ps. 60:1-3 [MT 3-5]; Lam. 4:11; Ezk. 5:15), and death (Ps. 88:6-7 [MT 7-8]; 90:7-12). What is involved is the understanding of all events as having their cause in the will of God (cf. Am. 3:6).

But because God had come to be known as the holy One who has called His people into a covenant relationship with Him, His wrath was distinguishable from the usual arbitrary maliciousness of deities of other ancient Near Eastern religions. It was understood as His response to sin, the antipathy of the holy toward that which is unholy, directed especially against Israel's breaches of the covenant (Dt. 11:17; 29:24-28 [MT 23-27]; Ezr. 8:22; Neh. 13:18; Ps. 78:21-31, 58-64; Jer. 21:12), but also against the hostility shown by other peoples toward the covenant people (Ps. 2; 79:6f.; Isa. 10:24-26; 63:3-6).

God's wrath is, therefore, a principle of rational retributive justice that explains the disasters which come upon individuals and nations. David's resort to mere chance in speaking of Uriah's death (2 S. 11:25) places the king for that moment outside the developing biblical pattern of thought. The covenant itself means that God's will is discernible and that the calamities which befall the covenant people must be understood as God's response to the sins of His people (Am. 3:2). (It is true, though, that ignorance of God is itself considered an inducement of the divine wrath [Job 42:7; Ps. 78:21f.; cf. Rom 1:18-25].) But retributive justice is not its own end in the OT; the basis of the covenant is God's desire to love a particular people, and a rational doctrine of reward and punishment did not exhaust Israel's understanding of its God (cf. Hos. 11:9; Mic. 7:18). Because of God's righteous upholding of His covenant with His people, He is able to turn His wrath away from them (Dnl. 9:16; cf. Ps. 78:38; 85:2f. [MT 3f.]; Isa. 48:9).

It is true, however, that God's wrath came to be thought of as especially concentrated in the eschatological future, which could be portrayed as a "day of wrath" (Zeph. 1:15, 18; 2:2f.; cf. Lam. 1:12). In this there is little resort to God's covenant love as the more fundamental divine characteristic. Just as human sin came to be thought of as a fixed state of affairs, divine wrath came to be thought of as a fixed state, waiting for the eschatological moment to be released in worldwide punishment. But even this thought was communicated as a call to repentance (as in Zeph. 2:3).

B. NT. The OT understanding of God's wrath is taken for granted by the NT writers. Paul states as axiomatic that God's wrath is universally revealed, now and always, against human impiety and injustice, inasmuch as these spring from human suppression of the truth concerning God's eternal power and divinity (Rom. 1:18-21). This revelation of wrath is an essential aspect of the revelation of God's righteousness, His justification of the ungodly through the coming of Christ (v. 17; 4:5). Paul adduces the vices of the gentile world as signs both of human sin and of God's abandonment of the human race to sin, which is itself an expression of His wrath (1:24, 26, 28). He also sees wrath as active in relation to the OT revelation: the Mosaic law itself produced wrath by defining transgression (4:15).

The coming of salvation in Christ does not mean that divine wrath has been eliminated. Rather, the gospel proclamation, in calling hearers to repentance, speaks of the wrath to come (Acts 17:30f.; Rev. 14:6f.). The salvation that comes through Christ is salvation from wrath (Rom. 5:9). The association of wrath and judgment specifically with the eschatological day of wrath is more definite in the NT (e.g., Mt. 3:7; Rom. 2:5; 5:9; 1 Thess. 1:10; Rev. 6:17), but wrath is in certain respects already resting on humankind (Jn. 3:36; 1 Thess. 2:16), because the eschaton has already been initiated by the coming of Jesus and the preaching of the gospel. In Revelation the eschatological wrath (*thymós*) of God is portrayed as wine (Rev. 14:10, 19; 19:15) or a cup (i.e., of wine, 16:19) — an image based on the intoxicating effect of wine which is also found in the OT (e.g., Ps. 60:3 [MT 5]; 75:8 [MT 9]; Jer. 25:15-27) — or as a series of seven bowls to be poured out (Rev. 15:7; ch. 16), an image which emphasizes the multiform character of the eschatological sufferings brought on by the wrath of God.

See also ANGER; FIERCE; FURY; INDIGNANT; JUDGMENT; RETRIBUTION.

Bibliography.–*APC*, pp. 147-154, 174-184; C. H. Dodd, comm. on Romans (*MNTC*, 1932), pp. 20-24; W. Eichrodt, *Theology of the OT*, I (Eng. tr., *OTL*, 1961), 258-269; Lactantius, "Treatise on the Anger of God," *Ante-Nicene Fathers*, VII (1886), 259-280; C. R. Schoonhoven, *Wrath of Heaven* (1966); R. V. G. Tasker, *Biblical Doctrine of the Wrath of God* (1951); *TDNT*, V, *s.v.* ὀργή κτλ. (Kleinknecht, *et al.*).

J. W. SIMPSON, JR.

WREATH [Heb. *g^{e}ḏilîm* (1 K. 7:17), *lōyâ* (1 K. 7:29f., 36); Gk. *stéphanos* (1 Cor. 9:25)]; AV also "addition," CROWN; NEB also FESTOON, SPIRAL DESIGN, SPIRAL WORK.

The OT references to wreaths concern various decorations in Solomon's temple. The exact nature of these decorations remains uncertain. According to J. Gray (*I & II Kings* [*OTL*, 2nd ed. repr. 1976], p. 185) Heb. *g^{e}ḏilîm* means "festoons" (so NEB), apparently a plaited design (cf. Dt. 22:12, where the same term refers to tassels on a garment). Heb. *lōyâ* is more problematic; many scholars propose reading *l^{e}wāyôṯ*, another term for "crown," for MT *lōyôṯ* (see comms. on Kings by J. Montgomery and H. Gehman [*ICC*, 1951], pp. 179f.; G. H. Jones [*NCBC*, 1984], p. 186; cf. J. Gray, p. 195).

Using an image from athletic contests, Paul exhorts his readers to strive for self-control in order to win an imperishable wreath, in contrast to the perishable wreath for which athletes strive (1 Cor. 9:24f.). The "perishable wreath" may be the crown of pine or celery (often already wilted) that victorious athletes received in the Isthmian games, which were held near Corinth (see G. Fee, *First Epistle to the Corinthians* [*NICNT*, 1987], pp. 433-37). Paul's point is that if athletes can discipline themselves and strive for such a perishable goal, so Christians should do the same for the imperishable — the coming kingdom of God (see *CD*, IV/2, 376f.; K. Barth, *Christian Life* [Eng. tr. 1981], p. 262).

G. A. L.

WRESTLE; WRESTLING [Heb. niphal of *pāṯal*] (Gen. 30:8); NEB "play a trick"; [hiphil of *'āḇaq*] (Gen. 32:24f. [MT 25f.]).

When her handmaid Bilhah bore a second son to Jacob (Gen. 30:7f.), Rachel named him NAPHTALI, a play on the root *ptl*, "twist" (see BDB, p. 836). Such wordplay in naming was common among the Hebrews (*see* NAMES, PROPER I.B.1.a); here Rachel sees the birth of this second son as a victory in her struggle with her sister Leah. (The NEB rendering reflects another development in the meaning of *ptl* — twisted in the sense of crooked, perverse, or wily; cf. Job 5:13; Ps. 18:26 [MT 27]; Prov. 8:8.)

On Jacob's famous wrestling match (Gen. 32:24-32), *see*

GAMES II.A; on wrestling in general in the ancient world, *see* GAMES. G. A. L.

WRINKLE [Gk. *rhytís*] (Eph. 5:27). Paul uses this rare Greek word (which occurs only here in the NT and not at all in the LXX) figuratively in referring to the Church as a bride "without spot or wrinkle." The emphasis here is not on youth (cf. *ISBE,* IV, *s.v.*) but on the cleansing and purifying of the Church that Christ has accomplished (see M. Barth, *Ephesians 4–6* [*AB,* 1974], pp. 627f.; F. F. Bruce, comm. on Ephesians [*NICNT,* 1984], pp. 389-391). G. A. L.

WRISTS [Heb. *ʾaṣṣîlê yāḏay*–'joints of my hands'] (Ezk. 13:18); AV "armholes." *See* ARMPIT.

WRITING.

I. Definition and Functions
II. Precursors of Writing
III. Writing Systems
  A. Criteria
  B. Logographic Systems
  C. Phonemic Systems
    1. Phonologization of Logographic Systems
    2. Syllabic Systems
    3. Alphabetic Systems
      a. Diacritical Signs for Phonemes
      b. Doubled Consonants and Long Vowels
      c. Aspiration
      d. Signs for Accents
      e. Indication of Vowels in West Semitic Alphabets
        (1) Special Letters for Vowels
        (2) Vowels Indicated by Letters for Related Consonants
        (3) Graphical Modification of Consonant Letters
        (4) Special Signs for Vowels
    4. Alphabet Tablets
  D. Graphical Signs Outside the Systems
IV. Writing Media
  A. Hard Writing Surfaces
    1. Stone
    2. Ceramics
    3. Plaster
    4. Metal
    5. Ivory
    6. Wood
  B. Soft Writing Surfaces
    1. Clay
    2. Wax
    3. Papyrus
    4. Paper
    5. Leather and Parchment
    6. Textiles
  C. Forms of Written Texts
    1. Clay Tablets
    2. Scrolls
    3. Books in Codex Form
  D. Writing Instruments and Techniques
    1. Stylus and Similar Instruments
    2. Brushes and Pens
    3. Stamps
    4. Writing Fluids
    5. Containers
V. Shapes of Graphical Signs
VI. Direction of Writing
VII. Text Divisions
  A. Division of Words
  B. Division of Verses and Sentences
VIII. Development of Writing Systems in the Ancient Near East and in the Greco-Roman World
  A. Sumerian Cuneiform
  B. Akkadian Cuneiform
  C. Cuneiform in Ebla
  D. Cuneiform in Syria and Palestine
  E. Hurrian and Hittite Cuneiform
  F. Egyptian Writing
  G. Hittite "Hieroglyphs"
  H. Cretan Writings: "Hieroglyphic" and Linear
  I. Iranian Writing Systems
  J. West Semitic Alphabet
    1. First Attempts
    2. Ugaritic Alphabet
    3. Phoenician Alphabet and Its Local Variants
      a. Palestine
      b. Aramaic
        (1) Aramaic Script in Judaism
        (2) Local Aramaic Scripts
        (3) Aramaic Script Adopted by Non-Aramaic Peoples
    4. South Arabian Alphabet
    5. Greek Alphabet and Derived Alphabets
IX. Study of Writing
  A. Subdisciplines
  B. Decipherment of Forgotten Writing Systems
    1. Successful Decipherments
    2. Ongoing Attempts at Decipherment
X. Writing in the Bible
  A. Biblical Words for Writing
  B. Ways of Writing
    1. Writing Media
    2. The Book
    3. Writing Procedures
    4. God and Writing
    5. Unusual and Metaphorical Writing
  C. Kinds of Written Documents
    1. Laws and Legal Documents
    2. Letters
    3. Lists
    4. Historical Records
    5. Literary Records
  D. Use of the Alphabet
  E. Quotations
    1. In the OT
    2. In the NT
  F. Writing in the NT

I. Definition and Functions.–A general definition of writing, based on that of Gelb, is *a system of human intercommunication by means of conventional visible signs associated with conventional word meanings and sounds of language*. In principle, writing has to be considered written language — at least in the biblical world — even if it does not reach the ideal, to be the exact counterpart of spoken language. The basic function of writing is to express the sounds of speech in visible, durable signs: speech is fixed in writing. In many writing systems certain signs express whole words (such as & or %); particularly common are special signs for numbers.

From ancient times, writing, which preserves the spoken word from forgetfulness or change, has served to make various economic and administrative records, to fix agreements between persons and communities, and, along with other special marks, to denote weights and volumes of vessels. Even in times when knowledge of writing was limited, written seals bearing the names of persons served for identification in place of handwritten signatures.

Ancient peoples used writing to identify buildings and their function, as well as to display publicly the names and functions of gods, achievement of rulers, and commemorations of the deceased for future generations. Many such public inscriptions are protected by special clauses at the end calling down curses against anyone who would destroy or change the monuments (see Rev. 22:18f.).

Later, literary works began to be fixed in writing. Literature, especially poetry, was transmitted in the ancient Near East for generations by oral tradition. Danger to the bearers of the traditions might have compelled them to secure the poems' survival by fixing them in written form.

Even texts placed where they could not be read (foundations of buildings, burial caves) were considered to have special value. Another kind of value was ascribed to writing in magical texts.

Another advantage of writing is that written messages can be transported to some distance. At a time when the ability to read and write was not as widespread as it is today, the role of the messenger was important. The formulas at the beginning of letters and also some other data show that the messenger read the letter aloud for the addressee. The written form of the letter could then be used to verify the message.

Some written remains indicate how beginners learned to write. Various texts in which an untrained hand repeated lists of letters and words or copied model texts show the care devoted to this learning. More complicated writing systems, such as cuneiform word-syllabic writing in Mesopotamia, or Egyptian hieroglyphic and its later variations, required many years of training for a professional scribe.

While in ancient Egypt and Mesopotamia the knowledge of writing was limited mostly to professional scribes and priests, the ability to use simple alphabetic writing was more widespread. Even so, this knowledge in ancient Israel was apparently limited. From Isa. 29:11f. it appears that not everyone was able to read; cf. also Ps. 71:15, and, for the Hellenistic period, Sir. 44:4 and 38:27.

The administrative records on ostraca found in Samaria, seals on jars, and especially occasional records and letters on sherds found in Lachish and Arad, attest to wide use of writing in the Israelite and Judean kingdoms, as do various funeral inscriptions. Graphical and orthographical imperfections in some of these written records show that they were not produced by professional scribes.

The knowledge of writing was more widespread in NT times. Reading and study of the Scripture required knowledge of Hebrew and Aramaic writing. The penetration of Greek culture was accompanied by wider knowledge of Greek writing. Contacts between Jewish and later Christian communities in the Diaspora were kept by frequent sending of letters.

The three languages of the inscription on the cross (Jn. 19:19-22) and information about "Syriac" (to be understood as Aramaic) additions to the book of Job in its Greek version (Job 42:17b) also demonstrate literacy in at least four languages for Palestine in Roman times.

II. Precursors of Writing.–Writing systems must be distinguished from communication by graphical signs not bound to a definite language. Such devices are known from various areas and times (e.g., the modern system of traffic signals).

Especially characteristic for this type of communication are the rock drawings (petroglyphs) of primitive peoples. To indicate more than one object of the same kind, the pictures were simply repeated as often as necessary; no special number signs were used. The term *ideographic* is used for this type of communication.

The ideographic signs can be understood and "read" (decoded) in different languages. Ideographic signs remain, as archaisms, even in writing systems developed to express words of a certain language. Ideographic features can be observed also in signs that do not belong to a writing system but that are used along with it, such as numerals.

Into this category come the small clay objects used for counting, sometimes impressed on clay tablets as used in prehistoric Mesopotamia and Elam; some have claimed that these are the actual precursors of writing (P. Amiet, D. Schmandt-Besserat). Other signs proposed are proprietors' marks (E. Speiser).

III. Writing Systems.–*A. Criteria.* Writing systems can be classified according to the language units expressed by individual graphical signs: (1) *logographic* systems, in which one sign expresses one word; (2) *phonemic* systems, in which one sign or *grapheme* may express either (a) groups of phonemes, mostly in syllabic systems, or (b) one phoneme, as in the alphabetic systems.

Writings of all systems have many inconsistencies. Often elements of more than one system appear together. Some features of an archaic system, such as signs for words (logograms), occur in phonemic syllabic or alphabetic writings (e.g., & = "and"). For one writing system several different systems of graphical signs could be used. For instance, the ancient Egyptian writing based on word units and groups of phonemes was written first in pictorial hieroglyphs (to which were added alphabetic or phonetic signs), later also in linear hieratic, then in demotic signs. Cuneiform signs were used for the ancient Sumerian logographic system, for later Mesopotamian and other syllabic writings, and also for the Ugaritic alphabet.

B. Logographic Systems. In such systems, one sign equaled one word. The sounds of a language thus cannot be recognized from a pure logographic system; only after some phonemic features are introduced can sounds be determined.

Some problems of the logographic system can be demonstrated from samples of ancient Sumerian pictorial and early cuneiform writing, as documented on clay tablets from Uruk, written *ca.* 3000 B.C.

The original signs depicted an object. For this purpose objects easily relatable to a noun were preferred. Then it was possible to use these noun signs for related nouns indicating entities or concepts not directly visible, e.g., the sign for "sun" was used also for "day," that for "star"

A clay tablet with pictorial writing. From Uruk, *ca.* 3000 B.C. (Iraq Museum, Baghdad; photo W. S. LaSor)

also for "sky," "heaven" also for "god" (DINGIR). The signs for nouns could be used for related verbs, e.g., the sign for "leg" (DU) could mean also "to stand" (GUB), "to go" (GIN), and "to carry off" (TUM). The meaning of signs could be modified, e.g., parallel strokes were added to the sign for "head" (SAG), and the resulting sign meant "mouth" (KA), or "foot" (ŠU), or "nose" (KIRI), or the verb "speak."

Two logograms were combined to indicate one word, either simple, e.g., "mouth" (KA) + "food" (GAR) = "to eat" (KU), or compound, e.g., "man" (LU) + "great" (GAL) = "king" (LUGAL).

Even on a logographic level, "determinatives" (semantic indicators) were introduced to distinguish words written by identical signs. The sign originally depicting a plow could be understood either as "plow" (APIN), if combined with the determinative for "wood" (GIŠ), while the same basic sign connected with that for "man" (LU) indicated "plowman" (ENGAR).

In a strictly logographic system, the number of graphical signs should equal the number of words, a requirement difficult to comply with. The number of word-signs attested in ancient Sumerian writing is estimated at two thousand.

Similar devices were used in ancient Egyptian writing.

C. Phonemic Systems. 1. Phonologization of Logographic Systems. Besides the semantic devices within the logographic system mentioned above, another much more effective device was introduced: a sign was used not only for the depicted object but also for a word of different meaning that was pronounced similarly. The Sumerian sign TI, "arrow," could be used also for the word "life," pronounced [ti]. Since in Sumerian many words were formed by one syllable, this "phonologization" led to a development of a syllabic kind of writing. The syllables, composed of consonants (C) and vowels (V), were of different types: CV, VC, CVC, or V only. Some signs contained more than one syllable, e.g., URU, "city," DINGIR, "god."

Syllabic signs were then used in the Sumerian writing as phonological complements to indicate the pronunciation of often ambiguous logograms: e.g., "crown" (MEN [+ EN]); the sign "leg" (DU) followed by BA had to be read GUB, "to stand"; similarly DU/GIN(NA), "to go," DU/TUM(MA), "to bring."

If a writing system developed for one language was adopted by another language, the logographic elements could be accepted without change in meaning, but they were pronounced differently. The Sumerian sign for "mountain" was pronounced [kur], while the same sign with the same meaning was pronounced [šadū] in Akkadian. The same sign was used in Akkadian in its syllabic value *kur*, e.g., in *iz-kur* "he said," *kur-ru*, a measure.

Phonological components were then used to avoid ambiguity in the meaning of some signs adopted from Sumerian, e.g., the Sumerian sign DINGIR, "god," was used in Akkadian with the same meaning; but to indicate that the sign should now be read *ilu*, the phonetic element *lu* could be added: DINGIR-*lu* = *ilu*. If the reading *šamē*, "heaven," was required for the same sign, the phonetic complement *ē* was added: DINGIR-*e*.

The phonologization of the Sumerian system led to the development of a prevalently syllabic system, even if many logographic signs were retained in their original function.

Since in the ancient Egyptian language the role of vowels was apparently less significant than that of consonants, the phonologization here led to the development of signs indicating consonants and their combinations, while vowels were not indicated.

2. Syllabic Systems. It seems appropriate to distinguish two kinds of syllabic systems, one developed from a logographic system in which various types of syllable signs coexist, and another "pure" syllabic system in which only CV combinations appear. The first kind is represented in the ancient Near East by the Sumerian system and its adaptations to other languages — Semitic Akkadian, Indo-European Hittite, and Hurrian. In all these languages, logograms were frequently used along with syllabic signs. The number of signs is large, more than six hundred in the Sumerian and more than three hundred in the Akkadian syllabary.

The second kind of syllabic system appears in Cretan Linear B and in the Cypriote syllabary. Both these related systems were used for archaic Greek dialects. The Cretan and Cypriote syllabic signs can be presented in a grid: on the left side the consonant (among them also zero for signs consisting of a vowel only), on the upper side the vowels. The number of signs of the type CV (or V) is in principle the multiple of the number of consonants times the number of vowels, in Cretan Linear B thirteen times five, i.e., sixty-five. Actually eighty-nine signs are known, some of them not yet determined. This general regularity was instrumental in the decipherment of Linear B by Michael Ventris.

3. Alphabetic Systems. The principle of any alphabetic system is the correspondence of grapheme (graphic sign) to one phoneme, i.e., a meaningful sound, either a consonant or a vowel. Accordingly, even systems in which not all phonemes are indicated by corresponding graphemes are considered alphabetic. The most important is the West Semitic alphabet, in which originally only consonants, not vowels, were indicated. Later, various devices for indicating vowels were introduced.

Even in simple alphabetic systems various inconsistencies can be detected. For instance, if a language adopted an alphabet from a language that had fewer consonantal phonemes than itself, some graphemes were ambiguous. This was the case in Early Aramaic, which had more consonantal phonemes than the twenty-two represented in the borrowed Phoenician alphabet. The use of two graphical signs for one phoneme is observable for the aspirates in some archaic Greek alphabets, *k* + *h*, *p* + *h*, and later for the spirant *ch* in Roman writing. On the other hand, two phonemes could be written by one sign, in Greek /k + s/ = ξ, /p + s/ = ψ; cf. Roman *x*.

The number of letters in the alphabetic system is much less than that of signs in logographic and syllabic systems. The Ugaritic alphabet had twenty-seven letters for consonants and three letters for vowels in combination with the glottal stop, altogether thirty letters. Because of a smaller number of consonantal phonemes, the number of letters in the Phoenician alphabet is only twenty-two. This number was preserved in the Hebrew and Aramaic alphabets, even when the number of phonemes was slightly higher in some dialects. The Old South Arabic alphabet has twenty-nine consonants (one more than the Classical Arabic alphabet). As the Greeks adopted the West Semitic alphabet, they omitted some letters and added some new ones; after a period of change lasting several centuries, the number of Greek letters stabilized at twenty-four. The same number eventually appeared for the ancient Roman alphabet, although not all of its letters corresponded to the Greek ones.

In various alphabets the letters had specific names. In the Phoenician and Hebrew alphabet the names are reminiscent of the original shapes of letters depicting certain objects, e.g., *aleph,* "ox," *beth,* "house," *ayin,* "eye." The principle of acrophony is applied here: the letter is named after the first consonant of the name. The West Semitic names were then adopted in a slightly changed form for the Greek alphabet. In the Roman alphabet the names of the letters consist of the named consonant or vowel with some addition (as in our alphabet); the same principle is used in the Arabic alphabet.

4. Alphabet Tablets. Alphabet sequences, complete or partial, are preserved both from various West Semitic areas and from countries where the Greek alphabet was used. Most of the complete series are written on tablets of stone or other hard material. There are also incomplete sequences of letters in alphabetical order, mostly from the first part of the alphabet.

The complete alphabets that are written very carefully probably served as models for students. To this category apparently belongs one of the oldest of such lists, on a small clay tablet from Ugarit (*ca.* 13th cent. B.C.). A clay tablet with cuneiform letters of the Ugaritic type but in the sequence of the South Arabic alphabet was found in excavations at Beth-shemesh in Palestine. A Greek alphabet very carefully written on the upper part of an ivory writing tablet, which could be filled with wax to form a writing surface, was found at Marsiliana d'Albegna in Italy. It served to transmit the Greek alphabet to the Etruscans.

Less careful and often incorrect alphabetic lists attest to attempts by students to imitate the models. Such exercises are preserved on clay tablets from Ugarit. Also, some stone tablets with carved letters may be mentioned here, e.g., the alphabet of 'Izbet Ṣarṭah near Aphek in Palestine (11th cent. B.C.), written from left to right, and several tablets and inscribed sherds from Phoenicia, Palestine, Syria, and Egypt, with letters of Phoenician, Palestinian, or Aramaic type.

Both Semites and Greeks also used letters of the alphabet for numerals. (*See* NUMBER.)

a. Diacritical Signs for Phonemes. If there were more phonemes in a language than in the adopted alphabet, it was customary in antiquity to endow unnecessary letters with new values or to create new letters (as in Greek, Coptic, Etruscan, Latin, Gothic, Old Church Slavonic). Diacritical signs for distinguishing two letters of the same shape were introduced either for graphical reasons (if two originally distinct letters became indistinguishable) or to indicate phonological values similar to that of the basic letter.

The first phenomenon appears in some later Semitic alphabets. In Aramaic, the originally different letters for *d* and *r* became identical; in Syriac, a later Aramaic dialect, a dot above the ambiguous letter indicated *r*; a dot below, *d*. The graphical simplification of Classical Arabic letters made necessary an elaborate system using one, two, or three dots above or below letters for distinguishing convergent shapes and phonological differences.

Diacritical signs were introduced in the Hebrew alphabet, probably in the 8th cent. A.D., for distinguishing the letter *shin* (שׁ) in its original value ("sh") from the variant *sin* (שׂ) that eventually merged in pronunciation with the consonant pronounced [s] (*samech,* ס). Originally small *shin* and *samech* letters were set above the basic letter; later they were replaced by a dot above the right upper corner for *shin* and a dot above the left upper corner for *sin*.

The Syriac plosive consonants *b, g, d, k, p,* and *t* were marked by a dot above the letter, their spirant variants by a dot below the letter. The Hebrew plosive consonants were marked by a dot in the center of the letters in the Tiberian tradition; the spirant variants were either left unmarked or were indicated by a horizontal stroke above the letter.

b. Doubled Consonants and Long Vowels. The doubling of consonants was indicated in some systems (Ugaritic rendering of Akkadian words, Greek, Latin) by writing the doubled consonant twice. In the Hebrew tradition the doubling consonant was marked by the sign *dagesh* (a dot in the middle of the letter), which was used also for the plosive pronunciation. In the Arabic alphabet a special sign for doubling is used.

The length of vowels in the Roman script was considered of lesser importance; in Greek new letters were introduced only for long *ē* and *ō*. Various diacritical signs for the length of vowels have developed only since the late Middle Ages.

c. Aspiration. Greek signs for distinguishing aspiration, /h/, or lack of aspiration with a vowel at the beginning of a word (so-called *spiritus asper* or *lenis*) were introduced in late antiquity.

d. Signs for Accents. Special signs for word stress in Hebrew and Syriac were introduced for the liturgical cantillation of sacred texts. In addition to marking stress, some of them also functioned as punctuation signs.

e. Indication of Vowels in West Semitic Alphabets. In the linear West Semitic alphabet originally only consonants were represented while the vowels were not indicated. Both ancient and modern readers of such texts had to supply the vowels from their knowledge of the word structure or from transliterations into other writing systems that indicated vowels.

In most instances the explicitly written consonant is implicitly followed by a vowel (CV). This situation led some scholars to classify the West Semitic alphabets among the syllabic systems (Gelb). But these languages also have closed syllables (CVC), written with two consonant letters; one consonant letter cannot be considered a sign for such a syllable.

The relationship between alphabetic and syllabic systems can be observed in Ugaritic words attested from the 13th cent. B.C. They are written mostly in alphabetic cuneiform, but many words are also represented in the quadrilingual vocabularies written in syllabic cuneiform. For the coincidence of consonantal letters with open syllables, see, e.g., *šmm* (alphabetic) and *ša-mu-ma* (syllabic), "heavens"; *lbn, la-ba-nu,* "white." The word for silver is written *ksp* alphabetically, *kas-pu* or *ka-as-pu* syllabically. The second person singular masculine pronoun "you," probably pronounced ['atta] or ['at], is written *at-ta* or, alphabetically, *at*.

Because the original West Semitic alphabet was limited — most probably following its Egyptian model — to indicating consonants only, various devices for completing this alphabet by signs for vowels were introduced. The strictly consonantal orthography was preserved only by the Phoenicians in their homeland and in their inscriptions in the eastern Mediterranean.

The principal devices for indicating vowels in the West Semitic and derived alphabets are as follows.

(1) Special Letters for Vowels. The first device was already tried in the Ugaritic cuneiform alphabet, the oldest major corpus of West Semitic alphabetic texts known to us. Ugaritic possessed, alongside twenty-seven letters for consonants, three letters expressing the vowels *a, i,* and *u* in combination with the glottal stop *aleph.* The introduction of these three signs — ascribed to an inventor whose name in Grecized from is given as Eisirios — is

Semitic Alphabets

Adapted from *BhHW,* cols. 1721f., with permission of the publisher, Vandenhoeck & Ruprecht.

SEMITIC, GREEK, AND LATIN ALPHABETS

Hebrew Name	Phoenician 8th Cent. B.C.		Ancient Greek 8th Cent. B.C.	Ancient Hebrew *ca.* 600 B.C.	Greek Name	Greek	Latin
ALEPH	𐤀	𐤀	Α	𐤀	ALPHA	Α	A
BETH	𐤁	𐤁	Β	𐤁	BETA	Β	B
GIMEL		𐤂	Γ	𐤂	GAMMA	Γ	G
DALETH	𐤃	𐤃	Δ	𐤃	DELTA	Δ	D
HE		𐤄	Ε	𐤄	EPSILON	Ε	E
WAW		𐤅	Ϝ	𐤅	(DIGAMMA)		V
ZAYIN	𐤆	𐤆	Ζ	𐤆	ZETA	Ζ	Z
HETH	𐤇	𐤇	Η	𐤇	ETA	Η	H
TETH			Θ	𐤈	THETA	Θ	
YODH	𐤉	𐤉	Ι	𐤉	IOTA	Ι	I
KAPH	𐤊	𐤊	Κ	𐤊	KAPPA	Κ	K
LAMEDH	𐤋	𐤋	Λ	𐤋	LAMBDA	Λ	L
MEM	𐤌	𐤌	Μ	𐤌	MU	Μ	M
NUN	𐤍	𐤍	Ν	𐤍	NU	Ν	N
SAMEKH	𐤎		Ξ	𐤎	XI	Ξ	
AYIN	𐤏	𐤏	Ο	𐤏	OMICRON	Ο	O
PE		𐤐	Π	𐤐	PI	Π	P
SADHE		𐤑	Ϻ	𐤑	(SAMPI)		
QOPH	𐤒	𐤒	Ϙ	𐤒	(KOPPA)		Q
RESH	𐤓	𐤓	Ρ	𐤓	RHO	Ρ	R
SHIN	𐤔	𐤔	Σ	𐤔	SIGMA	Σ	S
TAW	𐤕	𐤕	Τ	𐤕	TAU	Τ	T

Adapted from *BhHW,* cols. 285f., with permission of the publisher, Vandenhoeck & Ruprecht.

a violation of two principles of the West Semitic alphabet: its limitation to consonants and its strict one-to-one relationship between phonemes and graphemes. This was mitigated by the phonetic character of the consonantal component of the signs; the glottal stop ['] is an interruption of the sonation stream (corresponding to the definition of a "consonant"); it is usually audible only between vowels (cf. Eng. "co-operate," "re-enter").

With the destruction of the city of Ugarit and its culture *ca.* 1200 B.C., this device (aleph with its vowel) disappeared from the West Semitic alphabet. Much later a similar device was used in some late Punic inscriptions written in North Africa in the first centuries A.D., in which the letter for *aleph* was used for various long vowels at the ends of words.

Special letters for vowels were used consistently in the Greek alphabet from its very beginning. They were apparently inspired by their West Semitic (Aramaic, to be precise) models of so-called vowel letters (see below), but unlike them they were used exclusively for vowels, not for consonants as well. This use of special letters for vowels was then adopted, together with the Greek alphabet as a whole, by Etruscans, Romans, Copts, and other communities using the alphabet derived ultimately from the Greek (including our own).

(2) Vowels Indicated by Letters for Related Consonants. The indication of vowels by related consonants, especially long vowels at the end of words, was tried already in the Ugaritic alphabet. It was used sporadically in some late nonliterary texts and more regularly in alphabetic texts rendering Akkadian words. Probably this device was inspired by the practice in the Akkadian syllabary of writing the vowel sign in addition to signs ending in the same vowel, e.g., *la-a* for /lā/, *ki-i* for /kī/.

In Aramaic, from the oldest inscriptions on (from *ca.* 850 B.C.), some consonants were used for phonologically related vowels: *y* for *ī* and *ē*, *w* for *ū* and perhaps *ō*, *h* for final *ā* and *ē*, and perhaps *aleph* for *ā*. This system was used also in Hebrew and related inscriptions from Palestine, but less consistently. The frequency of vowel letters (*matres lectionis*) became higher in Hellenistic and Roman times, as attested by some Hebrew and Aramaic MSS from the Qumrân area. The only West Semitic writing system that reached consistency in indicating vowels in this way was Mandaic, an Eastern Aramaic dialect that has survived from ancient times to the present day.

(3) Graphical Modification of Consonant Letters. The indication of vowels by graphical modifications of the basic letter forms is used in the Ethiopic writing system. In the oldest Ethiopic inscriptions (3rd-4th cent. A.D.) only consonants are expressed. In the 6th cent. a new system was introduced in which the basic letter forms indicated Consonant + *a*, while for other Consonant + Vowel combinations modifications of the basic letter were introduced, such as extending or shortening of the letter on one side or adding a special graphical feature. Since this system corresponds to that used in the Indian writing system (itself developed indirectly from an Aramaic model), and since there were contacts between India and Ethiopia in late antiquity, it is probable that the Ethiopic system of indicating vowels was inspired by the Indian model.

(4) Special Signs for Vowels. The use of consonants for indicating vowels in the Northwest Semitic languages, especially Hebrew and Syriac, provided only partial help in attempts to ascertain the correct pronunciation of traditional texts in later times, when the original language was no longer spoken (Hebrew) or was exposed to the influence of the spoken dialect and its changes (Syriac and other Aramaic languages).

The first device, used in Syriac texts since *ca.* A.D. 400, was only a partial solution: words with full vowels, especially *a*, or with long vowels, especially *ā*, were marked by a supralinear dot, while words with the same consonants, but with short or no vowel in the corresponding positions, were left unmarked or marked with a sublinear dot.

This partial device was superseded by the introduction of specific signs for individual vowels set below or above the letters in Eastern Syriac texts. This innovation, attested since the beginning of the 7th cent. A.D., was followed shortly after by a similar system of the Western Syrians, who eventually adopted the Greek vowel capital letters, placed above or below the line, for the appropriate corresponding vowels.

The oldest attempts at indicating vowels in Hebrew texts imitated the Eastern Syriac system in principle and also in the shapes of some signs. It was introduced by Jewish scholars in Babylonia, where Jews spoke an Eastern Aramaic dialect similar to Syriac. This simple supralinear system was followed by a more complicated system that introduced additional signs, including those for reduced vowels.

The Babylonian supralinear vocalization was used in Babylonian centers of Jewish learning; later, in the Middle Ages, it was adopted by Jews in Yemen. The most ancient and most reliable MSS of the Aramaic Targums (translations or paraphrases of the Bible) are provided with Babylonian vocalization.

Another simple system for vocalization originated in Palestine *ca.* A.D. 800: the use of vowel signs was limited to some words. MSS using it are only sporadically preserved.

Both of these vocalization systems were superseded by the system introduced — probably *ca.* A.D. 850 — in the city of Tiberias at the Sea of Galilee. The Tiberian system is sublinear (for the most part): the signs, consisting of dots and short strokes, are put under the consonant letters. The system is more exact and consistent than its predecessor, indicating the qualities of the vowels and also the reduced vowels exactly according to the required pronunciation. The Tiberian scholars also consistently introduced signs for the exact pronunciation of consonants and musical accents; hence the correct recitation of the Hebrew biblical texts in accordance with old tradition has been ascertained. The results of the Tiberian school are present in Bible MSS, in the notes and collections accompanying them, and also in special treatises. The Tiberian vocalization system was eventually adopted by all Jewish communities; it was also used for nonbiblical texts, especially for poetry.

A vocalization system using vowel signs above or below consonant letters is also used in Arabic texts, especially in religious writings, Christian and Moslem, and in poetry.

D. Graphical Signs Outside the Systems. In different types of writing systems, besides syllabic or alphabetic signs indicating sounds, there are special graphical signs outside the system.

A specific system of its own is that of numbers. In the old Mesopotamian cuneiform texts special signs are based on the sexagesimal system — sixty lower units form a higher unit. In later Mesopotamian texts and also in the Ugaritic alphabet, cuneiform signs were used for the decimal system based on the number ten. Signs for the fractions 1/2 and 1/3 are also attested. In some alphabetic Phoe-

WRITING

A granite statue of Haremhab with a papyrus scroll unrolled in his lap. The statue pedestal is inscribed with prayers to various gods (18th Dynasty, probably from Memphis) (The Metropolitan Museum of Art, Gift of Mr. and Mrs. Everit Macy, 1923)

nician and Aramaic inscriptions and papyri special signs for the numbers one, ten, and one hundred were used. Among them were proprietary signs on various objects, masons' marks, and signs on weights (those in Palestine probably derived from Egyptian demotic signs).

Sometimes letters in alphabetical order were used to indicate a sequence. An old testimony of this practice was found on a Phoenician ship near the island of Motye (now Mozia) at the western shore of Sicily: wooden planks are marked by letters beginning with *aleph,* the first letter of the Phoenician alphabet. The same principle is applied in the alphabetic sequence of first letters of verses and verse groups in some Psalms (9–10; 25; 37; 111; 112; 119; 145), Lamentations (1–4), and some other biblical poems (Prov. 31:10-31; Nah. 1:1-8).

In Hellenistic times letters of the Greek alphabet began to be used for numbers. In order to cover all digits 1-9, all tens 10-90, and all hundreds 100-900, it was necessary to supplement the standard Greek alphabet by a few archaic letters. The Hebrew system had to manage with twenty-two letters of the alphabet: *'-ṭ* for 1-9, *y-ṣ* for 10-90; but only four letters *q-t* were left for 100-400; therefore higher hundreds were indicated by combinations of *t* (400) and the other hundred-signs. *See* NUMBER.

IV. Writing Media.–A. Hard Writing Surfaces. 1. Stone. Inscriptions were written on natural rocks, on stones in buildings, on the pedestals of stone statues, on stone vessels or on stone plates made especially to serve as writing surfaces. Most stone inscriptions were carved. In some inscriptions from northern Syria, in the Aramaic alphabetic writing, and in Hittite "hieroglyphs," the letters are not incised but sculpted as reliefs above the surface. Writings painted on stone have been found in Egypt and in western Asia.

Sometimes ordinary rock surfaces were preferred instead of especially prepared surfaces. The occasional rock inscriptions of Aramaic and Arabic nomads are often very sketchy. Inscriptions in funeral caves or in other subterranean rooms, such as that in the water tunnel at the Siloam spring in Jerusalem, are more carefully done. Even more carefully prepared were royal inscriptions, such as the sequence of inscriptions on a rock overlooking the Mediterranean at the river Eleutheros (Nahr el-Kelb) in Lebanon N of Beirut where various invaders glorified their conquests. Inscriptions of Persian Achaemenian kings at Behistun (Bisitun) are carved in large regular spaces high in the rocks.

Building inscriptions appear usually on visible places, to indicate who built the structure and why. They invoke the protection of gods against those who would destroy or alter the structure and the inscription. Egyptian hieroglyphic inscriptions on the walls of temples and tombs, carved or painted, accompany reliefs and paintings. Assyrian and Aramaic inscriptions were carved also on the stone statues of gods and kings, usually on their garment. In Greece and also later in the Near East, pedestals were used for dedicatory and other inscriptions.

Inscriptions on stone stelae (pillars) erected on graves are relatively frequent in antiquity. Thousands of them were found, with Punic inscriptions, in Carthage and in Punic cities in Sardinia.

Inscriptions on stone vessels and plates are carved or painted. Among those carved may be mentioned the Gezer calendar in Hebrew from *ca.* 1000 B.C. Painted Aramaic inscriptions are found on the bases of alabaster cultic vessels from Persepolis.

For inscriptions on stone, cooperation of two or more persons was necessary. A scribe drafted the shapes of the sign on the surface, and a craftsman chiseled or engraved them. Some inscriptions were engraved according to written models.

The quality of the stone affected both the techniques used and the durability of the writing. Hard stones such as granite or basalt were difficult for the engraver. It was easier to carve letters into limestone or sandstone, but inscriptions on them became less legible after a time due to weathering.

Special skills were required for engraving tiny letters in negative into small seals, cylindric or flat, made from stone — often precious stone — or sometimes metal.

2. Ceramics. Inscriptions may be carved, painted, or stamped onto a ceramic surface before burning, thus becoming part of the vessel, or they may be carved or painted on the vessel or its sherds after baking.

Inscriptions on potsherds have been found in Egypt, Mesopotamia, Syria, Palestine, and Greece. These sherds were the least expensive writing material available and were used for short occasional records and messages. Due to the durability of the material they survived longer than many contemporary formal written documents. These inscribed sherds are called OSTRACA (pl. of Gk. *óstrakon*).

The writing was sometimes carved, as on the archaic Greek sherds from Mt. Hymettos. More frequently signs were written in ink, as in the Demotic and Aramaic ostraca from Elephantine in southern Egypt, those found in Samaria, Lachish, Arad, and Beer-sheba in Palestine, and the seventh-century Aramaic ostraca from Asshur.

In Middle Kingdom Egypt the names of enemies were written on breakable clay figurines; destroying the figurines magically destroyed the enemies. In Mesopotamia, ceramic bowls from late antiquity have inner surfaces covered with Aramaic magical texts in a spiral or circular arrangement.

3. Plaster. Inscriptions on plaster covering stone are mentioned in the OT (Dt. 27:2-4). A long Aramaic inscription in black and red ink from *ca.* 700 B.C. on the plastered wall of a sanctuary was found at Tell Deir ʿallā E of the Jordan at the river Jabbok.

4. Metal. Bronze, silver, gold, and lead were used with some frequency for writing surfaces.

Bronze statues or plaques with reliefs were provided with inscriptions identifying images of gods or men, or giving the names and desires of those dedicating them. Because of their durability metal plaques were used for very important religious and secular laws and treaties, especially in Greece and Rome. Metal vessels were inscribed with the owners' names or dedications to the gods. Owners' names also appear on metal adzes, spearheads, and arrowheads from Syria and Palestine. Short inscriptions were written also on plaques, disks, jewelry, and amulets.

Inscriptions written on thin gold sheets are known, *inter alia,* from Pyrgi (Santa Severa) in central Italy, with inscriptions in Phoenician and Etruscan from the 5th cent. B.C. Greek religious texts in later times were written on such "lamellae." (*See ISBE,* I, Plate 5.)

Lead sheets, because of pliability and ease of writing, were used as writing surfaces. The oldest Mandaean texts and various magical writings were written on such scrolls.

Short inscriptions appear on various metal weights in geometric or in animal forms, usually indicating the weight units by letters or special signs.

A list of hidden treasures etched on a copper scroll was found in Qumrân Cave 3.

Inscriptions on coins of bronze, silver, and gold are particularly interesting. Their "legends" were first carved in hard dies; on the coins the letters appear generally in relief. Coins with Phoenician, Aramaic, and Hebrew inscriptions (often in archaic letters) generally indicate the name of the ruler or of the city, the monetary unit, sometimes the year, such as the "year of liberation" on Jewish coins from the time of the wars against the Romans (A.D. 66-70, 132-135). *See also* MONEY.

5. Ivory. Inscriptions appear on reliefs and carvings on ivory that adorned the royal furniture in Canaanite and Aramaic kingdoms. Some of them were found among the booty brought to Assyria from the conquered royal residences.

Ivory was also used for writing tablets. The tablet found at Marsiliana d'Albegna in central Italy has an archaic Greek alphabet at its top; in antiquity the surface in the center between the frames was filled with wax.

6. Wood. Wooden objects with inscriptions written in ink have been found in Egypt. In other countries wood did not survive. Wooden tablets were used as a writing surface in Egypt and elsewhere.

Tablets for which the wood itself did not serve as a writing surface but as a base and frame have also been found in Egypt. The writing was done not on the wood but — as on the ivory tablets — on a flat surface framed on borders and filled with wax. Some of these writing tablets (often only two of them) were bound together to form a kind of booklet.

B. Soft Writing Surfaces. 1. Clay. Clay tablets can be classified as both hard and soft writing material. The writing, with a stylus, was done when the clay was wet and soft; after the tablets dried or were baked in an oven, their surface hardened. Both this hardness and minimal usefulness for other purposes account for the survival of a great number of clay tablets.

Usually local clay was used. Sometimes, by chemical analysis and comparison of results, the provenance of tablets can be determined. An oven for baking cuneiform tablets was found in Ugarit; it was abandoned *ca.* 1200 B.C. with some tablets in it still unbaked.

Most common were flat clay tablets, generally oblong with rounded edges; often the rounded edges were also used as writing surfaces. Many of the smaller tablets were not flat but convex.

Clay tablets were used in Mesopotamia for pictorial writing in the archaic period, later for cuneiform writing. The dimensions varied considerably. The smallest have sides of only a few centimeters; the dimensions of a very large tablet could be 30 by 20 cm. (12 by 8 in.). The form and arrangement of clay tablets, along with cuneiform writing, were adopted in Syria and Asia Minor.

Flat clay tablets were also used for different scripts in other areas. At Tell Deir ʿallā clay tablets from the Iron Age with inscriptions in a still undeciphered script have been found.

Besides flat clay tablets, clay prisms and cylinders were used in Mesopotamia, often for historical records. Inscriptions on mushroom-like clay objects were set into building foundations.

Clay was also used as a writing surface in Bronze Age Crete. Pictorial signs were stamped on the clay disk of Phaestos. The clay tablets with Cretan Linear B were of

A clay prism from Babylon with an Akkadian inscription describing the restoration of the temple Esagila and the ziggurat Etemenanki at Babylon, 7th cent. B.C. (courtesy of the Trustees of the British Museum)

oblong form with rounded left and right ends; they were dried, not baked.

2. Wax. Wax writing surfaces were used for temporary records. The written surface could be easily flattened for reuse. The base and frame of the tablets were usually made of wood; expensive ones were made of ivory. Such writing surfaces are known from ancient Egypt and from the Greco-Roman world. The wax itself has survived only in traces, but its use is known from pictorial and literary sources.

3. Papyrus. Papyrus, a frequently used writing surface, survived only under especially favorable conditions. In the very dry climate of Egypt numerous papyrus texts in ancient Egyptian, Coptic, Aramaic, Greek, Phoenician, and Latin have been found. In the moister climate of other countries the organic fibers decomposed. They were preserved only under special circumstances, such as the Hebrew, Aramaic, and Greek papyri in the caves of the Judean desert and the Greek papyri carbonized by the eruption of Mt. Vesuvius in Herculaneum (Villa dei Papiri).

Papyrus was made in Egypt from the inner pith of the reed *Cyperus papyrus* (Heb. *sûp*), which grew abundantly in the river Nile in antiquity. Papyrus stems were cut and the pith cut into strips. They were put into parallel rows, and another layer of strips running at right angles was put over them. Both layers were then pressed together, probably without being pasted. The product was a smooth white writing material. For longer texts the strips of papyrus were pasted together and then rolled into scrolls.

The Greek word for papyrus as a writing material is *chártēs*; the word *pápyros* was used for the plant and some products from it. The word *papyrus* is derived from an Egyptian word meaning "that of the king (pharaoh)," indicating the royal monopoly on papyrus production. Papyrus was exported already in the 2nd millennium B.C. from Egypt to the Phoenician city of Gubla and from there re-exported further to Greece. From the Greek name of Gubla, Byblos, the Greek word *býblos*, later *bíblos*, for the papyrus plant, pith, and writing material itself is derived, as well as *byblíon* or *biblíon* for a sheet, scroll, or book.

Papyrus was often reused after the original writing was washed away. The term for such writing surface, derived from Greek, is "palimpsest" ("scraped again").

See also PAPYRUS.

4. Paper. The production of paper from rags was invented in China and brought to the Near East only in early Islamic times. Early medieval Jewish texts on paper were preserved in the Cairo Genizah. Only after *ca.* A.D. 1000 were biblical and other MSS written on paper, which was more durable than papyrus and less expensive than parchment.

5. Leather and Parchment. Animal skins were used for writing in ancient Egypt and in western Asia. Aramaic letters written on leather sent by the Persian governor Arshama (Arsames) in 408-407 B.C. from Persia or Mesopotamia have been found in Egypt, perserved because of the dry climate. Hundreds of Hebrew and Aramaic leather scrolls have been found in the Judean desert; they remained there from the 1st and 2nd cent. A.D. in the caves at Qumrân, in the vicinity of En-gedi, and in the ruins of Masada.

In general, the thinner skins of young goats were preferred. Sheets were sewn together into long scrolls, imitating those of papyrus. In dry climates leather survived relatively well, even when it became brittle. Many leather scrolls were damaged by parasites.

A special treatment of skins provided very thin, durable, and pliable white writing material. The name "parchment," Latin *pergamena (charta)*, is derived from the name of the city of Pergamon in western Asia Minor. The books of the famous library there of King Eumenes were written on parchment because it was difficult to get papyrus from Egypt. In the NT the word *membránai* (pl.; of Latin origin) is used.

See also LEATHER; PARCHMENT.

6. Textiles. Textiles were used only rarely as a writing surface. Some texts were written on linen in which mummies were wrapped in Egypt. On such linen is preserved the longest Etruscan inscription, now in the museum of Zagreb, Yugoslavia.

C. Forms of Written Texts. 1. Clay Tablets. See IV.B.1 above.

2. Scrolls. Scrolls for longer texts were made by pasting together sheets of papyrus or by sewing together leather sheets. They were most often written on one side, usually in columns. When rolled together, writing was on the inner side. Often empty sheets were used at the beginning of the scroll to protect it. In Greece and Rome the scrolls were rolled on a wooden rod. The Hebrew scrolls of the Law used in the Jewish synagogal services have two rods.

The scrolls had several disadvantages. They suffered from the constant rolling and unrolling. Damaged scrolls were mended by patches attached to the outer side (visible on some Qumrân scrolls). Another disadvantage was the difficulty in finding passages quickly; the scrolls were better suited for continuous reading than occasional reference.

See also SCROLL.

3. Books in Codex Form. The book in the form known to us (for which the Latin technical term *codex* is used) appeared only in the early Christian period, first in Egypt. Its predecessor and probable model was the *diptychon*, wax-coated wooden or ivory tablets joined together for easy opening and reading. The oldest books had their papyrus sheets put one on the other and then were sewn together in the center. This inconvenient arrangement was then improved by using shorter quires for a book. It cannot be said with certainty that the books in this practical form were introduced by Christians, but it proved very useful for them when it was necessary quickly to find various passages of Scripture for teaching or discussion.

Pages in codices were arranged in sequence corresponding to the direction of writing. In smaller codices one page contains only one column of text. In larger parchment codices two, three, or even four columns were written on a page.

D. Writing Instruments and Techniques. 1. Stylus and Similar Instruments. Chisels or similar sharp metal instruments were used for engraving signs into hard surfaces like stone, ceramic, or metal. Instruments of this kind preserved in Egypt and Greece are mostly of bronze. Sharp bronze writing instruments were also used for writing on wax tablets. Job 19:24 mentions iron as material for a stylus.

For inscriptions on very hard stones, such as granite or diorite, and also for fine stone seals, some kind of drilling instrument had to be used. Letters in relief were probably produced with the help of both chisel and drill.

The cuneiform signs on clay tablets were written with a stylus of angular shape, quadrangular or triangular in cross sections, made of wood or reed. The tablets were held in the left hand, probably on a 45 degree angle from the horizontal. With their triangular head, wedges had to begin on the left or upper side of the tablet.

2. Brushes and Pens. For writing with various fluids, brushes and pens were used. In Egypt brushes were made of rushes with an end split by chewing. Reed pens used by

Greeks were cut at the end to a point and split into two. Pens made from bird feathers (quills) were introduced only in the early Middle Ages.

Writing on a surface with a brush was similar to painting. Painting itself was used for inscriptions on vessels before firing, especially on Greek vases. The use of a soft brush was favorable to the rounded shapes of graphical signs.

The technique of painting or writing letters on plaster as attested in the Aramaic inscriptions from *ca.* 700 B.C. found at Tell Deir ʿallā was studied very carefully by J. van der Kooij. He was able to demonstrate the sequence and direction in which the traces of individual letters were written.

Scribes using a reed pen formed the signs according to the angle in which the pen was held and the direction of the writing. The requirement of fast writing led to connecting some letters together (ligature); this typical cursive feature can be seen in Western Syriac (Jacobite) *serto* and Eastern (Nestorian) writing, as well as in Arabic.

Writing of larger manuscripts required cooperation. One scribe wrote the basic text, others revised it and supplied signs for vowels and accents. Special scribes provided Masoretic notes.

Techniques prescribed for writing Hebrew scrolls of the Law (Torah) are presented in the post-Mishnaic treatise *Sopherim,* "Scribes." These regulations are followed until the present time.

See also PEN.

3. Stamps. The use of stamping was very limited. The only long text produced by stamping is the isolated clay disk of Phaestos (Crete) with stamped pictorial signs arranged in spirals. Smaller stamps served in ancient Israel for marking ceramic vessels containing deliveries, probably of oil or wine, "to the king," (*lmlk*). Impressions of stamps survived on clay. Stamps were used for clay bricks in ancient Mesopotamia and in the Roman empire.

4. Writing Fluids. Writing fluids were used mostly for soft surfaces such as papyrus and skin, rarely for writing on hard surfaces.

Black ink used for writing on papyrus in Egypt, western Asia, and the Greco-Roman world was made from carbon, probably a fine soot mixed with liquid glue, mostly gum of plant origin. Because of the chemical and physical stability of carbon, this type of ink survived well.

In Palestine some texts were written with ink made from ferrous salts and organic acids, roughly comparable to common modern inks. It preserved well on ceramic surfaces, such as the Lachish ostraca (see IV.A.2 above). But if writing on leather was exposed to moisture, the components of the ferrous ink reacted with it and damaged or even dissolved the leather. In the Aramaic scroll of the Genesis Apocryphon from Qumrân Cave 1 (1QapGen), some columns are visible only as empty contours after the skin under the ink had decomposed.

Red inks were used on papyrus scrolls in ancient Egypt, on the Aramaic plaster inscriptions found at Tell Deir ʿallā (see IV.A.3 above), and on some Qumrân scrolls.

See also INK.

5. Containers. The ancient Egyptian scribes used wooden palettes with two cavities, one for black ink and one for red. They also had cases for their writing instruments; such cases are also known from Assyrian reliefs and are mentioned in the OT (Ezk. 9:2f., 11).

Stone inkpots were found in the ruins of the scriptorium at Khirbet Qumrân, similar to the inkpots used in Roman times. Also in the scriptorium were found plaster tables that the scribes probably used. In other cases the scribes did not need special furniture. In Egypt they would sit with crossed legs while writing, as attested by statues (*see* picture in EDUCATION). Occasionally short scrolls or tablets were written while standing, as shown by Assyrian reliefs.

V. Shapes of Graphical Signs.–In ancient writing systems, the shapes of the graphical signs were determined by their original function, but then were often modified to conform to new writing techniques, surfaces, and instruments as they were developed.

In the oldest logographic systems (see III.B above), real objects are often clearly reflected, as in the oldest Sumerian writing in lower Mesopotamia and the oldest writing of Crete. The objects depicted on the oldest Sumerian tablets were gradually simplified as the linear signs were written with a sharply pointed instrument.

Real objects were depicted in considerable detail and with great care in the Egyptian hieroglyphic (the term means "sacred carving") writings carved on stone or written on papyrus scrolls. These shapes persisted for three thousand years without considerable change, to the very end of the use of the Old Egyptian writing system. For certain documents, the hieroglyphics were graphically simplified into *hieratic* ("priestly" writing), in which only a few signs remained of the original pictures. A further radical simplification of the sign in the *demotic* ("popular," "ordinary") script led to a set of graphically simple signs, some of them quite unlike their old models.

For the mostly syllabic Hittite writing, the term *hieroglyphic* is also used due to the external similarity — but not affinity — with the Egyptian signs. Real objects can also be recognized in some "pseudo-hieroglyphic" signs from Byblos and in some Proto-Sinaitic signs.

While the use of writing with pens or brushes on soft surfaces enhanced the tendency to form linear signs often with rounded features, writing or carving of letters on hard surfaces, such as stone, ceramics, or metal, required geometric forms, preferably straight strokes with sharp angles.

Even more demanding in this direction was the technique of writing on clay tablets with a stylus angular at the end, which left on the clay either short lines beginning with a wedge, or angle wedges only. The CUNEIFORM signs appear as combinations of a few basic wedge-formed elements, arranged in certain directions only. In this way, in nearly all cuneiform signs the connections to original pictures were obliterated.

In the fully developed Mesopotamian cuneiform writing, only two basic forms of wedges appear, the long stroke with a wedge at its beginning, and the angle wedge, in the form of an isosceles triangle pointing to the left. As the directions of the long wedge were more and more limited — vertical with wedge on top and horizontal, oblique with wedge on the left — the resulting signs had to be highly stylized. Very few relationships to the original pictograms can be observed.

For the Ugaritic cuneiform alphabet, only the minimal number of basic signs was selected and put together in simple combinations; the requirement of graphical simplicity prevailed.

A change of signs from prevalently pictorial to linear occurred in the West Semitic alphabet. Many ancient signs in the Proto-Sinaitic inscriptions reflect real objects, some of them according to their Egyptian hieroglyphic stylization. In the later West Semitic alphabets used in Palestine, Phoenicia, and Syria these original signs were simplified. A graphic simplification of the Proto-Sinaitic alphabet in a different direction led to the development of the ancient South Arabic letters.

A similar transition from pictorial "hieroglyphic" signs

Pictographs on a rock face at Serābîṭ el-Khâdim on the west side of the Sinai Peninsula (L. T. Geraty)

to linear writing systems (labeled A and B) can be observed also on Crete during the 2nd millennium B.C.

In the Aramaic alphabet, adopted also by the Jews and other Semitic communities in western Asia, linear letters were gradually simplified in a cursive direction. This eventually led to similar forms which had to be distinguished by diacritical marks (see III.C.3.a above).

In late antiquity and in the early Middle Ages, the Jews tried to shape their alphabetic letters of Aramaic origin into a square or quadrate frame. This writing, used for the Torah scrolls and other biblical MSS, is therefore called "square script." It has been adopted since the 15th cent. A.D. for printed Hebrew letters. A more cursive type of Hebrew writing was used for medieval biblical commentaries and MSS, later in printed books (the so-called Rashi script).

In Greek writing, adopted from the West Semitic alphabet, one can observe a tendency to make the letter more symmetrical; some are symmetrical to the vertical axis (e.g., A, Δ, Λ), some to the horizontal axis (e.g., B, Σ), and some to both (O, Ξ, X). Such a tendency is observable also in the Roman alphabet and in the South Arabic alphabet.

The tendency to symmetry was stronger in monumental inscriptions in which each letter was separated. In cursive writing the linking of letters and attempts to make the writing fluent and fast led again to some violation of symmetry. This can be observed in Greek and Latin minuscules in late antiquity and in the early Middle Ages.

In the time of the so-called Carolingian Renaissance (*ca.* A.D. 800) the return to classical forms led to more regularity. In the period of Gothic art the shapes of letters followed also the general tendency to more angular forms with accentuation of vertical strokes. In the late Middle Ages the distinction between capital and small letters was introduced.

Some changes in the shape of signs in various systems were caused by changes in writing direction, in writing technique, and in the arrangement of writing surfaces. As the writing direction in ancient Mesopotamia changed from vertical to horizontal, the signs were accordingly turned 90 degrees. Also the Greeks, after they adopted the West Semitic alphabet, turned some letters 90 degrees; thus the Greek A is symmetrical to the vertical axis, while the West Semitic *aleph,* pointing to the left, is symmetrical to the horizontal axis.

VI. Direction of Writing.–In most ancient Near Eastern writing, the signs were arranged in horizontal lines, in some writing systems going from left to right, in other systems usually from right to left. In the oldest Mesopotamian written documents the signs are arranged in a vertical direction from top to bottom of the written surface. The oldest Egyptian writing is also arranged vertically. The vertical arrangement reappeared much later, at the beginning of the Christian era, in Syriac rock inscriptions.

Most written texts from the biblical period are arranged in horizontal lines. The signs go mostly from right to left in ancient Egyptian texts, whether hieroglyphic, hieratic, or demotic. The same right-to-left direction was adopted for the West Semitic alphabet and used with very few exceptions by Phoenicians, Israelites and Judeans, and Arameans. The most ancient Greek inscriptions followed their West Semitic models in this respect.

A left-to-right arrangement in horizontal lines was used in nearly all kinds of cuneiform writing, by Sumerians and Akkadians in Mesopotamia, by Hurrians in northern Syria, and by Hittites in Asia Minor. This direction was also used in alphabetic cuneiform systems, either consistently, as in the Ugaritic alphabet, or partially, as in Old Persian.

There are a very few instances of the left-to-right direction for the West Semitic alphabet; one of them is the alphabet on the stone tablet dated *ca.* 1100 B.C. from ʿIzbet Ṣarṭah near Aphek (Antipatris), about 25 km. (15 mi.) E of Jaffa.

A combination of horizontal lines written alternatively from right to left and then left to right, like the furrows plowed in a field — hence called in Greek *boustrophēdón,* "as the ox turns" — was tried in the beginning of their alphabetic writing by the Greeks, but was soon abandoned. (The same practice is attested also in Hittite hieroglyphic writing and in some Old South Arabic inscriptions.) Eventually in the Greek alphabet and in the alphabets derived from it — Latin, Coptic, Gothic, and Old Slavonic — the left-to-right system prevailed.

A Hebrew abecediary found at ʿIzbet Ṣarṭah, 1200-1000 B.C., the oldest Hebrew inscription discovered (The Institute of Archaeology, Tel-Aviv University; photo M. Weinberg)

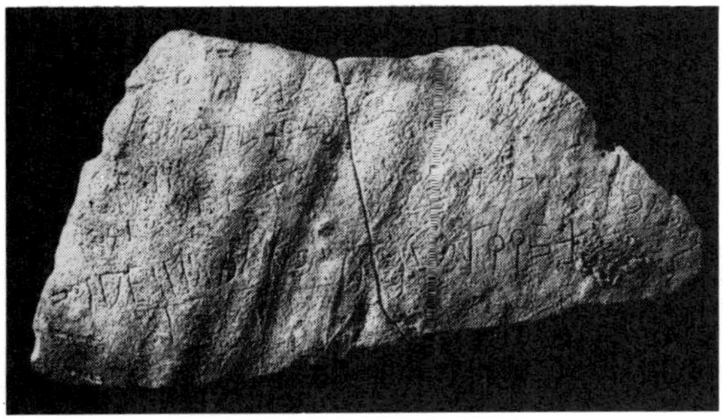

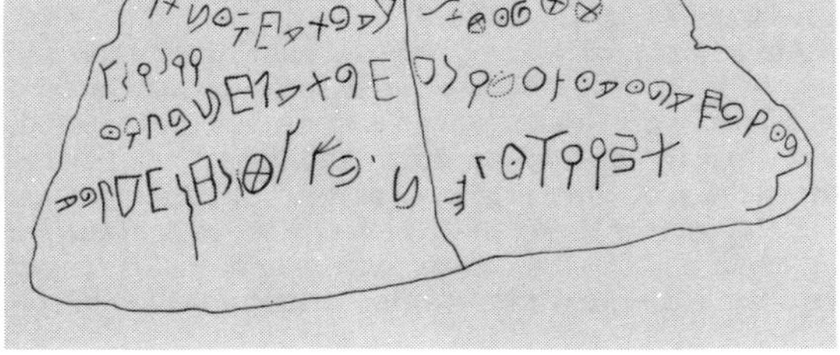

VII. Text Divisions.–A. Division of Words. In the oldest Mesopotamian and Egyptian writing systems, each word was expressed by a special word-sign (logogram; see III.B above).

In the Egyptian hieroglyphic writing, the phonological signs for consonants and their combinations were added as closely as possible to the logograms; no word dividers were used. (The names of gods and kings were written within a "cartouche," an oval frame.) In logographic, syllabic, and related writings the word boundaries could be recognized without the use of special dividers.

Dividers appeared in the oldest larger alphabetic texts. In the Ugaritic cuneiform alphabet small vertical wedges were used in nearly all written texts. Particles containing one consonant only were written together with the following word, although in some nonliterary texts they were separated by the word dividers.

A similar system was used in the oldest West Semitic alphabetic linear inscriptions. Words were divided by vertical strokes (Phoenician inscriptions from Byblos, 10th cent. B.C.; Aramaic inscriptions from Hamath, 8th cent. B.C.), or combinations of two or three dots arranged vertically (Aramaic inscription from Tell Fekherîyeh, *ca.* 850 B.C.). In the inscription of King Mesha of Moab (*ca.* 850 B.C.) words are separated by dots, while the vertical stroke served to separate sentences. In Phoenician and Aramaic inscriptions from Sam'al (Zenjirli) in north Syria (8th cent. B.C.) dots or very sharp vertical strokes were used as word dividers. In most Hebrew preexilic inscriptions and ostraca words are separated by dots, not always consistently. This system was continued in conservative postexilic Hebrew texts using preexilic types of letters, in some Qumrân scrolls, and even later in the Samaritan inscriptions and MSS.

In the Aramaean script adopted by the Judeans in the postexilic period, five letters (*k, m, n, p, ṣ*) have different forms when written at the end of a word.

In later Phoenician and Aramaic inscriptions word dividers were not used. This continuous writing (*scriptio continua*) makes the reading sometimes ambiguous.

Most of the ancient Greek texts written on stone, papyrus, and parchment from late antiquity are in continuous writing. Because a Greek word can end only on *n, r, s*, or a vowel, the reader could distinguish the words rather easily. (Cf. variants in Rom. 7:14; 1 Tim. 3:16.)

In the 1st cent. A.D. the words began to be divided by short spaces. This system was then gradually adopted for writing in the Greek and Latin alphabets, though some MSS in the 4th cent. A.D. (e.g., Vaticanus, Sinaiticus) still did not have word dividers. In the later scripts derived from the Greek and Latin alphabets, words are divided by spaces.

Neither in the Semitic alphabets nor in the ancient Greek and Roman alphabets were special forms developed for initial letters of words or sentences. This differentiation began only with Roman letters in the late Middle Ages, when texts were written in cursive minuscule writing and then only for special reasons — for the beginning of a sentence or section, proper names, etc. — were the large (majuscule) letters used.

Already in ancient Egyptian and cuneiform texts, and also in Hebrew and Greek texts, some corrections and additions were made. Incorrect signs were ereased, scratched, or marked by dots. Additions were put between lines, on the margins, or at the ends of paragraphs.

B. Division of Verses and Sentences. Already in ancient Egyptian and Mesopotamian texts, words that belonged together in a sentence were often written together in columns or lines, sometimes separated by thin lines drawn between them.

In Akkadian and then in Ugaritic cuneiform tablets, verses or cola were often set on separate lines. In some Akkadian poetic texts verses and half-verses were marked by vertical signs. In the Ugaritic poem about the wedding of two lunar deities (*UT,* 52) half-verses are marked by dividers while the words are mostly written together. Some psalms and some other poetic texts in the Qumrân Scrolls are written in lines reflecting the verse structure. In traditional Hebrew biblical MSS only some poetic passages, such as Dt. 32, are written in lines coinciding with poetic verses.

Major Greek biblical MSS from the 4th cent. A.D. present most poetic OT books in stichic arrangement, each verse on one line.

Certain accent signs used in the Hebrew biblical MSS since the 9th cent. A.D. can be conveniently used as help for delimiting clauses and sentences, even if they were not primarily meant for this purpose. The division of Hebrew biblical texts into so-called verses by a sign and into half-verses and their parts by a very elaborate system of accent signs serves primarily for the cantillation of biblical sections in synagogue worship.

Punctuation signs for indicating limits of sentences and their parts in Greek were introduced first in the Hellenistic period, but stabilized only in the late Middle Ages. An interrogative sign has been used only since *ca.* A.D. 800. The punctuation in the modern editions of the Greek NT was introduced by modern scholars; many of the variants listed in the apparatus of the critical editions affect the meaning significantly. The punctuation in Latin texts followed Greek models.

In MSS of the Masoretic Hebrew Bible additional information about words is given on margins, with longer remarks on the tops and bottoms of pages.

VIII. Development of Writing Systems in the Ancient Near East and in the Greco-Roman World.–The following survey presents those writing systems that are for various reasons important for the study of the Bible. In general their sequence is chronological. For the background of the OT the logographic systems of Mesopotamia and Egypt are important. The West Semitic alphabet and the Greek alphabet were used for writing the biblical books in their original languages. Writing systems in which the ancient versions of the OT and the NT were transmitted are also mentioned.

The following survey is in many points based on relatively little data. Only a fraction of the ancient written documents has survived until the present day and only a small fraction of them has been discovered. While the cuneiform texts on clay tablets survived well and thousands of them were accordingly unearthed, comparable papyrus and leather documents had less chance to survive.

The principles of the main writing systems — logographic, syllabic, and alphabetic — have been outlined above (III; see also Gelb).

A. Sumerian Cuneiform. The oldest written documents appeared in lower Mesopotamia at the end of the 4th millennium B.C. Since the original signs expressed entire words, while no phonological features were indicated, it is not immediately clear what language was fixed in these documents. Most probably it was Sumerian, the language that is contained in somewhat later texts, according to their phonological complements. Many of these archaic texts were found in the ruins of the city of Uruk (biblical Erech, now Warka), in the strata from the time shortly before 3000 B.C. These oldest written documents were purely logographic: one word, one sign. Additional signs were used as determinatives or semantic indicators (see III.B above).

Even a high number of logograms in the old Sumerian writing — about 2000 — did not suffice to express all words. Therefore the system was gradually phonologized, as described above (III.C.1).

Sumerian, which is not related to any other known language, is agglutinative, i.e., grammatical morphemes are added to the core words without changing them. A graphical system using both logograms and syllabograms was thus very convenient for this type of language. It seems that some rare consonants were not clearly distinguished from similar sounds. Since some syllabic signs consisted of one vowel only, this syllabic system had enough flexibility to indicate also words of foreign origin. This flexibility made it possible later to adapt this syllabic-logographic system for other languages. Even the retaining of logograms provided some convenience comparable to the use of graphical symbols (such as $ or &) or abbreviations. The use of the same type of writing contributed greatly to economical and cultural contacts between different areas and peoples of the ancient Near East.

But the cuneiform word-syllabic system was still very complicated. It was necessary to master several hundred signs, some of which were used for more than one word or syllable. Many of these signs could be read in more than one way. Although some simplification was reached through selective use of signs and their values in various local scribal schools and traditions, the ability to write and to read was always limited to a small segment of the population, especially to professional scribes and priests.

B. Akkadian Cuneiform. People who came in contact with the Sumerians began to adopt the Sumerian writing system on clay tablets, often with some adaptations. The inhabitants of ancient Elam discontinued use of their old syllabic linear writing in favor of the Sumerian cuneiform writing system.

The Semitic Akkadians who lived near or among the Sumerians used first not only the Sumerian writing but also the Sumerian language for their written records. Their identity is visible from their Semitic names, written mostly by syllabic signs.

The Akkadians accepted from the Sumerians both logographic and syllabic cuneiform signs, and gradually developed a principally syllabic form of writing (see III.C.2 above).

While in the Sumerian language the function of consonants and vowels in word formation was not in principle different, in the Semitic languages the consonants convey the basic meaning of words and the vowels serve to modify them. The number of consonantal phonemes in Old Akkadian and in later dialects was greater than in Sumerian. As Sumerian syllabic signs were adopted they often served indiscriminately for syllables with related but not identical Akkadian consonants; e.g., the dentals, voiced /d/, unvoiced /t/, and emphatic /ṭ/, were not always distinguished in syllabic signs used by Akkadians. But the vowel components of syllabic signs adequately expressed the Akkadian vowel system. Combinations of syllabic signs were also occasionally used for indicating long vowels and doubled consonants, which are important in the formation of Semitic words.

By the frequent use of syllabic signs and a more limited use of logograms the number of cuneiform signs used in different variants of Akkadian writing (Old Akkadian, and Old, Middle, and Late Babylonian and Assyrian) was more than five hundred. Thus in Akkadian cuneiform, elements of two systems, logographic and syllabic, and of two totally different languages, Sumerian and Akkadian, were mixed together.

The requirements for learning and using such a complicated system remained high; thus literacy remained limited. The difficulties were enhanced by the ambiguity of many signs that could be read either as words or as syllables with different values. For example, one sign, which originally depicted the rising sun, could be read as one of seventy different words, as an element in one of more than two hundred word-signs, or as one of several dozen different syllables (e.g., *ud, ut, uṭ, tu, du, ta, tam, ṭam, pir, par, laḫ-, liḫ-, maḫ-*; see G. R. Driver). On the other hand, one syllable could be represented by many different signs, e.g., for *du* not less than thirteen signs are attested.

Cuneiform syllabic writing was used for the Akkadian language until both came to an end. The last cuneiform Akkadian documents were written in the middle of the 1st cent. A.D.

The number of preserved Akkadian cuneiform texts, mostly on clay tablets, some on stone, amounts to many thousands. They have been found not only in the areas where the Akkadian language in its various dialects, Babylonian and Assyrian, was spoken, but also in colonies, such as Assyrian commercial settlements at Kanesh (Kültepe) in Cappadocia in the early 2nd millennium B.C., or where Akkadian and cuneiform writing were used for international contacts and local administration, as in Mari, Alalakh, and Ugarit in Syria during the 2nd millennium B.C. Akkadian letters, documents of various kinds, and even literary works were found in many sites outside Mesopotamia, in Asia Minor, Syria, Phoenicia, Palestine, and even Egypt.

C. Cuneiform in Ebla. Since 1974 many thousands of cuneiform tablets have been discovered by Italian archeologists at TELL MARDIKH in central Syria, in the ruins of ancient Ebla or Ibla, capital of a kingdom powerful in the middle of the 3rd millennium B.C. The language spoken in this kingdom was Semitic, but its precise character is not yet determined. It shares many features with the East Semitic Akkadian in its old stage, while some other features can be found in ancient West Semitic Canaanite languages. The main reason for the uncertainty is the use of Sumerian cuneiform in Ebla. In the texts published until 1983 the logographic signs are principally used, in some documents almost exclusively. The meaning of such texts can be recognized, but the very limited use of syllabic signs for indication of Semitic inflectional morphemes gives only partial information about the local Semitic language. More language is contained in Semitic personal, divine, and geographical names, written mostly by syllabic signs. This type of cuneiform writing for the Eblaite language was used only for a limited time, *ca.* 2500-2300 B.C.

D. Cuneiform in Syria and Palestine. In the 2nd millennium B.C. the Akkadian language, mostly in its Middle Babylonian dialect, served as a diplomatic, administrative, commercial, and cultural language in Syria and Palestine. It was written in Babylonian cuneiform, with some local peculiarities, some of which can be explained by the traditions of scribal schools, some by influence of the locally spoken Northwest Semitic languages of the Canaanite type. In these syllabic cuneiform texts many Northwest Semitic geographic, personal, and divine names are preserved, and also some general words (sometimes marked as glosses) and sentences.

From the first part of the 2nd millennium B.C., a great

number of cuneiform texts was preserved in the ruins of MARI (Tell el-Ḥarîrî) on the middle Euphrates in east Syria. These texts, unearthed by French archeologists, provide ample information about the history, administration, social structure, and religion of this area; also thousands of Amorite personal names are known from these sources. From the middle of the 2nd millennium B.C. cuneiform Akkadian texts from Alalakh (Tell ʿAtshânah) in northwest Syria (near Antioch) provide ample documentation about the local Canaanite kingdom.

The Akkadian language in syllabic cuneiform was used in the 14th cent. B.C. for correspondence between the kings of Egypt and their vassal kingdoms in Syria and Palestine and also with rulers of independent states in this area. About four hundred letters from places such as Ugarit, Byblos, Hazor, Megiddo, Shechem, Jerusalem, and Lachish were found at Tell el-Amarna in Middle Egypt (*see* AMARNA TABLETS). Some of these texts contain Canaanite forms and expressions. From the 14th and 13th cents. B.C. hundreds of syllabic cuneiform texts were preserved and excavated at Ugarit. Such texts attest to the international and local use of cuneiform syllabic writing for diplomatic, administrative, commercial, and religious purposes.

Assyrian and Babylonian domination of Syria and Palestine in the 8th to 6th cents. B.C. left a few texts there.

E. Hurrian and Hittite Cuneiform. Mesopotamian cuneiform writing was adopted by the Hurrians, a people living in the 2nd millennium B.C. in upper Mesopotamia and in north Syria. Hurrian texts using mostly syllabic signs are preserved mostly from the middle of the 2nd millennium B.C. A long Hurrian letter from the kingdom of Mitanni in north Syria was found at Tell el-Amarna in Egypt. A few Hurrian texts in local Ugaritic alphabetic writing were found at Râs Shamrah. The texts in both these writing systems can be read, but since Hurrian is a language unrelated to other languages except Urartian, the meaning of many words and texts remains unknown.

The Urartian language was used in the country called in antiquity Urartu (biblical Ararat, 2 K. 19:37; Jer. 51:27; also Gen. 8:4), modern Armenia. For this language cuneiform writing with mostly syllabic signs was used in the manner similar to the related Hurrian.

As the Indo-European Hittites settled in the center of Asia Minor in the middle of the 2nd millennium B.C., they adopted the cuneiform writing probably from their Hurrian neighbors. Syllabic signs were convenient for indicating Indo-European inflectional morphemes, while the logograms in Hittite texts provided the clue for determining the character of this language. Cuneiform was used for official documents of the Hittite empire and also for religious texts. Many texts of this kind were found at Ḫattušas (Boghazköy) in central Anatolia.

Syllabic-logographic cuneiform was used not only for Indo-European Hittite, called by the Hittites *nasili,* "Nesian," but also for the old Anatolian languages of this area called *ḫattili,* "Hattic."

Cuneiform was no longer used after the collapse of the Hittite empire *ca.* 1200 B.C., but syllabic pseudo-hieroglyphic writing, used for stone inscriptions, survived it for five centuries. These texts are in a language closely related to "cuneiform" Hittite and even more to Luwian, another language known from some Boghazköy cuneiform texts.

F. Egyptian Writing. The beginning of the Egyptian writing system can be dated shortly before 3000 B.C. It is probable that the general idea of expressing words of a language in writing was brought to Egypt from Sumerian Mesopotamia. The oldest written monuments attest the purely logographic stage, but in the oldest texts understandable to modern scholars, phonological signs appear in connection with the logograms.

Egyptian hieroglyphs from Abu Simbel, temple of Ramses II (1301-1234 B.C.) (D. H. Condit)

Egyptian logograms carefully depicted real objects. Very soon these signs were used also for other words or their parts that were pronounced with the same consonants. While these "phonological complements" in Sumerian writing were mostly syllabic, in Egyptian writing only vowelless consonants were indicated. This disregard of vowels was prompted by the structure of the Egyptian language, in which, as with the Semitic languages, the basic meaning of the words is expressed by consonants, while the vowels modify the basic concepts.

The number of logograms in the oldest stage of Egyptian writing was about one thousand; there were also determinatives, as in Sumerian, and signs for singular, dual, and plural, consisting of one, two, or three short strokes.

The phonological complements could repeat some or all consonants of the words written by word-signs, e.g., the word for "good" was written by the word-sign *nfr* with added complements for all its consonants: *nfr.n.f.r.*

Egyptian word-signs could contain one consonant — e.g., *r,* "mouth," probably pronounced [ra] — or two consonants — e.g., *pr,* "house," probably pronounced [paru] — or three consonants — e.g., *nfr,* "good." Many of these same logograms were also used for indicating consonants, individually or in groups of two or three. Although the Egyptians had in their inventory of signs more than twenty for individual consonants, they never took the opportunity to create a consonantal alphabet.

The Egyptian script took three forms: hieroglyphic, hieratic, and demotic (see V above).

Egyptian writing was not used for other languages. It even proved difficult for writing names and words of foreign origin; for this purpose signs for phonetically weak consonants were used to indicate some vowels.

In the kingdom of Meroë S of Egypt (now in north Sudan) a writing system imitating the Egyptian system in forms but using Greek alphabetic principles was in use from the 3rd cent. B.C. to the 4th cent. A.D.

Christians in Egypt replaced the ancient script by the Coptic script, which was derived from the Greek alphabet, with the addition of a few signs for specific Coptic sounds.

G. Hittite "Hieroglyphs." A system using syllabic signs with some word-signs, similar to hieroglyphs in shape, is preserved in Hittite texts since the middle of the 2nd millennium B.C. Most monuments were found in the late Hittite states of the 10th to 8th cents. in north Syria.

H. Cretan Writings: "Hieroglyphic" and Linear. On the island of Crete, during the 2nd millennium B.C., two writing systems were introduced: the so-called Cretan hieroglyphic writing and its successor, Linear writing A, which in turn was followed *ca.* 1500 B.C. by Cretan Linear writing B. The oldest written records of the Greek language used Linear B. The syllabic Linear B did not adequately express all sounds of archaic Greek. It does not indicate many syllable-closing consonants.

Linear B was used for economic and administrative records. In the upheavals after 1200 B.C. caused by the invasion of Peloponnesus and Crete by a new Greek wave, the Dorians, the knowledge of writing was virtually lost. It survived with some modifications on the island of Cyprus, where this syllabic system is represented by inscriptions from the 7th-3rd cents. B.C.

I. Iranian Writing Systems. Several writings systems were used for the Indo-European Iranian language and its dialects in antiquity. One imperfect attempt to overcome the complicated system of syllabic-logographic cuneiform was made by the Persians. The inscriptions of kings Darius (522-486 B.C.) and Xerxes (486-465 B.C.) are written in a system consisting of twenty-one syllabic signs and of thirteen signs indicating one consonant only to which a vowel can be added in reading; four special signs, such as for "king," are a relic of the logographic system. Three signs express vowels only: *a, i, u.* This type of writing, known only from royal inscriptions, was used only for a limited time. Most of these Old Persian inscriptions are accompanied by Elamite and Babylonian versions in syllabic cuneiform.

Greek letters were used by eastern Iranians in the Hellenistic period. The Persians in other areas utilized the Aramaic alphabet; the shapes of letters were considerably simplified, so that some were not sufficiently distinguished. In the Pahlavi writing in Persia (since the 3rd cent. B.C.) and in the Sogdian type used in areas E of the Caspian Sea, a new logography appeared: words written in Aramaic letters were read in Persian according to their meaning, e.g., *mlk,* Aram. *malkâ,* "king," was read as the Persian word for "king" (*šah*). Persian phonological complements indicated inflectional morphemes. In this type of writing the Zoroastrian sacred books (Avesta) were preserved, and it is still used by the Parsis.

J. West Semitic Alphabet. 1. First Attempts. A radical simplification of writing systems developed in an area where both the Egyptian and the Akkadian writing systems were known. From the Egyptian model the principle of graphical signs expressing one single consonant, and most probably some shapes of signs, was adopted; from the Mesopotamian cuneiform writing was derived the concept of adapting a writing system or its elements to another language.

About the middle of the 2nd millennium B.C. in Palestine and in the Canaanite cities on the western shore of the Mediterranean Sea several attempts were made to introduce a new, simple writing system. The ancient tradition preserved in Greek sources locates the invention of this new writing in Byblos. This important commercial center formed intensive connections at sea with Egypt and later also with the Aegean area. Inscriptions have been found that are probably remains of an attempt for a simple writing system with a limited number of signs. In inscriptions from the mid-2nd millennium B.C. more than one hundred signs are represented. This number may point to a syllabic system (see IX.B.2 below).

The largest set of inscriptions from the mid-2nd millennium B.C. in which an alphabetic writing with fewer than thirty consonantal letters may be sought, was found at the Egyptian turquoise mines at Serâbîṭ el-Khâdim in the western part of the Sinai Peninsula. Semites who worked in the mines probably made the inscriptions carved on rock and on stone statues. For these old inscriptions the term "Proto-Sinaitic" is used, in order to distinguish this writing from the much later Sinaitic Aramaic inscriptions.

Similar inscriptions from the mid-2nd millennium B.C. with signs similar to some Egyptian hieroglyphs or some letters of the West Semitic alphabet were found in Palestine, at Gezer, Lachish, Shechem, Hazor, and some other sites. Very old specimens of this type are short inscriptions from *ca.* 1600 B.C. found during the excavations of Gezer. The fragment of Lahav in southern Palestine may be a little older.

2. Ugaritic Alphabet. A West Semitic alphabet consisting of thirty letters was discovered at the excavation at Râs Shamrah on the north Syrian coast. While the previously mentioned alphabetic writings are of the linear type, the alphabet of the ancient city of Ugarit is written in cuneiform signs. It is attested, mostly on clay tablets, from the last two centuries of the existence of this wealthy Canaanite political and commercial center, destroyed *ca.* 1200 B.C. The first tablets were discovered in 1929, and the alphabet was deciphered one year later. The letters are written, as in the other cuneiform writings, from left to right, with very few exceptions. The identity of the letters was determined and confirmed due to the affinity of this north Canaanite language with other Semitic languages.

On several clay tablets all thirty letters of the Ugaritic alphabet are presented in their traditional order, which corresponds in general to the order of the twenty-two letters of the Hebrew alphabet. Five more consonants represent consonants not represented in the Phoenician and Hebrew inventory of consonants. As they are more or less evenly distributed throughout this alphabetic list, the Ugaritic alphabet and its order is obviously more original than that of twenty-two letters. Three letters at the end of the alphabet are clearly late additions. The very last one imitates by its form the West Semitic letter *s* (*samech*); it stands for the syllable /su/. The two signs preceding it indicate the glottal stop (Heb. *aleph*) plus the vowels /i/ and /u/: *i* and *u.* The first sign of this Ugaritic alphabet is used for the glottal stop plus the vowel /a/: *a.*

For more about the Ugaritic alphabet, see III.C.e above; *see also* CUNEIFORM; UGARIT.

A few short inscriptions in the Ugaritic cuneiform alphabet were found in Lebanon (Sarepta, Kumid el-Loz), in Palestine (Mt. Tabor, Taanach, Beth-shemesh), and on Cyprus (Hala Sultan Tekke near Larnaka-Kition).

3. Phoenician Alphabet and Its Local Variants. Phoenician and Palestinian inscriptions from the Iron Age (after *ca.* 1200 B.C.) are written in a linear alphabet consisting of twenty-two consonantal letters only. (Originally, Phoeni-

A receipt for grain on a tablet inscribed in alphabetic cuneiform. From Taanach, early 12th cent. B.C. (Taanach Expedition, courtesy A. Glock)

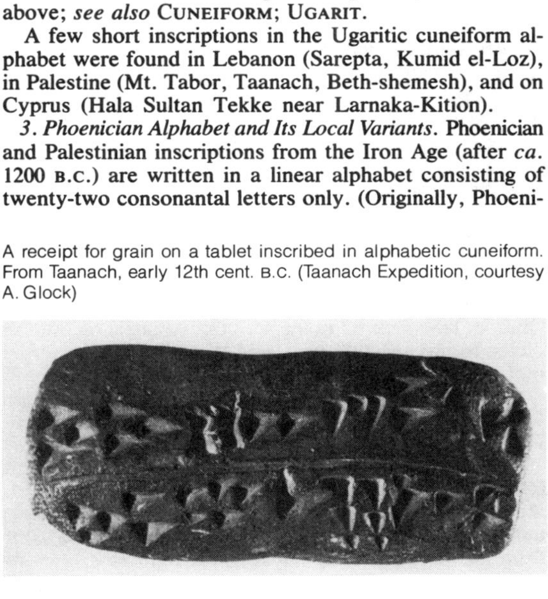

cian probably had twenty-seven consonantal phonemes.) From the 12th/11th cent. B.C. only a few short inscriptions on bronze arrowheads from Lebanon and from el-Khadr near Bethlehem are known.

The oldest Phoenician inscriptions were found in the ancient city of Byblos (Gubla). The inscription of the stone sarcophagus of King Aḥiram is now dated to *ca.* 1000 B.C. Inscriptions from later periods were found in Sidon, ʿAmrit, and other Phoenician sites at the coast and in their colonies on Cyprus. In the Phoenician colonies in the western Mediterranean, archaic writing is attested on the inscriptions from Sardinia (Nora) and Spain. A later type of writing used in Carthage is called Punic. The Phoenician language and alphabet were also used for inscriptions in areas where Phoenician merchants lived (Crete, Greece) and for official inscriptions in north Syria (Sam'al/Zenjirli) and Asia Minor (Karatepe).

a. Palestine. In Palestine the Phoenician alphabet was adopted with slight changes: the shapes of some letters were slightly modified, and at the end of some words "weak" consonants were used to indicate long final vowels.

The inscription from *ca.* 1100 B.C., found at ʿIzbet Ṣarṭah near Aphek, about 24 km. (15 mi.) E of Jaffa, contains an alphabet of twenty-two letters in the sequence known from later Hebrew tradition with a slight variant (*peh* before *ayin*), but written from left to right. From a slightly later time the so-called Gezer Calendar and texts written on sherds (ostraca) found at Tell el-Qasîleh on the northern outskirts of Tel Aviv are preserved.

For writing on sherds (ostraca) and on perishable media, cursive shapes of letters were developed, as the Samaria ostraca attest. On seals and letters, shapes similar to those on stone inscriptions were used. Most of the inscriptions on stone from Palestine are written in carelessly carved letters. Longer inscriptions are known from the vicinity of Jerusalem (Siloam spring, Silwan) and from the Negeb (Kuntillet ʿAjrūd). An ostracon found at Yavneh Yam, S of Jaffa, contains a complaint of a laborer named Hoshayahu against withholding of wages (cf. Dt. 24:15). Ostraca with a rather cursive Hebrew writing were found in greater numbers at Lachish (SW of Jerusalem), Arad (SE of Hebron), and Beer-sheba (in the Negeb). Their cursive writing is characterized by the rounded shapes of letters, with dots for word dividers. The long inscription of King Mesha of Moab from the middle of the 9th cent. B.C., found in Dibon in 1868, exhibits forms of letters corresponding to those in contemporary Palestine (*see* MOABITE STONE). Moabite and Edomite seals, too, were written in such letters.

The Palestinian type was used as the traditional script even in the postexilic period for special purposes. Coins of some Hasmonean kings were inscribed in the archaic Hebrew script, as were coins struck during the uprisings against Roman rule (A.D. 66 and 132). Among fragmentary scrolls found in Qumrân caves 4 and 11, those in old Hebrew (Paleo-Hebrew) script represent Genesis, Exodus, Leviticus, Deuteronomy, and Job. In some nonbiblical Qumrân MSS written in the script of Aramaic origin, the divine names *yhwh,* "Lord," and *'l,* "God," are written in archaic Hebrew letters.

Samaritans also have used this type of script since the Roman period for their inscriptions and their books in Hebrew and Aramaic.

b. Aramaic. When the Arameans adopted the Phoenician alphabet at the beginning of the 1st millennium B.C., they did not immediately change the shapes of the letters; only gradually did unique Aramaic types develop. But from the very beginning the Arameans introduced an innovation of great importance: they started to indicate vowels — at first long final vowels and later medial vowels as well — by letters used for phonetically related consonants (see III.C.e.[2] above). This violation of the alphabetic principle — one letter for one phoneme — was made easier by a similar inconsistency in writing the consonants: Early Aramaic possessed a few more consonantal phonemes than the twenty-two expressed by the same number of letters in the Phoenician alphabet.

This Aramaic stone inscription from Sfire (8th cent. B.C.) is part of the treaty between Mati'el king of Arpad and Bir-Ga'yah, a Mesopotamian suzerain (W. S. LaSor)

From the early period (10th-7th cents. B.C.) are preserved stone inscriptions from north Syria, Tell Fekherîyeh and Tell Ḥalâf in the northeast, Sfire near Aleppo, Hamath in central Syria, and Damascus in southern Syria. In the northern Syrian kingdom of Sam'al (Zenjirli in southern Turkey), Phoenician, standard Aramaic, and a local Aramaic dialect were all used for inscriptions, but the shapes of the letters did not differ significantly. Aramaic inscriptions are also known from the Jordan Valley, from Dan, from Ein Gev, and from Tell Deir ʿallā on the river Jabbok.

The forms of the Aramaic letters also influenced the Ammonites. A few short inscriptions in their language close to Hebrew are written in letters similar to the Aramaic type.

Aramaic language and writing were also used on ostraca and clay tablets in Mesopotamia. In the Neo-Babylonian empire during the 6th cent. B.C. the Aramaic language was also used for administrative purposes. When the Persians conquered Babylon, they made Aramaic the official language in major parts of their empire. This "Imperial (or Official) Aramaic" was used in many areas of the Persian empire, from India to Asia Minor, from Caucasus to Egypt. Aramaic inscriptions are known from areas where Aramaic was not commonly spoken, such as India, Afghanistan, Caucasus, Lydia, and Arabia; some of them are accompanied by parallel texts in other languages.

In Egypt official letters sent from Persia (the Arsham correspondence) and administrative Persian documents on leather and papyrus have been preserved, as well as private letters (e.g., the papyri from Hermopolis). The greatest number of Aramaic papyri and ostraca from the 5th cent. B.C. was found on the island of Yeb (called in Greek Elephantine, in the river Nile near Sewen, Greek Syene, now Aswân). In this Jewish military colony, which guarded the southern border of Egypt for the Persians, Aramaic was used for legal documents, private letters, and for religious purposes. *See* ELEPHANTINE PAPYRI.

(1) Aramaic Script in Judaism. In the Babylonian exile

Cuneiform tablets with Aramaic dockets and seal impressions of Darius II of Persia (courtesy of the University Museum, University of Pennsylania)

and after the return to Palestine, the Jewish community replaced their old Palestinian script with the Aramaic script.

This newer script is attested in some inscriptions and also in the papyri left by the Samaritans who were besieged by the soldiers of Alexander the Great in the caves of Wâdī Dâliyeh E of Nâblus. Jewish Hebrew and Aramaic scrolls left by the Jewish religious community in the Qumrân caves are written in this type of writing, with only a few exceptions, as are the texts left in the caves in the Judean desert from the Bar Cochba war (A.D. 132-135). Jewish inscriptions on ossuaries (bone boxes) and other funeral inscriptions in the vicinity of Jerusalem and in the necropolis of Beth-shearim (E of Haifa) as well as synagogal inscriptions from Palestine and other countries were written in a more formal type of writing that developed from the Aramaic type. The form that developed by regularizing cursive letters into square frames is called "square" script. It was used for rather formal purposes, in books and inscriptions.

(2) Local Aramaic Scripts. After the end of the Persian empire (332 B.C.), the uniformity of the Aramaic language and writing was no longer upheld by a central official use, and several local dialects and types of script developed. Some of them became very important for the further development and extension of alphabetic writing.

The NABATEANS, an Arabic people living in Hellenistic and Roman times E and SE of the Dead Sea, used the Aramaic language and script for their inscriptions. Later this type of writing was adopted by the other Arabs. The oldest Arabic inscription is preserved from the end of the 4th cent. A.D. The Arabs later simplified and schematized the shapes of letters. They developed various types for monumental inscriptions and a cursive that is very convenient for rapid writing.

Another local variant of Aramaic writing is attested by many inscriptions from the Roman period in the oasis of Tadmor (Palmyra) in the Syrian desert, an important commercial, administrative, and religious center.

Yet another local type of Aramaic language and script developed in Hatra in northern Mesopotamia. Inscriptions, mostly from the 2nd cent. A.D., offer much data about the religion of this city.

The local dialect and script of the city of Orhay (Greek Edessa, now Urfa in southeast Turkey) were well developed even before Christianity was adopted by the local rulers *ca.* A.D. 200. The Syriac dialect of Aramaic became the language of an important branch of Christianity. The old type of script (*estrangela*) developed in two directions, according to main trends and groups in which Syriac Christianity was divided, Eastern (Nestorian) and Western (Jacobite). Each of them developed a special type of writing with special systems for indicating vowels by signs below or above the letters. Besides a large number of MSS, Syriac inscriptions from pre-Christian and Christian times are preserved.

The Gnostic community of Mandeans that survived in small numbers in Iraq and adjacent areas of Iran used and preserved its own type of Aramaic alphabet. It is characterized by a consistent use of consonants for all vowels. Besides many MSS, old inscriptions on lead scrolls are also known.

Various types of Aramaic writing were used on magic bowls with inscriptions in various Eastern Aramaic dialects written in spirals or concentric circles on their inner sides (more rarely the outer); many such texts have been found in Iraq.

(3) Aramaic Script Adopted by Non-Aramaic Peoples. The Aramaic alphabet was also adopted by many non-Aramaic peoples for languages of various linguistic groups. These developments followed political and later religious lines. The Aramaic script was adopted in Hellenistic and later times by various Iranian peoples (see VIII.H above). After the conquest of Alexander the Great, the Aramaic script penetrated as far as India. In northwestern India it served as a model for the Brahmi script. In this system the vowels were indicated by graphical variants of basic forms of the consonants. From this ancient script many other scripts further developed that were used for the Indo-European and Dravidian languages in India and for various languages of India.

A kind of alphabet of Aramaic origin, perhaps Pahlavi, was used as model and source for the invention of the Armenian alphabet, ascribed to Mesrob. The Georgian alphabet was developed on a similar basis. Both the Indo-European Armenians and the Caucasian Georgians adopted Christianity in the 4th cent. A.D. The Bible translations and other religious texts in their respective languages deserve to be studied, as they preserve some old traditions otherwise lost.

Manichaean and later Christian (Nestorian) missions brought their sacred texts written in Syriac or related alphabets to various peoples of central and east Asia. Through the translations of religious literature and through imitations of the Aramaic alphabet, several new alphabetic scripts were developed, which were used at least temporarily by various Turkish peoples. Mongolian and Manchurian writing goes back to the Aramaic alphabet.

The Aramaic type of the West Semitic alphabet thus survived after the Phoenician and Palestinian types were long forgotten and served as the basis for many scripts, some of them important directly (Hebrew, Syriac, Armenian, Georgian) or indirectly (Mandean, Pahlavi of Avesta, Manichaean) for biblical studies.

4. South Arabian Alphabet. From a comparison of the forms of the letters and their number, it can be determined that the alphabetic writing attested in southern Arabia (now Yemen) developed from an older alphabetic writing similar to that known from the Proto-Sinaitic inscriptions. The number of consonantal letters is twenty-nine. The forms of the letters vary slightly according to the local types, Minaean, Sabean, Ḥimyaritic, and Hadramautic.

The inscriptions, mostly on stone buildings and statues, date from about the 8th cent. B.C. (or earlier) to the rise of Islam in the 7th cent. A.D. Very regular monumental letters are arranged from right to left, left to right, or both alternately in boustrophedon. *See* pictures in SABEANS.

This type of writing in cursive form was used from the 6th cent. B.C. by nomadic north Arabic tribes, Thamudaeans and Liḥyanites in the oases and Dedanites in the Ṣafa region. Those inscriptions carved on rocks provide information about their ancient religion.

The Ethiopians, who migrated from Arabia to Africa about the beginning of the Christian era, used at first the South Arabic consonants only. From the 3rd cent. A.D. they began to indicate vowels by graphical modification of the consonants. Christian Ethiopic literature preserved some pseudepigraphic books, such as the book of Jubilees and 1 Enoch.

5. Greek Alphabet and Derived Alphabets. Both ancient traditions and the comparison of the shapes and values of the alphabetic letters clearly indicate that the Greeks derived their alphabet from the Western Semites. They called these letters "Phoenician"; tradition connected them also with the name of Kadmos, the mythical newcomer from the east to Thebes. The oldest Phoenician written document found on Greek soil is a short inscription on a bowl found in a tomb at Tekke in south Crete, dated from the type of its letters to *ca.* 1000 B.C. The oldest Greek alphabetic texts can be dated to *ca.* 750 B.C. It is not clear when the Greeks adopted their alphabet, but it seems prudent not to go much beyond the oldest written texts.

Already the oldest Greek written alphabetic texts from the 8th cent. B.C., the inscription on a ceramic vase from Athens and the inscribed sherds from Mt. Hymettos, show consistent use of special letters for vowels. The Greek alphabet is based on the principle of "one sound, one letter"; its innovation against the West Semitic alphabet is the consistent use of letters for vowels in all positions in the word. Both short and long vowels were indicated in the beginning by the same letters; only later were additional letters for two long vowels, *ē* and *ō*, introduced (see III.C.3.e.[4] above).

The order of letters in the Greek alphabet derives from the West Semitic alphabet of twenty-two letters. The names of the letters are evidently of Phoenician (or Aramaic) origin; many of them were slightly modified to fit the Greek word structure. The shapes of the letters in most ancient Greek inscriptions are similar to those used in Phoenician texts of the northern periphery; most of these letters are also similar to those of Aramaic texts from north Syria.

While the Phoenicians in their homeland indicated only consonants, the Arameans already in the 9th cent. B.C. used some consonant letters for vowels (see III.C.3.e above). Some of these Aramaic vowel letters, *aleph, he,* and *yodh,* correspond to the Greek vowel letters *a, e,* and *i* in their form and value. This device was introduced by the Greeks to supplement the strictly consonantal alphabetic system, since in Greek the communicative function of vowels is higher than in the Semitic languages. Some letters not necessary for Greek were gradually omitted. Signs of Semitic origin were used for the combination of two sounds, [k] + [s] and for the aspirate [th]. Eventually a few additional signs were introduced, for [p] + [s] and [k] + [h] and for the long vowels [ē] and [ō]. The functions of some additional signs were different in various geographical variants of the Greek alphabet.

The introduction of the Greek alphabet coincides with the beginning of Greek colonization to the east and the west. In the oldest Greek colony in the western Mediterranean, Pithekoussai on the island of Ischia in the bay of Naples, besides Greek inscriptions, short Phoenician and Aramaic inscriptions have been found. The Greeks also came in contact with Phoenicians and Arameans in the commercial centers on the eastern shores of the Mediterranean. It is difficult to determine the place where the Greek alphabet was first conceived. Probably the tablets containing the twenty-two letters of the alphabet in the traditional sequence were instrumental in this process.

The Greek alphabet served as a model for the writing systems of several peoples of Asia Minor, the Phrygians, Lydians, Lycians, and Pamphylians.

The Etruscans introduced some minor changes in the shape and value of letters. Their alphabet was adopted by the Romans for their Latin language. Again some changes in the shape of letters, in values, and in the sequence of letters appeared.

Important biblical versions are preserved from antiquity in Coptic, the latest stage of the Egyptian language; in Gothic, a Germanic language used at the Black sea; and in Old Church Slavonic (Cyrillic letters), used in the Balkans and in central and eastern Europe. For the other alphabet used in Church Slavonic texts, "glagolitic," no pedigree could be determined.

IX. Study of Writing.–There is no generally accepted term for the study of writing. "Grammatology," the term introduced by I. J. Gelb and used also by J. Derrida (based on Gk. *grámma,* "letter"), fits well into the system of terms for various scientific disciplines. "Graphemics" has been proposed as a term for the study of graphical signs.

A. Subdisciplines. Among the special disciplines of the study of writing, paleography and epigraphy are important as tools for better understanding the Bible and its background. Both of these terms derive from Greek: *palaiós,* "ancient," *graphḗ,* "writing," *epigraphḗ,* "inscription." Their areas are not exactly determined and in practice often overlap.

Paleography is the study of ancient and medieval MSS. This term is sometimes limited to those in Greek and Latin, but this method can be applied to Hebrew MSS as well. Especially important is the comparison of the types of the letters and the tracing of their development. It is possible to establish a typological series; on the basis of them, if a document can be dated in terms of absolute chronology, it provides a fixed point for the other parts of the series. Reliable results have been reached in this way for dating the Hebrew and Aramaic Dead Sea Scrolls and of Greek and Coptic biblical papyri from Egypt.

Epigraphy is defined as the study of inscriptions, of records written on hard material. Sometimes its use is extended to clay tablets from Mesopotamia, Syria, and Crete. Epigraphic methods have been successfully applied to Hebrew and other inscriptions from the biblical period.

Several disciplines deal with inscriptions written on objects with a special function. Sphragistics is the study of seals. Numismatics is the study of coins and their inscriptions, called "legends." Recently the hybrid term "codicology" has been used for the study of MSS and printed books.

B. Decipherment of Forgotten Writing Systems. The writing systems used for the canonical texts of the Bible, Hebrew and Aramaic of the OT, Greek of the NT, were transmitted through copying, reading, and studying by religious communities, Jewish and Christian respectively, from antiquity until the present time. Also, the writings in which the most important ancient biblical versions were fixed have been used without interruption (Latin, Syriac, Coptic, Arabic, Ethiopic, Old Church Slavonic; an exception is Gothic).

Many writing systems used widely in the ancient Near East for long periods did not survive the end of their language or of the existence of their national or religious communities. The most recent documents in Egyptian hieroglyphs and in Akkadian cuneiform were written probably in the 1st cent. A.D. Other writing systems important for biblical studies went out of use even before that time. Some writing systems survived only in a form changed so considerably that they were no longer understood. In general, the survival of the understanding of a written system was conditional on the existence of a community using it actively or at least passively.

Some written monuments have been known and accessible since antiquity, even if no longer understood. Egyptian hieroglyphs on obelisks — several of them carried to Rome already in antiquity — and on temple walls remained the focus of interest. But inscriptions visible on rocks in remote areas of Syria, Asia Minor, and Persia were forgotten. Many written documents, especially smaller ones, were buried for many centuries and discovered, some by chance, some in systematic excavations only in modern times.

Most of the major writings of the ancient Near East have been successfully deciphered. Those writings that have defied decipherment are represented by a small number of monuments that do not allow a reliable confirmation of proposed readings or cannot be related to any known language.

1. Successful Decipherments. Since the 18th cent. various methods of decipherment have been successfully applied. Some attempts have been aided by the similarity of the unknown writing system with a better-known writing system. Most helpful has been the affinity of the new language with an already known language. Where neither graphical similarity nor related language was available, the decipherment did not succeed.

First among those forgotten writings deciphered were two West Semitic alphabets. The French scholar Jean-Jacques Barthélemy was able to determine the values of the alphabet used in the inscriptions in the Aramaic language in the Syrian oasis city Palmyra, written in the 1st-3rd cents. A.D. This successful decipherment in 1754 was followed four years later by his decipherment of the Phoenician alphabet, for which some partial results had previously been reached. Both these writing systems are alphabets of twenty-two signs corresponding in their values and their system to those of well-known related Semitic languages, Biblical Aramaic or Syriac and Hebrew, respectively, but they were deciphered with the help of parallel texts in Greek.

The writing of the Old South Arabic inscriptions from pre-Islamic times — some of them written already in the 8th cent. B.C. if not earlier — was identified in the 19th cent. with the help of its later descendant, the Ethiopic alphabet. The scripts derived from the South Arabic alphabet used by North Arabic tribes, Safaitic and Thamudic, were then deciphered by Enno Littmann at the beginning of the 20th century.

The decipherment of Egyptian hieroglyphic writing and its graphically simplified later stages was long hampered by the persuasion — based on Chinese writing studied in Europe since the 18th cent. — that the hieroglyphic pictorial signs expressed whole words only. The clue to the decipherment was provided by the inscriptions on the stone found at Rosetta in the Nile Delta during Napoleon's expedition in 1799. It contains three parallel texts: two Egyptian, one in hieroglyphic writing, the other in demotic writing, and their Greek version. It took François Champollion some twenty years to combine these data with those contained in Coptic alphabetic texts and achieve a successful decipherment, presented in 1822.

The first information about cuneiform writing reached European scholars in the 17th century. Copies of inscriptions of this type of rock were available only at the end of the following century. The first attempts — shortly after 1800 — to decipher Persian inscriptions in a very simple syllabic cuneiform system were presented by Georg Friedrich Grotefend, a high school teacher in Göttingen. He identified the names of some Persian kings known already from Greek sources, but did not fully succeed because of the then insufficient knowledge of the ancient Persian language that survived in the Avesta and other religious writings.

The cuneiform inscriptions and tablets from Mesopotamia became available in larger quantities only during the first half of the 19th cent. after they were excavated from the ruins of ancient Assyrian sites. The multiple values of many word-signs and syllable-signs, as well as the scripts from different periods, hindered the decipherment. But it was helped by ancient cuneiform lists in which the meaning of word-signs was indicated by syllabic signs. It was recognized that the language of most cuneiform tablets from Assyria and Babylonia was Semitic, and the comparison with Hebrew and Arabic words helped to determine the meaning of words of the ancient East Semitic language, later called Akkadian. Among the scholars who participated in the decipherment, shortly after 1850, the names of Edward Hincks and Henry Creswick Rawlinson are prominent.

Once the system of cuneiform word-syllabic writing used for Semitic Akkadian was established, it was possible to apply its syllabic and logographic values to cuneiform texts in other languages. This cannot be considered as a true decipherment of writing, but as the discovery of a previously unknown language and the determination of its structure and of word meanings.

This process led eventually to the understanding of the texts in the Sumerian language, spoken in lower Mesopotamia in the 3rd millennium B.C. and known as a sacred and literary language until the 1st millennium B.C. Names and loanwords appearing in both Sumerian and Akkadian helped in this effort. The task was difficult because Sumerian is not related to any other known language, and various dialects and systems of scribal devices appeared in the texts. Many translations or texts of Sumerian origin preserved in Akkadian helped to solve the problems and confirm the results. Only at the beginning of the 20th cent. was a fairly satisfactory understanding of Sumerian achieved, although some texts are still not understood.

Cuneiform tablets found at Boghazköy in central Asia Minor could be read but not understood. In 1915 B. Hrozný recognized that they render a language belonging to the Indo-European family. This discovery of Hittite provided the basis for the decipherment of "Hittite hieroglyphics," the other writing used in Hittite territories. The efforts of several scholars were summarized and extended by I. J. Gelb in the 1930's. Previous results were to a great extent confirmed after parallel texts in hieroglyphic Hittite and Phoenician were found at Karatepe in southeast Turkey in 1947.

Cuneiform texts in the Hurrian language from north Syria and adjacent countries can be read, but the structure of the language and the sense of the texts have been only partially determined, since this language is not related to any other better-known language.

The less complicated a writing system, the sooner it can be deciphered. This was demonstrated in the case of the cuneiform tablets found at Râs Shamrah (Ugarit) on the north Syrian coast in 1929. In the following year, three scholars, Hans Bauer, Paul (Edouard) Dhorme, and Charles Virolleaud, working independently but each using some results of the others, reached the conclusion that the cuneiform represented an alphabet of the West Semitic type. The affinity of Ugaritic to Hebrew, Arabic, and other Semitic languages made this rapid decipherment possible. The results were confirmed thirty years later by a tablet containing Ugaritic alphabetic letters provided with close syllabic cuneiform equivalents.

Bilingual texts can aid a rapid decipherment. Phoenician texts helped not only to confirm the decipherment of Hittite hieroglyphs after 1947, but seventy years before provided a clue to the decipherment of the Cypriote syllabary used by the Greeks. Inscriptions in this writing are preserved from the 7th-3rd cents. B.C. from various sites on Cyprus.

A relatively long time separated the find of the first inscriptions in Cretan Linear B, *ca.* 1900, from its decipherment, achieved in 1954 by British architect Michael Ventris. The names of places and persons known from Greek sources helped identify some syllabic signs. It was not expected that the language of these texts from the 15th-14th cent. B.C. found at Knossos on Crete would be identified as Greek, but with the help of classical philologist John Chadwick the structure of this most archaic Greek dialect was determined. The application of the results to documents in this writing found in Pylos on the Greek mainland confirmed the results.

2. Ongoing Attempts at Decipherment. Decipherments of several writings have been presented but not unanimously accepted. The consensus is stronger in some instances than in others.

The decipherment of the West Semitic Proto-Sinaitic inscriptions from the mid-2nd millennium B.C., begun by Alan Gardiner in 1915 and completed by W. F. Albright in 1948, can be supported by the similarity of the alphabetic signs with those of later Phoenician or Palestinian type; it is also possible to draw a line to the ancient South Arabic alphabet, which had twenty-nine consonants.

The so-called pseudo-hieroglyphic inscriptions from Byblos, which in general precede the alphabetic Phoenician inscriptions from the same site, can be considered syllabic because of the relatively large number of signs. The attempt to interpret them as being written in a rudimentary alphabet, presented by one of the decipherers of Ugaritic, Edouard Dhorme, in 1946, is now abandoned. After several preliminary announcements, G. E. Mendenhall published his decipherment in 1985. He presented a list of syllabic characters in which twenty-four consonants are combined with the vowels *a, i,* and *u*. The texts represent, according to Mendenhall, an archaic West Semitic language of the coastal area.

The writing attested on some documents from the Late Bronze Age found in Cyprus and also in Ugarit is called Cypro-Minoan, because of the similarity of some of its signs to the systems of the Aegean area. A decipherment presented by Emilie Masson seems to fit the requirements for a successful solution.

Even though the values of the Cretan Linear A writings correspond to those of Linear B, no attempts to interpret these texts in a Semitic or other language is considered successful. The difficulty lies probably not in the writing system but in the strange character of the language; the situation seems to be similar to that of cuneiform texts in Hurrian, or to that of Etruscan written in readable Greek letters.

Besides these not yet deciphered scripts, represented by a relatively large quantity of inscriptions, some monuments bear obviously graphical signs, which are either totally isolated or represented in very small quantities. Short and mostly fragmentary inscriptions on stone and ceramic from the Late Bronze Age found in southern Palestine contain some graphic signs similar to those of the Proto-Sinaitic inscriptions; some seem to be closer to the later standard West Semitic alphabet. From the area E of the Dead Sea a badly worn stone stele found near Bālūʿ, perhaps from the 11th cent. B.C., is known. Its characters are similar to the South Arabic alphabet. During Dutch excavations at Tell Deir ʿallā several clay tablets from about the 11th cent. B.C. were found, with graphical signs not similar to any hitherto known. Divisions by lines seem to indicate boundaries of words or sentences. In Late

A clay tablet from Tell Deir ʿallā, *ca.* 11th cent. B.C., inscribed in a presently undeciphered (though apparently alphabetic) script (Department of Antiquities, Jordan)

Bronze Age Crete, besides two types of linear writing (A and B) and two older "hieroglyphic" types, some isolated remains of other systems have been found. Very interesting is a clay disk from Phaestos on which the signs, in a spiral arrangement, are not written but stamped in clay.

*X. **Writing in the Bible.***–The writing used for the biblical books in their original languages is alphabetic: the West Semitic alphabet for the OT in Hebrew and Aramaic, and the Greek alphabet of the NT.

The heading "writing" covers both the activity and the results of it and also some terms relating to them, indicating the writing system — such as "alphabet" — or characteristic products of writing, such as "book" and "scroll."

A. Biblical Words for Writing. In the OT the English verb "write" reflects the Hebrew verb *kāṯaḇ*; verbs of similar meaning are *rāšam,* "record," and *ḥāraṯ,* "engrave." The root *ktb* also occurs in Biblical Aramaic. The original meaning of Hebrew and Aramaic *ktb* was apparently "to carve," as it indicated writing on hard surfaces with the help of a sharp instrument. The Greek equivalent *gráphō* and words derived from it appear in the LXX and in the NT.

In the OT the verb *kāṯaḇ* is used in connection with material on which someone writes (writing *on*), or with a document that is produced by writing (writing a letter, book, etc.), less frequently with the person to whom the writing is addressed (writing *to*). Often the person who writes is the author; scribes taking dictation from another person are also mentioned.

The use of the root *ktb* in the Aramaic passages of the OT corresponds to that in Hebrew; it is used for writing on the plaster of the wall (Dnl. 5:5), writing down of names (Ezr. 5:10) or of a dream (Dnl. 7:1), writing of edicts or letters (Dnl. 6:25 [MT 26]; Ezr. 4:8; cf. also Ezr. 5:7, 6:2). The Aramaic verb *rešam* also means "write," but specifically what is written or inscribed (Dnl. 6:8f. [MT 9f.]; 5:24f.). In Dnl. 10:21 (Hebrew) this verb is used in the same way.

In the Greek OT the verb *gráphō* is used regularly for *ktb*. In accordance with its original Greek meaning it can also be used for "carve," translating Hebrew *qlʿ* (cf. 1 K. 6:29). The use of *gráphō* for "write" in the apocryphal books corresponds to that in the books represented in the Hebrew canon: to write a document (Tob. 6:14; 13:1; 1 Macc. 10:17; 15:24), to write down in a list (1 Macc. 8:20).

In the Greek NT the verb is provided with prefixes in *engráphō,* "write in" (Lk. 10:20), and *prográphō,* "write before" in time (Rom. 15:4; Eph. 3:3) or publicly (Gal. 3:1).

Hebrew nouns derived from *ktb* are *keṯāḇ* and *miḵtāḇ,* indicating mostly "writing" as a written document. The word *keṯāḇ* is used for a kind of script in the Persian empire (Est. 1:22; 3:12; 8:9; cf. also Ezr. 4:7). The word *miḵtāḇ* can be used also for writing or ornaments engraved on some object (cf. Ex. 32:16; 39:30). Both these Hebrew words for written documents are translated in the AV by "writing," while the RSV tries to distinguish their various kinds, such as "edict" or "decree" (Est. 8:8; 4:8), "register" (Ezr. 13:9), "letter" (Ezr. 4:7).

Greek NT nouns related to *gráphō* are mostly translated into English by other words than "writing": *grámma,* "letter" — but "writings (of Moses)" Jgs. 5:47; *graphḗ,* "scripture(s)"; cf. also *grammateús,* "scribe."

B. Ways of Writing. 1. Writing Media. Specific writing surfaces are mentioned in the Bible. The stone tablets (pl. *lûḥôṯ*) on which the Decalogue was written are understood as simple stone surfaces in which the writing (*miḵtāḇ*) was carved (pass. part. *ḥārûṯ*); cf. Ex. 32:16. According to Dt. 27:2-4 the laws were to be written on big stones covered with plaster on which the letters were written (*ktb*). A large writing tablet (*gillāyôn*) is mentioned in Isa. 8:1.

In the NT, the priest Zechariah wrote the name John for his son on a writing tablet (*pinakídion,* Lk. 1:63). Writing tablets made of wood also appear in the Latin apocryphal book 4 Ezr. (2 Esdras) 14:24; rapid scribes had to use these tablets to write ninety-four books at Ezra's dictation in forty days.

The tool for engraving letters on hard surfaces, probably a piece of metal with a sharp point, is indicated by the Hebrew word *ḥereṭ* (Isa. 8:1); see also Ex. 32:5, "stylus" (cf. NEB mg. on Isa. 8:1; "pen" is not an adequate rendering). Another Hebrew word for this instrument is *ʿēṭ* (Jer. 17:1; Job 19:24; cf. also Ps. 45:1 [MT 2]). In the Greek translation general terms for writing instruments are used: *graphís* (Isa. 8:1) and *grapheíon* (Job 19:24). Since in Hellenistic times reed pens were used by scribes (*graphikós kálamos,* 3 Macc. 4:20), the term *kálamos,* "reed/pen," is also used in rendering Ps. 45:1 (MT 2; LXX 44:2) and in the NT (3 Jn. 13). A "diamond point" (*ṣippōren šāmîr*), mentioned in parallel with "stylus" in Jer. 17:1, served for engraving (*ḥrš*) hard surfaces.

The function of lead (*ʿōpereṯ*) mentioned in Job 19:24 together with the iron stylus is not clear. Probably the carved letter shapes were filled with lead, as it is done in a small part of King Darius's inscription at Behistun. In later times lead sticks were used for writing on soft surfaces, like pencils much later.

For black ink the word *deyō* is used in the OT (Jer. 36:18), *mélan* in the NT (1 Cor. 5:11; 2 Jn. 12; 3 Jn. 13). Red ink was used in OT times, in the Aramaic Deir ʿallā inscription, and in some Qumrân scrolls, but the Hebrew word *šāšar* is used only for red paint in the OT (Jer. 22:14; Ezk. 23:14).

The scribes had their tools in a writing case (*qeseṯ*), which could be fastened at their waist (Ezk. 9:2). This Hebrew word is derived from the Egyptian word for the scribe's palette, *gst(y)*.

2. The Book. The Hebrew word most frequently translated as "book," *sēper,* indicates any written document. It can be a document of divorce (Dt. 24:3; Isa. 50:1), a genealogical list (Neh. 7:5), or a historical record or book (Mal. 3:16; Est. 6:1).

The book is characterized by its content, e.g., of the words of the Lord (Nu. 21:14), of the words of Solomon (1 K. 11:41), of the covenant (2 K. 23:2); often the book of the law (Dt. 28:61; Josh. 8:34), or of the law of God (Josh. 24:26; cf. Neh. 8:18), or of the law of Moses (Josh. 8:31), or simply the book of Moses (Neh. 13:1). In the postexilic books these expressions refer to the canonical books of the Law; this reference is clear in 2 Macc. 2:23, where five books are mentioned. In many instances the word "book" refers to those represented in the Hebrew biblical canon, such as books of Kings (2 Ch. 16:11) or the Kings of Judah and Israel (2 Ch. 25:26); cf. also the book of Lamentations (2 Ch. 35:25).

The Greek equivalent of "book," *biblíon,* is used in the Apocrypha also for the book of the law or of Moses (1 Macc. 1:56f.; Tob. 7:12f.) or for the apocryphal books themselves (cf. Tob. 1:1; Bar. 1:3; and esp. the translator's prologue to Sirach).

The scroll as a special form of a written document, especially a book, is mentioned many times in Jer. 36 (cf. also Ps. 40:7 [MT 8]; Ex. 2:9). As poetic metaphors the flying scroll (Zec. 5:1f.) and a scroll that must be eaten (Ezk. 3:1-3) are mentioned. The Hebrew word for scroll, *megillâ,* which indicates something that can be rolled, is rendered in Greek as *chartíon* or *chártēs* (Jer. 36, LXX 43; cf. also 2 Jn. 12), the word for papyrus. Another writing material, parchment (*membrána*) is mentioned in 2 Tim. 4:13.

In the NT the words for "book," *biblíon* and *bíblos,* indicate OT books (Mk. 12:26; Lk. 4:17; 20:42), the books of the NT (cf. Jn. 20:30; 21:25; Rev. 1:11; 22:7, 18f.; cf. also Mt. 1:1), "the book of life" (cf. Rev. 13:8; 20:15), and books of judgment (Rev. 20:12).

3. Writing Procedures. Usually writing was put on only one side of the writing surface; rarely are instances of the use of both sides mentioned (Ex. 32:15; Jer. 36:2; Rev. 5:1).

A detailed description of how the writing was done and even how it could be destroyed is recorded in Jer. 36; the prophet Jeremiah dictated "from his mouth" to his friend Baruch who wrote on a book in the form of a scroll (*megillaṯ sēper*). The book was then read by the king's counselors and then by King Jehoiakim himself. As he did not like the message, he cut the columns of the book with the scribe's knife and then burned them in the fire. The material may have been papyrus, which smells pleasant when burnt, while leather would have produced a bad odor. The destroyed book was then replaced by a new one.

4. God and Writing. While the Egyptians credited the god Thoth with the invention of writing and the Babylonians ascribed it to the god Nabû, writing is not considered a divine gift in the Bible. God used it as an instrument in revealing His law to Israel, written on stone tablets (*lûḥōṯ hā'eḇen,* Ex. 24:12). The book (*sēper*) written by God is mentioned in Ex. 32:32.

5. Unusual and Metaphorical Writing. Besides regular writing materials, such as stone tablets and books in the form of scrolls, some unusual writing surfaces for special purposes are mentioned.

Writing on doorposts (Dt. 6:9) had to be perhaps performed on their wood; this biblical prescription was later obeyed by fixing small scrolls with biblical quotations in small boxes on the doorposts (cf. Heb. *mezûzâ*). Writing on rods is also mentioned (Nu. 17:2f. [MT 17f.]). In Isa. 44:5 writing on the hand (or by hand?) is mentioned.

Not only in the framework but also in the narrative sections of the book of Revelation writing appears frequently: the names of the faithful are written down (19:12), they bear the name of God on their foreheads (14:1; 17:5; cf. 3:12) and also on their robes (19:6).

Metaphorical uses include writing on the tablet of the heart (Prov. 3:3 and 2 Cor. 3:2; Jer. 31:33 and He. 8:10).

Writing on earth (Jer. 17:13) indicates something futile. Jesus' writing on sand is mentioned in the adulteress pericope (Jn. 8:6), perhaps symbolizing the impermanence of the particular word.

In the Hebrew OT a code called *'aṯbaš* was used to conceal some names. Instead of the first letter of the alphabet, the last was written; instead of the second, the next-to-last; etc. Thus the name *ššk* (*šēšāḵ*), "Sheshak," in Jer. 25:26; 51:41 stands for *bbl* (*bāḇel*), "Babylon," and *lb qmy* (*lēḇ qāmāy*), "heart/midst of them that rise against me," in Jer. 51:1 for *kśdym* (*kaśdîm*), "Chaldeans." Thus the name of the enemy was presented in cipher. *See also* ATHBASH.

By a device called *not(a)rikon* the consonants of a word could be understood as initial letters of other words. Such interpretation of *'yk* (*'ēḵ*), "how," in Jer. 3:19 as *'[āmēn] y[hwh] k[î],* "so be it Lord, for," is attested in the LXX *génoito kýrie hóti.* In Jer. 7:4, *hmh,* "they," could be interpreted as *h[am]m[āqôm] h[azzeh],* "this place."

Later Hebrew poetry has examples of the acrostic arrangement, in which the initial letters of lines in a passage can be read together as a name or other word. Aside from alphabetical acrostics, the attempts to find examples in the Hebrew OT (e.g., Psalm 4) may be considered unsuccessful. *See* ACROSTIC.

By a device called in Hebrew *gemaṭreyā'* (from Gk. *geōmetría*) numerical values of letters were used for interpretation of some numbers in Hebrew biblical texts. The number 603,550 for the Israelites in Nu. 1:46 is explained as the numerical value of *bny yśr'l kl r'š,* "sons of Israel, every head/person" (cf. Nu. 1:2). According to talmudic tradition the number of Abraham's servants (318) gives the numerical value of the name of his chief servant *'ly'zr,* "Eliezer" (cf. Gen. 14:14). Another interpretation of the same number 318 (Gk. TIH) is given in the Greek Epistle of Barnabas: T (300) indicates the cross, and I (10) and H (8) are the first two letters of the name of Jesus, ΙΗΣΟΥΣ.

The Solomonic collection has 375 proverbs (cf. Prov. 10:1–22:16). This number can be explained as the numeric value (300 + 30 + 40 + 5) of the letters in the name *šlmh* (*šelōmō[h]*), "Solomon" (Prov. 10:1).

C. Kinds of Written Documents. 1. Laws and Legal Documents. Among the documents written by human beings, the laws appear as very important. The law of Moses was written on stones by Joshua (Josh. 8:32) and by the king in a book (Dt. 17:18). Various legal documents were written: covenant (Neh. 10:1 [MT 9:38]), judgment (Ps. 149:9), bill of divorce (Dt. 24:1, 3; cf. Mk. 10:4), marriage contract (Tob. 7:14). Also the edicts of the Persian kings were written to be sent out (cf. Ezr. 1:1-4; Est. 3:12-15).

Edicts of foreign kings, Babylonian and especially Persian, were written in the form of letters (Dnl. 3:29; 4:1; Est. 3:12-15; 8:5, 8-10, 13f.). Such edicts of Persian kings are preserved in the book of Ezra, in their Aramaic text, from Artaxerxes (4:17-22; 7:12-26) and Darius (6:6-12) or, in Hebrew, like the edict of Cyrus (1:1-4).

2. Letters. Letters were carried by messengers (2 K. 19:9, 14) and were read by them to the addressee (cf. Ezr. 4:33). As already mentioned, the decrees of Persian kings were formulated as letters. They were often issued as answers to letters from officials in the provinces (cf. Ezr. 4:7-16; 5:6-17).

Letters were also used for religious purposes, for announcing festivals such as Purim (Est. 9:20-32), Passover (2 K. 24:21), and celebration of the purification of the temple of Jerusalem (cf. 2 Macc. 1:1–2:18). An Aramaic letter concerning the date and the manner of the celebration of Passover was found at Elephantine.

Letters as religious messages could be issued in the name of an assembly (Bar. 1:3f.), to be read in another place in a Jewish religious assembly. This custom, which was continued in Judaism in NT times, is beyond the function of most NT epistles.

Many letters are mentioned or quoted in the apocryphal books: of King Demetrius and to the Jewish nation (2 Macc. 10:25-45; 15:1-9), of King Alexander to Jonathan (1 Macc. 10:59); of Jonathan to the Spartans (12:5-18) and the answer (12:19-23); letters of the Roman consul (15:15-24); letters of Jews in Jerusalem to Jews in Egypt (2 Macc. 1:1–2:18).

In NT times communication by letters was common between Romans (cf. Acts 23:24-30), Jews (Acts 9:2; 22:5), and Christians. Very important was the letter sent out at the council of the apostles to Christians in Antioch and other cities (Acts 15:20, 23-29).

Paul wrote some letters with his own hand (Philem. 19). At the end of the letter to the Galatians (6:11), he indicated that he wrote it in very large letters. For other letters Paul used the help of scribes to whom he dictated; Tertius wrote the letter to the Romans (16:22). In many other passages in which Paul mentions that he wrote or is writing (cf., e.g., 1 Cor. 5:9, 11; 14:37; 2 Cor. 2:3; 9:1) the authority of the sender is implied (cf. also Eph. 3:3).

The Pastoral Epistles have relatively less mention of writing (cf. 1 Tim. 3:14, similar to 2 Cor. 9:1). The Catholic Epistles also mention writing: the scribe Sylvanus is named in 1 Pet. 5:12; cf. also 2 Pet. 3:11, 15; Jude 3.

See also EPISTLE; LETTERS.

3. Lists. The OT has many lists of different kinds that attest intensive scribal activity. The detailed description of tribal territories with indications of their boundaries in Josh. 15–19 is probably based on ancient administrative records. There were various kinds of lists of persons (cf. 1 Ch. 4:41), such as court officials (e.g., 2 S. 8:16-18; 20:23-26; 23:8-39), priests and Levites (1 Ch. 24–26; cf. Neh. 12:22f.), and exiles who returned (Ezr. 2:1-70). Genealogical records were considered very important; large parts of the books of Numbers and Chronicles are devoted to them; cf. also NT genealogies in Mt. 1:1-17; Lk. 3:23-28. There are many references to written registers of different kinds (cf. Nu. 11:26; Ps. 87:6). In Elephantine lists of persons who contributed to the local Jewish temple are preserved.

4. Historical Records. Historical events were recorded as a memorial in a book (cf. Ex. 17:14; cf. also Mal. 3:16). Kings of Israel and Judah held court records or chronicles for which a special scribe was responsible; cf. those of Solomon (1 K. 11:41), of the kings of Israel (1 K. 14:19), and of Judah (1 K. 14:29).

5. Literary Records. A song of Moses was put in writing and taught to the people of Israel (Dt. 31:19). The proverbs were also written (Prov. 22:20). In the Book of Jashar ancient poems were collected (Josh. 10:13; 2 S. 1:18). Writing was also important for the preservation of prophecies. Prophets were summoned to write their visions (Hab. 2:2; cf. Rev. 1:11) or dreams (Dnl. 7:1). The individual prophecies were fixed in writing (cf. Jer. 45:1). The writing down of Jeremiah's prophecies (Jer. 30:2; 51:60) was mentioned above (X.B.3).

See also SCRIBES.

D. Use of the Alphabet. The concept of the alphabet as a series of letters was used in the Bible for various purposes.

The series of twenty-two Hebrew letters served to mark the beginning of verses or verse groups in an ACROSTIC or alphabetic poem: half-verses (Pss. 111; 112); verses (Pss. 25; 145; Prov. 31:10-31; cf. also Nah. 1:2-8 and Sir. 51:13-30); two verses (Pss. 9–10; 37; Lam 4); three verses (Lam. 1; 2); each of three subsequent verses (Lam. 3); each of eight subsequent verses (Ps. 119). In some of these poems the sequence of letters differs slightly from common use: *peh* precedes *ayin* in Ps. 10 and in Lam. 2, 3, and 4 (see VIII.I.3.a above on the 'Izbet Ṣarṭah inscription). The alphabetic arrangement could serve as help for the memory; perhaps its original purpose was to indicate that the poem is as complete as the alphabet.

The original meaning of the words *'ûrîm* (Ex. 28:30; 1 S. 28:6) and *tummîm* (Lev. 8:8; Ezr. 2:63), used as a tool for obtaining instructions from God, is not clear; the first of these words begins with the first letter of the Hebrew alphabet, the other with the last one; perhaps alphabetic completeness was thereby indicated.

Similar use of the first and last letter of the alphabet appears in the Greek NT; Christ is the *alpha* and the *omega* (Rev. 1:8; 21:6; 22:13), beginning and end.

E. Quotations. 1. In the OT. Already in the OT references to the "book of the law," "law of the Lord," or "law of Moses" appear (e.g., Ezr. 3:2; Neh. 8:13-15; 2 Ch. 16). Quotations from the book of the law are introduced by fixed formulas, e.g., "it is written" (2 Ch. 25:4; 10:35; Dnl. 9:13; cf. Josh. 8:31, 34). Also, some prophecies and prophetic books refer to written texts from which the written form of the source is sometimes visible (2 Ch. 32:32), but not always (cf. Jer. 26:18, 20f.; Ezr. 1:1).

2. In the NT. Most introductory formulas for biblical quotations in the Greek NT are similar in style to the contemporary Jewish formulas and quotations, as attested in the Hebrew MSS from the Qumrân caves. In some NT formulas for quoting Scripture words for speaking are used (e.g., *légō*), even when the quotation does not point to God or a person who spoke but to a written source (e.g., Jas. 4:5f.).

Frequently these formulas expressly mention that a written text is quoted. Passive forms of the Greek verb *gráphō,* "write," are used, the perfect *gégraptai,* "it was/is written," or perfect participle *gegramménon,* "written," corresponding to the passive participle *kāṯûḇ* in contemporary Hebrew formulas.

Most frequent, attested already in the Greek OT (2 K. 14:6), is *kathṓs gégraptai,* "as it is written," e.g., Lk. 2:23; Acts 15:15; Rom. 1:17; 1 Cor. 1:31; cf. also similar formulas in Mk. 7:6; 1 Cor. 10:7; Rom. 3:4. Formulas with the passive participle appear in the LXX in Dnl. 9:13; in the NT in 2 Cor. 4:13 and Jn. 6:31. Similar formulas with an explanatory particle such as *gégraptai gár,* "for it was written," appear, e.g., in Mt. 4:6; Acts 1:20; Gal. 4:27; cf. also v. 22.

Some quotations mention the source: the book of Moses (Mk. 12:26; cf. Gal. 3:10; Jn. 10:34); "the book of the prophets" (Acts 7:42; cf. also Mk. 1:2; Jn. 6:45), "the book of the words of Isaiah the prophet" (Lk. 3:4), the Book of Psalms (Lk. 20:42). Sometimes even texts that are not part of the canonical OT are introduced by a formula used for quotation of the Scriptures, e.g., Mt. 2:23; 1 Cor. 2:9; Eph. 5:14; Jas. 4:5.

F. Writing in the NT. The use of the verb "write" in the Greek NT is very similar to that in the Hebrew OT.

As the author of a Gospel, Luke writes about his purpose (1:3; cf. also Acts 1:1), and mentions previous attempts to compile a narrative from the traditions (Lk. 1:1f.).

The notion of writing is more visible in John's Gospel: the disciple has written the events (21:24); in this book the signs and things could be written only in part (20:30f.; 21:25). The stress on writing appears characteristic for the other NT books marked with the name of John. In the Epistles occur expressions like "I am writing" (e.g., 1 Jn. 2:1), "I write to you" (1 Jn. 2:12f.; cf. 2 Jn. 1; 3 Jn. 13). This graphical character is stressed in 2 Jn. 12, where the writing media papyrus (*chártēs*) and ink (*mélan*) are mentioned. The written character of the message is stressed in the book of Revelation. The letters in chs. 2–3 were to be written (cf. 2:1 to 3:14) to the seven churches, and further the instructions to write are given several times (e.g., 1:11; 10:4; 21:5). Especially important appears the blessing for those keeping what is written therein (1:3) and the formula of protection for what was written in this book (22:18f.); nothing is to be added and nothing taken away. This formula is very similar to those used for protection of Phoenician and Aramaic inscriptions from the beginning of the 1st millennium B.C.

The inscription giving the reason for Jesus' crucifixion is mentioned in the Gospels (Mk. 15:33; Mt. 27:37; Jn. 19:19-22). According to Jn. 19:20 this inscription was written in three languages, Hebrew, Latin, and Greek.

The notion of a book in which the names of the faithful are written is mentioned in Lk. 10:20. *See also* BOOK OF LIFE.

See also INSCRIPTIONS.

Bibliography.–*General Works:* M. L. Carter and K. N. Schoville, eds., *Sign, Symbol, Script* (1984); D. Diringer, *The Alphabet* (3rd ed. 1968); *The Book Before Printing* (2nd ed. 1982); G. R. Driver, *Semitic Writing: From Pictograph to Alphabet* (1954, 3rd ed. 1976); I. J. Gelb, *Study of Writing* (2nd ed. 1963); *Visible Language*, 8/4 (1974), 293-318; C. H. Gordon, *Forgotten Scripts* (1968); J. Naveh, *Early History of the Alphabet* (1982); M. Pope, *The Story of Decipherment: From Egyptian Hieroglyphic to Linear B* (1975).

Origins: G. Buccellati, "The Origin of Writing and the Beginning of History," in G. Buccellati and C. Speroni, eds., *The Shape of the Past: Studies in Honor of Franklin D. Murphy* (1981), pp. 2-13; R. Claiborne, *Birth of Writing* (1974); G. E. Mendenhall, *Syllabic Inscriptions from Byblos* (1985); E. Puech, *RB*, 93 (1986), 162-213; D. Schmandt-Besserat, *Syro-Mesopotamian Studies*, 1 (1977), 31-70.

Special Studies: Y. Aharoni, *Arad Inscriptions* (1981); W. F. Albright, *Proto-Sinaitic Inscriptions and Their Decipherment* (repr. 1969); A. Barucq, *et al.*, *Écrits de l'Orient ancien et sources bibliques* (1986); S. A. Birnbaum, *Hebrew Scripts* (1971); J. Černý, *Paper and Books in Ancient Egypt* (1952); J. Chadwick, *Decipherment of Linear B* (1958); F. M. Cross, "Development of the Jewish Scripts," in *BANE*, pp. 133-202; F. M. Cross and D. N. Freedman, *Early Hebrew Orthography* (1952); J. C. de Moor, J. Hoftijzer, and G. Mussies, "Systems of Writing," in S. van der Woude, ed., *World of the Bible* (1986), pp. 75-120; D. Diringer, "The Biblical Scripts," in *Cambridge History of the Bible*, I (1970), 11-29; H. Donner, and W. Röllig, *Kanaanäische und aramäische Inschriften* (3 vols, 1966-1969); J. Finegan, *Encountering NT Manuscripts* (1974); A. Gardiner, *JEA*, 3 (1916), 1-16; J. C. L. Gibson, *Textbook of Syrian Semitic Inscriptions* (3 vols, 1971-1982); M. Guarducci, *Epigraphia greca*, I (1967); J. Hoftijzer and G. van der Kooij, eds., *Aramaic Texts from Deir 'Alla* (1976), pp. 21-167; L. Jeffery, *Local Scripts of Archaic Greece* (1961); A. Lemaire, *Les Écoles et la formation de la Bible dans l'ancien Israel* (1981); P. McCarter, *Antiquity of the Greek Alphabet and the Early Phoenician Scripts* (1976); G. Mendenhall, *Syllabic Inscriptions from Byblos* (1985); B. M. Metzger, *Manuscripts of the Greek Bible: An Introduction to Greek Paleography* (1981); F. Muzika, *Die schöne Schrift in der Entwicklung des lateinischen Alphabets*, I (1965); J. Naveh, *IEJ*, 23 (1973), 206-208; M. Noth, *OT World* (1966), pp. 202-223; S. Segert, *Klio*, 41 (1963), 38-57; *Writing in Focus* (1983), pp. 131-156; *JNES*, 37 (1978), 111-14; C. Virolleaud, *Syria*, 12 (1931), 304-310; D. J. Wiseman and C. H. Roberts, "Books in the Ancient World," in *Cambridge History of the Bible*, I (1970), 30-66; E. Würthwein, *Text of the OT* (Eng. tr. 1979).

S. SEGERT

WRITING CASE [Heb. *qeseṯ (hassōp̄ēr)* (Ezk. 9:2f., 11)]; AV INKHORN; NEB PEN AND INK. Hebrew *qeseṯ* is apparently a loanword from Egyp. *gst(y)*, "palette." *See* WRITING X.B.1.

WRITING TABLET [Gk. *pinakídion égrapsen*] (Lk. 1:63); AV WRITING TABLE; [Lat. *buxos*] (2 Esd. 14:24); AV "box tree."

Immediately following the birth of his son, Zechariah, who had been struck dumb because he did not believe Gabriel's announcement that Elizabeth would bear a son (Lk. 1:13-20), responded to the people's inquiries about the name of his son by writing on a small tablet (Gk. *pinakídion* is the diminutive of *pinakís*), which was probably covered with wax (*see* WRITING IV.A.6; B.2). He thus confirmed his wife's naming of the child, in accordance with Gabriel's instructions, and hence regained his speech (see K. Barth, *Great Promise: Luke I* [Eng. tr. 1963]).

In 2 Esd. 14:24 the AV's apparently nonsensical "box trees" is a literal translation of Lat. *buxos*, but here *buxos* probably translates Gk. *pyxíon*, which refers to a tablet made of box-wood (see *APOT*, II, 622).

G. A. L.

WYCLIF BIBLE. *See* ENGLISH VERSIONS II.C.

X

XANTHICUS zan'thi-kəs [Gk. *Xanthikos*] (2 Macc. 11:30, 33, 38). The name of a month that corresponds to Nisan (March/April) of the calendar used by the Jews. *See* CALENDAR II.A.2.

XERXES zûrk'sēz [Old Pers. *xšayāršan*; Elamite *ik-še-ir-iš-ša*; Akk. *ḫi-ši-ʾ-ar-ša*; Heb. *ʾaḥašwērôš*; Gk. *Xerxēs*]. The name of two Persian kings.

1. Xerxes I, son of Darius the Great and Atossa, the daughter of Cyrus the Great and sister of Cambyses. Xerxes was designated heir-apparent by his father and served as satrap of Babylon from 498 B.C. to his accession in 486. He is portrayed with his father on the reliefs at Persepolis, where Darius sits on his throne in his robe of state and behind him stands the crown prince (*see* picture in FOOTSTOOL). The winged Ahura-Mazda floats above the scene. This sculpture confirms Xerxes's statement that his father "made me the greatest after himself."

Xerxes lacked the toleration and sensitivity of CYRUS and the foresight of DARIUS (2). Soon after his accession he brutally crushed revolts in Egypt and Babylon. Xerxes did not have the military ability of his predecessors, but urged on by bad advisers he began an assault on Greece in 480 B.C. Herodotus's description of Xerxes' army (vii.56-99) is a most valuable ethnographic document; although he exaggerated the number of soldiers (1,700,000, excluding naval forces), his figure of 1200 ships is confirmed by Aeschylus. Xerxes' preparations included digging a canal near Athos and having a bridge built over the Hellespont by Phoenician and Egyptian engineers. When a storm destroyed the bridge Xerxes ordered the engineers' heads cut off and the waters of the Hellespont given three hundred lashes. A new double bridge was built, and the army crossed over. After being delayed by the Greeks at Thermopylae, the Persians pushed on to Athens and burned the city. Later that year the Persian fleet suffered a disastrous defeat at Salamis, and Xerxes ordered the execution of the Phoenician admiral; after this both the Phoenician and Egyptian fleets deserted him. Xerxes withdrew from Greece, leaving the army in the hands of his general Mardonius. In 479 the Greeks defeated the Persian army at Plataea and, on the same day, the Persian fleet at Mycale. In 466 the Persians were defeated again and forced to give up all the territory that Darius had gained outside of Asia Minor. Xerxes returned home and concentrated on building at Persepolis and Susa. Construction attributed to him at Persepolis includes the completion of the Apadana, his own palace, and the harem (*See* pictures in ARCHEOLOGY OF IRAN).

Xerxes inherited an empire that was basically sound, but he was not equal to the task of maintaining its vitality. The description of his character in Esther (where he is called King AHASUERUS [1]) agrees with evidence from other sources. His undisciplined temper and moral weakness cost him everything he had gained. He died by the hand of an assassin in 465 B.C.

See also PERSIA III.E.

The three main pillars of the gatehouse of Xerxes at Persepolis (L. A. Willis)

Part of the audience hall at Persepolis, begun by Darius and finished by Xerxes (W. S. LaSor)

2. Xerxes II son of Artaxerxes and Damaspia, who was killed after a reign of forty-five days (424 B.C.) by his half-brother Secydianus.

Bibliography.–R. Collins, *Medes and Persians* (1974), pp. 138-148; W. Culican, *Medes and Persians* (1965), pp. 80-82; B. Dicks, *The Ancient Persians: How They Lived and Worked* (1979), pp. 45-47; R. Ghirshman, *Iran* (1954), pp. 190-94; A. T. Olmstead, *History of the Persian Empire* (1948), pp. 230-288. R. E. HAYDEN

Y

YAHWEH. *See* GOD, NAMES OF II.C.

YARMUK yär'mək. The chief river of Transjordan. It is not mentioned in any Jewish writings until Mishnaic times. The first literary appearance of the name is in Pliny *Nat. Hist.* (1st cent. A.D.). Its lack of mention in the OT may be explained by Israel's early loss of control over the plateau of BASHAN. Hence the Yarmuk did not serve as a frontier for Israel, even though in times of strength Israel's territory reached the river or even beyond (cf. mention of Ashtaroth in 1 Ch. 6:71 [MT 56]).

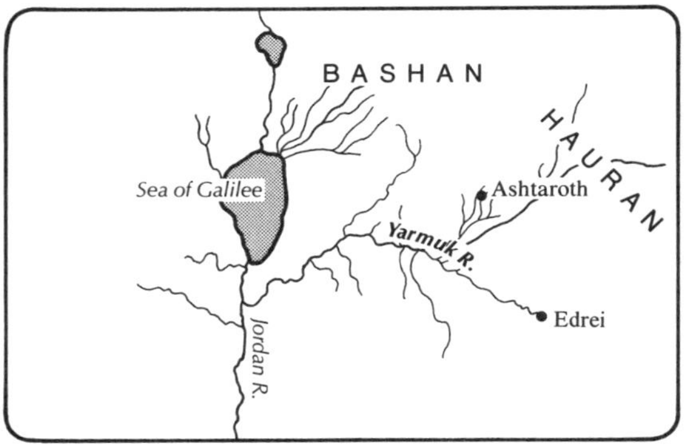

The Yarmuk's tributaries drain virtually the whole of Bashan and Hauran. Like the Jabbok, Arnon, and Zered rivers the Yarmuk has cut a deep gorge through the Transjordanian plateau (*see* PALESTINE IV.A.7). Where the Yarmuk joins the Jordan about 6.5 km. (4 mi.) S of the Sea of Galilee, they are both about 9 m. (30 ft.) wide although the Yarmuk is deeper. The two main towns of the Yarmuk basin were Ashtaroth and Edrei (cf. Dt. 1:4 [LXX, Vulg., RSV, NEB]; Josh. 12:4). H. L. ELLISON

The gorge of the Yarmuk River through the Transjordan plateau (W. Braun)

YA'UDI yä-ōō'dē [Assyr. *ya-ú-du, ya-ú-di, ya-u-di*; Zenjirli inscription *y'dy*], **YA'UDIANS** [Assyr. *ya-ú-da-a-a* (read *yaudaya*)]. A place mentioned in the inscriptions of Tiglath-pileser III and Sargon II of Assyria, and those of Panammu and Barrakib from Zenjirli, and the people of that place. In 2 K. 14:28 the NEB reads JAUDI rather than Judah.

I. Language.–The inscriptions from Zenjirli are written in a language or dialect that has been classified as Phoenician (J. Friedrich, *Phönizisch-Punische Grammatik* [1951], pp. 2f., 153-162) and as Old Aramaic (G. A. Cooke, *Text-Book of North-Semitic Inscriptions* [1903], pp. 159-185, and many scholars since; F. M. Cross, and D. N. Freedman, *Early History Orthography* [1952], p. 29, describe it as the standard Aramaic of the day). Some elements in the language are closer to Phoenician than to Aramaic, and other elements are clearly Aramaic, as both Friedrich (p. 153) and Cooke (p. 185) recognized. It probably should be described as a local dialect (the term is used by both Friedrich and Cooke), neither Phoenician or Aramaic but closely related to both.

II. Location.–Zenjirli, also known as Samal (Assyr. *samallu* (*ARAB*, II, § 197], is located in the KaraSu, a valley N of Antioch-on-the-Orontes and E of the mountains that separate Karatepe from Zenjirli. Certain kings are known:

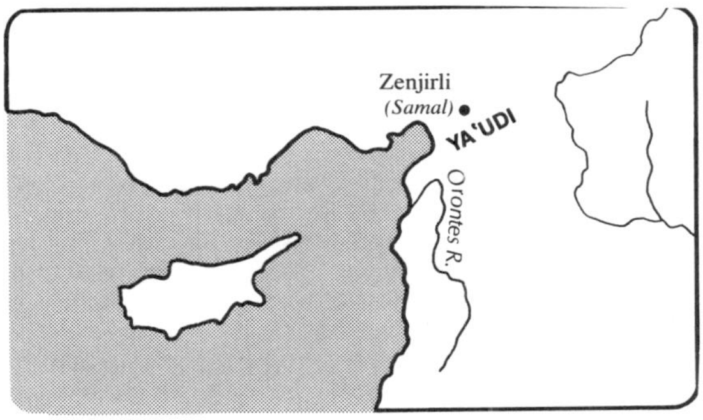

Kilamuwa (840-830) Panammu I, Panammu II (? - 733), and Barrakib, from their own inscriptions; Khaianu (858-853) and Panammu II from Assyrian, Urartian, or Babylonian sources. Samal became an Assyrian province in the days of Sargon II.

III. The Biblical Problem.–According to an inscription of Tiglath-pileser, he concluded a campaign in Ulluba, near Bitlis and a source of the Tigris, in order to strengthen his eastern border. At that time the Syrian states attempted to break loose from Assyria. One of the leaders of this revolt was "Azriyau of Yaudaya" (*ARAB,* I, § 770; *ANET,* pp. 282f.). This has provoked a long discussion about his identity. Some claim that he was Azariah of Judah, also known as Uzziah, whose reign, including co-regencies, extended from 790 to 740 (cf. *BHI* [2nd ed. 1972], p. 268; and H. Tadmor, "Azriyau of Yaudi," in *Scripta Hierosolymitana,* 8 [1961], 232-271). For a period this was the commonly held view. More recently, some scholars have returned to the conclusion set forth by H. Winckler (*Altorientalische Forschungen,* 1 [1897], 1ff.), that Azriyau was a king of a small city-state (cf. *CAH,* III/1 [2nd ed. 1982], 410-12 and the footnotes), perhaps to be identified with Samal, which is also called *y'dy.*

The arguments supporting the identification with Azariah of Judah can be reduced to the simple statement that there would likely not be two rulers with similar names ruling over two kingdoms with similar names at the same time. Moreover, the word *ya-ú-da-a-a* is precisely the word used for Judah or Judean (cf. Sennacherib's account of his attack on Jerusalem, Taylor Cylinder, iii, 12; *ARAB,* II, § 240; *ANET,* p. 287). This appears to be a weighty argument.

The arguments against this identification, however, are also weighty. (1) The distance between Judah and Samal is great, and would stretch the lines of communication exceedingly. Moreover, the northern kingdom lay in the way, and at that time it was quite likely a tributary of Tiglath-pileser. (2) In an inscription on a statue honoring his father Panammu, Barrakib refers to the conspiracy in his father's house, the death of his father and the destruction of his house and devastation of the land which resulted, and it was Tiglath-pileser the king of Assyria, named in the inscription, who placed him, Barrakib, on the throne. (3) The city-state is called *y'dy* and also *sm'l* in the two inscriptions (Cooke, nos. 62, 63). (4) Sargon,

An inscription of King Kilamuwa telling of his accomplishments as king over Ya'udi. From the entrance to the large palace at Zenjirli, *ca.* 825 B.C. (Staatliche Museen zu Berlin, DDR)

in his Nimrûd inscription, refers to himself as the subduer of the land of Yaudu (often taken to mean Judah; cf. *ARAB,* II, § 137). but in a parallel account he calls the city "Samalla" (taken by some to refer to Samaria, but this is rather unlikely; cf. *ARAB,* II, § 197). (5) Ya'udi uses the *hê* in all other words where the same character would occur in Hebrew. We should therefore expect "Judah/Judean" to be written *yhdy* in Ya'udi. The reason why Assyrian represents both words in the same form is due to the fact that ' is regularly used for *h,* since there is no orthographic way of representing *h* in any of the Akkadian dialects.

See also INSCRIPTIONS II.D; TIGLATH-PILESER III.

Bibliography.–In addition to the works mentioned above, see P. E. Dion, *La langue de Ya'udi* [1974]; E. R. Thiele, *MNHK* (2nd ed. 1965), pp. 93f. and bibliography in n.7.

W. S. LASOR

YEA; YES. "Yea" is an archaic form of "yes." Both denote affirmation or assent (like Ger. *ja*). Biblical Hebrew has no single word meaning simply "yes," though *kēn* ("surely," Isa. 53:4; "even so" or "behold," Ex. 39:43), *gam* ("yes," e.g., Gen. 27:33), *'aḇ* ("yea," e.g., Dt. 33:3), *kî* ("yes," e.g., Jgs. 18:10), and *w^e* (lit. "and"; "yea," e.g., Ex. 6:1) convey direct affirmation. Simple affirmation in the OT is often expressed by a declarative sentence ("yes," 1 S. 9:12a, NEB), often repeating a portion of the question or assertion just uttered (1 K. 20:32f.). Most of the appearances of "yea" and "yes" in the RSV OT, including the thirty occurrences in the Psalms, serve a rhetorical purpose, to emphasize and elaborate through parallel repetition, rather than to give mere neutral assent.

In the NT Gk. *naí* has the nearest meaning to modern English "yes," and is usually so translated in modern versions (e.g., Mt. 5:37; 9:28; Jn. 11:27; 2 Cor. 1:17-20; Jas. 5:12). Other Greek terms and expressions translated "yea" or "yes" include *kaí ge* (lit. "and indeed," "even," Acts 2:18) and *éti* (lit. "still, yet"; "yes" in Lk. 14:26; AV "yea"). In some contexts Gk. *allá* (lit. "but") conveys a positive assertion ("yes," Lk. 24:21; 2 Cor. 3:15; Phil. 1:19). Similarly, Gk. *mállon dé* (lit. "but more," "but rather") can introduce an expression "that supplements and thereby corrects what has preceded" (Bauer, rev., p. 489), as in Rom. 8:34. C. D. LINTON

YEAR [Heb. *šānâ,* also *yāmîm*–'days' (e.g., Josh. 13:1); Aram. *š^{e}nâ*; Gk. *étos, eniautós*]. *See* CALENDAR.

YEARS, SEVENTY. *See* SEVENTY YEARS.

YELLOW. *See* COLOR V.J.

YIRON yir'ən [Heb. *yir'ôn*]; AV, NEB, IRON. A fortified city belonging to the tribe of Naphtali (Josh. 19:38). It has been identified with modern Yārûn in northern Galilee, about 10 km. (6 mi.) WSW of Tell Qades (Kedesh, v. 37).

YODH yōd [י]. The tenth letter of the Hebrew alphabet, transliterated in this encylcopedia as *y*. It came also to be used for the number ten, and it stands at the beginning of the tenth section of Ps. 119 (cf. AV). *See* WRITING.

YOKE; YOKE-BAR [(nouns) Heb. *'ōl,* also *môṭâ*–'pole,' 'collar' (Isa. 58:6, 9; Jer. 27:2; 28:10, 12), *môṭ* (Nah. 1:13), *k^{e}lî*–'equipment' (2 S. 24:22; 1 K. 19:21), *ṣemeḏ* (1 S. 11:7; 1 K. 19:19, 21; Job 1:3; 42:12), (vbs.) niphal of *ṣāmaḏ*–'join,' 'attach oneself to' (Nu. 25:3, 5), *'āsar*–'bind' (1 S. 6:7, 10), hiphil of *rāḵaḇ* ("put to the yoke," Hos. 10:11); Gk. *zygós* (Mt. 11:29f.; Acts 15:10; etc.), *zeúgos* (Lk. 14:19)]; AV also INSTRUMENT (*k^{e}lî*), HEAVY (Isa. 58:6), TIE (*'āsar*), JOIN (niphal of *ṣāmaḏ*), "make to ride" (Hos. 10:11), etc.; NEB also THRESHING-SLEDGE (2 S. 24:22), WOODEN GEAR (1 K. 19:21), "join in the worship of" (Nu. 25:3, 5), etc. In Lam. 5:5 "with the yoke" is supplied by the RSV (cf. AV, RSV mg.). The text of Hos. 11:7 is obscure and may be corrupt; the RSV has emended MT *'al* to read *'ōl* (see comms.).

The noun denotes a shaped wooden bar placed across the necks of two oxen (or other draft animals) and connected by a beam to a plow or cart. As the animals pull, the weight of the load is carried by their shoulders. The verb means "join with a yoke." The noun *ṣemeḏ,* derived from the verb *ṣāmaḏ,* denotes a team of two oxen yoked together (cf. also Gk. *zeúgos,* Lk. 14:19). *Ṣemeḏ* can also be used to denote the land area that can be plowed by a team of oxen in one day (*see* ACRE).

The term is used infrequently in the literal sense (e.g., Nu. 19:2; Dt. 21:3; 2 S. 24:22; 1 K. 19:21). Most often it is used as a symbol for slavery or political oppression (e.g., Dt. 28:48; 1 K. 12:4, 9-11, 14 par. 2 Ch. 10:4, etc.; Isa. 47:6; Jer. 28:14; Lam. 5:5; Sir. 33:26; 1 Macc. 8:18, 31; 1 Tim. 6:1). Breaking or removing the yoke thus symbolizes liberation from oppression and servitude (e.g., Gen. 27:40; Lev. 26:13; Isa. 9:4; 10:27; 14:25; 58:6, 9; Jer. 30:8; Ezk. 34:27; Nah. 1:13; 1 Macc. 13:41). Jeremiah was told by the Lord to make and wear "thongs and yoke-bars" as a demonstration that Judah and surrounding nations were to submit to the authority of Nebuchadnezzar king of Babylon (Jer. 27:1f.). This may have been an actual yoke such as those borne by oxen, or it is possible that the Babylonians had designed a special yoke to constrain slaves or captives. Most likely, however, Jeremiah constructed a small-scale model of an ox-yoke that he could

An Assyrian relief showing captives in yokes straining with a heavy burden (from a palace at Khorsabad, 8th cent. B.C.) (CNMHS/ARS, NY/SPADEM)

carry around for dramatic effect. To emphasize his rejection of Jeremiah's message and dramatize his call for rebellion against Babylon, the false prophet Hananiah broke the yoke that Jeremiah had been carrying (28:1-11). God vindicated Jeremiah, however, and reemphasized His somber message (vv. 12-17).

The yoke can also represent bondage to sin (Lam. 1:14). In Sirach it sometimes refers to sufferings produced by slander (28:19f.) or other hardships (26:7; 40:1). Such sufferings can have the value of producing self-discipline (cf. Lam. 3:27).

The yoke is also a symbol for obedience to the law of God (Sir. 51:26) or to Wisdom (6:30). Thus rebellion against God's law can be pictured as "breaking the yoke" (Jer. 2:20; 5:5). The "yoke of the law" was a common expression in rabbinic literature (e.g., *Pirke Aboth* 3.6; see SB, I, 608-610). With their legalism the Pharisees of NT times made the law of God a very heavy yoke (Acts 15:10; Gal. 5:1). By contrast, Jesus stated that the yoke of His discipline was refreshing and easy to bear (Mt. 11:29f.).

The verb "yoke" can be used as a graphic symbol of a close alliance or union. The Israelites were severely punished for yoking themselves to (i.e., worshiping) Baal of Peor (Nu. 25:3, 5). In 2 Cor. 6:14 Paul warns believers not to be "mismated" (Gk. *heterozygéō*; AV, lit., "unequally yoked") with unbelievers. Paul is not encouraging aloofness from unbelievers, which he sees as neither possible nor God's will (1 Cor. 5:9f.), but he is warning against alliances in matters where important Christian principles would be compromised. In his first letter he had mentioned some such instances: marrying an unbeliever (7:12-15), eating in the homes of unbelievers meat that had been offered to idols (10:27f.), and taking legal matters involving fellow believers before secular courts (6:5-8). Believers are never to forget the radical difference between the dynamic of their life in Christ and the operating principles governing the world. Forming alliances that unite these two alien motivations is like plowing a field with an ox (a "clean" animal) and an ass (an "unclean" animal) yoked together (see Dt. 22:10; cf. 14:3-8).

G. A. VAN ALSTINE N. J. O.

YOKEFELLOW [Gk. *sýzygos* (for *sýnzygos*)–'yoked with']; NEB COMRADE. In extrabiblical Greek, a companion in any enterprise: a marriage partner, a comrade in arms, a business associate. The only NT occurrence is in Phil. 4:3, where Paul addresses a person residing or ministering at Philippi and encourages him to help solve a conflict between two women in that church, Euodia and Syntyche. The identity of the "true yokefellow" addressed by Paul is unknown. Various conjectures have been made.

Some have suggested that the "true yokefellow" was one of several persons known to have been connected with the church at Philippi. The most prominently mentioned are: Epaphroditus, who was a messenger between Paul and the Philippian church (Phil. 2 25; 4:18); Luke, who seems to have stayed in Philippi after the "we" section of Acts (Acts 16); and Lydia, in whose home the church at Philippi probably held worship services (16:40). Clement of Alexandria insisted that this strong term of kinship could refer only to Paul's wife. In the mid-19th cent. E. Renan revived this view, identifying Paul's spouse as Lydia (*Saint Paul* [4th ed. 1866], p. 148). Two facts argue against this suggestion, however: (1) clear biblical indications that Paul was not married (1 Cor. 7:8; 9:5), and (2) the use of the masculine form of the adjective "true."

Other scholars have suggested that Gk. *sýzygos* is really a proper name. Westcott and Hort's Greek NT includes this possibility as a marginal reading. Synzygus is nowhere found as a Greek name, although Zygus is. If Paul is here addressing an otherwise unknown church leader by the name of Synzygus, he may be reminding him of the meaning of his name and asking him to express it in action: "Synzygus, here is a chance to live up to your name. Be a *true* yokefellow and bring back together these two women who have in the past worked side by side with me in the gospel yoke." For a similar application of the meaning of an individual's name, see Paul's evaluation of the runaway slave Onesimus (meaning "useful") as formerly "useless," but now "useful" because of his conversion to Christ (Philem. 11).

G. A. VAN ALSTINE

YOM KIPPUR yōm ki-po͞or', yom kip'ər. *See* ATONEMENT, DAY OF.

YOUNG(ER) (MAN) [Heb. *bāḥûr* (Dt. 32:25; Jgs. 14:10; Ruth 3:10; etc.), *naʿar* (Gen. 14:24; Nu. 11:27; etc.), *yeleḏ* (Gen. 4:23; 1 K. 12:8, 10, 14); Gk. *neanías* (Acts 7:58; 20:9; 23:17), *neanískos* (Mt. 19:20, 22; Mk. 14:51; 16:5; Lk. 7:14; Acts 2:17 [Joel 3:1, LXX]; 5:10; 23:18, 22; 1 Jn. 2:13f.), *neṓteros* (Lk. 15:12f.; Jn. 21:18; Acts 5:6; 1 Tim. 5:1; Tit. 2:6; 1 Pet. 5:5; "youngest," Lk. 22:26]; AV also LAD, BOY, etc.; NEB also YOUNG SON, YOUNG WARRIOR, ARMY, SERVANT, BOY, CHILD, MAN, etc.; **YOUNG(ER) (WOMAN)** [Heb. *naʿarâ* (Dt. 22:15; Ruth 4:12; etc.), *ʿalmâ* (Gen. 24:43; Isa. 7:14; etc.); Gk. *néa* (Tit. 2:4), *neṓtera* (1 Tim. 5:2, 11, 14)]; AV also DAMSEL, MAID(EN), VIRGIN; NEB also GIRL, MAIDEN, LADY-IN-WAITING, etc.; **YOUTH** (abstract noun) [Heb. *beḥûrôṯ* (Eccl. 11:9; 12:1), *neʿûrîm* (Gen. 8:21; 1 S. 12:2; 2 S. 19:7 [MT 8]; etc.), *nōʿar* (Job 36:14; Ps. 88:15 [MT 16]; Prov. 29:21; "youthful vigor," Job 33:25), *neʿurôṯ* (Jer. 32:30), *ṣeʿîrâ* (Gen. 43:33), *yalḏûṯ* (Ps. 110:3; Eccl. 11:9f.); Gk. *neótēs* (Mk. 10:20; Lk. 18:21; Acts 26:4; 1 Tim. 4:12)]; AV also CHILDHOOD; A CHILD('S); NEB "his/their prime," BOYHOOD, "so on down to the youngest"; **YOUTHFUL** [Gk. *neōterikós* (2 Tim. 2:22)]; NEB OF YOUTH. Words used in the Bible for young persons are not clearly delineated from each other and do not signify the age of a person with exactness.

Hebrew *naʿar* and its feminine counterpart, *naʿarâ*, are quite broad in their application. *Naʿar* is used of Moses at three months (Ex. 2:6; AV and RSV "babe"), of Samuel as a small child (1 S. 1:22, 24) and as a boy receiving God's revelation (2:11, 18, 21), of Jacob and Esau as boys growing up (Gen. 25:27), of Ishmael as a lad of more than fourteen years (21:17), of Joseph at seventeen (37:2), and of Joshua as a young adult in service to Moses (Ex. 33:11). The *naʿar* was often but not always an adult.

Naʿarâ appears as a qualifier of *beṯûlâ*, a term for young women of marriageable age generally translated "virgin," in which case *naʿarâ* is translated "young" (Jgs. 21:12; 1 K. 1:2; Est. 2:2). By itself *naʿarâ* can be used of a virgin (Gen. 24:14, 16, 28; Dt. 22:15ff.), a married woman (Ruth 4:12), or a concubine (Jgs. 19:3ff.; RSV "girl").

Like *naʿar*, *bāḥûr* was used of one in the prime of manhood (1 S. 9:2; Prov. 20:29), but, unlike *naʿar*, not of a person any younger. It appears paralleled with *beṯûlâ*, "virgin" (e.g., Dt. 32:25; Ps. 148:12; Ezk. 9:6), and seems, therefore, to be a term for unmarried young men of marriageable age (cf. Isa. 62:5). Where both *naʿar* and *bāḥûr* appear, *naʿar* represents the younger group (Ps. 148:12; Jer. 51:22).

Hebrew *ʿalmâ* refers to a young woman of marriageable age (e.g., Prov. 30:19) and possibly a girl of less than marriageable age. Heb. *ʿelem*, the masculine counterpart of *ʿalmâ*, occurs only twice in the OT and apparently refers to boys who have not reached or who have just reached adulthood (1 S. 17:56; 20:22; AV "stripling," "young man"; RSV "stripling," "youth"; NEB "lad"). Heb. *yeleḏ* normally referred to a child, even an infant (e.g., Ex. 2:9), but could be used of a young man as an insult (Gen. 4:23; 1 K. 12:8, 10, 14).

Hebrew *neʿûrîm, nōʿar,* and *neʿûrôṯ* are abstract nouns related to *naʿar* that can be translated "youth." They are often used as a reference point for what one claims to have practiced or experienced during all of one's responsible life (e.g., Gen. 46:34; Ps. 88:15 [MT 16]; Ezk. 4:14; cf. Prov. 29:21; Jer. 32:30) and in referring to the strength and vigor of youth as opposed to old age (e.g., Job 33:25; Ps. 103:5).

The value of young men to society was, indeed, found mainly in their physical strength, that of older men in their experience and ability to give counsel and guide the affairs of the community (Prov. 20:29). Youth was thought to be characterized by inexperience (Jgs. 8:20; 1 S. 17:33; 1 Ch. 22:5; 2 Ch. 13:7; Jer. 1:6) and lack of wisdom (Prov. 1:4; 7:7; 22:15) in contrast to old age. This conception of youth is the basis for hyperbolic use of *naʿar* in Solomon's prayer (1 K. 3:7) and stands behind the account of the beginning of Rehoboam's reign — not only did the young king reject the natural wisdom of age, he also adopted the reckless forcefulness of youth (1 K. 12:6-14; cf. Isa. 3:4f.).

The frequent use of "young man" as equivalent to "soldier" (e.g., Gen. 14:24; 1 S. 30:17; 2 Ch. 36:17; Jer. 11:22) shows how vital the strength and daring of youth were. (According to Nu. 1:3 a man could be a soldier from the age of twenty.) The use of *naʿar* for servants (Jgs. 7:10; 1 K. 18:43) also reflects an emphasis on the physical strength of young people. Youth was also expected to be the time of intense enjoyment of life's pleasures (Eccl. 11:9), and of intense devotion (Jer. 2:2; Ezk. 16:43).

In the NT the Greek comparative *neṓteros* is used of adult or nearly adult persons, but usually with some contrast between such persons and those who are older (Lk. 15:12; Jn. 21:18; 1 Tim. 5:1f., 11, 14 [cf. v. 9]; Tit. 2:6 [cf. v. 2]; 1 Pet. 5:5). The same can be observed concerning the use of the feminine absolute (non-comparative) form of the word (*néa*) in Tit. 2:4 (cf. v. 3). When Jesus said that the greatest should become as the youngest (Lk. 22:26, *neṓteros*), He had in mind the usual obligation of the young to perform more humble tasks (cf. Acts 5:6, 10).

That Paul was a *neanías* when Stephen was stoned (Acts 7:58) is probably mentioned to explain the secondary role he takes in the stoning. He was, however, apparently a young adult rather than a child, ready soon after to take on great responsibilities (8:3; 9:1f.). Eutychus, on the other hand, is described not only as a *neanías* (20:9) but also as a *país* (a child, v. 12; RSV "lad") and so was apparently not an adult. Paul's nephew was a *neanías* and a *neanískos* at the time of Paul's Jerusalem imprisonment (23:17f., 22); that the tribune took him by the hand before questioning him (v. 19) may indicate that Paul's nephew was still a child. But a man whom Luke called "rich" and a "ruler" (Lk. 18:18, 23) was a *neanískos* according to Mt. 19:20, 22. (Matthew also omits the man's reference back to the time of his "youth" [cf. Mk. 10:20; Lk. 18:21, *neótēs*], which may show a particular interest on the part of Matthew in portraying the man as young.) Other uses of *neanískos* give no more exactness to the term except to distinguish those designated by it from those older or younger (Acts 2:17; 1 Jn. 2:13f.).

See also CHILD; VIRGIN.

See H. W. Wolff, *Anthropology of the OT* (Eng. tr. 1974), pp. 120-23. D. B. PECOTA J. W. S.

Z

ZAANAIM zā-ə-nā'əm (Jgs. 4:11, AV). *See* ZAANANNIM.

ZAANAN zā'ə-nan [Heb. *ṣa*^{a}*nān*; Gk. *Sennaar*] (Mic. 1:11). A fortress city mentioned only in Micah's lament mourning the Assyrian army's systematic seizure of Judah's main lines of defence in the Shephelah. (see *LBHG* [2nd ed. 1979], p. 392). It has often been identified with Zenan (Heb. *ṣ*^{e}*nān*) of Josh. 15:37, since both are in the Shephelah and named along with Lachish. On the basis of the Arabic version reading (el-ʿAraq), F.-M. Abel located it at ʿArâq el-Kharab (*GP*, II, 455); but this identification has not been generally accepted.

J. E. MCKENNA W. S. L. S.

ZAANANNIM zā-ə-nan'im, **OAK IN** [Heb. *K 'ēlôn b*^{e}*ṣa*^{ʿa}*n-nayim* or *baṣʿannîm, Q 'ēlôn b*^{e}*ṣa*^{ʿa}*nannîm*]; AV ALLON TO ZAANANNIM (Josh. 19:33), PLAIN OF ZAANAIM (Jgs. 4:11); NEB ELON-BEZAANANNIM. A place on the southern border of Naphtali in the vicinity of the Jabneel valley (Josh. 19:33); possibly the same as the site of Heber the Kenite's encampment near Kedesh (Jgs. 4:11).

Textual problems make the reading difficult. The RSV reads Heb. *'ēlôn* as a noun ("oak") and *b*^{e} as a preposition ("in"), but *'ēlôn* could also be read either as a place name in its own right (cf. AV "Allon") or as a construct, in which case *b*^{e} would be read as part of the name Bezaanannim (cf. LXX B *Besemiim*, A *Besenanim* in Josh. 19:33; in Jgs. 4:11 the LXX translates *pleonektoúntōn* [B] or *anapauoménōn* [A], assuming the Hebrew root to be *bṣʿ*), or as the first element of a compound name (so NEB). The absence of the definite article before *'ēlôn* favors reading "oak of Bezaanannim" or "Elon-bezaanannim." The place may have been a cultic center (see B. Mazar, *JNES*, 24 [1965], 297-303; *LBHG* [rev. ed. 1979], p. 227).

The exact location of the site is unknown; the problem is complicated by uncertainty about the identification of Kedesh in Jgs. 4:11. Some have identified Bezaanannim with Lejjun, about 4 km. (2½ mi.) N of Taanach, between Megiddo and Tell Abû Qedeis (*see* KEDESH 2). Others have argued for an identification with Khirbet Bessûm on the plateau W of the Sea of Galilee, about 5 km. (3 mi.) NE of Tabor, not far from Khirbet Qedish. Based on a derivation of the name *ṣa*^{ʿa}*nannîm* from the root *ṣʿn* ("pack up"; thus "of the caravanners"), and a tentative identification of the other places mentioned in Josh. 19:33, still others have favored an identification with Khan et-Tujjar, a caravan station on the road from Beth-shan to Damascus, located about 6.5 km. (4 mi.) SE of Adam (Khirbet Dâmiyeh).

Bibliography.–*GP*, II, 64, 239; *GTTOT* §§ 333f., 554; *HGHL*, pp. 394, 395 n.1.

D. E. WARING

ZAAVAN zā'ə-van [Heb. *za*^{ʿa}*wān* < *zāwa*ʿ–'tremble'(?)]; AV also ZAVAN; NEB ZAVAN. Son of Ezer; a Horite clan chief who descended from Seir (Gen. 36:27; 1 Ch. 1:42).

ZAB, GREATER AND LESSER zāb [Assyr. *zabu šupalu* (Lower Zab) and *zabu elu* (Upper Zab); Lat. *Lycus* and *Absithris* (Pliny *Nat. hist.* vi.30); Gk. *Lykos* and *Kapros* (Strabo *Geog.* xvi.1.4)]. Two tributaries of the TIGRIS River which, flowing from the east, join it in upper Mesopotamia. The Greater (Upper) Zab rises in the snowy Zagros mountains along the Turkish-Iranian border midway between Lake Van and Lake Urmiah. Its 425 km. (265 mi.) journey through southeastern Turkey and northeastern Iraq passes first through rugged, forested mountain canyons and past occasional waterfalls, then through wide, fertile river valleys. It meets the Tigris near Calah (ancient Nimrud) about 32 km. (20 mi.) S of Nineveh (modern Mosul). The Lesser (Lower) Zab originates in

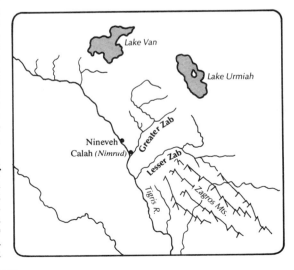

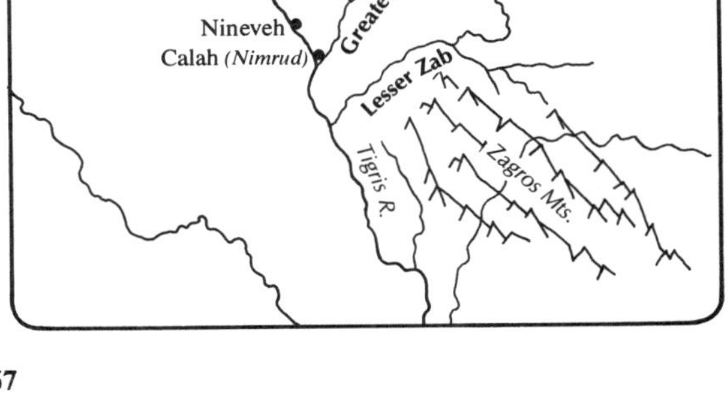

the mountains of western Iran near Lake Urmiah and courses through similar terrain parallel to the Greater Zab. It joins the Tigris about 80 km. (50 mi.) S of the Greater Zab after a journey of about 400 km. (250 mi.).

Though not mentioned in the Bible, the Zab rivers played a crucial role in the birth of the Mesopotamian civilizations from which Abram later came. Indeed, if the Tigris-Euphrates valley is "the cradle of civilization," the upper regions of the Zab rivers are its womb and their river valleys its birth canal. Skeletons of a Neanderthal type have been found in the Shanidar cave near the Greater Zab, and prehistoric rock inscriptions at Zaban (modern Altun Kupri) on the Lower Zab. The inhabitants of these sites lived in caves and fed themselves by hunting and gathering food. But sites like Zawi Chemi Shanidar (*ca.* 8500 B.C.), 5 km. (3 mi.) from the cave on the east bank of the Greater Zab, and Jarmo (*ca.* 5000 B.C.) S of the Lesser Zab, reflect a radically different life-style. Their inhabitants had learned to build their own houses, farm their own crops, and breed their own livestock. This development, the so-called neolithic revolution, formed the basis of civilization. The migration of these farmers down the river valleys of the two Zabs to the Mesopotamian plain (*ca.* 5000 B.C.) gave birth to the later Sumerian, Akkadian, and Assyrian cultures.

In historical times the Zab rivers are periodically mentioned in Assyrian records. Kings reported crossing them enroute to and returning from their battles. Shalmaneser III (*ca.* 860 B.C.) apparently used the Greater Zab for his advance into Urartu. At times the rivers served as informal borders of the Assyrian empire during its many periods of expansion and contraction. Sargon II (*ca.* 700 B.C.) cited the Lesser Zab as the northern frontier of one of his provinces. No doubt Shalmaneser I (mid-13th cent. B.C.) founded the city of Calah where the Greater Zab meets the Tigris because of the natural moat provided by the two rivers. Later Ashurnasirpal II (*ca.* 680 B.C.) tapped the Greater Zab with a canal 10 km. (6 mi.) long to water his newly planted orchards outside Calah.

Bibliography.–M. A. Beek, *Atlas of Mesopotamia* (1962); A. T. Olmstead, *History of Assyria* (1951); *ANET*, pp. 275, 304, 558, 628; R. L. Solecki, *An Early Village Site at Zawi Chemi Shanidar* (1981).

R. L. HUBBARD, JR.

ZABAD zā'bad [Heb. *zāḇaḏ*, perhaps a contraction of *zᵉḇaḏyâ*–'Yahweh has given,' or of *zaḇdî'ēl*–'God is my gift'(?); *see* ZABDIEL].

1. Son of Nathan, a Jerahmeelite of the tribe of Judah (1 Ch. 2:36f.).

2. An Ephraimite; son of Tahath and father of Shuthelah (1 Ch. 7:21).

3. Son of Ahlai; one of David's mighty men (1 Ch. 11:41).

4. Son of Shimeath the Ammonitess (2 Ch. 24:26); one of the men who assassinated King Joash in revenge for the stoning death of Zechariah the son of Jehoiada (cf. vv. 20-22, 25). In 2 K. 12:21 (MT 22) he is called Jozacar, although some MSS have *yôzāḇāḏ* (Jozabad; see *BHS*).

5. [Gk. Apoc. *Sabathos*]; AV Apoc. SABATUS; NEB Apoc. SABATHUS. Son of Zattu; one of the Israelite laymen who divorced the foreign wives they had married during the Exile (Ezr. 10:27; 1 Esd. 9:28).

6. [Gk. Apoc. A *Sabannaious*, B *Bannaious*]; AV Apoc. BANNAIA; NEB Apoc. BANNAEUS. Son of Hashum; another layman who divorced his foreign wife (Ezr. 10:33; 1 Esd. 9:33).

7. [Gk. Apoc. *Zabadaias*]; AV Apoc. ZABADAIAS; NEB Apoc. ZABADAEAS. Son of Nebo; another layman who divorced his foreign wife (Ezr. 10:43; 1 Esd. 9:35).

See *IP*, pp. 22, 46f.

N. J. O.

ZABADAEAS zab'ə-dā'əs (1 Esd. 9:35, NEB); **ZABADAIAS** (1 Esd. 9:35, AV). *See* ZABAD **7.**

ZABADEANS zab-ə-dē'ənz [Gk. *Zabadaioi*]. An Arab tribe (or Arab inhabitants of a town Zabad or Zabadai) who were "crushed" and "plundered" by Jonathan in his campaign against Demetrius (1 Macc. 12:31). Since Jonathan's campaign took him to "the region of Hamath" (v. 25), and the forces of Demetrius escaped by crossing the Eleutherus River (v. 30), then after plundering the Zabadeans Jonathan went on to Damascus (v. 32), the Zabadeans must have been NW of Damascus. According to Y. Aharoni and M. Avi-Yonah (*Macmillan Bible Atlas* [rev. ed. 1977], map 203) the Zabadeans were located at Beth-zabdai (ez-Zebdani) in the land of Chalcis, about 30 km. (18 mi.) NW of Damascus. Josephus apparently referred to the same people as "Nabateans" (*Ant.* xiii.5.9 [179]), an impossible identification since at that time the Nabateans were located considerably farther south. Oesterley inexplicably read Gabadeans, though he noted that the versions read Zabadeans (*APOT*, I, 112). See also J. Goldstein, *I Maccabees* (*AB*, 1976), pp. 464f.

W. S. L. S.

ZABBAI zab'ī [Heb. *zabbay*; Gk. Apoc. B *Zabdos*, A *Iōzabados*]; AV Apoc. JOSABAD; NEB Apoc. OZABADUS.

1. Son of Bebai; one of the Israelite laymen who divorced the foreign wives they had married during the Exile (Ezr. 10:28; 1 Esd. 9:29).

2. Father of a certain Baruch who repaired a section of the wall of Jerusalem in the time of Nehemiah (Neh. 3:20). The *qere* reads *zakkay* (Zaccai).

ZABBUD zab'ud (Ezr. 8:14, AV, NEB). *See* ZACCUR **5.**

ZABDAEUS zab-dā'əs (1 Esd. 9:21, NEB); **ZABDEUS** zab-dē'əs (1 Esd. 9:21, AV). *See* ZEBADIAH **9.**

ZABDI zab'dī [Heb. *zaḇdî*–'(Yahweh) has given'(?), 'gift (of Yahweh)'(?); *see* ZABAD].

1. A Judahite of the family of Zerah; ancestor of Achan (Josh. 7:1, 17f.). In 1 Ch. 2:6 (and also some LXX MSS of Josh. 7:1, 17f.) he is called Zimri, probably due to confusion in transmission (Heb. *b* and *m* are easily confused phonetically, *d* and *r* graphically). *See* ZIMRI **3.**

2. Son of Shimei; head of a Benjaminite family (1 Ch. 8:19).

3. One of David's officers, called a SHIPHMITE; he was in charge of "the produce of the vineyards for the wine cellars" (1 Ch. 27:27).

4. A Levite of the family of Asaph; ancestor of Mattaniah (Neh. 11:17). In 1 Ch. 9:15 he is called Zichri, probably due to confusion between Heb. *b* and *k* and between *d* and *r*.

N. J. O.

ZABDIEL zab'di-əl [Heb. *zaḇdî'ēl*–'El (God) is my gift' (?) or 'God has given'(?); Gk. Apoc. *Zabdiēl*].

1. Father of Jashobeam and descendant of Perez (1 Ch. 27:2; cf. v. 3).

2. Son of HAGGEDOLIM; overseer of a division of priests (Neh. 11:14).

3. An Arabian who beheaded Alexander Balas and sent his head to Ptolemy (1 Macc. 11:17). Josephus calls him a chieftain (*Ant.* xiii.4.8 [118]).

See *IP*, pp. 33-35, 46f.

ZABUD zā'bud [Heb. *zāḇûḏ*–'bestowed'] (1 K. 4:5). One of Solomon's administrative officials. He is called the son of Nathan, who may have been Nathan the prophet

(2 S. 7) or one of David's sons (cf. 2 S. 5:14). If the latter, Zabud would have been Solomon's nephew. Zabud is described as priest and king's friend. The title "king's friend" is thought to represent an office — a counselor — rather than an honorific title. *See* FRIEND OF THE KING. Textual variants (some Hebrew MSS *zakkûr*, Lucian Gk. *Zachour*, Syr. *Zakur*) have led some commentators (e.g., J. Gray [*OTL*, rev. ed. 1970], pp. 131, 133) to read the more common name Zakur rather than Zabud (the two names would have looked quite similar in ancient Hebrew script).

Bibliography.–T. N. D. Mettinger, *Solomonic State Officials* (*Coniectanea biblica, OT,* 5, 1971), pp. 63-69; A. van Selms, *JNES*, 16 (1957), 118-123.

A. HICKCOX

ZABULON zab'ū-lən [Gk. *Zaboulon*]. The AV form of ZEBULUN in Mt. 4:13, 15; Rev. 7:8, following the Greek spelling.

ZACCAI zak'ī [Heb. *zakkay*–'Yahweh has remembered'(?); perhaps a shortened form of Zechariah]. Head of a family of 760 people who returned from exile with Zerubbabel (Ezr. 2:9; Neh. 7:14).

See *IP*, pp. 39, 187.

ZACCHAEUS za-kē'əs [Gk. *Zakchaios* < Heb. *zakkāy*–'pure, righteous']; AV also ZACCHEUS (2 Macc. 10:19).

1. An officer in the army of Judas Maccabeus, one of a group given the task of besieging two towers in which Idumean forces had taken refuge (2 Macc. 10:19).

2. A wealthy "chief tax collector" at whose house in Jericho Jesus stayed (Lk. 19:1-10). Zacchaeus was most likely a collector of tolls on merchandise moving through Jericho. He may have been the one who held the contract from the Roman government for the collection of these tolls, and he probably made use of a number of subcontractors in the collecting of them. At any rate, his position made him wealthy, but it also subjected him to a large measure of the contempt that fell on collectors of Roman taxes from most Jews in Palestine. (Zacchaeus's name indicates that he himself was Jewish, as would be expected.)

What caused Zacchaeus to attempt to see Jesus was apparently simple curiosity, but this curiosity, coupled with his short stature, was enough to cause him to sacrifice his dignity to the point of climbing a tree in the attempt (vv. 3f.). Jesus' response to Zacchaeus and His going to the tax collector's house prompted the usual negative response to Jesus' contact with those bearing little respect in society (vv. 5-7; cf. 5:29f.; 15:1f.). As in similar situations, Jesus made this negative response the occasion for teaching concerning the nature of His mission (19:9f.; cf. 5:31f.; 15:3-32). What is notable in the encounter with Zacchaeus is that Jesus very clearly takes the initiative in going into Zacchaeus's home. Jesus' unambiguous statement concerning the salvation of Zacchaeus (19:9) is probably intended by Luke as a reflection of, and partial answer to, the question raised earlier concerning the possibility of a rich man being saved (18:24-28).

Zacchaeus indicated his own response to Jesus' receiving him by promising to rid himself of much of his wealth and give it to those who could most benefit from it (the poor) and those to whom some of it rightfully belonged (those who had lost it to Zacchaeus through his dishonest means — not surprising in one of his profession). His multiple restoration to the latter is in line with both OT-Jewish (e.g., Ex. 22:1 [MT 21:37]) and Roman legal practices. For Zacchaeus, however, the fourfold restitution is not required by a judicial procedure but made voluntarily in response to Christ's coming to him.

See also TAX COLLECTOR.

See W. P. Loewe, *CBQ*, 36 (1974), 321-331.

J. W. SIMPSON, JR.

ZACCHUR zak'ər (1 Ch. 4:26, AV). *See* ZACCUR **2.**

ZACCUR zak'ər [Heb. *zakkûr*–'remembered'(?)].

1. Father of Shammua the Reubenite spy (Nu. 13:4).

2. A Simeonite, descendant of Mishma (1 Ch. 4:26).

3. A Levite of the family of Merari; son of Jaaziah (1 Ch. 24:27).

4. A Levitical singer descended from Asaph (1 Ch. 25:2, 10; Neh. 12:35).

5. [Heb. *K zāḇûḏ, Q zakkûr*]; AV, NEB, ZABBUD. A descendant of Bigvai who accompanied Ezra on the return to Jerusalem from Babylon (Ezr. 8:14). In 1 Esd. 8:40 he is called Istalcurus and is named as the father of Uthai.

6. Son of Imri; one of those who helped to rebuild the wall of Jerusalem (Neh. 3:2).

7. A Levite who signed the covenant under Nehemiah (Neh. 10:12 [MT 13]).

8. Son of Mattaniah and father of a certain Hanan who was appointed as an assistant to the treasurers by Nehemiah (Neh. 13:13).

9. [Gk. Apoc. *Bakchouros*]; AV, NEB, BACCHURUS. A temple singer who divorced his foreign wife in the time of Ezra (1 Esd. 9:24).

N. J. O.

ZACHARIAH zak-ə-rī'ə. The AV rendering of two names: ZECHARIAH **(1)** the king of Israel (2 K. 14:29; 15:8, 11) and ZECHARIAH **(2)** the grandfather of King Hezekiah (2 K. 18:2 par. 2 Ch. 29:1).

ZACHARIAS zak-ə-rī'əs. The AV Apoc. and NT rendering of ZECHARIAH and once (1 Esd. 5:8) of SERAIAH.

ZACHARY zak'ə-rē (2 Esd. 1:40, AV). *See* ZECHARIAH **19.**

ZACHER zā'kər (1 Ch. 8:31, AV, NEB). *See* ZECHER.

ZADOK zā'dok [Heb. *ṣāḏôq*–'righteous]; AV also SADDUC (1 Esd. 8:2), SADOC (2 Esd. 1:1).

1. One of David's high priests. His ancestry is uncertain, for there are apparent discrepancies among the texts that record it. 2 S. 8:17 lists "Zadok the son of Ahitub and Ahimelech the son of Abiathar" as priests when David began to reign over all Israel (cf. 1 Ch. 18:16). But other texts record Abiathar as the son of Ahimelech (1 S. 22:20; 23:6; 30:7), and Ahitub as the father of Ahijah/Ahimelech (1 S. 14:3; 22:9, 11, 20). If these references are considered accurate and 2 S. 8:17 and 1 Ch. 18:16 are corrupt, then Zadok is left without genealogy. But genealogies in 1 Ch. 6:1-8 (MT 5:27-34); 6:50-53 (MT 6:35-38); and Ezr. 7:2-5 all speak of Zadok as a son of Ahitub and, more significantly, as a descendant of Aaron. Some scholars suppose that these genealogies merely repeat the error of 2 S. 8:17. The problem is to determine whether 2 S. 8:17 and corroborating texts are accurate historically or whether they are ill-fated attempts to provide a genealogy for Zadok that goes back to Aaron. Several attempts have been made to solve this puzzle.

One influential theory posits that Zadok did not have any Israelite ancestry (see Hauer, Rowley). Rather, he was the priest of the Jebusite sanctuary in Jerusalem when David captured the city. By appointing him priest David sought to unite the old city with its conquerors. Evidence for this view is found in the association of names similar to

Zadok in Jerusalem's history: the king during the time of Joshua was Adoni-zedek (Josh.10:1, 3), and Melchizedek was priest-king during the time of Abraham (Gen. 14:17-20). Criticisms of this position, however, are cogent. Thus, if Melchizedek was Zadok's ancestor, why did the later Zadokites recognize Aaron as their ancestor instead of Melchizedek? Also, it seems unlikely that David would appoint a non-Israelite to the most important position in Israelite religion.

F. M. Cross's reconstruction of 2 S. 8:17 salvages Zadok as an Aaronide and posits his origin in Hebron among the Aaronides as their leader. David brought him to Jerusalem as priest, after Zadok had shown his faithfulness to David in Hebron. Cross's assumptions and the complexity of his reconstruction are problematic, but his thesis has much to commend it.

In 1 Ch. 12:26-28 a Zadok appears as "a young man mighty in valor," who was among those men of war who declared David king in Hebron (1 Ch. 12:38-40). Some have suggested that the solution to Zadok's ancestry is found if he is considered to be a successful military adventurer whom David raised to the rank of priest. The problem with this theory is that the identification of this Zadok with Zadok the high priest is uncertain; if the identification is accepted, then 1 S. 2:27-36 would have been composed as a *vaticinium ex eventu* to justify the replacement of Abiathar and the house of Eli by Zadok.

The biblical texts emphasize the faithfulness of Zadok to David, and the name Zadok ("righteous") implies the character of the man. During the rebellion of Absalom, Zadok showed unswerving loyalty to David, as did his son (2 S. 9:11-14; 15:24-29, 36; 17:17-20: 18:19, 22, 27). David appointed Zadok to serve in the tabernacle at Gibeon (1 Ch. 16:39). He sided with Solomon against Adonijah (1 K. 1), while Abiathar supported Adonijah.

After David, Zadok and his sons became the ruling priestly line in Jerusalem (cf. 1 K. 4:2; 2 Ch. 31:10). The descendants of Zadok are listed in 1 Ch. 6:1-15 as follows: Zadok, Ahimaaz, Azariah, Johanan, Azariah, Amoriah, Ahitub, Zadok, Shallum, Hilkiah, Azariah, Seraiah, Jehozadak. This genealogy seems to differ from similar material recorded in Kings/Chronicles. But no detailed chronological checks should be attempted with a stylized list such as this.

It is generally accepted that the descendants of Zadok held the priesthood in Jerusalem till the Exile. Four references to sons/family of Zadok in Ezekiel (40:46; 43:19; 44:15; 48:11) highlight the future service that the sons of Zadok will have at the restored sanctuary because of their faithfulness to Yahweh.

2. A "young man mighty in valor," apparently a Levite, who came to Hebron to make David king (1 Ch. 12:26-28, 38). Josephus identified him with Zadok the priest (*Ant.* vii.2.2 [56]); see **1** above.

3. Son of Ahitub and father of Shallum, a descendant of Zadok the priest (1 Ch. 6:12 [MT 5:38]). See also **1** above.

4. Son of Meraioth and father of Meshullam (1 Ch. 9:11; Neh. 11:11); perhaps the same as **3** above; see also **1** above.

5. Father of Jerusha(h), who was mother of King Jotham of Judah (2 K. 15:33; 2 Ch. 27:1); perhaps the same as **3** or **4** above.

6. A scribe whom Nehemiah appointed as one of the three treasurers over the storehouses (Neh. 13:13).

7. One of the chiefs of the people who signed Nehemiah's covenant (Neh. 10:21 [MT 22]); perhaps the same as **4** above.

8. A descendant of Baana who helped repair the wall of Jerusalem in Nehemiah's time (Neh. 3:4; cf. Ezr. 2:2).

9. A descendant of Immer who helped repair the wall of Jerusalem in Nehemiah's time (Neh. 3:29; cf. Ezr. 2:37).

10. [Gk. *Sadōk*]; AV SADOC. Son of Azor and father of Achim, an ancestor of Joseph the husband of Mary (Mt. 1:14).

Bibliography.–A. Cody, *History of OT Priesthood* (1969), pp. 88-93; F. M. Cross, *Canaanite Myth and Hebrew Epic* (1973), pp. 195-215; R. de Vaux, *Ancient Israel* (Eng. tr. repr. 1965), II, 372-76; C. E. Hauer, *JBL*, 82 (1963), 89-94; H. H. Rowley, *JBL*, 58 (1939), 113-141; "Melchizedek and Zadok," in W. Baumgartner, *et al.*, eds., *Festschrift Alfred Bertholet* (1950), pp. 461-472.

E. E. CARPENTER

ZADOKITE FRAGMENTS zā'də-kīt. Two copies of a Hebrew document (or documents) discovered in the Genizah (a storage place for Scriptures that were no longer usable but too sacred to destroy) of the Ibn Ezra Synagogue in Old Cairo in 1896-97 and taken to the library at Cambridge University. Solomon Schechter published them in 1910, and Chaim Rabin reedited them in 1954 (*Zadokite Documents*).

I. Name.–Various names have been given to these MS fragments. Schechter published them as *Fragments of a Zadokite Work*. Because of their description of a sect that sojourned for a time at Damascus, the MSS were given the name Damascus Document. When the DSS were discovered, the relationship between the Zadokite Fragments and the Qumrân scrolls became apparent, and the former were called the Cairo Damascus Document, and given the symbol CDC. Later, when the *sigla* for the Qumrân documents were standardized, the Cairo MSS were given the symbol CD and fragments of the same document that were found at Qumrân were given the symbols 4QD, 5QD, and 6QD, indicating that they came from Qumrân caves 4, 5, and 6.

The sect responsible for CD placed emphasis on Zadok, high priest under Solomon (2 S. 8:17), and the "sons of Zadok," described by Ezekiel as the priests who will minister in the new temple (Ezk. 40:46; 44:15; CD 3:21–4:5). For this reason, Schechter used the name "Zadokite." The use of the term "sons of Zadok," with reference to the Qumrânians, led some to identify them with the Sadducees, but most scholars have rejected this identification.

II. The Fragments.–The fragments were parts of two different MSS, conveniently labeled A and B, A being dated on paleographic grounds to the 10th cent. A.D. and B to the 11th-12th cent. A.D. According to C. Rabin, MS A consists of two entirely different writings, the admonitions, preserved almost in their entirety, and the laws, of which both the beginning and ending are lacking (p. x). The admonitions are contained in cols. 1-8 of A, supplemented by cols. 19-20 of B. The laws constitute cols. 9-16 of A. Efforts to conflate the two documents have resulted in several "editions," as well as various methods of numbering that are unnecessarily confusing. C. Rabin has published the English translation and Hebrew text on facing pages, and his system of dual numbering where A and B are commingled is reasonably clear. The vocalized text published by A. M. Haberman (*m^e^gillôṯ miḏbar y^e^hûḏâ* [1959]), on the other hand, has been completely renumbered, making it difficult to locate passages from standard references.

The A document consists of eight folios of parchment (sixteen pages), approximately 21.5 by 19 cm. (8½ by 7½ in.), with twenty-one to twenty-three lines of text, written on both sides. The B document is a single folio with two pages of thirty-five lines each. These columns were arbitrarily numbered 19 and 20. Column 19 parallels in part and complements in part cols. 7-8 of A, whereas B 20 is almost entirely additional material.

The B document of the Zadokite MSS (11th-12th cent. A.D.) (by permission of the Syndics of Cambridge University Library)

III. Relation to the DSS.–Immediately following the publication of the first scrolls from Qumrân, the relationship between the two sets of documents was recognized. But it was not until fragments of the same writings were discovered at Qumrân (caves 4, 5, and 6) that identification of the originators of the Zadokite Fragments with the Qumrânians was established beyond doubt. (For references to these Qumrân fragments, see J. A. Fitzmyer, *Dead Sea Scrolls: Major Publications and Tools for Study* [2nd ed. 1977].)

All the problems concerning this relationship have not yet been solved. The Zadokite Fragments were found in a Qaraïte synagogue. The Qaraïtes (Karaïtes) were a Jewish sect that flourished in the Middle Ages, characterized by their rejection of talmudic tradition and their study of the Scriptures alone. What was the link between Qumrân and the Qaraïtes? Possibly the protests against the "builders of the wall," the priests of the Jerusalem cult, may offer some explanation. But a study of Rabin's work, particularly his notes, seems to show a relationship between Qumrân teachings, particularly as contained in the Damascus Document, and talmudic law. We must keep in mind that the Talmud did not come into existence until several centuries after Qumrân was a flourishing community. But according to rabbinic tradition the materials of the Mishnah and the Gemara already existed in oral form. Again, the laws in the second half of document A (CD 9–16) appear to be a kind of legalism. But it was partly because of the difference between mishnaic teachings and Qumrân that S. Zeitlin so strongly insisted that the DSS were a product of the Middle Ages. Evidence of several kinds has proved him wrong in his dating the DSS, but the schism between Qumrân Judaism and Jerusalem Judaism of the closing days of the second temple is clear.

The only direct evidence for the origins of the Qumrân community, the importance of the Teacher of Righteousness in its formative days, and certain specifics of membership is found in CD, supplemented by 1QS and 1QSa. These works, the Manual of Discipline (1QS), the Rule of the Congregation (1QSa), and the Damascus Document (CD) form the basis for most of our knowledge of the Qumrânians. Much of the rest of what has been written about the Qumrânians is hypothetical, ranging from conclusions based on careful critical study to the fantastic.

We must still face the facts that (1) the Zadokite Fragments were part of the literature of the Qumrân community. This is demonstrated by the number of fragments of the Damascus Document that were found in caves 4, 5, and 6 of Qumrân, indicating the importance that the Qumrânians placed on this work. And (2) the Zadokite Fragments were found in a Cairo Genizah. We can therefore conclude that some person or group of persons took the document (or, more likely, documents) of which the Zadokite Fragments were copies (or copies of copies) to Cairo. That the agents were refugees from Qumrân at the time of its destruction, who escaped possibly with those who made their way to Masada (cf. Y. Yadin, *Masada* [1966], pp. 187-190), seems unlikely. Because of the Qumrânian rule against making known the truth to those outside the community (1QS 9:17f.), we may not assume that Qumrân missionaries had gone out from Qumrân.

Evidence indicates that some scrolls were discovered in a cave in the neighborhood of the Dead Sea *ca.* A.D. 800 (cf. O. Eissfeldt, *TLZ,* 74 [1949], cols. 597ff.; H. H. Rowley, *Zadokite Fragments and the Dead Sea Scrolls* [1952], p. 22 n. 4). Further, Qirqisani (Ḳirḳisani), a Qaraïte of the 10th cent. A.D. refers to a Jewish sect called "al-Maghariya" ("cave sect"), which may provide a link between the Qumrân writings and the Qaraïtes (cf. Rowley, pp. 23-29). But if a scroll or scrolls were found in a Qumrân cave *ca.* A.D. 800 and made their way to the Qaraïte community in Cairo, it would require some continuity of the community making use of the document(s) to account for copies made in the 10th-12th cents. A.D. We may therefore assume some kind of link between the Qaraïte community in Cairo and the Qumrân community, but it remains unclear whether it was anything more than an attraction to the views presented in CD.

IV. Research on the Zadokite Fragments.–Between the time Schechter published the fragments and the discovery of the Qumrân scrolls, scholars produced much work on the fragments. (For a thorough bibliography, see L. Rost, *Die Damaskusschrift* [1933]; H. H. Rowley, *Zadokite Fragments and the Dead Sea Scrolls* [1952].) Since the discovery of the Qumrân materials, research on CD has been fully integrated with that on the DSS. It is therefore needless to discuss it separately in this article. For subsequent bibliography, see W. S. LaSor, *Bibliography of the Dead Sea Scrolls 1948-1957* (1958); Ch. Burchard, *Bibliographie zu den Handschriften vom Toten Meer,* II (*BZAW,* 89, 1965).

One or two points, however, should be emphasized. The relationship of the Teacher of Righteousness to the origin of the Qumrân community is clearly spelled out in the Zadokite Fragments — and often overlooked by scholars working on the DSS. The Teacher of Righteousness was not the founder of the sect, although this is often asserted. CD 1:1-6 speaks of the sinful nature of Israel and the remnant that remained. Then God visited them and caused a "root" to possess His land, but they were like the blind "for twenty years" (1:10). Then God "raised for them a Teacher of Righteousness to lead them in the way of His heart and to make known to the last generations that which He would do to the last generation, the congregation of the faithless" (1:10-12). The sect was already conscious of its existence for two decades before the Teacher appeared. For the origins of the Qumrân community, see H. H. Rowley, *BJRL*, 49 (1966), 203-232. For the relationship of the Teacher of Righteousness to the Qumrân community, see W. S. LaSor, *Dead Sea Scrolls and the NT* [1972], chs. 8–9; H. H. Rowley, *BJRL*, 40 [1957/58], 114-146.

See also DEAD SEA SCROLLS.

Bibliography.–S. Schechter, *Documents of Jewish Sectaries, I. Fragments of a Zadokite Work* (1910; repr. 1970); S. Zeitlin, *Zadokite Fragments* (1952); C. Rabin, *Zadokite Documents* (1954); *APOT*, II, 785-834 (seriously out of date). W. S. LASOR

ZAHAM zā'ham [Heb. *zaham*–'loathsome']. A son of King Rehoboam by Mahalath (2 Ch. 11:19).

ZAIN zä'yin. *See* ZAYIN.

ZAIR zā'ēr, zā'ər [Heb. *ṣā'îr*–'little, insignificant'; Gk. *Siōr*]. A place to which Joram "passed over" with all his chariots when Edom revolted against Judah (2 K. 8:21). It is possibly to be located in Edom, and some have suggested reading "Seir." There are textual points to consider, however. The parallel passage (2 Ch. 21:9) has "with his commanders" (*'im-śārāyw*) instead of "to Zair." The LXX of 2 K. 8:21 reads *Siōr*, which has led some to identify Zair with ZIOR, modern Sa'îr or Si'îr, 8 km. (5 mi.) NE of Hebron. But this site does not fit well with the context (Joram "passed over" to Zair). Moreover, the suggestion that *ṣā'îr* is related to Sā'îr ignores the fact that in Arabic as well as in Hebrew *ṣ* and *ś* (= Arab. *š*) do not sound at all alike; they merely look similar in transliteration. W. S. L. S.

ZALAPH zā'laf [Heb. *ṣālāp*–'caper-plant']. Father of a certain Hanun who helped to repair the well of Jerusalem in the time of Nehemiah (Neh. 3:30).

ZALMON zal'mən [Heb. *ṣalmôn*–'dark'(?)]. An Ahohite, one of David's thirty mighty men (2 S. 23:28). In 1 Ch. 11:29 he is called Ilai. See W. Rudolph, *Chronikbücher* (*HAT*, 1955), p. 100.

ZALMON zal'mən [Heb. *ṣalmôn*–'dark'(?); Gk. *Selmōn*, some MSS *Ermōn* (Jgs. 9:48)]; AV also SALMON (Ps. 68:14 [MT 15]).

1. A mountain near Shechem (Jgs. 9:48). Some have identified it with Mt. Ebal; but its modern name, Jebel Eslāmîyeh, bears only superficial resemblance to *ṣalmôn*. Other scholars have identified it with et-Tenanir at the foot of Mt. Gerizim, immediately S of Balâṭah (the site of ancient Shechem), where a Middle Bronze Age villa has been discovered (cf. *AP*, fig. 17); but any identification can be only tentative.

Bibliography.–E. Sellin, *ZAW*, 50 (1932), 305-307; J. Nagele, *JPOS*, 12 (1932), 152-161.

2. A mountain mentioned in Ps. 68:14 (MT 15), in a very difficult context. Some scholars have identified it with **1** above; but since Bashan is mentioned in the next verse, others have looked for it in the Hauran region, where Ptolemy located a mountain *Asalmanos*.

Bibliography.–J. G. Wetzstein, *Reisebericht über Hauran und die Trachonen* (1860), p. 90; W. F. Albright, *HUCA*, 23 (1950/51), 23. A. VAN SELMS

ZALMONAH zal-mō'nə [Heb. *ṣalmōnâ*–'dark, gloomy']. The site of an Israelite encampment in the wilderness, between Mt. Hor and Punon (Nu. 33:41f.). Its identification is uncertain, although some have suggested Bir Madhkur, E of Harun. *See* WANDERINGS OF ISRAEL.

ZALMUNNA. *See* ZEBAH AND ZALMUNNA.

ZAMBIS zam'bis. The AV transliteration of Gk. *Zambris* in 1 Esd. 9:34. The RSV emends the text to read Amariah in harmony with Ezr. 10:42 (see RSV mg.). *See* AMARIAH **7.**

ZAMBRI zam'brī (1 Macc. 2:26, AV). *See* ZIMRI **1.**

ZAMBRIS zam'bris. The NEB transliteration of Gk. *Zambris* in 1 Esd. 9:34. The RSV emends the text to harmonize with Ezr. 10:42. *See* AMARIAH **7.**

ZAMOTH zā'moth (1 Esd. 9:28, AV, NEB). *See* ZATTU.

ZAMZUMMIM zam-zum'əm [Heb. *zamzummîm;* Gk. *Zochommin, Zomzommein, Zommein*; cf. Arab. *zamzama*–'talk gibberish']. A name given to the REPHAIM by the Ammonites who dispossessed them (Dt. 2:20). If the Arabic etymology is accepted (cf. *BDB*, p. 273), it may be assumed that they spoke another language that sounded like gibberish to the Ammonites, who spoke a Semitic language. They have often been identified with the ZUZIM (Gen. 14:5), but this has no firm basis. The Rephaim, who occupied Transjordan and parts of Palestine prior to the coming of the Semites, were divided into various groups: the Emim (Dt. 2:10), Anakim (v. 11), and Zamzummim (v. 20), and possibly others (Horites, v. 12; Avvim, v. 23). These peoples were described as tall, 6 or 7 cubits in height (3-3.5 m., 9-10½ ft.) (F.-M. Abel, *GP*, I, 325-29, also 277f.). Outside the Bible the Zamzummim are unknown. See *GTTOT*, § 211. W. S. LASOR

ZANOAH zə-nō'ə [Heb. *zānô(a)ḥ*].

1. A town listed in the northernmost district of the Judean Shephelah (Josh. 15:34), along with identifiable towns such as Zorah (Ṣar'ah) and Eshtaol (Eshwa'). It was also occupied in the postexilic period (Neh. 11:30); its association with Jarmuth (Khirbet Yarmûk) and Adullam (esh-Sheikh Madhkûr) strengthens the location in the northern Shephelah.

Inhabitants of Zanoah repaired the Valley Gate of Jerusalem during Nehemiah's great building project (Neh. 3:13). In the NT period the fine flour from this town (Heb. *zᵉnôḥā'*, with textual variants) was of the highest quality and like that of Michmash was used for the sacred loaves of the bread of the Presence (Mish. *Menahoth* viii.1).

Eusebius and Jerome indicated that Zanoah was on the northeastern border of the metropolitan district of Eleutheropolis (Beit Jibrîm) (*Onom.* 92.13f. and 93.13f. respectively). Robinson noted the presence of Khirbet Zānû', which stands on the west side of Wâdī en-Nejîl; Albright noted also the pronunciation *Zānûḥ*. The presence of not only Byzantine but also late Iron Age pottery on the surface of this site strengthens its identification with Zanoah.

Bibliography.–*GP*, II, 489; W. F. Albright, *BASOR*, 18 (Apr. 1925), 11; E. Robinson, *Biblical Researches* (1856), II, 61; *SWP*, III, 404.

2. A place in the southeastern district of the Judean hill country, facing the wilderness (Josh. 15:56); it was founded by Jekuthiel (1 Ch. 4:18). The MT of Josh. 15:56, which distinguishes Zanoah from Cain (prob. Khirbet Benī Dâr, formerly known as Khirbet Yaqîn), is preferable to the corrupt rendering of LXX B (Gk. *Zakanaim*), which seems to conflate the two names. The proposed identification with Khirbet Zānûtā, 16 km. (10 mi.) SW of Hebron, would place the town too far W and in the wrong district; the name is also phonetically suspect. The alternate suggestion, Khirbet Beit ʿAmrā' about 2 km. (1¼ mi.) NW of Jutah (modern Yaṭṭā), is also without archeological support, although the section of Wâdī el-Khalîl on which it is situated, called Wâdī Abū Zennâkh, may preserve an echo of the biblical name Zanoah.

Bibliography.–*GP*, II, 489; *SWP*, III, 351, 410f.

A. F. RAINEY

ZAPHENATH-PANEAH zaf-ə-nath-pə-nē'ə [Heb. *ṣāpᵉnaṯ paʿᵃnē(a)ḥ*]; AV ZAPHNATH-PAANEAH. The name given to Joseph by Pharaoh when he appointed Joseph to a position of high authority over the land of Egypt (Gen. 41:45). The conferring of a new name commonly accompanied promotions of this sort. Discussion about the meaning of the name has produced widely divergent theories. Many favor G. Steindorff's suggestion that it represents Egyp. *ḏd-p3-nṯr-w.f-ʿnh* ("the god speaks and he [Joseph] lives"), although names of this type were not common until at least the 12th cent. B.C. (see comms. on Genesis, e.g., J. Skinner [*ICC*, 2nd ed. 1930]; G. von Rad [*OTL*, Eng. tr. 1972]). For another interpretation *see* JOSEPH II.D.

N. J. O.

ZAPHON zā'fon [Heb. *ṣāpôn*–'north'; Gk. B *Saphan*, A *Saphōn*]. A city E of the Jordan in Gad (Josh. 13:27). There the men of Ephraim met with Jephthah to rebuke him but were struck down by Jephthah and the other men of Gilead (Jgs. 12:1; the AV translates "northward" instead of "to Zaphon").

The Talmud (T.P. *Shebuoth* ix.2) identified Zaphon with ʿAmmata, which the *Onomasticon* places 21 Rom. mi. (30 km., 19 mi.) S of Pella. This identification has been followed by several scholars, although Abel declared it "inadmissible" (*GP*, II, 448). Glueck, however, showed in detail that the Talmud was not far wrong, for Zaphon is almost certainly to be identified with Tell el-Qôs, which is less than 1.2 km. (¾ mi.) from ʿAmmata. Asophon, a town mentioned by Josephus (*Ant*. xiii.12.5 [338]), and located N of ʿAmmata and less than 2.5 km. (1½ mi.) from Tell el-Qôs, appears to preserve the name Zaphon. For full discussion see Glueck, *AASOR*, 25 (1951), 297-300, 350-55.

W. S. L. S.

ZAPHON zä-fōn', zā'fon, **MOUNT.** In Ugaritic literature the term *ṣapānu* refers to a specific location, Mt. Casius (Jebel el-'Aqraʿ), about 40 km. (25 mi.) NNE of Râs Shamrah. It also refers to the cosmic mountain where Baal reigns (cf. Isa. 14:13). According to Kapelrud, the tower in a temple dedicated to Baal may have been named Zaphon in order to enhance its sacredness. Since this mountain was in the north, *ṣapānu* came to have the secondary meaning of "north." This became the primary meaning of Heb. *ṣāpôn*. In a few OT texts, however, this term carries its mythopoetic meaning, i.e., the highest mount where God reigns. Thus the NEB renders Ps. 89:12a (MT 13a), "Thou didst create Zaphon and Amanus" (RSV "The north and the south, thou hast created them"); this means that Yahweh has created even the most distant, ominous places and, therefore, no place lies beyond His rule. In Ps. 48:2 (MT 3) the psalmist lauds Zion as the center of Yahweh's universal reign by comparing it to the utmost heights of Zaphon (see NEB mg., NIV). A few scholars have advocated that *ṣāpôn* be rendered Zaphon in two other texts: Isa. 14:13, which speaks of the highest mountain in the north where the supreme God rules over the assembly, and Job 27:6, which speaks of God spreading out *ṣāpôn* over chaos.

See also NORTH.

Bibliography.–R. J. Clifford, *Cosmic Mountain in Canaan and the OT* (1972); C. Grave, *Orientalia*, 51 (1982), 161-182; A. S. Kapelrud, *Baal in the Ras Shamra Texts* (Eng. tr. 1952); J. Roberts, *Bibl.*, 56 (1975), 554-57; A. Robinson, *VT*, 24 (1974), 118-123; J. de Savignac, *VT*, 3 (1953), 95f.; *THAT*, II, *s.v.* צפון (W. H. Schmidt).

J. E. HARTLEY

ZARA zâr'ə (Mt. 1:3, AV). *See* ZERAH **2**.

ZARACES zâr'ə-sēz (1 Esd. 1:38, AV). *See* ZARIUS.

ZARAH zâr'ə (AV Gen. 38:30; 46:12; NEB Mt. 1:3). *See* ZERAH **2**.

ZARAEAS zə-rā'əs (NEB); **ZARAIAS** zə-rī'əs, zə-rā'əs (AV).

1. (1 Esd. 5:8, NEB). *See* SERAIAH **8**.

2. The NEB and AV renderings of Gk. *Zaraias* (LXX A) in 1 Esd. 8:2. The RSV omits, following LXX B.

3. (1 Esd. 8:31, NEB, AV). *See* ZERAHIAH **2**.

ZARATHUSTRA zar-ə-thōōs'trə. *See* RELIGIONS OF THE BIBLICAL WORLD: PERSIA V.

ZARDAEAS zâr-dā'əs (1 Esd. 9:28, NEB). *See* ZERDAIAH.

ZAREAH zâr'ē-ə (Neh. 11:29, AV). *See* ZORAH.

ZAREATHITES zâr'i-ə-thīts (1 Ch. 2:53, AV, NEB). *See* ZORATHITES.

ZARED zâr-ed (Nu. 21:12, AV, NEB). *See* ZERED.

ZAREPHATH zar'ə-fath [Heb. *ṣārᵉpaṯ*; Gk. *sarepta*; Akk. *ṣariptu* < vb. *ṣarāpu*–'to dye'] (1 K. 17:9f.; Ob. 20; Lk. 4:26); AV NT, NEB NT, SAREPTA. A city-state situated near the tip of a promontory along the Lebanese Mediterranean some 13 km. (8 mi.) S of Sidon and 21 km. (13 mi.) N of Tyre. From its earliest occupation near the beginning of the Late Bronze Age, Zarephath enjoyed a prosperous and relatively peaceful existence for more than two millennia. An inscription recovered near the site indicates that its name is preserved in the modern village Sarafand, located in the hills immediately to the SE of the somewhat inconspicuous tell.

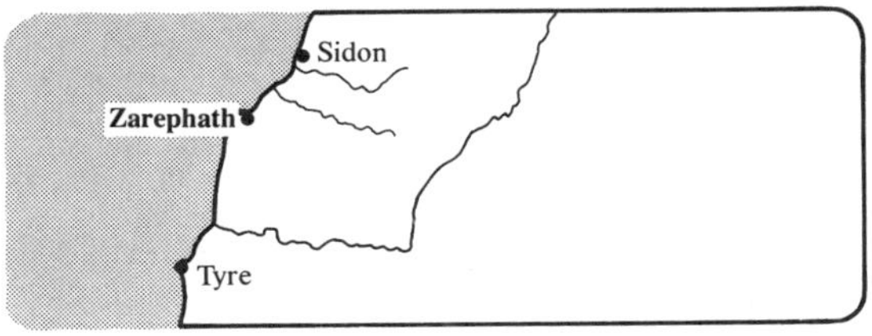

Zarephath is listed in a thirteenth-century B.C. Egyptian papyrus as the site of a Phoenician harbor (see *ANET*, p. 477). When Zarephath surrendered peaceably to Sennacherib's vast hordes in 701 B.C., he described it as a walled city belonging to the king of Sidon (spelled Zaribtu, *ANET*, p. 287). In the time of Esarhaddon (*ca*. 680-669 B.C.) the city was transferred to Tyre's control. Located only some 80 km. (50 mi.) N of Mt. Carmel, Zarephath was

A wall painting from the Dura-Europos synagogue depicting Elijah reviving the widow's child at Zarephath (Yale University Art Gallery, Dura-Europos Collection)

the city to which Elijah went during the severe drought that occurred in Ahab's reign (1 K. 17:9). There he found lodging with a widow, miraculously provided her with a constant supply of oil, and eventually revived her dying son (1 K. 17:10-24). This latter event is commemorated in a mural painting in a third-century A.D. synagogue at DURA-EUROPOS on the Euphrates. The prophet Obadiah identified Zarephath as the northern extremity of Canaan (Ob. 20). Reading in the synagogue at Nazareth, Jesus referred to the Zarephathite widow to illustrate that a prophet is unwelcome in his own land (Lk. 4:26).

From as early as the late 4th cent. A.D. pilgrims journeyed to Zarephath. A tower was erected to mark the "upper chamber," in which Elijah had lived. Later, Theodosius (*PPTS*, II, 16) spoke of a large church in the city, and Antoninus Martyr of Placentia (*PPTS*, II, 3) described it as "a very Christian city." Still later a text delineating a Crusaders' route mentioned Zarephath as a walled city (*PPTS*, XII, 13).

Recent archeological excavations have shown that Zarephath was a sizable commercial city during both the Phoenician and Roman occupations. It possessed residential, religious, and industrial quarters; the latter was predominantly concerned with the production of textiles and ceramics. A highly developed maritime industry exported grain, wine, oil, and above all the red-purple dye extracted from shellfish (cf. Pliny *Nat. hist.* v.70) for which both the city and Phoenicia ("red-purple") itself were named. A large and technically sophisticated Roman port was discovered, dating from the 1st to 6th cents. A.D. Overlooking this port was found a shrine of the goddess Tanit (= Astarte?); some scholars have associated this shrine with ceremonies involving child sacrifices, a practice strongly condemned by Scripture (Jer. 7:31f.; 19:3-6; 2 K. 23:10).

See also PHOENICIA II.

Bibliography.–PPTS = Palestine Pilgrims' Text Society (14 vols., 1897); J. B. Pritchard, *Expedition*, 14 (1971), 14-23; "Sarepta in Tradition and History," in J. Reumann, ed., *Understanding the Sacred Text* (1972), pp. 101-114; *Recovering Sarepta: A Phoenician City* (1978).

B. J. BEITZEL

ZARETAN zâr'ə-tən (Josh. 3:16, AV). *See* ZARETHAN.

ZARETHAN zâr'ə-than [Heb. *ṣarᵉṯān*–'great (or lofty) rock' (?); Gk. *Sarthan, Sirdathai*]; AV ZARETAN, ZARTANAH, ZARTHAN; NEB also ZARTANAH. A city located in the central Jordan Valley E of the Jordan River in the neighborhood of ADAM (Tell ed-Dâmiyeh), mentioned in connection with the blockage of the Jordan when Joshua and the Hebrews crossed into Canaan (Josh. 3:16). 1 K. 4:12 states that Zarethan was "beside" Beth-shean and "below Jezreel." In Solomon's time the valley between Zarethan and Succoth was the region where the bronze vessels were cast for the Jerusalem temple (7:46). In the par. 2 Ch. 4:17 Zarethan is called "Zeredah" (AV "Zeredathah"). Jgs. 7:22 states that Gideon pursued the Midianites "as far as Beth-shittah toward Zererah" (AV "Zererath"), which is probably a misreading of "Zeredah" resulting from the similarity of the Hebrew letters *dāleṯ* (*d*) and *rēš* (*r*).

Scholars have debated the exact identification of Zarethan. J. Simons (*GTTOT*, pp. 565f.) placed it W of the Jordan River, while others have located it on the eastern side. A. Mazar and Y. Aharoni have supported Tell Umm Ḥamîd, a large site between Adam (Tell ed-Dâmiyeh) and Succoth (Tell Deir ʿallā). N. Glueck and J. B. Pritchard have preferred Tell es-Saʿīdîyeh, a site that W. F. Albright and Aharoni identified as Zaphon.

Pritchard conducted four seasons of excavations at Tell es-Saʿīdîyeh from 1964-1967. His efforts revealed artifacts or structures from the Chalcolithic to the Iron Age periods. Numerous copper objects of the 13th-12th cents. B.C. support this site as a bronze-working center, perhaps in later use during Solomon's time (cf. 1 K. 7:46). Extensive

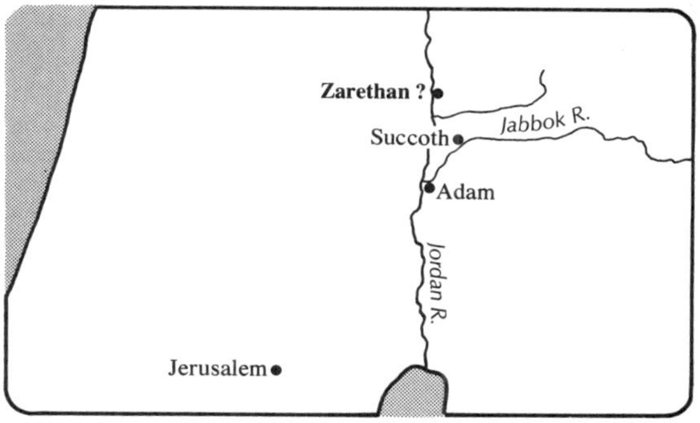

remains of an Israelite city (10th-8th cents. B.C.) have been uncovered, including a 17-ft.-thick casemate wall, a weaving room, and an elaborate covered water system. Tombs from the E.B., L.B., and E.I. periods were also discovered. Although there is no agreement about the location of Zarethan, the evidence suggests Tell es-Sa'īdîyeh as a likely candidate.

Bibliography.–Y. Aharoni, *LBHG*, (rev. ed. 1979), pp. 34, 123, 284 n. 222; *EAEHL*, IV, *s.v.* "Tell es-Sa'idiyeh" (J. B. Pritchard), N. Glueck, *AASOR*, 25-28 (1951), 340-47; *GP*, II, 448; *GTTOT*, pp. 462, 565f., 839; A. Mazar, *Eretz-Israel*, 3 (1954), 26.

W. L. THOMPSON, JR.

ZARETH-SHAHAR zâr'eth shā'här (Josh. 13:19, AV). *See* ZERETH-SHAHAR.

ZARHITES zär'hīts (AV, NEB, Nu. 26:13, 20; etc.). *See* ZERAHITES.

ZARIUS zâr'i-əs [Gk. B *Zarios*, A *Zarakēs*]; AV ZARACES. Brother of King Jehoiakim of Judah, according to 1 Esd. 1:38 (LXX 36), which appears to be a confused account of the events recorded in 2 Ch. 36:4. In Chronicles Neco takes Jehoahaz to Egypt; in 1 Esdras Jehoiakim takes his brother Zarius out of Egypt.

ZARTANAH zär-tan'ə, zär'tan-ə (1 K. 4:12, AV, NEB). *See* ZARETHAN.

ZARTHAN zär'than (1 K. 7:46, AV). *See* ZARETHAN.

ZATHOE zath'ō-i (1 Esd. 8:32, AV, NEB). *See* ZATTU.

ZATHUI zath'o͞o-i (1 Esd. 5:12, AV, NEB). *See* ZATTU.

ZATTHU zath'o͞o (Neh. 10:14, AV). *See* ZATTU.

ZATTU zat'o͞o [Heb. *zattû'*; Gk. Apoc. *Zathoui* (1 Esd. 5:12), *Zathoēs* (8:32), *Zamoth* (9:28)]; AV also ZATTHU; AV Apoc., NEB Apoc., ZATHUI, ZATHOE, ZAMOTH. Head of a lay family of which some members returned to Jerusalem from Babylon (Ezr. 2:8 par. Neh. 7:13; 1 Esd. 5:12; Ezr. 8:5 par. 1 Esd. 8:32). Some of the men of this family divorced the foreign wives that they had married during the Exile (Ezr. 10:27 par. 1 Esd. 9:28). Zattu himself was one of the chiefs who signed the covenant under Nehemiah (Neh. 10:14).

ZAVAN zā'van (1 Ch. 1:42, AV, NEB). *See* ZAAVAN.

ZAYIN zä'yin [ז]. The seventh letter of the Hebrew alphabet, transliterated in this encyclopedia as *z*. It came also to be used for the number seven, and it stands at the beginning of the seventh section of Ps. 119 (cf. AV). *See* WRITING.

ZAZA zā'zə [Heb. *zāzā'*]. Son of Jonathan, a descendant of Jerahmeel (1 Ch. 2:33).

ZEAL [Heb. *qin'â*] (2 K. 10:16; 19:31; Ps. 69:9 [MT 10]; 119:139; etc.); AV also ENVY (Isa. 26:11); NEB also "bitter enemies," RESENTMENT; [*qānā'*] (2 S. 21:2); [Gk. *zēlos*] (Jn. 2:17; Rom. 10:2; 2 Cor. 7:7, 11; 9:2; Phil. 3:6); AV also "fervent mind"; NEB also "long for," EAGERNESS; [*haplótēs*] (Rom. 12:8); AV SIMPLICITY; NEB "exert yourself"; [*spoudḗ*] (Rom. 12:11; 2 Cor. 7:12); AV BUSINESS, CARE; NEB ENERGY, DEVOTED; **(BE) ZEALOUS** [Gk. *zēlōtḗs*] (Acts 21:20; 22:3; Gal. 1:14; Tit. 2:14; 1 Pet. 3:13); AV also FOLLOWER; NEB STAUNCH UPHOLDER, ARDENT, etc.; [*spoudázō*] (2 Pet. 1:10; 3:14); AV GIVE DILIGENCE, BE DILIGENT; NEB EXERT ONESELF, DO ONE'S UTMOST; [*zēleúō*] (Rev. 3:19); NEB "be on your mettle." Impassioned devotion to a person or cause, which may be either worthy or unworthy. At times the orginal term would be better translated "jealousy"; under certain conditions jealousy is justified (e.g., God's jealousy for His people), but selfish jealousy is sinful (*see* JEALOUS).

Isaiah 9:6f. attributes the realization of the messianic hope, from the birth of the King to the consummation of His kingdom, to "the zeal of the Lord of hosts." According to Jn. 2:17, Jesus' cleansing of the temple so strongly impressed the disciples that they came to associate His act with Ps. 69:9 (MT 10), "Zeal for thy house has consumed me" (the quotation in John follows the LXX, which reads "will consume"). Some interpreters have understood this as a prediction that Jesus' zeal would lead to His death at the hands of the authorities He had antagonized by His action; others have taken it simply as a messianic prophecy peculiarly fitting as a description of Jesus' motivation for the act.

According to Paul the Jewish people in NT times were zealous for God (Acts 22:3), but unfortunately they failed to understand that the righteousness of God was attained through Jesus Christ (Rom. 10:2-4). In his early days Paul himself was zealous to master the traditions handed down by the great teachers of Judaism and to order his life accordingly (Gal. 1:14). Loyal to this cause, he saw Jesus' followers as a dangerous rival to his own faith, and so his zeal took a negative and violent form (Phil. 3:6). But when his confrontation with the risen Lord disclosed the better way of trust in an all-sufficient Savior, the zealot for Judaism was transformed into a zealot for Christ and the gospel.

See also ZEALOT. E. F. H.

ZEALOT [Gk. *zēlōtḗs*]; AV ZELOTES. A designation of the disciple Simon in Luke's lists of the twelve (Lk. 6:15; Acts 1:13), where it serves to differentiate him from Simon Peter. In the parallel lists he is designated the "Cananaean" (Gk. *Kananaios*, Mt. 10:4; Mk. 3:18; AV "Canaanite"; NEB "a member of the Zealot party"), which is clearly a Greek transliteration of *qn'n'*, the Aramaic equivalent of *zēlōtḗs*. The word-group to which *zēlōtḗs* belongs refers to a passionate devotion to a person or a cause, combining within its semantic range senses both of "jealousy" and of "zeal" (*see* JEALOUS; ZEAL). The LXX uses *zēlōtḗs* only in the former sense and only of God (e.g., Ex. 20:5). In the NT it is used in a general way of those who are "eager" for manifestations of the Spirit (1 Cor. 14:12; AV "zealous"), or "zealous" for good deeds (Tit. 2:14; NEB "eager") or for what is right (1 Pet. 3:13; AV "followers"; NEB "devoted"). It also appears in the more specifically Jewish sense of one who is "zealous" for the Torah and the traditions of Judaism (Acts 21:20

[NEB "staunch upholders"]; 22:3 [NEB "ardent"]; Gal. 1:14 [NEB "devotion"]).

In popular usage "Zealot" has come to be used of all who participated in Jewish resistance to the Roman rule of Palestine from the time of Judas of Galilee (A.D. 6) through to the war of 66-70. Such usage, however, is inaccurate and misleading. On the one hand, "Zealot" does not appear as the designation of an identifiable rebel group until sometime after the outbreak of the war, and even then it refers to only one of several rebel factions. There is no real evidence of a Zealot party in the pre-war period. On the other hand, the zealot ideal — willingness both to use and to suffer violence for the sake of the Torah — was widespread within Judaism from Maccabean times. Even in the 1st cent. A.D. the term did not necessarily designate one as an advocate of rebellion against Rome. Popular usage, then, is both too broad and, in another sense, too narrow.

- I. "Zeal" in Second Temple Judaism
- II. The Rebellion Against Rome
  - A. The Popular View Reconsidered
  - B. Identifiable Resistance Groups
  - C. Common Motives and Features
- III. Zealots and the NT
  - A. Simon the Zealot
  - B. Jesus
  - C. Paul
  - D. Jerusalem "Torah Christians"

***I. "Zeal" in Second Temple Judaism* (ca. 500 B.C.–A.D. 10).**–By adopting the name "Zealots" as a self-designation, the Jewish revolutionaries described in *BJ* iv.3.9 (160f.) were identifying with a widely held Jewish ideal and laying claim to an honored tradition. Farmer was probably right in his assertion that the Maccabean revolt was responsible for the prominence of this ideal in subsequent history. Certainly the Maccabees embodied central features of the ideal: both the willingness to use violence to defend the Torah and the hope that God would reward such faithfulness with success. Moreover, the language of zeal was explicitly linked with Mattathias and his sons by the author of 1 Maccabees, who was evidently an admirer and close associate of the Hasmonean regime. Not only does he describe Mattathias's original resistance to the edict of Antiochus as an act of zeal (2:24, 26), but he attributes zeal language to Mattathias himself. "Let everyone who is zealous for the law and supports the covenant come out with me" was Mattathias's rallying cry (2:27), and later on his deathbed he urged his sons to "show zeal for the law and give your lives for the covenant of our fathers" (v. 50). The concept of zeal did not originate with the Maccabees, however. It appears in earlier literature of the Hellenistic period (Sir. 45:23; 48:2), and it is deeply rooted in the OT, especially in connection with Phinehas (Nu. 25, esp. vv. 11, 13) and Elijah (1 K. 18–19, esp. 19:10, 14), both of whom, along with Simeon and Levi, served as prototypes for the developing tradition. Nor was the ideal limited to the descendants of the Maccabees and their supporters. As the texts cited in this section amply illustrate, the zealot ideal appears across a broad spectrum of the Judaism of the period.

As has been mentioned, the developing zeal tradition looked to several OT figures as models and prototypes. Phinehas's reputation for zeal stems from his violent opposition to Baal worship as recounted in Nu. 25: to purge Israel of this contamination he slew Zimri the Israelite and the Midianite woman with whom he was "playing the harlot" (cf. v. 1), as they were engaged in the very act (vv. 6-8). Elijah's zeal was demonstrated in his slaughter of the prophets of Baal and of Asherah, who had induced Israel to forsake the covenant, throw down the altars of Yahweh, and kill Yahweh's prophets (1 K. 19:10, 14). Both Phinehas and Elijah were held up as exemplars of zeal, and of the divine reward accompanying such faithfulness, in Mattathias's deathbed speech (1 Macc. 2:54, 58) and elsewhere in the literature of the Second Temple Period (on Phinehas, see Sir. 45:23f.; 1 Macc. 2:26; 4 Macc. 18:12; cf. Pseudo-Philo 47:1; Mish. *Sanhedrin* ix.6; on Elijah, see Sir. 48:1f.). The Genesis account of the vengeance that Simeon and Levi wreaked on the men of Shechem in retaliation for the rape of their sister Dinah (Gen. 34) is somewhat critical of their actions, and the language of zeal appears in neither the MT nor the LXX of this passage. In the Second Temple Period, however, the slaughter of the Shechemites was seen as an act of zeal, qualifying Simeon and Levi for full membership in the ranks of the zealous (Jub. 30:18; T.Levi 6:3; Jth. 9:2-4). This reinterpretation of Gen. 34 probably resulted from the confluence of two factors: the glorification of the house of Levi, characteristic of the Hasmonean period; and the priestly orientation of much of the zeal tradition (both Levi [Jub. 30:18; T.Levi 5:2] and Phinehas [Nu. 25:12f.; Sir. 45:24; 1 Macc. 2:54] were awarded the hereditary priesthood as a reward for their zeal). The fact that Jth. 9:2-4 attributes zeal only to Simeon, however, demonstrates that zeal was not exclusively a priestly tradition (cf. Gal. 1:14; Acts 22:3; 2 Bar. 66:5).

It should be clear from these OT prototypes that the developing zealot tradition was characterized by more than just a fervent devotion to the Torah and the traditions of Judaism. While this was certainly its starting point (2 Macc. 4:2; 1QS 4:4), a zealot was one whose fervent devotion involved him or her (in the case of Judith) in violence. In the first instance, a zealot was one prepared to use violence against those who were contravening, subverting, or opposing the law, whether these were Jews

A sherd inscribed "ben-Ya'ir" (possibly Eleazar ben-Ya'ir) found at Masada. It may have been one of the lots used for the rebels' mass suicide (The Estate of Yigael Yadin)

(e.g., Phinehas; 1 Macc. 2:23f., 26; 2 Bar. 66:1-8; Mish. *Sanhedrin* ix.6; cf. *Ant.* xviii.1.6 [23]), Gentiles (e.g., Simeon and Levi; Judith; 1 Macc. 2:25), or the wicked in general (e.g., T.Ash. 4:2-5; 1QS 9:23; 1QH 14:4; Philo *De Specialibus Legibus* ii.253). In addition, the zealot ideal embraced a willingness to suffer and die for the sake of the Torah (1 Macc. 2:50-60; 2 Macc. 7:2; 8:21; 4 Macc. 18; cf. 1 Macc. 1:63; 2:32-41; *Ant.* xviii.1.6 [23f.]), even to the point of committing suicide (2 Macc. 14:37-46; cf. *BJ* vii.8.6–9.1 [320-401]).

Such zealous activity was undergirded and motivated by a compelling theology of zeal. It was believed that God would reward such faithfulness with honor, righteousness, and renown (1 Macc. 2:50-64; Jub. 30:18-20; 2 Bar. 66:6; 4 Macc. 18). Further, it was believed that divine assistance would be forthcoming to those who took up the sword in defense of the Torah: "It is not on the size of the army that victory in battle depends, but strength comes from Heaven" (1 Macc. 3:19; cf. *Ant.* xviii.1.1 [5]). But perhaps the most significant motivating factor was belief in the atoning value of zeal. Those who "burned with zeal for the law as Phinehas did" (1 Macc. 2:26) did so in the expectation that they too would "turn back [God's] wrath from the people of Israel" (Nu. 25:11). Zeal itself would atone for the sins of Israel (cf. 4 Macc. 17:20-22; Midr. *Nu. Rabbah* xxi.3).

It should be clear, then, that in the 1st cent. A.D. the term "zealot" (e.g., Simon the Zealot) would not necessarily refer to someone advocating the overthrow of Roman rule. Certainly many would have seen such rebellion as an expression of zeal, in keeping with the inherited tradition; it is not surprising that revolutionaries would adopt the term as a self-designation. But as the case of Paul demonstrates (Gal. 1:14; Phil. 3:6), one could be a zealot for the tradition without being a revolutionary. Indeed, that Paul could use the term *zēlōtēs* of himself without further explanation demonstrates that the term did not at this time refer exclusively to revolutionaries, just as Luke's casual use of the term in the post-war period (Acts 21:20; 22:3) suggests that the emergence of the Zealot party during the war did not completely obliterate the older sense of the term.

II. The Rebellion Against Rome.–*A. The Popular View Reconsidered.* According to the popular view the "Zealots" were a clearly identifiable party of national liberation, founded by Judas of Galilee in A.D. 6, which agitated for resistance to Roman rule until it succeeded in provoking the populace to widespread revolt. The various terms used by Josephus in connection with revolutionary activity ("Zealots," "fourth philosophy," Sicarii, "brigands") are to be taken as references to a single religio-political movement. This view developed as a result of the work of such nineteenth-century scholars as Graetz, Jost, and especially Schürer (*HJP*), and it continues to find scholarly advocates (e.g., with differences in detail, Cullmann, Hengel, Brandon, Merkel, the revised Schürer).

The validity of this synthetic approach is open to serious question, however, as has been demonstrated by a growing number of scholars (e.g., Jackson and Lake, Smith, Rhoads, Borg, Horsley and Hanson). The question is more than just one of terminology. This newer approach goes beyond the recognition that there is no evidence of "zealot" being a party designation in the pre-war period, to assert that there was no single, cohesive revolutionary party in this period at all. Rather, it is argued, the evidence points to widespread social unrest and discontent, directed not only at Rome but also at the ruling Jewish elite, which gave rise to a variety of spontaneous and unconnected social movements and events, which ultimately precipitated open revolt.

The older reconstruction rests on a foundation provided by two aspects of Josephus's account. The first is the statement in *Ant.* xviii.1.1 (9) that Judas of Galilee, who with Saddok the Pharisee started "an intrusive fourth school of philosophy," was thereby responsible for "planting the seeds of those troubles which subsequently overtook" Judea. While this statement mentions no organic or organizational link between the "fourth philosophy" and the later rebel groups, the older view understands this lack to be supplied by a second aspect of Josephus's account, namely, the participation of other members of Judas's family in rebel activity. Two sons, James and Simon, were put to death by Tiberius Alexander (A.D. 46-48) for unspecified crimes (*Ant.* xx.5.2 [102]). Menahem, another son (or grandson), led a band of supporters, armed with weapons plundered from Masada, into Jerusalem in the early days of the revolt; he proceeded to play a leading role until he was assassinated by followers of Eleazar the son of the high priest, who objected to his royal pretensions (*BJ* ii.17.8f. [433-448]). Another relative, Eleazar the son of Jairus, led the remnant of Menahem's followers to Masada (ii.17.9 [447]), where they remained throughout the war. It is argued that these references supply evidence not only of the continued existence of the party founded by Judas but also of the basic equivalence of Josephus's terms. The link between "Zealots" and Sicarii is argued on the basis of the Menahem account. His followers are in one instance described as "armed zealots" (*BJ* ii.17.9 [444]), but once they retreat to Masada they are referred to consistently as Sicarii (e.g., vii.8.1 [252]). Since Menahem at one point acted as "the leader of the revolution" (ii.17.8 [434]), it is argued that the Sicarii were a sub-group that separated from the larger Zealot party to which it had formerly belonged. Some would go further and posit a link between the brigands and the "fourth philosophy" by identifying Judas of Galilee with Judas the son of the brigand chief Hezekiah, who according to *BJ* ii.4.1 (56) followed in his father's footsteps.

But the evidence will not support the weight of the hypothesis. There is nothing to suggest that Menahem's followers used the term "zealot" as a self-designation; the term is Josephus's, and it means no more than "ardent follower." Nor can Judas be identified with the son of Hezekiah. Josephus made no connection between them; indeed, he described them quite differently ("sophist" and "brigand"). While a link between Judas's "fourth philosophy" and the Sicarii is probable, the brigands and the Zealots were separate phenomena. Josephus's statement blaming the whole rebellion on Judas of Galilee must be read in the context of his apologetic purpose: to convince the Romans that the Jewish war was the responsibility of a small fanatical minority, not of the people as a whole. He may have meant to say only that Judas was the first to call for resistance to Roman rule and that he had an influence on all who followed. But if it is argued that Josephus wanted his readers to see Judas as the founder of a single party, it must be replied that his actual narrative shows no evidence of its existence. He provided no name for such a group, no evidence of coordinated rebel activity between A.D. 6 and 44, and no indication that the moderate party that set out to organize for war had to deal with another organized group. What does emerge from his narrative is a situation of widespread social unrest that gave rise to a variety of groups and movements.

B. Identifiable Resistance Groups. 1. Brigands. Both the NT and Josephus provide evidence for the widespread activity of brigands during the period. While Josephus's account presents them as ordinary robbers with purely mercenary motives, they are more accurately seen as a socio-political phenomenon of a type frequently found in peasant societies when the perceived injustice of the social system reaches a certain intensity. It is clear from Josephus's account that they were popular with the common people and that their brigandage was directed mainly against the ruling Jewish elite. As well as adding to the general social unrest, they made two specific contributions to the rebellion against Rome. The brigands and common people who fled to Jerusalem after the collapse of Galilee helped to overthrow the moderate revolutionary government under Ananus (*BJ* iv.3.3ff. [135ff.]). And a brigand chief, Simon bar Giora, became the dominant figure in the later stages of the war.

2. Sicarii. In contrast to the brigands, the Sicarii were a largely urban group who engaged in terrorist tactics of selective assassination, plunder of the wealthy, and kidnapping for ransom. Emerging in the time of Felix, their name derives from the short dagger (Lat. *sica*) that they used in their activity. Probably linked with Judas of Galilee through hereditary leadership and ideology ("no lord but God"), they contributed to the revolt mainly by aiding in the initial overthrow of the pro-Roman establishment in A.D. 66 (*BJ* ii.17.6-9 [425-443]). When their leader Menahem was himself assassinated, the Sicarii retreated to Masada, where they sat out the war until they fell to the Romans in A.D. 73 or 74.

3. Zealots. An identifiable Zealot party is an integral element in Josephus's narrative from the winter of A.D. 67-68 to the end of the war. Brigands from Galilee and the countryside of Judea fled to Jerusalem where, with the help of the Idumeans, they overthrew the moderate government, assassinated the high priest Ananus, and set up a revolutionary government with a new high priest chosen by lot. This Zealot party was joined for a while by John of Gischala, but it eventually broke with him and continued as a smaller rebel faction under the leadership of Eleazar son of Simon. Smith, followed by Horsley and Hanson, saw the Zealots as composed mainly of brigand refugees. But there are several reasons to believe that the group also contained a Jerusalem component with strong priestly orientation. First, Eleazar, the main Zealot leader and a priest, was a major player in the initial defeat of Cestius's

A rare coin from Year 4 of the Second Jewish Revolt (The Estate of Yigael Yadin)

Roman troops, and was thus not a refugee. Further, even before the incursion of the brigands the term "zealot" was used of the radical faction in Jerusalem in a way that suggests a party name ("so-called Zealots," *BJ* ii.22.1 [651]). It is possible that the Zealot party went through three phases: (1) a group of Jerusalem radicals with a strong element of lower-status priests, formed in reaction against the moderate party, which had excluded them from power (cf. *BJ* ii.20.3 [564]); (2) a coalition with the brigand refugees; (3) a continuing group, smaller in number, after the break with John of Gischala and his followers.

4. John of Gischala. John, a prominent Galilean with highly placed Jerusalem friends, resented the appointment of Josephus as commander of Galilee and worked to undermine his authority. After the fall of Galilee he fled to Jerusalem, where he initially aligned himself with the moderate government of Ananus. Apparently desirous of power, he forged secret alliances with the Zealots, identifying with them fully once the moderate party had been overthrown. Unwilling to share power with the Zealot leaders, he broke away and formed his own group, which strove with the Zealots and with Simon bar Giora for supremacy within Jerusalem. Captured by the Romans, he was sentenced to life imprisonment.

5. The Idumeans. A contingent of Idumeans played an important part in the power struggles within Jerusalem during the war. Initially invited in by the Zealots, they provided decisive assistance in the overthrow of the moderate government of Ananus. Distressed by the subsequent reign of terror, many of them returned home. Those who remained sided at first with John of Gischala, but later they joined some of the remaining chief priests in attempting to wrest control of Jerusalem from John and the Zealots by inviting Simon bar Giora into the city. The identity and motives of this group are not clear. Perhaps there was some connection with Eleazar the son of the high priest, who had precipitated the revolt by refusing to offer the usual sacrifice on behalf of the emperor, and who was later appointed commander of Idumea (*BJ* ii.20.4 [566]).

6. Simon bar Giora. This brigand chief first appears in Josephus's account in connection with the rout of Cestius's army. During the early years of the war he gained a following among the lower classes, who were attracted by his attacks on the wealthy and his promise of benefits for the poor. He was aligned with the Sicarii at Masada for a time, and his power grew until he controlled much of southern Judea and Idumea. Invited into Jerusalem, he engaged in a year-long power struggle with John and the Zealots for control of the city. During the Roman siege he demonstrated strong and disciplined leadership, and he emerged as the acknowledged commander of the defense of the city. He was executed in Rome after being put on display in Titus's triumphal parade.

C. Common Motives and Features. Despite the evident differences among the groups, there were common elements that should not be overlooked. First, much of the rebel activity appears to have had a socio-economic basis; the revolt was as much a reaction against perceived oppression by the ruling Jewish elite as it was a revolt against Roman rule. It is not incidental that one of the first acts of the Jerusalem insurgents in A.D. 66 was to destroy the debt records held in the public archives (*BJ* ii.17.6 [427]). Violence against the wealthy, the nobility, and the higher-status priestly circle was carried out by the Sicarii, the brigands, and the Zealots alike. Further, despite Josephus's obvious contempt for the rebels, it is possible to perceive common religious motivations. All groups showed an evident concern for Torah and temple and saw themselves as acting to defend both from "contamination," confident that God would vindicate their faithfulness (e.g., *BJ* ii.16.4 [391-93]); i.e., they were motivated by the ideals of zeal. In addition, several aspects of Josephus's account — e.g., the rebels' confidence that God would come to their aid (ii.16.4 [391]; v.9.4 [403]) and the role of eschatological prophets in stirring up revolutionary fervor (ii.13.4f. [258-263]) — suggest the presence of an eschatological motivation as well: the expectation that the war would culminate in the arrival of the Kingdom.

III. Zealots and the NT.–A. *Simon the Zealot.* If the preceding analysis is correct, Simon's nickname in no way identifies him as "a member of the Zealot party" (NEB). During the time of Jesus' ministry such a party did not exist, nor was the term *zēlṓtēs/qn'n'* necessarily linked with revolutionary activity. The nickname originated, undoubtedly in Christian circles, because of Simon's identification with the type of zealous adherence to Israel's tradition described in section I above. The presence of zeal language in Christian usage (Jn. 2:17; Acts 21:20) suggests that the characteristics that gave rise to the nickname were not necessarily restricted to his pre-disciple days. The precise form in which his zeal came to expression, however, is open to speculation.

B. Jesus. From the time of Reimarus down to the present (notably the work of Brandon) there have been attempts to demonstrate that Jesus, if not a Zealot, was at least in fundamental sympathy with the goals and methods of the anti-Roman rebels. The main foundations for such hypotheses are the following: (1) Jesus' execution by Rome on a charge of political sedition ("the King of the Jews"); (2) Jesus' triumphal entry into Jerusalem, with its royal overtones, followed by an assault on the temple; (3) Jesus' identification with the common people, criticism of the wealthy, and conflict with the powerful; (4) the presence within Jesus' band of disciples of at least one "Zealot." Other aspects of Jesus' ministry are then appealed to in a secondary way, e.g., the command to procure a sword (Lk. 22:36) and the statement "not peace but a sword" (Mt. 10:34). Since there is also much in the Gospels' depiction of Jesus that does not conform to this picture, such hypotheses contend that the Gospels were written in part to disguise and conceal the true nature of Jesus' mission.

Although the discussion is still going on, it is clear to most scholars that the Zealot hypothesis cannot be sustained. (1) The strongest piece of favorable evidence is the execution of Jesus as a royal pretender. But its significance is virtually nullified by the fact that the Romans showed no interest whatsoever in rounding up Jesus' disciples or curtailing the activity of the early Church. They apparently viewed the Jesus movement as posing no military or revolutionary threat. The execution of Jesus does not in and of itself identify Him as an advocate of armed revolt. Anyone in the flammable political environment of first-century Palestine who proclaimed a kingdom, gathered crowds, and annoyed the power elite was courting death. (2) No one seriously contemplating revolution would have thought of attacking the temple, which had impregnable fortifications, with anything less than a full-scale military assault. Jesus' entry into Jerusalem and His subsequent activity in the temple are much more plausibly seen as prophetic signs than as revolutionary actions. (3) While Jesus shared the social orientation of the revolutionaries, His message — centered on a kingdom established by God, and a kingdom ethic demanding love even of enemies — cannot possibly be construed in terms of armed insurrection. (4) The argument from Simon's nickname is, as has been demonstrated, without value.

To dissociate Jesus from political revolution is not, however, to dissociate Him from Israel's zeal tradition. Like other "zealots" (cf. Jn. 2:17), He identified fully with Israel's history, plight, and hope. He was not a teacher of timeless truths who just happened to be Jewish. Rather, His mission was to announce to "the lost sheep of the house of Israel" the dawning of the long awaited era of salvation. Like other exhibitors of zeal, He was willing to suffer violence and death for the sake of God's cause and even to see such suffering as having atoning value (Mk. 10:45; cf. 4 Macc. 17:20-22). Jesus' mission cannot be understood solely in terms of the zeal tradition, of course. But this tradition may serve to provide sharper definition to some facets of it.

C. Paul. Paul described his violent persecution of the Church as an act of "zeal" (Phil. 3:6), and this clearly conforms to the traditional use of the term. He felt that "the traditions of the fathers" were threatened by this movement, and as a "zealot" for those traditions (Gal. 1:13f.) he resorted to violence to defend them. The nature of the perceived threat, however, is not clear. Was the Church already admitting uncircumcised Gentiles? Were Jewish Christians criticizing Torah observance in the name of Christ? Or was the message of a crucified Messiah in itself seen as an affront to Torah (cf. Dt. 21:23; Gal. 3:13)? Since Paul's reasons for objecting to the Christian faith must be seen as the starting point for his developing theology once he became convinced that the crucified Jesus was indeed God's Messiah, an answer to this question should shed light on his subsequent thought concerning the law, the Gentiles, and the cross.

D. Jerusalem "Torah Christians." The Jerusalem church included many Christians who advocated circumcision of Gentiles (Acts 15:1; Gal. 2:3-5) and who resisted any weakening of Torah observance among Jewish Christians (Acts 21:20). With some justification, Luke calls them "zealots for the law" (Acts 21:20), but there is no evidence that their zeal included the use or advocacy of violence.

Bibliography.–General: S. Applebaum, *Journal of Roman Studies,* 61 (1971), 155-170; G. Baumbach, *Bibel und Liturgie,* 41 (1968), 2-25; M. Borg, *JTS,* 22 (1971), 504-512; *Encyclopedia Judaica Suppl.* (1972), *s.v.* "The Zealots," (M. Stern); W. R. Farmer, *Maccabees, Zealots, and Josephus* (1956); M. Hengel, *Die Zeloten* (1961); R. A. Horsley and J. S. Hanson, *Bandits, Prophets, and Messiahs* (1985); *HJP*², II, 598-606; F. J. F. Jackson and K. Lake, *BC,* I, 421-25; H. P. Kingdon, *NTS,* 17 (1970/71), 68-72; 19 (1972/73), 74-81; D. Rhoads, *Israel in Revolution* (1976); M. Smith, *HTR,* 64 (1971), 1-19; M. Stern, "Sicarii and Zealots," in M. Avi-Yonah and Z. Baras, eds., *World History of the Jewish People,* VIII (1977), 263-301; Y. Yadin, *Masada* (1966); S. Zeitlin, *JBL,* 81 (1962), 395-98.

Jesus and Zealotism: E. Bammel and C. F. D. Moule, eds., *Jesus and the Politics of His Day* (1984); S. G. F. Brandon, *Jesus and the Zealots* (1967); J. Carmichael, *Death of Jesus* (1962); O. Cullmann, *Jesus and the Revolutionaries* (Eng. tr. 1970); R. Eisler, *Messiah Jesus and John the Baptist* (Eng. tr. 1931); M. Hengel, *Was Jesus a Revolutionist?* (Eng. tr. 1971); H. S. Reimarus, *The Goal of Jesus and His Disciples* (Eng. tr. 1970).

T. L. DONALDSON

ZEBADIAH zeb-ə-dī'ə [Heb. *zeḇaḏyāhû, zeḇaḏyâ*–'Yahweh has given'; Gk. Apoc. *Zabdaios* (1 Esd. 9:21)]; AV Apoc. ZABDEUS; NEB Apoc. ZABDAEUS.

1. Son of Beriah; head of a Benjaminite family (1 Ch. 8:15).

2. Son of Elpaal; head of a Benjaminite family (1 Ch. 8:17).

3. Son of Jeroham of Gedor; a Benjaminite recruit of David's at Ziklag (1 Ch. 12:7 [MT 8]).

4. Third son of Meshelemiah; a gatekeeper of the Levitical family of Korah during the reign of David (1 Ch. 26:2).

5. Son and successor of Asahel as the officer in charge of one of the twelve divisions of David's army (1 Ch. 27:7).

6. One of the Levites sent by King Jehoshaphat to teach the law in the towns of Judah (2 Ch. 17:8).

7. Son of Ishmael; described as "the governor of the house of Judah" (2 Ch. 19:11), which may mean simply that he was the leading person in the tribe of Judah. He was appointed by Jehoshaphat to preside over civil cases at a court of appeal in Jerusalem.

8. Son of Michael; head of a family that returned from Babylon to Jerusalem with Ezra (Ezr. 8:8). He is called Zeraiah in 1 Esd. 8:34.

9. Son of Immer; one of the priests who divorced his foreign wife in Ezra's reform (Ezr. 10:20 par. 1 Esd. 9:21).

N. J. O.

ZEBAH zē'bə [Heb. *zeḇaḥ*–'sacrifice' or 'victim of sacrifice'] **AND ZALMUNNA** zal-mun'ə [Heb. *ṣalmunnāʿ*–'protection refused']. Two Midianite kings slain by Gideon in revenge for their murder of his brothers (Jgs. 8:5-21; Ps. 83:11 [MT 12]). The original Midianite names were probably distorted in the Hebrew to form word-plays alluding to the two kings' fate, i.e., abandonment by their god. The first element in "Zalmunna" (*ṣalm*) may represent the name of an Arabic deity; cf. the name *ṣlmšzb* ("Salm has delivered"), which was discovered in a north Arabian inscription at Teima.

Zebah and Zalmunna were presumably the leaders of the camel-riding bedouin who had been making raids on Israelite farms for seven years (Jgs. 6:1-6). (*See also* MIDIAN.) The story of their encounter with GIDEON follows the account of Gideon's successful surprise attack on the Midianites with a band of only three hundred Israelite warriors (7:19-25). Pursuing the two kings and the remnant of the Midianite army (which according to 8:10 had been reduced from 135,000 to 15,000), Gideon and his men crossed the Jordan and requested supplies from the elders of Succoth and Penuel (8:4-9). These officials refused, probably because of fear of Midianite reprisals, saying sarcastically: "Are the palms of Zebah and Zalmunna already in your hand, that we should give bread to your army?" (v. 6). The RSV and NEB emend the MT *hᵃḵap* ("the palm") to the interrogative particle *ha'ap*; but the MT should probably be retained (so AV) in the light of evidence from Egypt and Râs Shamrah that the hands of captured enemies were often cut off as a trophy of victory (see Nötscher; Gray, p. 295).

Vowing vengeance against Succoth and Penuel, Gideon and his famished soldiers continued their pursuit and caught the Midianite army off guard at Karkor (8:10f.). Taking Zebah and Zalmunna with him as captives, Gideon returned to carry out his retribution against Succoth and Penuel (vv. 12-17).

Gideon then addressed himself to avenging the murder of his brothers (8:18-21). The words of Zebah and Zalmunna in vv. 18, 21 show them to have been proud warriors who were ready to meet their death. Gideon offered his son Jether the privilege of avenging his uncles' death, but the boy shrank from the task, sparing Zebah and Zalmunna the ignominy of having been slain by a boy. Instead they died an honorable death at the hands of Gideon himself.

Bibliography.–G. A. Cooke, *Text-Book of North Semitic Inscriptions* (1903), pp. 195-99; J. Gray, *Joshua, Judges, Ruth* (*NCBC*, 3rd. ed. 1986), pp. 295-98; G. F. Moore, *ICC* on Judges (1895), pp. 217-228; F. Nötscher, *Das Buch der Richter* (*Echter Bibel*, 2nd ed. 1955), p. 35.

N. J. O.

ZEBAIM zə-bā'əm (AV Ezr. 2:57; Neh. 7:59). *See* POCHERETH-HAZZEBAIM.

ZEBEDEE [Gk. *Zebedaios* < Aram. *zaḇday*; Heb. *zᵉḇaḏyā*–'gift of Yah(weh)'] (Mt. 4:21 par.; 10:2 par.; 20:20 par.; 26:37; 27:56; Jn. 21:2). A Galilean fisherman; the father of James and John, two of Jesus' twelve disciples. Zebedee and his sons were partners with Peter and Andrew in the fishing trade (Lk. 5:10). The fragmentary Gospel of the Nazarenes (fol. 35ʳ; see H-S, I, 152) calls him a "poor" fisherman, but the reference to hired servants in Mk. 1:20 suggests that more likely he was fairly well-to-do. There is no record that he protested his sons' decision to leave the business and follow Jesus.

The close parallelism between Mt. 27:56 and Mk. 15:40 suggests that the "mother of the sons of Zebedee" was Salome, although the mention by both Gospels of other unnamed women at the cross makes this equation less than certain. If it is accepted, then Salome was Zebedee's wife. The parallel in John (19:25) refers to a sister of Jesus' mother, and some have equated her with Zebedee's wife as well; in this event Zebedee would have been an uncle of Jesus by marriage. But in light of the many differences between John's Gospel and the Synoptics, this additional equation is more dubious.

See also JAMES, 1; JOHN THE APOSTLE.

C. L. BLOMBERG

ZEBIDAH zə-bī'də, zeb'i-də [Heb. *K zᵉḇîḏâ, Q zᵉḇûḏâ*–'gifted']; AV ZEBUDAH. Daughter of Pedaiah of Rumah, and mother of King Jehoiakim (2 K. 23:36). In 2 Ch. 36:5 the MT lacks the name, but the LXX has Gk. *Zechōra,* which in Hebrew would be *zᵉḵûrâ* (Heb. *k* is easily confused with *b,* and *r* with *d*). This fact, and also the occurrence of the masculine form *zāḇûḏ* (*see* ZABUD), suggest that the *qere* (Zebudah) may be the preferred form.

ZEBINAH zə-bī'nə [Aram. *zᵉḇînā'*–'bought' (i.e., a child bought from his parents)]. Son of Nebo; one of those who divorced their foreign wives in the reform of Ezra (Ezr. 10:43). The name does not appear in 1 Esd. 9:35. See *IP,* p. 231.

ZEBOIIM [Heb. *ṣᵉḇōyim, ṣᵉḇōyyim, ṣᵉḇō'yim*] (Gen. 10:19; 14:2, 8; Dt. 29:23 [MT 22]; Hos. 11:8); AV also ZEBOIM; NEB ZEBOYIM. One of the five CITIES OF THE VALLEY. In Gen. 10:19 Zeboiim and the other four cities are listed as defining the southeastern boundary of Canaan. In the time of Abraham, Shemeber king of Zeboiim joined his four fellow kings in an abortive rebellion against a Mesopotamian coalition led by Chedorlaomer king of Elam (14:1-12). Later Yahweh destroyed Zeboiim along with Sodom, Gomorrah, and Admah in a fiery overthrow (19:24-29). Both Moses (Dt. 29:23 [MT 22] and Hosea (Hos. 11:8) cited Zeboiim as an example of Yahweh's judgment. Its precise site is unknown, but it was likely S or SE of the Dead Sea. *See* SIDDIM, VALLEY OF.

D. M. HOWARD, JR.

ZEBOIM zə-bō'əm [Heb. *ṣᵉḇōʿîm*–'hyenas'].

1. A Benjaminite town occupied after the return from the Exile, listed between Hadid and Neballat (Neh.

11:34). Khirbet Sabieh in the maritime plain N of Lydda has been suggested as a possible site of this town.

2. A valley located in Benjamin NE of Jerusalem and SE of Michmash. A company of Philistine raiders followed a route overlooking this valley (1 S. 13:18). Several valleys are named after the hyena; most are associated with the Wâdī Qelt and its tributaries. The Wâdī Abū Dabāʿ, "Valley of the Father of the Hyenas," and the Sheikh ed-Dabāʿ, "Ravine of the Hyenas," both join the Wâdī Qelt. Running parallel to the Wâdī Qelt is the Wâdī Dabāʿ, "Valley of the Hyenas." The exact location of the biblical reference is unknown though Sheikh ed-Dabāʿ is most probable. K. L. C. R. BURTON

ZEBUDAH zə-bōō'də (2 K. 23:36, AV). *See* ZEBIDAH.

ZEBUL zē'bul [Heb. *zᵉḇul*–'exalted,' 'lord' (?); Gk. *Zeboul*] (Jgs. 9:28, 30, 36, 38, 41). The deputy of Abimelech the son of Gideon at Shechem. After murdering his half-brothers, Abimelech had had himself made "king" of the city-state of Shechem and its territory. Abimelech himself lived at Arumah (Jgs. 9:31, 41), and Zebul governed Shechem as his *pāqîḏ* ("officer," v. 28) or *śar-hāʿîr* ("ruler of the city," v. 30; cf. the same title, rendered "governor of the city," in 1 K. 22:26 par. 2 Ch. 18:25; 2 K. 23:8; 2 Ch. 34:8).

When a certain Gaal and his clan moved into Shechem and fomented rebellion against Abimelech, Zebul informed his master of the sedition and suggested a plan for drawing Gaal and his followers into combat in the open fields (Jgs. 9:26-33). Following Zebul's plan, Abimelech came by night and concealed his troops in the fields near the city. The next morning they arose from their ambush and advanced toward the city. Gaal spotted the troops and reported his discovery to Zebul, but the latter attributed their distant movements to Gaal's imagination (vv. 35f.). When they had approached closer however, and Gaal could see that they were coming from different directions, Zebul taunted him by reminding him of his previous boasts against Abimelech (vv. 37f.); thus Gaal was compelled to go out and fight or lose face with the Shechemites. The rebels were routed in the ensuing battle, and Gaal was forced to flee for his life. Thus Gaal and his clan were banished from Shechem, and Zebul continued to govern the city as Abimelech's deputy (v. 41).

N. J. O.

ZEBULONITE zeb'yə-lə-nīt (AV Nu. 26:27; Jgs. 12:11f.). *See* ZEBULUNITE.

ZEBULUN zeb'ū-lən [Heb. *zᵉbûlûn*; Gk. *Zaboulōn*]; AV NT ZABULON (Mt. 4:13, 15; Rev. 7:8). The tenth son of Jacob, the sixth borne by Leah in Paddan-aram; and the tribe named for him. Gen. 30:20 suggests two derivations of the name: Leah exclaims, "God has endowed [*zāḇaḏ*] me with a good dowry"; now my husband will honor [*zāḇal*] me."

I. The Patriarch.–Nothing is known of this patriarch's life, except insofar as it coincides with that of his brothers. Targum Pseudo-Jonathan says that he was first of the five brothers presented to Pharaoh by Joseph when Israel and his house arrived in Egypt (Gen. 47:2). Three sons, Sered, Elon, and Jahleel, were born to Zebulun in Canaan and went to Egypt with him during the famine; these became the ancestors of the three main divisions of the tribe (46:14).

II. The Tribe.–The position of Zebulun in the wilderness was E of the tabernacle, next to Issachar in the division of Judah (Nu. 2:7). This division led the march (v. 9). At the first census Zebulun numbered 57,400 men of war (1:30); the leader of the tribe was Eliab the son of Helon (2:9). At the second census the men of war numbered 60,500 (26:27); but *see* NUMBERS, BOOK OF III. Zebulun was represented among the spies by Gaddiel son of Sodi (13:10). Elizaphan the son of Parnach was the Zebulunite chosen to assist in the division of the land (34:25). During the covenant renewal ceremony at Shechem, Zebulun (the descendants of Leah's youngest son) stood with Reuben (whose personal disgrace [Gen. 35:22] attached to his tribe) and the tribes descended from Jacob's concubine to hear the curses, while the other six tribes, who traced their descent to Rachel and Leah, stood on Mt. Gerizim for the blessing (Dt. 27:12f.).

III. Its Territory.–At the second division of territory the lot of Zebulun came up third, and the tribe was assigned a beautifully diversified stretch of country in the north (Josh. 19:10-16). Although the general area of its possession is clear enough, the boundaries cannot be defined exactly. According to S. Yeivin two lists have been combined, as in the case of other tribes' allotments: one describes the boundaries, the other lists the towns within the territory. The northwestern part of the Valley of Esdraelon was, in any case, within the territory, as was the western part of southern lower Galilee. An important town on the southern border of Zebulun was Sarid (Tell Shadûd). From there the border ran W toward the lower course of the Kishon in the direction of Jokneam (Tell Qeimûn); and E from Sarid the border ran toward Chesulloth (modern Iksâl) and Daberath (Debûriyeh) up to Mt. Tabor. From there it turned N to Japhia and then, in a broad easterly sweep, to Gath-hepher (which Yeivin identified with the village of Mašad). From there the border ran to Rimmon in the Valley of Netophâh and then to Hannathon (Tell el-Bedeiwîyeh) at the western end of the valley. The western border is not mentioned at all in the OT.

Zebulun's territory is said to have included twelve towns (v. 15); since only five are mentioned, part of the list must have been lost.

See also TRIBES, TERRITORIES OF THE.

IV. Its Later History.–Elon the judge is the only Israelite leader from the tribe of Zebulun of whom there is any record (Jgs. 12:11f.). But the Zebulunites were brave and skillful in war, and for the battle against Sisera they provided, according to the Song of Deborah, "those who bear the marshal's staff" (5:14). They sent fifty thousand dedicated, experienced, and well-equipped warriors, to David at Hebron (1 Ch. 12:33); and from their rich land they brought stores of provisions (v. 40). The tribe's chief officer in David's time was Ishmaiah son of Obadiah (27:19). By Hezekiah's time the Zebulunites had fallen away from God, but some of them responded to the king's summons and went to Jerusalem to celebrate the Passover (2 Ch. 30:10f., 18f.). Although Zebulun is not named in 2 K. 15:29, its people were probably taken captive with those of Naphtali in the invasion of Tiglath-pileser.

In intertestamental times the men from these breezy uplands lent strength and enterprise to the Jewish armies. Jotapata (Khirbet Jefât), the scene of Josephus's heroic defense, was in Zebulun, as was Sepphoris (Ṣaffûriyeh), which for a time was the capital of Galilee (Josephus *Ant.* xviii.2.1 [27]; *BJ* vii; iii.2.4 [30-34]). Nazareth, Jesus' boyhood home, is sheltered among the lower hills of Zebulun.

Bibliography.–K. H. Sethe, *Abhandlungen der Preussischen Akademie der Wissenschaften,* 5 (1926); R. Dussaud, *Syria* 8

(1927), 221-233; W. F. Albright, *JPOS*, 8 (1928), 239, 253; 16 (1936), 17f.; M. David, *VT*, 1 (1951), 59ff.

A. Alt, *PJ*, 21 (1925), 42 n. 4; 22 (1926), 59ff.; *ZAW*, 45 (1927), 59-81; 25 (1929), 39ff.; M. Noth, *ZDPV*, 58 (1935), 215-230; *Das Buch Josua* (1938), pp. 84ff.; *GP*, II, 62ff.; S. Yeivin, *Encyclopedia Miqraith*, II (1954), cols. 695-900 (in Hebrew).

A. A. SAARISALO

ZEBULUNITE zeb'yə-lə-nīt [Heb. *hazzᵉḇûlōnî*] (Nu. 26:27; Jgs. 12:11f.); AV ZEBULONITE. A member of the tribe of ZEBULUN.

ZECHARIAH zek-ə-rī'ə [Heb. *zᵉḵaryâ, zᵉḵaryāhû*– 'Yahweh remembers'; Gk. *Zacharias*]; AV also ZACHARIAH (2 K. 14:29; 15:8-12), Apoc. and NT ZACHARIAS, ZACHARY (2 Esd. 1:40); NEB Apoc. also ZACHARIAS.

1. Son of Jeroboam II (2 K. 14:29), and king of Israel for six months during the thirty-eighth year of Azariah (Uzziah) king of Judah (15:8). His reign was characterized by a continuation of his father's practices (v. 9) at a time when the southern kingdom was enjoying a partially righteous reign (cf. vv. 3f.). Zechariah was assassinated by the usurper Shallum son of Jabesh (v. 10). As foretold to Jehu (10:30) and threatened by Amos during the days of Jeroboam II (Am. 7:8f.), Zechariah was the fifth and last king in the line of Jehu (2 K. 15:12). R. J. WAY

2. The father of Abi the mother of King Hezekiah (2 K. 18:2 par. 2 Ch. 29:1).

3. Head of a Reubenite family (1 Ch. 5:7).

4. First son of Meshelemiah; a Korahite Levite appointed by King David to serve as gatekeeper at the entrance of the tent of meeting (1 Ch. 9:21; 26:2). In 26:14 he is called "a shrewd counselor."

5. A Benjaminite (1 Ch. 9:37). In a parallel list in 8:31 he is called Zecher.

6. A Levite appointed by David to play the harp before the ark of the Lord as it was brought to Jerusalem (1 Ch. 15:18, 20) and later when it was stationed in the tabernacle (16:5).

7. A priest appointed to blow the trumpet before the ark as it was brought to Jerusalem (1 Ch. 15:24).

8. A Levite, son of Isshiah (1 Ch. 24:25).

9. Fourth son of Hosah; a Merarite Levite appointed by King David to serve as a gatekeeper at the house of the Lord (1 Ch. 26:11).

10. A Manassite of Gilead; father of Iddo (1 Ch. 27:21).

11. One of the lay officials ("princes") sent by Jehoshaphat to teach the law in the town of Judah (2 Ch. 17:7).

12. A Levite of the family of Asaph; son of Benaiah and father of Jahaziel who prophesied in the time of Jehoshaphat (2 Ch. 20:14).

13. Fourth son of King Jehoshaphat (2 Ch. 21:2). He and his other brothers were granted cities and treasures by Jehoshaphat, but they were all slain by their oldest brother Jehoram when the latter ascended to the throne (vv. 3f.).

14. Son of Jehoiada the priest. During the reign of King Joash he was led by the Spirit of God to rebuke the people publicly for their apostasy. As a result of this he was stoned by the people at Joash's command (2 Ch. 24:20f.). As Zechariah was dying he called upon the Lord to "see and avenge" (v. 22). His death was avenged by two servants who assassinated Joash (vv. 25f.). As 2 Chronicles is the last book of the Hebrew OT, Zechariah was regarded as the last of the OT martyrs. In Mt. 23:35 par. Lk. 11:51 Jesus cites Zechariah as one of the martyrs for whose blood the scribes and Pharisees (who were in Jesus' day rejecting and murdering those sent by God) would be judged. In Mt. 23:35 the words "son of Barachiah" may have been a marginal note that at some point became incorporated into the text (based on a mistaken identification with the postexilic prophet [see **19** below]; cf. Zec. 1:1); or they may represent a conflation by Matthew of the two Zechariahs for literary-theological reasons (cf. the citation of Zec. 11:12f. in Mt. 27:3-10; see R. H. Gundry, *Matthew: A Comm. on His Literary and Theological Art* [1982], p. 471).

15. A man who instructed King Uzziah "in the fear of the Lord" in the early years of Uzziah's reign (2 Ch. 26:5); probably a prophet. As long as he followed Zechariah's instruction, the king prospered.

16. A Levite of the line of Asaph who assisted in the cleansing of the temple in the time of Hezekiah (2 Ch. 29:13).

17. A Kohathite Levite who was one of the overseers in the repair of the temple under King Josiah (2 Ch. 34:12).

18. One of three high-ranking priests who donated animals for the celebration of the Passover during the reign of Josiah (2 Ch. 35:8; 1 Esd. 1:8).

19. A postexilic prophet, contemporary with Zerubbabel and the prophet Haggai (1 Esd. 7:3; 2 Esd. 1:40). He was a grandson of Iddo (Ezr. 5:1; 6:14; and 1 Esd. 6:1 call him the "son of Iddo," but "son" often means "descendant") and the son of Berechiah (Zec. 1:1, 7). If, as seems likely, this Iddo is the same person who is listed as head of a family of priests who returned from exile with Zerubbabel (Neh. 12:4), then Zechariah was a priest as well as a prophet (v. 16). His recorded prophetic activity took place during the reign of Darius I (Zec. 7:1, 8). (On Mt. 23:35, see **14** above.) *See* ZECHARIAH, BOOK OF.

20. Son or descendant of Parosh; head of a family that returned from exile with Ezra (Ezr. 8:3; 1 Esd. 8:30).

21. Son or descendant of Bebai; head of another family that returned from exile with Ezra (Ezr. 8:11; 1 Esd. 8:37).

22. One of the "leading men" sent by Ezra to obtain Levites from Casiphia (Ezr. 8:16; 1 Esd. 8:44); probably the same as **24,** and possibly the same as **20** or **21.**

23. A layman of the family of Elam; one of those who divorced their foreign wives in the reform of Ezra (Ezr. 10:26; 1 Esd. 9:27).

24. One of the men who stood at Ezra's left hand at the public reading of the law (Neh. 8:4; 1 Esd. 9:44); probably the same as **22.**

25. A Judahite, son of Amariah; ancestor of a family that lived in Jerusalem after the Exile (Neh. 11:4).

26. Another Judahite, son of "the Shilonite"; ancestor of a family that lived in Jerusalem after the Exile (Neh. 11:5).

27. Son of Pashhur; a priest, some of whose descendants lived in Jerusalem after the Exile (Neh. 11:12).

28. Son of Jonathan and descendant of Asaph; a Levite who blew the trumpet at the dedication of the wall of Jerusalem in the time of Nehemiah (Neh. 12:35).

29. A priest who blew the trumpet at the dedication of the wall of Jerusalem (Neh. 12:41).

30. Son of Jeberechiah; one of two "reliable witnesses" called upon by Isaiah to attest the time at which he disclosed the name Maher-shalal-hash-baz (Isa. 8:2), so that when its message proved true they could support the prophet's claim to have foretold the defeat of Syria and Ephraim (cf. Dt. 18:22).

31. The name of one of the three leaders of the temple singers, according to 1 Esd. 1:15. In 2 Ch. 35:15 (cf. also 1 Ch. 15:17; 25:1; 2 Ch. 5:12) he is called HEMAN **(1).**

32. Father of the Joseph who was one of the commanders of the Maccabean forces (1 Macc. 5:18, 56).

N. J. O.

ZECHARIAH (NT) zek-ə-rī'ə [Gk. *Zacharias*].

1. The father of John the Baptist. Zechariah appears exclusively in Luke's nativity account as the first person to witness the dawn of the messianic age (Lk. 1:5, 12f., 18, 21, 40, 59, 67). His image recalls that of the elderly Elkanah and Hannah, who gave birth to the prophet Samuel at an advanced age (1 S. 1). Zechariah and his wife Elizabeth are similarly older and without child; but God promises them a son whose name will be John. As Samuel anointed Israel's King Saul (1 S. 10:1) and King David (16:13), so John will anoint Israel's messianic king (Lk. 3:15-22).

The organization of priests in the 1st cent. followed the OT order of twenty-four families (1 Ch. 24:7-18). Even though only four of these families returned from the Exile (Ezr. 2:36-39), Nehemiah implies that the twenty-four OT names and divisions were reinstituted (Neh. 12:1-7). Hence Zechariah was of the eighth division (called "Abijah," Lk. 1:5), which like the other divisions served the temple for one week every six months. (Jeremias estimates that there was a total of 18,000 priests and Levites in first-century Jerusalem [*Jerusalem in the Time of Jesus* (Eng. tr. 1969), pp. 200f.].)

Lots were cast among the priests to select who would burn the twice daily incense offering on the golden altar within the inner temple (cf. Ex. 30:1-10; 37:25-29; 1 Macc. 1:21; 4:49; Mish. *Tamid* iii.6, 9; vi.3). Zechariah was chosen. While he was serving at the altar, an angel (later identified as Gabriel, Lk. 1:19) appeared to him revealing that God had heard his prayers and that he and Elizabeth would have a son named John. The song of Gabriel in Lk. 1:14-17 indicates John's character ("filled with the Holy Spirit," and "great before the Lord" [v. 15]) and his task of preparing the people in the power of Elijah.

Zechariah was incredulous at all of this and sought a sign to confirm the reality of the promise (1:18), which Gabriel provided: the priest was struck dumb for the duration of Elizabeth's pregnancy (1:20). This judgment on Zechariah was fulfilled, to the amazement of those who greeted him when he left the temple.

Following Elizabeth's conception of John (1:24) and the visit of Mary (1:39), Luke recorded John's birth (1:57). On the eighth day it was customary to circumcise a boy (Gen. 17:12) and in Hellenistic times the child was also given a name that was the same as that of his father or grandfather. Elizabeth and Zechariah employed a new name and broke with custom. In fact, once Zechariah publicly embraced the instructions of Gabriel ("His name is John," 1:63), his silence was lifted. The "fear" of the crowds (1:65) is a typical reaction in Luke to God's intervention (cf. 5:26; 7:16; 8:25, 37). In this case God removed Elizabeth's barrenness in her old age as well as loosened Zechariah's tongue. Zechariah's first audible words were a hymn of praise (1:67-79) extolling God for His saving visitation.

Zechariah appears in the apocryphal Protoevangelium of James (chs. 23–24) in an interesting passage where he is slain in the temple forecourt as a result of Herod's wrath. But this story is a conflation of the Zechariah of Lk. 1 with the OT reference in 11:51 (see below). (Christian tradition has sometimes identified Zechariah's tomb in Jerusalem's Kidron Valley, but this is a 2nd cent. B.C. tomb of the priestly family of the Bene Hezir.)

2. The son of Jehoiada. Matthew and Luke record detailed criticisms that Jesus voiced against the Jewish authorities during His ministry. Jesus denounced the crimes of murder in Israel, which spilled "righteous blood" whenever God's messengers spoke. As an illustration he referred to "Zechariah . . . , whom you murdered between the sanctuary and the altar" (Mt. 23:35; Lk. 11:51). The story comes from 2 Ch. 22–24. During the reign of King Joash, the high priest's son (Zechariah, son of Jehoiada) was filled with the Spirit and as a result denounced the apostasy and disobedience of the people. Zechariah was killed on the instigation of the king; but since Jehoiada had originally aided Joash's accession to power (ch. 23), the priest avenged the death of his son by taking Joash's life (24:25).

For Jesus this was a poignant reminder of God's judgment upon sin, especially the sin of Jerusalem, which murders God's messengers. The judgment upon Joash will be the judgment of Jerusalem: it too will be destroyed (Mt. 24). (Matthew calls Zechariah "the son of Barachiah," thus making the martyr the postexilic minor prophet [see Zec. 1:1]. Jesus' illustration, however, is clearly from 2 Ch. 24. Some have resolved this historical problem by identifying Zechariah as the "son of Baruch," who was killed in the temple by Zealots in A.D. 67 [Josephus *BJ* iv.5.4 (334-344)]. Thus the murders of Judaism are chronicled up to contemporary times. But this solution is not compelling.)

G. M. BURGE

ZECHARIAH zek-ə-rī'ə, **BOOK OF.** The next-to-last book of the Minor Prophets.

I. Title
II. Historical Background
III. Contents
IV. Composition
V. Character
VI. Place in the Canon
VII. Text
VIII. Message
IX. Zechariah in the NT

I. Title.–The book is named after the prophet Zechariah, who prophesied after the Exile. In Zec. 1:1, 7 he is called "the son of Berechiah" and grandson of Iddo. This is probably the same Iddo who is listed among the priests who returned with Zerubbabel in 536 B.C. (Neh. 12:4, 16); if so, Zechariah was both priest and prophet, like Ezekiel and Jeremiah. In Ezr. 5:1; Neh. 12:16 Zechariah is called the son of Iddo rather than his grandson; but this is not contradictory to Zec. 1:1, since the expression "son of" is sometimes used for a descendant rather than an actual son.

II. Historical Background.–Two definite dates are mentioned in connection with Zechariah's prophesying, namely, the second year of the reign of Darius Hystaspis, 520 B.C. (1:1, 7), and the fourth year of his reign, 518 (7:1). It is probable, however, that the prophet was active before 520 and long after 518.

The book of Zechariah is best understood in its historical context. In 538 B.C. (eighteen years before Zechariah's recorded prophecy) the mighty and glorious kingdom of the Babylonians was destroyed by Cyrus (Heb. *kôreš*, Isa. 45:1) the Great. Uninterested in ruling his people, Nabonidus king of Babylon had given the responsibility to his son Bel-shar-usur (called Belshazzar in Daniel). Babylon was taken without any major military operation because of the weakness of its rulers. The new king, Cyrus, was tolerant toward the religions of other nations, especially those who had been oppressed. Some scholars have suggested that the Jews were allowed to return in order to strengthen Palestine against Egypt and to form a buffer state. Meanwhile the Persian king gained control over almost the entire Near East. Cyrus died in 528, possibly of a wound inflicted by nomads during a campaign.

He was succeeded by his son Cambyses II. Cambyses was not nearly as successful as his father. He lacked Cyrus's strong personality and magnanimity, and had he not reigned so briefly he would have destroyed the Persian empire. His greatest achievement was defeating Psammetichus III of Egypt and occupying that country. But this action was contrary to the usually tolerant Persian policy, and it was never forgotten or forgiven by the Egyptians. As a result of his cruel policy, the Egyptians continually tried to overthrow the Persian overlords.

During Cambyses's reign the situation was no better at home. He murdered his brother Bardiya (Smerdis) but kept the deed secret. After he went to Egypt resentment grew at home. A Magian named Gaumata arose, claiming to be Bardiya, and gained popular support. A rebellion started Mar. 11, 522. Afterward Cambyses died, but, according to the chronicle of Darius, confessed on his deathbed to his brother's murder, hoping thereby to unmask the pretender and ensure that the new king would come from the ranks of the Achaemenians. His hopes were not in vain. A young officer named Darius returned to Persia from Egypt and killed Gaumata in a carefully planned conspiracy. Darius, who was somehow linked to the family of Cambyses, succeeded in gaining control on Sept. 29, 522.

The change of ruler caused widespread confusion, for only two satraps were loyal to Darius. Media formed its own government; Parsa, homeland of Darius, became unfaithful; and Elam declared its independence. Darius turned against Babylon, which had rebelled under the so-called Nebuchadnezzar III (Nidintu-Bel), and defeated the rebels on Dec. 18, 522. Early in 521 he was in control of the entire empire. Later that year another Babylonian pretender tried to gain control, but he was defeated and the rebel leaders were impaled.

This situation and the accompanying confusion aroused new hopes of liberty among the smaller nations. To the returned Jews at Jerusalem it gave new hope for accomplishing the rebuilding of the temple, which had been interrupted. The prophets Haggai and Zechariah played a very important role in kindling enthusiasm for this work. The whole episode of the building and the protest of the governor of the western part of the kingdom are vividly described in Ezr. 5–6. When the original document of Cyrus was found, Darius commanded the governor to withdraw his accusation (Ezr. 6:6f.; cf. F. Rundgren, *ZAW*, 70 [1958], 213). The Jews were allowed to continue their work, and in the sixth year of Darius (516/15) they completed it. Zechariah's night vision played a particularly important role in this outstanding accomplishment.

This historical background throws some light on the first part of Zechariah, chs. 1–8; but the second part, 9–14, is very difficult to associate with any definite period, as will be shown.

III. Contents.–The prophecies of Zechariah can be subdivided in three sections: chs. 1–8, 9–11, and 12–14.

A. Chs. 1–8. 1. General Introduction (1:1-6). These verses issue a special message of repentance to the Jews. According to 1:1, Zechariah delivered it in the eighth month of the second year of Darius, i.e., 520 B.C.

2. Eight Visions of the Night (1:7–6:15). The date attached to this part is the twenty-fourth day of the eleventh month of the second year of Darius — three months after the first prophecies and two months after the cornerstone of the temple had been laid (1:7; cf. Hag. 2:18). All these visions encourage the people to rebuild the temple.

a. The Four Horsemen and the Man Among the Myrtle Trees (1:7-17). In this first vision the horsemen announce that the world is at peace (in 520). But this is not a promising message, because Jerusalem is still oppressed. The comforting news, however, is that Yahweh is again turning to Jerusalem in compassion and the temple will be built (v. 16).

b. The Four Horns and Four Smiths (1:18-21 [MT 2:1-4]). The horns symbolize the world powers that carried the Jews into exile. The smiths are sent by God to destroy these powers.

c. Man with a Measuring Line (2:1-5 [MT 5-9]); Appendix (2:6-13 [MT 10-17]). The vision of a man with a measuring line indicates that Jerusalem will be rebuilt. No wall is necessary because the Lord Himself will protect the inhabitants (cf. also Dt. 32:10). The second part of the vision can be subdivided into two parts: vv. 6-9, which refer to the Exile and the impending punishment of Judah's oppressors; and vv. 10-13, which promise that the Lord will dwell in the midst of His people as soon as the temple is built.

d. Trial of Joshua the High Priest (3:1-10). In the fourth vision Joshua the high priest, with filthy garments indicating his sins and those of his people, is accused by Satan and acquitted by the Lord.

e. The Lampstand and the Two Olive Trees (4:1-14). This vision can be subdivided into three parts: vv. 1-5, which give the vision of the lampstand and two olive trees, referring to the restoration of the temple service; vv. 6-10, which show that nothing will stop Zerubbabel from rebuilding the temple; and vv. 11-14, in which the prophet is told that the vision refers to the two anointed ones (generally thought to be Zerubbabel and Joshua).

f. The Flying Scroll (5:1-4). The outsized scroll announces that sinners will be cut off from Judah.

g. The Woman in the Ephah (5:5-11). The woman, symbolizing the nation's sins, is carried away to Babylon, the seat of sins.

h. The Four Chariots (6:1-8). This vision stands in close connection with the first. The difference is that the horses return in the first vision, while the chariots do not.

3. Miscellaneous Prophecies and Historical Events (6:9–8:23). a. Coronation of Joshua (6:9-15). The crowning of the high priest symbolizes the beginning of the messianic age and the rebuilding of the temple.

b. True Righteousness Superior to Fasting (ch. 7). In 7:1 a new date is given, the fourth day of the ninth month of the fourth year of Darius, thus 518 B.C. A historical exposition of Jewish history stresses that unrighteousness will be punished. Zechariah delivered this message after a deputation came to the priests and prophets to ask about fasting over the fallen city and the ruined temple.

c. Promise of Glorious Blessings (8:1-23). This prophecy sketches a glorious future for the remnant of Israel. When the messianic age dawns on Judah and Jerusalem, there will be manifold blessings (vv. 1-17). Then the Jews will hold their fasts in great joy and the heathen will join them in seeking the Lord (vv. 18-23).

B. Chs. 9–11. 1. God's Judgment on the Nations N and W of Judah (9:1-8).

2. The Messianic Kingdom and the King's Triumphant Procession (9:9-17).

3. God Alone the Giver of Rain (10:1f.).

4. The Triumphant Deliverance and Return from Exile (10:3–11:3). These verses emphasize that God's anger is turned against the oppressors of Israel. 11:1-3 describes their fall.

5. Good and Bad Shepherds (11:4-17). In symbolic words and acts, this enigmatic passage prophesies the judgment of God's unfaithful people.

C. Chs. 12–14. 1. Future Deliverance and Blessing (12:1-14). In the far future enemies of God's people will march against Jerusalem, but God will obliterate them (cf. Ezk. 38–39).

2. The Rooting Out of Idolatry and False Prophecy (13:1-6).

3. National Purification (13:7-9). The death of the shepherd (leader) will lead to the scattering of but a faithful remnant will remain.

4. Last Battle of the Host of Yahweh (14:1-21). Foreign nations will march against Jerusalem on "a day of the Lord," but they will be defeated by God. The people of God will live in peace in Jerusalem, and other nations will come to celebrate with them the Feast of Tabernacles.

IV. Composition.–Most modern scholars do not regard Zechariah as a unity. Only the first part, chs. 1–8, is commonly ascribed to the propeht Zechariah son of Berechiah. Some scholars have thought that a redactor contributed to this part, but this is very difficult to prove. Both 1:1 and 7:1 ascribe the prophecies of this part to Zechariah.

The real difficulty lies with the second part, chs. 9–14. Mt. 27:9 quotes Zec. 11:12f. but attributes the passage to Jeremiah. This point was noticed by J. Mede (1586-1638), who ascribed the whole of the second part to Jeremiah. At the end of the 19th cent. this view was commonly accepted (e.g., by F. Hitzig, S. Davidson, C. A. Bruston, C. von Orelli, H. L. Strack), on the grounds that the great powers of Egypt and Assyria are frequently mentioned and that the northern kingdom seems still to have existed. The theory is still advocated by a few scholars (see *SQE*, no. 335, lines 15f.).

In 1824 J. G. Eichhorn, the famous critical scholar of the OT, wrote that 9:1-8 might refer to the conquest of Alexander the Great (*Einl. in das AT* [1824], pp. 444ff.). This view was not immediately accepted. In the first issue of *ZAW* (1881/82) B. Stade demonstrated that the second part of Zechariah must definitely be placed after Ezekiel; this assumption led to the commonly accepted view that chs. 9–14 are much later than 1–8. But there is considerable variety of opinion about the exact date of chs. 9–14. Proposals include the days of Alexander the Great, the wars of the Diadochi, the Ptolemaic period in Palestine, the time of Antiochus the Great's invasion of Palestine, and the age of the Maccabees. The dates range, therefore, from 330 to 166. The latter date, 166, commonly accepted by scholars, is very improbable because already in 190 B.C. Sirach (49:10) wrote of the Book of the Twelve (Minor Prophets). This illustrates how dangerous it is to make any far-reaching conclusions from vague expressions in certain chapters.

Some scholars have dated 9:1-12 to the time of Alexander the Great's siege of Tyre. According to C. C. Torrey, an event of such importance must have left some impression on the literature of the OT. But this argument does not prove the point, because many important events in world history are never mentioned in the OT, although contemporaneous with the writers. Since scholars have disagreed on the dating of almost every part of chs. 9–14, possibly the utterances are from anonymous persons and were affixed to the book of Zechariah later. But such assumptions can hardly be based on internal evidence, because no definite historical event is mentioned in these chapters.

Some arguments for certain dates are built on stylistic and linguistic differences. But the short and fragmentary character of the various utterances makes final conclusions difficult. Moreover, some places use the idiom of apocalyptic writings, which is difficult, strange, and basically the same over a long period; thus drawing conclusions from the cryptic allusions in this literature is very dangerous.

It is far better to abstain from hypotheses on a possible date for these utterances. They might postdate Zechariah, or possibly they were written by Zechariah after he recorded the prophecies of the first part. There is some connection in style between 6:9–8:23 and the second part. Zechariah may have written the second part in two consecutive sections: first chs. 9–11, and then chs. 12–14. It is also possible that Zechariah used earlier prophecies, e.g., those of Jeremiah, and blended them with his own. This assertion lacks proof, however, and a definite conclusion must await the discovery of new evidence.

V. Character.–Zechariah is one of the few OT books with definite apocalyptic characteristics. Various visions are described in other prophetic books, but Zechariah's eight night visions must be regarded as unique. They are written in language that is symbolic and sometimes almost cryptic. There are horses with different colors, an outsized book or scroll, an ephah, a mysterious lampstand, and two olive trees; sometimes an explanation is offered, but sometimes it is withheld. All these visions symbolize important expectations. The symbolism is artificial, however, as is common in apocalyptic literature. Frequent reference is made to angels, and the role of an interpreting angel is especially emphasized; these features are common in later apocalyptic literature. Zechariah differs from apocalyptic literature, however, in that Babylonian and Persian influences are almost completely absent (see Rignell's convincing illustration). Mythological material is also sparse.

When Zechariah is compared with other apocalyptic literature, it is obvious that this book had a very great influence on the formation of the apocalyptic tradition. Zec. 1–8 originated in a time of uncertainty and danger for the Jewish nation. The Jews did not know what attitude they might expect from Darius, the new king. Thus it was better to speak in symbols than in unambiguous terms; most other apocalyptic literature, significantly, also originated in dangerous times (e.g., Daniel).

VI. Place in the Canon.–Zechariah forms part of the Twelve Minor Prophets (Heb. *šᵉnê ʿāśār*), which are the fourth collection in the Latter Prophets. The order in the Greek Bible is different from that in the Hebrew Bible, which is roughly chronological but by no means accurate. The place of Zechariah in both the LXX and MT is the same: it comes after Haggai and is the second to last of the Minor Prophets.

VII. Text.–There are no major difficulties with the text and versions of the book of Zechariah. The text of the Twelve Minor Prophets discovered in the caves of Wâdī Murabbaʿât near the Dead Sea is unfortunately quite mutilated, and Zechariah is represented only by the beginnings of six lines up to 1:4. The consistent characteristic of this damaged scroll is its close affinity to the MT, as F. M. Cross pointed out (*Ancient Library of Qumran and Modern Biblical Studies* [1958], p. 14 n. 33).

VIII. Message.–The prophecies of Zechariah brought a powerful message to the people of his time. They were a small group of disappointed Jews who went to Jerusalem to rebuild their sanctuary but were stopped before completing the work. According to Ezr. 5:1; 6:14, Zechariah and Haggai were responsible for new hope and renewed activity among the Jews. Typically Zechariah began by calling the Jewish people to repent, saying that their dilemma was due to their sins and unfaithfulness (cf. also Jer. 3:14, 22, etc.). With vigor and faith he fired the hopes of his people; his night visions especially stirred them to recommence building.

One of the main strands in Zechariah's message is the expectation of salvation for the Jewish nation. Sometimes employing apocalyptic language, the prophet sketched the final war between the people of God and the hostile powers. In this war God alone will defeat the enemy. To an oppressed nation that had become almost resigned to servitude, this message brought new hope for a blissful future. Messianic expectation also plays a very important role and should be noticed in the NT references to Zechariah. The prophet was a staunch believer in the power of the almighty God and His control of world affairs, even of the acts of mighty kings.

IX. Zechariah in the NT.–Reference has already been made to the quotation of Zec. 11:12f. in Mt. 27:9 and the ascription of it to Jeremiah. The NT contains forty-one other citations and allusions to Zechariah, which reveal the book's important role in eschatological literature. Revelation echoes Zechariah twenty-one times, and some of its symbols resemble those of the OT book, e.g., horses of different colors (Rev. 6:1-8). It is not always clear to what extent Revelation uses the symbols of Zechariah or borrows common apocalyptic terminology that was influenced by Zechariah.

The NT refers in a very few instances to the OT for predictions of the passion of Christ; e.g., Jn. 19:37 and Rev. 1:7 cite Zec. 12:10. From these few examples it is clear that Zechariah exercised a profound influence on NT thought, especially on its eschatology.

Bibliography.–Comms. by S. Amsler (*Commentaire de l'AT,* 1981); J. Baldwin (*Tyndale OT Comms.,* 1972); W. E. Barnes (*CBSC,* 1917); P. C. Craigie (*Daily Study Bible,* 1985); A. H. Edelkoort (1945); F. C. Fensham (1958); K. Marti (1892); H. G. T. Mitchell (*ICC,* 1937); D. L. Petersen (*OTL,* 1984); R. L. Smith (*Word Biblical Comm.,* 1984); D. W. Thomas and R. C. Dentan (*IB*). In addition, see comms. on Minor Prophets in Bibliography of AMOS.

P. R. Ackroyd, *Exile and Restoration* (*OTL,* 1968), pp. 171-217; P. Benoit, J. T. Milik, and R. de Vaux, *Les Grottes de Murabba'at* (1961); S. B. Frost, *OT Apocalyptic* (1952); P. D. Hanson, *Dawn of Apocalyptic* (rev. ed. 1979), pp. 240-401; E. Lipiński, *VT,* 20 (1970), 25-55; R. G. Rignell, *Die Nachtgesichte des Sacharja* (1950); E. Sellin, *Serubbabel* (1898).

F. C. FENSHAM

ZECHER zē'kər [Heb. *zeḵer,* pausal *zāḵer*]; AV, NEB, ZACHER. A Benjaminite (1 Ch. 8:31). In 9:37 he is called Zechariah.

ZEDAD zē'dad [Heb. *ṣᵉḏāḏ*; Sam. Pent. *ṣᵉrāḏ*; Gk. B *Saradak,* A *Sadadak* (Nu. 34:8), B *Seldamma,* A *Eldamma* (Ezk. 47:15)]. A place on the northern border of Canaan (Nu. 34:8; Ezk. 47:15). Two sites have been suggested. A few scholars (following the Sam. Pent. and LXX) identify Zedad with Khirbet Ṣerādā, N of Dan and E of Merj 'Ajûn; but this would place the border too far south. Most scholars identify it with the village of Ṣadâd, 56 km. (35 mi.) NE of Lebweh (Lebo-hamath; cf. NEB; RSV "entrance of Hamath"), near the Damascus-Homs highway (*LBHG* [rev. ed. 1979], pp. 72f.).

D. E. WARING

ZEDECHIAS zed-ə-kī'əs (1 Esd. 1:46, AV). *See* ZEDEKIAH **2.**

ZEDEKIAH zed-ə-kī'ə [Heb. *ṣiḏqîyāhû, ṣiḏqîyâ*–'Yah(weh) is my righteousness'; Gk. *Sedekias*]; AV also ZIDKIJAH (Neh. 10:1), SEDECIAS (Bar. 1:1, 8), ZEDECHIAS (1 Esd. 1:46).

1. Son of Chenaanah. Zedekiah was the leader of a band of four hundred prophets attached to the court of Samaria whom Ahab and Jehoshaphat consulted as they prepared their military campaign against Ramoth-gilead. These prophets in unison supported Ahab's intention to attack, and Zedekiah dramatically depicted the prophecy by placing horns of iron on his head to signify how Ahab would defeat the Arameans (1 K. 22:11; 2 Ch. 18:10). When Jehoshaphat insisted on hearing from another prophet of Yahweh (1 K. 22:7; 2 Ch. 18:7), Micaiah the son of Imlah was summoned, and he opposed the campaign. In response Zedekiah slapped Micaiah and asked sarcastically, "How did the Spirit of the Lord go from me to speak to you?" (1 K. 22:24; cf. 2 Ch. 18:23).

2. The last king of Judah (*ca.* 597-587 B.C.), third son of Josiah (1 Ch. 3:15), whom Nebuchadrezzar established as king in the place of his exiled nephew Jehoiachin (2 K. 24:8-17; Jer. 29:3).

According to 2 K. 24:17 his original name was Mattaniah (as in Lachish Letter no. 1; see J. Gibson, *Syrian Semitic Inscriptions* [1975], I, 36); he received the name Zedekiah from Nebuchadrezzar as a sign of vassalage (cf. Ezk. 17:12-14). The AV and RSV designate him the "brother" of Jehoiakin in 2 Ch. 36:10, but the NIV correctly translates Heb. *'āḥ* by the more general designation "relative" (the NEB emends to "father's brother").

Little is known of Zedekiah's kingdom from historical records. Babylonian materials (*ANET,* pp. 301-308; *see* picture in CAPTIVITY) provide a few details of contemporary events from a Babylonian perspective. The biblical historical books deal with the king in an abbreviated manner. Royal annals incorporated into the earlier portions of Kings and Chronicles were apparently unavailable for this period. Kings merely evaluates him as an evil ruler and turns directly to the fall of Jerusalem (2 K. 24:18–25:21). The Chronicler adds only a few details not found in the Kings account (2 Ch. 36:11-21).

For these reasons the primary sources for reconstructing the events of Zedekiah's reign are the books of Jeremiah and Ezekiel. Jeremiah viewed the king from the vantage point of one residing in Jerusalem, and Ezekiel from the perspective of one in Babylon. The prophets shared similar outlooks on the king. Their descriptions of Zedekiah's reign include his initial appointment by Nebuchadrezzar (Jer. 24; Ezk. 11:15; 17:12-14), disappointing events associated with the beginning of his reign (Jer. 27–29), and prophecies given at different points in the period (Jer. 21; 34:1-7; 51:59; Ezk. 4–7; 8–12; 17:11-21). The siege and eventual defeat of Jerusalem is a particular focus in both books (Jer. 32; 37; 38; 39:1-10; Ezk. 24:1-2; 33:21f.).

Zedekiah ruled under difficult circumstances. He was only twenty-one years old when he became king of Judah. He took power after Nebuchadrezzar had deported most of the nobility to Babylon, leaving a vacuum of wise counsel for the king (Jer. 24; cf. 2 K. 24:14-17; Ezk. 17:13f.). These factors, along with serious flaws in his character, contributed to making him a deceitful and inept king. His negative qualities can be seen in his dealings both with the prophet Jeremiah and with King Nebuchadrezzar.

Zedekiah's relationship with Jeremiah is a mixed picture. He frequently sought the prophet's direction but often lacked the fortitude to carry it out. In response to prophetic warnings of divine judgment, Zedekiah promised the release of Hebrew slaves in accordance with Mosaic legislation; nevertheless, he did not fulfil his promise and was condemned by the prophet (Jer. 34:8-22). He also feared public knowledge of his interest in Jeremiah's advice (37:17; 38:24-26). He allowed the prophet to be mistreated and imprisoned (37:15; 38:4-6). It is no wonder that the prophetic outlook on the king was negative. Ezekiel called him "unhallowed wicked one, prince of Israel" (Ezk. 21:25).

The other major source of conflict in Zedekiah's life was Nebuchadrezzar. Zedekiah was king of Judah solely by the decree of Nebuchadrezzar: he was a vassal sworn to full allegiance in the name of God (2 Ch. 36:13; Ezk. 17:13; 1 Esd. 1:48). Yet he was unfaithful to this oath. Babylonian records indicate that Nebuchadrezzar had to deal with a revolt in Babylonia and other disturbances in his empire during the early years of Zedekiah's reign. Very likely the emperor's preoccupation with these matters aroused the Judeans' hope for the rapid demise of the Babylonian empire. As a result, in the fourth year of his reign Zedekiah contemplated breaking his oath of loyalty by joining an alliance with Edom, Moab, Ammon, Tyre, and Sidon (Jer. 27:1-12). False prophets had assured victory (chs. 37–38), but Jeremiah warned against the coalition (28:1). This rebellion never materialized, but it surely called Zedekiah's loyalty into question in Babylon.

In 589 B.C., however, Zedekiah openly rebelled against Nebuchadrezzar. This event is particularly noted in the historical accounts of his reign (2 Ch. 36:13; 2 K. 24:20), since it constitutes the historical impetus for the destruction of Jerusalem. In response to this rebellion the Babylonian army laid siege to Jerusalem. Zedekiah asked Jeremiah if God would intervene on his behalf, but the prophet responded that defeat was sure (Jer. 21). Zedekiah sought to appease God by promising to release all Hebrew slaves; but when the Babylonians temporarily lifted the siege due to the approach of the Egyptian army (cf. 37:5), he refused to keep his agreement (34:8-22). As a result, the Babylonians returned and continued the siege.

Although Jeremiah continued to advise submission to Babylon (e.g., Jer. 21:9; 38:2, 17f.), Zedekiah and his army refused to surrender. In the summer of 587 B.C. the food supply in Jerusalem was depleted and the wall was breached by the Babylonians (2 K. 25 1-21; Jer. 39:2-20; 52:1-10). Zedekiah fled during the night, but he and his sons were captured (Jer. 39:4f.). On the orders of Nebuchadrezzar Zedekiah's sons were executed before their father's eyes; Zedekiah was subsequently blinded and taken captive to Babylon, where he died (39:6f.; 52:1-11).

Bibliography.–*BHI* (3rd ed. 1981), pp. 327-330; *WBA*, pp. 177-182.

3. An otherwise unknown son of Jehoiakim (1 Ch. 3:16).

4. Son of Maaseiah; one who prophesied falsely in the days of Jeremiah (Jer. 29:21-23). He and another false prophet, Ahab the son of Kolaiah, predicted a quick return of the captives from Babylon. Jeremiah accused them of false prophecy and immoral living and prophesied that they would die at the hands of Nebuchadrezzar.

5. Son of Hananiah (Jer. 36:12); a prince of Judah before whom Jeremiah's scroll was read by Baruch and later by Jehudi (vv. 14-21).

6. One of the prominent leaders of Judah who sealed the covenant in the time of Nehemiah (Neh. 10:1 [MT 2]).

7. An ancestor of Baruch (Bar. 1:1).

8. Son of Josiah king of Judah. According to Bar. 1:8 he made silver vessels for the temple after Nebuchadrezzar took into captivity Jeconiah (Jehoiachin) and the leading men of Judah. R. L. PRATT, JR.

ZEEB zē'əb, zēb [Heb. *ze'ēḇ*–'wolf']. A Midianite prince captured and killed by the Ephraimites after Gideon's surprise attack had routed the Midianite forces (Jgs. 7:25; 8:3). The Ephraimites, summoned by Gideon to cut off the retreat of the Midianites, seized the two Midianite princes OREB and Zeeb, beheaded them, and presented their heads to Gideon. The winepress at which Zeeb was slain was apparently named after him (7:25); its location is not known. This Israelite victory is recalled in Ps. 83:11 (MT 12), which petitions God to make Israel's enemies "like Oreb and Zeeb."

ZELA zē'lə [Heb. *ṣēla'*–'rib' (?)]. One of a group of fourteen cities of Benjamin (Josh. 18:28), named between Taralah and Ha-eleph; the burial place of Saul and Jonathan (2 S. 21:14). Some scholars have favored joining Zela with the following name in Josh. 18:28, reading "Zela haeleph." This reading has the support of the LXX (*Selaleph*), but the list would not then add up to "fourteen cities" (v. 28).

Since the tomb of Saul's father Kish was located in Zela (2 S. 21:14), this town was probably Saul's birthplace. Both passages require a location in the region NW of Jerusalem. One suggested site is Khirbet Salah between Jerusalem and the high place of Gibeon (L. Grollenberg, *Atlas of the Bible* [Eng. tr. 1965], p. 165). *See also* ZELZAH. W. S. L. S.

ZELEK zē'lek [Heb. *ṣeleq*]. An Ammonite who was one of David's mighty men (2 S. 23:37; 1 Ch. 11:39).

ZELOPHEHAD zə-lō'fə-had [Heb. *ṣᵉlop̄ḥāḏ*–'shadow (protector) from terror'(?)]. Son of Hepher; a Manassite who died in the wilderness without a male heir (Nu. 26:33; 1 Ch. 7:15). Upon his death his five daughters came to Moses and Eleazar and successfully pleaded for recognition as heirs (Nu. 27:1, 7; Josh. 17:3). This became the occasion for a law providing that in the case of a man who died without sons, the inheritance passed to his daughters so that his name would be perpetuated. Most likely this law did not abrogate the law of levirate marriage (*see* MARRIAGE IV.A.2) but rather provided for situations in which the wife had also died or there was no brother to marry the widow. A further regulation, stipulating that daughters who had inherited property must marry within the same tribe as their father, averted the danger that tribal possessions might be lost to another tribe (Nu. 36:1-9). The daughters of Zelophehad complied with this regulation, and Zelophehad's inheritance remained in the tribe of Manasseh (vv. 10-12).

Bibliography.–P. J. Budd, *Numbers* (*Word Biblical Comm.*, 1984), pp. 299-303, 387-390; *IP*, p. 256. N. J. O.

ZELOTES zə-lō'tēz (AV Lk. 6:15; Acts 1:13). *See* ZEALOT; SIMON (NT) **3.**

ZELZAH zel'zə [Heb. *ṣelṣaḥ*–'leaping'(?); Gk. *alloménous megála*–'leaping mightily'(?); Vulg. *in meridie*–'at noon,' 'in the south'] (1 S. 10:2). The location of the first of three signs given to Saul to confirm Samuel's annunication that he was to be prince over Israel. Zelzah was "by Rachel's tomb in the territory of Benjamin" (v. 2). From there Saul was to go on to the oak of Tabor for the second sign (vv. 3f.) and then to Gibeath-elohim for the third sign (vv. 5f.); finally he was to go to Gilgal (v. 8). For a map of this circuit, see Y. Aharoni and M. Avi-yonah, *Macmillan Bible Atlas* (rev. ed. 1977), Map 86. This route would rule out any site such as Beit Jala or the traditional RACHEL'S TOMB just N of Bethlehem (cf. Gen. 35:19), requiring instead a location N of Jerusalem.

Because of the variant readings in the LXX and Vulgate, and because no satisfactory site has been proposed for Zelzah, some scholars have suggested emending the text to read ZELA. But another possibility, in view of these readings, is that Heb. *ṣelṣaḥ* may not be a place name at all. W. S. L. S.

ZEMARAIM zem-ə-rā'əm [Heb. *ṣᵉmārayim*; Gk. A *Semrim*, B *Sara* (Josh. 18:22), *Somorōn* (2 Ch. 13:4)]. The name of a place and of a mountain, probably in the same region.

Zemaraim was one of the cities of Benjamin, named between Beth-arabah and Bethel (Josh. 18:22). In 2 Ch. 13:4, however, Zemaraim is the name of a mountain: in a war against Jeroboam of Israel, Abijah of Judah "stood up on Mount Zemaraim which is in the hill country of Ephraim" and rebuked Israel and its king. In 25:13 "Samaria" should probably be emended to "Zemaraim," based on geographical references in the context (*GTTOT*, §§ 996f.).

F.-M. Abel suggested that the border between Ephraim and Benjamin followed approximately a line between Attaroth Addar and Beth-horon (*GP*, II, 256), and that the city of Zemaraim gave its name to the nearby summit of the "mountain [Heb. *har*] of Ephraim" (RSV "hill country of Ephraim"). According to Y. Aharoni, the border between Judah and Israel after the division of the monarchy extended from Mizpah to Zemaraim-Bethel (*LBHG* [rev. ed. 1979], p. 315; cf. VT, 9 [1959], 232-34). The "mountain of Ephraim" consisted of a chain extending from Shechem to Bethel, a branch of which lay between Jericho and Bethel; a summit of this branch was Mt. Zemaraim (*GP*, I, 359). Thus a city of Benjamin could quite readily give its name to a mountain "in the hill country of Ephraim."

An earlier identification of Zemaraim with Khirbet es-Samrah is now generally rejected. Abel thought Clermont-Ganneau's suggestion of Râs ez-Zeimara, between eṭ-Ṭaiyibeh and Rammûn, "more likely" (*GP*, II, 454), and J. Simons accepted it (*GTTOT*, § 77). Aharoni, however, preferred Râs eṭ-Ṭaḥûneh (*LBHG* [rev. ed. 1979], p. 443), at or near el-Bîreh, E of Ramallah and S of Beitîn (Bethel).

W. S. L. S.

ZEMARITE [Heb. *ṣᵉmārî*; cf. Akk. *Ṣimirra*; Am.Tab. *Ṣumur*]. Descendants of Canaan and "brothers" of the Arvadites and Hamathites (Gen. 10:18 par. 1 Ch. 1:16). The Zemarites settled on the Phoenician coast near the mouth of the Eleutheros River (Nahr el-Kebir) at the site of the modern hamlet of Sumra, located between Arvad and Tripolis just N of the Syrian-Lebanese border. Assyrian and Egyptian records show that in the biblical period the site was a strategic provincial city within the Amurru district and represented a vital Egyptian base prior to the battle of Kadesh (1285 B.C.; cf. references to Simirra and Simyra in *ANET*, pp. 239, 282-85, 477).

See *LBHG* [rev. ed. 1979], pp. 7, 75, 158, 164, 171-73.

B. J. BEITZEL

ZEMIRAH zə-mī'rə [Heb. *zᵉmîrâ*]; AV, NEB, ZEMIRA. A Benjaminite, son of Becher (1 Ch. 7:8). Some scholars have suggested that the names in this passage originally belonged to the genealogy of Zebulun, which is otherwise lacking. This is unlikely, however, due to the extensive emendations that this theory would require.

ZENAN zē'nan [Heb. *ṣᵉnān*–'place of flocks']. A town in the Shephelah of Judah (Josh. 15:37); probably the same as ZAANAN.

ZENAS [Gk. *Zēnas*, contraction of *Zēnodōros*–'gift of Zeus']. A person mentioned only in Paul's concluding instructions to Titus: "Do your best to speed Zenas the lawyer and Apollos on their way; see that they lack nothing" (Tit. 3:13). The verb *propémpō* can mean either "accompany, escort" (as in Acts 20:38; 21:5) or "send on one's way" with the idea of equipping the traveler with the things necessary for the journey (as in 3 Jn. 6; Rom. 15:24; 1 Cor. 16:6, 11). While it is possible that Paul was instructing Titus to bring Zenas and Apollos with him to Nicopolis (cf. v. 12), Paul's instructions were to equip them for continuing their missionary journey to an undisclosed destination. Possibly Zenas and Apollos carried Paul's letter to Titus as part of a larger mission to Crete.

The description of Zenas as a "lawyer" (*nomikós*) does not make clear whether he was an expert in Jewish or non-Jewish (prob. Roman) law. The other NT uses of this term refer to experts in Jewish law. In the papyri and inscriptions, however, the term is used frequently for anyone from an eminent jurist (see Plutarch *Sulla* 36) to a humble notary (see MM, pp. 428f.), and the historical setting in which the reference occurs suggests that the term may refer to a jurist. Those who hold that Zenas was an expert in Jewish law point to Paul's instruction in Tit. 3:9 to avoid "quarrels over the law" (*máchas nomikás*), which is understood as referring to the Mosaic law. They also argue that if Zenas, like Apollos (assuming this to be the same Apollos mentioned in Acts 18:24), was a converted Jew, he may have retained his former designation as an expert in Torah. Zenas's association with Apollos in no way requires that Zenas was a converted Jew, however; and if Zenas was a Gentile, the law he practiced would have been Greek or Roman law. Furthermore, it seems unlikely that Paul would have referred to Zenas as an expert in Torah when the retention of rabbinic methods was apparently anything but a recommendation in Paul's eyes (cf. 1 Tim. 1:7, where *nomodidáskalos* has a negative connotation). Thus Zenas may well have been a practicing jurist rather than an expert in Torah. His profession may have been mentioned here for the purpose of distinguishing him from another Zenas.

Some have attempted to identify Zenas with Zenon the son of Onesiphorus (cf. 2 Tim. 1:16f., 4:19), who according to the apocryphal Acts of Paul lived in Iconium. Later tradition identified Zenas as the first bishop of Diospolis (NT Lydda) and the author of the apocryphal Acts of Titus; but this tradition has little credibility.

Bibliography.–Comms. on the Pastoral Epistles by M. Dibelius and H. Conzelmann (Eng. tr., *Hermeneia*, 1972), D. Guthrie (*Tyndale NT Comms.*, 1957), J. N. D. Kelly (*HNTC*, 1963), E. F. Scott (*MNTC*, 1936); T. Zahn, *Intro. to the NT* (1953), p. 54.

W. H. GLOER

ZEND-AVESTA zen-də-ves'tə. The Avesta and commentary. *See* RELIGIONS OF THE BIBLICAL WORLD: PERSIA III.B.

ZEPHANIAH zef-ə-nī'ə [Heb. *ṣᵉpanyâ, ṣᵉpanyāhû*–'Yahweh has treasured'; Lat. Apoc. *Sofoniae*]; AV Apoc. SOPHONIAS (2 Esd. 1:40).

1. Son of Maaseiah; the second priest in rank in the days of Jeremiah. Twice he was part of a delegation sent by King Zedekiah to consult the prophet Jeremiah (Jer. 21:1; 37:3). He was apparently not hostile to Jeremiah, for he received from the exiled prophet Shemaiah a letter rebuking him for not having imprisoned Jeremiah (29:24-28). Zephaniah read this letter to Jeremiah and did not imprison him (v. 29). Moreover, Zephaniah is not listed among those who demanded Jeremiah's execution (38:1-4). After the fall of Jerusalem he was among the leaders of Israel who were taken to the king of Babylon at Riblah and put to death (2 K. 25:18-21; Jer. 52:24-27).

2. A Kohathite Levite; ancestor of the singer Heman (1 Ch. 6:36 [MT 21]).

3. Son of Cushi; a prophet during the reign of King

Josiah (Zeph. 1:1; 2 Esd. 1:40). *See* ZEPHANIAH, BOOK OF.

4. Father of Josiah, one of the exiles who returned from Babylon (Zec. 6:10, 14). N. J. O.

ZEPHANIAH, APOCALYPSE OF. A Jewish pseudepigraphal work written originally in Greek, probably sometime between 100 B.C. and A.D. 70. Like several other apocalyptic writings (e.g., *see* APOCALYPTIC LITERATURE III.A.F; APOCRYPHAL APOCALYPSES II.D), the work consisted of the seer's description of a cosmic journey on which he witnessed the splendors of heaven as well as the torments of sinners receiving their just punishment.

Although the complete text has been lost, the work is known from its mention in three ancient lists and from three fragments that have been preserved. It is listed as an apocryphal work in the *Stichometry* of Nicephorus, the *Synopsis scripturae sacrae* of Pseudo-Athanasius, and the *Catalogue of the Sixty Canonical Books*; in each list it is closely associated with the Apocalypse of Elijah. The only fragment preserved in Greek is a short quotation by Clement of Alexandria that describes the seer's visit to the fifth heaven (*Stromata* v.ii.77). Two Coptic MSS, one in the Akhmimic dialect from the end of the 4th cent. and another in the Sahidic dialect from the beginning of the 5th cent., contain the text of the Apocalypse of Elijah as well as fragments of the Apocalypse of Zephaniah. The short Sahidic fragment describes the seer's vision of a soul being tormented in Hades, followed by a vision of a "broad place." The much longer Akhmimic fragment contains various travel scenes, including a visit to Hades in which the seer observes a sea of fire (6:1-3; 10:3). Much discussion has focused on the problem of the relationships among these documents, since the fragments do not overlap and there appear to be some contradictions in details between the Clement quotation and the Coptic fragments.

See O. S. Wintermute, "Apocalypse of Zechariah," in J. H. Charlesworth, ed., *OT Pseudepigrapha,* I (1983), 497-507. N. J. O.

ZEPHANIAH, BOOK OF. Zephaniah (Heb. *ṣᵉpanyâ*; LXX *Sophonias*) is the last of the nine minor prophets written before the Exile. Its main features are clear, so that there has been relatively little scholarly debate over the book. Nevertheless, this brief book is well worth careful study for its vigorous prophecy and for its sensitive depiction of the mystery of God's judgment and redemption joined.

- I. Background
  - A. Date
  - B. The Prophet
  - C. Authenticity
- II. The Book Itself
  - A. Text
  - B. Style
  - C. Structure
  - D. Themes
  - E. Canonicity
- III. Interpretation

I. Background.–A. *Date.* Little mystery obscures the dating of Zephaniah. Despite an occasional proposal to redate it to another era, most scholars have accepted a date within the period stated in 1:1, namely, the reign of King Josiah (640-609 B.C.). Many scholars have suggested that Zephaniah can be dated more specifically within that thirty-one-year reign. G. A. Smith and others have argued that the widespread degeneracy Zephaniah depicts in Judah is possible only in the early years of Josiah's rule, before 622 B.C., when Josiah began refurbishing the temple and reinstating the rule of the Torah (2 K. 22–23). Yet Keil and others have argued that the phrase "the remnant of Baal" (Zeph. 1:4) points to a time when Josiah had already decimated Baal's people, namely, after 622 B.C. The evidence is insufficient to decide this debate. The phrase "remnant of Baal" is appropriate not only to historical description but also to emphatic threats of future judgment.The sins Zephaniah condemns persisted through Josiah's reign (cf. Jer. 44). Surely the prophet approved of Josiah's reforms, and he did not include Josiah among the leaders deserving condemnation. Still, Zephaniah's perspective seems to have been more like that of Huldah and the compiler of Kings (2 K. 22:14-20), namely, that Josiah's reforms were a glorious respite that came too late in Judah's mad rush to ruin. The royal reforms did not reach the heart of the sin depicted by Zephaniah's prophecy–sin that continued before, despite, and after Josiah's reign.

B. The Prophet. All that is known about the prophet himself is also contained in 1:1, and it is very little. It is not known how old Zephaniah was when he prophesied, what his profession was, or what friends or enemies he had. His description of Jerusalem's quarters (1:10f.) suggests that he probably lived in the city, but even that is not certain. In short, the prophet's personality is not presented; only his message is put forward. Nor should it be assumed that Zephaniah's character can be perceived through the coloring of his prophecy; for even in instances where more is known about a prophet (e.g., Jeremiah), the prophecy may run strongly counter to the prophet's own preference and character.

The only aspect of Zephaniah's biography that is given in detail is his lineage: 1:1 names his forefathers to the fourth generation. This genealogy, unique for a prophet, has led many interpreters to suppose that Zephaniah's ancestors must have been very important; in particular, many have concluded that Zephaniah's great-grandfather must have been King Hezekiah. Other explanations have been offered (cf. Rudolph, *in loc.*); but they have all been too contrived, and none has convinced many scholars. In support of this theory, enough time elapsed between King Hezekiah and Zephaniah for four generations (Amon and Josiah were both quite young when their successors were born). Also, King Hezekiah would bring not only prestige but also justice and true religion to Zephaniah's lineage. The major problems are that the text does not call Hezekiah "king" and that none of the early interpreters identified him as the king, even as late as the 4th cent. A.D. In fact, Ibn Ezra (d. 1167) seems to have been the first to suggest that Zephaniah's ancestor was the king. With such gaps in the evidence the identification can be only probable, not certain.

C. Authenticity. From time to time some scholars have questioned the authenticity of various parts of the book. Some early modern scholars (e.g., Wellhausen, 1892) interpreted Zephaniah's message as a consistent one of doom for Judah and thus questioned the more hopeful passages, such as 2:8-11; 3:9-20. More recently G. Krinetzki (*Zefanjastudien* [1977]) attempted to delineate several stages of editing and various smaller interpolations (e.g., 1:12a; 2:5f.; 2:9i-j; 3:10b).

Yet virtually all of Zephaniah is intelligible as spoken in Josiah's reign. Although many scholars have judged that Zephaniah underwent later editing, there has been no convincing convergence of their views on any large number of verses. While there seems to be a critical consensus that the references to the scattered ones, the exiles, or the Diaspora (e.g., 2:7, 9; 3:10, 19f.) were added during or after the Exile, there is otherwise a growing tendency to see Zephaniah himself as the composer of longer passages

A papyrus of Zeph. 1:11–3:6 found in a cave of Wâdī Murabbaʿât (*ca.* A.D. 135) (courtesy, Israel Department of Antiquities and Museums)

or even of the whole book (cf. Kapelrud, van der Woude).

II. The Book Itself.*–*A. Text. The MT of Zephaniah seems to have come to us in good condition. The LXX is occasionally helpful for recovering an earlier reading (as in 1:4, where "with the priests" could be a gloss), but there are not many such passages. The MT is the best form of the text available, and it is probably the basis of all the versions.

B. Style. Zephaniah's style is relatively plain. He did not use extended metaphors or very detailed descriptions. In fact, his work contains only remnants of the standard prophetic speech forms that are discernible in Amos or in Nathan's speeches. Instead Zephaniah constructed longer passages by the accumulation of charges and threats, borne along by the constantly recurring *qînâ* (3,2) rhythm. He added emphasis and interest to several shorter sections by the use of repetition, either identical (e.g., *beṭerem* three times in 2:2f.) or slightly varied (e.g., day of the Lord, day of wrath, day of distress and of anguish, etc., in 1:14-16), and by the use of wordplay (e.g., "Gaza [*ʿazzâ*] shall be deserted [*ʿazûḇâ*]," 2:4). Only once does the work use moderate speech, when it urges that perhaps the humble may be hidden on the day of wrath (2:3). Apart from this, every sentence is a direct and forceful assertion, whether of accusation, judgment, or promise. The hearer is driven along and challenged down to the final verse.

C. Structure. The book's structure is a matter of controversy among scholars. For instance, within a few years of each other Kapelrud, Rudolph, and van der Woude published three careful and significantly different analyses. Some of these controversies, particularly among the early critical scholars, arose from insoluble debates about the book's authenticity and editing. But another cause of disagreement is that two kinds of structure are observable in Zephaniah.

The first and most apparent ordering principle is the following schema: (1) prophecy against Israel (1:2–2:3); (2) prophecy against the nations (2:4-15); (3) prophecy of salvation (3:9-20). This schema fits the bulk of the passages. It is observable in the major prophets, and it may have been traditional for prophecy by Zephaniah's time. Crossing through this traditional form, however, is another structure that is more particularly Zephaniah's. This structure may be outlined as follows:

- 1:2–2:3 Judgment on all, especially Judah
  - 1:2-18 Mingled threats and accusations
    - 1:2-3 Universal destruction
    - 1:4-13 Destruction of Judah and various sinners within
    - 1:14-18 Variations on "the Day of the Lord"
  - 2:1-3 Response to the threat: call to repentance
- 2:4–3:13 Purging of the nations, including Judah
  - 2:4-15 Destruction of foreign powers
  - 3:1-8 Against the powers in Jerusalem
  - 3:9f. Purification of the nations
  - 3:11-13 Purification of Israel
- 3:14-20 Response to the purification: call to rejoice

D. Themes. In important respects Zephaniah's prophecy stands in the mainstream of Israel's prophecy and repeats several of its most insistent themes (*see* PROPHET IV.C). Yet there are also several themes to which this work brings a new or distinctive word. The most prominent example is its treatment of the Day of the Lord (1:7-18). Zephaniah confounds the popular hope that that day will be simple joy for all Israelites (cf. Am. 5:18-20) and then drives the message of disaster home with powerful rhythmic repetition. After Zephaniah's prophecy this phrase will always be associated with a vast (1:2f.) and complete (1:8f.) judgment on Israel as well as on other peoples.

Next, it is striking that Zephaniah speaks of the purification of the nations, not merely their obliteration: the book depicts all the peoples calling on the Lord with pure speech (3:9). In speaking of their purification — even as Israel must become pure — Zephaniah reminds readers of the Lord's openness to the Gentiles as well as Israelites.

The prophet Zephaniah brought a particular insight to the spiritual struggle between pride and humility. Many prophets were indignant about the oppression of the poor, and Zephaniah especially turned the worldly values upside down. He declared that the poor and humble might be the only ones to live and be blessed (2:3; 3:12). While he did not require literal poverty, he did urge his hearers to care for the humble and to seek humility. Pride, however, he damned and mocked. He compared the proud with the sludge in a wine vat (*see* LEES), too stupid to care or to respond to what the Lord required (1:12f.); their elimination would purify Israel (3:11-13). Significantly, he depicted the judgment of the Gentiles as reaching a climax against the blasphemous pride of Nineveh, which left no option but complete desolation (2:13-15). Thus Zephaniah showed both the stupidity of self-confidence and the confidence that the humble may have in God.

A related but smaller topic in Zephaniah's prophecy is the vanity of trust in wealth. The foreign fashions are an offense (1:8); the goods of the proud will be plundered (v. 13). Their silver and gold will be useless to save them (v. 18), and the traders will be no more (v. 11). Even the difficult phrase *lōʾ niḵsāp̄* in 2:1 (RSV "shameless") makes sense as a play on *kesep* ("silver," "money") in 1:18, suggesting (in modern terms) that those who live for the dollar aren't worth a nickel.

Finally, the book persistently portrays the holiness and grace of God. God's holiness appears in the contrasts between Him and the proud sinners: they pretend to rule, but God judges with inexorable power; they hold office, but the Lord gives unfailing justice (3:1-5). God's grace appears chiefly in the two passages (2:1-3; 3:11-20) that offer hope and salvation to a nation (and possibly even Gentiles) that has just been rightly condemned to complete desolation.

E. Canonicity. Zephaniah probably had canonical authority from the time of its composition — at least among a significant group of Judeans. Initially preserved as a word of the Lord, within thirty years it was confirmed when Jerusalem fell on a terrible "day of the Lord." O. Eissfeldt (*The OT: An Intro.* [Eng. tr. 1965], p. 425) remarked that Zephaniah "gives a good impression of the purity and depth of the movement which led to the reform of Josiah." This is surely true, and probably members of that movement were the first to treasure this book. When the reform dissolved, Zephaniah remained, because it was more than simply a tract for a national religious policy. Its author saw to the heart of the matter. In G. A. Smith's memorable phrase, Zephaniah saw that "the elements were loose" (p. 49) — that no human rearranging could save Israel. Although Zephaniah supported religious reforms, his book urges hope in the Lord, not in movements. It thus has permanent value as well as an occasional value for Israel. By the end of the Exile apparently the whole Jewish people had acknowledged Zephaniah as canonical.

III. Interpretation.–The earliest extant perspective on Zephaniah appears in the NT. The four NT passages that allude to Zephaniah (Mt. 13:41 [cf. Zeph. 1:3]; Rev. 6:17 [cf. Zeph. 1:14-18]; 14:5 [cf. Zeph. 3:13]; 16:1 [cf. Zeph. 3:8]) all deal with the Last Judgment, when God's wrath will remove the causes of sin and gather the pure. Thus it appears that Matthew and John saw Zephaniah primarily as an announcement of the Last Day. Although Zephaniah's contemporaries had surely referred "the Day of the Lord" to Jerusalem's fall in 587 B.C., later generations — including the NT writers — saw that Zephaniah's prophecies still awaited a complete fulfillment that God would effect at the end of the age. Parallelling this NT usage, the apocalyptic interpretation of Zephaniah shows up in a late apocalypse attributed to Zephaniah and also in some rabbinic usage (*Pesikta Rabbathi* 8; T. B. *Baba Bathra* 10).

Apocalyptic interpretation of Zephaniah continues to this day, but the book has been used in other ways as well since the early cents. A.D. Clement (*Paed.* ii.13) cited Zeph. 1:18 to warn against pride and idolatry in silver and gold jewelry, counseling instead simplicity and care for the poor. Cyprian repeatedly drew on Zephaniah as proof that flagrant sinners, even apostates, should be called to penitence (cf. Zeph. 2:1ff.; 3:1-3), and that the faithful should not seek early or private vengeance, for the Lord will avenge all evil (*Treatise on Patience* 21; *Testim.* iii.47, 106). The Talmud made a similar moral use of Zephaniah in its statement that the Messiah will not come until there are no conceited men in Israel (T. B. *Sanhedrin* 98a). Thus Zephaniah has provided not only an announcement of the Last Judgment but also practical help for present life in anticipation of that Day.

Augustine also quoted Zephaniah (2:11; 3:9-12) to support the doctrine that salvation comes to the Gentiles (*Civ. Dei* xviii.33). This became commonplace in Christian commentaries; but it is also worth emphasizing that Jewish tradition had affirmed this interpretation of Zeph. 3:9 in its own way (T. B. *Berakoth* 57b).

The medieval Latin hymn *Dies Irae*, composed by Thomas of Celano on the basis of Zeph. 1:14ff., echoes some of the terror of that passage and offers a reflective Christian response; it provides a sober note of hope in the requiem mass and has been translated into many hymnals.

From the Renaissance to the present, preachers have also related Zephaniah to contemporary institutions, calling upon the authorities to make sweeping and effective reforms lest the judgment threatened by Zephaniah befall the present government. This use of the book is scattered through Calvin's comm. on Zephaniah and it is also observable in G. A. Smith's vigorous preaching (ch. 3).

Bibliography.–Comms. by J. Calvin, G. A. Smith (*Expos.B.*, 1928), W. Rudolph (*KZAT*, 1975), A. S. van der Woude (1978), R. L. Smith (*Word Biblical Comm.*, 1984), P. C. Craigie (*Daily Study Bible*, 1985), and E. Achtemeier (*Interpretation*, 1986); also K. Sullivan, *Worship*, 31 (1957), 130-39; A. S. Kapelrud, *Message of the Prophet Zephaniah* (Eng. tr. 1975); see also the bibliographies in Kapelrud, Rudolph, and van der Woude.

D. A. SCHNEIDER

ZEPHATH zē'fath [Heb. *ṣ^{e}paṯ*]. A Canaanite city in the Negeb of Judah near Arad (Jgs. 1:17). The tribes of Judah and Simeon totally destroyed the city and renamed it HORMAH ("destruction").

ZEPHATHAH zef'ə-thə, **VALLEY OF** [Heb. *gê' ṣ^{e}paṯâ*]. A valley near Mareshah in which King Asa of Judah defeated Zerah the Ethiopian (2 Ch. 14:10 [MT 9]). Mareshah may have been only one of a chain of cities along this valley fortified by Rehoboam in the 9th cent. B.C. (cf. 11:5-10). As pointed in the MT the *hê* appears to be adverbial ("toward Zephath"); the LXX *katá borrán* supports the adverbial reading with the emendation of *ṣ^{e}paṯâ* to *ṣapônâ* ("toward the north," i.e., N of Mareshah). On this basis J. Simon identified this valley with the valley of the Terebinth (Wâdī es Sanṭ; RSV "valley of Elah," 1 S. 17:2, 19; 21:9 [MT 10]; see *GTTOT*, § 254). Other scholars have identified it with Wâdī Ṣâfiyeh (see *WHAB*, p. 130).

This Zephath(ah) should not be confused with the city of Zephath mentioned in Jgs. 1:17.

J. E. MCKENNA
W. S. L. S.

ZEPHI zē'fī [Heb. *ṣ^{e}pî*; LXX *Sōphar*] (1 Ch. 1:36); **ZEPHO** zē'fō [Heb. *ṣ^{e}pô*; LXX *Sōphar*] (Gen. 36:11, 15). Third son of Eliphaz; an Edomite chief.

ZEPHON zē'fon [Heb. *ṣ^{e}pôn* < *ṣāpâ*–'watch'(?)]; **ZEPHONITES** zē'fə-nīts [Heb. *haṣṣ^{e}pônî*]. The oldest son of Gad (called ZIPHION in Gen. 46:16) and the family descended from him (Nu. 26:15).

ZER zûr [Heb. *ṣēr*; Gk. *Tyros*–'Tyre' (assuming Heb. *ṣōr* instead of *ṣēr*)]. A fortified town in Naphtali. In Josh. 19:35 it is listed between Ziddim (near Ḥaṭṭîn?) and Hammath (Ḥammâm Ṭabarîyeh), just W of the Sea of Galilee. Some have suggested that Zer be identified with Madon (Qarn Ḥaṭṭîn), but this identification is uncertain. A Zer is mentioned, along with sixty-four other place names, in the Egyptian Execration Texts (*LBHG* [rev. ed. 1979], p. 146); but this Zer is in Bashan and thus cannot be the Zer of Josh. 19:35. The exact location of the site is unknown.

D. E. WARING

ZERAH zē'rə [Heb. *zeraḥ*–'shining forth' (?); Gk. *Zara* (Mt. 1:3)]; AV also ZARA (Mt. 1:3), ZARAH (Gen. 38:30; 46:12); NEB NT ZARAH.

1. An Edomite chief; son of Reuel and grandson of Esau and Basemath the daughter of Ishmael (Gen. 36:13, 17; 1 Ch. 1:37).

2. Father of an early Edomite king named Jobab; a resident of Bozrah (Gen. 36:33; 1 Ch. 1:44).

3. One of the twin sons born to Judah and his daughter-in-law Tamar (Gen. 38:30; 46:12; 1 Ch. 2:4; Neh. 11:24).

His name is attributed to something that happened at his birth: his hand was the first to appear and the midwife tied a scarlet thread around it; but then he withdrew his hand and his brother Perez was born first (Gen. 38:28-30). It is difficult to establish a linguistic link between the name and "scarlet," however. Zerah was ancestor of a family called the Zerahites (Nu. 26:20; cf. 1 Ch. 2:6), which included Achan (Josh. 7:1, 18, 24; 22:20) and Pethahiah (1 Ch. 9:6). His name appears in a genealogy of Jesus (Mt. 1:3).

4. A son of Simeon and head of a Simeonite family called the Zerahites (Nu. 26:13; 1 Ch. 4:24). In Gen. 46:10; Ex. 6:15 he is called Zohar.

5. A Levite of the family of Gershom (1 Ch. 6:21, 41 [MT 6, 26]).

6. An "Ethiopian" (so AV, RSV; NEB "Cushite"; Heb. *hakkûšî*) military leader who invaded Judah with a large army ("million" may simply be an expression for a huge number) and was completely routed by King Asa at Mareshah (2 Ch. 14:9).

Various theories have been proposed regarding his place of origin. Although Heb. *kûš* (*see* CUSH) usually denotes a region of Africa (Nubia or Ethiopia), some scholars have proposed that *hakkûšî* here refers to an Arabian who led a band of Bedouins in a raid against Judah in order to gain better pasture land for themselves. The mention of tents and camels in v. 15 is cited in support of this theory. The association with Libyans in 16:8, however, strongly suggests an origin in Africa. The theory that identified Zerah with the Libyan pharaoh Osorkon I (or Osorkon II; see, e.g., *ISBE* [1929]) has been discredited on both linguistic and historical grounds (see *FSAC*, pp. 46f.). It is possible, however, that Zerah was an Ethiopian general leading an army of Ethiopian and Libyan mercenaries on behalf of Osorkon I, who was attempting to duplicate the earlier success of his father Sheshonq (Shishak, 2 Ch. 12:2-4).

Bibliography.–K. A. Kitchen, *Third Intermediate Period in Egypt* (1973), p. 309; H. G. M. Williamson, *1 and 2 Chronicles* (*NCBC*, 1982), pp. 263-65.

N. J. O.

ZERAHIAH zer-ə-hī'ə [Heb. *zeraḥyâ*–'Yahweh has shone forth'; Gk. Apoc. *Zaraia*]; AV Apoc. ZARAIAS; NEB Apoc. ZARAEAS.

1. A priest, son of Uzzi and descendant of Eleazar (1 Ch. 6:6, 51 [MT 5:32; 6:36]); an ancestor of Ezra (Ezr. 7:4; AV, NEB, 1 Esd. 8:2 [omitted by RSV, following LXX B]). He is called Arna in 2 Esd. 1:2.

2. Father of Eliehoenai, whose family returned from exile with Ezra (Ezr. 8:4; 1 Esd. 8:31).

ZERAHITES zer'ə-hīts [Heb. *hazzarḥî*]; AV ZARHITES; NEB ZARHITE FAMILY, CLAN (or FAMILY) OF ZERAH.

1. The family of a Simeonite named Zerah (Nu. 26:13). *See* ZERAH **4**.

2. The family of Zerah the son of Judah (Nu. 26:20). Achan (Josh. 7:17) and two of David's mighty men (1 Ch. 27:11, 13) belonged to this family. *See* ZERAH **3**.

ZERAIAH zə-rā'yə [Gk. *Zaraias*]; AV ZARAIAS; NEB ZARAEAS. Son of Michael; head of a family that returned from exile with Ezra (1 Esd. 8:34). He is called Zebadiah in Ezr. 8:8.

ZERDAIAH zər-dī'ə [Gk. *Zerdaias* (Rahlfs), B *Zeralias* A *Zardaias*]; AV SARDEUS; NEB ZARDAEAS. One of the sons of Zamoth who had married foreign wives, apparently the same person as AZIZA in Ezr. 10:27.

ZERED zer'ed [Heb. *zered*; LXX B *Zaret*, A *Zare*]; AV also ZARED (Nu. 21:12); NEB ZARED. The wadi that marked the end of the Israelites' wanderings (Dt. 2:13f.), and the valley where they camped before reaching the Arnon (Nu. 21:12). Earlier authorities identified it with a tributary of the Wâdī Kerak or of the Arnon, but scholars now usually identify it with the Wâdī el-Ḥesā, the larger stream flowing into the southeast corner of the Dead Sea that formed the boundary between Edom and Moab. The identification depends in part on the interpretation of the details of Israel's route. *See* WANDERINGS OF ISRAEL V.

The "Brook of the Willows" in Isa. 15:7, the "Brook of the Arabah" in Am. 6:14, and the "dry streambed" in 2 K. 3:16 (cf. v. 22) are probably all to be identified with the Zered (see *GB*, pp. 62f. [2 K. 3]; see comms.).

H. L. ELLISON

ZEREDAH zer'ə-də [Heb. *ṣerēḏâ*]; AV ZEREDA, ZEREDATHAH.

1. The birthplace of Jeroboam the son of Nebat, and his residence prior to his revolt against Solomon (1 K. 11:26; omitted by LXX). The identification of Jeroboam as an "Ephraimite" indicates that the town was in the hill country region between Jerusalem and Shechem. Several sites have been proposed for its location, including the modern Deir Ghassâneh (about 24 km. [15 mi.] SW of Shechem) and the nearby ʿAin Ṣeridah, which are both located in Wâdī Deir Balluṭ (but cf. W. F. Albright, *JPOS*, 5 (1925), 33 n. 37, 37 n. 41).

2. A variant spelling of ZARETHAN in 2 Ch. 4:17 (cf. par. 1 K. 7:46). Most scholars also believe that "Zeredah" is also the correct spelling of ZERERAH in Jgs. 7:22.

W. L. THOMPSON, JR.

ZEREDATHAH zer-ə-dā'thə (2 Ch. 4:17, AV). *See* ZEREDAH **2**.

ZERERAH zer'ə-rə [Heb. *ṣerērâ* (MT *ṣerērāṯâ*–'toward Zererah')]; AV ZERERATH. A place to which the Midianite army fled after their defeat by Gideon (Jgs. 7:22). Some MSS read *ṣerēḏâ*; thus the correct spelling may be ZEREDAH (**2**) (cf. 2 Ch. 4:17), which is probably a variant of ZARETHAN.

ZERESH zer'esh [Heb. *zereš*–'gold' (from Pers.)]. The wife of Haman (Est. 5:10). She was apparently one of his chief advisers (5:14; 6:13).

ZERETH zer'eth [Heb. *ṣereṯ*]. A Judahite; first son of Helah the wife of Asshur (1 Ch. 4:7).

ZERETH-SHAHAR zer'eth shā'hār [Heb. *ṣereṯ haššaḥar*; Gk. B *Serada kaí Siōr*, A *Sarth kaí Siōn*]; AV ZARETH-SHAHAR. A town originally ruled by Sihon king of the Amorites, assigned by Moses to the tribe of Reuben (Josh. 13:19). It is described as "on the hill of the valley" (Heb. *behar hāʿēmeq*), possibly designating one of the hills overlooking the eastern shore of the Dead Sea. Scholars have cautiously accepted the identification with ez-Zārât, the hot springs of Callirhoë near Machaerus. See *GP*, II, 457.

W. S. L. S.

ZERI zer'ī [Heb. *ṣerî*–'mastic' (*IP*, p. 223)]; NEB IZRI. One of the sons of Jeduthun who prophesied with the lyre in the temple (1 Ch. 25:3). He may be the man called Izri (cf. NEB) in v. 11.

ZEROR zē'rôr [Heb. *ṣ^e^rôr*]. Son of Becorath and father of Abiel; an ancestor of King Saul (1 S. 9:1).

ZERQĀ zer'kə The Arabic name (meaning "blue") of three streams in Palestine and Transjordan.

1. The Zerqā Māʿîn, a small stream that flows into the Dead Sea on its eastern side about halfway between the Arnon and the Jordan. Like the other streams flowing into the Dead Sea from the east, it has cut a gorge for its waters; it is remarkable for its cataract of hot water. Some scholars have identified it with NAHALIEL, a stopping place of the Israelites on their journey to the Promised Land (Nu. 21:19).

2. Wâdī or Nahr ez-Zerqā, the JABBOK.

3. The Crocodile River (Nahr ez-Zerqā), which rises in the Carmel range W of Megiddo and flows into the Mediterranean between Dor and Caesarea. It is not mentioned in the Bible. H. L. ELLISON

ZERUAH zə-ro͞o'ə [Heb. *ṣ^e^rûʿâ*–'leprous' (*IP*, pp. 227f.)]. Mother of King Jeroboam I (1 K. 11:26).

ZERUBBABEL zə-rub'ə-bəl [Heb. *z^e^rubbāḇel*; Akk. *zēr-bābili*–'seed (descendant) of Babylon' (cf. J. J. Stamm, *Die akkadische Namengebung* [1939], pp. 40ff., 269f.; *CAD*, XXI, 95); Gk. *Zorobabel*]; AV Apoc. and NT ZOROBABEL. Descendant of David and grandson of Jehoiachin; governor of postexilic Judah during the restoration of the temple.

I. Family and Birth.–Zerubbabel is usually called the son of Shealtiel, Jehoiachin's eldest son (Ezr. 3:2, 8; 5:2; Neh. 12:1; Hag. 1:1, 12, 14; 2:2, 23; Mt. 1:12; Lk. 3:27), but in 1 Ch. 3:19 he appears as the son of Pedaiah, Jehoiachin's third son. Since Chronicles is dated later than Haggai and yet puts Zerubbabel in a less exalted position, both traditions should probably be taken seriously. Several suggestions have been advanced to harmonize these traditions; all of them make Zerubbabel the literal son of Pedaiah and link him with Shealtiel by some legal device such as levirate marriage (cf. Dt. 25:5-10).

The Jehoiachin Tablets (cf. *DOTT*, pp. 84-86) suggest that Zerubbabel's father may have been born early in Jehoiachin's captivity. If so, Zerubbabel himself could have been born any time after *ca.* 575 B.C., which would have made it quite possible for him to lead a return from Babylon to Jerusalem in the first year of Cyrus (538) or soon after.

II. Suggested Identity with Sheshbazzar.–Josephus (*Ant.* xi.i.3 [13f.]) identified Zerubbabel with SHESHBAZZAR (Ezr. 1:8-11; 5:14-16), and some scholars have followed this suggestion, since both men appear to have performed similar functions at the same time although they are never mentioned together: each is given the title *peḥâ*, "governor" (Ezr. 5:14; Hag. 1:1; 2:2), has led a return from Babylon to Jerusalem in 538 B.C. (Ezr. 1:11; 2:1f.), and each is said to have played a role in supervising the laying of the foundations of the temple (Ezr. 3:8; 5:16).

This identification is to be rejected, however, for two main reasons. (1) Although some individuals were known by two names (e.g., Daniel/Belteshazzar, Dnl. 1:7; 2:26), it is highly unlikely that a member of the Jewish royal line would have had two Babylonian names. (2) Ezr. 5 seems to distinguish the two men. According to vv. 2f. Zerubbabel was personally involved in the controversy with Tattenai over the rebuilding of the temple, but vv. 14-16 refer to Sheshbazzar in language designed to introduce him as someone not known to Tattenai and not present at the time. (Against the further attempt to identify Sheshbazzar with Shenazzar, Zerubbabel's uncle, see P. -R. Berger, *ZAW*, 83 [1971], 98-100.)

III. His Life.–No question concerning Zerubbabel raises more difficulties than the date of his journey to Jerusalem. Two main views are possible.

(1) According to the traditional approach, Ezr. 1–6 is read as a straightforward account of the following events: Zerubbabel led the first return to Jerusalem, as authorized by Cyrus in 538 B.C. (chs. 1–2); soon after his arrival the rebuilding of the temple was begun, but this was abandoned because of opposition (chs. 3–4); the work was not resumed and completed until many years later, under the stimulus of the preaching of Haggai and Zechariah (chs. 5–6).

(2) A second approach has attempted to do greater justice to the variety of source materials in Ezr. 1–6. This approach notes, e.g., that the list of returned exiles in ch. 2 is composite, and that several features suggest that it was intended as a summary of all who returned during 538-515 B.C. Ezr. 3:1–4:5 is regarded as a separate unit, again without any absolute date; its main purpose, indicated by allusions in the passage, is to parallel the building of the second temple with the building of the first under Solomon. 4:4f. has been identified as a "summary notation," a literary device that "recapitulate[s] the contents, and thus also delineate[s] the extent of a preceding textual unit" (cf. *IDBSupp.*, p. 322 [S. Talmon]). If this is so, then the reference in 4:4 to the "people of the land" making the Jews afraid to build is a recapitulation of 3:3 rather than a further development of the narrative, and 4:4f. indicates that building did not begin until the reign of Darius. 3:8-13 can then be read as parallel with, not prior to, the Aramaic account in chs. 5–6. According to this view the date of Zerubbabel's journey to Jerusalem could have been later than 538.

It is extremely difficult to decide between these two approaches, and the issue cannot be argued in full here. Both approaches come together, however, on the most important point, namely, that Zerubbabel in association with Joshua the high priest led the intensive work of rebuilding the temple in 520-515 B.C. The two men were encouraged by the prophets Haggai and Zechariah, whose oracles accord well with Ezr. 5–6, and no doubt also by the financial assistance of the Persian authorities, who conformed to Cyrus's decree of some twenty years earlier. The successful completion of this work (6:13-15) undoubtedly constitutes Zerubbabel's chief historical significance (cf. Sir. 49:11f.).

The biblical records are silent about Zerubbabel's life after the completion of the second temple. Undoubtedly, considerable excitement attended the rebuilding, and the people may well have drawn parallels between the work of this descendant of David and the earlier work of (and promises to) Solomon. Moreover, Hag. 2:20-23, a prophecy directed to Zerubbabel, seems to have messianic overtones; and many scholars have contended that Zec. 6:11-14 originally described the symbolic coronation of Zerubbabel rather than of Joshua (see comms., e.g., *IB*, VI, 1079f.). Coupling these passages with the lack of references to Zerubbabel at the dedication of the temple (Ezr. 6:16-22) or thereafter, some have conjectured that he became involved in a messianic conspiracy and was removed from office, or even executed, by Darius.

Several factors, however, indicate that such speculations are unwarranted. (1) All such arguments are based entirely on silence. The weakness of these arguments is shown by the fact that there is also no mention of Joshua the high priest at the dedication of the temple, but nobody has contended that he was removed from office. (2) Darius confirmed Zerubbabel in his role as governor and temple builder despite the inquiry of Tattenai and his associates (Ezr. 6:6f.). Darius would not have granted this permission had there been any suspicion of seditious activity. (3) Ch. 4 implies that "the adversaries of Judah and Benjamin" waited until the reign of Artaxerxes before accusing the city and its inhabitants of being "rebellious and wicked." This delay would be hard to explain had there been earlier occasion for such an accusation. (4) Several commentators have rejected the former view that Zechariah entertained royal or messianic hopes for Zerubbabel (see esp. W. Rudolph's interpretation of Zec. 6:12f. in *Haggai — Sacharja 1–8/9–14 — Maleachi* [1976]).

One may thus conclude that Zerubbabel himself kept well clear of any politically questionable involvement; indeed, the biblical material gives the impression that he did not seek to advance himself but rather waited for others to motivate him to act. It is thus appropriate that nothing of his personal history is known after his significant role in rebuilding the second temple.

IV. Other Traditions.–Historical knowledge about Zerubbabel is confined to the sources already discussed — principally Ezr. 1–6 with the support of Hag. 1:1–2:9 and Zec. 4:6-10, which record how the prophets prompted and encouraged him in his task of temple building. In addition, the messianic title "signet ring" (cf. Jer. 22:24) and the anticipated overthrow of the nations in Hag. 2:20-23 suggest that Haggai may have entertained what proved to be exaggerated hopes of Zerubbabel. Naturally enough, he was not followed in this by subsequent writers, but there is evidence that Zerubbabel continued to be held in high esteem in early Jewish tradition.

1 Esdras is an apocryphal work based largely on 2 Ch. 35–36, Ezra, and Neh. 8. Its relationship with the canonical texts is disputed. One of its major deviations from the biblical record is the insertion (1 Esd. 3:1–5:6) of the story of a dispute at the court of Darius in which three of the king's bodyguards contest "what one thing is strongest" (3:5). The third bodyguard, who turns out to be Zerubbabel, wins the contest with his proposition that "women are strongest, but truth is victor over all things" (3:12); he is thus granted permission to lead a return to Jerusalem.

It is generally agreed today that this story is among the latest elements to be included in 1 Esdras and that in the process of its inclusion the name of Zerubbabel was added to what was originally an independent wisdom tale. It is thus unwise to use the story as evidence for the date of Zerubbabel's journey to Jerusalem (cf. III above). Together with added references in 1 Esd. 5:7f., 14; 6:27, however, it is valuable as evidence of the honor in which Zerubbabel continued to be held as an influential leader of his people and indeed as one who (unlike at Sir. 49:11f.) is put on a pedestal above Joshua the high priest. The influence of such figures as Daniel and Nehemiah is also apparent. Since in his account of the postexilic restoration Josephus (*Ant.* xi) followed 1 Esdras rather than the biblical book of Ezra, it is not surprising to find that Josephus continued this process even further (cf. S. Japhét, *ZAW*, 95 [1982], 218-229).

Bibliography.–Comms. on Ezra-Nehemiah, Haggai, and Zechariah; also S. A. Cook, "Age of Zerubbabel," in H. H. Rowley, ed., *Studies in OT Prophecy* (1950), pp. 19-36; F. I. Andersen, *Australian Biblical Review*, 6 (1958), 1-35; J. S. Wright, *Building of the Second Temple* (1958); K. Galling, *Studien zur Geschichte Israels im persischen Zeitalter* (1964); A. Gelston, *VT*, 16 (1966), 232-35; P. R. Ackroyd, *Exile and Restoration* (1968), pp. 138-152; K. -M. Beyse, *Serubbabel und die Königserwartungen der Propheten Haggai und Sacharja* (1972); S. Japhét, *ZAW*, 94 (1982), 66-98; H. G. M. Williamson, *JTS*, N.S. 34 (1983), 1-30; W. D. Davies and L. Finkelstein, eds., *Cambridge History of Judaism*, I (1984).

H. G. M. WILLIAMSON

ZERUIAH zə-ro͞o'yə [Heb. *ṣ^erûyâ, ṣ^eruyâ* (2 S. 14:1; 16:10) –'perfumed with mastic' (*IP*, p. 227)]. Mother of Joab, Abishai, and Asahel, three commanders of David's army (1 S. 26:6; 2 S. 2:13, 18; 3:39; 8:16; etc.). These men are always identified as sons of Zeruiah and never by the name of their father. This may have been due to her husband's early death (although it does not mention his name, 2 S. 2:32 states that his tomb was in Bethlehem), or it may indicate that she was the stronger personality. Some scholars have seen here a preservation of the ancient custom of tracing descent through the line of the mother. In 1 Ch. 2:16 Zeruiah and ABIGAIL (2) are called sisters of David; but they may have been only his half-sisters by the same mother, since 2 S. 17:25 calls Abigail the daughter of Nahash. Perhaps Nahash the father of Zeruiah and Abigail died, and his widow then became the wife of Jesse.

N. J. O.

ZETHAM zē'thəm [Heb. *zēṯām*–'olive tree' (*IP*, p. 242)]. A Gershonite Levite, called the son of Ladan in 1 Ch. 23:8 but the son of Jehieli in 26:22. Possibly the MT of 26:22 should be repointed to read, "Jehiel and his brothers Zetham and Joel . . . " (so NEB). Zetham and his brother(s) were in charge of the treasuries of the temple.

ZETHAN zē'thən [Heb. *zêṯān*–'olive tree' (*IP*, p. 242)]. Son of Bilhan; a Benjaminite (1 Ch. 7:10). *See* ZEMIRAH.

ZETHAR zē'thär [Heb. *zēṯar* < Pers. *zaitar*–'conqueror' (?) (BDB, p. 285)]. One of the seven eunuchs of King Ahasuerus (Est. 1:10).

ZEUS zo͞os [Gk. *Zeus*, genitive *Dios*] (Acts 14:12f.); AV, NEB, JUPITER. One of the principal deities in the Greco-Roman pantheon. To the Romans he was known as Jovis or Jupiter.

Of Indo-European origin, Zeus was originally associated with the sky and atmospheric phenomena. He was not the ancestor of gods or people, but as the supreme deity, ruler of gods and humanity, he functioned among the Greeks as benefactor, especially to those engaged in agricultural pursuits (see, e.g., the anonymous *Hymn to Zeus Diktaios*, so termed from the Cretan mountain Dicte, E. Diehl, ed., *Anthologia Lyrica* [1925], II, 279-281). Identified as "Father," a term applied to kings in their role of concern for the needs of their subjects, Zeus served as the protector especially of the suppliant and the guest (cf. the title "Friend of Strangers," 2 Macc. 6:2). He was recognized as the god of the courtyard and of the household. Closely associated is his interest in political freedom, which earned him such titles as Soter and Eleutherios. Homer celebrated his majestic authority in *Iliad* i.528-530: "Then nodded Kronos' son with darkened brow and from his head immortal rolled in waves ambrosial locks, and great Olympus trembled at his bidding." Hesiod, recognizing Zeus as the protector of laws and morals, invoked him as a champion of justice (*Opera et dies* 213-285). From Zeus emanated all revelation.

Ancient Christian writers were quick to refer to variations of a story about Zeus's alleged grave. Callimachus, whose *Hymnus in Jovem* rivals that by Cleanthes as one of the loftiest expressions of piety in the history of devotion, had centuries earlier exposed the story as a Cretan deception. Aeschylus expressed an idea that was echoed in

The temple to Olympian Zeus built in the 2nd cent. B.C. beneath the acropolis at Athens. Originally surrounded by over one hundred Corinthian columns, this was the largest temple in Greece (Philip Gendreau, NY)

the reference to an "Unknown God" (Acts 17:23): "Zeus, whoever He may be, if that name please Him well, by this I now address Him" (*Agamemnon* 160-62). In the Hellenistic age Zeus's name was freely bestowed on the chief deity of any non-Greek tribe or region (cf. 2 Macc. 6:2). Through the cultic fusion of Greek and Egyptian piety initiated by Ptolemy I Soter (*ca.* 301-286 B.C.), Zeus gradually gave way — as did numerous other Greek deities — to Sarapis.

Acts 14:13 appears to suggest that a statue of Zeus was stationed at the gate of Lystra. Codex Bezae (D) here reads *toú óntos Dios pró póleōs,* "of the Zeus that is known as '[Zeus] Before-the-city.'" This reading appears to be secondary, reflecting knowledge of a locative title, *Zeus pró póleōs* (for inscriptions with such usage, see Wikenhauser, p. 363). A third-century A.D. inscription attests the association of Zeus with Hermes in Lycaonia (at Sedasa, about 40 km. [25 mi.] SW of Lystra). In harmony with Greco-Roman writers, Luke's account associates oxen and garlands with the cult of Zeus (see Wettstein, p. 543).

In Acts 19:35 the AV renders Gk. *diopetḗs* (used of meteorites or other objects sent from the skies) with the paraphrase, "fell down from Jupiter" (RSV "sacred stone"; NEB "fell from heaven"). *See* SACRED STONE.

Bibliography.–W. M. Calder, *Classical Review,* 24 (1910), 77; A. B. Cook, *Zeus,* I-III (1914-1940); W. H. Roscher, ed., *Ausführliches Lexikon der griechischen und römischen Mythologie* (1924-1937), VI, *s.v.*; J. Wettstein, *Novum Testamentum Graecum,* II (1752, repr. 1962), 542f.; A. Wikenhauser, *Die Apostelgeschichte und Ihr Geschichtswert* (1921), pp. 362-63.

F. W. DANKER

ZIA zī'ə [Heb. *zî(a)*ʿ–'trembler' (?) (*IP,* p. 242)]. Head of a Gadite clan (1 Ch. 5:13).

ZIBA zī'bə [Heb. *ṣîḇā',* *ṣiḇā'* (2 S. 16:4)–'planting' or 'branch' (?)] (2 S. 9:2-4, 9-12; 16:1-4; 19:17, 29). A former servant of Saul who managed his estate after his master's death, assisted perhaps by his fifteen sons and twenty servants (2 S. 9:10). When David inquired if any member of Saul's family was left to whom he might show kindness for Jonathan's sake (cf. Jonathan's request and David's oath, 1 S. 20:14-17), Ziba informed him of Jonathan's crippled son Mephibosheth, who was thereupon given Saul's estate with Ziba continuing as manager (2 S. 9).

Later, during Absalom's revolt, when David was fleeing from Jerusalem, Ziba met him near the Mt. of Olives and gave him provisions and transport for the journey (16:1f.). When asked about his master Ziba accused Mephibosheth of treachery, saying that he was remaining in Jerusalem to take the kingdom (v. 3). This probably was untrue. But David, always fearing a threat from Saul's house, believed Ziba and gave him his master's estate (v. 4). When David was returning to Jerusalem, Ziba, assisted by his sons and servants, helped him cross the Jordan River (19:17f.). Soon after, Mephibosheth was able to give his version of the story, whereupon David, perhaps not knowing whom to believe, divided the property between them (vv. 24-30). J. A. BALCHIN

ZIBEON zib'ē-ən [Heb. *ṣiḇʿôn*–'hyena']. Third son of Seir, and father of Aiah and Anah; a Horite clan chief (Gen. 36:2, 14, 20, 24, 29; 1 Ch. 1:38, 40). The MT calls him a "Hivite" in Gen. 36:2; this should be emended to read "Horite" (cf. NEB) with vv. 20, 29 (*see* HIVITES; HORITES). In vv. 2, 14 the AV follows the MT in referring to Anah as the "daughter" of Zibeon. The RSV and NEB correctly follow the LXX, Sam. Pent., and Syr. in reading "son" (cf. also vv. 24, 29; 1 Ch. 1:40).

ZIBIA zib'ē-ə [Heb. *ṣiḇyā'*–'gazelle' (*IP,* p. 230)]. A Benjaminite; one of the sons that Shaharaim had by his wife Hadesh in the land of Moab (1 Ch. 8:9).

ZIBIAH zib'ē-ə [Heb. *ṣiḇyâ*–'gazelle' (*IP,* p. 230)]. Mother of King Joash of Judah; a native of Beer-sheba (2 K. 12:1 [MT 2]; 2 Ch. 24:1).

ZICHRI zik'rī [Heb. *ziḵrî*–'remembrance' (?); possibly a shortened form of ZECHARIAH (see *IP,* pp. 38, 187)].

1. A Kohathite Levite of the family of Izhar (Ex. 6:21).
2. A Benjaminite, son of Shimei (1 Ch. 8:19).
3. A Benjaminite, son of Shashak (1 Ch. 8:23).
4. A Benjaminite, son of Jehoram (1 Ch. 8:27).
5. A Levite of the family of Asaph (1 Ch. 9:15). He is called ZABDI (4) in Neh. 11:17.
6. A Levite descended from Eliezer; son of Joram and father of Shelomoth (1 Ch. 26:25).
7. A Reubenite; father of the Eliezer who was chief officer for his tribe in the time of David (1 Ch. 27:16).
8. A Judahite; father of the Amasiah who served as a commander of Jehoshaphat's army (2 Ch. 17:16).
9. Father of the Elishaphat who was a commander in the army in the time of Jehoiada (2 Ch. 23:1).
10. A "mighty man of Ephraim" in the army of King Pekah of Israel. He is reported to have slain King Ahaz's son and two of his high officials as punishment for Ahaz's idolatry (2 Ch. 28:7).
11. A Benjaminite, father of Joel (Neh. 11:9).
12. Head of the priestly family of Abijah in the days of Joiakim, following the return from exile (Neh. 12:17).

N. J. O.

ZIDDIM zid'im [Heb. *ṣiddîm*–'sides']. A fortified town in Naphtali, W of the Sea of Galilee. It is mentioned in Josh. 19:35 along with Zer and Hammath. The Talmud identifies Ziddim with Caphar Hittaia (modern Ḥaṭṭîn el-Qadim), which is N of Qarn Ḥaṭṭîn (the "Horns of Ḥaṭṭîn") and about 8 km. (5 mi.) WNW of Tiberias; but this identification is not certain. The exact location of the site is unknown.

See *GP,* II, 460f. D. E. WARING

ZIDKIJAH zid-kī'jə (Neh. 10:1, AV). *See* ZEDEKIAH **6**.

ZIDON zī'dən; **ZIDONIANS** zī-dō'nē-ənz. *See* SIDON.

ZIF zif (1 K. 6:1, 37, AV). *See* ZIV.

ZIHA zī'hə [Heb. *ṣîḥā', ṣiḥā'* (Neh. 7:46); Gk. Apoc. *Esau* (1 Esd. 5:29)]; AV Apoc., NEB Apoc., ESAU. Head of a family of temple servants that returned from the Exile (Ezr. 2:43; Neh. 7:46; 1 Esd. 5:29). He is probably the same person that is called an overseer of the NETHINIM in Neh. 11:21.

ZIKLAG zik'lag [Heb. *ṣiqlag, ṣiqlāg* (2 S. 1:1), *ṣîqlag* (2 Ch. 12:1, 20); Gk. *Sekelak, Sikelag,* etc.]. A town in the western Negeb.

According to Josh. 19:5 Ziklag was assigned to Simeon (within the territory of Judah, v. 9), but later it was apparently absorbed into the tribe of Judah (1 Ch. 4:30f.; cf. Josh. 15:31). In the time of Saul, however, it was within the territory occupied by the Philistines. During his flight from Saul, David found refuge with the Philistines, and Achish king of Gath gave him Ziklag as a fief (1 S. 27:6). David and his men lived in Ziklag for a year and four months (v. 7), during which time they were joined by warriors from Benjamin and Judah (1 Ch. 12:1-8 [MT 9]). David used his fighting men in aggressive defense of the southern districts of Judah by attacking the hostile tribal elements in northern Sinai and the highlands S of the Negeb (1 S. 27:8f.), but he reported to Achish that he was raiding the settled areas of Judah and its satellite tribes (v. 10). While David was at the Philistine assembly point in Aphek, the Amalekites raided the Negeb and destroyed Ziklag (30:1-3). After an exhausting pursuit David and four hundred men took the Amalekites by surprise and rescued the women and children (vv. 4-20). Under the monarchy Ziklag remained royal property (27:6). During the postexilic period Ziklag was resettled by returning Jews and listed among the cities of Judah (Neh. 11:28).

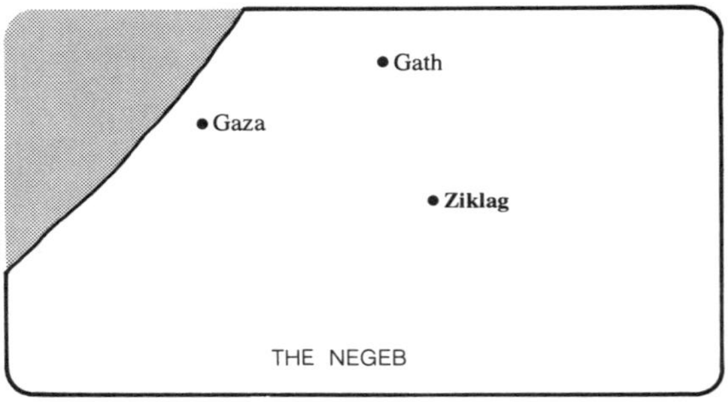

The location of Ziklag is still uncertain. It must have been in the western Negeb, because at one time it belonged to the Philistines (1 S. 27:6). Moreover, it could not have been in the central or eastern Negeb where the Judeans, Jerachmeelites, and Kenites lived, because David was ostensibly making war on them. Therefore Tell el-Khuweilfeh — often proposed as the site of Ziklag — is out of the question, since it is too far east. More likely is Tell esh-Sherî'ah (Tel Seraʿ), about 33 km. (20 mi.) ESE of Gaza on the Wâdī esh-Sherî'ah (Naḥal Gerar). Excavations there have shown that it was occupied in the periods during which Ziklag appears in the historical record. A stratum of Philistine occupation is especially noteworthy. No conclusive proof for this identification has been discovered, however.

Bibliography.–W. F. Albright, *BASOR,* 17 (Feb. 1925), 6; A. Alt, *JPOS,* 15 (1935), 294-324; I. Press, *Topographical-Historical Encyclopaedia of Palestine,* IV (1955), 806f. (Hebrew); A. F. Rainey, *Eretz-Israel,* 12 (1975), 71f.; *EAEHL,* IV, *s.v.* "Esh-Shari'a, Tell" (E. D. Oren); E. Oren, *BA,* 45 (1982), 155-166; A. F. Rainey, "Early Historical Geography of the Negeb," in Z. Herzog, ed., *Beer-sheba,* II (1984), 100-102. A. F. RAINEY

ZILLAH zil'ə [Heb. *ṣillâ*–'shadow']. The second wife of Lamech (Gen. 4:19, 23); mother of Tubal-cain and Naamah (v. 22).

ZILLETHAI zil'ə-thī [Heb. *ṣillᵉṯay*–'(Yahweh is) a shadow (i.e., protection)' (*IP,* pp. 39, 152)]; AV, NEB, ZILTHAI.

1. A Benjaminite, son of Shimei (1 Ch. 8:20).

2. A Manassite who joined David at Ziklag (1 Ch. 12:20 [MT 21]).

ZILPAH zil'pə [Heb. *zilpâ*]. Mother of Gad and Asher (Gen. 30:10-13; 35:26; 46:16-18). Laban gave her to Leah as a maid (Gen. 29:24; 46:18), and Leah gave her to Jacob as his "wife" (concubine) after Leah herself had stopped bearing children (30:9; cf. 37:2).

ZILTHAI zil'thī (AV, NEB, 1 Ch. 8:20; 12:20). *See* ZILLETHAI.

ZIMMAH zim'ə [Heb. *zimmâ*–'(Yahweh has) planned' (see *IP*, pp. 39, 176)]. A Gershonite Levite (1 Ch. 6:20, 42 [MT 5, 27]; 2 Ch. 29:12).

ZIMRAN zim'ran [Heb. *zimrān*]. A son of Abraham and Keturah (Gen. 25:2; 1 Ch. 1:32), understood as a gentilic for a tribe or region by that name. Since the other names in Gen. 25:2-4 are probably to be located in Arabia, this is a likely place for Zimran. LXX B of 1 Ch. 1:32 reads Gk. *Zembran,* possibly the Zembram of Ptolemy (*Geog.* vi.7.5), a region of Cinaidocolpites on the Red Sea not far from Mecca, or the Zamareus of Pliny (*Nat. Hist.* vi.158). The Latin texts of both these references can be found in K. Conti Rossini, *Chrestomathia arabica meridionalis epigraphica* (1931), pp. 20, 32. Zimran has been identified with Zimri in Jer. 25:25, but while v. 25 mentions "the kings of Zimri" after "the kings of Arabia and all the kings of the mixed tribes that dwell in the desert" (v. 24), v. 25 groups "the kings of Zimri" (omitted by LXX) more closely with "the kings of Elam, and all the kings of Media" (v. 25); hence the identification with Zimri is not fully convincing. W. S. LASOR

ZIMRI zim'rī [Heb. *zimrî*; Gk. *Zambri, Zambrei*]; AV Apoc. ZAMBRI (1 Macc. 2:26). Apparently a Semitic name, perhaps a truncated form of Zimri-el on the analogy of Zimri-lim at Mari (see Huffmon; cf. *zkr'l* in Jackson) or Zimri-yahu (cf. Diringer). The exact etymology of the name is uncertain. Some have proposed that it means "my protection," based on the Arabic root *ḏmr* (cf. Job 35:10). Noth (*IP*, p. 176) attributed the name to the Hebrew and Aramaic root *zmr,* "sing" (hence Zimri means "my song"; cf. Ex. 15:2; Isa. 12:2; 25:5; Ps. 118:14). J. Gray suggested that the ending *-î* may merely signify a nickname (p. 361). G. B. Gray related the name to *zmrn,* "mountain sheep" (cf. *zemer,* Dt. 14:5; Zimran, Gen. 25:2; 1 Ch. 1:32).

1. Son of Salu; a Simeonite elder who shamelessly committed adultery with Cozbi, a Midianite princess (Nu. 25:14). By slaying both Zimri and Cozbi, Phinehas stayed the plague that God had sent upon Israel (cf. 1 Macc. 2:26; 1 Cor. 10:8).

2. King of Israel for seven days in Tirzah, and successor of Elah son of Baasha, whom he assassinated. Zimri was the commander of half the Israelite chariotry, and he usurped the throne while Elah was in a drunken stupor in Tirzah and the remainder of the Israelite army was besieging Gibbethon (1 K. 16:9f., 15; cf. 15:27). Upon establishing himself as king, Zimri systematically exterminated all potential rivals from the extended family of Baasha in accordance with the oracle of the prophet Jehu (16:11f.). The persistent idolatry of Baasha and Elah was cited as the reason for God's judgment (v. 13; cf. vv. 1-4, 7). Zimri's assassination of Elah was later alluded to by Jezebel, who greeted Jehu with the words: "Is it peace, you Zimri, murderer of your master?" (2 K. 9:31).

When the Israelite troops at Gibbethon heard of the coup in Tirzah they immediately installed Omri, the commander-in-chief, as a rival king (presumably with the support of "all Israel," 1 K. 16:16). Then Omri withdrew from Gibbethon and besieged Tirzah (v. 17). Seeing Omri's certain victory, Zimri went into the citadel of the palace and burned the building down over him, thereby committing suicide (v. 18).

These events are dated to the twenty-seventh year of Asa's reign (16:10). Some scholars, e.g., J. Gray (p. 64) and E. Theile (*MNHK*, pp. 62-64), assuming synchronism between the records of Judah and Israel, have placed Zimri's brief reign in 885 B.C. Others, e.g., W. F. Albright, followed by J. Bright (*BHI* [3rd ed. 1981], p. 239), have regarded the synchronism as a secondary factor (since it is omitted in the LXX) and have placed Zimri's rebellion in Asa's thirty-eighth year (*ca.* 876 B.C.). (*See* CHRONOLOGY OF THE OT V.A, B.)

Like the other kings of Israel, Zimri was judged by the biblical author as evil for perpetuating the bull-god cult of Jeroboam (16:19f.). While Zimri probably had little opportunity to "walk in the way of Jeroboam," given his one-week reign, he may have issued a formal statement of adherence to Jeroboam's religious policy.

3. Son of Zerah and grandson of Judah and Tamar (1 Ch. 2:6). In Josh. 7:1, 17f. he is called ZABDI (1).

4. Son of Jehoaddah (1 Ch. 8:36; called Jarah in 9:42); a descendant of King Saul through Jonathan and Meribaal (Mephibosheth).

Bibliography.–W. F. Albright, *BASOR,* 100 (Dec. 1945), 16-22; D. Diringer, *Le iscrizioni antico-ebraiche Palestinesi* (1934), pp. 25, 43 n.18, 211; G. B. Gray, *Studies in Hebrew Names* (1896), p. 154; J. Gray, *I & II Kings* (*OTL,* 2nd ed. 1970), pp. 361-65; H. B. Huffmon, *Amorite Personal Names in the Mari Texts* (1965), pp. 187f.; K. P. Jackson, *Ammonite Language of the Iron Age* (*Harvard Semitic Monographs,* 27; 1983), no. 43; J. M. Miller, *JBL,* 86 (1967), 76-88; J. A. Montgomery, *ICC* on 1 and 2 Kings (1951), pp. 283-290. A. E. HILL

ZIMRI zim'rī [Heb. *zimrî*]; NEB ZAMRI. A region or tribal district of uncertain location, listed with Elam and Media in Jer. 25:25. The phrase "all the kings of Zimri" is lacking in the LXX. The records of Sargon of Assyria (*ARAB,* II, §§ 20, 155) mention a Mt. Zimur somewhere on the border of Urartu and Mannai, perhaps SE of Lake Urmiah. *CAH,* III, Map 5 locates Zimri directly S of Lake Urmiah and between the Lower Zab and Adhan Rivers. Some commentators (e.g., J. A. Thompson, *Book of Jeremiah* [*NICOT,* 1980], p. 518) have even suggested reading "Zimki," an athbash for Elam (cf. Jer. 49:34-39). A. E. HILL

ZIN zin [Heb. *ṣin*]. An area of "wilderness" (Heb. *miḏbār*) through which the Israelites passed on their way from Egypt to Canaan. The wilderness of Zin was the locale of

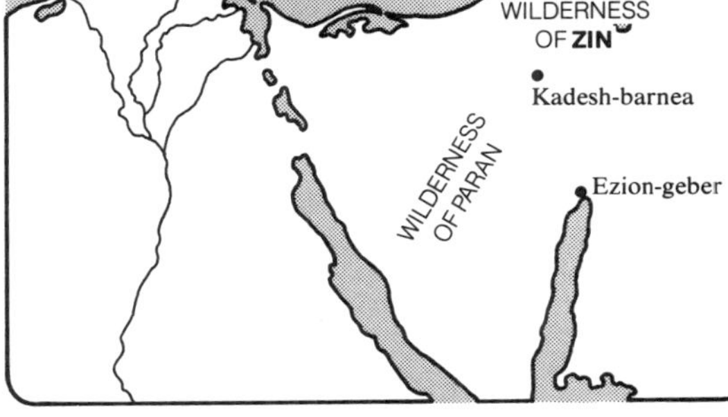

several biblical events. Moses sent the twelve spies to reconnoiter the land "from the wilderness of Zin to Rehob, near the entrance of Hamath" (Nu. 13:21). Kadesh-barnea was in the wilderness of Zin (e.g., 33:36; but cf. 13:26, which places this oasis in the wilderness of PARAN). Miriam's death (20:1) and the incident at Meribah for which Moses was denied entrance to the Promised Land (27:14; Dt. 32:51) are both placed at KADESH (1) in the wilderness of Zin.

These references indicate that the wilderness of Zin was located S of Canaan in an area including Kadesh-barnea. Its location is further defined in a description of the southern boundary of the tribe of Judah (Josh. 15:1-4; cf. Nu. 34:3f.). Unfortunately, the precise location of the ascent of Akrabbim is disputed. In the itinerary of Nu. 33 the Israelites journey into the wilderness of Zin from Ezion-geber, located at the tip of the Gulf of Aqabah. Thus the wilderness of Zin appears to have been located W of the Arabah, S of the Salt Sea, and NW of the Gulf of Aqabah.

T. V. BRISCO

ZINA zī'nə. *See* ZIZAH.

ZION zī'ən [Heb. *ṣîyôn*; Gk. *Siōn*]; AV also SION. An ancient name attached to different sites within JERUSALEM in various periods of the city's history.

- I. Origin
- II. Semantic Development in the OT
  - A. Geographical Designation
    - 1. Jebusite Fortress
    - 2. Temple Mount
    - 3. Jerusalem
  - B. Soteriological Application
- III. Semantic Development in Greco-Roman and Byzantine Times
  - A. Intertestamental Period
    - 1. Temple Mount
    - 2. "Citadel"
  - B. First Century A.D.
  - C. Later Developments
- IV. Modern Research

I. Origin.–The etymology of the ancient Hebrew term is uncertain, but among the several proposals two are particularly attractive. J. Wetzstein derived it from the Semitic root preserved in Arabic as *ṣâna*, "protect" — i.e., from a hypothetical *ṣîyân, "fortress," or the like (see F. Delitzsch, *Genesis* [4th ed. 1872], p. 578). G. A. Smith took as his starting point the Arabic name for Mt. Zion, Jebel Ṣahyûn. He did not mention Syr. *Ṣehyôn*, which probably gave rise to the Arabic form; but he cited Arab. *ṣahweh*, "tower on top of a mountain," and noted the well-fortified site on the edge of a hill in Lebanon called *Ṣehyûn*. The following derivation might thus be posited: Heb. *ṣîyôn ("fortified tower") < *ṣîyân < *ṣihyân.

II. Semantic Development in the OT.–*A. Geographical Designation.* Whatever its etymology, "Zion" was primarily a topographical designation.

1. Jebusite Fortress. It was David who conquered the "stronghold of Zion" (Heb. *mᵉṣûḏaṯ ṣîyôn*) and there established his own royal residence, calling it "the city of David" (2 S. 5:7, 9 par. 1 Ch. 11:5, 7). This stronghold was lower than the temple and palace complex built by Solomon, since it was necessary to "bring up the ark of the covenant of the Lord out of the city of David, which is Zion" (1 K. 8:1 par. 2 Ch. 5:2). Pharaoh's daughter also "went up from the city of David to her own house which Solomon had built for her" (1 K. 9:24; cf. 2 Ch. 8:11, which alludes to the ark's former presence in the city of David). Furthermore, the "city of David" must have been above the Gihon spring; i.e., it was apparently identical with the Ophel (Heb. *ʿōpel*), the ridge extending S from the temple mount (2 Ch. 33:14).

2. Temple Mount. With the establishment of the ark first in the Jebusite fortress and then in the newly built temple, Zion became known as the sacred dwelling place of Israel's Lord, the One "who dwells in Zion" (Ps. 9:11 [MT 12]). The divine oath to establish the Davidic dynasty is linked with His choice of Zion as His abode (Ps. 132, esp. vv. 13f.); and though these oracular pronouncements originally referred to Salem, the pre-Israelite city (cf. Gen. 14:18), as Yahweh's residence (Ps. 76:2 [MT 3]), the emphasis soon changed to "Zion, my holy hill" (Ps. 2:6). The Lord of Hosts dwells at Mt. Zion (Ps. 74:2; Isa. 8:18; 18:7) and reigns from there (Mic. 4:7b). Mt. Zion and Jerusalem are sometimes named together (Isa. 10:12; 24:23; Joel 2:32 [MT 3:5]; Zec. 1:14), but whether the terms are synonymous or refer to separate entities is hard to decide. Zion is called "the city of our appointed feasts" (Isa. 33:20); the capital, Jerusalem, is evidently meant here, since it was the focal point for the three great annual pilgrimages. Nevertheless, in the postexilic era the City of David was limited to that lower part of the ridge on the south (Neh. 3:15f.).

3. Jerusalem. Eventually the term "Zion" was extended to include the entire city, but this synecdoche usually occurs in poetic passages. "Zion" can stand in juxtaposition to the "cities of Judah" (Ps. 69:35 [MT 36]), or it can occur in parallelism with "Jerusalem" (Isa. 4:3f.; 52:1f.), most notably in Ps. 48, where "the city of our God, his holy mountain" is "Mount Zion, . . . the city of the great King" (vv. 1f. [MT 2f.]). Mt. Zion is even exalted to the status of the mysterious *yarkᵉṯê ṣāpôn*, literally, "the remotenesses of the North" (v. 2 [MT 3]) — a figurative allusion to the old West Semitic abode of Baal in the recesses of Mt. Zaphon, attested in Ugaritic literature of the 14th cent. B.C. (*ṣrrt ṣpn* or *mrym ṣpn*).

More frequently, however, the city itself is called the "daughter of Zion" as distinct from the actual "mount." For example, the approaching foe will "shake his fist at the mount of the *daughter* [MT *K* and versions] of Zion, the hill [LXX "hills"!] of Jerusalem" (Isa. 10:32; see also 16:1).

Besides "daughter of Zion" (Isa. 1:8; 52:2; 62:11; Jer. 4:31; 6:2, 23; Mic. 1:13; 4:10, 13; etc.), the city is known as "the virgin daughter of Zion" (2 K. 19:21; Isa. 37:22; Lam. 2:13) and "inhabitant of Zion" (*yôšeḇeṯ ṣîyôn*, Isa. 12:6; Jer. 51:35). The Lord calls the citizenry of Jerusalem "sons of Zion" (Lam. 4:2; Joel 2:23; Zec. 9:13) and "daughters of Zion" (Isa. 3:16f.; 4:4). The senior members of the society are called "the elders of the daughter of Zion" (Lam. 2:10).

That the "daughter of Zion" means the city of Jerusalem is clear from allusions to her wall (Lam. 2:8) and gates (Ps. 9:14 [MT 15]). Zion itself is sometimes characterized as a fortified city with gates (Ps. 87:2), towers, ramparts, and citadels (Ps. 48:12f. [MT 13f.]). These latter expressions are somewhat uncertain, however, since the palace-temple complex that Solomon built within the city itself was also a fortified citadel with the same architectural elements.

B. Soteriological Application. The sociological application of the term "Zion" to the population of Jerusalem is naturally extended to denote the people of God. The basis for this development is Zion's position as the focal point of God's soteriological activity, His deliverance of His holy abode from many adversaries (Isa. 33:5; 34:8; 52:8).

Development of this usage received special impetus from the Exile, particularly since it was the captive population of Jerusalem (and Judah) that produced the prophetic and literary spokesmen who used the term (cf. Ps. 126:1; 129:5).

III. Semantic Development in Greco-Roman and Byzantine Times.–*A. Intertestamental Period. 1. Temple Mount.* In this period "Zion" clearly designates the height occupied by the temple, which was cleansed by Judas Maccabeus (1 Macc. 4:36-61, esp. vv. 37, 60; cf. also 5:54; 6:48, 62; 7:33; 10:11; 14:27; apparently also Jth. 9:13; Sir. 24:10). Undoubtedly only the eastern hill is meant, since the Seleucid enemy was holding a strong point on the western side of the Tyropoeon Valley, opposite the temple.

2. "Citadel." In 167 B.C. the Seleucid army built a heavily fortified enclosure around what was now called the City of David; this fortress they called Acra ("citadel"; Gk. *ákra,* 1 Macc. 1:33-36). The liberation of the temple mount by Judas leaves no doubt that the Acra was on the western hill; Judas had to employ some of his troops against the Seleucids in the citadel during the cleansing of the temple area (1 Macc. 4:41). Thus the city of David cannot have been in its former position on Ophel, for otherwise the Jewish forces could hardly have gained access to the temple.

The construction of a fortress on the western ridge may have coincided with the attempt to establish there a Hellenistic polis or city-state (2 Macc. 4:7-17). V. Tcherikover noted that the Jewish hellenizers' request for Antiochian citizenship and the founding of Hellenic institutions such as the gymnasium point to the organization of such a municipal entity with all the civil and religious status that entailed; he was probably correct in assuming that the new polis was to be called "Antiochia in Jerusalem." Only in 141 B.C. was the troublesome citadel conquered by Simon Maccabeus (1 Macc. 13:49-53). The surrender of the fortress gave the anti-Hellenist Jews access to the former polis on the western ridge, which by then was firmly established in local parlance as the City of David (1 Macc. 14:36). The dismantling of the Seleucid stronghold was evidently carried out by one of the later Hasmonean rulers (Josephus *BJ* v.4.1 [137-39]) and not by Simon himself (cf. *BJ* i.2.2 [50]; *Ant.* xiii.6.7 [215-17]). On the site of the Acra the Hasmoneans built their own palace which was later taken over by the Herodian dynasty (*Ant.* xx.8.11 [189f.]). This must have been where Herod Antipas resided during the Passover season when Jesus was led before him (Lk. 23:6-12).

B. First Century A.D. Josephus placed the City of David, also known in his day as the Upper City, unequivocally on the western ridge. He asserted that here was the "fortress" (Gk. *phroúrion,* his rendering for Heb. *m*^{e}*ṣûḏâ*) that David had occupied, but that his own contemporaries called the place "the upper market." This "Davidic" fortress-market area he clearly distinguished from the promontory projecting E from the western ridge toward the temple mount, i.e., the Acra of the former Seleucid citadel (*BJ* v.4.1 [137-39]).

The monumental "tomb of David" is usually (though not unanimously) presumed to have been on the western ridge, just as one of Herod's mighty towers, named after his brother Phasael (*BJ* v.4.3 [166-69]), is still popularly known as "David's Tower." Josephus recorded that the impressive Tomb of David was deprived of its treasures by Hyrcanus (*BJ* i.2.5 [61]; *Ant.* vii.15.3 [392f.]; xiii.8.4 [249]) and later by Herod (*Ant.* xvi.7.1 [179, 181, 188]). None of these passages (nor Acts 2:29) states that the tomb was actually on the western hill. On the contrary, a rabbinic testimony contends that the tombs of the prophetess Huldah and King David both had underground channels (Heb. *m*^{e}*ḥillôṯ*) that carried their uncleanness down to the Kidron (Rabbi Akiba in Tosefta *Baba Bathra* i.11f.). Since Huldah's tomb was presumably near the two gates on the temple enclosure's south side (which are named after her, Mish. *Middoth* i.3), the Davidic funerary monument thus should also be on the eastern ridge, S of the temple mount. Rabbi Akiba's statement that both tombs were connected with the Kidron via subterranean channels strengthens the impression that the eastern location of David's tomb was still recognized at the end of the 1st cent. A.D.; i.e., the biblical tradition (Neh. 3:16) was still alive. The structure fell into ruin during the Bar Cochba revolt (A.D. 135), as reported by Dio Cassius (*Hist.* lxix.14), and Christians long tended to place David's burial site in Bethlehem.

Remarkably, Josephus did not use the term "Zion." He may have been influenced by the sharp distinction between the temple mount (i.e., the eastern ridge) as Zion and the western ridge as the City of David — a distinction already in vogue during the Hasmonean period (see III.A above).

The NT writers usually referred to Zion only in quotations from the OT, e.g., Mt. 21:5 and Jn. 12:15 (= Zec. 9:9); Rom. 9:33 and 1 Pet. 2:6 (= Isa. 28:16; cf. 8:14f.); Rom. 11:26 (= Isa. 59:20; note Heb. *l*^{e}*ṣîyôn* rendered by Gk. *ek Siōn,* "from Zion," perhaps reflecting an ancient prepositional usage). None of these passages implies a connection with any particular ridge or hill within Jerusalem. On the other hand, twice in the NT "Zion" has a spiritual meaning. In He. 12:22 it represents the Christian fold as the abode of the living God, i.e., the "heavenly Jerusalem," and Rev. 14:1 makes Mt. Zion the focal point of the messianic reign. This latter concept is also expressed in contemporary Jewish apocalyptic (e.g., Jub. 1:28), which considered Zion the navel of the earth (8:19).

C. Later Developments. Origen continued to identify Zion with the temple mount (*In Ioannem* iv.19f.), and Jerome may have done the same in one passage (*In Esai* xxii.1f.). Eusebius stated merely that *Siōn* was "a mountain in Jerusalem" (*Onom.* 162.12), but Jerome translated "*the* mountain *of* Jerusalem" (*Onom.* 163.14); the Greek original may imply that Zion was considered separate from the temple hill, but the evidence is tenuous. The Bordeaux Pilgrim (A.D. 333) clearly called the western ridge *Sion,* referring to both the southern portion outside the city wall of his day and also the northern part inside the city. Epiphanius (d. A.D. 392), reputedly basing his statement on Hegesippus (2nd cent. A.D.; though perhaps a work by Aristo of Pella stands behind the tradition), claimed that when Hadrian came to Jerusalem (A.D. 130) he found the entire city, including the temple mount, in ruins, except for Zion. This testimony makes good sense, in view of Josephus's statement that Titus had left only Herod's three towers (beside the present-day Jaffa Gate) and part of the western wall (*BJ* vi.9.1 [413]; vii.1.1 [1-4]); the 10th Legion camped on the western ridge. Therefore both Epiphanius and the Bordeaux Pilgrim have transferred the name Zion to the western ridge. Epiphanius referred to the "little church of God" commemorating the site where the disciples had assembled after the Ascension; subsequent church writers were unanimous in this testimony.

Apparently several factors led to the transfer of the name "Zion" to the western hill. First, in Hasmonean times the "City of David" was located on the western hill in contradistinction to the temple mount, which remained Mt. Zion. Then the Romans destroyed the entire city on the eastern ridge, including the temple. The western ridge survived the disaster of A.D. 70 and after 135, when Hadrian expelled the Jews from the city and defiled the temple mount with his pagan shrine, the Christians were left with the southern promontory of the western ridge as the focal point for their own worship; meanwhile they kept alive the tradition that the site of the crucifixion was N of the northern extremity of the same ridge. Their own apologetic needs led them to interpret various passages (e.g., Isa. 2:3 and 59:20 as reflected in Rom. 11:26) as proof that their community was the new Zion, the center of revelation and redemption for the world.

Since the 10th cent. A.D. the tomb of David has also been located on the southwest spur of the western ridge. Moslem writers of the 10th and 11th cents. alluded to Christian (and Jewish) traditions in this regard. In the 12th cent. Benjamin of Tudela recorded the story of the tomb's "discovery" during excavations for repairs on the church on that site. The present structure houses the Cenaculum or "upper room," evidently the building shown on the Madeba Map as attached to the basilica of Mt. Zion. Archeological investigation has shown that the original structure was a late Roman synagogue that was subsequently converted into a mosque.

IV. Modern Research.–After his second visit to Jerusalem, the nineteenth-century scholar E. Robinson asserted that the identification of Zion with the western ridge was unassailable (*Later Biblical Researches,* p. 206). Others were already beginning to question this point, however, and during the ensuing decades many scholars contributed to a lively debate on the subject. F. F. Birch (*PEQ,* 1878ff.) published a series of articles in which he argued strongly for the location of the City of David and Zion on the Ophel, i.e., the eastern ridge. Many others followed suit, including C. Wilson and C. Warren, two leading investigators of Jerusalem's topography. Significant among Catholic scholars was the definitive essay by M. J. Lagrange (*RB,* 1 [1892], 17-38), whose expert knowledge of the city and its historical sources was unimpeachable. He demonstrated the prior claims of the eastern ridge and explained the transfer of the name in early Christian times as a natural outgrowth of the contemporary physical situation in the new Aelia Capitolina and of the Church's spiritual aspirations. Thus both the demands of historical topography and the respect for ecclesiastical tradition were satisfied.

From 1948 to 1967 the southern spur of the western ridge was the only part of Old Jerusalem occupied by the Israelis. Because the Israelis were denied access to their holy places in the Jewish quarter, the Tomb of David became the focal point for pilgrimage and prayer. Modern Jews, Christians, and Moslems still use the name "Mt. Zion" for this southwest spur, and the gate opening onto it is known as the "Zion Gate." The associations of Zion with the northern continuation of the western ridge, so fundamental to E. Robinson and others in the 19th cent., are practically forgotten. Scholarly circles generally acknowledge the claims regarding the eastern ridge as reflected in the biblical sources. Though archeological excavations shed new light on problems of Jerusalem's topography from year to year, the most significant point for the location of Zion on the Ophel is the conclusive evidence that the pre-Israelite city, i.e., the Jebusite citadel conquered by David, was on the eastern ridge.

The southwestern hill of "Zion" showing the mosque built over the crusader church on the traditional site of David's tomb and the Last Supper (W. S. LaSor)

Bibliography.–E. Robinson, *Biblical Researches* (1856), I, 229-231, 241-43, 263-65; *Later Biblical Researches* (1856) pp. 177-189, 199f., 206-211; M. J. Lagrange, *RB,* 1 (1892), 17-38; G. A. Smith, *Jerusalem from the Earliest Times to A.D. 70* (1908), I, 134-169; S. Yeivin, *JNES,* 7 (1948), 30-45; H. Z. Hirschberg, *Eretz-Israel,* 3 (1954), 213-220; M. Avi-Yonah, *Madeba Mosaic Map* (1954), pp. 55f.; V. Tcherikover, *Hellenistic Civilization and the Jews* (Eng. tr. 1959), pp. 161ff., 404-409; D. R. Ap-Thomas, "Jerusalem," in *AOTS,* pp. 276-295; K. M. Kenyon, *Jerusalem: Excavating 3000 Years of History* (1967); B. Mazar, *et al.,* "Jerusalem," in *EAEHL* (1970) I, 211-241; M. Avi-Yonah, *IEJ,* 21 (1971), 168f.; *EAEHL,* II, *s.v.* "Jerusalem" (O. Bar-Yoseph, *et al.*).

A. F. RAINEY

ZIOR [Heb. *ṣî'ōr*–'little, insignificant'; Gk. LXX A *Siōr,* B *Sōrth*]. A town in the hill country of Jodah, part of a district of nine cities that apparently extended to the SW of Hebron (Josh. 15:52-54). The site cannot be identified with confidence. The common association of biblical Zior with modern Si'īr is beset with numerous difficulties: the location of the modern village, 8 km. (5 mi.) NE of Hebron, appears to be more consonant with the district described in Josh. 15:58f. (Halhul, modern Ḥalḥûl, is located between Hebron and Si'īr); the confirmed spelling of the Arab. *Si'īr* (not *Ṣâ'īr,* as in BDB, p. 859; cf. *GTTOT,* §319 B/9) is phonetically dissimilar to the Heb. *ṣî'ōr*; finally, the modern village lies in a valley, an uncharacteristic site for biblical cities, and shows no clear evidence of pre-Byzantine settlement.

See also ZAIR.

Bibliography.–W. F. Albright, *BASOR,* 18 (Apr. 1925), 6-9; F. M. Cross and G. E. Wright, *JBL,* 75 (1956), 202-226.

J. T. BUTLER

ZIPH zif [Heb. *zîp*].

1. Son of MARESHAH (1) (or Mesha; cf. RSV mg., AV, NEB) and grandson of Caleb (1 Ch. 2:42). Although listed in the context of Caleb's genealogy, Ziph probably refers here to a town in Judah "founded" (cf. NEB) by Mareshah or Mesha. *See* ZIPH (place) 1.

2. Son of Jehallelel and head of a clan in Judah (1 Ch. 4:16); possibly a reference to a town in Judah (*see* ZIPH [place] 1).

ZIPH (place) [Heb. *zîp̱*; Gk. LXX A *Ziph,* B *Ozeib*].

1. A town in the easternmost district of the hill country of Judah, adjacent to the wilderness region leading down to the Dead Sea. The "wilderness of Ziph" figures prominently in the accounts of David's flight from Saul: here David receives a renewed pledge of loyalty from Saul's son Jonathan (1 S. 23:14-18); he is betrayed by the Ziphites, who send to Saul at Gibeah to disclose David's whereabouts (1 S. 23:19-24; 26:1; cf. the title of Ps. 54 [MT 1f.]); when Saul comes in pursuit of him, David wins his blessing

by sparing his life (1 S. 26:2-25). The town is also mentioned as one of fifteen fortified by Rehoboam in order to secure Judah and Benjamin after the defection of the northern tribes (2 Ch. 11:8). Ziph is one of four place names occurring in an extensive series of stamped jar-handles, recovered from a number of southern sites, which bear the expression *lmlk* ("pertaining to the king"); although the precise significance of these stamps is disputed, they suggest that Ziph was of importance during the 7th and early 6th cents. as a center of administrative or economic activity under royal sponsorship.

Ziph is almost certainly to be located in the vicinity of modern Tell Zîf, an imposing mound 7 km. (4 mi.) SE of Hebron. The site has strategic significance for protecting the southeast approach to Hebron and central Judah, and the fertile plain to the west was undoubtedly of agricultural importance in antiquity. No excavations have been conducted, but pottery shards typical of Iron II (monarchical period) have been found.

Bibliography.–H. J. Stoebe, *ZDPV,* 80 (1964), 9f.; P. Welten, *Die Königs-Stempel* (1969).

2. A town in the Negeb of Judah (Josh. 15:24). Although it is sometimes identified with ez-Zeifeh (SW of Kurnub/Mampsis), the site cannot be located with certainty (cf. *GTTOT,* §317, 10). J. T. BUTLER

ZIPHAH zīf'ə [Heb. *zîpâ*]. Son of Jehallelel and head of a clan in Judah (1 Ch. 4:16).

ZIPHIMS zif'imz (superscription of Ps. 54, AV). *See* ZIPHITES.

ZIPHION zif'ē-ən [Heb. *ṣipyôn*]. First son of Gad (Gen. 46:16). The Sam. Pent. and LXX support the reading "Zephon," which occurs at Nu. 26:15.

ZIPHITES zif'īts [Heb. *(haz)zîpîm, (haz)zipîm*]; AV also ZIPHIMS (superscription to Ps. 54; NEB omits). Inhabitants of ZIPH (1) in the hill country of Judah. When David was hiding from Saul in the wilderness of Ziph, the Ziphites informed the king about his hiding place and offered to assist in his capture (1 S. 23:19f.). Saul requested that they provide more exact information (vv. 21-24), and they fulfilled this request by returning later with a further report on David's hiding place (26:1). The superscription to Ps. 54 appears to be a later addition to a psalm that pleads for God's protection from enemies that seek the psalmist's life. N. J. O.

ZIPHRON zif'ron [Heb. *ziprôn*]. A place on the northern boundary of the Promised Land, between Zedad and Hazar-enan (Nu. 34:9). Its exact location is unknown.

ZIPPOR zip'ôr [Heb. *ṣippôr*–'bird']. The father of Balak king of Moab (Nu. 22:2, 4, 10, 16; 23:18; Josh. 24:9; Jgs. 11:25).

ZIPPORAH zi-pôr'ə, zip'ə-rə [Heb. *ṣippōrâ*–'sparrow' or 'swallow']. Daughter of Reuel/Jethro the priest of Midian; Moses' wife (Ex. 2:21). The Midianites were descendants of Abraham by Keturah (Gen. 25:1f.). They lived in Sinai and northern Arabia in the area around the Gulf of Aqabah. Moses met the daughters of Reuel while fleeing from the wrath of Pharaoh (Ex. 2:15f.).

Zipporah was the mother of Moses' sons Gershom (Ex. 2:22) and Eliezer (18:2-4). As Moses was returning to Egypt to liberate the Hebrews, he (or possibly his son) was attacked by the Lord (4:24). The reason for this attack is not clear, but Zipporah perceived that somehow the Abrahamic covenant had been violated (Gen. 17:14); so she circumcised her son (Ex. 4:25), and God's judgment stopped.

Zipporah is mentioned a third time in Ex. 18:2, which states that she and her sons had been sent back to her father's home but now, after the exodus from Egypt, were rejoining Moses. The narrative does not disclose the circumstances that led to Zipporah's return to Midian, but probably her safety was the concern.

Some scholars think that during Zipporah's absence Moses married another woman, the CUSHITE WOMAN who was the object of Aaron and Miriam's scorn (Nu. 12:1f.). The fact that "Cushite" usually refers to Nubians or Ethiopians supports this view. In Hab. 3:7, however, "Cushan" and "Midian" occur in parallelism, which suggests that the terms could be synonyms. Since the peoples of Nubia and Ethiopia were black-skinned, possibly the term was applied to other darker-skinned nomadic peoples like the Midianites. Therefore the "Cushite" woman of Nu. 2:1f. could well have been the Midianite Zipporah.

See also MOSES II.B, E. J. K. HOFFMEIER

ZITHRI zith'rī (Ex. 6:22, AV). *See* SITHRI.

ZIV ziv [Heb. *ziw*] (1 K. 6:1, 37); AV ZIF. The second month of the Canaanite calendar. *See* CALENDAR II.A.2.

ZIZ, ASCENT OF [Heb. *ma'alēh haṣṣîṣ*]. A pass used by a coalition of Moabites, Ammonites, and Meunites to ascend from the shore of the Dead Sea at En-gedi against the forces of Jehoshaphat at Jerusalem (2 Ch. 20:16). This route through the difficult terrain of the Judean wilderness has traditionally been identified with the course of the Wâdī Ḥaṣâṣah, by which there is access from En-gedi to the road connecting with Tekoa, Bethlehem, and Jerusalem. A survey of this ascent found evidence of an ancient road from Israelite times with some Roman improvements. The road rises 328 m. (1076 ft.) from En-gedi, and with its cutbacks it is 1680 m. (5512 ft.) long. The natural 45 percent gradient of the slope is improved by the road to an average of 19.5 percent.

See M. Harel, *IEJ,* 17 (1967), 18-26. J. T. BUTLER

ZIZA zī'zə [Heb. *zîzā'*, prob. a name of endearment, using reduplication of a shortened form of the name (see *IP,* pp. 40f.)].

1. A Simeonite chief whose family participated in their tribe's expansion toward Geder (1 Ch. 4:37; cf. vv. 38-41).

2. A son of King Rehoboam by Maacah (2 Ch. 11:20).

ZIZAH zī'zə [Heb. *zîzâ; see* ZIZA]. A Gershonite Levite, son of Shimei (1 Ch. 23:11). In v. 10 he is called Zina (Heb. *zînā'*), but this is probably a transcriptional error. The LXX and Vulgate have *Ziza* in both verses, and one Hebrew MS has *zîzā'* in v. 10. Thus "Ziza" should be read in both verses (cf. NEB).

ZOAN zō'an [Heb. *ṣō'an*; Gk. *Tanis*; Copt. *Djaane,* etc.; Egyp. *Ḏ'nt, Djane(t)*]. An Egyptian city in the northeastern Delta, identified with Ṣân el-Ḥagar, which J. Yoyotte labeled "the most famous site in the Delta" (*Encyclopedia of Egyptian Civilization* [1959], p. 279).

I. Other Names and Identifcations.–The site has had a plethora of names and identifications. It was once commonly regarded as the site of Avaris, the capital of the Hyksos, but most scholars now identify Avaris with Tell el-Dab'a (see Baines and Málek, pp. 175f.). Many also identify it with Pi-Ra'messe, the Delta residence of Ramses II, and with Rameses, the store-city built for the Egyptians by Israelite slave labor (Ex. 1:11), although Qanṭîr is now the generally accepted site of Pi-Raʿmesse (see Baines and Málek, pp. 175f.).

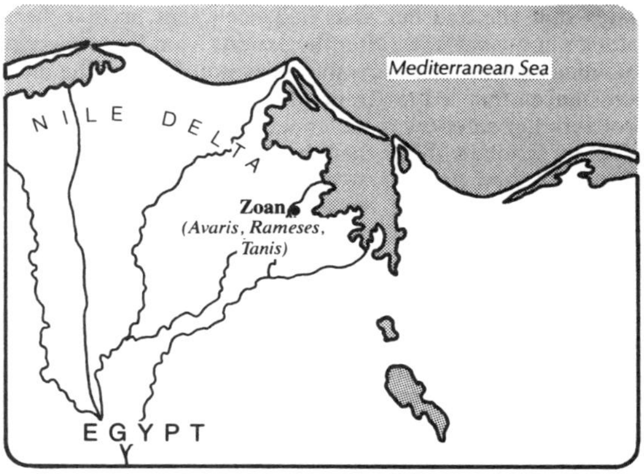

The name Zoan constitutes a minor biblical textual problem, for the Egyp. *Ḏʿnt* is not known before the 21st Dynasty (*ca.* 1085-945 B.C.); if this is truly the earliest date for the name, attributable to the 21st Dynasty builders at Ṣân, its presence in the biblical text may be explained by a copyists's updating of a place name.

II. Biblical References.–Zoan is mentioned in the Pentateuch only in Nu. 13:22, which says, "Hebron was built seven years before Zoan in Egypt." Unfortunately, the date of the founding of neither city is known, but the evidence indicates that both cities were very ancient.

In an oracle concerning Egypt (Isa. 19) Isaiah asserted, "the princes of Zoan are utterly foolish" (v. 11; cf. v. 13). Chapter 30 graphically portrays the futility of Israel's trusting in Egypt rather than in the Lord; although Pharaoh's officials are at Zoan, reliance upon Egypt will lead only to disgrace and humiliation (vv. 4f.).

Ezekiel also pronounced a prophecy against Egypt, and in 30:14 the Lord declares: "I will make Pathros a desolation, and will set fire to Zoan, and will execute acts of judgment upon Thebes."

The only other biblical reference to Zoan is the expression "the fields of Zoan" (Ps. 78:12, 43), referring to the place where God wrought the miracles and plagues that preceded the Exodus. Parallels to this expression are found in Egyptian sources.

III. Archeological History.–Modern archeological interest in Ṣân el-Ḥagar dates to the expedition of Napoleon (1798) and the work of the savants who produced the *Description de l'Égypte*. In the 19th cent. the antiquities hunters were at work, and monuments from this site began to appear in the museums of western Europe. J. F. Champollion recognized the importance of the place, and the early investigators felt that this city was the residence of the pharaoh who persecuted the Israelites. In 1860 A. Mariette undertook excavations with brilliant results, including the finding of colossi, sphinxes, and stelae (one of which was the celebrated 400-Year Stele), as well as a granite edifice of Ramses II. In 1884 W. M. F. Petrie worked at this site for the Egypt Exploration Fund. The results were published in two memoirs, which included descriptions of many of the objects unearthed by Mariette but incompletely published. The most extensive investigation of Ṣân el-Ḥagar was conducted by P. Montet, who began excavating in 1929 and continued for more than twenty seasons, with remarkable finds to reward his efforts.

IV. History of the City.–The site is an excellent example of how monuments were reused or usurped in antiquity. The oldest remains date to the time of Pepi I of the 6th Dynasty (*ca.* 2300 B.C.), but Petrie argued convincingly that they were brought to Zoan from another site at a later date. There was beautiful statuary of the Middle Kingdom, mostly 12th Dynasty (*ca.* 1991-1786 B.C.). Among the remains of colossi are parts of a statue of Amenemhet II, which Petrie regarded as in some respects the finest Egyptian statue known. The striking red granite sphinxes (now at Cairo and the Louvre) were later appropriated by Merneptah and Sheshonq I (Shishak). Many of the works of this period were usurped by later kings, particularly of the 19th Dynasty (esp. Ramses II). The crude craftsmanship of the later period contrasts markedly with the fine work of the Middle Kingdom.

In the 19th Dynasty Ramses II (*ca.* 1304-1227 B.C.) did much building at Ṣân. He constructed a large temple and appropriated many of the monuments of his predecessors, but no remains of a palace or royal residence have been found. The site of the Delta residence (Pi-Raʿmesse) of Ramses II is uncertain; the leading alternatives appear to be Ṣân el-Ḥagar (supported by Montet, Gardiner, Albright, *et al.*) and Qanṭîr (favored by M. Hamza, W. C. Hayes, P. Courroyer, L. Habachi, *et al.*), about 19 km. (12 mi.) to the south. J. Yoyotte stated that the claims are about even and wisely suggested that further excavation at both sites is necessary. It has been proposed that Pi-Raʿmesse took in both sites, with Qanṭîr having the palace and Ṣân being the religious center (see A. Alt, *Festschrift für Friedrich Zucker* [1954]. pp. 3-13; cf. Gardiner, *Ancient Egyptian Onomastica,* II, 175).

Yoyotte also observed that Ramses II built so many cities bearing his name that it is not certain which was the biblical Rameses (Ex. 1:11). On the other hand, propo-

The granite statue of Ramses II uncovered at Ṣân el-Ḥagar, the site of Zoan (J. Finegan)

nents of the early date of the Exodus do not regard Ramses II as the king for whom the store-city was built. The identification of the biblical site is of interest not only to biblical geography but also to the chronology of biblical events, especially of the Exodus (*see* EXODUS, DATE OF THE).

Tanis flourished until Roman times. In the 21st Dynasty (*ca.* 1085-945 B.C.) it was the seat of government, contemporaneous with the priest-kings of Thebes; it was also the capital of the 14th nome of Lower Egypt. In the southwestern corner of the great temple Montet found the undisturbed burials of a number of kings, including Psusennes I of the 21st Dynasty. This was an opulent burial, with sarcophagi of pink granite, black granite, silver, and silver overlaid with gold, and with many other items of metal, stone, and pottery. Also discovered were impressive burials of Psusennes II and Amenemopet of the 21st Dynasty, and Osorkon II and Sheshonq III of the 22nd Dynasty.

See also EGYPT VIII.G.

Bibliography.–J. Baines and J. Málek, *Atlas of Ancient Egypt* (1980), esp. pp. 176f.; J. von Beckerath, *Tanis und Theben* (1951); A. H. Gardiner, *Ancient Egyptian Onomastica* (1947), II, 171-75, 199-201; *JEA*, 5 (1918), 127, 179, 242; 10 (1929), 87-96; P. Montet, *Les Nouvelles fouilles de Tanis (1929-1932)* (1933); *Tanis, douze années de fouilles dans une capitale oubliée du delta égyptien* (1942); *Le Necropole royal de Tanis*, I-III (1947-1960); *Les Énigmes de Tanis* (1952); W. M. F. Petrie, *Tanis*, I (2nd ed. 1889); *Tanis*, II (1888). C. E. DEVRIES

ZOAR zō'är [Heb. *ṣō'ar, ṣô'ar*–'little'; Gk. *Sēgōr,* also *Zogor, Zogora*]. The only one of the five CITIES OF THE VALLEY that was not destroyed in the fiery upheaval described in Gen. 19:24-28; the city to which Lot escaped from Sodom (vv. 20-23, 30). It was apparently less significant than the other four cities. It is the only one whose king is not named in 14:2, which lists the five kings who fought unsuccessfully against a coalition of four Mesopotamian kings (vv. 1-12). Furthermore, 19:20 describes Zoar as "little"; indeed, its name is related to Heb. *ṣ'r,* a root meaning "be small, insignificant." The MT of 14:2, 8 also calls it Bela. (Some have proposed emending the MT so that Bela would be the name of Zoar's ruler. This emendation is unnecessary, however, because of the plain sense of the MT and Zoar's already-mentioned insignificance.)

As with its four sister cities, the exact site of biblical Zoar is unknown, although it is likely S or SE of the Dead Sea. The description of the lands that Moses saw from Mt. Nebo (Dt. 34:1-3) places Zoar in the same relationship to the "plain, the valley of Jericho," that Dan had to Gilead; i.e., just as Dan was far N of Gilead (and not visible from Mt. Nebo), so Zoar was far S of the "plain, the valley of Jericho" (and likewise not visible from Nebo). Isa. 15:5 and Jer. 48:34 associate Zoar with cities of Moab. The RSV and NEB also mention Moab and Zoar together in Jer. 48:4, following the LXX (*eis Zogora,* "as far as Zoar"; cf. AV "her little ones," following the MT).

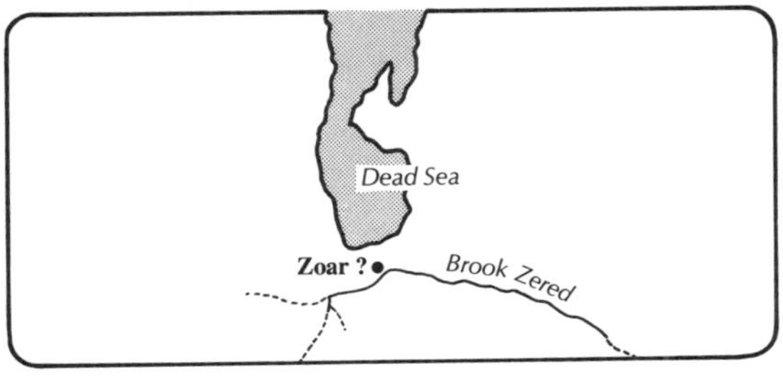

Zoar is mentioned frequently in postbiblical sources, and this evidence also suggests a southern location. Josephus (*BJ* iv.8.4 [482]) placed *Zoara* at the south end of the Dead Sea and stated that it was still called *Zoōr* in his own day (*Ant.* i.11.4 [204]). Other Jewish sources refer to the destruction of the cities and mention Zoar as having survived this (cf. Midr. *Gen. Rabbah* xlii.5). The Mishnah (*Yebamoth* xvi.7) calls it "the City of Palms." Ptolemy (*Geog.* v.17.5) stated that it was part of Arabia Petraea. Eusebius also placed it S of the Dead Sea and stated that it had a garrison of Roman soldiers and was known for its balsam and date palms (*Onom.* 231, 261). It apparently had some ecclesiastical significance around this time, for it had a bishop in the 4th cent. and was represented at the Council of Chalcedon (A.D. 451).

Since Byzantine times Zoar has been identified with eṣ-Ṣâfī, a site on the Wâdī el-Ḥesā (Brook Zered), about 8-9 km. (5-5 1/2 mi.) S of the Dead Sea. The sixth-century Madeba Map pictures it as a fortress city surrounded by palm trees, lying SE of the Dead Sea. Medieval Arab geographers often referred to it (by the name *Zughar*) as an important commercial center S of the Dead Sea, two days from Jericho on the well-traveled trade route between Jericho and the Gulf of Aqabah; it was known for its dates, indigo, and sugar. At eṣ-Ṣâfī the remains of a flourishing medieval town still exist, including ruins of old sugar mills and slag from old smelting operations. The Crusaders also mentioned encountering a pleasant town of *Segor* (cf. LXX *Sēgōr*), which had many palm trees.

This medieval town is apparently not the exact site of biblical Zoar, since soundings there have revealed only Byzantine and Arabic ruins. Eṣ-Ṣâfī is a large site, however, and it has not yet been fully excavated. Thus biblical Zoar was very likely at another area of the site, since there are indications that parts of the site were occupied in biblical times (in both the Early Bronze Age and the Iron Age). It is also possible that biblical Zoar was not on the Wâdī el-Ḥesā at all but rather on one of the other perennial streams nearby that flow into the southeastern end of the Dead Sea.

See also SIDDIM, VALLEY OF.

Bibliography.–F.-M. Abel, *RB*, 40 (1931), 380-400; 41 (1932), 255-57; W. F. Albright, *BASOR*, 14 (Apr. 1924), 4f.; M. Avi-Yonah, *Madeba Mosaic Map* (1954); *HDB*, IV, *s.v.* (S. R. Driver); D. M. Howard, Jr., *JETS*, 27 (1984), 385-400; E. Power, *Bibl.*, 11 (1930), 49-62, 149-182; W. E. Rast and R. T. Schaub, *ADAJ*, 19 (1974), 9-11, 15-17. D. M. HOWARD, JR.

ZOBAH zō'bə [Heb. *ṣōḇâ, ṣôḇā', ṣōḇâ*; Gk. *Souba*; Akk. *Ṣubiti* < *ṣubītu*–'dyeing (cloth),' 'soaking (fields)']; AV also ZOBA; **ARAM-ZOBAH** âr'əm zō'bə [Heb. *'ᵃram ṣôḇâ*] (superscription to Ps. 60 [MT 60:2]); NEB omits. A dominant Aramean city-state in the central Lebanese Beqa' valley, established in the 11th cent. B.C. At its apex its boundaries extended from the upper Euphrates to the Yarmuk, and it encompassed much of central Lebanon. Moreover, it was rich in vineyards, grain fields, and valuable minerals, particularly copper (cf. 2 S. 8:8).

It was inevitable that Zobah, situated along Israel's northern perimeter and ruled by aggressive kings, should come into conflict with Israel's nascent monarchy. Saul first encountered Zobah and won an Israelite victory (1 S. 14:47). David warred against Hadadezer king of Zobah (2 S. 8:3-12 par. 1 Ch. 18:3-11), and his stunning victory brought important natural resources under Israel's control; the superscription to Ps. 60 refers to this event. Later David's commander Job defeated a massive Ammonite coalition that included 20,000 mercenaries from Zobah (2 S. 10:6-8; cf. 1 Ch. 19:6-9). David's defeat of

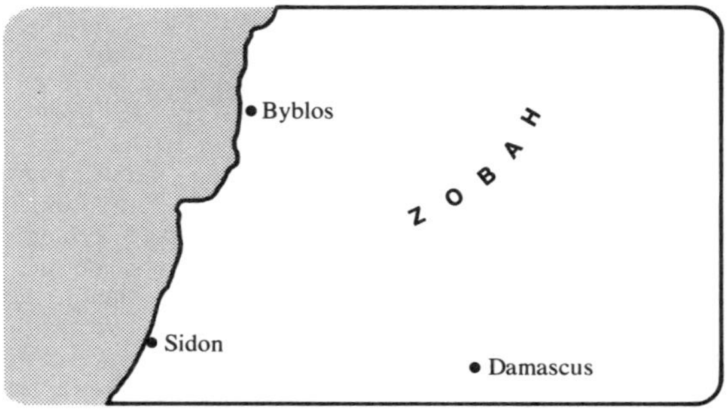

Hadadezer marked the end of Aram-Zobah's hegemony in Syria; but in Solomon's time Rezon, a fugitive from the king of Zobah, founded the kingdom of Aram-Damascus and became a powerful adversary to the Jerusalem monarch (1 K. 11:23-25).

According to 2 S. 23:36 one of David's thirty mighty men was "Igal the son of Nathan of Zobah." The LXX, however, has *dynámeōs* instead of *Souba*; thus some have suggested that the MT *ṣōḇâ* should be emended to read *ṣāḇā'*, "army" (see P. K. McCarter, Jr., *II Samuel* [*AB*, 1984], p. 493).

B. J. BEITZEL

ZOBEBAH zō-bē'bə [Heb. *haṣṣōḇēḇâ*]. A family of the tribe of Judah (1 Ch. 4:8). The name has the definite article prefixed.

ZOHAR zō'här [Heb. *ṣōḥar* < *ṣāhōr*–'tawny, yellowish-red' (?)].

1. Father of Ephron the Hittite (Gen. 23:8; 25:9).

2. A son of Simeon (Gen. 46:10; Ex. 6:15). In Nu. 26:13; 1 Ch. 4:24 he is called ZERAH (**4**).

ZOHELETH zō'hə-leth, **STONE OF** (1 K. 1:9, AV). *See* SERPENT'S STONE.

ZOHETH zō'heth [Heb. *zôḥēṯ*–'proud' (*IP*, p. 229)]. A Judahite, son of Ishi (1 Ch. 4:20).

ZOOLOGY. The Bible makes frequent reference to various species of animals that do or did live in the region of Palestine. Zoology or the study of animals deals with living organisms ranging from simple forms such as sponges, corals, and worms to more complex invertebrates, such as insects and spiders, to what are commonly called animals, the birds and mammals. The fauna of the Bible lands has been treated in several books and numerous articles, but most references are incomplete or have numerous inaccuracies.

I. Animals in Relation to Human Beings
II. Problems of Identification
  A. General
  B. Faunal Changes
III. Fauna of the Bible
  A. Phylum *Porifera*
  B. Phylum *Cnidaria,* Class *Anthozoa*
  C. Worms
  D. Phylum *Mollusca*
  E. Phylum *Arthropoda*
    1. Class *Arachnida*
    2. Class *Insecta*
  F. Phylum *Chordata:* Vertebrates
    1. Class *Osteichthyes:* Fish
    2. Class *Amphibia:* Frogs and Toads
    3. Class *Reptilia:* Lizards, Snakes, and Crocodiles
    4. Class *Aves:* Birds
    5. Class *Mammalia:* Mammals
IV. Fiery Serpent

I. Animals in Relation to Human Beings.–Animals hold a special place in the biblical writings because of their creation by God and because of their role in relation to people. God views animals as representatives of His marvelous creative activities (Job 40:15–41:34 [MT 41:26]). He created them to have a special relationship with human beings, and so brought them to Adam to be named (Gen. 2:19).

Animals were not originally intended as food; in the garden God mentioned only plants as food (Gen. 2:9, 16) and did not give animals as food until after the flood (9:3). The Bible enjoins proper care for the needs of domestic animals (Prov. 12:10), helping an enemy's animal with its load if it cannot bear it (Ex. 23:5), allowing animals to rest on the sabbath (Dt. 5:14), and not taking both a mother bird and her eggs for food (22:6f.).

The most important distinctions among animals according to the OT are between "clean" and "unclean" animals (*see* CLEAN AND UNCLEAN) and between domesticated and wild animals. Animals considered clean, i.e., suitable for human consumption, include mammals that have a split hoof and chew the cud and animals in general that do not feed on fecal matter or other animals. Most insects are considered unclean, though grasshoppers and their relatives are acceptable because their posterior legs are bent for jumping. Domesticated animals considered clean, among which were cattle and sheep, were raised for food and other products such as wool. Wild animals considered clean include many fish and birds, some insects, and wild mammals, especially deer, ibex, and gazelles.

Unclean domesticated animals include beasts of burden (e.g., the ass, camel, and horse) and pets (e.g., dogs). Other unclean animals, such as swine, were domesticated or hunted for food by peoples living around the Israelites. Some unclean wild animals were common and well known to those living in Palestine, and are frequently mentioned in the OT. Some of these are mentioned most in connection with the harm they can cause, such as damage to crops by locusts, birds, and rodents, damage to fabrics by moths and rodents, and more direct harm to human beings and their domestic animals by lions, leopards, bears, wolves, snakes, crocodiles, scorpions, hornets, and leeches. In most cases the relationship between human diseases and animals that carried diseases was not known, but the relationship of rats to bubonic plague apparently was (see III.F.5.d below).

II. Problems of Identification.–*A. General.* Almost one hundred eighty Hebrew and over fifty Greek words are used in the Bible for various animals. Many of the identifications of these names with precise animal species are best considered "uncertain." Each translation, commentary, or faunal study has sought to apply names to the animals in the biblical accounts with varying degrees of accuracy. In many cases the biblical name is simply not understood, so that any designation is guesswork. Other names are used in a very general sense and applied to any of a number of related species of animals.

Furthermore, most biblical authorities have had no training in zoology. Names used are often those that a given author is familiar with and refer, therefore, to animals common in Europe rather than in Palestine. The complex fauna of Palestine includes representatives of European, Asian, and African faunas. Mistaken names or misunderstandings of zoological literature have resulted in some misinterpretations.

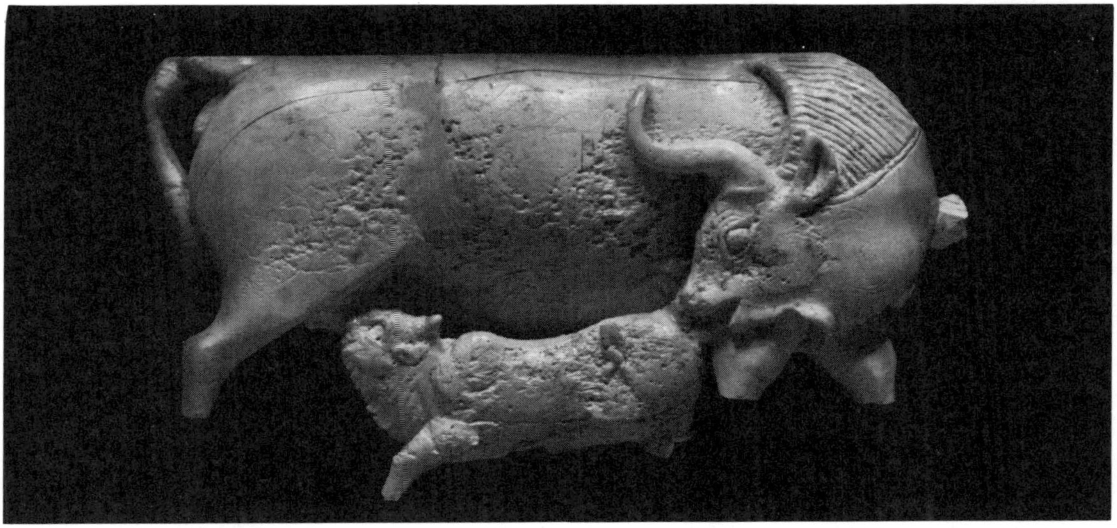

A cow and suckling calf. A Phoenician ivory furniture carving from Arslan Tash, Syria, 9th cent. B.C. (The Metropolitan Museum of Art, Fletcher Fund, 1957)

B. Faunal Changes. The great diversity of animal species and the faunal changes that have taken place also make certain identification difficult. Species that formerly occurred have become extinct in the area, and other species have become established since biblical times.

Faunal changes occurred already during the time of the Bible (*see* FLORA II). A fauna typical of African savannahs and grassland, including lions, leopards, hyenas, and gazelles, is presented in the early OT. Later, particularly in the NT, the large mammal fauna is more characteristic of deserts and arid grasslands. This process has continued since NT times and has been accelerated in the 20th cent., though attempts in the latter half of this century to protect wild animals in Israel may help reverse this decline.

The reasons for this faunal change are now understood to include possible minor changes in weather patterns and human encroachment on and destruction of animal habitats. Shifting weather patterns have probably contributed to the desertification of northern Africa and the Middle East. While these shifts have not been as strong as those of the Pleistocene Epoch (the glacial age, *ca.* 1,000,000–9000 B.C.), the climate has continued to undergo constant slow change.

The development of sedentary agriculture brought human beings into contact with animals in new ways. Animals that fed on crops or livestock were decimated and pushed into restricted habitats. The development of cities also restricted animal habitats. Desertification has also been partly a result of agriculture and settlement. By deforestation (cf. Josh. 17:14-18), overgrazing, and other misuses of the land, some of which could have been kept in check by observation of the Sabbatical Year and the Jubilee, the soil was exposed to wind and rain erosion, thus destroying the habitats of many animals. Modern Christian scientists and theologians are urging a return to "earthkeeping," i.e., a biblically based stewardship of the environment.

Another cause of faunal change is the increase in species and numbers of domesticated animals and wild animals that flourished in an environment shaped by human settlement. In addition to those raised for food, other domesticated animals have become established during and since biblical times. Cats were almost unknown in Palestine, though revered in Egypt, but in the past several centuries they have become widespread in the Middle East. Dogs and camels were familiar but not common, and both increased following NT times. The brown rat, usually found in human settlements, has become widespread, and has diminished the population of black rats, which were more common during OT times.

III. Fauna of the Bible.–An outline of the fauna of the Bible follows, but reference should be made to articles on specific animals and general categories of animals for additional information.

Goat herdsmen depicted in a wall painting (facsimile) from the tomb of Ipuy, 19th Dynasty. At lower left a man untangles a goat from some branches (The Metropolitan Museum of Art)

A relief on the stairs at Persepolis depicting a lion attacking a bull (W. S. LaSor)

A. Phylum Porifera. A sponge (Gk. *spóngos*) was used to offer vinegar to Jesus on the cross (Mt. 27:48 par.). This is the dried protein remains of a simple marine animal that has been used throughout history to soak up and hold fluids until the development of modern rubber reduced its popularity.

B. Phylum Cnidaria, *Class* Anthozoa. CORAL is the limestone produced by small, simple animals that thereby form reefs in warm sea and ocean waters. Several types of black and red coral were used as semiprecious stone for jewelry (Ezk. 27:16).

C. Worms. Terms translated "worm" may refer to any of a number of animals including worms from several phyla or the larvae of insects (*see* WORM). Larvae (maggots) of houseflies or of one of the bluebottle flies are commonly found living on dead animal matter; texts that mention worms of the phylum *Nematoda* that frequently live in the larvae (Job 7:5; Isa. 14:11), though these references may also indicate internal parasitic worms, especially roundworms of the phylum Nematoda that frequently live in the intestines of human beings (see also IV below). Many parasitic worms are common in the area of Palestine including the following nematodes: *Ascaris lumbricoides* (the intestinal roundworm), several species of hookworm, *Enterobius vermicularis* (the pinworm), *Dracunculus medinensis* (the guinea worm), and *Trichuris trichiura* (the whipworm). Each of these is a widespread cause of disease. Parasitic worms of the phylum *Platyhelminthes*, including tapeworms and flukes, may have been common causes of disease.

The worms that afflicted and ate Herod Agrippa (Acts 12:23) could have been some form of ascarid nematodes. Since his death was sudden it appears more likely to have been a case of intestinal blockage, such as that caused by ascarids, rather than myiasis caused by fly larvae, which normally feed only on dead tissue and are usually found only on the exterior of the body.

One of the many types of earthworms (phylum *Annelida*, class *Oligochaeta*) is probably in view where humankind is likened to a worm (e.g., Job 25:6). Earthworms are widespread and common in moist soils and in piles of organic matter. They burrow into soil and were probably quite common when the topsoil of Palestine was still thick, but have been greatly reduced by the loss of topsoil that has occurred since OT times. The LEECH (phylum *Annelida*, class *Hirudinea;* Prov. 30:15) attaches itself to animals when they walk in or drink from water in order to suck their blood for its own sustenance. It does not reproduce internally as some sources indicate.

D. Phylum Mollusca. Snails (class *Gastropoda*) of genera *Murex* and *Purpura* from the Phoenician coast of the Mediterranean were the sources of the economically important purple and blue or violet dyes (e.g., Ex. 25:4; 39:29, 31). Pearls are formed from secretions of various oysters or clams that are mollusks of class *Bivalvia*. The secretions are normal protective mechanisms to surround a foreign object in the shell to render it harmless. *See also* DYE; PEARL.

E. Phylum Arthropoda. *1. Class* Arachnida. This class includes both scorpions and spiders. Scorpions are common inhabitants of desert and tropical areas and are represented by over a dozen species in Palestine and surrounding areas. Most references allude to the pain and danger associated with being stung by the tail of the scorpion. While the sting of scorpions is painful, it is not deadly except in persons weakened by other diseases. Spiders are very common worldwide. Their habit of spinning silk webs is mentioned in Job 8:14; 27:18; Isa. 59:5f. *See* SCORPION; SPIDER'S WEB.

2. Class Insecta. Insects occur everywhere on earth and are referred to often in the Bible. Flies (order *Diptera*) are mentioned as the fourth plague of Egypt (Ex. 8:21-24 [MT 17-20]) and as a nuisance in general. The third plague (vv. 16-18 [MT 12-14]) has been thought to consist of gnats (i.e., small flies; so RSV), or lice (order *Anoplura;* so AV), which are wingless, strictly parasitic insects, or ticks (class *Arachnida*), which are also external parasites. Most likely this was a plague of small members of order *Diptera*, such as biting flies (families *Psychodidae*, the sand flies, or *Simuliidae*, the blackflies or buffalo gnats) or mosquitoes (family *Culicidae*), which would be a nuisance and explains why they occurred on man and beast. It has also been suggested that this plague consisted of a midge (family *Chironomidae*) that may have caused problems simply by their huge numbers and annoying habit of flying into the faces, mouths, and noses of the Egyptians. The "gnats" strained out of wine to prevent ritual defilement (Mt. 23:24) were small flies similar to what we call fruit flies that were attracted to sweet alcoholic wine. Words translated "worm" frequently refer to fly larvae. *See* FLY; GNAT; PLAGUES OF EGYPT.

Order *Lepidoptera* includes the clothes moth, which is mentioned as destroying clothes and possessions (Job 13:28; Mt. 6:20; Lk. 12:33). Members of order *Hymenoptera*, bees and wasps, are common insects. Particularly referred to are the honey bee and hornet. The Bible often refers to locusts and grasshoppers (order *Orthoptera*) and their destruction to crops. *See also* ANT; BEE; HORNET; LOCUST; MOTH.

F. Phylum Chordata: *Vertebrates. 1. Class* Osteichthyes: *Fish*. Palestine has a limited amount of suitable habitats for fish. A wide variety of fish species, many of them edible, occurs in the Mediterranean. Several lakes and ponds, excluding the Dead Sea, and the few rivers of Palestine support fish, including edible species. Heb. *dāg(â)* and *dā'g*, "fish," were also used to refer to other aquatic animals (e.g., shrimp and clams) and aquatic mammals (e.g., seals). *See also* FISH; FISHING.

2. Class Amphibia: *Frogs and Toads*. Amphibians require an aquatic habitat for the development of their eggs and normally must keep their skins moist. Thus they are usually found only in areas where there is standing fresh water for at least part of the time. Palestine has, therefore, few amphibians, with two frog species and one species each of toads, salamanders, and newts. Frogs are mentioned as the second plague of Egypt. *See also* FROG.

3. Class Reptilia: *Lizards, Snakes, and Crocodiles*. These land-dwelling animals are fairly common in the

Locusts in Palestine (W. Braun)

Middle East with over eighty different species recorded. Because of the small, secretive nature of many reptiles and the fear that many, especially snakes, engender, they were poorly observed and understood. Names and species are frequently confused. Eighteen Hebrew names are thought to represent reptiles, though many of these can be assigned only with great uncertainty.

Hebrew *liwyāṯān*, RSV "Leviathan," should probably be identified with the Nile crocodile, which occurred not only in the Nile but also along the Mediterranean in biblical times, and is primarily aquatic. Though tortoises and turtles occurred in the area, they do not appear to be mentioned in the Bible. *See also* LEVIATHAN.

A number of Hebrew words for lizards appear in Lev. 11:29f.: *ṣāḇ*, probably large spiny-tailed lizards of the genus *Uromastix;* *'ănāqâ*, possibly the gecko or any of several species of small lizards that occur on buildings and in many natural settings; *kō(a)ḥ*, possibly the common chameleon of Palestine, which is able to change color and blend well against backgrounds so that it is hard to see (not to be confused with the American chameleon, which is not a true chameleon); *leṭā'â*, probably the lacertids, which are typical lizards; *ḥōmeṭ*, perhaps the skink; and *tinšemeṯ*, another term for the chameleon. *See also* LIZARD. For snakes *see* DRAGON; SERPENT (cf. IV below).

4. Class Aves: *Birds*. Many of the biblical references to birds cannot be assigned with any certainty to any of the over four hundred species of birds identified in Palestine. All birds lay eggs for reproduction and most are able to fly using their wings. *See also* ABOMINATION, BIRDS OF; BIRDS; BIRDS OF PREY; BIRDS, UNCLEAN; BUZZARD; CHICKEN; COCK; CORMORANT; CRANE; DOVE; EAGLE; FALCON; FOWL; HAWK; HERON; HOOPOE; IBIS; KITE; NIGHTHAWK; OWL; PEACOCK; PELICAN; PIGEON; QUAIL; RAVEN; SEA GULL; SPARROW; STORK; SWALLOW; VULTURE; WATER HEN.

A terra-cotta libation vessel with incised depictions of fish and a turtle. From Larsa, 2nd millennium B.C. (RMN/ARS, NY/SPADEM)

a. Order Struthioniformes: *Ostrich*. The ostrich, the largest bird in the world, occurred in Palestine and was familiar to the OT writers. Two certain terms for ostrich are Heb. *yāʿēn* (Lam. 4:3) and *rᵉnānîm* (Job 39:13). Other terms have also been so translated.

b. Order Pelecaniformes: *Pelicans and Cormorants*. The cormorant and the pelican are large fish-eating birds (Heb. *šālāḵ* and *qāʾāṯ*) that are listed among the unclean birds (Lev. 11:17f.).

c. Order Ciconiiformes: *Herons, Bitterns, Storks, Ibises*. Heb. *ḥᵃsîḏâ* refers to storks and *ʾᵃnāpâ* to herons. These are listed among the unclean birds (Lev. 11:19), and the migrations of the first are noted by Jeremiah (Jer. 8:7). The AV has "bittern" for Heb. *qippōḏ* (Isa. 14:23; Zeph. 2:14), but a more likely identification is the hedgehog. The RSV has "ibis" for Heb. *yanšûp* (Lev. 11:17), but "owl" (so RSV in Dt. 14:16; Isa. 34:11) is a more likely identification.

d. Order Anseriformes: *Swans, Geese, Ducks*. Over two dozen types of swans, ducks, and geese pass through Palestine on their migrations. The people of biblical times were probably familiar with them, but there is no clear mention of any of them in the Bible.

e. Order Falconiformes: *Vultures, Hawks, Eagles, Falcons, Kites*. All birds of prey were considered unclean, and many are mentioned, though it is difficult to assign definite species to the Hebrew names. See the discussions under the specific names.

f. Order Galliformes: *Grouse, Quail, Peacock, Chicken*. The chicken or cock was a domesticated source of food. Peacocks (Heb. *tukkîyîm*) were brought to Solomon (1 K. 10:22). The quail is a migratory bird that was widely used for food and was familiar to the Israelites (Heb. *śᵉlāw*, Nu. 11:31).

A heron depicted on a mosaic from the Benedictine Church of the Multiplication of the Loaves and Fishes at Tabgha, 4th cent. A.D. (J. Finegan)

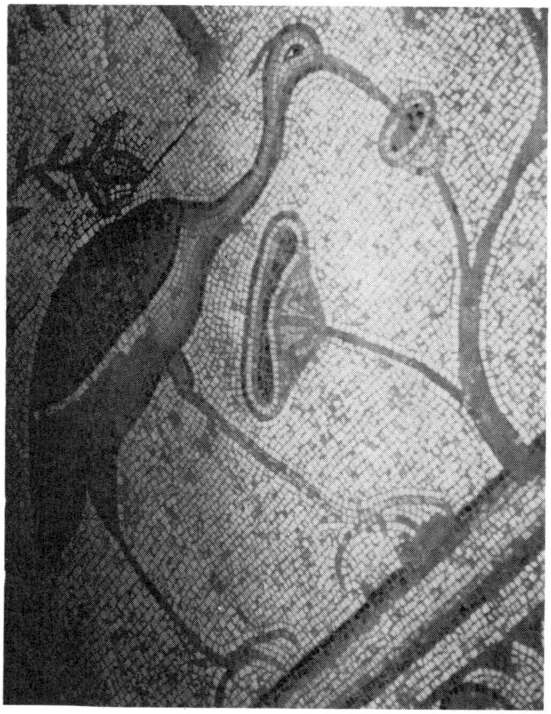

g. Order Gruiformes: *Cranes*. The crane is probably represented by Heb. *ʿāgûr*, and its migrations may be mentioned by Jeremiah (Jer. 8:7). Cranes may have sometimes remained in the southern portions of Palestine for the winter. As a noncarnivore it is not listed among the unclean birds. Its loud voice is mentioned in Isa. 38:14.

h. Order Charadriiformes: *Sandpipers, Plovers, Curlews, Gulls, Terns*. The gull and tern group is migratory with some species nesting in Palestine. They feed on many sources, including refuse and carrion; thus they might be included in the list of unclean animals (as Heb. *šaḥap*). The wading birds (e.g., the sandpipers and plovers), also migratory, have over forty representatives in Palestine, but are probably not represented by any of the biblical words for birds.

i. Order Columbiformes: *Pigeons, Doves*. Doves and pigeons are known by a number of Hebrew and Greek names. *See* DOVE; PIGEON.

j. Order Strigiformes: *Owls*. Heb. *kôs* and *yamšûp* are clearly owls. Other Hebrew words have also been taken to represent owls in general or specific species, but with less certainty. Owls are listed among the unclean birds because of their predatory habits. They were not familiar birds because of their nocturnal habits.

k. Order Caprimulgiformes: *Nightjars*. Nightjars are similar to swifts and might have been mistaken for them.

l. Order Apodiformes: *Swifts*. Swifts are probably represented by Heb. *sûs* (Isa. 38:14; Jer. 8:7 [*Q sîs*]), but the designation "swallow" (so RSV in both passages) may be correct; the two species are easily confused.

m. Order Coraciiformes: *Kingfishers, Hoopoes, Bee-eaters*. These birds were considered unclean due to their diets, including, for the hoopoe, worms from refuse and garbage.

n. Order Passeriformes: *Songbirds*. This is the largest group of birds and includes many familiar species. Sparrows and swallows are two groups of birds that were common in Palestine and were regarded favorably. The raven and its relatives were not looked upon as favorably because of their scavenging habits and their being a cause of damage to crops.

5. *Class* Mammalia: *Mammals*. These animals, which includes human beings, are those that have hair and in which the fetal development occurs inside the mother with a placental connection.

a. Order Insectivora. Heb. *qippōḏ* represents the HEDGEHOG, or, as has also been suggested, the porcupine, which is a rodent.

b. Order Chiroptera. Over twenty species of bats (Heb. *ʿᵃṭallēp*) are known in Palestine. They are nocturnal and feed on insects or fruit. *See also* BAT.

c. Order Carnivora. These flesh-eating mammals are often mentioned in the Bible because of their ability to harm human beings and domestic animals. Included is the dog family, *Canidae*, of which the domestic DOG, FOX, HYENA, JACKAL, and WOLF are all members. The brown BEAR is in the family *Ursidae*. Weasels and badgers are in the *Mustelidae* (*see* ROCK BADGER; WEASEL). The CAT, cheetah, LEOPARD, and LION belong to the *Felidae*.

d. Order Rodentia. Mice and rats are common rodents that live in close association with human settlement. Together under Heb. *ʿaḵbār* they are mentioned as unclean animals (Lev. 11:29; *see* MOUSE). Rats of the genus *Rattus* were the principle carriers of bubonic plague, which is transferred by the flea *Xenopsylla cheopis*. Five golden "mice," actually rats, were offered by the Philistines (1 S. 6:4f., 11, 18) in response to bubonic plague that afflicted them when they had the Ark of the Covenant, causing tumors (buboes) and death. *See also* MOLE.

A Great Owl in Palestine (W. Braun)

e. Order Lagomorpha. The hares and rabbits belong to this order, not with the rodents. Several species of hares (Heb. *'arneḇeṯ*) occur in the Middle East. They were considered unclean because they ingest their own feces (*see* HARE). Rabbits do not occur in Palestine, and references in translations to rabbits, badgers, or coneys (an old name for rabbits) should probably be to the rock hyrax, which belongs to a small separate order.

f. Order Proboscidea. The use of elephants in warfare is mentioned in 1, 2, and 3 Maccabees (e.g., 1 Macc. 11:56). Ivory from elephant tusks is referred to often in the Bible. *See* ELEPHANT; IVORY.

g. Order Perissodactyla. These hoofed mammals with odd numbers of toes include three that were domesticated as beasts of burden, the HORSE, the Ass or donkey, and the MULE, which is a hybrid of the horse and donkey.

h. Order Artiodactyla. These even-toed hoofed mammals include many species of large domestic and wild animals. Domesticated forms include camels, cattle, oxen, goats, sheep, and swine (*see* BULL; CAMEL; CATTLE; COW; GOAT; OX; SHEEP). Wild forms mentioned in the Bible include the ANTELOPE, BOAR, DEER, FALLOW DEER, IBEX, MOUNTAIN-SHEEP, and WILD OX (*see also* BEHEMOTH; ROEBUCK; STAG).

i. Order Primates. Human beings are classified in this order, as are monkeys, baboons, and apes. *See* APE.

IV. Fiery Serpent.–During the wilderness wanderings the Israelites rebelled against God for prolonging their travels. In response to the rebellion, the Lord sent fiery serpents (Heb. *nāḥāš śārāp*) among them (Nu. 21:6f.). While this is normally interpreted to mean a poisonous snake, an alternative interpretation might provide a better understanding.

Nāḥāš usually means "snake" ("serpent") but may also mean any crawling or snakelike animal. The fiery serpent may indicate a nematode parasite known as the Guinea worm (*Dracunculus medinensis*). This parasite is acquired from drinking water that contains the immature stages of the worm, and the developed form eventually finds its

Jackals in Palestine (W. Braun)

A Hyrax or Syrian Hare in En-gedi, Israel (Anat Rotem)

way into the skin of the arms or legs and causes a sore to develop. If the sore becomes infected, a burning pain results that could easily be recognized as fiery. Removal of the worm requires rolling it gently onto a stick intermittently over a period of days. The bronze serpent erected by Moses would then be less likely to act as an idol, but would instead represent the healing power of God as demonstrated in those individuals to whom He gave the knowledge and skill to remove the worms (Nu. 21:8f.; cf. Jn. 3:14).

Bibliography.–F. S. Bodenheimer, *Animal Life in Palestine* (1935); *Animal and Man in Bible Lands* (Eng. tr. 1960); G. S. Cansdale, *Animals of Bible Lands* (1970); R. Pinney, *Animals in the Bible* (1964).

R. J. WOLFF

ZOPHAH zō'fə [Heb. *ṣôpaḥ*–'bellied jug' (*IP*, p. 226)]. Head of a family in the tribe of Asher (1 Ch. 7:35f.).

ZOPHAI zō'fī [Heb. *ṣôpay*]. A Kohathite Levite; an ancestor of Elkanah and of Samuel (1 Ch. 6:26 [MT 11]). In 1 S. 1:1, 1 Ch. 6:35 (MT 20) he is called ZUPH.

ZOPHAR zō'fär [Heb. *ṣōpar*, *ṣôpar*; Gk. *Sōphar*] (Job 2:11; 11:1; 20:1; 42:9). The third of Job's friends, who came to "condole with him and comfort him" (Job 2:11). His name, like Bildad's, is of uncertain meaning, although some have suggested "young bird" (cf. *ṣippôr*, "bird"). Nor can his home, Naamah, be identified with certainty; the Judean Naamah (Josh 15:41) can be ruled out, however (*see* NAAMATHITE). Like Job's other two friends, Zophar was almost definitely from Transjordan, but there are no definite grounds for linking him with Edom, unless the LXX reading in Gen. 36:11, 15 (Gk. *Sōphar*) be accepted in place of the MT (*ṣ^{e}pô*; RSV "Zepho").

Although Zophar, like Eliphaz and Bildad, is presented primarily as a wise man, he was doubtless a rich chief. His being mentioned always last and his merciless attitude toward Job both suggest that he may have been the youngest of the three. He was a man of common sense, suspicious of words (Job 11:2) and of undue interest in the mysteries of God (vv. 7f.). He was the first to charge Job openly with wickedness, going so far as to suggest that his punishment had been reduced (v. 6). Although he too held out to Job the hope of restoration (vv. 13-19), the bitter gibe of v. 12 betrays his true feelings.

As the text of Job stands, Zophar speaks only twice (chs. 11, 20); it is usually assumed that his common sense held him back from further argument, once he saw that Job was incorrigible. There can be little doubt, however, that the text of chs. 25–27 is in some confusion, and part of it may have been lost. Perhaps 27:7-23, or else vv. 13-23, is Zophar's last speech, in whole or in part. Certainly the words suit him far better than Job, whose views it flatly contradicts. Both here and especially in ch. 20 Zophar typifies the man of common sense for whom facts take second place to preconceived ideas.

H. L. ELLISON

ZOPHIM zō'fim, **FIELD OF** [Heb. *ś^{e}ḏēh haṣṣōpîm*–'field of the watchers']; NEB FIELD OF THE WATCHERS. The place near or on the top of PISGAH to which Balak took Balaam to curse Israel (Nu. 23:14). Possibly the Hebrew should be translated "field of the watchers" and not as a proper name (cf. LXX *agroú skopía*), although some have suggested that modern Talʿat eṣ-Ṣafa may preserve the name.

For Ramathaim-zophim (1 S. 1:1), *see* RAMAH **2**; ZUPH (place).

W. S. L. S.

ZORAH zôr'ə [Heb. *ṣorʿâ*; Gk. *Saraa*]; AV also ZOREAH, ZAREAH. A city in the Shephelah; the home of Manoah the father of Samson (Jgs. 13:2). Zorah (modern Ṣarʿah) was located in the northernmost district of the Shephelah, 2.5 km. (1½ mi.) W of Eshtaol (Eshwaʿ) and 6 km. (4 mi.) S of Latrun. Overlooking the valley of Sorek (Wâdī eṣ-Ṣarâr), it was important to the defense of Judah throughout the history of Israel. Zorah, originally a Canaanite city, is mentioned in the Amarna Letters as one of

An elephant and a rhinoceros, painted on the last section of the animal frieze in tomb 1 at Maresha, Israel, probably from the Seleucid era (from the archives of the Palestine Exploration Fund)

the cities ruled by the king of Gezer (*LBHG* [rev. ed. 1979], p. 174).

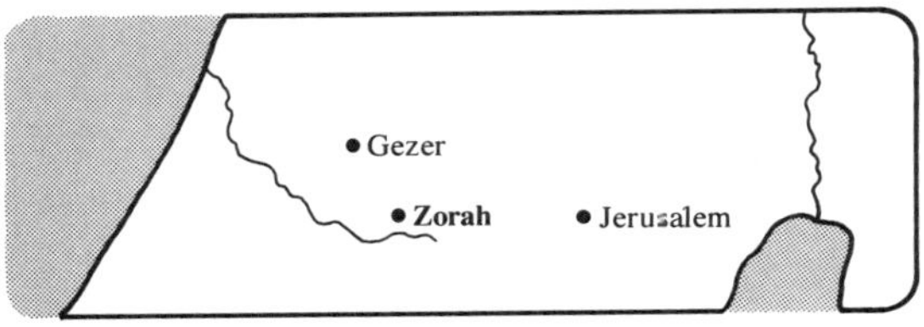

According to Josh. 15:33 Zorah was allotted to Judah when the Israelites invaded Canaan. Apparently, however, it was assigned first to the tribe of DAN (Josh. 19:41), which encountered stiff opposition from the Amorites (and later the Philistines) when it attempted to occupy the region (Jgs. 1:34f.). The story of Samson, a Danite born in Zorah, is set in this region (13:2, 24f.). After struggling his entire life against the Philistines, Samson was buried in the city of his birth (16:31). Eventually the Danites decided to migrate north, and they sent out spies from Zorah to survey the land (18:2, 8, 11).

Centuries later, Rehoboam fortified Zorah as part of Judah's western line of defense (2 Ch. 11:10). This line of fortresses served as an effective defense system for Judah in several wars during the next two or three generations (*LBHG* [rev. ed. 1979], pp. 330-33). When the Jews returned from exile in Babylon they occupied the site once again. Even the Crusaders found it an important site for their campaigns in Palestine. Located 335 m. (1100 ft.) above sea level and 244 m. (800 ft.) above the valley of Sorek, Zorah (Arab. *Ṣarʿah*) has retained its strategic value throughout the centuries. J. E. MCKENNA

ZORATHITES zôr'ə-thīts [Heb. *ṣorʿāṯî*; Gk. *Sarathaioi*]; AV, NEB, ZAREATHITES. A clan listed in the genealogy of Judah as having descended from Shobal (1 Ch. 2:53; 4:2). They were inhabitants of the city of ZORAH.

ZOREAH zôr'ē-ə (Josh. 15:33, AV). *See* ZORAH.

ZORITES zôr'īts [Heb. *ṣorʿî*]. A family of Judahites descended from Salma (1 Ch. 2:54); possibly the same as half the clan of the MANAHATHITES. The Zorites were probably not the same as the Zorathites of v. 53.

ZOROASTRIANISM zôr-ō-as'tri-ən-izm. *See* RELIGIONS OF THE BIBLICAL WORLD: PERSIA.

ZOROBABEL zə-rob'ə-bəl (AV Mt. 1:12f.; Lk. 3:27). *See* ZERUBBABEL.

ZORZELLEAS zôr-zel'i-əs (1 Esd. 5:38, NEB). *See* BARZILLAI **1, 2.**

ZUAR zo͞o'är [Heb. *ṣûʿār*–'little one']. Father of the Nethanel who was head of the tribe of Issachar in the wilderness (Nu. 1:8; 2:5; 7:18, 23; 10:15).

ZUPH zo͞of [Heb. *ṣûp̱*–'honeycomb'(?), also *K ṣîp̱* (1 Ch. 6:35 [MT 20]). An ancestor of Elkanah and SAMUEL, identified as an Ephraimite in 1 S. 1:1 and as a Kohathite Levite in 1 Ch. 6:35 (MT 20) (also in v. 26 [MT 11], where he is called Zophai). Various attempts have been made to explain this discrepancy. Perhaps Zuph was a Levite by descent but an Ephraimite in the sense that he resided in Ephraim. Alternatively, many scholars have suggested that Zuph was an Ephraimite by descent (*see* ZUPH [place]), but that in later times Samuel and his ancestors were adopted into the Levitical genealogy because of Samuel's priestly functions.

ZUPH zo͞of [Heb. *ṣûp̱*]. A region in which Saul searched for his father's asses (1 S. 9:5) and found the home of Samuel (vv. 6-14). Elkanah the father of Samuel was a descendant of an Ephraimite named Zuph (1:1; *see* ZUPH above). It may be assumed, therefore, that the region had once belonged to Elkanah's ancestor and was in Ephraim. In 1:1 J. Simons and other scholars have emended the MT *ṣôp̱îm* (in "Ramathaim-zophim") to *ṣûp̱î*, i.e., "the Zuphite Ramathaim" (assuming that the *m* is due to dittography from the following word; cf. LXX *Armathaim Zipha*). Simons suggested that Ramathaim-zuphi was so called to distinguish the Ramah/Ramathaim of Samuel from the Ramah in Benjamin. Following Eusebius (*Onom.* 288.11f.), he identified Ephraimite Ramah with Rentîs, 14 km. (8½ mi.) NE of Lydda (Ludd). He suggested that this was confirmed by the existence, until recently, of a clan named *riğâl ṣûfā* about 5 km. (3 mi.) N of Rentîs (*GTTOT*, §§ 646f.; see also *WHAB*, pp. 42, 65, 126). W. S. L. S.

ZUPHITE zo͞o'fīt (1 S. 1:1, NEB). *See* ZUPH (place).

ZUR zûr [Heb. *ṣûr*–'rock'].

1. A Midianite chief; father of Cozbi, the Midianite woman who was slain with the Israelite Zimri by Phinehas (Nu. 25:15). This event was followed by a war in which Midian was punished for having led Israel into religious apostasy (cf. vv. 16-18; 31:1-3). According to Nu. 31:8 Zur was one of five Midianite kings slain in this war. Josh. 13:21 links the slaying of these kings with the campaign against Sihon king of the Amorites.

2. A Benjaminite from Gibeon; son of Jeiel and brother of Kish the father of Saul (1 Ch. 8:30; 9:36).

ZURIEL zoo'ri-əl [Heb. *ṣûrî'ēl*–'my ROCK is God (El)']. Son of Abihail; head of the clan of Merari during the journey through the wilderness (Nu. 3:35).

ZURISHADDAI zoo-ri-shad'ī [Heb. *ṣûrîšadday*–'my ROCK is Shaddai' (*see* GOD, NAMES OF II.B.1)]. Father of the Shelumiel who was the leader of the tribe of Simeon during the journey through the wilderness (Nu. 1:6; 2:12; 7:36, 41; 10:19).

ZUZIM zo͞o'zim [Heb. *zûzîm*; LXX *éthnē ischyrá*–'strong nations']. One of the peoples subdued by Chedorlaomer and the three kings allied with him (Gen. 14:5). According to the Hebrew text they were located in "Ham" (Heb. *bᵉhām*), which is named between Ashteroth-karnaim and Shaveh-kiriathaim. Ham has been identified with the *huma* mentioned in the list of Thutmose III (*ANET*, p. 242), and with modern Hâm, 6 km. (4 mi.) SW of Beth-arbel (Irbid) in Gilead on the King's Highway (see *LBHG*, pp. 55, 435; *GP*, II, 36). This identification has been questioned, however (*see* HAM). Some have suggested emending Zuzim to read ZAMZUMMIM. This idea gained some support from 1QapGen 21:29, which reads *bʿmn*, "in Ammon," in place of MT *bᵉhām*; but this was probably influenced by Dt. 2:20, which states that the Rephaim (cf. Gen. 14:5) were former residents of Ammon and were called Zamzummim by the Ammonites (see J. Fitzmyer, *Genesis Apocryphon of Qumran Cave I* [rev.ed. 1971], pp. 164f.). There is no basis for this emendation in any text of Genesis; moreover, the *Genesis Apocryphon* is in places quite fanciful and therefore hardly a valid textual witness. The Zuzim are otherwise unknown. W. S. LASOR